# Writing and Reading Across the Curriculum

*Canadian Edition*

## Laurence Behrens

University of California
Santa Barbara

## Leonard J. Rosen

Harvard University

## Jaqueline McLeod Rogers

University of Winnipeg

## Catherine Taylor

University of Winnipeg

Longman

*To Bonnie and Michael—*
*and to L.C.R., Jonathan, and Matthew*
                                    *—LB and LJR*

*To Hartley, Morgan, and Warren*
                          *—JMR*
*and to Janice*
            *—CT*

**National Library of Canada Cataloguing in Publication Data**

Main entry under title:
    Writing and reading across the curriculum

Canadian ed.
Includes index.
ISBN 0-321-10572-9

1. College readers.  2. Interdisciplinary approach in education—Problems, exercises, etc.
3. English language—Rhetoric—Problems, exercises, etc.  4. Academic writing—Problems, exercises, etc.  I. Behrens, Laurence.

PE1417.W73 2003  808'.0427     C2002-900945-6

ISBN 0-321-10572-9

Vice-President, Editorial Director: Michael J. Young
Acquisitions Editor: Jessica Mosher
Marketing Manager: Toivo Pajo
Developmental Editor: Dawn du Quesnay
Senior Production Editor: Joe Zingrone
Copy Editor: Ann McInnis
Proofreaders: Sharon Kirsch, Karen Bennett
Senior Production Coordinator: Peggy Brown
Page Layout: Jansom
Art Director: Mary Opper
Cover/Interior Design: Sarah Battersby, Michelle Bellemare

  2 3 4 5    06 05 04

Printed and bound in Canada.

# Contents

## ■ PART II
### *Elements of Academic Essays 81*

## 5 Representing Others: Summary, Paraphrase, and Quotation 82

## Psychology

## 9 Obedience to Authority 268

## Education

### 11  Power and Privilege in School Culture  416

## Film Studies

# Preface

This is the first Canadian edition of *Writing and Reading across the Curriculum*, a book that is designed to prepare university and college students to write essays and to familiarize them with both academic and popular readings across the disciplines. Like other Canadian instructors who have been using the U.S. Seventh Edition alongside their American counterparts for many years, we found the approach and topics were fascinating to us and to our students, but they were often drawn from American culture and appealed to American perspectives. The current volume retains the strengths of the American version, but it has been substantially revised to incorporate Canadian references and readings that our students will find more relevant to their studies.

## STRUCTURE

Without attempting to reproduce the detail of a handbook, Part I, Aspects of the Writing Process, provides a focus on key stages of essay writing: The first chapters present a transdisciplinary overview of a recursive writing process, with an emphasis on developing a thesis, and on shaping the paragraphs that elaborate it. Some of this material has been relocated from Chapter 3 of the Seventh Edition. Its new place of prominence in Chapters 1 (Process and Thesis) and 2 (Paragraphs) is intended to signal several things. Most obviously, we wanted to start with the big picture of essay writing before heading into specific elements or types of assignments. We also wanted to indicate that thesis and argument are relevant considerations to every form of academic writing covered in the book, including the work of summary. And most importantly, we wanted to make the related assertion of the primacy of the student's own inquiring spirit in all kinds of academic work.

Academic texts, whether one is reading a journal article or writing a research essay, routinely require a bold, engaged effort not only to understand powerful ideas but to make and shape them, something beyond the level of confidence or aspiration of many new post-secondary students. In the face of unfamiliar subjects, erudite professors, and formidable libraries, many students shy away from venturing a bold thesis and taking control of an argument, judging it more prudent to remain non-committal in their views, and performing poorly in essays as a result. This attitude is all the more evident in the context of compulsory writing courses.

Subsequent chapters in Part I, which cover some of the options available for research (Chapter 3) and documentation (Chapter 4), make amply clear the importance to academic writers of sound knowledge and due respect for outside sources. This edition reflects a new level of attention to the by-now firmly established importance of developing competence in computer-based research. To this end, the research chapter has been revised from one that counseled a largely print-oriented research process to one that gives more emphasis to online sources. We include new coverage of topics such as writing search statements and retain material on the judicious assessment of Web sources. The documentation section of the Seventh Edition is presented for convenience of consultation as a separate chapter that begins with a brief discussion of the role of documentation in academic method.

Part II, Elements of Academic Essays, takes up the key elements of essay writing: the ways in which we represent our own knowledge and ideas can interact with those of others. Chapters 5 (Representing Others: Summary, Paraphrase and Quotation), 6 (Critiquing Others: Textual Analysis and Response) and 7 (Synthesizing Self and Others: Research Essays) emphasize representing outside sources accurately, critiquing those sources fairly, and synthesizing them in a way that expresses one's own voice and view. While summaries and critiques are sometimes assignments in themselves, our overall aim in devoting a chapter to each is to provide opportunities for students to practise the elements brought forward in that most common of all academic writing assignments, the research essay. By covering summary, critique, and synthesis in Part II, we have maintained the structure of the Seventh Edition which has been popular with instructors and students.

Part III is an anthology of readings drawn from various subject areas, grouped thematically. We have kept many of the readings that students have found most engaging in the U.S. Seventh Edition, but we have incorporated many changes. Chapter 8 still covers the discipline of political science, but is now centred around the theme of "Homelessness in the Just Society" and looks at this issue from a Canadian perspective. The chapter on the American legal system has been replaced by Chapter 11, Power and Privilege in School Culture—a topic in which most students have an immediate investment, not just those who are prospective teachers. Students who are intrigued by the psychology readings on group mentality will find important connections with the new readings on school as an instrument of normalization and with those on the link between the bullying and school shootings that concern us all. We have also incorporated Canadian readings into several popular chapters (Psychology, Biology/Genetics, Folklore, and Film Studies) and retained Chapter 10, on the Book of Job.

## NOTE TO FORMER USERS OF THE U.S. SEVENTH EDITION

We have made every effort to build on the strengths of the Seventh Edition in revising it for a Canadian context, and we hope that you will find the new material well suited to your own teaching needs. Instructors who want to use the Canadian edition but still follow the sequence of topics in the Seventh Edition could follow this order of chapters:

Chapter 5 — Representing Others: Summary, Paraphrase, and Quotation (Seventh ed. Ch. 1)

Chapter 6 — Critiquing Others (Seventh ed. Ch. 2)

Chapter 1 — Process and Thesis (Seventh ed. Ch. 3)

Chapter 2 — Paragraphs: Forming and Shaping Ideas (Seventh ed. Ch. 3)

Chapter 7 — Synthesizing Others into your own Work (Seventh ed. Ch. 4)

Chapter 3 — Research (Seventh ed. Ch. 5)

Chapter 4 — Documenting Sources (Seventh ed. Ch. 5)

## SUPPLEMENT TO THE TEXT

An Instructor's Manual has been written to accompany this text. It includes sample syllabi and notes and teaching suggestions for the anthology readings.

## ACKNOWLEDGMENTS

We would like to thank the reviewers who helped us to revise this book by providing valuable feedback on the needs of Canadian writing instructors: Anthony Sisti (Concordia University), Dianne Bateman (Champlain College), Ruth Panofsky (Ryerson Polytechnic University), Ritva Seppanen, (Concordia University), T.G. Ezzy (Dawson College), and Marie Dowler (Ryerson Polytechnic University).

In the early stages of manuscript preparation, Marta Tomins provided always congenial editorial advice. Our thanks to the ever-patient Dawn du Quesnay, who helped us to get the complicated manuscript organized and to Amanda McCormick who handled the process of acquiring permission to use the many new readings in this edition. We were grateful for the careful work of copy editor Ann McInnis and for Joe Zingrone's shepherding of the manuscript through the final production editorial process.

The University of Winnipeg generously provided us with a work study grant that enabled us to employ the assistance of Jo Snyder in preparing the manuscript. Our colleagues in the Centre for Academic Writing have enriched our pedagogical and curricular thinking in countless ways. Finally, we would both like to thank students in our Academic Writing courses who, over many years, have helped us develop insight into the interests and needs of Canadian students.

# Introduction to The Art of Essay Writing

First-year students are sometimes told by their more experienced peers that essays are easy, that they can be written almost according to formula and still fetch reasonable marks from most professors. And it is true that all essays have in common a basic structure: each has an introduction, followed by an orderly series of claims and support, in turn followed by a conclusion, all held together by devotion to an overarching claim or thesis. Though the details change from subject to subject and occasion to occasion, we can be fairly confident of our work if we keep in mind Aristotle's simple description of another complex form of text—essays, like Greek tragedies, must have a beginning, a middle, and an end, or they don't work.

However, if the art of writing essays could be adequately mastered simply by following some such structural principles, essays would not be the challenging enterprise their name (from the Old French *essaier*, to try, to test—not necessarily to succeed) suggests they are.

First, the people who take a formulaic approach underestimate the central role that must be played by the essayist him- or herself. The essayist must use his or her own imagination to find an interesting angle on the topic, develop a thesis or insight that makes sense of it, and explore that thesis through a paper that carefully unpacks and tests its logic. Writing about any topic, whether one has a personal interest in it or not, requires the probing, connecting, questioning, shaping activity of the individual mind, not only "essaying" previously unfamiliar ideas and connections between ideas, but reflecting on whether they make sense of the topic.

## READING WELL AND WRITING WELL

Of course, this demand that the essay actually make sense of things further complicates the task. Not only must the essay be a well-crafted line of argument with its own structural integrity; it must also accurately represent that portion of the universe that is its topic. Depending on the topic, the need for accurate representation might require essay writers to observe with extreme attentiveness the behaviour of grizzly bears first-hand (though seldom in first year), or examine distant galaxies through a telescope, or recollect a 10-year-old experience in detail, or intently read and reread a poem or philosophical treatise, or conduct interviews with survivors of a natural disaster. Care is required because essays collapse if they are based on faulty observation. For example, an eloquently argued essay on Shakespeare's *Macbeth* is no good if its claims are based on misquotations and misreadings; an essay on the safety of genetically modified foods, no matter how beautifully constructed as a fluid series of logically connected claims, cannot work if it has the facts wrong, or relies on faulty sources, or fails to consider important aspects of the issue. Essays, then, demand a dual focus—on both claims and support, writing and reading, expression and impression, the mind's eye and what it sees.

In an undergraduate university or college program, students are not often asked to find support for their claims by doing "primary research" (first-hand observation of the phenomenon under discussion), except for humanities topics such as "Emmanuel Kant's ethics" or "sprung rhythm in Canadian poetry" where it can be done by reading primary sources: in these cases, Kant's philosophical works or Margaret Atwood's poetry. Other essay topics, such as "the environmental impact of hydroelectric megaprojects" or "gang activity among middle-class suburban adolescents" probably won't require the student to do primary research (in these examples, that would involve visiting megaprojects or interviewing gang members) but supporting claims about these topics most certainly will involve reading "secondary" texts: articles and books written about the topic. It is by reading much more than by any other activity that students become knowledgeable about their topics and support their ideas.

Take a look at the table of contents of this book and you will find that every chapter on aspects of the writing process (whether on accurate representation, insightful criticism, or synthesizing sources) contains material on successful reading processes. Readings feature prominently in this book because the art of essay writing stems, in large part, from the art of active reading. This can be a daunting realization for people who are accustomed to the visually and acoustically stimulating modern world of the Web, DVDs, and big-screen TV, where money is poured into the attempt to make information-gathering that entertaining and consumerist process suggested by the recently evolved terms "edutainment" and "infomercials." Post-secondary study, in contrast, is largely textual, making for an atmosphere that can seem eerily silent and plain. When computers are used for research, the purpose is usually to locate texts, either online, or still more likely, in the library. Sensory stimulation is limited to variations in print style and paper quality. Any course that requires essays is almost certain to require substantial time spent in this quiet world. You are asked to read texts, texts in abundance, texts in a range of forms from articles and books written for scholars with PhDs in the subject, to course textbooks like this one that are designed to be accessible to you at the beginning of your university or college career.

## THE READINGS

If you scan the table of contents for Part III of this book you will get a sense of the range of readings included. Each chapter of readings covers a theme typical of the topics studied in different "disciplines" or subject areas—for example, the social dangers of obedience in the Psychology chapter, the power structures of school culture in the Education chapter, and the popular appeal of horror films in the Film Studies chapter.

But leaving the broad subject divisions aside, the readings differ from each other in another way, as well. They differ in *genre* or type: they reflect the purposes, audiences, and publications for which they were written. The range includes student essays and scholarly articles, and many texts drawn from non-scholarly sources, such as newspaper editorials and magazine articles, short stories, and government documents.

As a general rule, professors ask students to use scholarly texts as their research sources, not popular texts. That is because scholars have developed research methods appropriate for their subjects that permit a high degree of confidence that the claims they make are sound and offer genuine insight into the topic under discussion. Before scholarly writing is accepted for publication, it is usually reviewed for originality, importance, and methodological soundness by several scholarly experts in a process known as "peer review" or "blind review" (because the identities of the authors and reviewers are not revealed to each other). A popular source might make similar claims, and might even express them more engagingly (the purpose of popular writing is, after all, to appeal to people). It might even have been written by someone who is also a successful scholarly writer. But a popular source cannot offer the same degree of confidence as a scholarly one. However, we have a few reasons for including popular sources such as well-written newspaper editorials even though they are not likely to be accepted as research sources in other courses.

Our first reason is that scholarly articles demand a specialized knowledge base that students cannot be assumed to have just because they are enrolled in a writing course, any more than a specialized knowledge base about essay writing could be assumed of students enrolled in a history course. Trying to produce that knowledge base would take too much time away from the main focus in either course.

Second, hard work and good thinking are not the exclusive business of university professors; even though newspaper editorials would not be appropriate for a research source for a sociology essay, they may spark thinking in the reader that will lead to a good essay topic and the subsequent search for acceptable scholarly sources. Students, like professors, are wise to pay attention to intelligent speech wherever they find it, rather than reserving their critical faculties exclusively for hard-core scholarly reading. (Seeing connections between course work and other aspects of your life is a sign that you are developing new analytical and critical abilities.) Sometimes scholars' best ideas develop not from research articles written for other specialists, but from their non-specialized, "popular" reading.

## WRITING AND READING ACROSS THE CURRICULUM

In this book, we introduce questions about academic writing that arise whenever you are assigned an essay: how personal or neutral your voice should be, how argumentative the thesis should be, how best to design the structure of claim and support, which types of evidence are appropriate, which secondary sources are relevant. First-year university students, perhaps more than scholars at any other level of education, need to develop a sure grasp of these key concepts—and develop it rather quickly—because they need to be able to recognize the different applications of those concepts in so many different subject areas. (Once a major is selected, the same issues of evidence, design, alternate perspectives, and so on remain important, and the writer still needs to think about how best to meet the demands of a particular topic. However, at least the writer with a major or declared program gets to concentrate on writing appropriately for an increasingly familiar audience.)

In this book, you will have the opportunity to examine a range of texts to see how writers in various situations, both scholarly and non-scholarly, have handled these issues to suit their own purposes. You will be able to examine articles written in different scholarly "disciplines"—the areas of study that students know as "departments"—to get a sense of how differences between the overall purposes and methods of disciplines influence particular writers' decisions about appropriate approaches to key writing issues. In each of your other courses, you will have the opportunity to read many scholarly articles produced by specialists within a particular discipline. As you read such articles, pay attention to how these questions are answered in different subjects, and especially in your major, because disciplinary methods influence the requirements for essays that students are expected to write.

## Reading Exercise 1

In groups, compare several scholarly articles from Part III of this book:

> Anne McGillivray, "Civilizing Childhood" and "Education and Normalization: The Residential School"
>
> Diana Baumrind, "Review of Stanley Milgram's Experiments on Obedience"
>
> Cecie Starr and Ralph Taggart, "Recombinant DNA and Genetic Engineering"
>
> Kay Stone, "And She Lived Happily Ever After?"
>
> Analyze them to see how essays in various disciplines (education, psychology, biology, film studies, religion) reflect disciplinary values in the following categories: use of a voice that is neutral or one that it highly expressive of the writer's personality, level of argumentativeness, and types of evidence used. Be prepared to back up your observations with specific details.

## Reading Exercise 2

> Select a chapter from Part III and examine all the readings in the chapter. First, decide which ones are probably "scholarly" and which ones are written for other audiences such as the popular press or government

documents. Then comment on how the scholarly texts are similar to, and different from, the other kinds of writing on the same subject in their approach to authorial voice, nature of evidence, what sources are used, how sources are documented, writing style, and so on. Be prepared to back up your observations with specific details.

## Reading Exercise 3

Select a chapter from Part III and find a scholarly journal in the library (or on the Web) that contains articles on related subjects. For example, if you choose the Horror Films chapter you would look for a journal on film studies. Examine the articles in the journal using the categories of analysis in Exercise 2 and try to generalize about the common qualities and range of variations shown in articles in the journal.

## Writing Exercise 1

Select a topic such as stem-cell research or homelessness in your home town (if you are having trouble thinking of one, scan the table of contents for Part III or think about the topics discussed in your other courses) and develop a thesis on it: the main claim or central insight that you would want to make about this topic. Then write a one-page mini-essay in which you develop that thesis into an argument that a university professor would find convincing. How are your writing choices influenced by knowing that the intended audience is academic?

## Writing Exercise 2

Rewrite the essay in the previous exercise for two of the following audiences: the student newspaper, the *National Enquirer*, your city newspaper, an e-zine on the web, or *Maclean's* magazine. How do these changes of audience affect your presentation of the essay?

## Writing Exercise 3

Rewrite the essay in Writing Exercise 1 for two other subject areas. To do this, think about what you already know about differences in those subject areas in such terms as level of personality or neutrality in writing style, what kind of evidence is considered valuable, and the kind of language used.

# FORMS OF ACADEMIC WRITING

In Part II of this book we introduce three kinds of writing that students encounter in essay assignments: representation, criticism, and synthesis:

- Representational writing is devoted to accurately expressing the content of an outside source—typically an article or a book—by summary, paraphrase, and quotation. Insofar as writing is representational, it does not include personal comment: the writer is entirely at the service of the outside source. Many a representational assignment has wrecked on the shoals of uncalled-for critical content. Examples of representational assignments include annotated bibliographies where the task is to supply a brief summary of each source in the list, paragraph-length abstracts for your own or others' essays, and lengthier summaries of complicated texts such as philosophical arguments.
- Critical writing, unlike representational writing, aims to offer an interpretation or assessment of the argument made by an outside source. Typical assignments include source assessments, critiques, and book reviews.
- Synthesis writing can be thought of as entering into (scholarly) conversation on a topic. The writer pulls together different sources to explore a topic and makes connections between them, all the while orchestrating the conversation to make sure that sources are accurately represented and thoughtfully criticized. This is the kind of analytical writing assignment that students encounter in the form of a research essay.

Of the three types of writing in this list, only representation (in the form of summary) exists as a separate form that does not involve one or both of the others. Critical writing assignments invariably rely on a platform of accurate representation, and sometimes even include long summary sections. Synthesis writing assignments involve accurate representation and thoughtful criticism in the process of orchestrating multiple sources on a topic. The three types of writing show up in various mixes depending on the discipline and the specific assignment. For example, an Education course assignment might involve *representational writing* in requiring summaries of relevant theories on the power dynamics of school culture, *critical writing* in requiring an assessment of which theories have greatest explanatory power, and *synthesis writing* in that the essay is governed by a thesis that orchestrates multiple sources.

# PART I

# Aspects of the Writing Process

# 1

# Process and Thesis

The process of writing a successful essay involves much more time than students often expect—particularly if, as is often the case, you became accustomed in high school to getting good grades for "night-before" efforts that were short on research and contemplation but perhaps graced by a spirited manner. The single most important advice we can give you for doing well on university and college writing assignments is to give them the time they demand, and to spend that time productively.

## THE RECURSIVE WRITING PROCESS

Keep in mind that an essay is not finished when the required number of pages is full: On the contrary, essay-writing is a "recursive" process—one that goes over the same territory many times in the interests of shaping the best possible expression of the material. The intense concentration involved is more akin to that of painting a canvas or carving a sculpture than that of running a 100-metre race. Although successful writers vary in the particular techniques they employ and the amount of time they devote to each one, generally the recursive process involves three main stages:

**1. Planning or pre-writing.** In this stage writers analyze the requirements of the writing challenge before them. They might have to decide on a topic if it is not supplied, or choose one from a limited selection. They try to find an angle that interests them and work at "unpacking" the topic to explore possible approaches to writing about it. Sometimes they use techniques such as freewriting or pro-con lists at this stage.

### Focused Freewriting: Writing to Explore a Topic

1. Don't STOP.
2. Don't worry about CORRECTNESS.

Let's say you are asked to write about biotechnology in a biology class, and you are uncertain about how to start. Freewriting can often help you to narrow your topic and identify a "real" subject that interests you.

*What to say about biotech ... I never think about it very much why would I since I don't need any radical cures thank goodness and my family is OK so we don't have experience with transplants or whatever extremes they experiment with. I did hear about operations on embryos and how Canada needs to pass laws to make it illegal to do stem cell research, like they just passed laws in Britain I think. But there's GM foods, too—that's something that affects me, all the alterations they are doing to crops and animals, at least to animals through the sort of feed they get, so that they say kids are maturing earlier with all the hormones or steroids that are in the feed that cows eat and that get into the meat and the milk. That doesn't sound quite right. That could be a place to start looking . . .*

## Point/Counterpoint Outline

Another way to get started is to outline ideas. On the informal level, there are scratch outlines, containing key words and ideas that the writer wants to explore. More formal outlines often list out all the main points of support. The following represents the start of a three-column outline. This kind of outlining helps you to generate ideas, since it invites you to list your points of support, arguments running counter to each of these and justifications explaining why your points prevail or how they can be modified to reflect the counter position.

Working Thesis: Canada needs to continue developing GM foods to enable our agriculture industry to continue expanding and our government to continue supplying the growing needs of developing countries.

| Point in support | Counterpoint | Justification/Modification of point |
| --- | --- | --- |
| Financial gains for small farmers | Expense of buying these patented seeds | After start-up costs, the returns should grow |
| Testing guarantees safety | Experimental stages aren't safe | Regulations can ensure sufficient testing |
| Growing population means higher demands for food supply | Possible use of people in need as guinea pigs | People need food to live: we need to produce more |

After they have done some research, writers can often develop quite a detailed point-counterpoint table, as the next example demonstrates in its use of evidence from the Wal-Mart readings in Chapter 7.

Working Thesis: People have the right to shop wherever they choose, but they should not let convenience and cheap prices win out over supporting the Canadian economy and maintaining a sense of individuality.

| SUPPORTING POINTS | OPPOSING POINTS | DEFENCES |
| --- | --- | --- |
| "Everything's starting to look the same, everybody buys all the same things" (Ortega 134). | People will buy what they like at a cheap price, regardless of how many other people have the same product. | I hated driving around at Christmas time last year and seeing everyone's house decked out with icicle lights that they most likely bought at Wal-Mart. |
| People who are against Wal-Marts are regular people. "People aren't poor because they are paying 15 cents more for a pair of underwear" (Ortega 135). | Supporters of Wal-Mart call protesters "elitists for opposing a purveyor of low-priced goods" (Ortega 135). | Other things are more important to some consumers, such as being environmentally friendly. |

| | | |
|---|---|---|
| Wal-Marts are taking too much money from other businesses. | Many businesses are not run efficiently or competitively, and are blaming Wal-Mart for their shortcomings. | Businesses must find ways to become more competitive or unique. |
| Local businesses are noted for giving generously to the community and charities. It is seen as a way to thank the community for supporting the business. | Wal-Mart does give to the community. | "Except for one high school scholarship per year, Wal-Mart gives very little back to the community" (Norman 136). |
| Shoppers should support Canadian businesses. | Wal-Mart takes money out of the community. | Many other non-Canadian businesses take money out of the community. |

As in the above examples, writers usually develop a working thesis (though they continue to fine-tune it in the next, drafting, stage) and they try to find whatever research sources they need. If they can not find the sources they need to support their preliminary thesis, or if their view of the topic changes unexpectedly as a result of information and ideas encountered in the research process, they revise the thesis. (We discuss this important process of finding a topic and developing a thesis later in this chapter.) Some writers develop a detailed formal outline that is almost a point-form version of their whole essay before they go on to the drafting stage; others use mind-maps or quite minimal lists of the five or six main points. Whatever the particular techniques employed, the overall aim of the pre-writing stage is to put oneself in an excellent position to begin drafting.

**2. Drafting and redrafting or revising.** Again, successful writers approach this phase in different ways. For some, the first draft is very drafty indeed; it is written quickly and intensely, with the writer trying to plough through from beginning to end, knowing that there will be ample time for radical revision. Other writers work and rework each paragraph or block of paragraphs as they go along rather than separating their drafts out into different sittings, and then do one last reworking of the whole essay. The important thing at this stage is to ensure that the final draft ends up being the best possible execution of your thesis for your particular audience.

It is obvious that revising well involves effective rewriting of material; what is less obvious perhaps is that it involves particular troubleshooting skills such as looking for gaps or repetitions in the argument, and identifying unsupported claims. Instructors are providing you with an excellent opportunity to develop these troubleshooting skills when they set up peer feedback workshops. Such workshops also provide you with the opportunity to hear from real, live readers of your work before you submit it to be graded.

**3. Editing and proofreading.** Time should be reserved at the end to attend to such micro-level issues as style (Is the language used always appropriate for the audience? Is it as clear and dynamic as you can make it?), correct usage (Are comma splices and sentence fragments avoided? Is everything spelled correctly?), typing (Are there any keyboarding errors?), and complete documentation (Is there a citation for every single usage of every single source, and a reference list at the end?). Because it is often hard to see your own mistakes, particularly if you have been working on an essay so long that you're feeling a bit stale about it, writing instructors often set up peer-editing workshops that focus only on this final stage of the writing process.

At this stage, access to a well-thumbed writing handbook that goes over stylistic options and grammatical issues can be helpful, as can the writing tools available in word processors (spell checker, thesaurus, grammar checker), though they are neither infallible in error-detection nor always wise in their counsel. All of these editing aids, including peer feedback, should be used as sources of possible improvements rather than correct answers. Writers know their work best and should always weigh their options carefully rather than obediently following advice.

In Chapter 7 on synthesizing source material into a research essay, we go over several examples of writing assignments as they move through some of these stages.

## THESIS AND THE STRUCTURE OF ARGUMENTS

The goal of this careful recursive process is to produce an essay that communicates its thesis in a well-crafted structure of claim and support. Crudely put, an academic essay usually looks something like this:

Thesis (X) in an introduction
Claim 1 (often a claim that the opposition doesn't count)
Claim 2 (a reason for believing X)
Claim 3 (another reason for believing X)
Conclusion where X is reasserted in a larger context

Sometimes academic writing is so blatantly structured this way that the whole line of argument—the structure of claim and support that develops the thesis—can be picked up simply by reading the first sentence of each paragraph and stringing them together. But even if the argument is not so readily apparent, a successful academic essay will invariably have a solid structure of claim and support on closer inspection. As the novelist Virginia Woolf says about painting, even if an essay is, "on the surface, feathery and evanescent, one colour melting into another like the colours on a butterfly's wing . . . beneath it must be clamped together with bolts of iron" [1]—or else it's a failed attempt because it can't carry the weight of the thesis.

[1] Virginia Woolf, *To the Lighthouse* (Harmondsworth, U.K.: Penguin, 1968), 194.

# WRITING A THESIS

*A thesis is a one-sentence summary of a paper's content.* It is similar, actually, to a paper's conclusion (see page 21) but lacks the conclusion's concern for broad implications and significance. For a writer in the drafting stages, the thesis establishes a focus, a basis on which to include or exclude information. For the reader of a finished product, the thesis anticipates the author's discussion. *A thesis, therefore, is an essential tool for both writers and readers of academic material.*

This last sentence is our thesis for this section. Based on this thesis, we, as the authors, have limited the content of the section; and you, as the reader, will be able to form certain expectations about the discussion that follows. You can expect a definition of a thesis; an enumeration of the uses of a thesis; and a discussion focused on academic material. As writers, we will have met our obligations to you only if in subsequent paragraphs we satisfy these expectations.

## The Components of a Thesis

Like any other sentence, a thesis includes a subject and a predicate, which consists of an assertion about the subject. In the sentence "Sir John A. Macdonald and Louis Riel were equally key figures in Canadian Confederation," "Sir John A. Macdonald and Louis Riel" is the subject and "were equally key figures in Canadian Confederation" is the predicate. What distinguishes a thesis from any other sentence with a subject and predicate is that *the thesis presents the controlling idea of the paper.* The subject of a thesis must present the right balance between the general and the specific to allow for a thorough discussion within the allotted length of the paper. The discussion might include definitions, details, comparisons, contrasts—whatever is needed to illuminate a subject and carry on an intelligent conversation. (If the sentence about Macdonald and Riel were a thesis, the reader would assume that the rest of the paper contained comparisons and contrasts between the two leaders.)

Bear in mind when writing thesis statements that the more general your subject and the more complex your assertion, the longer your paper will be. For instance, you could not write an effective 10-page paper based on the following:

Democracy is the best system of government.

Consider the subject of this sentence ("democracy") and the assertion of its predicate ("is the best system of government"). The subject is enormous in scope; it is a general category composed of hundreds of more specific subcategories, each of which would be appropriate for a paper 10 pages in length. The predicate of our example is also a problem, for the claim that democracy is the best system of government would be simplistic unless accompanied by a thorough, systematic, critical evaluation of *every* form of government yet devised. A 10-page paper governed by such a thesis simply could not achieve the level of detail expected of college and university students.

# Limiting the Scope of the Thesis

To write an effective thesis and thus a controlled, effective paper, you need to limit your subject and your claims about it. Two strategies for achieving a thesis of manageable proportions are (1) to begin with a working thesis (this strategy assumes that you are familiar with your topic) and (2) to begin with a broad area of interest and narrow it (this strategy assumes that you are unfamiliar with your topic).

## BEGIN WITH A WORKING THESIS

Professionals thoroughly familiar with a topic often begin writing with a clear thesis in mind—a happy state of affairs unfamiliar to most college and university students who are assigned term papers. But professionals usually have an important advantage over students: experience. Because professionals know their material, are familiar with the ways of approaching it, are aware of the questions important to practitioners, and have devoted considerable time to study of the topic, they are naturally in a strong position to begin writing a paper. Not only do professionals have experience in their fields, but also they have a clear purpose in writing; they know their audience and are comfortable with the format of their papers.

Experience counts—there's no way around it. As a student, you are not yet an expert and therefore don't generally have the luxury of beginning your writing tasks with a definite thesis in mind. Once you choose and devote time to a major field of study, however, you will gain experience. In the meantime, you'll have to do more work than the professional to prepare yourself for writing a paper.

But let's assume that you *do* have an area of expertise, that you are in your own right a professional (albeit not in academic matters). We'll assume that you understand your non-academic subject—say, backpacking—and have been given a clear purpose for writing: to discuss the relative merits of backpack designs. Your job is to write a recommendation for the owner of a sporting-goods chain, suggesting which line of backpacks the chain should carry. Since you already know a good deal about backpacks, you may already have some well-developed ideas on the topic before you start doing additional research.

Yet even as an expert in your field, you will find that beginning the writing task is a challenge, for at this point it is unlikely that you will be able to conceive a thesis perfectly suited to the contents of your paper. After all, a thesis is a summary, and it is difficult to summarize a presentation yet to be written—especially if you plan to discover what you want to say during the process of writing. Even if you know your material well, the best you can do at the early stages is to formulate a *working thesis*—a hypothesis of sorts, a well-informed hunch about your topic and the claim to be made about it. Once you have completed a draft, you can evaluate the degree to which your working thesis accurately summarizes the content of your paper.[2] If the match is a good one, the working thesis becomes the thesis. If, however, sections of the paper drift from the focus set out in the working thesis, you'll need to revise the thesis and the paper itself to ensure that the presentation is unified. (You'll know that the match between the content and thesis is a good one when every paragraph directly refers to and develops some element of the thesis.)

## BEGIN WITH A SUBJECT AND NARROW IT

Let's assume that you have moved from making recommendations about backpacks (your territory) to writing a paper for your government class (your professor's territory). Whereas you were once the professional who knew enough about your subject to begin writing with a working thesis, you are now the student, inexperienced and in need of a great deal of information before you can begin to think of thesis statements. It may be a comfort to know that your political science professor would likely be in the same predicament if asked to recommend backpack designs. She would need to spend several weeks, at least, backpacking to become as experienced as you; and it is fair to say that you will need to spend several hours looking for sources before you are in a position to choose a topic suitable for an undergraduate paper.

Suppose you have been assigned a 10-page paper in Political Science 104, a course on social policy. Not only do you not have a thesis—you don't have a subject! Where will you begin? First, you need to select a broad area of interest and make yourself knowledgeable about its general features. What if no broad area of interest occurs to you? Don't despair—usually there's a way to make use of discussions you've read in a text or heard in a lecture. The trick is to find a topic that can become personally important, for whatever reason. (For a paper in your biology class, you might write on the digestive system because a relative has stomach troubles. For an economics seminar, you might explore the factors that threaten banks with collapse because your great-grandparents lost their life savings during the Great Depression.) Whatever the academic discipline, try to discover a topic that you'll enjoy exploring; that way, you'll be writing for yourself as much as for your instructor. Some specific strategies to try if no topics occur to you: Review material covered during the semester, class by class if need be; review the semester's readings, actually skimming each assignment. Choose any subject that has held your interest, if even for a moment, and use that as your point of departure.

Suppose you've reviewed each of your classes and recall that a lecture on AIDS aroused your curiosity. Your broad subject of interest, then, will be AIDS. At this point, the goal of your research is to limit this subject to a manageable

---

[2] Some writers work with an idea, committing it to paper only after it has been fully formed. Others begin with a vague notion and begin writing a first draft, trusting that as they write they'll discover what they wish to say. Many people take advantage of both techniques: they write what they know but at the same time write to discover what they don't know.

scope. Although your initial, broad subject will often be more specific than our example, "AIDS," we'll assume for the purposes of discussion the most general case (the subject in greatest need of limiting).

A subject can be limited in at least two ways. First, a general article such as an encyclopedia entry may do the work for you by presenting the subject in the form of an outline, with each item in the outline representing a separate topic (which, for your purposes, may need further limiting). Second, you can limit a subject by asking several questions about it:

Who?
What aspects?
Where?
When?
How?

These questions will occur to you as you conduct your research and see the ways in which various authors have focused their discussions. Having read several sources and having decided that you'd like to use them, you might limit the subject "AIDS" by asking *who*—AIDS patients; and *which* aspect—civil rights of AIDS patients.

Certainly, "the civil rights of AIDS patients" offers a more specific focus than does "AIDS"; still, the revised focus is too broad for a 10-page paper in that a comprehensive discussion would obligate you to review numerous particular rights. So again you must try to limit your subject by posing a question. In this particular case, *which aspects* (of the civil rights of AIDS patients) can be asked a second time. Six aspects may come to mind:

- Rights in the workplace
- Rights to hospital care
- Rights to insurance benefits
- Rights to privacy
- Rights to fair housing
- Rights to education

Any *one* of these aspects could provide the focus of a 10-page paper, and you do yourself an important service by choosing one, perhaps two, of the aspects; to choose more would obligate you to too broad a discussion and you would frustrate yourself: Either the paper would have to be longer than 10 pages or, assuming you kept to the page limit, the paper would be superficial in its treatment. In both instances, the paper would fail, given the constraints of the assignment. So it is far better that you limit your subject ahead of time, before you attempt to write about it. Let's assume that you settle on the following as an appropriately defined subject for a 10-page paper:

the rights of AIDS patients in the workplace

The process of narrowing an initial subject depends heavily on the reading you do. The more you read, the deeper your understanding of a topic. The deeper your understanding, the likelier it will be that you can divide a broad and complex topic into manageable—that is, researchable—categories. In the AIDS example, your reading in the literature suggested that the civil rights of AIDS patients was an issue at the centre of recent national debate. So reading allowed you to narrow the subject "AIDS" by answering the initial questions—the *who* and *which* aspects. Once you narrowed your focus to "the civil rights of AIDS patients," you read further and quickly realized that civil rights in itself was a broad concern that also should be limited. In this way, reading provided an important stimulus as you worked to identify an appropriate subject for your paper.

## MAKE AN ASSERTION

Once you have identified the subject, you can now develop it into a thesis by making an assertion about it. If you have spent enough time reading and gathering information, you will be knowledgeable enough to have something to say about the subject, based on a combination of your own thinking and the thinking of your sources. If you have trouble making an assertion, try writing your topic at the top of a page and then listing everything you now know and feel about it. Often from such a list you will discover an assertion that you then can use to fashion a working thesis. A good way to gauge the reasonableness of your claim is to see what other authors have asserted about the same topic. In fact, keep good notes on the views of others; the notes will prove a useful counterpoint to your own views as you write, and you may want to use them in your paper.

Next, sketch several different versions of a thesis, looking for one that best fits your present perspective on the topic.

1. During the past few years, the rights of AIDS patients in the workplace have been debated by national columnists.
2. Several columnists have offered convincing reasons for protecting the rights of AIDS patients in the workplace.
3. The most sensible plan for protecting the rights of AIDS patients in the workplace has been offered by columnist Anthony Jones.

Keep in mind that these are *working thesis statements*. Because you haven't written a paper based on any of them, they remain *hypotheses* to be tested. After completing a first draft, you would compare the contents of the paper to the thesis and make adjustments as necessary for unity. The working thesis is an excellent tool for planning broad sections of the paper, but—again—don't let it prevent you from pursuing related discussions as they occur to you.

Notice how the three statements in our example differ from one another in the forcefulness of their assertions. The third thesis is *strongly argumentative*. "Most sensible" implies that the writer will explain several plans for protecting the rights of AIDS patients in the workplace. Following the explanation would come a comparison of plans and then a judgment in favour of Anthony Jones's plan. Like any working thesis, this one helps the writer plan the paper. Assuming the paper follows the three-part structure we've inferred, the working thesis would become the final thesis, on the basis of which a reader could anticipate sections of the essay to come.

The first of the three thesis statements, by contrast, is *explanatory*:

> During the past few years, the rights of AIDS patients in the workplace have been debated by national columnists.

In developing a paper based on this thesis, the writer would assert only the existence of a debate, obligating himself merely to a summary of the various positions taken. Readers, then, would use this thesis as a tool for anticipating the contours of the paper to follow. Based on this particular thesis, a reader would *not* expect to find the author strongly endorsing the views of one or another columnist. The thesis does not require the author to defend a personal opinion.

The second thesis *does* entail a personal, intellectually assertive commitment to the material, although the assertion is not as forceful as the one found in statement 3:

> Several columnists have offered convincing reasons for protecting the rights of AIDS patients in the workplace.

Here we have an *explanatory, mildly argumentative* thesis that enables the writer to express an opinion. We infer from the use of the word *convincing* that the writer will judge the various reasons for protecting the rights of AIDS patients; and, we can reasonably assume, the writer herself believes in protecting these rights. Note the contrast between this second thesis and the first one, in which the writer committed himself to no involvement in the debate whatsoever. Still, the present thesis is not as ambitious as the third one, whose writer implicitly accepted the general argument for safeguarding rights (an acceptance she would need to justify) and then took the additional step of evaluating the merits of those arguments in relation to each other.

As you can see, for any subject you might care to explore in a paper, you can make any number of assertions—some relatively simple, some complex. It is on the basis of these assertions that you set yourself an agenda in writing a paper—and readers set for themselves expectations for reading. The more ambitious the thesis, the more complex will be the paper and the greater will be the readers' expectations.

## Using the Thesis

Different writing tasks require different thesis statements. The *explanatory thesis* often is developed in response to short-answer exam questions that call for information, not analysis (e.g., "List and explain recent modifications to Canadian legislation on the rights of same-sex couples."). The *explanatory but mildly argumentative thesis* is appropriate for organizing reports (even lengthy ones), as well as essay questions that call for some analysis (e.g., "In what ways are the recent modifications to Canadian legislation about same-sex couples significant?"). The *strongly argumentative thesis* is used to organize papers and exam questions that call for information, analysis, *and* the writer's forcefully stated point of view (e.g., "Evaluate recent modifications to the legal status of same-sex couples.").

The strongly argumentative thesis, of course, is the riskiest of the three, since you must unequivocally state your position and make it appear reasonable—which requires that you offer evidence and defend against logical objections. But such intellectual risks pay dividends, and if you become involved enough in your work to make challenging assertions, you will provoke challenging responses that enliven classroom discussions. One of the important objectives of a university education is to extend learning by stretching, or challenging, conventional beliefs. You breathe new life into this broad objective, and you enliven your own learning as well, every time you adopt a thesis that sets a challenging agenda both for you (as writer) and for your readers. Of course, once you set the challenge, you must be equal to the task. As a writer, you will need to discuss all the elements implied by your thesis. If you can't do it, change your thesis to one you can fulfill.

To review: A thesis (a one-sentence summary of your paper) helps you organize and your reader anticipate a discussion. Thesis statements are distinguished by their carefully worded subjects and predicates, which should be just broad enough and complex enough to be developed within the length limitations of the assignment. Whereas "topic" (from *topos*, the Greek word for "place") is a neutral description of the territory you explore in an essay, thesis is opinionated: it is the main claim—or, if you will, the central organizing insight—you make about that territory:

> Topic: Modifications to the legal status of same-sex couples
> Thesis: Same-sex couples are still far from enjoying the same legal rights as heterosexual couples.

The thesis is not always stated conveniently in one sentence or in one place, but a successful argument always has an implicit thesis that can be deduced from the argument itself. Both novices and experts in a field typically begin the initial draft of a paper with a working thesis—a statement that provides writers with structure enough to get started but with latitude enough to discover what they want to say as they write. Once you have completed a first draft, you should test the "fit" of your thesis with the paper that follows. Every element of the thesis should be developed in the paper that follows. Discussions that drift from your thesis should be deleted, or the thesis changed to accommodate the new discussions.

## BUILDING A STRONG THESIS STATEMENT

*There is no one formula for writing a strong thesis statement, but the following approach is well suited to any essay in which you are expected to develop a thesis that takes alternative views into account. In this approach, the writer starts with his or her basic claim about the topic, then expands on it to provide the rationale for the claim, then incorporates the likeliest opposition to the claim:*

*Simple*—just state your main claim about the topic:

- a one-clause sentence: X

  "College and university students are the hardest-working demographic group in Canada today."

  *Expanded*—better for you and the reader because it *forecasts* your argument by providing the rationale for your main claim:

- a two-clause sentence: X *because* Y

  "College and university students are the hardest-working demographic group in Canada today because they typically work part-time or even full-time while going to school."

  Or use another clause (Z) to acknowledge the opposition to X. This works well in an argumentative essay where the position taken is likely to be attacked.

- *Although* Z, X or *Even though* Z, X

  "Even though being a student is generally regarded as easier than working for a living, college and university students are the hardest-working demographic group in Canada today." Better yet, do both.

  Acknowledge the opposition right away, and then support your claim:

- *Even though* Z, X *because* Y

  "Even though being a student is generally regarded as easier than working for a living, college and university students are the hardest-working demographic group in Canada today because they typically work part-time or even full-time while going to school."

*This one forecasts the movement of a whole essay. In this case, the thesis promises that the essay will compare the workloads of students to those of other demographic groups. The essay will support the main claim that students are the hardest-working group by showing that they are unique in combining the double workload of employment and study, and it will refute the common perception that being a student is easier than working.*

*Now, ask yourself: If I prove this thesis, will my reader be persuaded that X is true—that students are the hardest-working people in Canada? If not, revise the thesis. Finally, ask yourself, "So what?" If you say this to your thesis statement and no good answer comes to mind, it still needs work.*

## ■ EXERCISES

1. Choose one of the chapters from Part III and try to identify the thesis in the first paragraphs of each of the readings.
2. Choose a topic and write a thesis statement for it. Now get some practice at expanding your options by writing three more thesis statements on the same topic, all of them significantly different in perspective and purpose from the first.
3. Read the following thesis statements and decide whether each one is weak or strong. Consider the criteria discussed in this chapter in making your decision:
   • Is it clear? Is it brief enough to be held in mind while writing a paper? Is it logical? Does it avoid careless or sensationalistic language?
   • Does it go beyond mere topic description to make a claim about a topic?
   • Can that claim be proved? Would it be hard to research?
   • Is the claim ambitious enough to need an essay? On the other hand, is it so ambitious that its promises could not be fulfilled in the time and space typically available for an essay?
   • So what? What difference does it make whether it's true or not? Why would anyone care?

If you have time, explain your evaluation and propose a better version.

1. This essay will examine the health risks of eating potatoes.
2. We have come a long way since human beings first crawled out of caves.
3. College and university students are the hardest-working demographic group in Canada today.
4. Although Canada's anti-Jewish immigration policy during the Nazi Holocaust has been blamed on the prejudice of a few officials, the main reason for its adoption can be found in Mackenzie King's sensitivity to the political climate of his country: anti-Semitism was a vote-getter.
5. Margaret Laurence's writing is full of hot sex scenes.
6. Princess Diana was murdered by the Royal Family.
7. There is no need to be overly concerned about street gangs. After all, human beings have gathered into groups based on shared interests since the dawn of time.
8. Globalization of the economy is happening all around the world. More and more governments take their orders from big business. Some companies have more influence on the course of history than governments do. Students have been in the forefront of demonstrations against globalization. One of these demonstrations was at Quebec City, where anyone who approached the security fence was tear-gassed.
9. Same-sex couples are still far from enjoying the same legal rights in Canada as heterosexual couples.
10. Although they are typically organized around ideals of love and compassion, religions sadly also produce intolerance and hatred for others.

# 2

# Paragraphs: Forming and Shaping Ideas

## WHAT PARAGRAPHS DO

Paragraphs are made up of sentences that focus on one topic or idea and develop it fully. The indentation that marks the start of a new paragraph is like a pause to tell your readers that there is some separation between the idea you have been developing and the one that you will develop in the paragraph ahead. Of course, the new paragraph is related to the previous one because both are concerned with some aspect of your thesis, but it is common for each paragraph to offer a fresh or altered approach.

As you have probably noticed when you are reading, paragraphs vary in length and complexity. Paragraph variety is often recommended as a way to appeal to readers. Yet the length of a paragraph is not entirely arbitrary, since it is often governed by the complexity of the concepts you are treating. Complex ideas sometimes require a long paragraph or even several paragraphs in order to explore their components. If several paragraphs are needed to treat one idea, a shift to a new paragraph means that the writer is refocusing to take a new angle or present a new stage of thought.

The following sections provide some guidelines to help you think about shaping paragraphs and make choices about developing details. Some writers are conscious of forming paragraphs even in early drafting stages. These writers often work from an outline of main, or topic, ideas, and thus approach essay writing by building a series of paragraphs that address different elements of the thesis. Other writers are more concerned with using their draft to explore ideas and they do not worry about paragraph structure until returning to the draft to make revisions.

At some stage in the writing process, it can be useful to remember that most projects require these three types of paragraphs—introductory, concluding, and middle paragraphs that build the body of the essay—and that there are helpful guidelines for shaping each of these. You also need to remember that these guidelines are not rules, and should be applied to each writing situation with flexibility, depending on your purpose and the material you are working with. Many visual artists whose work is eventually free-form and original began by first learning to draw human and still-life figures. Analogously, once you have an understanding of the basic forms of paragraphs, you will probably want to explore modifications or variants in order to decide what is suitable in a given writing situation.

## INTRODUCTIONS: SOME GENERAL GUIDELINES

Frequently, the purpose of the introductory paragraph is to announce your topic and identify how you intend to approach it, and often to do this, you need to include your thesis sentence. This enables readers to understand your intention from the outset—whether it is, for example, to explore, illustrate, or demonstrate your idea. Like other paragraphs, introductions usually contain some generalizations alongside more specific details. What makes an introduction different from the paragraphs of development following it is that its purpose is to announce the main argument or the "big idea."

## WRITING INTRODUCTIONS: A BASIC APPROACH

Although in the next section we will present several alternative ways to build opening paragraphs, you may find it helpful in the drafting process to have a basic or conventional pattern in mind. Perhaps the most basic organizational pattern is to move from general to specific. You begin on relatively general grounds, often by telling the reader what the topic area is, what book you will examine, what controversy you will enter, or what situation you will analyze. The next sentence or two often narrow in to focus or restrict your topic, so that you clarify some of your decisions about how to take a specific approach to your topic; this sometimes involves sorting out now from then, or this from that, so that you are pinpointing your topic in a chronological or ideational context. Finally, the last sentence of your opening paragraph often gives your thesis.

As a figure, a general-to-specific introduction can be compared to a funnel or top-heavy triangle, since in common these things all begin broadly, and narrow in toward a point.

One of the biggest problems with writing an opening paragraph occurs if you try to cover too much. Remember that an introductory paragraph needs to familiarize readers with your focus and approach, and that substantive commentary presenting your evidence should come in the paragraphs to follow, which aim at developing your thesis idea. Yet length of introduction is largely a matter of personal or corporate style: there is no rule concerning the correct length of an introduction. If you feel that a short introduction is appropriate, use one. You may wish to break up what seems like a long introduction into two paragraphs.

## Statement of Thesis

Although we have suggested that the most conventional spot for the thesis is at the end of the introductory paragraph, in the final sentence, perhaps a more direct method of introduction is to begin immediately with the thesis:

> Computers are a mixed blessing. The lives of North Americans are becoming increasingly involved with machines that think for them. "We are at the dawn of the era of the smart machine," say the authors of a cover story on the subject in *Newsweek*, "that will change forever the way an entire nation works," beginning a revolution that will be to the brain what the industrial revolution was to the hand. Tiny silicon chips already process enough information to direct air travel, to instruct machines how to cut fabric—even to play chess with (and defeat) the masters. One can argue that development of computers for the household, as well as industry, will change for the better the quality of our lives: computers help us save energy, reduce the amount of drudgery that most of us endure around tax season, make access to libraries easier. Yet there is a certain danger involved with this proliferation of technology.

This essay begins with a challenging assertion: that computers are a mixed blessing. It is one that many readers are perhaps unprepared to consider, since they may have taken it for granted that computers are an unmixed blessing. The advantage of beginning with a provocative (thesis) statement is that it forces the reader to sit up and take notice—perhaps even to begin protesting. The paragraph goes on to concede some of the "blessings" of computerization but then concludes with the warning that there is "a certain danger" associated with the new technology—a danger, the curious or indignant reader has a right to conclude, that will be more fully explained in the paragraphs to follow.

Yet sometimes it is difficult to begin with your thesis, particularly when you are writing a first or early-stage draft. The section that follows points out that few writers are prepared to articulate their position and focus right off the bat, and presents a variety of ways to organize opening paragraphs.

## WRITING INTRODUCTIONS: SOME OPTIONS

A classic image: The writer stares glumly at a blank sheet of paper—or a blank screen. Usually, however, this is an image of a writer who hasn't yet begun to write. Once the piece has been started, momentum often helps to carry it forward, even over the rough spots, which can always be fixed later. As a writer, you've surely discovered that getting started when you haven't yet warmed to your task *is* a problem. What's the best way to approach your subject? With high seriousness, a light touch, an anecdote? How best to engage your reader?

Many writers avoid such agonizing choices by putting them off—productively. Bypassing the introduction, they start by writing the body of the piece; only after they're finished the body do they go back to write the introduction. There's a lot to be said for this approach. Because you have presumably spent more time thinking about the topic itself than about how you're going to introduce it, you are in a better position to begin directly with your presentation. And often, it's not until you've actually seen the piece on paper and read it over once or twice that a "natural" way of introducing it becomes apparent. Even if there is no natural way to begin, you are generally in better psychological shape to write the introduction after the major task of writing is behind you and you know exactly what you're leading up to.

Perhaps, however, you can't operate this way. After all, you have to start writing *somewhere*, and if you have evaded the problem by skipping the introduction, that blank page may loom just as large whenever you do choose to begin. If this is the case, then go ahead and write an introduction, knowing full well that it's probably going to be flat and awful. Set down any kind of pump-priming or throat-clearing verbiage that comes to mind, as long as you have a working thesis. Assure yourself that whatever you put down at this point (except for the thesis) "won't count" and that when the time is right, you'll go back and replace it with something that's fit for eyes other than yours. But in the meantime, you'll have gotten started.

The *purpose* of an introduction is to prepare the reader to enter the world of your essay. The introduction makes the connection between the more familiar world inhabited by the reader and the less familiar world of the writer's particular subject; it places a discussion in a context that the reader can understand.

You have many ways to provide such a context. We'll consider just a few of the most common.

## Quotation

Here is an introduction to a paper on democracy:

> "Two cheers for democracy" was E. M. Forster's not-quite-wholehearted judgment. Most Americans would not agree. To them, our democracy is one of the glories of civilization. To one American in particular, E. B. White, democracy is "the hole in the stuffed shirt through which the sawdust slowly trickles . . . the dent in the high hat . . . the recurrent suspicion that more than half of the people are right more than half of the time" (915). American democracy is based on the oldest continuously operating written constitution in the world—a most impressive fact and a testament to the farsightedness of the founding fathers. But just how farsighted can mere humans be? In *Future Shock*, Alvin Toffler quotes economist Kenneth Boulding on the incredible acceleration of social change in our time: "The world of today . . . is as different from the world in which I was born as that world was from Julius Caesar's" (13). As we move into the 21st century, it seems legitimate to question the continued effectiveness of a governmental system that was devised in the 18th century; and it seems equally legitimate to consider alternatives.

The quotations by Forster and White help set the stage for the discussion of democracy by presenting the reader with some provocative and well-phrased remarks. Later in the paragraph, the quotation by Boulding more specifically prepares us for the theme of change that will be central to the essay as a whole.

## Historical Review

In many cases, the reader will be unprepared to follow the issue you discuss unless you provide some historical background. Consider the following introduction to an essay on the film-rating system:

> Sex and violence on the screen are not new issues. In the Roaring Twenties there was increasing pressure from civic and religious groups to ban depictions of "immorality" from the screen. Faced with the threat of federal censorship, the film producers decided to clean their own house. In 1930, the Motion Picture Producers and Distributors of America established the Production Code. At first, adherence to the Code was voluntary; but in 1934 Joseph Breen, newly appointed head of the MPPDA, gave the Code teeth. Henceforth all newly produced films had to be submitted for approval to the Production Code Administration, which had the power to award or withhold the Code seal. Without a Code seal, it was virtually impossible for a film to be shown anywhere in the United States, since exhibitors would not accept it. At about the same time, the Catholic Legion of Decency was formed to advise the faithful which films were and were not objectionable. For several decades the Production Code Administration exercised powerful control over what was portrayed in American theatrical films. By the 1960s, however, changing standards of morality had considerably weakened the Code's grip. In 1968, the Production Code was replaced with a rating system designed to keep younger audiences away from films with high levels of sex or violence. Despite its imperfections, this rating system has proved more beneficial to American films than did the old censorship system.

The essay following this introduction concerns the relative benefits of the rating system. By providing some historical background on the rating system, the writer helps readers to understand his arguments. Notice the chronological development of details.

## Review of a Controversy

A particular type of historical review is the review of a controversy or debate. Consider the following introduction:

> The *American Heritage Dictionary*'s definition of civil disobedience is rather simple: "the refusal to obey civil laws that are regarded as unjust, usually by employing methods of passive resistance." However, despite such famous (and beloved) examples of civil disobedience as the movements of Mahatma Gandhi in India and the Reverend Martin Luther King, Jr., in the United States, the question of whether or not civil disobedience should be considered an asset to society is hardly clear cut. For instance, Hannah Arendt, in her article "Civil Disobedience," holds that "to think of disobedient minorities as rebels and truants is against the letter and spirit of a constitution whose framers were especially sensitive to the dangers of unbridled majority rule." On the other hand, a noted lawyer, Lewis Van Dusen, Jr., in his article "Civil Disobedience: Destroyer of Democracy," states that "civil disobedience, whatever the ethical rationalization, is still an assault on our democratic society, an affront to our legal order and an attack on our constitutional government." These two views are clearly incompatible. I

believe, though, that Van Dusen's is the more convincing. On balance, civil disobedience is dangerous to society.[1]

The negative aspects of civil disobedience, rather than Van Dusen's essay, are
the topic of this essay. But to introduce this topic, the writer has provided quotations that represent opposing sides of the controversy over civil disobedience, as well as brief references to two controversial practitioners. By focusing
at the outset on the particular rather than the abstract aspects of the subject,
the writer hoped to secure the attention of her readers and to involve them in
the controversy that forms the subject of her essay.

## From the General to the Specific

Another way of providing a transition from the reader's world to the less
familiar world of the essay is to work from a general subject to a specific
one. The following introduction to a discussion of the 1968 massacre at
My Lai, Vietnam, begins with general statements and leads to the particular
subject at hand:

> Though we prefer to think of man as basically good and reluctant to do evil, such
> is not the case. Many of the crimes inflicted on humankind can be dismissed as
> being committed by the degenerates of society at the prompting of the abnormal
> mind. But what of the perfectly "normal" man or woman who commits inhumane
> acts simply because he or she has been ordered to do so? It cannot be denied that
> such acts have occurred, either in everyday life or in war-time situations.
> Unfortunately, even normal, well-adjusted people can become cruel, inhumane,
> and destructive if placed in the hands of unscrupulous authority. Such was the case
> in the village of My Lai, Vietnam, on March 16, 1968, when a platoon of
> American soldiers commanded by Lt. William Calley massacred more than 100
> civilians, including women and children.

## From the Specific to the General: Anecdote, Illustration

Consider the following paragraph:

> In late 1971 astronomer Carl Sagan and his colleagues were studying data trans-
> mitted from the planet Mars to the earth by the *Mariner 9* spacecraft. Struck by the
> effects of the Martian dust storms on the temperature and on the amount of light
> reaching the surface, the scientists wondered about the effects on earth of the dust
> storms that would be created by nuclear explosions. Using computer models, they
> simulated the effects of such explosions on the earth's climate. The results astound-
> ed them. Apart from the known effects of nuclear blasts (fires and radiation), the
> earth, they discovered, would become enshrouded in a "nuclear winter." Following
> a nuclear exchange, plummeting temperatures and pervading darkness would
> destroy most of the Northern Hemisphere's crops and farm animals and would

---

[1] Michele Jacques, "Civil Disobedience: Van Dusen vs. Arendt." [Unpublished paper. Used
by permission.]

eventually render much of the planet's surface uninhabitable. The effects of nuclear war, apparently, would be more catastrophic than had previously been imagined. It has therefore become more urgent than ever for the nations of the world to take dramatic steps to reduce the threat of nuclear war.

The previous introduction went from the general (the question of whether humankind is basically good) to the specific (the massacre at My Lai); this one goes from the specific (scientists studying data transmitted from a space probe) to the general (the urgency of reducing the nuclear threat). The anecdote is one of the most effective means at your disposal of capturing and holding your reader's attention. For decades, speakers have begun their general remarks with a funny, touching, or otherwise appropriate story; in fact, there are plenty of books that are nothing but collections of such stories, arranged by subject.

## Question

Frequently, you can provoke the reader's attention by posing a question or a series of questions:

> Are gender roles learned or inherited? Scientific research has established the existence of biological differences between the sexes, but the effect of biology's influence on gender roles cannot be distinguished from society's influence. According to Michael Lewis of the Institute for the Study of Exceptional Children, "As early as you can show me a sex difference, I can show you the culture at work." Social processes, as well as biological differences, are responsible for the separate roles of men and women.[2]

Opening your essay with a question can be provocative, since it places the reader in an active role: He or she begins by considering answers. *Are* gender roles learned? *Are* they inherited? In this active role, the reader is likely to continue reading with interest.

## CONCLUSIONS: SOME GENERAL GUIDELINES

One way to view the conclusion of your paper is as an introduction worked in reverse, a bridge from the world of your essay back to the world of your reader. A conclusion is the part of your paper in which you restate and (if necessary) expand on your thesis. If the form of an introduction at its most basic is like a funnel or top-heavy triangle, the conclusion can be pictured as an inversion of this—as inverted funnel or bottom-heavy triangle. Usually the first sentence offers a recap of the thesis idea. This can be relatively brief, since your readers should be fairly clear about your main contention and expect the conclusion to offer a general reminder of the gist.

---

[2] Tammy Smith, "Are Sex Roles Learned or Inherited?" [Unpublished paper. Used by permission.]

Important in most conclusions is the summary, which is not merely a repetition of the thesis but a restatement that takes advantage of the material you've presented. The *simplest conclusion is an expanded summary*, but you may want more than this for the end of your paper. Depending on your needs, you might offer a summary and then build onto it a discussion of the paper's significance or its implications for future study, for choices that individuals might make, for policy, and so on. You might also want to urge the reader to change an attitude or to modify behaviour. Certainly, you are under no obligation to discuss the broader significance of your work (and a summary, alone, will satisfy the formal requirement that your paper have an ending); but the conclusions of better papers often reveal authors who are "thinking large" and want to connect the particular concerns of their papers with the broader concerns of society.

Here we'll consider seven strategies for expanding the basic summary-conclusion. But two words of advice are in order. First, no matter how clever or beautifully executed, a conclusion cannot salvage a poorly written paper. Second, by virtue of its placement, the conclusion carries rhetorical weight. It is the last statement a reader will encounter before turning from your work. Realizing this, writers who expand on the basic summary-conclusion often wish to give their final words a dramatic flourish, a heightened level of diction. Soaring rhetoric and drama in a conclusion are fine as long as they do not unbalance the paper and call attention to themselves. Having laboured long hours over your paper, you have every right to wax eloquent. But keep a sense of proportion and timing. Make your points quickly and end crisply.

## Statement of the Subject's Significance

One of the more effective ways to conclude a paper is to discuss the larger significance of what you have written, providing readers with one more reason to regard your work as a serious effort. When using this strategy, you move from the specific concern of your paper to the broader concerns of the reader's world. Often, you will need to choose among a range of significances: A paper on the Wright brothers might end with a discussion of air travel as it affects economies, politics, or families; a paper on contraception might end with a discussion of its effect on sexual mores, population, or the church. But don't overwhelm your reader with the importance of your remarks. Keep your discussion well focused.

The following paragraphs conclude a paper on George H. Shull, a pioneer in the inbreeding and crossbreeding of corn:

> . . . Thus, the hybrids developed and described by Shull 75 years ago have finally dominated U.S. corn production.
>
> The adoption of hybrid corn was steady and dramatic in the Corn Belt. From 1930 through 1979 the average yields of corn in the U.S. increased from 21.9 to 95.1 bushels per acre, and the additional value to the farmer is now several billion dollars per year.
>
> The success of hybrid corn has also stimulated the breeding of other crops, such as sorghum hybrids, a major feed grain crop in arid parts of the world. Sorghum yields have increased 300 percent since 1930. Approximately 20 percent

of the land devoted to rice production in China is planted with hybrid seed, which is reported to yield 20 percent more than the best varieties. And many superior varieties of tomatoes, cucumbers, spinach, and other vegetables are hybrids. Today virtually all corn produced in the developed countries is from hybrid seed. From those blue bloods of the plant kingdom has come a model for feeding the world.[3]

The first sentence of this conclusion is a summary, and from it the reader can infer that the paper included a discussion of Shull's techniques for the hybrid breeding of corn. The summary is followed by a two-paragraph discussion on the significance of Shull's research for feeding the world.

## Call for Further Research

In the scientific and social scientific communities, papers often end with a review of what has been presented (as, for instance, in an experiment) and the ways in which the subject under consideration needs to be further explored. If you raise questions that you call on others to answer, however, make sure you know that the research you are calling for hasn't already been conducted.

This next conclusion comes from a sociological report on the placement of elderly men and women in nursing homes.

> Thus, our study shows a correlation between the placement of elderly citizens in nursing facilities and the significant decline of their motor and intellectual skills over the ten months following placement. What the research has not made clear is the extent to which this marked decline is due to physical as opposed to emotional causes. The elderly are referred to homes at that point in their lives when they grow less able to care for themselves—which suggests that the drop-off in skills may be due to physical causes. But the emotional stress of being placed in a home, away from family and in an environment that confirms the patient's view of himself as decrepit, may exacerbate—if not itself be a primary cause of—the patient's rapid loss of abilities. Further research is needed to clarify the relationship between depression and particular physical ailments as these affect the skills of the elderly in nursing facilities. There is little doubt that information yielded by such studies can enable health care professionals to deliver more effective services.

Notice how this call for further study locates the author in a large community of researchers on whom she depends for assistance in answering the questions that have come out of her own work. The author summarizes her findings (in the first sentence of the paragraph), states what her work has not shown, and then extends her invitation.

## Solution/Recommendation

The purpose of your paper might be to review a problem or controversy and to discuss contributing factors. In such a case, it would be appropriate, after summarizing your discussion, to offer a solution based on the knowledge

[3] From "Hybrid Vim and Vigor" by William L. Brown from pp. 77–78 in *Science* 80–85, November 1984. Copyright 1984 by the AAAS. Reprinted by permission.

you've gained while conducting research. If your solution is to be taken seriously, your knowledge must be amply demonstrated in the body of the paper.

(1) . . . The major problem in college sports today is not commercialism—it is the exploitation of athletes and the proliferation of illicit practices which dilute educational standards.

(2) Many universities are currently deriving substantial benefits from sports programs that depend on the labor of athletes drawn from the poorest sections of America's population. It is the responsibility of educators, civil rights leaders, and concerned citizens to see that these young people get a fair return for their labor both in terms of direct remuneration and in terms of career preparation for a life outside sports.

(3) Minimally, scholarships in revenue-producing sports should be designed to extend until graduation, rather than covering only four years of athletic eligibility, and should include guarantees of tutoring, counseling, and proper medical care. At institutions where the profits are particularly large (such as Texas A & M, which can afford to pay its football coach $280,000 a year), scholarships should also provide salaries that extend beyond room, board, and tuition. The important thing is that the athlete be remunerated fairly and have the opportunity to gain skills from a university environment without undue competition from a physically and psychologically demanding full-time job. This may well require that scholarships be extended over five or six years, including summers.

(4) Such a proposal, I suspect, will not be easy to implement. The current amateur system, despite its moral and educational flaws, enables universities to hire their athletic labor at minimal cost. But solving the fiscal crisis of the universities on the backs of America's poor and minorities is not, in the long run, a tenable solution. With the support of concerned educators, parents, and civil rights leaders, and with the help from organized labor, the college athlete, truly a sleeping giant, will someday speak out and demand what is rightly his—and hers—a fair share of the revenue created by their hard work.[4]

In this conclusion, the author summarizes his article in one sentence: "The major problem in college sports today is not commercialism—it is the exploitation of athletes and the proliferation of illicit practices which dilute educational standards." In paragraph 2, he continues with an analysis of the problem just stated and follows with a general recommendation—that "concerned educators, parents, and civil rights leaders" be responsible for the welfare of college athletes. In paragraph 3, he makes a specific proposal, and in the final paragraph, he anticipates resistance to the proposal. He concludes by discounting this resistance and returning to the general point, that college athletes should receive a fair deal.

## Anecdote

An anecdote is a briefly told story or joke, the point of which in a conclusion is to shed light on your subject. The anecdote is more direct than an allusion.

---

[4] From Mark Naison, "Scenario for Scandal," *Commonweal* 109 (16), September 24, 1982. Reprinted by permission.

With an allusion, you merely refer to a story ("Too many people today live in Plato's cave . . ."); with the anecdote, you actually retell the story. The anecdote allows readers to discover for themselves the significance of a reference to another source—an effort most readers enjoy because they get to exercise their creativity.

The following anecdote concludes an article on homicide. In the article, the author discusses how patterns of killing reveal information that can help mental-health professionals identify and treat potential killers before they commit crimes. The author emphasizes both the difficulty and the desirability of approaching homicide as a threat to public health that, like disease, can be treated with preventive care.

> In his book, *The Exploits of the Incomparable Mulla Nasrudin*, Sufi writer Idries Shah, in a parable about fate, writes about the many culprits of murder:
> "What is Fate?" Nasrudin was asked by a scholar.
> "An endless succession of intertwined events, each influencing the other."
> "That is hardly a satisfactory answer. I believe in cause and effect."
> "Very well," said the Mulla, "Look at that." He pointed to a procession passing in the street.
> "That man is being taken to be hanged. Is that because someone gave him a silver piece and enabled him to buy the knife with which he committed the murder; or because someone saw him do it; or because nobody stopped him?"[5]

The writer chose to conclude the article with this anecdote. She could have developed an interpretation, but this would have spoiled the dramatic value for the reader. The purpose of using an anecdote is to make your point with subtlety, so resist the temptation to interpret. Keep in mind three guidelines when selecting an anecdote: It should be prepared for (readers should have all the information they need to understand it), it should provoke the reader's interest, and it should not be so obscure as to be unintelligible.

## Quotation

A favourite concluding device is the quotation—the words of a famous person or an authority in the field on which you are writing. The purpose of quoting another is to link your work to theirs, thereby gaining for your work authority and credibility. The first criterion for selecting a quotation is its suitability to your thesis. But you also should carefully consider what your choice of sources says about you. Suppose you are writing a paper on the American work ethic. If you could use a line by comedian David Letterman or one by the current minister of labour to make the final point of your conclusion, which would you choose and why? One source may not be inherently more effective than the other, but the choice certainly sets a tone for the paper. Here's an example of a conclusion that employs quotation:

[5] From "The Murder Epidemic" by Nikki Meredith from pp. 42–48 in *Science* 80–85. December 1984. Copyright by AAAS. Reprinted by permission of the author.

> There is no doubt that machines will get smarter and smarter, even designing their own software and making new and better chips for new generations of computers. . . . More and more of their power will be devoted to making them easier to use—"friendly," in industry parlance—even for those not trained in computer science. And computer scientists expect that public ingenuity will come up with applications the most visionary researchers have not even considered. One day, a global network of smart machines will be exchanging rapid-fire bursts of information at unimaginable speeds. If they are used wisely, they could help mankind to educate its masses and crack new scientific frontiers. "For all of us, it will be fearful, terrifying, disruptive," says SRI's Peter Schwartz. "In the end there will be those whose lives will be diminished. But for the vast majority, their lives will be greatly enhanced." In any event, there is no turning back: if the smart machines have not taken over, they are fast making themselves indispensable—and in the end, that may amount to very much the same thing.[6]

Notice how the quotation is used to position the writer to make one final remark.

Particularly effective quotations may themselves be used to end an essay, as in the following example. Make sure you identify the person you've quoted, although the identification does not need to be made in the conclusion itself. For example, earlier in the paper from which the following conclusion was taken, Maureen Henderson was identified as an epidemiologist exploring the ways in which a change in diet can prevent the onset of certain cancers.

> In sum, the recommendations describe eating habits "almost identical to the diet of around 1900," say Maureen Henderson. "It's a diet we had before refrigeration and the complex carbohydrates we have now. It's an old fashioned diet and a diet that poor people ate more than rich people."
>
> Some cancer researchers wonder whether people will be willing to change their diets or take pills on the chance of preventing cancer, when one-third of the people in the country won't even stop smoking. Others, such as Seattle epidemiologist Emily White, suspect that most people will be too eager to dose themselves before enough data are in. "We're not here to convince the public to take anything," she says. "The public is too eager already. What we're saying is, 'Let us see if some of these things work.' We want to convince ourselves before we convince the public."[7]

There is a potential problem with using quotations: If you end with the words of another, you may leave the impression that someone else can make your case more eloquently than you can. The language of the quotation will put your own prose into relief. If your own prose suffers by comparison—if the quotations are the best part of your paper—you'd be wise to spend some time revising. The way to avoid this kind of problem is to make your own presentation strong.

---

[6] From "And Man Created the Chip," *Newsweek*, June 30, 1980. Copyright © 1980 by Newsweek, Inc. All rights reserved. Reprinted by permission.

[7] Reprinted by permission. From the September issue of *Science* '84. Copyright © 1984 by the American Association for the Advancement of Science.

# Question

Questions are useful for opening essays, and they are just as useful for closing them. Opening and closing questions function in different ways, however. The introductory question promises to be addressed in the paper that follows. But the concluding question leaves issues unresolved, calling on the readers to assume an active role by offering their own solutions:

> How do we surmount the reaction that threatens to destroy the very gains we thought we had already won in the first stage of the women's movement? How do we surmount our own reaction, which shadows our feminism and our femininity (we blush even to use that word now)? How do we transcend the polarization between women and women and between women and men to achieve the new human wholeness that is the promise of feminism, and get on with solving the concrete, practical, everyday problems of living, working and loving as equal persons? This is the personal and political business of the second stage.[8]

Perhaps you will choose to raise a question in your conclusion and then answer it, based on the material you've provided in the paper. The answered question challenges a reader to agree or disagree with your response and thus also places the reader in an active role. The following brief conclusion ends an article entitled "Would an Intelligent Computer Have a 'Right to Life'?"

> So the answer to the question "Would an intelligent computer have the right to life?" is probably that it would, but only if it could discover reasons and conditions under which it would give up its life if called upon to do so—which would make computer intelligence as precious a thing as human intelligence.[9]

# Speculation

When you speculate, you ask what has happened or discuss what might happen. This kind of question stimulates the reader because its subject is the unknown.

The following paragraph concludes "The New Generation Gap" by Neil Howe and William Strauss. In this essay, Howe and Strauss discuss the differences among Americans of various ages, including the "GI Generation" (born between 1901 and 1924), the "Boomers"(born 1943–1961), the "Thirteeners" (born 1961–1981), and the "Millennials" (born 1981–2000):

> If, slowly but surely, Millennials receive the kind of family protection and public generosity that GIs enjoyed as children, then they could come of age early in the next century as a group much like the GIs of the 1920s and 1930s—as a stellar (if

---

[8] Betty Friedan, "Feminism's Next Step" in *The Second Stage*. New York: Summit Books, 1981.
[9] Robert E. Mueller and Eric T. Mueller, "Would an Intelligent Computer Have a 'Right to Life'?" *Creative Computing*. August 1983.

bland) generation of rationalists, team players, and can-do civic builders. Two decades from now Boomers entering old age may well see in their grown Millennial children an effective instrument for saving the world, while Thirteeners entering midlife will shower kindness on a younger generation that is getting a better deal out of life (though maybe a bit less fun) than they ever got at a like age. Study after story after column will laud these "best damn kids in the world" as heralding a resurgent American greatness. And, for a while at least, no one will talk about a generation gap.[10]

Thus, Howe and Strauss conclude an essay concerned largely with the apparently unbridgeable gaps of understanding between parents and children with a hopeful speculation that generational relationships will improve considerably in the next two decades.

## MIDDLE PARAGRAPHS: PARAGRAPHS OF SUPPORT

While it is important to write carefully crafted introductions and conclusions because they catch readers both coming and going, paragraphs in the body or middle of the essay make up the remaining 98% of your essay and are therefore worth some consideration. Middle paragraphs are sometimes called paragraphs of support because they typically demonstrate or support some element of the thesis or main idea. Yet common general purpose aside, middle paragraphs do many things—raise questions, provide examples, analyze arguments, develop interpretations—and take different shapes. Those that work best tend to reflect these three principles: unity, coherence, and completeness.

### Unity

A paragraph should be about one thing. It should discuss one point, rather than several or, if the point is complex, one aspect of the point. Paragraphs that try to cover too much ground can seem thin or underdeveloped, conveying the impression that the writer's thoughts have ranged far and wide but have not been deep.

One way to ensure that a paragraph is unified is to develop it from a topic sentence—a sentence that announces the general paragraph idea. This sentence controls the paragraph, since everything that follows it offers some level of support. For example, after announcing the paragraph topic in the topic sentence, the next sentence often restates the topic, in a more refined or restricted version. From there we get the specific support—the facts, illustrations, statistics—that serve as evidence.

It helps some writers to think about the topic sentence as an umbrella sentence that "covers" the paragraph. In this way, it works like a small version

---

[10] Excerpt from "The New Generation Gap" by Neil Howe and William Strauss. Originally appeared in *Atlantic*, December 1992. Reprinted by permission of Raphael Sagalyn, Inc.

of the thesis sentence, which can be seen as the umbrella sentence that covers the essay as a whole.

Many paragraphs do not state a topic sentence directly, but convey what they are about tacitly, by implication. If one of your paragraphs seems unmanageable and appears to lack unity, you might try to summarize it in a sentence, which can then function as an organizing topic sentence. You can decide whether to build this sentence into the paragraph directly or use it to help you focus and redirect the paragraph.

In the following example, the first paragraph builds from a direct topic statement, while the second paragraph implies the topic idea.

## DIRECT TOPIC SENTENCE

Narrative writing has become increasingly influential across the curriculum in the last 10 years. Before that time, most disciplines favoured an objective tone and the recital of facts, but using the personal voice to treat the realm of material experience became more popular with the spread of postmodern skepticism toward the possibility of knowing truth. In the social sciences, ethnographies and case studies began to appear alongside more traditional quantitative studies, and personal essays began to be published with more frequency in journals in the humanities. In their recent text examining *Narrative Inquiry,* Clandinin and Connelly point out that while a narrative approach is appropriate to education research because it grants a human dimension to studying how humans think and learn, they have "read in other social sciences and humanities for insights"[11] into how narrative inquiries can work.

## TACIT TOPIC SENTENCE

About 10 years ago, ethnographies and case studies began to appear alongside more traditional quantitative studies in the social sciences, and personal essays began to be published with more frequency in journals in the humanities. In their recent text examining *Narrative Inquiry,* Clandinin and Connelly point out that while a narrative approach is appropriate to education research because it grants a human dimension to studying how humans think and learn, they have "read in other social sciences and humanities for insights"[11] into how narrative inquiries can work.

You also need to consider that sometimes complex topic sentences are multi-layered and control several paragraphs. To demonstrate in more detail the topic sentence idea from the same paragraphs above that narrative inquiry is being used in many disciplines, a writer might decide to use three paragraphs to explore how there is evidence of this in the humanities, the social sciences, and, finally, the sciences.

---

[11] D. Jean Clandinin and F. Michael Connelly. *Narrative Inquiry: Experience and Story in Qualitative Research.* San Francisco: Jossey-Bass, 2000.

## Completeness

You have already been asked to consider paragraph variety as a strategy to engage readers. For a paragraph to be complete, there is no formula to govern length. You may find it helpful, however, to remember that for a paragraph to develop an idea fully usually requires a blend of general and specific information. On a general level, you state your topic sentence or paragraph point. More specific-level information follows this, serving as evidence to demonstrate your general point. For example, after an assertion, you might offer examples, facts and/or statistics as supporting detail.

While there are no litmus tests to see whether a paragraph is complete, many undergraduate writers struggle with the problem of leaving their ideas underdeveloped. It can sometimes help to remind yourself that two examples are probably more convincing than one and that readers expect you to explain or interpret the way in which an example demonstrates your point. Moreover, it is also a good strategy to use a variety of evidence, so that you can strengthen the effect of an example or observation from experience by giving it alongside a relevant statistic or a supportive quotation from an expert. In the sample paragraph demonstrating the use of a direct topic sentence, the writer's observations and interpretations gain resonance because they are echoed in "the expert testimony" of Clandinin and Connelly.

### COHERENCE

Coherence refers to whether paragraph ideas are smoothly connected, so that readers understand how one thing leads to another. You can write about one topic in a unified way, and still be incoherent so that your readers are left wondering how your ideas fit together and why one sentence follows another.

### USING TRANSITIONS

To ensure coherence, you need to clarify the connections between ideas, which can be done using several devices. Probably using transition words and phrases —words that specify the nature of relation between sentence parts—is the best way to help readers to see how one thing leads to another. Transitions signal shifts and connections in writing. The following sample sentences begin to illustrate how transition words work:

### USING TRANSITION WORDS

Wayne and Shuster pioneered a new form of comedy. They defined our sense of humour.

Wayne and Shuster pioneered a new form of comedy AND they defined our sense of humour.

ALTHOUGH Wayne and Shuster pioneered a new form of comedy, they defined our sense of humour.

Music teachers differ. Some emphasize theory, some practice.

Music teachers differ; FOR EXAMPLE, some emphasize theory, some practice.

Music teachers differ, BECAUSE some emphasize theory WHILE others emphasize practice.

Music teachers differ. ON THE ONE HAND, some emphasize theory, WHILE ON THE OTHER, some emphasize practice.

As these examples indicate, adding transition words can alter the direction of your idea, so you need to be sure that the connecting words you choose are those that best specify the relation you have in mind. It makes a big difference, for example, if something happens and then something else happens after this, or if a causal pattern of development replaces sheer chronology so that something happens because something else preceded it. Using transitions can also prompt you to add more information, so that the connections between your ideas are clarified. This happens, for example, when the subordinator "although" helps the reader to understand the contrastive relationship between the notion that Wayne and Shuster were innovators and the notion that they had a definitive influence on how we think about comedy.

## ■ EXERCISE

Make this paragraph more coherent by adding transition words.

```
Many programs require students to write an autobiogra-
phy as part of the admission application. The School of
Journalism requires this. I know two students who wrote
autobiographies to get into Medicine. You need to write
an autobiography for admission to Education. These can
be short. An autobiography should highlight your acade-
mic achievements. You should talk about life experiences
that have prepared you for the field of study.
```

### USING PARALLEL STRUCTURE

You can also help readers to understand how your ideas are connected if you remember to replicate the grammatical form of ideas that have equal value or that belong to a series. The following sentences illustrate how parallel structure can be used to build in coherence:

She liked walking and to run.
She liked to walk and run.
PARALLEL: She liked walking and running.

He couldn't stop practising his speech, whether locked in his room, watching TV, on the way to the lake, or shopping.
PARALLEL: He couldn't stop practising his speech, whether sitting in his room, looking at the TV, driving to the lake, or shopping at the mall.

## REPEATING KEY WORDS OR PHRASES

While needless or awkward repetition can spoil sentence rhythm and aggravate readers, when you repeat key words you can draw attention to the way in which the paragraph connects or coheres around a core point. Rather than having each sentence take off in fresh flight, you can use repetition to create an echoing effect and thus to streamline the development of sentences within a paragraph.

In the following paragraph, key words that build paragraph coherence are highlighted.

Being able *to read* well is important *throughout our lives.* As *children in elementary school,* we begin to define ourselves by how quickly we can advance from *one reading series to another,* and often we are placed in groups according to *reading ability.* By *junior high, students* who *cannot read* are those who are struggling with school and often overwhelmed by homework in the form of leftover classroom chores. By the *end of high school, readers* look forward to some form of future study, while those who *don't read* well can only hope to avoid being confronted with *books.* People who *love reading* take a comforting hobby with them into their *adult and senior years.*

# 3

# Research

## GOING BEYOND THIS TEXT

In this chapter we'll discuss how you can use the skills you've learned in writing summaries, critiques, and syntheses to compose research papers and reports. A research paper is generally considered to be a major academic endeavour. But even a paper based on only one or two sources outside the scope of assigned reading has been researched. Research requires you (1) to locate and take notes on relevant sources and organize your findings; (2) to summarize or paraphrase these sources; (3) to critically analyze them for their value and relevance to your subject; and (4) to synthesize information and ideas from several sources that both support and challenge your own critical viewpoint.

As you'll see, each chapter in Part III of *Writing and Reading Across the Curriculum* consists of a group of related readings on a particular subject; for example, obedience to authority, biotechnology, Biblical literature. The readings in a chapter will give you a basic understanding of the key issues associated with the subject. For a deeper understanding, however, you'll need to go beyond the relatively few readings included here. A paper based on even two or three additional sources will have a breadth missing from a paper that relies exclusively on the text readings.

Of course, you may be asked to prepare a research paper of some length. Each chapter in Part III concludes with a number of research activities on the subject just covered. In some cases, we suggest particular sources; in others, we provide only general directions. Your instructor may ask you to work on at least one of these assignments during the term. But whether you are preparing an in-depth research paper or just locating a few additional sources on your subject (or something in between), it's essential to know your way around a university library, to be able to locate quickly and efficiently the information you need. It's becoming equally important to know your way around the Web. In this chapter, we'll give you some important research tips. For more comprehensive information (e.g., annotated lists of specialized reference tools), consult a text on research papers or the research section of a handbook.

# RESEARCH PAPERS IN THE ACADEMIC DISCIPLINES

Though most of your previous experience with research papers may have been in English classes, you should be prepared for instructors in other academic disciplines to assign papers with significant research components. Here, for example, is a sampling of research topics that have been assigned recently in a broad range of undergraduate courses:

*Anthropology:* Identify, observe, and gather data pertaining to a particular subculture within the campus community; describe the internal dynamics of this group, and account for these dynamics in terms of theories of relevant anthropologists and sociologists.

*Canadian Studies:* Address an important socio-psychological issue for inner-city communities and/or individuals—for example, the effects of racial and ethnic stereotypes, poverty, discrimination, schooling, or cultural norms and conflicts. Review both the theoretical and research literature on the issue, conduct personal interviews, and draw conclusions from your data.

*Environmental Studies:* Choose a problem or issue of the physical environment at any level from local to global. Use both field and library work to explore the situation. Include coverage of the following: (1) the history of the issue or problem; (2) the various interest groups involved, taking note of conflicts among them; (3) critical facts and theories from environmental science necessary to understand and evaluate the issue or problem; (4) impact and significance of management measures already taken or proposed; (5) your recommendations for management of the solution.

*Film Studies:* Pick a particular period of British film and discuss major film trends or production problems within that period.

*History:* Write a paper analyzing the history of a public policy (example: the Canadian government's role in severely restricting Jewish immigration before, during, and after the Holocaust), drawing your sources from the best, most current scholarly histories available.

*Physics:* Research and write a paper on solar cell technology, covering the following areas: basic physical theory, history and development, structure and materials, types and characteristics, practical uses, state of the art, and future prospects.

*Political Science:* Explain the contours of Canada's policy on fishing rights and quotas in the last few decades and then, by focusing on one specific controversy, explain and analyze the way in which policy was adapted and why. Consider such questions as Aboriginal claims, international agreements, replenishment of fish stocks, and impact on fishing economies.

*Psychology:* Explore some issue related to the testing of mental ability; for example, the effects of time limits upon test reliability.

*Religious Studies:* Select a particular religious group or movement present in Canada for at least 20 years and show how its belief or practice has changed since members of the group have been in the country or, if the group began in Canada, since its first generation.

*Sociology:* Write on one of the following topics: (1) a critical comparison of two (or more) theories of deviance; (2) field or library research study of a specific deviant career: thieves, drug addicts, prostitutes, corrupt politicians, university administrators; (3) portrayals of deviance in popular culture—e.g., television "accounts" of terrorism, incest, spouse abuse; (4) old age as a form of deviance; (5) the relationship between homelessness and mental illness.

As you can see, essay topics vary greatly both within disciplines and from one discipline to another. Some of these research papers allow students a considerable range of choice (within the general subject); others are highly specific in requiring students to address a particular issue. Most of these papers call for some library research; a few call for a combination of library and field research; others may be based entirely on field research. In the humanities—subjects such as history or philosophy—you are often expected to do *primary research*; that is, you make your own direct observations of the phenomenon under study and report these in an essay that integrates your observations and analysis with those of published scholars. Primary research is more commonly required in the humanities than in the sciences because the phenomena under study are readily available in book form: the novels of Margaret Laurence; the books of the Bible, Koran, or Talmud; the philosophical works of Hannah Arendt. Primary research is less often required in the sciences since it is less practical for university students because it involves lab or field research: interviews, lab experiments, archaeological digs, etc.

In any case, most essays will involve *secondary* research; that is, you read other people's reports, in article and book form, of their primary research.

## ■ EXERCISE

Working in groups, analyze the essay topics listed above and identify the elements of primary research involved in each one. For those topics that do not require primary research, imagine what kind of primary research could be done, given the resources of time and money.

## WRITING THE RESEARCH PAPER

Here is an overview of the main steps involved in writing research papers. Keep in mind that as with other synthesis projects, writing research papers is a recursive process: You may not necessarily follow these steps in the order below, and you will find yourself backtracking and looping. This is not only normal, it is essential to carefully developed research.

- **Find a subject.** Decide what subject you are going to research and write about.
- **Develop a research question.** Formulate an important question that you would like to answer through your research.

- **Conduct preliminary research.** Consult knowledgeable people, general and specialized encyclopedias, overviews and bibliographies in recent books, and credible Web sources (see pp. **45–48**).
- **Conduct focused research.** Conduct keyword searches of book, periodical, and Web catalogues to find sources on your topic. Consult biographical indexes, general and specialized dictionaries, government publications, and other appropriate sources in print and online. Conduct interviews and surveys, as necessary.
- **Develop a working thesis.** Based on your initial research, formulate a working thesis that attempts to respond to your research question.
- **Develop a working bibliography.** Keep a working bibliography (either paper or electronic) of potential sources. Make this bibliography easy to sort and rearrange.
- **Evaluate sources.** Attempt to determine the relevance and reliability of potential sources; use your critical reading skills.
- **Take notes from sources.** Paraphrase and summarize important information and ideas from your sources. Copy down important quotations. Note page numbers from sources of this quoted and summarized material.
- **Arrange your notes according to your outline.** Develop a working outline of topics to be covered in your paper. Arrange your notes according to this outline.
- **Write your draft.** Write the preliminary draft of your paper, working from your notes, according to your outline.
- **Avoid plagiarism.** Take care to cite all quoted, paraphrased, and summarized source material, making sure that your own wording and sentence structure differ from those of your sources.
- **Cite sources.** Use in-text citations and a "Works Cited" or "References" list, according to the conventions of the discipline (e.g., MLA, APA, CBE).
- **Revise your draft.** Use transitional words and phrases to ensure coherence. Check for style. Make sure that the research paper reads smoothly, logically, and clearly from beginning to end. Check for grammatical correctness, punctuation, and spelling.

## FINDING A SUBJECT

In your present writing course, finding a general subject shouldn't be a problem, since your research likely will concern one of the subjects covered in this text. And, as we've suggested, your instructor may assign you one of the research activities at the end of each chapter, for which some focus will be provided in our directions. Or your instructor may specify his or her own particular directions for your research activity. In other cases, you'll be asked simply to write a paper on some aspect of the subject.

Which aspect? Review the readings, the questions following the readings, and your responses to these questions. Something may immediately (or eventually) spring to mind. Perhaps while reading the chapter from Aldous Huxley's enormously influential *Brave New World* you wonder how the book was received by critics and general readers when it first appeared in 1932. Maybe while reading the selections on the Milgram experiment in the chapter on obedience to authority you become curious about later experiments that also tested obedience to authority, or about a recent event that demonstrated the malign effects of obedience to unlawful or immoral authority. Consider the readings on biotechnology. What has been written on this subject since these selections appeared? To what extent have the terms of the debate on genome research changed?

## THE RESEARCH QUESTION

Research handbooks generally advise students to narrow their subjects as much as possible. A 10-page paper on the modern feminist movement would be unmanageable. You would have to do an enormous quantity of research (a preliminary computer search of this subject would yield several thousand items), and you couldn't hope to produce anything other than a superficial treatment of such a broad subject. But a paper on the contemporary reception of *Brave New World* or on its relationship to other 20th-century dystopias should be quite manageable. It's difficult to say, however, how narrow is narrow enough. (A literary critic once produced a 20-page article analyzing the first paragraph of Henry James's *The Ambassadors*.)

Perhaps more helpful as a guideline on focusing your research is to seek to answer a particular question, a *research question*. For example, how did the Trudeau government respond to the demands of Quebec separatists? To what extent is Canada perceived in other countries as an annex of the United States? Did Exxon behave responsibly in handling the *Valdez* oil spill? How has the debate over genetic engineering evolved during the past decade? To what extent do contemporary cigarette ads encourage children to smoke? Or how do contemporary cigarette ads differ in message and tone from cigarette ads in the 1950s? Focusing on questions such as these and approaching your research as a way of answering such questions is probably the best way to narrow your subject and ensure focus in your paper. The essential answer to this research question eventually becomes your *thesis*, and in the paper you present evidence that systematically supports your thesis.

## PRELIMINARY RESEARCH

Once you have a research question, you want to see what references are available. You want to familiarize yourself quickly with the basic issues and to generate a preliminary list of sources. There are many ways to go about doing this; some of the more effective ones are listed in the box below. We'll consider a few of these suggestions in more detail.

## HOW TO FIND PRELIMINARY SOURCES AND NARROW THE SUBJECT

- Ask your instructor to recommend sources on the subject.
- Ask your university librarian for useful reference tools in your subject area.
- If you're working on a subject from this text, use some of the sources we've mentioned in the research activities section.
- Read an encyclopedia article on the subject and use the bibliography following the article.
- Read the introduction to a recent book on the subject and review that book's bibliography.
- If you need help in narrowing a broad subject, consult one or more of the following:
  - a search by subject (not keywords) in an electronic database (the subject will be broken down into its components)
  - the subject heading in an electronic periodical catalogue, such as *InfoTrac*, or in a print catalogue, such as the *Readers' Guide to Periodical Literature*
  - the *Library of Congress (LOC) Subject Headings* catalogue (in the reference section of any library organized by the LOC system; also online at **kcweb.loc.gov**)

## Consulting Knowledgeable People

When you think of research, you may immediately think of libraries or the Web. But don't neglect a key reference source—other people. Your *instructor* probably can suggest fruitful areas of research and some useful sources, and the vast majority will appreciate your initiative in asking. Try to see your instructor during office hours, however, rather than immediately before or after class, so that you'll have enough time for a productive discussion. One word of caution: Don't claim that nothing has been written on your topic; instead, ask for help in identifying appropriate keywords and particular sources.

Once you get to the library, ask a *reference librarian* which reference sources (e.g., bibliographies, specialized encyclopedias, periodical indexes, statistical almanacs) you need for your particular area of research. Librarians won't do your research for you, but they'll be glad to show you how to research efficiently and systematically.

You can also obtain vital information from people when you interview them, ask them to fill out questionnaires or surveys, or have them participate in experiments. We'll cover this aspect of research in more detail below.

## Encyclopedias

Reading an encyclopedia entry about your subject will give you a basic understanding of the most significant facts and issues. Whether the subject is First Nations land claims or the mechanics of genetic engineering, the encyclopedia article—written by a specialist in the field—offers a broad overview that may serve as a launching point to more specialized research in a particular area. The article may illuminate areas or raise questions that you feel motivated to pursue further. Equally important, the encyclopedia article frequently concludes with an *annotated bibliography* describing important books and articles on the subject.

Encyclopedias have certain limitations. First, most professors don't accept encyclopedia articles as legitimate sources for academic papers. You should use encyclopedias primarily to familiarize yourself with (and to select a particular aspect of) the subject area and as a springboard for further research. Also, because new editions appear only once every five or ten years, the information they contain—including bibliographies—may not be current. The latest editions of the *Encyclopaedia Britannica* (in print or online), for instance, may not include information about the most recent developments in biotechnology.

Keep in mind that the library also contains a variety of *specialized encyclopedias*. These encyclopedias restrict themselves to a particular disciplinary area, such as chemistry, law, or film, and are considerably more detailed in their treatment of a subject than general encyclopedias.

## Overviews and Bibliographies in Recent Books

If your professor or one of your bibliographic sources directs you to an important recent book on the subject, skim the introductory (and possibly the concluding) material to the book, along with the table of contents, for an overview of the key issues. Look also for a bibliography. For example, Zvi Dor-Ner's 1991 book *Columbus and the Age of Discovery* includes a four-page annotated bibliography of important reference sources on Columbus and the age of exploration.

Keep in mind that authors are not necessarily objective about their subjects, and some have particularly biased viewpoints that you may unwittingly carry over into your paper, treating them as objective truth.[1] However, you

---

[1] Bias is not necessarily bad. Authors, like all other people, have certain preferences and predilections that influence the way they view the world and the kinds of arguments they make. As long as they inform you of their biases, or as long as you are aware of them and take them into account, you can still use these sources judiciously. (You might gather valuable information from a book about the Trudeau era, even if it were written by former Prime Minister Trudeau or one of his chief cabinet ministers, as long as you make proper allowance for their understandable biases.) Bias becomes a potential problem only when it masquerades as objective truth or is accepted as such by the reader. For suggestions on identifying and assessing authorial bias, see the material on persuasive writing (pp. 129–138) and evaluating assumptions (pp. 140–141) in Chapter 6.

may still be able to get some useful information out of biased sources. For example, some scholars argue that to treat Columbus's explorations as an age of discovery suggests an imperialist bias that ignores the perspective of First Nations people, who lived in the Americas long before Europeans "discovered" and claimed those lands. Sources biased towards a Eurocentric view of Columbus could still contain useful factual information. Alert yourself to authorial biases by looking up the reviews of your book in the *Book Review Digest* (described on p. 43). Additionally, consult biographical indexes for information about the author, whose previous writings or professional associations may suggest a predictable set of attitudes on the subject of your book.

## ■ EXERCISES

1. After reviewing the following section on "Focused Research," visit the website of your university or college library to determine what kinds of resources are available to you online in the following categories: reference works, such as dictionaries and encyclopedias; library book holdings; indexes to journal articles, indexes that contain complete text of journal articles, and entire online journals; federal, provincial, and municipal government documents; newspapers; and scholarly websites.

2. Working in a small group of students who share your likely major, find out what key reference works and journal indexes exist for research on topics in your area, both in your university library and online.

## FOCUSED RESEARCH

Once you've narrowed your scope to a particular subject and a particular research question (or set of research questions), you're ready to undertake more focused research. Your objective now is to learn as much as you can about your particular subject and ultimately to find sources that you will actually use in your essay. Only in this way will you be qualified to make an informed response to your research question. This means you'll have to become something of an expert on the subject—or, if that's not possible, given time constraints, you can at least become someone whose critical viewpoint is based solidly on the available evidence. In the following pages we'll suggest how to find sources for this kind of focused research. In certain cases, your research may be based partially or even primarily on *interviews* and *surveys.* But most university essays rely heavily on textual research: *books, articles,* and specialized *reference* sources such as government documents. To find any of these efficiently, you need to become adept at using search engines.

### Using Search Engines

Researchers find the documents they need by using "search engines": computer programs that scan large databases to locate documents that correspond to the researchers' search terms. To find books housed in a particular library, the search engine they use is the library catalogue. To find journal and magazine articles, they use periodical indexes. To find documents housed on the Web, they use Web search engines.

These engines do not always offer links to the documents themselves. Instead, they provide you with the information you need to find the documents. For books, that information is the Library of Congress or Dewey Decimal System call number that librarians stamp on the spine of the books. For articles, that information is the name, volume, and issue number of the journal or magazine where the article appears (sadly, your library may not subscribe to the periodical, and you will need to find articles in periodicals it does subscribe to). Increasingly, though, journal articles are being made available within journal indexes.

All search engines—whether the book catalogue of your own university library, or a periodical index for thousands of journals your library may have only a few hundred of, or a Web search engine that tries (never with complete success) to find all relevant documents on the whole "World Wide Web"— work basically the same way: through search statements.

## WRITING SEARCH STATEMENTS

If you know exactly what document you are looking for, the search statement will consist of the author's name, or the title of the document. Book catalogues and periodical indexes offer both of these search options. If you know the subject heading or "descriptor" used by the catalogue or index, you might choose a "subject" search instead, which will offer you a list of all those documents classified under the subject you are searching for. (Hint: If you don't know how your subject is classified, try a keyword search as described below, and then look for the subject descriptor area in one of the document records. Clicking on a highlighted descriptor, such as "Bilingual Education," will take you to a listing of all documents classified under the subject.)

However, by far the most common and useful type of search statement is the keyword search: a combination of terms that you would expect to find in the citations or descriptions of the documents that would be relevant to your research needs. Many students underutilize the power of search statements by choosing inappropriately general or inappropriately narrow terms, and then give up, concluding there is nothing available on the topic. When deciding on keywords, ask yourself, "what are the various keywords that might be used by writers on my topic?" and try the range. For example, if nothing results from a search for "bullying in schools," try "peer pressure" and "violence" instead.

Searchers also underutilize the power of search statements by not using the various operators available to help them zero in on as many relevant documents as possible, or on the most relevant documents. Different search engines permit the use of many of the following operators. To find out which ones can be used with a particular search engine, check the "Search Tips" or "Help" link that is normally found on the home page of the engine. These are the most common:

### Boolean Operators

Keywords can be combined using Boolean operators to shape the results of the search:

**AND** (the document must contain both words that are joined by the operator),

**NOT** (must not contain the word following the operator), and

**OR** (must contain at least one of the words joined by the operator)

For example:

- St. John's AND cod (would find documents containing both terms)
- St. John's OR Conception Bay (would find documents containing one or both terms)
- St. John's NOT comedy (would find documents containing one but not the other—particularly useful when lots of irrelevant documents would contain the excluded term)

Parentheses can be used to shape the phrase still better:

(St. John's OR Conception Bay) AND cod NOT comedy

### Plus and Minus Signs

In some engines (e.g., Excite), **plus** and **minus** signs can be used to require or exclude a word: +*cat* –*wild* requests results that definitely contain the exact word "cat" and definitely do not contain the exact word "wild."

### Truncating

Some search engines use **wildcards** to find variations of a keyword. A symbol, commonly an asterisk, is used; e.g., librar* to find library, libraries, librarian, librarianship, etc. Other search engines such as *Excite* automatically look for these variations.

Truncation is very useful for any keywords that have multiple relevant endings:

universit* for university and universities
(retain as much of the original as possible to avoid mismatches)
univers* would get the above, but also universe, universal, etc.)
feminis* for feminism and feminist and feminists
(femini* would fetch the above, but also feminine and femininity)

Some databases offer additional ways of shaping a search, such as naming a particular publication year. Check the home page or main menu for links to a help screen.

## Books

Scholarly books often are useful in providing both breadth and depth of coverage of a subject. Because they generally are published at least a year or two after the events treated, they also tend to provide the critical distance that is sometimes missing from articles. (Of course, books also may be shallow, inaccurate, outdated, or hopelessly biased; for help in making such determinations, see *Book Review Digest*, below.) You can locate relevant books through the library catalogue. When using this catalogue, you may search in four ways: (1) by *author*, (2) by *title*, and (3) by *subject* and, in the online version, (4) by *word* or *keyword*. Entries include the call number (a classification number printed on the spine of the book that determines where the book will be located in the library), the publication information, and frequently, a summary of the book's contents. Larger libraries use the Library of Congress (LOC) cataloguing system for call numbers (example: E111/C6); smaller ones use the Dewey Decimal System (example: 970.015/C726). For a full listing of the LOC classification categories and their corresponding call numbers, see the website at **kcweb.loc.gov**, where you will also find a tutorial on how to decipher the call number.

### BOOK REVIEW DIGEST

Perhaps the best way to determine the reliability and credibility of a book you may want to use is to look it up in the annual *Book Review Digest*. These volumes list (alphabetically by author) the most significant books published during the year, supply a brief description of each, and, most importantly, provide excerpts from (and references to) reviews. If a book receives bad reviews, you don't necessarily have to avoid it (the book still may have something useful to offer, and the review itself may be unreliable). But you should take any negative reaction into account when using that book as a source.

## Periodicals: Popular Press

### MAGAZINES

Because many more periodical articles than books are published every year, you are likely (depending on the subject) to find more information in periodicals than in books. By their nature, periodical articles tend to be more current than books (the best way, for example, to find out about the federal government's current policy on welfare reform is to look for articles in periodicals and newspapers). However, periodical articles may have less critical distance than books, and they also may date more rapidly—to be superseded by more recent articles.

General periodicals (such as *Maclean's* and *Saturday Night*) are intended for non-specialists. Their articles, which tend to be highly readable, may be written by staff writers, freelancers, or specialists. But usually they do not provide citations or other indications of sources and so are of limited usefulness for scholarly research, beyond giving you ideas for topics to research in scholarly journals.

Professors often require that you use only scholarly articles as sources for research essays.

Increasingly, the whole texts or at least abstracts of articles are available in online databases, such as CBCA, EBSCOhost, ProQuest, and JStor. These texts may be downloaded to your computer or a diskette, printed, or e-mailed to your e-mail address.

NEWSPAPERS

News stories, features, and editorials (even letters to the editor) may be important sources of information. Your library website may provide a link to the
*Canadian News Disk* database, which offers access to newspaper articles
written since 1998; it may provide The *Globe and Mail* index, and indexes to
other important newspapers, such as the *New York Times* and the *Christian
Science Monitor*. Current editions of most major newspapers are available
online, either by going directly to the website for the particular newspaper, or
by going to the *American Journalism Review* website at **ajr.newslink.org/
news.html** and following the links. New items can also be found by linking to
the news category that is found on the home page of many search engines such
as Hotbot and Excite: check to see if you can broaden the search to the past
week or month. If newspaper holdings are on microfilm, you will need to use
a microprinter/viewer to get hard copies.

As an alternative to print-based news providers, check out the online version of news channels such as CNN (**www.cnn.com**), CBC (**www.cbc.ca**), and
Canadian Aboriginal (**www.canadianaboriginal.com**).

## Periodicals: Scholarly Press

JOURNALS

Many professors will expect at least some of your research to be based on articles in specialized scholarly periodicals, which are commonly called journals
instead of magazines. So instead of (or in addition to) relying on an article
from the popular press magazine *Psychology Today* for an account of the
effects of crack cocaine on mental functioning, you might (also) rely on an
article from the *Journal of Abnormal Psychology*. If you are writing a paper
on the satirist Jonathan Swift, you may need to locate a relevant article in
*Eighteenth-Century Studies*. Articles in such journals normally are written by
specialists and professionals in the field, rather than by staff writers or freelancers, and the authors will assume that their readers already understand the
basic facts and issues concerning the subject.

To find articles in specialized periodicals, you'll use specialized indexes—
that is, indexes for particular scholarly disciplines. As explained earlier, many
indexes are now available online or onsite at university library computers and
often include *abstracts* or summaries of the articles listed. Abstracts can save
you a lot of time in determining which articles you should read and which
ones you can safely skip.

## Other Sources/Government Publications

You also may find useful information in other sources. For current informa-
tion on a subject as of a given year, consult an *almanac* (example: *World
Almanac*). For annual updates of information, consult a *yearbook* (example:
*The Statesman's Yearbook*). For maps and other geographic information,

consult an *atlas* (example: *New York Times Atlas of the World*). (Often, simply browsing through the reference shelves for data on your general subject—such as biography, public affairs, psychology—will reveal valuable sources of information.) And of course, much reference information is available on government sites on the Web.

Many libraries keep pamphlets in a *vertical file* (i.e., a file cabinet). For example, a pamphlet on AIDS might be found in the vertical file, rather than in the library stacks. Such material is accessible through the *Vertical File Index* (a monthly subject and title index to pamphlet material).

## The World Wide Web

The *Web* offers "hyperlinks" to related material in numerous sources. To access these sources, you can either browse (i.e., follow your choice of paths or links wherever they lead) or type in a site's address.

For example, to get information on recent employment statistics, you could go to the StatsCan or Human Resources and Development website and follow the links to the statistics of interest to you.

To search for Web information on a particular topic, try using one of the more popular *search engines:*

*Northern Lights:* **www.nlsearch.com/**
*Yahoo:* **www.yahoo.com/**
*AltaVista:* **altavista.digital.com/**
*Lycos:* **www-att.lycos.com/**
*Google:* **google.com**

And remember, if at first you don't succeed, revise your search and/or try another search engine.

### THE BENEFITS AND THE PITFALLS OF THE WORLD WIDE WEB

In the late nineties, the Web became not just a research tool, but a cultural phenomenon. The pop artist Andy Warhol once said that in the future everyone would be famous for 15 minutes. He might have added that everyone would also have a personal website. People use the Web not just to look up information, but also to shop, to make contact with long-lost friends and relatives, to grind their personal or corporate axes, to advertise themselves and their accomplishments.

The Web makes it possible for people sitting at home, work, or school to gain access to the resources of large libraries, and to explore corporate and government databases. In her informative book *The Research Paper and the World Wide Web*, Dawn Rodrigues quotes Bruce Dobler and Harry Bloomberg on the essential role of the Web in modern research:

> It isn't a matter anymore of using computer searches to locate existing documents buried in some far off library or archive. The Web is providing documents and resources that simply would be too expensive to publish on paper or CD-ROM.

Right now—and not in some distant future—doing research without looking for resources on the Internet is, in most cases, not really looking hard enough. . . . A thorough researcher cannot totally avoid the Internet and the Web.[2]

And indeed, websites are increasingly showing up as sources on both student and professional papers. But like any other rapidly growing and highly visible cultural phenomenon, the Web has created its own backlash. First, as anyone who has tried it knows, systematically searching the Web is not possible on some subjects. For all the information that is on the Internet, there's a great deal more that has not been and may never be converted to digital format. The *Globe and Mail* is available on the Web, but the online edition includes only a fraction of the content of the print edition, and online versions of the articles generally are abridged.

Moreover, locating what *is* available is not always easy, since there's no standardized method—like the Library of Congress subheading and call number system—of cataloguing and cross-referencing online information. The tens of thousands of websites and millions of Web pages, together with the relative crudity of search engines such as Yahoo, AltaVista, and WebCrawler, have made navigating an ever-expanding cyberspace an often daunting and frustrating procedure.

Second, it is not a given that people who do research on the Web will produce better papers as a result. David Rothenberg, a professor of philosophy at New Jersey Institute of Technology, believes that "his students' papers had declined in quality since they began using the Web for research" (Steven R. Knowlton, "Students Lost in Cyberspace," *Chronicle of Higher Education*, 2 Nov. 1997: 21). Neil Gabler, a cultural critic, writes:

> The Internet is such a huge receptacle of rumor, half-truth, misinformation and disinformation that the very idea of objective truth perishes in the avalanche. All you need to create a "fact" in the web world is a bulletin board or chat room. Gullible cybernauts do the rest.[3]

Another critic is even blunter: "Much of what purports to be serious information is simply junk—neither current, objective, nor trustworthy. It may be impressive to the uninitiated, but it is clearly not of great use to scholars."[4]

Of course, print sources are not necessarily objective or reliable either, and in Chapter 6, under "Critical Reading," we discuss some criteria by which readers may evaluate the quality of information and ideas in *any* source (pp. 127–141). Web sources, however, present a special problem. In most cases, material destined for print has to go through one or more editors and fact checkers before being published, since most authors don't have the resources to

---

[2] Galen and Latchaw, 1997.

[3] "Why Let Truth Get in the Way of a Good Story?" *Los Angeles Times*, "Opinion," 26 Oct. 1997: 1.

[4] William Miller, "Troubling Myths About On-Line Information," *Chronicle of Higher Education*, 1 Aug. 1997: A44.

publish and distribute their own writing. But anyone with a computer and a modem can "publish" on the Web; and those with a good Web authoring program and graphics software can create sites that, outwardly, at least, look just as professional and authoritative as those of the top academic, government, and business sites. These personal sites will appear in search engine listings—generated through keyword matches, rather than through independent assessments of quality or relevance—and uncritical researchers, using their information as a factual basis for the claims they make in their papers, do so at their peril.

We certainly don't mean to discourage Web research. There are thousands of excellent sites in cyberspace. The websites of most university libraries will provide lists of such sites, arranged by discipline, and the most useful sites also are listed in the research sections of many handbooks. Most people locate websites, however, by using search engines and by "surfing" the hyperlinks. And for Web sources, more than print sources from university libraries, where professional librarians and faculty have selected the titles to be purchased by the library, the warning *caveat emptor*—let the buyer beware—applies. There are solid scholarly documents on the Web, and very often they are published on a scholarly website such as an online journal, which gives you some confidence that they are appropriate research sources. If you find documents on non-scholarly sites, you need to be able to figure out on your own whether they are appropriate.

In their extremely useful site "Evaluating Web Resources" (**www. science.widener.edu~withers/webeval.htm**), reference librarians Jan Alexander and Marsha Tate offer some important guidelines for assessing Web sources. First, they point out, it's important to determine what *type* of Web page you are dealing with. Web pages generally fall into one of six types, each with a different purpose: (1) entertainment, (2) business/marketing, (3) reference/information, (4) news, (5) advocacy of a particular point of view or program, (6) personal page. The purpose of the page—informing, selling, persuading, entertaining—has a direct bearing upon the objectivity and reliability of the information presented.

Second, when evaluating a page, one should apply the same general criteria as are applied to print sources: (1) accuracy, (2) authority, (3) objectivity, (4) currency, (5) coverage. As we've noted, when assessing the *accuracy* of a Web page, it's important to consider the likelihood that its information has been checked by anyone other than the author. When assessing the *authority* of the page, one considers the qualifications of the author to write on the subject and the reputability of the publisher. In many cases, it's difficult to determine not just the qualifications, but the very identity of the author. When assessing the *objectivity* of a Web page, one considers the bias on the part of the author or authors and the extent to which the authors are trying to sway the opinion of their readers. Many Web pages passing themselves off as informational are in fact little more than "infomercials." When assessing the *currency* of a Web page, one asks whether the content is up-to-date and whether the publication date is labelled clearly. Dates on Web pages often are missing or are not indicated clearly. If a date is provided, does it refer to the date the page was written, the date it was placed on the Web, or the date it was last revised? Finally, when assessing the *coverage* of a Web page, one considers what topics are included (and not included) in the work and whether the topics are covered in depth. Depth of coverage has generally not been a hall-mark of Web information.

Other pitfalls of websites: Reliable sites may include links to other sites that are inaccurate or outdated. Web pages also are notoriously unstable, frequently changing or even disappearing without notice.

Finally, the ease with which it's possible to surf the Internet can encour-age intellectual laziness and make researchers too dependent upon Web resources. Professors are increasingly seeing papers largely or even entirely based upon information from non-scholarly websites when stronger, more rel-evant print sources were readily available in the library (or from links on the library website). While Web sources are indeed an important new source of otherwise unavailable information, there's often no substitute for library or other research, such as interviews or field study. The vast majority of printed material in even a small college or university library—much of it essential to informed research—does not appear on the Web, nor is it likely to in the near future. Much of the material you will research in the next few years remains bound within covers. You may well learn of its existence through electronic search engines, but at some point you'll probably need to pull out a book or journal, and turn printed pages.

## ■ EXERCISE: ASSESSING THE SCHOLARLY STRENGTH OF WEB DOCUMENTS

Find a Web document that addresses a topic you are currently researching and assess its strength as a credible secondary source for an essay that requires scholarly references. You should be prepared to explain your assessment in terms of the apparent purpose of the article and of the five criteria for schol-arly strength discussed in this chapter: accuracy, authority, objectivity, cur-rency, and coverage.

## Interviews and Surveys

Depending on the subject of your paper, some or all of your research may be conducted outside the library. You may pursue primary research in science labs, in courthouses, in city government files, in shopping malls (if you are observing, say, patterns of consumer behaviour), in the quad in front of the humanities building, or in front of TV screens (if you are analyzing, say, situ-ation comedies or commercials, or if you are drawing on documentaries or interviews—in which cases you should try to obtain transcripts or tape the programs). Whenever your research involves people instead of texts, you need to determine what ethical guidelines your university requires you to follow to ensure confidentiality, informed consent, and anonymity.

You may want to *interview* your professors, your fellow students, or other individuals knowledgeable about your subject. Before interviewing your subject(s), become knowledgeable enough about the topic that you can ask intelligent questions. You also should prepare most of your questions before-hand. Ask "open-ended" questions designed to elicit meaningful responses, rather than "forced choice" questions that can be answered with a word or two, or "leading questions" that presume a particular answer. (Example: Instead of asking, "Do you think that men should be more sensitive to women's concerns for equality in the workplace?" ask, "To what extent do you see evidence that men are insufficiently sensitive to women's concerns for equality in the workplace?") Ask follow-up questions to elicit additional insights or details. If you record the interview (in addition to or instead of taking notes), get your subject's permission, preferably in writing.

*Surveys* or *questionnaires*, when well prepared, can produce valuable information about the ideas or preferences of a group of people. Before preparing your questions, determine your purpose in conducting the survey, exactly what kind of information you want to obtain, and whom you are going to ask for the information. Decide also whether you want to collect the questionnaires as soon as people have filled them out or whether you want the responses mailed back to you. (Obviously, in the latter case, you have to provide stamped, self-addressed envelopes and specify a deadline for return.) Keep in mind that the larger and the more representative your sample of people, the more reliable the survey. As with interviews, it's important to devise and word questions carefully, so that they (1) are understandable and (2) don't reflect your own biases. If you're surveying attitudes on capital punishment, for example, and you ask, "Do you believe that the state should endorse legalized murder?" you've loaded the questions to influence people to answer in the negative, and thus you've destroyed the reliability of your survey.

Unlike interview questions, survey questions should be short answer or multiple choice; open-ended questions encourage responses that are difficult to quantify. (You may want to leave space, however, for "additional comments.") Conversely, "yes" or "no" responses or rankings on a 5-point scale are easy to quantify. For example, you might ask a random sample of students in the cafeteria the extent to which they are concerned that genetic information about themselves might be made available to their insurance companies—on a scale of 1 (unconcerned) to 5 (extremely concerned). For surveys on certain subjects (and depending on the number of respondents), it may be useful to break out the responses by as many meaningful categories as possible—for example, gender, sexual orientation, age, ethnicity, religion, education, geographic locality, profession, and income. Obtaining these kinds of statistical breakdowns, of course, means more work on the part of your respondents in filling out the surveys and more work for you in compiling the responses. If the survey is too long and involved, some subjects won't participate or won't return the questionnaires.

# FROM RESEARCH TO WORKING THESIS

The search strategy we've just described isn't necessarily a straight-line process. In other words, you won't always proceed from the kinds of things you do in "preliminary research" to the kinds of things you do in "focused research." You may not formulate a research question until you've done a good deal of focused research. And the fact that we've treated, say, book sources before specialized periodical articles does not mean that you should read books before you read articles. We've described the process as we have for convenience; and, *in general*, it is a good idea to proceed from more general sources to more particular ones. In practice, however, the research procedure often is considerably less systematic. You might begin, for example, by reading a few articles on the subject, continue by looking up an encyclopedia article or two. Along the way, you might consult specialized dictionaries, book review indexes, and a guide to reference books in the area. Or, instead of proceeding in a straight line though the process, you might find yourself moving in circular patterns—backtracking to previous steps and following up leads you missed or ignored earlier. There's nothing wrong with such variations of the basic search strategy, as long as you keep in mind the kinds of resources that are available to you, and as long as you plan to look up as many of these resources as you can—given the constraints on your time.

One other thing you'll discover as you proceed: Research is to some extent a self-generating process. That is, one source will lead you—through references in the text, citations, and bibliographic entries—to others. Your authors will refer to other studies on the subject; and, frequently, they'll indicate which ones they believe are the most important, and why. At some point, if your research has been systematic, you'll realize that you've already looked at most of the key work on the subject. This is the point at which you can be reasonably assured that the research stage of your paper is nearing its end.

As your work progresses, you may find that your preliminary research question undergoes a change. Suppose you are researching bilingual education. At first, you may have been primarily interested in the question of whether bilingual education is a good idea. During your research, you come across Quebec's controversial law requiring all immigrant children to attend French school only, and you decide to shift the direction of your research toward this particular debate. Or, having made an initial assessment that bilingual education is a good idea, you conclude that the idea is desirable but unworkable. Be prepared for such shifts: They're a natural—and desirable— part of the research (and learning) process. They indicate that you haven't made up your mind in advance, that you're open to new evidence and ideas.

You're now ready to respond to your modified research questions with a *working thesis*—a statement that controls and focuses your entire paper, points toward your conclusion, and is supported by your evidence. See our earlier discussion, in Chapter 1 (pp. 6–10), on the process of devising and narrowing a thesis.

# THE WORKING BIBLIOGRAPHY

As you conduct your research, keep a working bibliography—that is, a set of bibliographic information on all the sources you're likely to use in preparing the paper. Compile full bibliographic information as you consider each source. It's better to spend time during the research process noting information on a source you don't eventually use than to have to go back to the library to retrieve information—such as the publisher or the date—just as you're typing your final draft.

An efficient way to compile bibliographic information is on 3" × 5" cards or on a word processor. You can easily add, delete, and rearrange sources as your research progresses. For each source record:

A.  the author or editor (last name first)
B.  the title (and subtitle) of the book or article
C.  the publisher and place of publication (if a book) or the title of the periodical
D.  the date of publication; if periodical, volume and issue number
E.  the inclusive page numbers (if article)
F.  the Web address and date you read it (if a Web document)

You also may want to include the following:

G.  a brief description of the source (to help you recall it later in the research process)
H.  the library call number (to help you relocate the source if you haven't checked it out)
I.  a code word or number, which you can use as a shorthand reference to the source in your notecards

Your final bibliography, known as "Works Cited" in Modern Language Association (MLA) format and "References" in American Psychological Association (APA) format, consists of the sources you have actually summarized, paraphrased, or quoted in your paper, arranged in alphabetical order.

Here is an example of a working bibliography card for a book:

---

*Sale, Kirkpatrick. The Conquest of Paradise: Christopher Columbus and the Columbian Legacy. New York: Knopf, 1990.*

*Attacks Columbian legacy for genocide and ecocide. Good treatment of Columbus's voyages (Chaps. 6–8).*

---

Here is an example of a working bibliography card for an article:

---

*Axtell, James. "Europeans, Indians and the Age of Discovery in American History Textbooks." <u>American Historical Review</u>, 92.3 (1987), 621–32.*

*Finds treatments of subjects in title of article inadequate in most university-level American history texts. Specific "errors," "half-truths" and "misleading assertions." Recommends changes in nine areas.*

---

Some instructors may ask you to prepare—either in addition to or instead of a research paper—an *annotated bibliography*. This is a list of relevant works on a subject, with the contents of each briefly described or assessed. The bibliography cards shown provide examples of two entries in an annotated bibliography on the Columbian legacy. Annotations are different from *abstracts* in that they do not claim to be comprehensive summaries; they indicate, rather, how the items may be useful to the prospective researcher.

## EVALUATING SOURCES

As you sift through what seems a formidable mountain of material, you'll need to work quickly and efficiently; you'll also need to do some selecting. This means, primarily, distinguishing the more important from the less important (and the unimportant) material. The hints in the box below can simplify the task.

---

### HOW TO EVALUATE SOURCES

- **Skim** the source: With a book, look over the table of contents, the introduction and conclusion, and the index; zero in on passages that your initial survey suggests are important. With an article, skim the introduction and the headings.
- Be on the alert for **references** in your sources to other important sources, particularly to sources that several authors treat as important.
- Other things being equal, the more **recent** the source, the better. Recent work often incorporates or refers to important earlier work.
- If you're considering making multiple references to a book, look up the **reviews** in the *Book Review Digest* or the *Book Review Index*. Also, check the author's credentials in a source such as *Contemporary Authors* or *Current Biography*.
- Draw on your **critical reading** skills to help you determine the reliability and value of a source (see Chapter 6).

---

# NOTE-TAKING

People have their favourite ways of note-taking. Some use cards; others use legal pads or spiral notebooks; yet others type notes into a laptop computer. We prefer computer entry or 4" × 6" cards for note-taking. Such methods have some of the same advantages as 3" × 5" cards for working bibliographies: They can easily be added to, subtracted from, and rearranged to accommodate changing organizational plans. Also, discrete pieces of information from the same source can easily be arranged (and rearranged) into subtopics—a difficult task if you have three pages of handwritten notes on an entire article.

Whatever your preferred approach, we recommend including, along with the note itself,

A. a page reference
B. a topic or subtopic label, corresponding to your outline (see below)
C. a code word or number, corresponding to the word or number assigned the source in the working bibliography

Here is a sample notecard for an article by Charles Krauthammer entitled "Hail Columbus, Dead White Male" (*Time*, May 27, 1991) and coded:

---

*Defences of Columbus (III B)*         3

*Defends Columbus against what he calls revisionist attacks. Our civilization "turned out better" than that of the Incas. "And mankind is the better for it. Infinitely better. Reason enough to honor Columbus and 1492" (74).*

---

Here is a notecard for the specialized periodical article by Axtell (see bibliography card on page 52):

---

*Problems With Textbooks (II A)*         Axtell

*American history textbooks do not give adequate coverage to the Age of Discovery. An average of only 4% of the textbook pages covering first-semester topics is devoted to the century that accounts for 30% of the time between Columbus and Reconstruction after the U.S. Civil War 300 years later. "The challenge of explaining some of the most complex, important, and interesting events in human history—the discovery of a new continent, the religious upheavals of the sixteenth century, the forging of the Spanish empire, the Columbian biological exchange, the African diaspora—all in twenty or twenty-five pages—is one that few, if any, textbook authors have met or are likely to meet" (623).*

The notecard is headed by a topic label followed by the tentative location in the paper outline where the information will be used. The number or word in the upper right corner is coded to the corresponding bibliography card. The note itself in the first card uses *summary* ("Defends Columbus against revisionist attacks") and *quotation*. The note in the second card uses *summary* (sentence 1), *paraphrase* (sentence 2), and *quotation* (sentence 3). Summary was used to condense important ideas treated in several paragraphs in the sources; paraphrase, for the important detail on textbook coverage; quotation, for particularly incisive language by the source authors. For general hints on when to use each of these three forms, see p. 123.

## ARRANGING YOUR NOTES: THE OUTLINE

Recall that your research originally was stimulated by one or more *research questions*, to which you may have made a tentative response in your *working thesis* (see p. 7). As you proceed with your research, patterns should begin to emerge that substantiate, refute, or otherwise affect your working thesis. These patterns represent the relationships you discern among the various ideas and pieces of evidence that you investigate. They may be patterns of cause and effect, of chronology, of logical relationships, of comparison and contrast, of pro and con, of correspondence (or lack of correspondence) between theory and reality. Once these patterns begin to emerge, write them down as the components of a preliminary outline. This outline indicates the order in which you plan to support your original working thesis or a new thesis that you have developed during the course of research.

For example, on deciding to investigate new genetic technologies, you devise a working thesis focused on the intensity of the debate over the applications of such technologies. Much of the debate, you discover, focuses on arguments about the morality of (1) testing for genetic abnormalities in the fetus, (2) using genetic information to screen prospective employees, and (3) disrupting the ecosystem by creating new organisms. Based on this discovery, you might create a brief outline, numbering each of these three main categories (as examples of the pro-con debates) and using these numbers on your notecards to indicate how you have (at least provisionally) categorized each note. As you continue your research, you'll be able to expand or reduce the scope of your paper, modifying your outline as necessary. Your developing outline becomes a guide to continuing research.

Some people prefer not to develop an outline until they have more or less completed their research. At that point they will look over their notecards, consider the relationships among the various pieces of evidence, possibly arrange their cards into separate piles, and then develop an outline based on their perceptions and insights about the material. They will then rearrange (and code) the notecards to conform to their newly created outline.

In the past, instructors commonly required students to develop multi-levelled formal outlines (complete with Roman and Arabic numerals) before writing their first drafts. But many writers find it difficult to generate papers from such elaborate outlines, which sometimes restrict, rather than stimulate, thought. Now, many instructors recommend only that students prepare an *informal outline*, indicating just the main sections of the paper, and possibly one level below that. Thus, a paper on how the significance of Columbus's legacy has changed over the years may be informally outlined as follows:

```
Intro: Different views of Columbus, past and present;
    —thesis: view of Columbus varies with temper of
    times
Pre-20th-century assessments of Columbus and legacy
The debate over the quincentennial in 1992
    —positive views
    —negative views
Conclusion: How to assess Columbian heritage
```

Such an outline will help you organize your research and should not be unduly restrictive as a guide to writing.

The *formal outline* (a multi-levelled plan with Roman and Arabic numerals, capital- and small-lettered subheadings) may still be useful, not so much as an exact blueprint for composition—although some writers do find it useful for this purpose—but rather as a guide to revision. That is, *after* you have written your draft, outlining it may help you discern structural problems: illogical sequences of material; confusing relationships between ideas; poor unity or coherence; sections that are too abstract or underdeveloped. Some instructors also require that formal outlines accompany the finished research paper to show that you have tested the logical flow of your essay.

The formal outline should indicate the logical relationships in the evidence relating to your particular subject (see example below). But it also may reflect the general conventions of presenting academic ideas. Thus, after an *introduction*, papers in the social sciences often proceed with a description of the *methods* of collecting information, continue with a description of the *results* of the investigation, and end with a *conclusion*. Papers in the sciences often follow a similar pattern. Papers in the humanities generally are less standardized in form. In devising a logical organization for your paper, ask yourself how your reader might best be introduced to the subject, be guided through a discussion of the main issues, and be persuaded that your viewpoint is a sound one.

Formal outlines are generally of two types: *topic* and *sentence outlines*. In the topic outline, headings and subheadings are indicated by words or phrases —as in the informal outline above. In the sentence outline, each heading and subheading are indicated in a complete sentence, making the logical flow of the whole evident. Both types are generally preceded by the thesis statement.

Here is an example of a sentence outline:

*Thesis*: How Columbus, his voyages, and his legacy are assessed varies, depending on the values of the times.

   I. Early 19th-century and late 20th-century assessments of Columbus are 180 degrees apart.

     A. 19th-century commentators idolize him.

     B. 20th-century commentators often demonize him.

     C. Shifting assessments are based less on hard facts about Columbus than on the values of the culture that assesses him.

  II. In the 16th and 17th centuries, Columbus was not yet being used for political purposes.

     A. In the early 16th century, his fame was eclipsed by that of others.

       1. Amerigo Vespucci and Vasco da Gama were considered more successful mariners.

       2. Cortés and Pizarro were more successful in bringing back wealth from the New World.

     B. In the next century, historians and artists began writing of the achievements of Columbus, but without an overt political purpose.

       1. The first biography of Columbus was written by his son Fernando.

       2. Plays about Columbus were written by Lope de Vega and others.

     C. An important exception was that in 1542 the monk Bartolomé de las Casas attacked the Spanish legacy in the Americas—although he did not attack Columbus personally.

 III. In the 18th and 19th centuries, Columbus and his legacy began to be used for political purposes.

     A. During the late 18th century, Columbus's stature in North America increased as part of the attempt to stir up anti-British sentiment.

       1. Columbus was opposed by kings, since he "discovered" a land free of royal authority.

       2. Columbus, the bold visionary who charted unknown territories, became symbolic of the American spirit.

    B. During the 19th century, Columbus's reputation reached its peak.
       1. For some, Columbus represented geographical and industrial expansion, optimism, and faith in progress.
       2. For others, Columbus's success was the archetypal rags-to-riches story at the heart of the American Dream.
       3. After the U.S. Civil War, Catholics celebrated Columbus as an ethnic hero.
       4. The 400th anniversary of Columbus's landfall both celebrated the past and expressed confidence in the future. Columbus became the symbol of American industrial success.

IV. By the quincentennial of Columbus's landfall, the negative assessments of Columbus were far more evident than positive assessments.
    A. Historians and commentators charged that the consequences of Columbus's "discoveries" were imperialism, slavery, genocide, and ecocide.
    B. The National Council of Churches published a resolution blasting the Columbian legacy.
    C. Kirkpatrick Sale's *The Conquest of Paradise* also attacked Columbus.
    D. Native Americans and others protested the quincentennial and planned counter-demonstrations.

V. Conclusion: How should we judge Columbus?
    A. In many ways, Columbus was a man of his time and did not rise above his time.
    B. In his imagination and boldness and in the impact of his discoveries, Columbus stands above others of his time.
    C. When we assess Columbus and his legacy, we also assess our confidence in American culture, our optimism about it, and our faith in "progress."

# WRITING THE DRAFT

Your goal in drafting your paper is to support your thesis by clearly and logically presenting your evidence—evidence that you summarize, critique, and synthesize. (For an overview of the techniques of summary, critique, and synthesis, see Chapters 5, 6, and 7.) In effect, you are creating and moderating a conversation among your sources that supports the conclusions you have drawn from your exploration and analysis of the material. The finished paper, however, should not merely represent an amalgam of your sources; it should present your own particular critical perspective on the subject. Just as in personal writing, your own voice should remain prominent (though the "sound" of your voice should be suitable to the occasion). Your job is to select and arrange your material in such a way that your conclusions seem inevitable (or at least reasonable). You also must select and arrange your material in a way that is fair and logical. Try not to be guilty of such logical fallacies as hasty generalization, false analogy, and either/or reasoning (see pp. 137–138).

As we suggested in the section on introductions (pp. 16–21), when writing the first draft it's sometimes best to skip the introduction (you'll come back to it later when you have a better idea of just what's being introduced) and to start with the main body of your discussion. What do you have to tell your audience about your subject? It may help to imagine yourself sitting opposite your audience in an informal setting like the student centre, telling them what you've discovered in the course of your research, and why you think it's interesting and significant. The fact that you've accumulated a considerable body of evidence (in your notecards) to support your thesis should give you confidence in presenting your argument. Keep in mind, too, that there's no one right way to organize this argument; any number of ways will work, provided each makes logical sense. And if you're working on a computer, it is easy to move whole paragraphs and sections from one place to another.

Begin the drafting process by looking at your notes. Arrange the notes to correspond to your outline. Summarize, paraphrase, and quote from your notes as you draft. If necessary, review the material on explanatory and argument syntheses (pp. 157–196). In particular, note the table "How to Write Syntheses" (pp. 155–156 and **inside back cover**) and "Developing and Organizing the Support for Your Arguments" (pp. 193–199). When presenting your argument, consider such rhetorical strategies as counterargument, concession, and comparison and contrast. The sample student papers in the synthesis chapter may serve as models for your own research paper.

As you work through your notecards, be selective. Don't provide more evidence or discussion than you need to prove your point. Resist the urge to use *all* of your material just to show how much research you've done. (One experienced teacher, Susan M. Hubbuch, scornfully refers to papers with too much information as "memory dumps"—consisting of nothing but "mindless regurgitation of everything you have read about a subject.") Also avoid going into extended discussions of what are essentially tangential issues. Keep focused on your research questions and on providing support for your thesis.

At the same time, remember that you *are* working on a rough draft—one that will probably have all kinds of problems, from illogical organization to awkward sentence structure to a banal conclusion. Don't worry about it; you can deal with all such problems in subsequent drafts. The important thing now is to get the words on paper (or on your disk).

# 4

# Documenting Sources

Documentation of outside sources is the most immediately identifiable footprint of scholarly work. Commonly understood as a courtesy or perhaps legality by which we acknowledge our indebtedness to other writers, documentation is actually far more important than that: It is the system by which we anchor our claims in the existing body of worldwide scholarship on the topic. By making use of other scholars' work, we ensure that our own work builds from where we are now rather than reinventing the wheel. By documenting our use of others' work, we provide assurance to our own readers that we have drawn on sources that followed sound scholarly method, and we give them the means to trace our research back to our original sources. Documentation is a scholar's way of saying, "You can trust my claims. I didn't just make this stuff up." Acknowledging debts is the least we are doing in that gesture—it's the scholarly equivalent of putting your shoes on before you leave the house. However, it is also completely compulsory.

## AVOIDING PLAGIARISM

Plagiarism generally is defined as the attempt to pass off the work of another as one's own. Whether born out of calculation or desperation, plagiarism is the least tolerated offence in the academic world. The fact that most plagiarism is unintentional—arising from ignorance of conventions rather than deceitfulness—makes no difference to many professors.

You can avoid plagiarism and charges of plagiarism by following the basic rules below:

### RULES TO AVOID PLAGIARISM

- Cite (a) *all* quoted material and (b) *all* summarized and paraphrased material, unless the information is common knowledge (e.g., Pierre Elliott Trudeau was Prime Minister of Canada during the 1970s).
- Make sure that both the *wording* and the *sentence structure* of your summaries and paraphrases are substantially your own.

Following is a passage of text about Joseph R. McCarthy, the U.S. senator who led an inquisition-style purging of suspected Communists from government, education, and the film industry during the Cold War in the 1950s, along with several student versions of the ideas represented. (The passage is from Richard Rovere's April 30, 1967, *New York Times Magazine* article, "The Most Gifted and Successful Demagogue This Country Has Ever Known.")

> McCarthy never seemed to believe in himself or in anything he had said. He knew that Communists were not in charge of American foreign policy. He knew that they weren't running the United States Army. He knew that he had spent five years looking for Communists in the government and that—although some must certainly have been there, since Communists had turned up in practically every other major government in the world—he hadn't come up with even one.

One student version of this passage reads as follows:

```
McCarthy never believed in himself or in anything he
had said. He knew that Communists were not in charge of
American foreign policy and weren't running the United
States Army. He knew that he had spent five years
looking for Communists in the government, and although
there must certainly have been some there, since
Communists were in practically every other major gov-
ernment in the world, he hadn't come up with even one.
```

Clearly, this is intentional plagiarism. The student has copied the original passage almost word for word.

Here is another version of the same passage:

```
McCarthy knew that Communists were not running U.S.
foreign policy or its Army. He also knew that although
there must have been some Communists in the U.S. gov-
ernment, he hadn't found a single one, even though he
had spent five years looking.
```

This student has attempted to put the ideas into her own words, but both the wording and the sentence structure still are so heavily dependent on the original passage that even if it *were* cited, most professors would consider it plagiarism.

In the following version, the student has sufficiently changed the wording and sentence structure, and she properly credits the information to Rovere, so that there is no question of plagiarism:

```
According to Richard Rovere, McCarthy was cynical
enough to know that Communists were running neither
the government of the United States nor its Army. He
```

```
also knew that he hadn't found a single Communist in
government, even after a lengthy search (192).
```

Remember too, that quite apart from questions of plagiarism, it is essential to quote accurately. You are not permitted to change or omit any part of a quotation without using brackets or ellipses (see pp. 120–122).

## CITING SOURCES

When you refer to or quote the work of another, you are obligated to credit or cite your source properly. There are two types of citations, and they work in tandem.

If you are writing a paper in the humanities, you probably will be expected to use the Modern Language Association (MLA) format for citation. This format is fully described in the *MLA Handbook for Writers of Research Papers*, 5th ed. (New York: Modern Language Association of America, 1998). A paper in the social sciences will probably use the American Psychological Association (APA) format. This format is fully described in the *Publication Manual of the American Psychological Association*, 5th ed. (Washington, D.C.: American Psychological Association, 2001).

In the following section, we will focus on MLA and APA styles, the ones you are most likely to use in your academic work. Keep in mind, however, that instructors often have their own preferences. Some require the documentation style specified in the *Chicago Manual of Style*, 14th ed. (Chicago: University of Chicago Press, 1993). This style is similar to the American Psychological Association style, except that publication dates are not placed within parentheses. Instructors in the sciences often follow the Council of Biology Editors (CBE) format. Or they may prefer a number format: Each source listed on the bibliography page is assigned a number, and all text references to the source are followed by the appropriate number within parentheses. Some instructors, especially in history, like the old MLA style, which calls for footnotes and endnotes. Check with your instructor for the preferred documentation format if this is not specified in the assignment itself.

---

### TYPES OF CITATIONS

- Citations that indicate the source of quotations, paraphrases, and summarized information and ideas—these citations appear *in text*, within parentheses, like this: (Zhang 193).
- Citations that appear in an alphabetical list of "Works Cited" or "References" following the paper. These give the full details for all the sources cited in the essay.

## In-Text Citation

Because it involves interrupting your essay to insert information in a pair of brackets, the general rule for in-text citation is to make the interruption as brief as possible. Include only enough information to alert the reader to the source of the reference and to the location within that source. Normally, this information includes the author's last name and page number. But if you have already named the author in the preceding text, and have not named any other author since, just the page number is sufficient.

## Content Notes

Most citation styles use in-text citations instead of endnotes or footnotes, but occasionally, you may want to provide a footnote or an endnote as a *content* note—one that provides additional information bearing on or illuminating, but not directly related to, the discussion at hand. For example:

[1] Equally well known is Forster's distinction between story and plot: in the former, the emphasis is on sequence ("the king died and then the queen died"); in the latter, the emphasis is on causality ("the king died and then the queen died of grief").

Content notes are numbered consecutively throughout the paper; do not begin renumbering on each page. This and other details are handled automatically by the endnote or footnote function in most word processors.

## References Page

In MLA format, your list of sources is called "Works Cited." In APA format, it is called "References." Entries in this listing should be double-spaced, with second and subsequent lines of each entry indented—five spaces; use the "hanging indent" function in the paragraph format menu of your word processor. In both styles, a single space follows the period or colon.

### MLA AND APA COMPARED

- In MLA style, the date of the publication follows the name of the publisher at the very end of the item; in APA style, the date is placed within parentheses immediately following the author's name.
- In APA style, only the initial of the author's first name is indicated. In MLA style, the full name is given.
- In APA style, only the first word (and any proper noun) of a book or article title and subtitle is capitalized. In MLA style, all the words following the first word (except articles and prepositions) are capitalized; in APA, only journal titles are capitalized this way. The first letter of any word after the colon in a title is capitalized in both styles.

- For APA style, do *not* place quotation marks around journal/magazine article titles. Do use "p." and "pp." to indicate page numbers of newspaper articles.
- In both MLA and APA styles, publishers' names should be abbreviated; thus, "Random House" becomes "Random"; "William Morrow" becomes "Morrow."
- While the hanging indent (second and subsequent lines indented) is the recommended format for APA style references in student papers, manuscripts intended for publication follow paragraph indent format in which the first line of each reference is indented.

*Note:* In both MLA and APA format, italicized titles may be underlined instead (though the latter is becoming less common).

Provided below are some of the most commonly used citations in both MLA and APA formats. For a more complete listing, consult the MLA *Handbook,* the APA *Manual,* or whichever style guide your instructor has specified.

## MLA STYLE

### In-Text Citation

Here are sample in-text citations using the MLA system:

> From the beginning, the AIDS antibody test has been "mired in controversy" (Bayer 101).

If you have already mentioned the author's name in the text, it is not necessary to repeat it in the citation:

> According to Bayer, from the beginning, the AIDS antibody test has been "mired in controversy" (101).

In MLA format, you must supply page numbers for summaries and paraphrases, as well as for quotations:

> According to Bayer, the AIDS antibody test has been controversial from the outset (101).

Notice that in the MLA system there is no punctuation between the author's name and the page number. Notice also that the parenthetical reference is placed *before* the final punctuation of the sentence unless it refers to more than one preceding sentence. In such cases, the citation follows the period ending the last paraphrased sentence, and it is your responsibility to make clear how many of the preceding sentences are involved. For example, you might use the source author's name at the beginning of the paraphrased material and use signal phrases ("she argues," "she goes on to say") to make it easy for the reader to identify all paraphrased material.

For block (indented) quotations, however, always place the parenthetical citation *after* the period:

> Amit Srivastava points towards troubling developments in her account of a recent visit to Canada:
>> Flying in from the San Francisco area where I live, I was on my way to give a speech about human rights and the environment in Calgary. I didn't get past the immigration desk. (A25)

If the reference applies only to the first part of the sentence, the parenthetical reference is inserted at the appropriate point *within* the sentence:

> While Baumrind argues that "the laboratory is not the place to study degree of obedience" (421), Milgram asserts that such arguments are groundless.

There are times when you must modify the basic author/page number reference. Depending on the nature of your sources, you may need to use one of the following citation formats:

QUOTED MATERIAL APPEARING IN ANOTHER SOURCE

(qtd. in Milgram 211)

AN ANONYMOUS WORK

("Obedience" 32)

TWO AUTHORS

(Woodward and Bernstein 208)

A PARTICULAR WORK BY AN AUTHOR, WHEN YOU LIST TWO OR MORE WORKS BY THAT AUTHOR IN THE "WORKS CITED"

(Butler, *Bodies*, 96–97)

TWO OR MORE SOURCES AS THE BASIS OF YOUR STATEMENT (ARRANGE ENTRIES IN ALPHABETIC ORDER OF SURNAME)

(Giannetti 189; Sklar 194)

**A Multi-volume Work**

> (2: 88) [volume: page number]

**The Location of a Passage in a Literary Text**

> (224; ch. 7) [Page 224 in the edition used by the writer; the chapter number, 7, is provided for the convenience of those referring to another edition.]

**The Location of a Passage in a Play**

> (1.2.308–22) [act.scene.line number(s)]

**The Bible**

> (1 Chron. 21.8) [book.chapter.verse]

## In-Text Citation of Electronic Sources (MLA)

Websites, CD-ROM data, and e-mail generally do not have numbered pages. Different browsers may display and printers may produce differing numbers of pages for any particular site. You should therefore omit both page numbers and paragraph numbers from in-text citations to electronic sources, unless these page or paragraph numbers are provided within the source itself.

## Examples of MLA Citations in "Works Cited" List

## Books (MLA)

**One Author**

> Rose, Mike. *Lives on the Boundary.* New York: Penguin, 1989.

**Two or More Books by the Same Author**

> Butler, Judith. *Bodies That Matter: On the Discursive Limits of "Sex."* New York: Routledge, 1993.
> ——. *Gender Trouble: Feminism and the Subversion of Identity.* New York: Routledge, 1990.
>
> *Note:* For MLA style, references are listed in alphabetical order of title.

## Two Authors

Ristock, Janice and Joan Pennell. *Community Research as Empowerment: Feminist Links, Postmodern Interruptions.* Toronto: Oxford UP, 1996.

## Three Authors

Skrobanek, Siriporn, Nataya Boonpakdee, and Chutima Jantateero. *The Traffic in Women: Human Realities of the International Sex Trade.* London: Zed Books, 1997.

## More Than Three Authors

Maimon, Elaine, et al. *Writing in the Arts and Sciences.* Boston: Little, 1982.

## Book With an Editor

Sweetman, Caroline, ed. *Gender and Migration.* Oxford: Oxfam GB, 1998.

## Later Edition

Kyi, Aung San Suu. *Freedom from Fear: and Other Writings.* 2nd ed. London: Penguin Books, 1995.

## Republished Book

Lawrence, D. H. *Sons and Lovers.* 1913. New York: Signet, 1960.

## One Volume of a Multi-volume Work

Nodeco. *Hibernia Development Project Platform Construction Site: Environmental Protection Plan.* 4 vols. St. John's, Nfld.: Hibernia Management and Development Company Ltd., 1992. Vol. 1.

## Separately Titled Volume of a Multi-volume Work

Churchill, Winston. *The Age of Revolution.* Vol. 3 of *A History of the English Speaking Peoples.* New York: Dodd, 1957.

## TRANSLATION

Champlain, Samuel de. *The Voyages and Explorations
    of Samuel de Champlain, 1604-1616*. Trans. Annie
    Nettleton Bourne. Toronto: Courier Press, 1911.

## SELECTION FROM AN EDITED COLLECTION (OR ANTHOLOGY)

Ng, Roxanna. "Finding Our Voices: Reflections on
    Immigrant Women's Organizing." *Women and Social
    Change: Feminist Activism in Canada*. Ed. Jeri D.
    Wine and Janice L. Ristock. Toronto: James
    Lorimer, 1991. 184-97.

## REPRINTED MATERIAL IN AN EDITED COLLECTION

McGinnis, Wayne D. "The Arbitrary Cycle of
    *Slaughterhouse-Five*: A Relation of Form to Theme."
    *Critique: Studies in Modern Fiction* 17. 1 (1975):
    55-68. Rpt. in *Contemporary Literary Criticism*.
    Ed. Dedria Bryfonski and Phyllis Carmel Mendelson.
    Vol. 8. Detroit: Gale, 1978. 530-31.

## GOVERNMENT PUBLICATION

Canada. Health Canada. *1994 Youth Smoking Survey*.
    Ottawa: Queen's Printer, 1996.

## THE BIBLE

*The New English Bible*. New York: Oxford UP, 1972.

## SIGNED ENCYCLOPEDIA ARTICLE

Lack, David L. "Population." *Encyclopaedia
    Britannica: Macropaedia*. 1998 ed.

## UNSIGNED ENCYCLOPEDIA ARTICLE

"Louis Riel." *Canadian Encyclopedia*. Toronto:
    McClelland & Stewart. 2000 ed.

# Periodicals (MLA)

## CONTINUOUS PAGINATION THROUGHOUT ANNUAL CYCLE

Riger, Stephanie. "What's Wrong With Empowerment."
    *American Journal of Community Psychology* 21
    (1993): 279-92.

### Separate Pagination Each Issue

Rockhill, Kathleen. "The Chaos of Subjectivity in the Ordered Halls of Academe." *Canadian Woman Studies* 8.4 (1987): 12-17.

### Monthly Periodical

Rooke, Leon. "Painting the Dog." *Toronto Life* Aug. 2000: 84-87.

### Signed Article in Weekly Periodical

Krotz, Larry. "Caseload." *Saturday Night* 17 June 2000: 21-27.

### Unsigned Article in Weekly Periodical

"Notes and Comment." *New Yorker* 20 Feb. 1978: 29-32.

### Signed Article in Daily Newspaper

Landsberg, Michele. "Tory Policies Slowly Poison Public Education." *Toronto Star* 18 June 2000: A2.

### Unsigned Article in Daily Newspaper

"Report Says Crisis in Teaching Looms." *Philadelphia Inquirer* 20 Aug. 1984: A3.

### Review

Maddocks, Melvin. "A Most Famous Anthropologist." Rev. of *Margaret Mead: A Life*, by Jane Howard. *Time* 27 Aug. 1984: 57.

## Other Sources (MLA)

### Interview

Emerson, Robert. Personal interview. 10 Oct. 1998.

### Dissertation (Abstracted in Dissertation Abstracts International)

Gans, Eric L. "The Discovery of Illusion: Flaubert's Early Works, 1835-1837." *DA* 27 (1967): 3046A. Johns Hopkins U.

*Note:* If the dissertation is available on microfilm, give University Microfilms order number in parentheses at the conclusion of the reference. Example, in MLA format: "Ann Arbor; UMI, 1993. 9316566."

## LECTURE

> Rossborough, Hans. "The Great Man Theory: Caesar."
> Lecture. History 1541. University of Alberta,
> Edmonton, 5 Nov. 1999.

## PAPER DELIVERED AT A PROFESSIONAL CONFERENCE

> Worley, Joan. "Texture: The Feel of Writing."
> Conference on College Composition and
> Communication. Cincinnati, 21 Mar. 1992.

## FILM

> *Howard's End.* Dir. James Ivory. Perf. Emma Thompson
> and Anthony Hopkins. Merchant/Ivory and Film
> Four International, 1992.

## TV PROGRAM

> *Legacy of the Hollywood Blacklist.* Videocassette.
> Dir. Judy Chaikin. Written and prod. Eve
> Goldberg and Judy Chaikin, One Step Productions.
> Public Affairs TV. KCET, Los Angeles. 1987.

## RECORDING

> Beatles. "Eleanor Rigby." *The Beatles 1962-1966.*
> Capitol, 1973.
> Schumann, Robert. *Symphonies Nos. 1 & 4.* Cond.
> George Szell, Cleveland Orchestra. Columbia, 1978.

# Electronic Sources (MLA)

Full guidelines for the documentation of electronic sources in MLA and APA format can be found on Longman's *The English Pages* at **www.abacon.com/ compsite/resources/citation.html**.

In general, follow the format for analogous print sources (a journal article for an online journal article, a book for an online book). That is, put quotation marks around titles that are part of a larger website, and italicize titles of the website itself; include the names of the document author and the website editor if available. Also follow these additional guidelines:

- Follow the regular information for print sources with the URL in angle brackets and the date on which you accessed the document.
- Use the date the document was posted or updated as the publication date.
- If information such as author or date of publication or revision is missing, leave it out and go on to the next piece of information.

## A DOCUMENT ON A WEBSITE

> Burka, Lauren P. "A Hypertext History of Multi-User Dimensions." *The MUDdex*. 1993. 5 Dec. 1994 <http://www.apocalypse.org/pub/u/lpb/muddex/essay/>.

## AN ONLINE BOOK

> Whitman, Walt. *Leaves of Grass*. Philadelphia: McKay, 1891-2. *The Walt Whitman Hypertext Archive*. Ed. Kenneth M. Price and Ed Folsom. 16 Mar. 1998. 3 Apr. 1998 <http://jefferson.village.virginia.edu/whitman/works/leaves/1891/text/title.html>.

This book is an online version of one already published in print, so the full print information is given first. This is followed by the name of the website on which it appears online, the editors of the website, and the date it was published online. Finally, your date of access and the http address are given.

## AN ARTICLE IN A SCHOLARLY JOURNAL

> Jackson, Francis L. "Mexican Freedom: The Idea of the Indigenous State." *Animus* 2.3 (1997). 4 Apr. 1998 <http://www.mun.ca/animus/1997vol2/jackson2.htm>.

## A PERSONAL OR PROFESSIONAL SITE

> Winter, Mick. *How to Talk New Age*. 6 Apr. 1998. <http://www.well.com/user/mick/newagept.html>.

This entry is short because there is no print version of the web document, and some information is not available. We have only the document author's name and title of the document, followed by the access date and URL.

## ELECTRONIC PUBLICATIONS SUCH AS CDs

> Zieger, Herman E. "Aldehyde." *The Software Toolworks Multimedia Encyclopedia*. Vers. 1.5. Software Toolworks. Boston: Grolier, 1992.

In this case, the document is published on CD, not online, so city and publisher are given instead of URL, and no access date is required because the document is not subject to change.


## APA STYLE

### In-Text Citation

Here are the sample in-text citations using the APA system:

> From the beginning, the AIDS antibody test has been "mired in controversy" (Bayer, 1989, p. 101).

If you have already mentioned the author's name in the text, it is not necessary to repeat it in the citation:

> According to Bayer (1989), from the beginning, the AIDS antibody test has been "mired in controversy" (p. 101).

or:

> According to Bayer, from the beginning, the AIDS antibody test has been "mired in controversy" (1989, p. 101).

When using the APA system, provide page numbers only for direct quotations, not for summaries or paraphrases. If you do not refer to a specific page, simply indicate the date:

> Bayer (1989) reported that there are many precedents for the reporting of AIDS cases that do not unduly violate privacy.

Notice that in the APA system, there is a comma between the author's name and the page number, and the number itself is preceded by "p." or "pp." Notice also that the parenthetical reference is placed *before* the final punctuation of the sentence (except, as explained for MLA, when the reference applies to more than the one preceding sentence).

For block (indented) quotations, however, place the parenthetical citation *after* the period:

> Amit Srivastava points towards troubling developments in her account of a recent visit to Canada:
>
>> Flying in from the San Francisco area where I live, I was on my way to give a speech about human rights and the environment in Calgary. I didn't get past the immigration desk. (2000, p. A25)

If the reference applies only to the first part of the sentence, the parenthetical reference is inserted at the appropriate point *within* the sentence:

While Baumrind (1963) argued that "the laboratory is not the place to study degree of obedience" (p. 421), Milgram asserted that such arguments are groundless.

There are times when you must modify the basic author/page number reference. Depending on the nature of your source(s), you may need to use one of the following citation formats:

## QUOTED MATERIAL APPEARING IN ANOTHER SOURCE

(cited in Milgram, 1974, p. 211)

## AN ANONYMOUS WORK

("Obedience," 1974, p. 32)

## TWO AUTHORS

(Woodward and Bernstein, 1974, p. 208)

## A PARTICULAR WORK BY AN AUTHOR, WHEN YOU LIST TWO OR MORE WORKS BY THAT AUTHOR IN THE "WORKS CITED"

(Butler, 1993, pp. 96–97)

## TWO OR MORE SOURCES AS THE BASIS OF YOUR STATEMENT (ARRANGE ENTRIES IN ALPHABETIC ORDER OF SURNAME)

(Giannetti, 1972, p. 189; Sklar, 1974, p. 194)

## A MULTI-VOLUME WORK

(Vol. 2, p. 88)

# In-Text Citation of Electronic Sources (APA)

Web sites, CD-ROM data, and e-mail generally do not have numbered pages, and different printers may produce different numbers of pages for any particular site. You should therefore omit both page numbers and paragraph numbers from in-text citations to electronic sources, unless these page or paragraph numbers are provided within the source itself.

## Examples of APA Citations in "References" List

## Books (APA)

### ONE AUTHOR

> Rose, M. (1989). *Lives on the boundary.* New York:
> Penguin.

### TWO OR MORE BOOKS BY THE SAME AUTHOR

> Butler, J. (1990). *Gender trouble: Feminism and the
> subversion of identity.* New York: Routledge.
> —. (1993). *Bodies that matter: On the discursive
> limits of "sex."* New York: Routledge.
> *Note:* For APA style, references are listed in
> chronological order of publication.

### TWO AUTHORS

> Ristock, J., & Pennell, J. (1996). *Community
> research as empowerment: Feminist links, post-
> modern interruptions.* Toronto: Oxford.

### THREE AUTHORS

> Skrobanek, S., Nataya, B., & Jantateero, C. (1997).
> *The traffic in women: Human realities of the
> international sex trade.* London: Zed Books.

### MORE THAN THREE AUTHORS

> Maimon, E., Belcher, G. L., Hearn, G. W., Nodine,
> B. N., & O'Connor, F. W. (1982). *Writing in the
> arts and sciences.* Boston: Little.

### BOOK WITH AN EDITOR

> Sweetman, C. (Ed.). (1998). *Gender and Migration.*
> Oxford: Oxfam GB.

### LATER EDITION

> Kyi, A. S. (1995). *Freedom from fear and other
> writings* (2nd ed.). London: Penguin Books.

## REPUBLISHED BOOK

Lawrence, D. H. (1960). *Sons and lovers.* New York:
Signet. (Original work published 1913).

## ONE VOLUME OF A MULTI-VOLUME WORK

Nodeco. *Hibernia development project platform con-*
*struction site: Environmental protection plan.*
4 vols. St. John's, Nfld.: Hibernia Management
and Development Company Ltd., 1992. Vol 1.

## SEPARATELY TITLED VOLUME OF A MULTI-VOLUME WORK

Churchill, W. (1957). *A history of the English*
*speaking peoples: Vol. 3. The age of revolution.*
New York: Dodd.

## TRANSLATION

Champlain, S. de. (1911). *The voyages and explo-*
*rations of Samuel de Champlain, 1604–1616.* (A.
N. Bourne, Trans.). Toronto: Courier Press.

## SELECTION FROM AN EDITED COLLECTION (OR ANTHOLOGY)

Ng, Roxanna (1991). Finding our voices: Reflections
on immigrant women's organizing. In J. D. Wine
and J. L. Ristock (Eds.), *Women and social*
*change: Feminist activism in Canada (pp. 184–97).*
Toronto: James Lorimer.

## REPRINTED MATERIAL IN AN EDITED COLLECTION

McGinnis, W. D. (1975). The arbitrary cycle of
*Slaughterhouse-five*: A relation of form to
theme. In D. Bryfonski and P. C. Mendelson
(Eds.), *Contemporary literary criticism* (Vol. 8,
pp. 530–531). Detroit: Gale. Reprinted from
*Critique: Studies in modern fiction,* 1975 (Vol.
17, No. 1), pp. 55–68.

## GOVERNMENT PUBLICATION

Canada. Health Canada. (1996). *1994 youth smoking*
*survey.* Ottawa: Queen's Printer.

### SIGNED ENCYCLOPEDIA ARTICLE

Lack, D. L. (1974). Population. *Encyclopaedia
    Britannica: Macropaedia.*

### UNSIGNED ENCYCLOPEDIA ARTICLE

"Louis Riel." (2000). *Canadian Encyclopedia.*

## Periodicals (APA)

### CONTINUOUS PAGINATION THROUGHOUT ANNUAL CYCLE

Riger, S. (1993). What's wrong with empowerment.
    *American Journal of Community Psychology, 21,*
    279-92.

### SEPARATE PAGINATION EACH ISSUE

Rockhill, K. (1987). The chaos of subjectivity in
    the ordered halls of academe. *Canadian Woman
    Studies, 8* (4), 12-17.

### MONTHLY PERIODICAL

Rooke, L. (2000, August). Painting the dog. *Toronto
    Life,* 84-87.

### SIGNED ARTICLE IN WEEKLY PERIODICAL

Krotz, L. (2000, June 17). Caseload. *Saturday
    Night,* 21-27.

### UNSIGNED ARTICLE IN WEEKLY PERIODICAL

Notes and Comment. (1978, February 20). *The New
    Yorker,* 29-32.

### SIGNED ARTICLE IN DAILY NEWSPAPER

Landsberg, M. (2000, June 18). Tory policies slowly
    poison public education. *Toronto Star,* A2.

### UNSIGNED ARTICLE IN DAILY NEWSPAPER

Report says crisis in teaching looms. (1984, August
    20). *Philadelphia Inquirer,* p. A3.

## REVIEW

Maddocks, M. (1984, August 27). A most famous anthropologist [Review of the book *Margaret Mead: A life*]. *Time,* 57.

# Other Sources (APA)

### INTERVIEW

Emerson, R. (1989, October 10). [Personal interview].

### DISSERTATION (ABSTRACTED IN DISSERTATION ABSTRACTS INTERNATIONAL)

Pendar, J. E. (1982). Undergraduate psychology majors: Factors influencing decisions about college, curriculum and career. *Dissertation Abstracts International, 42,* 4370A–4371A.

*Note:* If the dissertation is available on microfilm, give University Microfilms order number in parentheses at the conclusion of the reference. In APA format, enclose the order number in parentheses: "(University Microfilms No. AAD93-15947)."

### LECTURE

Rossborough, H. (1999, January). The self in social interactions. Sociology 2100 lecture, University of British Columbia, Vancouver.

### PAPER DELIVERED AT A PROFESSIONAL CONFERENCE

Worley, J. (1992, March). Texture: The feel of writing. Paper presented at the Conference on College Composition and Communication. Cincinnati, OH.

### FILM

Thomas, J. (Producer), & Cronenberg, D. (Director). (1991). *Naked lunch* [Film]. 20th Century Fox.

### TV PROGRAM

Chaikin, J. (Co-producer, director, & co-writer), & Goldberg, E. (Co-producer & co-writer). One Step Productions. (1987). *Legacy of the Hollywood blacklist* [videocassette]. Los Angeles, Public Affairs TV, KCET.

## RECORDING

```
Beatles. (Singers) (1973). Eleanor Rigby. The
    Beatles 1962-1966. (Cassette Recording No. 4X2K
    3403). New York: Capitol.
Schumann, R. (Composer). (1978). Symphonies nos. 1
    & 4 (Cassette recording No. YT35502). New York:
    Columbia.
```

# Electronic Sources (APA)

As with MLA, full guidelines for documenting electronic sources in APA format can be found on The English Pages at **www.abacon.com/compsite/ resources/citations.html**.

If the electronic source includes a previously published printed source for which you have given the date, do not include the date of electronic publication. Do not include the date of your access. As with MLA citation, follow the regular order of information for print sources, including as much of the pertinent information as is available.

The general APA format for online periodical sources is as follows:

Author, I. (date). Title of article. *Name of Periodical.* [Online]. *xx.* Available: Specify http address

Remember: For online sources do not add periods or other punctuation immediately following the address; such extra marks may prevent the instructor reading your references from being able to access the source.

### A DOCUMENT ON A WEBSITE

```
Burka, L. P. (1993). A hypertext history of multi-
    user dimensions. The MUDdex. [Online]. 5 Dec.
    1994. Available: http://www.apocalypse.org/pub/u/
    lpb/muddex/essay/
```

### A PERSONAL OR PROFESSIONAL SITE

```
Winter, M. How to talk new age. Retrieved Apr. 6,
    1998. Available: http://www.well.com/user/mick/
    newagept.html
```

This entry is short because there is no print version of the Web document, and some information is not available. We have only the document author's name and title of the document, followed by the access date and URL.

## A Book

> Whitman, W. (1891-92). *Leaves of grass.*
> Philadelphia: McKay. In K. M. Price & E. Folsom
> (Eds.), *The Walt Whitman hypertext archive.*
> [Online]. Retrieved 3 April 1998. Available:
> http://jefferson.village.virginia.edu/whitman/
> works/leaves/1891/text/title.html

## A Journal Article

> Jackson, F. L. (1997). Mexican freedom: The idea of
> the indigenous state. *Animus, 2* (3). [Online].
> Retrieved 4 April 1998. Available: http://www.
> mun.ca/animus/1997vol2/jackson2.htm

## Electronic Publications Such as CDs

> Zieger, H. E. (1992). Aldehyde. *The Software
> Toolworks multimedia encyclopedia.* Vers. 1.5.
> Software Toolworks. Boston: Grolier.

In this case, the document is published on CD, not online, so city and publisher are given instead of URL, and no access date is required because the document is not subject to change.

## ◼ Exercise

Figure out whether each of the following is a book, chapter of a book, journal article in print or on the Web, or personal website. Turn the unordered list into an alphabetized "Works Cited" list in proper MLA form. Then recast it as an APA "References" list.

- James Miller, Is Bad Writing Necessary?
  in Lingua Franca, 2000, volume 9 number 9
  on the Web at http://www.linguafranca.com/9912/writing.html

- Judith Butler, Bodies That Matter: On the Discursive Limits of "Sex."
  New York, Routledge, 1993.

- Beverly Daniel Tatum, Lighting Candles in the Dark.
  on pages 56–63 in Becoming and Unbecoming White, edited by
  Christine Clark and James O'Donnell. Westport, Connecticut and
  London, Bergin & Garvey, 1999.

- Diane Elam and Robyn Wiegman, editors, Feminism Beside Itself.
  New York, Routledge, 1995.

- Peter Newman, Living Dangerously.
  in Maclean's, December 20, 1999, pages 50–6

- Mabel Maney, The Case of the Not-So-Nice Nurse.
  New York, Cleis Press, 1991.

- Andrew Ross, Uses of Camp.
  in his No Respect: Intellectuals and Popular Culture.
  London, Routledge, 1989, pages 135–70.

- MTC Cronin, Look for It Here.
  in Atlantis: A Women's Studies Journal, 1998, volume 23, number 1,
  page 68 only.

# PART II

# Elements of
# Academic Essays

# 5

# Representing Others: Summary, Paraphrase, and Quotation

## THE ROLE OF REPRESENTING OTHERS

If asked to name the most important issues in essay-writing, many writers would say "thesis" or "representing my own perspective on the topic," or, more elaborately, "developing an idea that's powerful enough to account for the topic in all its complexity." All of these answers emphasize the creative activity of the mind working to invent an argument that makes sense of a challenging topic: "What accounts for the popularity of social conservatism in some provinces and not others?" "What should be done to protect the City of Winnipeg from the next flooding of the Red River?" "To what extent can Margaret Atwood's *The Handmaid's Tale* be read as a logical prediction based on current social trends?" And the thesis that guides the writer through an adequate response to such questions is, without doubt, the heart and soul of an essay.

All intellectual work is a form of the human mind trying to understand the universe. In the course of doing this, the mind ventures a great many opinions, theories, hunches, claims, theses, some of them dead ends, others of them well worth following through on, but they are worth nothing if they are not grounded in an attempt to get it right—to see accurately and to represent what we see accurately. Without accurate representation of others' work on the subject, an essay is, at best, an intriguing rant, a series of unsupported claims that have not been tested against the phenomena they describe (a Mars launch, a short story, a three-toed sloth) or the studies of those phenomena done by other scholars. It is in fact by representation of the work of other scholars that academic writing distinguishes itself from other kinds of writing. By situating our own perspectives in the existing body of scholarly work on the topic, rather than speaking as one, possibly brilliant, individual thinker, we work collaboratively toward the best possible understandings of our topic. (And by documenting our representations of others as shown in Chapter 4, we make sure that our representations of others can be checked for accuracy by our readers; in this way scholarly writing provides a system of quality assurance that is quite unique in the publishing world.)

Representation of others' work can be of two kinds: That work might be a primary source that constitutes the topic of your paper (such as Leonard Cohen's *Beautiful Losers* or Virginia Woolf's *A Room of One's Own*) or it might be a secondary source drawn from the existing body of scholarship on the topic (such as a critic's interpretation of *Beautiful Losers*). Whether the work is primary or secondary, it can be represented in three forms—summary, paraphrase, and quotation. The three forms cover a wide range from complete fidelity to the original, quoting it word for word, to drastic changes to the source, summarizing a whole book in a few sentences. Nevertheless, all three are forms of the original version and a faithful *re*-presentation of it. Though summarizing is the most ethically demanding of the three since it undertakes such a radical transformation of the original, all three require that writers put themselves completely and conscientiously at the service of the source they undertake to represent.

Together, summary, paraphrase, and quotation can occupy 50% or more of a research essay. For examples of the extent of representation in scholarly writing, look at the student essay "A Vote for Wal-Mart." Even though it has a strong thesis that clearly controls the development of the argument, a large portion of the essay consists of representations of others' work on the topic. But representing others is not just a humble rite of passage demanded of students: Scan the pages of any scholarly journal for the tell-tale footnote numbers or in-text citations that signify a representation of someone else's work and you will see how seriously professional scholars take this aspect of academic writing. The methods used vary with the disciplines: psychologists mainly use summary and paraphrase rather than quotation, and literary scholars mainly use quotation for primary sources and paraphrase for secondary ones, but all scholars use some form of representation in order to test their claims and integrate their work with that of others.

## WHAT IS A SUMMARY?

The best way to demonstrate that you understand the information and the ideas in any piece of writing is to compose an accurate and clearly written summary of that piece. By a *summary* we mean a *brief restatement, in your own words, of the content of a passage* (a group of paragraphs, a chapter, an article, a book). This restatement should focus on the *central idea* or thesis of the passage. The briefest of all summaries (one or two sentences) will do no more than this. A longer, more complete summary will indicate, in condensed form, the main points in the passage that support or explain the central idea. It will reflect the order in which these points are presented and the emphasis given to them. It may even include some important examples from the passage. But it will not include minor details. It will not repeat points simply for the purpose of emphasis. And it will not contain any of your own opinions or conclusions. It will simply extract the main line of argument of the passage. A good summary, therefore, has three central qualities: *brevity, completeness,* and *objectivity*. Although summarizing seems a humble task in comparison to criticizing, representing a source accurately without letting your judgments surface is tough intellectual work that calls for extreme attentiveness and self-control.

## Can a Summary Be Objective?

Consider, for example, how difficult objectivity might be to achieve in a summary. By definition, writing a summary requires you to select some aspects of the original and to leave out others. Since deciding what to select and what to leave out calls for your personal judgment, your summary is really a work of *interpretation*. And, certainly, your interpretation of a passage may differ from another person's. One factor affecting the nature and quality of your interpretation is your *prior knowledge* of the subject. For example, if you're attempting to summarize an anthropological article and you're a novice in the field, then your summary of the article might be quite different from that of your professor, who has spent 20 years studying this particular area and whose judgment about what is more significant and what is less significant is undoubtedly more reliable than your own. By the same token, your personal or professional *frame of reference* may also affect your interpretation. A union representative and a management representative attempting to summarize the latest management offer would probably come up with two very different accounts. Still, we believe that in most cases it's possible to produce a reasonably objective summary of a passage if you make a conscious, good-faith effort not to allow your own feelings on the subject to distort your account of the text.

## Form of Summary

Writing a summary is sometimes required as an assignment in itself. For example,

- Find 10 books and articles on the topic of lesbian and gay rights legislation in Canada and produce a 100-word summary of each. (This is a form of annotated bibliography; see pp. 51–52.)
- Write a 200-word summary of your research essay and insert it between the title page and page 1 of your essay. (This is an abstract.)
- Write a five-page summary of Michel Foucault's "Discourse on Language."

A summary shows up in scholarly writing by professors, too:

- as an abstract of a proposed conference presentation
- as an abstract of a journal article, inserted between the title and first paragraph of the article.

But a summary is most common as an element of a larger piece of work, the research essay that requires the writer to synthesize many outside sources. A summary allows writers to do this efficiently without sacrificing accuracy.

## Using the Summary

In some quarters, the summary has a bad reputation—and with reason. Summaries often are provided by writers as substitutes for analyses. As students, many of us have summarized books that we were supposed to *review* critically. The point is that the summary does have an important place in respectable university work. First, writing a summary is an excellent way to understand what you read, because it forces you to put the text into your own words. Practice with writing summaries also develops your general writing habits, since a good summary, like any other piece of good writing, is clear, coherent, and accurate.

Second, summaries are useful to your readers. Suppose you're writing a paper about the rise of Naziism in German villages in the 1930s, and in part of that paper you want to discuss Ursula Hegi's *A Stone From the River* as a fictional treatment of the subject. A summary of the plot would be helpful to a reader who hasn't seen or read—or who doesn't remember—the novel. (Of course, if the novel is on the reading list your professor gave you, you can safely omit the plot summary.) Or perhaps you're writing a paper about the creation of the territory of Nunavut in Canada's Arctic. If your reader isn't familiar with the Acts of Parliament by which the territory was created, it would be a good idea to summarize these provisions at some early point in the paper. In many cases (a test, for instance), you can use a summary to demonstrate your knowledge of what your professor already knows; when writing a paper, you can use a summary to inform your professor about some relatively unfamiliar source.

## Underestimating the Summary

It may seem to you that being able to tell (or to retell) exactly what a passage says is a skill that ought to be taken for granted in anyone who can read at the high school level. Unfortunately, this is not so: For all kinds of reasons, people don't always read carefully. In fact, it's probably safe to say that usually they don't. Either they read so inattentively that they skip over words, phrases, or even whole sentences or, if they do see the words in front of them, they see them without registering their significance.

When a reader fails to pick up the meaning and the implications of a sentence or two, usually there's no real harm done. (An exception: You could lose credit on an exam or paper because you failed to read carefully a crucial direction by your instructor.) But over longer stretches—the paragraph, the section, the article, or the chapter—inattentive or haphazard reading creates problems, for it will thwart your efforts to perceive the shape of the argument, to grasp the central idea, to determine the main points that compose it, to relate the parts of the whole, and to note key examples. This kind of reading takes more energy and determination than casual reading. But, in the long run, it's an energy-saving method because it enables you to retain the content of the material and to use that content as a basis for your own responses. In other words, it allows you to develop an accurate and coherent written discussion that goes beyond summary.

## How to Write Summaries

Every article you read will present a different challenge as you work to summarize it. As you'll discover, saying in a few words what has taken someone else a great many can be difficult. But like any other skill, the ability to summarize improves with practice. Here are a few pointers to get you started. They represent possible stages, or steps, in the process of writing a summary. These pointers are not meant to be ironclad rules; rather, they are designed to encourage habits of thinking that will allow you to vary your technique as the situation demands. Overall, the goal is to read carefully and extract the thesis and line of argument from the original text.

---

### HOW TO WRITE SUMMARIES

- *Read* the passage carefully. Start looking for its structure of claims and support: the thesis and the main points (or in a longer passage, stages of thought) used to advance that thesis.
- *Reread*. This time divide the passage into sections or stages of thought. If you are summarizing a very short article, you might consider each paragraph to be a "stage of thought." If you are summarizing a longer article or a book, you will need to treat whole groups of paragraphs as stages of thought. In social science writing, the commencement of a new stage of thought is often indicated by a subtitle; in other forms of writing, you can often identify where one stage ends and another begins by asking, "where could a subtitle be inserted?" *Label,* on the passage itself, each section or stage of thought. *Underline* key ideas and terms.
- Write *one-sentence summaries,* on a separate sheet of paper, of each stage of thought.
- *Write a thesis: a one- or two-sentence summary of the entire passage.* The thesis should express the central idea of the passage, as you have determined it from the preceding steps. You may find it useful to keep in mind the information contained in the lead sentence or paragraph of most newspaper stories—the *what, who, why, where, when,* and *how* of the matter. For persuasive passages, summarize in a sentence the author's conclusion. For descriptive passages, indicate the subject of the description and its key feature(s). *Note:* In some cases, especially in scholarly writing, *a suitable thesis may already be in the original passage.* If so, you may want to quote it directly in your summary.
- *Write the first draft of your summary* by (1) combining the thesis with your list of one-sentence summaries or (2) combining the thesis with one-sentence summaries *plus* significant details from the passage. In either case, eliminate repetition and less important information. Disregard minor details or generalize them (e.g., Mulroney and Chrétien might be generalized as "recent prime ministers"). Use as few words as possible to convey the main ideas.
- *Check your summary against the original passage* and make whatever adjustments are necessary for accuracy and completeness.
- *Revise your summary,* inserting transitional words and phrases where necessary to ensure coherence. *Avoid a series of short, choppy sentences.* Combine sentences for a smooth, logical flow of ideas.

## Demonstration: Summary

To demonstrate these points at work, let's go through the process of summarizing a passage of expository material. Read the following passage carefully. Try to identify its parts (there are four) and to understand how these parts work together to create a single, compelling idea.

## *For the Infertile, a High-Tech Treadmill*

SHERYL GAY STOLBERG

On a frigid Sunday morning in February 1995, Nancy Alisberg and Michael   1
Albano took a stroll on a windswept beach. They had fled their Brooklyn
apartment for the Hamptons, holing up in a quaint bed-and-breakfast for the
weekend. But this was no ordinary getaway.

It was, rather, a funeral of sorts. After three unsuccessful attempts at con-   2
ceiving a test-tube baby, the Brooklyn couple had come to the seashore to
bury their dream of having a biological child.

Bundled up in their heavy winter coats, they settled in near a log to pro-   3
tect themselves from the wind. There, Ms. Alisberg and Mr. Albano, both
lawyers, both in their early 40's, pulled lists from their pockets on which each
had written characteristics of the other that they would miss in not having a
baby from their own eggs and sperm. They read the lists aloud and then,
because it was too windy to burn them, as they had planned, they buried them
in the sand.

The ceremony, Ms. Alisberg said recently, "was to say goodbye and then   4
to try to work on the moving on." But moving on was easier said than done.

The couple began investigating adoption as soon as they returned home,   5
and they are now the parents of a 2-year-old girl from Korea. But at the same
time they plunged back into the seductive, emotionally wrenching world of
reproductive medicine, signing up for egg donation, in which Ms. Alisberg
might become pregnant using another woman's eggs.

"The technology," Mr. Albano said, "has given us so many options that   6
it is hard to say no."

For infertile couples, saying no to reproductive technology has become a   7
vexing problem. Every month, it seems, there is another stride in the science
of making babies. And while public attention inevitably focuses on the latest
accomplishment—the McCaughey septuplets, the California woman who
gave birth at 63 and other recent feats—the reality is that the high-tech path
to parenthood yields failure far more often than success, about three out of
four times.

Thousands of couples are riding the infertility merry-go-round, many   8
unable to get off for fear that the next expensive procedure is the one that will
finally work.

"My patients are always saying to me, 'How can I stop?'" said Dr. Alice    9
Domar, who directs the behavioral medicine program for infertility at the
Beth Israel Deaconess Medical Center in Boston. "I've got this 42-year-old
woman in my group who is just about at the end. She says they are ready to
move on, and then she hears about this cytoplasm stuff," in which doctors
mingle the core genetic blueprint of one egg with the surrounding fluid, or
cytoplasm, from another.

"Where," Dr. Domar asked, "do you get to the point where you say, 'I    10
can't do this anymore?'"

The question carries as much angst for infertility specialists as it does for    11
their patients. "This is the hardest part of my job," said Dr. Jamie A. Grifo,
director of the division of reproductive endocrinology at New York University
Medical Center. "I have patients whom I tell, point blank, 'You should stop,'
and they say to me, 'Well, I want to give it one more try.' I say: 'Here, look
at the data. Your chance is one percent.' And they say, 'Well, I'm going to be
that one, Doc.'"

The National Center for Health Statistics says that in 1995, the most    12
recent year for available figures, the United States had 60.2 million women of
reproductive age, and that 10 percent—or 6.1 million of them—were infertile.
Of these, about 600,000 had at some point tried assisted reproductive technology, participating in what Pamela Madsen, who runs a New York support
group for infertile women, calls "the ovarian Olympics."

New terms are entering the popular lexicon, from "assisted hatching," in    13
which researchers slit open the shells of embryos, to a veritable alphabet
soup of techniques. There is IVF, for in vitro fertilization, in which sperm and
egg are combined in a laboratory dish and then implanted into the uterus as
embryos. There is GIFT, for gamete intrafallopian transfer, in which eggs and
sperm are inserted into the fallopian tubes in the hope they will unite into
embryos. There is ZIFT, for zygote intrafallopian transfer, in which fertilized
embryos are transferred to the tubes. There is ICSI, for intracytoplasmic
sperm injection, in which male infertility is treated by sifting through a man's
sperm and injecting a single strong one into a woman's egg. And of course,
there is egg donation.

The procedures take place over the course of a month and are therefore    14
called cycles. The American Society for Reproductive Medicine estimates that
in 1994, the most recent year for which figures are available, infertility clinics attempted 42,509 cycles of high-tech conception, resulting in 9,573 births,
some multiple, for an overall success rate of 22.5 percent. A couple's chances
of success depend on a variety of factors, including the woman's age and the
quality of her eggs, as well as her husband's sperm count.

For in vitro fertilization, the most common technique, the success rate was    15
20.7 percent. Egg donation has a much higher success rate—46.8 percent—but
it means that a woman must give up a genetic connection to her child. Some,
like Mr. Albano, have a difficult time with that. "It didn't sit well with me that
I wouldn't have a pairing of my genetic material with hers," he said. "But
Nancy was very much desirous of wanting to experience pregnancy and birth."

Critics have suggested that there is an element of subtle coercion in all this   16
state-of-the-art medicine, with infertility clinics making emotional appeals to couples at a particularly vulnerable point in their lives. Moreover, they fear that
couples in their baby-making fervor are not thinking through the moral implications of having children whose genetic roots are different from their own.

"This is not just a science problem; it's a marketing problem," said Barbara   17
Katz Rothman, professor of sociology at City University of New York. "Once
you are buying these services, there is a never-ending next service."

The treatments are expensive. In vitro fertilization costs, on average,   18
$7,800 per cycle. And some patients are going heavily in debt to pay for them,
taking second and even third mortgages on their homes. While doctors who
treat fertility consider it a disease, only 12 states require insurance companies
to cover the treatments, which often can drag on for years.

"We pay $550 a month for our own insurance," said Heather Higgins,   19
28, of Billerica, Mass., a small town near the New Hampshire border. She and
her husband, Eric, who drives a canteen truck, have spent more than six
years trying to have a baby. "I would have the cheapo accident insurance if it
weren't for the infertility. With $8,000 a cycle, I could never do it."

By her own estimation, Mrs. Higgins has attempted in vitro fertilization   20
more than 20 times. "I lost count at 21," she said.

Her physician, Dr. Vito Cardone of the Fertility Center of New England   21
in Reading, Mass., says the multiple attempts are necessary because Mrs.
Higgins is a "poor producer," meaning the fertility drugs he gives her prompt
her body to create only one or two eggs at a time, and sometimes none at all.
He is pressing her to try egg donation, but Mrs. Higgins is not ready.

"I'm going to exhaust all efforts," she said, "emotionally, physically and   22
financially, until I can't."

She works part time as a medical assistant, but her days are governed by   23
the rhythm of her in vitro fertilization cycles: 16 days of fertility drugs, which
her husband injects into her buttocks (he practiced on an orange); vaginal
ultrasound probes to check egg development; egg retrieval, in which doctors
remove her eggs, mix them with sperm in a laboratory dish to create embryos
that will be inserted into her uterus when they are no bigger than eight cells,
and then 10 days of anxious waiting to find out if she is pregnant. She spends
much of her time at the computer, chatting electronically with infertile friends
in far-flung places.

"I probably sign on five or six times a day," she said. "Some of the mes-   24
sages are very sad."

Indeed, experts have long suspected that infertility causes depression,   25
and while there is little research on the topic, they are just beginning to learn
that depression can also contribute to infertility.

Dr. Domar, the counselor, said infertile women were twice as likely to be   26
depressed as those who are fertile. In 1993, she published research that found
women with infertility had the same levels of depression as those with cancer,
heart disease or the virus that causes AIDS.

But she said the last time anyone examined the link between treatment     27
failure and depression was 1984, when a study showed that 64 percent of
women who had undergone an unsuccessful in vitro fertilization cycle demonstrated symptoms of clinical depression. The results did not surprise her.

"Unsuccessful treatment is going to cause depression," she said. "That's     28
just common sense. The problem is that women who have the resources or
insurance bounce right back and do more cycles."

Indeed, Nancy Alisberg and Michael Albano said they would have continued their attempts at in vitro fertilization had it not been for genetic screening that showed Ms. Alisberg's eggs contained chromosomal anomalies,     29
meaning the infant would be born with birth defects.

The discovery, which prompted their trip to the Hamptons, came after     30
three emotionally grueling years of trying to conceive, including an unsuccessful effort to correct Mr. Albano's low sperm count by removing an enlarged
vein in his scrotum; two artificial inseminations, and three in vitro fertilizations,
including one that resulted in a "biochemical pregnancy," in which a blood test
suggested that Ms. Alisberg was pregnant. But the embryo failed to implant.

The discovery of the genetic defects left the couple with a difficult deci-     31
sion: Would they move on to egg donation, which might enable Ms. Alisberg
to fulfill her desire to carry a baby? Or would they choose adoption, which
would virtually guarantee a child? Cost was an issue; while their health insurance covered in vitro fertilization, it did not cover egg donation. If they spent
$15,000 for donated eggs, the couple reasoned, they might lose the money
they had saved for adoption. While adoption agencies discourage it, they
decided to push ahead on both fronts.

Jumping back on the infertility merry-go-round was no picnic. To test the     32
likelihood that she would get pregnant with a donated egg, Ms. Alisberg had
to go through a "mock cycle" in which she took fertility drugs, underwent
blood tests, ultrasound scans and biopsies, all the while knowing that no
embryos would be transferred into her uterus.

"Everybody I know who has gone through IVF and then started doing     33
donor egg has a real visceral reaction to being back in that waiting room,"
Ms. Alisberg said. "You don't want to feel those things again."

On Dec. 27, 1995, Sophie Sang Ah Albano-Alisberg arrived from Korea,     34
4 months old, long and lean, with fuzzy black hair and beautiful clear skin.
Her new parents met her at La Guardia Airport, after two months of gazing
at her picture. "I recognized her immediately," Mr. Albano said.

Not quite two weeks later, he and his wife received a call from their infer-     35
tility clinic, which had matched them with an egg donor. They spent a few
days considering the offer, but finally rejected it. "It was not fair to Sophie,"
Ms. Alisberg said. "She had just arrived."

But she and her husband cannot bring themselves to eliminate the possi-     36
bility of egg donation entirely. Today, two years later, their names remain on
the donor candidate list.

■ ■ ■

## Reread, Underline, Divide into Stages of Thought

Let's consider our recommended pointers for writing a summary.

As you reread the passage, consider its significance as a whole and its stages of thought. What does it say? How is it organized? How does each part of the passage fit into the whole?

Many of the selections you read for your courses will have their main sections identified for you by subheadings. When a passage has no subheadings, as is the case with "High-Tech Treadmill," you must read carefully enough that you can identify the author's main stages of thought.

How do you determine where one stage of thought ends and the next one begins? Assuming that what you have read is coherent and unified, this should not be difficult. (When a selection is unified, all of its parts pertain to the main subject; when a selection is coherent, the parts follow one another in logical order.) Look, particularly, for transitional sentences at the beginning of paragraphs. Such sentences generally work in one or both of the following ways: (1) they summarize what has come before; (2) they set the stage for what is to follow.

For example, look at the sentence that opens paragraph 16: "Critics have suggested that there is an element of subtle coercion in all this state-of-the-art medicine, with infertility clinics making emotional appeals to couples at a particularly vulnerable point in their lives." Notice how the first part of this sentence, with its reference to "*this* state-of-the-art medicine" (italics added), asks the reader to recall information from the preceding section. The second part of the transitional sentence announces the topic of the upcoming section: 13 paragraphs devoted to the emotional vulnerability of couples involved in assisted reproductive technology.

Each section of an article will take several paragraphs to develop. Often between paragraphs, and almost certainly between sections of an article, you will find transitions that help you understand what you have just read and what you are about to read. For articles that have no subheadings, try writing your own section headings in the margins as you take notes. Then proceed with your summary.

The sections of Stolberg's article may be described as follows:

*Section 1:* Introduction—the difficulty of stepping off the high-tech treadmill of fertility medicine—with a lead-in example (paragraphs 1–10).

*Section 2:* The technology—a brief review of the techniques and statistics associated with assisted reproductive technology (paragraphs 11–15).

*Section 3:* Emotional vulnerability—the lengths, financial and emotional, to which some will go in order to conceive, with an extended example (paragraphs 16–28).

*Section 4:* Difficult decision based on genetic diagnosis and the choice to adopt rather than conceive—with the introductory example continued (paragraphs 29–36).

Here is how the first of these sections might look after you had marked the main ideas, by underlining and by marginal notations:

On a frigid Sunday morning in February 1995, Nancy Alisberg and Michael Albano took a stroll on a windswept beach. They had fled their Brooklyn apartment for the Hamptons, holing up in a quaint bed-and-breakfast for the weekend. But this was no ordinary getaway. 1

*Example: Emotional difficulty of failed ART,[1] no biological children*

It was, rather, a funeral of sorts. After three unsuccessful attempts at conceiving a test-tube baby, the Brooklyn couple had come to the seashore to bury their dream of having a biological child. 2

Bundled up in their heavy winter coats, they settled in near a log to protect themselves from the wind. There, Ms. Alisberg and Mr. Albano, both lawyers, both in their early 40's, pulled lists from their pockets on which each had written characteristics of the other that they would miss in not having a baby from their own eggs and sperm. They read the list[s] aloud and then, because it was too windy to burn them, as they had planned, they buried them in the sand. 3

The ceremony, Ms. Alisberg said recently, "was to say goodbye and then to try to work on the moving on." But moving on was easier said than done. 4

The couple began investigating adoption as soon as they returned home, and they are now the parents of a 2-year-old girl from Korea. But at the same time they plunged back into the seductive, emotionally wrenching world of reproductive medicine, signing up for egg donation, in which Ms. Alisberg might become pregnant using another woman's eggs. 5

*Main Pt. of Article: Hard to say no to ART*

"The technology," Mr. Albano said, "has given us so many options that it is hard to say no." 6

*High-publicity success, but most often failure*

For infertile couples, saying no to reproductive technology has become a vexing problem. Every month, it seems, there is another stride in the science of making babies. And while public attention inevitably focuses on the latest accomplishment—the McCaughey septuplets, the 7

---

[1] "ART," used in margin notes on this and subsequent pages, is an abbreviation for "assisted reproductive technology."

*Only 25% success rate*

California woman who gave birth at 63 and other recent feats—the reality is that the high-tech path to parenthood yields <u>failure</u> far more often than success, <u>about three out of four times.</u>

*the "treadmill" of title*

Thousands of couples are <u>riding the infertil-</u> 8 <u>ity merry-go-round,</u> many unable to get off for fear that the next expensive procedure is the one that will finally work.

*Not even multiple*
*failures can keep*
*patients from hope*

"My patients are always saying to me, 'How 9 can I stop?'" said Dr. Alice Domar, who directs the behavioral medicine program for infertility at the Beth Israel Deaconess Medical Center in Boston. "I've got this 42-year-old woman in my group who is just about at the end. She says they are ready to move on, and then she hears about this cytoplasm stuff," in which doctors mingle the core genetic blueprint of one egg with the surrounding fluid, or cytoplasm, from another.

*It's always the next*
*new procedure that*
*will work (finally)*

*For patients, when to*
*quit is very hard*

"<u>Where,</u>" Dr. Domar asked, "<u>do you get to</u> 10 <u>the point where you say, 'I can't do this any-</u> <u>more?'</u>"

## Write a One-Sentence Summary of Each Stage of Thought

The purpose of this step is to wean you from the language of the original passage, so that you are not tied to it when writing the summary. Here are one-sentence summaries for each stage of thought in the "Treadmill" article's four sections:

*Section 1:* Introduction—the difficulty of stepping off the high-tech tread-mill of fertility medicine—with a lead-in example (paragraphs 1–10).

```
Infertile couples face difficult emotional problems as
they consider abandoning their efforts to become preg-
nant through assisted reproductive technologies (ART).
```

*Section 2:* The technology—a brief review of the techniques and statistics associated with assisted reproductive technology (paragraphs 11–15).

```
ART is a broad term describing a set of complex labo-
ratory procedures in which eggs are fertilized outside
the body and then implanted in women who, otherwise,
have been unable to become pregnant.
```

*Section 3:* Emotional vulnerability—the lengths, financial and emotional, to which some will go in order to conceive, with an extended example (paragraphs 16–28).

```
The costs of these treatments are high both financial-
ly (roughly $8000 per attempted pregnancy) and emo-
tionally: couples trying to conceive ride a roller
coaster of hope with each ART attempt and despair with
each ART failure (failures occur three out of every
four attempts).
```

*Section 4:* Difficult decision based on genetic diagnosis and the choice to adopt rather than conceive—with the introductory example continued (paragraphs 29–36).

```
After three ART failures, Nancy Alisberg and Michael
Albano chose to adopt a child but still hope to under-
go yet another ART procedure.
```

## Write a Thesis: A One- or Two-Sentence Summary of the Entire Passage

To ensure clarity for the reader, the first sentence of your summary should begin with the author's thesis, regardless of where it appears in the article itself.

A thesis consists of a subject and an assertion about that subject. How can we go about fashioning an adequate thesis for "High-Tech Treadmill?" Probably no two proposed thesis statements for this article would be worded identically, but it is fair to say that any reasonable thesis will indicate that the subject is assisted reproductive technology (ART) and the emotionally difficult decision of whether or not to continue fertility clinic treatments. What issues, specifically, does Stolberg believe are raised by ART? For a clue, look at the beginning of paragraph 7: "For infertile couples, saying no to reproductive technology has become a vexing problem." As Stolberg's title suggests, ART can be a "high-tech treadmill" that couples find difficult to leave. Mindful of Stolberg's subject and the assertion she makes about it, we can write a thesis statement *in our own words* and arrive at the following:

```
Infertile couples face emotional difficulties as they
consider abandoning their efforts to become pregnant
through assisted reproductive technologies (ART).
```

To clarify for our readers the fact that this idea is Stolberg's and not ours, we'll frame the thesis as follows:

```
In her article "For the Infertile, a High-Tech
Treadmill," Sheryl Gay Stolberg reports that infertile
couples face emotional difficulties as they consider
```

abandoning their efforts to become pregnant through
assisted reproductive technologies (ART).

The first sentence of a summary is crucially important, for it orients readers by letting them know what to expect in the coming paragraphs. The preceding example sentence provides the reader both with a direct reference to an article and a thesis for the upcoming summary. And lest you become frustrated too quickly, realize that writing an acceptable thesis for a summary takes time—in this case, three drafts, or roughly seven minutes of effort spent on one sentence and another few minutes of fine-tuning after a draft of the entire summary was completed. That is, the first draft of the thesis was too vague; the second draft was too cumbersome; and the third draft needed refinements.

Draft 1: Sheryl Gay Stolberg reports on the emotional and financial costs associated with assisted reproductive technologies.

*(Too vague— what about the costs?)*

Draft 2: Sheryl Gay Stolberg reports that when *infertile* ∨ couples ~~who want biological children~~ give up on efforts to become pregnant through measures associated with assisted reproductive technologies (ART), the couples face emotional difficulties.

*(cumbersome)*

Draft 3: In her article "For the Infertile, a High-Tech Treadmill," Sheryl Gay Stolberg reports that f~~o~~r infertile couples ~~the decision to end attempts~~ *as they consider abandoning their attempts to become* ~~at~~ pregnan~~cy~~*t* through assisted reproductive technologies (ART) / is *face* emotional~~ly~~ difficult *ies)*

```
Final: In her article "For the Infertile, a

       High-Tech Treadmill," Sheryl Gay

       Stolberg reports that infertile

       couples face emotional difficulties as

       they consider abandoning their efforts

       to become pregnant through assisted

       reproductive technologies (ART).
```

## Write the First Draft of the Summary

Let's consider two possible summaries of the example passage: (1) a short summary, combining a thesis with one-sentence section summaries, and (2) a longer summary, combining thesis, one-sentence section summaries, and some carefully chosen details. Again, realize that you are reading final versions; each of the following summaries is the result of at least two full drafts.

## (1) Short Summary: Combine Thesis Sentence with One-Sentence Section Summaries

```
In her article "For the Infertile, a High-Tech
Treadmill," Sheryl Gay Stolberg reports that infertile
couples face emotional difficulties as they consider
abandoning their efforts to become pregnant through
assisted reproductive technologies (ART). ART is a
broad term describing a set of complex laboratory pro-
cedures in which eggs are fertilized outside the body
and then implanted in women who, otherwise, have been
unable to become pregnant. The treatments, which fail
three out of every four attempts, are expensive, cost-
ing roughly $8000 per attempted pregnancy. Emotionally,
the costs are high as well, as couples trying to con-
ceive ride a roller coaster of hope with each ART
attempt and despair with each ART failure. Stolberg
illustrates this emotional turmoil with the story of
a couple who adopted an infant from Korea after three
```

```
ART failures but who still hope for a biological
child by undergoing yet another ART procedure. Many
who use ART become frustrated and depressed; still,
they're eager to try again, hoping to beat the odds
and give birth.
```

## Discussion

This summary consists essentially of a restatement of Stolberg's thesis plus the section summaries, altered or expanded a little for stylistic purposes. The first sentence encompasses the summary of section 1 and is followed by the summaries of sections 2, 3, and 4. Notice in the summary of section 4 the decision to refer to Alisberg and Albano as "a couple" and to conclude with a sentence that uses the general outline of their story to reemphasize the article's main point: that despite the failures, couples want to continue high-tech efforts to conceive.

## (2) Longer Summary: Combine Thesis Sentence, Section Summaries, and Carefully Chosen Details

The thesis and one-sentence section summaries also can be used as the outline for a more detailed summary. Most of the details in the passage, however, won't be necessary in a summary. It isn't *necessary* even in a longer summary of this passage to discuss either of Stolberg's examples—Higgins or Alisberg and Albano; it would be *appropriate*, though, to provide a bit more detail about Alisberg/Albano and, perhaps, about Higgins (who isn't mentioned in the first summary). In a more extended summary, concentrate on a few carefully selected details that might be desirable for clarity. For example, in "High-Tech Treadmill" you could mention that 600 000 women visit fertility clinics each year, and you could name a few of the ART procedures. You might also develop the notion that stepping off the "treadmill" of ART is difficult.

How do you know which details may be safely ignored and which ones may be advisable to include? The answer is that you won't always know. Developing good judgment in comprehending and summarizing texts is largely a matter of reading skill and prior knowledge (see pp. 84–85). Consider the analogy of the chess player who can plot three separate winning strategies from a board position that to a novice looks like a hopeless jumble. In the same way, the more practised a reader you are, the more knowledgeable you become about the subject, and the better able you will be to make critical distinctions between elements of greater and lesser importance. In the meantime, read as carefully as you can and use your own best judgments as to how to present your material.

Here's one version of a completed summary, with carefully chosen details. Note that we have highlighted phrases and sentences added to the original, briefer summary.

*Thesis*
*Section 1*
*Summary of*
*¶s 1–10*

*Section 2*
*Summary of*
*¶s 11–15*

*Section 3*
*Summary of*
*¶s 16–28*

In her article "For the Infertile, a High-Tech Treadmill," Sheryl Gay Stolberg reports that infertile couples face emotional difficulties as they consider abandoning their efforts to become pregnant through assisted reproductive technologies (ART). ART is a broad term describing a set of complex laboratory procedures in which eggs are fertilized outside the body and then implanted in women who, otherwise, have been unable to become pregnant. These techniques include in vitro fertilization, gamete intrafallopian transfer, and intracytoplasmic sperm injection. Some 600 000 infertile women a year (as of 1995) visit fertility specialists in an effort to become pregnant. The treatments are expensive, costing roughly $8000 per attempted pregnancy. Emotionally, the costs are high as well, as couples attempting to conceive ride a roller coaster of hope with each ART attempt and despair with each ART failure. Unfortunately, disappointment is all too common since ART fails roughly in three out of every four attempts. Still, couples persist. One woman, who "lost count" of the number of procedures she had after 21 attempts, claimed that she would exhaust herself "emotionally, physically and financially" before resigning herself to never having a biological child. Fuelled by their intense emotional need and by rapidly evolving techniques that promise improved results, infertile couples feel justified in staying on the "high-tech [reproductive] treadmill," even after multiple failures. Stolberg illus-

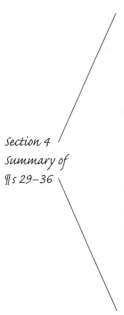

*Section 4*
*Summary of*
*¶s 29–36*

trates the emotional difficulties of life
on the treadmill through the story of a
couple who adopted an infant from Korea
after three ART failures and the discovery that the woman's eggs were genetically flawed. Two years after adoption, the
couple still hopes for a biological
child, this time through a procedure that
would allow the wife to become pregnant
using another woman's eggs. The successes
of complex procedures such as egg donation, when they occur, are dazzling. But
a great many infertile couples who turn
to ART become frustrated and depressed;
even so, they're eager to try again,
hoping to beat the odds and give birth.

## Discussion

The structure of this summary generally reflects the structure of the original—
with one notable departure. Stolberg splits her discussion of Alisberg and
Albano between the beginning and end of the article, a useful strategy for
bracketing the piece with a related introduction and conclusion. After the
thesis, this summary omits reference to the Alisberg/Albano example in favour
of defining assisted reproductive technology in terms the reader can understand. The definition is followed with a section that lays out the emotional difficulties of infertile couples—the main point of Stolberg's article—and only
then introduces Alisberg/Albano, to help make the point. For the sake of efficiency, the Alisberg/Albano example is discussed in only one place—at the end
of the piece.

Compared to the first, briefer summary, this effort adds details about
Stolberg's second example, Ms. Higgins; adds a figure for the number of
women who visit fertility clinics annually; identifies three ART techniques;
and adds one sentence on why infertile couples feel justified in continuing to
seek ART even after multiple failures.

## Summary Length

How long should a summary be? This depends on the length of the original
passage. A good rule of thumb is that a summary should be no longer than
one-fourth of the original passage. Of course, if you were summarizing an
entire chapter or even an entire book, it would have to be much shorter than

that. The summary above is about one-fifth the length of the original passage. Although it shouldn't be very much longer, you have seen (pp. 96– 97) that it could be quite a bit shorter.

The length of a summary, as well as the content of the summary, also depends on its *purpose*. Let's suppose you decided to use Stolberg's piece in a paper that dealt with the motivation of couples who persist with assisted reproductive technologies in the face of overwhelming odds. In this case, you might summarize *only* Stolberg's two examples—Higgins and Alisberg/Albano—to provide your paper with some poignant material. If, instead, you were writing a paper in which you argued against ART on the grounds that it was expensive and too prone to failure, you might omit reference to the examples and focus, instead, on Stolberg's use of statistics and basic information about ART. Thus, depending on your purpose, you would summarize either selected portions of a source or an entire source, as we will see more fully in the chapter on syntheses.

## SUMMARIZING A NARRATIVE

A narrative is a story, a retelling of a person's experiences. That person and those experiences may be imaginary, as is the case with fiction, or they may be real, as in biography. Summarizing a narrative presents special challenges. You have seen that an author of an argument (such as Stolberg's "High-Tech Treadmill") follows assertions with examples and statements of support. Narrative presentations, however, usually are less direct. The author relates a story—event follows event—the point of which may never be stated directly. The charm, the force, and the very point of the narrative lies in the telling; generally, narratives do not exhibit the same logical development of writing designed to convey information or present an argument. They do not, therefore, lend themselves to summary in quite the same way. Narratives do have a logic (as Coleridge explained, "Poetry has a logic as severe as that of science)," but that logic may be emotional, imaginative, or plot-bound. The writer who summarizes a narrative is obliged to represent that logic through an overview—a synopsis—of the story's events and an account of how these events affect the central character(s).

The following narrative begins Paulette Bates Alden's *Crossing the Moon: A Journey Through Infertility*. As the title suggests, the book is a memoir that recounts the author's experiences in attempting to become pregnant with the help of fertility clinics. If you were writing a paper on assisted reproductive technologies, you might reasonably want to include references to women (and men) who could offer accounts from a patient's point of view. You could quote parts of such narratives, and you could summarize them. (While Alden does not mention fertility clinics in this excerpt, the moment she describes here prompted her and her husband to become clinic patients.)

# Crossing the Moon:
## A Journey Through Infertility

PAULETTE BATES ALDEN

It's an unseasonably warm afternoon in April, 1986, and I'm sitting on a     1
stone bench outside a Dairy Queen near our house in Minneapolis, considering the two mothers and three children who share my table. I'm about to turn
thirty-nine years old, which is why I'm so interested in mothers and children.

I haven't always been so interested. In fact, for most of my adult life I've     2
behaved as if mothers and children had nothing to do with me, which, on the
whole, they haven't. But lately I can't take my eyes off them. I'm in the
process of making (for me) a mind-boggling discovery: women have children. It's what women *do*. A lot of them, it seems. Most of them, from what
I can tell. Now that the blinders have dropped from my eyes, I'm amazed,
dazzled, puzzled, and afraid.

One of the mothers is younger than I, the first detail I note about her.     3
Blond hair, good teeth, and I wonder if she works outside the home, since it's
the middle of the afternoon and she's in Bermuda shorts. For all I know she's
the president of IBM, but something tells me her job is raising the little girl
beside her who is eating an ice cream cone dipped in waxy-looking butter-
scotch. The ice cream is running down the child's hands, grasped around the
cone in a double-fisted grip, dripping onto her shorts and bare legs, which are
covered in downy hair so fair it is translucent. There is a pasty white ring
around her mouth, which I would love to wipe off. The mother has a handful
of cheap paper napkins, which she's going through in a desultory way—she's
been to Dairy Queen before—while issuing a soft series of admonitions I seem
vaguely to remember from my own childhood: "Why don't you lick around
the cone to keep it from dripping? . . . here . . . let me help you . . . won't you
let me hold it for you? . . . oh, Sarah! . . . now look what you've done!"

I try to imagine these mother-words issuing from my own lips. I can't     4
imagine keeping up the constant murmuring that motherhood requires. But I
have felt how my hand, of its own volition, wanted to reach out and wipe that
child's mouth.

The other mother at the table is actually as old as I, but of course she     5
already has her children. We arrived in the parking lot at the same time. I
simply got out of my car and went in. While I waited in line, I watched this
mother get out, go around to the trunk, get the stroller out, open it, lift the baby
into it, buckle him in, help the other child, a boy about three, out of the car,
push the stroller to the glass door, open it, maneuver the stroller into the
crowded space while trying to keep track of her little boy, who made a bee-
line for the condiments bar, where he happily began fishing dill pickle slices
out with his fingers.

I felt dizzy with relief that I was not a mother. I got my hamburger    6
wrapped in gold foil and hurried out to sit in the sun, tired, hungry, and wild
to be alone.

But the only spot available was at the table with the young blond mother    7
and little girl. And then when the older mother had her order, she pushed the
stroller out the glass door and looked around for a place to sit. Naturally she
pushed it right up next to me. And in spite of myself, I smiled and moved over
to make room.

By now the little girl has ice cream pretty much all over her. "Oh well, I'll    8
just have to throw her in the bathtub when I get home anyway," the younger
mother says, and laughs self-deprecatingly, as if the joke were on her. I am
touched by her—to say the mundane, the unremarkable thing. The two mothers begin conversing, exchanging information about the children's ages and
such, but what I want to know is, *What is it like to be a mother?* I want the
skinny, the good and the bad, the sublime and the tedious.

But it's a warm spring afternoon at Dairy Queen and I'm not about to    9
rend the social fabric by asking such a question. Besides, I know what they'd
probably say, once they recovered from the shock of someone so out of it.
They might start with a little humor, but then if I pressed them on it, go on to
say that children change your life, but that they are worth it. Which doesn't
really speak to the uninitiated. So what I must really want to know is something neither they nor anyone else can tell me: Should *I* be a mother?

I had a Little Ricky doll when I was ten years old. He was the son of Lucy    10
and Ricky Ricardo, and I loved him intensely the summer our family took a
Western trip in our '57 Chevy station wagon. I gave him his little bottle,
changed his clothes out of his own little suitcase, showed him the passing cacti
and red rock mesas out the window, made sure he got his naps, tucked him
in in our motel room at night. The first thing I thought of in the morning was
Ricky—his round plastic face, his hard blue crystal eyes that blinked open, his
shapely limbs, like pale link sausages, his pleasingly plump torso, his intoxi-
cating rubber smell. He completely filled my senses. The sight, the smell, the
feel of him gave me deep pleasure. All I wanted or needed—then—was Ricky.

Still, I remember how relieved I was when I moved on to plastic horses.    11
Cathy Meyers from up the road had a black stallion and I had a buckskin one,
and we'd race them for hours across the wide-open expanse of our basement
floors. The horses were always having to escape captivity, a plot we never
tired of, until we discovered boys. We were twelve by then, going on thirteen,
and perhaps we sensed what was waiting for us up ahead. It would have nothing to do with wild horses.

I ponder the three children at our table, lost as they are in their revelry of    12
cold sweet cream. In a way they're adorable, and then again, just the usual
young of the species. I try to imagine what it would be like if I had a little
child, if I had brought him or her to Dairy Queen today.

About the closest I can come to imagining what it would be like to have    13
a child is with our cat, Cecil. For Cecil I feel the most delicious love, but also

the most anxious responsibility. My husband, Jeff, loves Cecil too, but he can go to sleep at night if Cecil isn't in. I have to get up every fifteen minutes or so to check for him. When he finally does appear, I sweep him up in my arms, burying my nose in his cold fur that smells of our neighbor's arborvitae bush. He's always on my mind, even when I'm not thinking about him.

How much worse would it be with a child? How much worse, that is, would *I* be? I'm not sure I want to unleash all that maternal instinct. Would I ever feel free again? Would I ever be *alone*? I don't just mean by myself; it isn't as if I haven't heard of babysitters. I know that other women do it—have selves and babies, too. But I'm not sure I can be one of them. I remember Ricky-love. **14**

The children, having finished their ice cream, have begun a game of chase around our table, catching onto their mothers' hips as round and round they go. The baby in the stroller regards these antics with wide-eyed amazement, as if seeing such a sight for the first time, which perhaps he is. But suddenly the little boy trips and falls, and after a moment of stunned silence in which he checks himself over to see if he's okay, lets out a bawl. We three women rise as one, but his mother is there first, hoisting him whimpering into her arms: "Does it hurt? Mama make it better," and she kisses the tiny finger he holds out, sweetly, to her lips. **15**

And before I can stop it, I'm filled with a sudden anguish: *I might never have a child!* A grief worthy of a death wells in me, before there has even been a life. *I might never have a child,* and the irony is not lost on me, that I'm not even sure I want one. And alongside that is another shape just coming into focus, which I don't want to see, but which is drawing closer every day: I might not be able to. It might already be too late, I might already be too old, there might be something wrong. **16**

It's true that Jeff and I are not using birth control. We haven't been for quite some time (I won't let myself remember how long). But I tell myself we're not really *trying*. Trying is for people who want a child, and I'm not sure. Jeff is leaving it mainly up to me. He says he can be happy either way, and besides, he has his hands full, dealing with the barely contained insanity of a small law firm, something they didn't teach him in law school. We both know it would be my life that would change the most if we had a child. Maybe it doesn't have to be that way, but that's the way it is. Jeff would still get dressed in a suit every day, and go off to his office downtown, and I would be mainly responsible for baby. **17**

I believe in making a conscious choice where having a child is concerned. But in the meantime, I've been hoping nature would just take its course. But nothing has ever happened. I haven't gotten pregnant. I'm not going to be let off the hook. If we do want a child, if we're ever going to have one, we've got to do something about it. **18**

■  ■  ■

Alden provides a glimpse into an extraordinarily private moment—the moment of recognition that she and her husband might never have a child. This first-person account could be valuable in a paper otherwise dependent on newspaper and journal articles and on books explaining the more technical elements of reproductive technology. You might reasonably pause in your explanations to acknowledge the tumultuous emotions of those who want children but who need the help of fertility clinics. How would you refer to this passage from Alden's memoir?

When you summarize a narrative, bear in mind the principles that follow, as well as those listed in the box.

---

## HOW TO SUMMARIZE NARRATIVES

- Your summary will *not* be a narrative, but rather the synopsis of a narrative. Your summary will likely be a paragraph at most.
- You will want to name and describe the principal characters of the narrative and describe the narrative's main actions or events.
- You should seek to connect the narrative's characters and events: describe the significance of events for (or the impact of events on) the character: what is the "logic" of the story?
- Don't offer mere plot summary when you should be analyzing; your summary should be a platform for your critical observations, not a substitute for them.

---

To summarize events, reread the narrative and make a marginal note each time you see that an action advances the story from one moment to the next. The key here is to recall that narratives take place *in time*. In your summary, be sure to re-create for your reader a sense of time flowing. Name and describe the characters as well. (For our purposes, *character* refers to the person, real or fictional, about whom the narrative is written.) The trickiest part of the summary will be describing the connection between events and characters. Earlier (p. 84) we made the point that summarizing any selection involves a degree of interpretation, and this is especially true of summarizing narratives. What, in the case of Alden, is the impact of the events described? An answer belongs in a summary of this piece, yet developing an answer is tricky. Five readers would interpret the narrative's significance in five distinct ways, would they not? Yes and no: yes, in the sense that these readers, given their separate experiences, will read from different points of view; no, in the sense that readers should be able to distinguish between the impact of events as seen from a main character's (i.e., Alden's) point of view and the impact of these same events as seen from their (the readers') points of view. We should be able to agree that Alden experienced a breakthrough realization.

At times, you will have to infer from clues in a narrative the significance of events for a character; at other times, the writer will be more direct. In either case, remember that it is the narrative's main character, real or imaginary, whose perspective should be represented in the summary. Here is a one-paragraph summary of Alden's narrative. (The draft is the result of two prior drafts.)

Paulette Bates Alden begins her memoir *Crossing the Moon: A Journey Through Infertility* by recalling the panic with which she realized she might never have a child. On an ordinary spring day at a Dairy Queen in Minneapolis, Alden finds herself sharing a picnic table with two mothers and their young children. As the children eat ice cream (making sticky messes of themselves) and the mothers trade stories and information, Alden suddenly realizes that, at 39, "I might not be able to [have a child]. It might already be too late, I might already be too old, there might be something wrong." Her grief at the thought is "worthy of a death," she writes, which strikes her as ironic in that she had valued her independence and never wanted children. Although she no longer uses birth control, getting pregnant never "happened" by itself, and Alden understands that if she and her husband want a child they will need to take deliberate action—which leads them to a fertility clinic and reproductive medicine.

## Summarizing Figures and Tables

In your reading in the sciences and social sciences, often you will find data and concepts presented in non-text forms—as figures and tables. Such visual devices offer a snapshot, a pictorial overview, of material that is more quickly and clearly communicated in graphic form than as a series of (often complicated) sentences. The writer uses a numbered "figure" to present the quantitative results of research as points on a line or a bar, or as sections ("slices") of a pie. Pie charts show relative proportions, or percentages. Graphs, especially effective in showing patterns, relate one variable to another: for instance, income to years of education or a university student's grade point average to hours of studying.

## HOW TO SUMMARIZE FIGURES (CHARTS AND TABLES)

- Study the figure to identify its logic and main claims, including general trends and striking results. (Even though the data are not presented in sentence form, figures, like paragraphs, do make claims.)
- If the summary will be included in an essay, focus on the claims that relate to your topic, even if they do not support your perspective.
- Write the summary and check it against the figure for fairness and accuracy.
- Revise the summary for logical flow. Frame it properly by naming the source either in the summary itself or in a citation.

The figures and tables that follow appeared in a national study on assisted reproductive technology (ART), conducted by the U.S. federal government's Centers for Disease Control, located in Atlanta, Georgia, and based on data collected from 281 fertility clinics in 1995.

In Figure 5.1, a *pie chart* relates the percentage of ART pregnancies (from fresh—non-frozen—embryos resulting from non-donor eggs) that led to the live births of a single child or multiple children. Study this pie chart to identify its main claims.

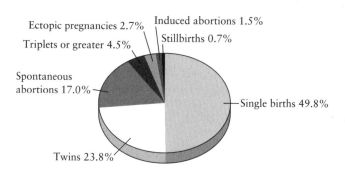

FIGURE 5.1   **Outcomes of Clinical Pregnancies Resulting from ART, 1995**

Here is a summary of the information presented:

By far, the most common outcome of a pregnancy that results from ART using fresh embryos and non-donor eggs is a single birth (roughly 50 percent of live births). Twins are born nearly one quarter of the

```
time and triplets (or greater) only 4.5 percent.
Roughly 22 percent of such ART pregnancies do not
lead to a live birth.
```

The points on the *graph* in the next figure, 5.2, relate the age of women undergoing ART and the success rates of their procedures, as measured by live births. ("Cycle" refers to a specific attempt at pregnancy, using ART). Here is the summary that accompanied the graph in the national report:

A woman's age is the most important factor affecting the chances of a live birth when the woman's own eggs are used. Figure [5.2] shows the live birth rate for women of a given age who had an ART procedure in 1995. Rates were relatively constant at about 25 percent among women aged 34 years and younger but declined with age after 34. Success rates were zero among women aged 47 years and older.

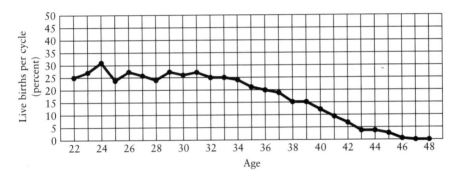

**FIGURE 5.2    ART Live Birth Rates by Age of Woman, 1995**

Sometimes a single graph will present information on two populations, or data sets, both of which are tracked with the same measurements. In Figure 5.3, the graph tracks the live birth rate of (1) ART for women whose own eggs are fertilized outside their bodies and implanted (that is, transferred from the test tube to the patient), and (2) women who receive *another* woman's (a donor's) egg that has been fertilized. Here is the summary that accompanied the graph in the national report:

Figure [5.3] shows that the age of the woman undergoing ART treatment does not affect success rates for cycles using embryos formed from donor eggs as it affects success rates for cycles using embryos from a woman's own eggs. The likelihood of a fertilized egg implanting is related to the age of the woman who produced the egg. As a result, the success rate for cycles using donor embryos is nearly constant (around 30 percent) across all age groups from 25 to 50. This graph illustrates that women age 36 and older are more likely to have success with ART using donor eggs.

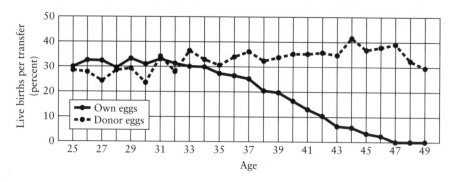

FIGURE 5.3   Live Births per Transfer for Fresh Embryos from Own and Donor Eggs by Age of Recipient, 1995

A *table* presents numerical data in rows and columns for quick reference. Tabular information can be incorporated into graphs, if the writer chooses. Graphs are preferable when the writer wants to emphasize a pattern or relationship; tables are used when the writer wants to emphasize numbers. Table 5.1 provides an overview of the entire 1995 national summary on assisted reproductive technologies.

Explanation of some terms and symbols will be useful in understanding this table. The mathematical symbols for "less than" (<) and "greater than" (>) indicate the age brackets of women in the study: younger than 35; 35 through 39; and older than 39. A "cycle" is a single attempt at pregnancy, using ART. Eggs fertilized in a laboratory—via in vitro fertilization (IVF)—can be transferred immediately into a woman's uterus or fallopian tubes (a so-called fresh embryo transfer) or can be frozen for later implantation (a "frozen" transfer). A woman can have her own fertilized egg transferred from the test tube to her uterus, or those of a donor. A "retrieval" is a collection of eggs contained in the ovaries and then fertilized for implantation. A "cancellation" is an ART cycle that is stopped before eggs are retrieved or a frozen embryo is implanted.

A summary of such a comprehensive table will necessarily be selective, depending on which information from the table is pertinent to the task.

- In writing a paper on ART, you could draw on the data in this table to report on the number of women undergoing treatment.
- You could compare numbers of women receiving their own fertilized eggs for transplantation as opposed to donor eggs, noting that the non-donor transfer is by far the more common (53 371 transfers of non-donor eggs versus 3 352 transfers of donor eggs).
- You could report on the high success rate of cycles using donor eggs as compared to the success rate of a woman's attempting pregnancy using her own eggs.

TABLE 5.1   1995 ART Pregnancy Success Rates

|  | AGE OF WOMEN | | | |
|---|---|---|---|---|
|  | <35 | 35–39 | >39 | TOTAL |
| CYCLES USING FRESH EMBRYOS FROM NONDONOR EGGS |  |  |  |  |
| Number of Cycles | 21,019 | 16,728 | 8,159 | 45,906 |
| Pregnancies per cycle (%) | 29.7 | 23.4 | 13.2 | 24.4 |
| Live births per cycle[a] (%) | 25.3 | 18.2 | 8.0 | 19.6 |
| Live births per retrieval[a] (%) | 28.0 | 21.5 | 10.2 | 22.8 |
| Live births per transfer[a] (%) | 30.6 | 23.6 | 11.6 | 25.1 |
| Cancellations (%) | 9.1 | 14.8 | 21.5 | 13.6 |
| Avg. number embryos transferred | 4.0 | 4.0 | 4.1 | 4.0 |
| Multiple birth rate per transfer |  |  |  |  |
| Twins | 9.8 | 6.6 | 1.9 | 7.4 |
| Triplets or greater | 2.6 | 1.2 | 0.3 | 1.7 |
| CYCLES USING FROZEN EMBRYOS FROM NONDONOR EGGS |  |  |  |  |
| Number of transfers | 3,724 | 2,433 | 1,001 | 7,465 |
| Live births per transfer[a] (%) | 16.4 | 14.8 | 11.0 | 15.1 |
| Avg. number embryos transferred | 3.5 | 3.4 | 3.4 | 3.4 |
| CYCLES USING DONOR EGGS |  |  |  |  |
| Number of fresh transfers | 572 | 668 | 2,112 | 3,352 |
| Live births per transfer[a] (%) | 30.8 | 35.8 | 36.7 | 35.5 |
| Avg. number embryos transferred | 4.0 | 4.0 | 4.2 | 4.1 |

[a] Pregnancies resulting in one or more children born alive; therefore, multiple births are counted as one.

From: Centers for Disease Control. *1995 Assisted Reproductive Technology Success Rates: National Summary and Fertility Clinic Reports.*

- From the numbers in the table you could infer that women seeking ART vastly prefer to have their own biological offspring.
- You might be interested in summarizing the age breakdown of women undergoing IVF and in noting that older women have higher success rates with donor eggs than do younger women. But for non-donor cycles, the younger the ART recipient, the better the likelihood of success.

You could glean other information from this table as well, depending on your research needs.

## Paraphrase

In certain cases, you may want to *paraphrase* rather than to summarize material. Writing a paraphrase is similar to writing a summary: It involves recasting a passage into your own words, and so it requires your complete understanding of the material. The difference is that while a summary is a shortened version of the original, the paraphrase is approximately the same length as the original.

Why write a paraphrase when you can quote the original? The main reason is to keep your own voice in control of the essay. Research essays typically involve so many representations of outside sources that always quoting instead of paraphrasing would result in the reader's hearing more from your sources than from you, resulting in jarring, confusing shifts of tone and terminology. The result could be chaotic, especially if the quotations do not share a common set of key terms with you, or assume a familiarity with specialized terms that is inappropriate for your own purpose and audience.

You may decide, then, to offer a paraphrase of material written in language that is dense, abstract, archaic, or possibly confusing. For example, suppose you were writing a paper on some aspect of human progress and you came across the following passage by the Marquis de Condorcet, a French economist and politician, written in the late 18th century:

> If man can, with almost complete assurance, predict phenomena when he knows their laws, and if, even when he does not, he can still, with great expectations of success, forecast the future on the basis of his experience of the past, why, then, should it be regarded as a fantastic undertaking to sketch, with some pretense to truth, the future destiny of man on the basis of his history? The sole foundation for belief in the natural science is this idea, that the general laws directing the phenomena of the universe, known or unknown, are necessary and constant. Why should this principle be any less true for the development of the intellectual and moral faculties of man than for the other operations of nature?

You would like to introduce Condorcet's idea on predicting the future course of human history, but you also don't want to slow down your essay with this somewhat abstract quotation. You may decide to attempt a paraphrase, as follows:

> The Marquis de Condorcet believed that if we can predict such physical events as eclipses and tides, and if we can use past events as a guide to future ones, we should be able to forecast human destiny on the basis of history. Physical events, he maintained, are determined by natural laws that are knowable and predictable. Since humans are part of nature, why should their intellectual and moral development be any less predictable than other natural events?

Each sentence in the paraphrase corresponds to a sentence in the original. The paraphrase is somewhat shorter, owing to the differences of style between 18th- and 21st-century prose (we tend to be more brisk and efficient, although not more eloquent). But the main difference is that we have replaced the language of the original with our own language. For example, we have used the term "humans" instead of "man," since the latter is an outdated usage that could seem sexist to contemporary readers. We have paraphrased Condorcet's "the general laws directing the phenomena of the universe, known or unknown, are necessary and constant" with "Physical events, he maintained, are determined by natural laws that are knowable and predictable." To contemporary readers, "knowable and predictable" might be clearer than "necessary and constant" as a description of natural (i.e., physical) laws. Note that we added the specific examples of eclipses and tides to clarify what might have been a somewhat abstract idea. Note also that we included two attributions to Condorcet within the paraphrase to credit our source properly.

When you come across a passage that you don't understand, the temptation is strong to skip over it. Resist this temptation! Use a paraphrase as a tool for explaining to yourself the main ideas of a difficult passage. By translating another writer's language into your own, you can clarify what you understand and pinpoint what you don't. The paraphrase therefore becomes a tool for learning the subject.

The following pointers will help you write paraphrases.

---

## HOW TO WRITE PARAPHRASES

- Make sure that you understand the source passage.
- Substitute your own words for those of the source passage; look for synonyms that carry the same meaning as the original words.
- Use a different sentence pattern from that of the source; avoid using the source as a fill-in-the-blanks template for your paraphrase.
- Rearrange and connect your own sentences so that they read smoothly.
- Note: Don't paraphrase passages that you analyze closely, such as lines of poetry or parts of a speech. Quote them directly instead.
- *Always* provide a citation so that the reader knows what is being paraphrased. See Chapter 4, "Documenting Sources," for citation styles.

---

Let's consider some other examples. If you were investigating the ethical concerns relating to the practice of in vitro fertilization, you might conclude that you should read some medical literature. You might reasonably want to hear from the doctors themselves who are developing, performing, and questioning the procedures that you are researching. In professional journals and bulletins, physicians write to one another, not to the general public. They use specialized language. If you wanted to refer to a technically complex selection, you might need to write a paraphrase:

## IN VITRO FERTILIZATION: FROM MEDICAL
## REPRODUCTION TO GENETIC DIAGNOSIS

### DIETMAR MIETH

[I]t is not only an improvement in the success-rate that participating research scientists hope for but rather, developments in new fields of research in in-vitro gene diagnosis and in certain circumstances gene therapy. In view of this, the French expert J. F. Mattei has asked the following question: "Are we forced to accept that in vitro fertilization will become one of the most compelling methods of genetic diagnosis?" Evidently, by the introduction of a new law in France and Sweden (1994), this acceptance (albeit with certain restrictions) has already occurred prior to the application of in vitro fertilization reaching a technically mature and clinically applicable phase. This may seem astonishing in view of the question placed by the above-quoted French expert: the idea of embryo production so as to withhold one or two embryos before implantation presupposes a definite "attitude towards eugenics." And to destroy an embryo merely because of its genetic characteristics could signify the reduction of a human life to the sum of its genes. Mattei asks: "In face of a molecular judgment on our lives, is there no possibility for appeal? Will the diagnosis of inherited monogenetic illnesses soon be extended to genetic predisposition for multi-factorial illnesses?"[2]

Like most literature intended for physicians, the language of this selection is somewhat forbidding to an audience of non-specialists, who have trouble with phrases such as "predisposition for multi-factorial illnesses." As a courtesy to your readers and in an effort to maintain a consistent tone and level in your essay, you could paraphrase this paragraph of the medical newsletter. First, of course, you must understand the meaning of the passage, perhaps no small task. But, having read the material carefully (and perhaps consulting a dictionary), you might eventually prepare a paraphrase such as this one:

> Writing in the *Newsletter of the European Network for Biomedical Ethics,* Dietmar Mieth (1996) reports that fertility specialists today not only want to improve the success rates of their procedures but also to diagnose and repair genetic problems before they implant fertilized eggs. Since the result of the in vitro process is often more fertilized eggs than can be used in a procedure, doctors may examine test-tube embryos for genetic defects and "withhold one or two" before implanting them. The practice of selectively implanting embryos raises concerns about eugenics and the rights of rejected embryos. On what genetic

[2] From: *Biomedical Ethics: Newsletter of the European Network for Biomedical Ethics,* Vol. 1, No. 1, 1996.

```
grounds will specialists distinguish flawed from
healthy embryos and make a decision whether or not to
implant? The appearance of single genes linked direct-
ly to specific, or "monogenetic," illnesses could be
grounds for destroying an embryo. More complicated
would be genes that predispose people to an illness
but in no way guarantee the onset of that illness.
Would these genes, which are only one factor in
"multi-factorial illnesses" also be labelled undesir-
able and lead to embryo destruction? Advances in fer-
tility science raise difficult questions. Already,
even before techniques of genetic diagnosis are fully
developed, nations are writing laws governing the
practices of fertility clinics.
```

We begin our paraphrase with the same "not only/but also" logic of the original's first sentence, introducing the concepts of genetic diagnosis and therapy. The next four sentences in the original introduce concerns of a "French expert." Rather than quoting Mieth quoting the expert and imme- diately mentioning new laws in France and Sweden, we decided (first) to explain that in vitro fertilization procedures can give rise to more embryos than needed. We reasoned that non-medical readers would appreciate our making explicit the background knowledge that the author assumes of other physicians. Then we quote Mieth briefly ("withhold one or two" embryos) to provide some flavour of the original. We maintain focus on the ethical questions and wait until the end of the paraphrase before mentioning the laws to which Mieth refers. Our paraphrase is roughly the same length as the original, and it conveys the author's concerns about eugenics. As you can see, the paraphrase requires a writer to make some decisions about the pre- sentation of material. In many, if not most, cases, you will need to do more than simply "translate" from the original, sentence-by-sentence, to write your paraphrase.

Finally, let's consider a passage written by a fine writer that may, nonethe- less, best be conveyed in paraphrase. In "Identify All Carriers," an article on AIDS, the ultra-conservative American editor and columnist William F. Buckley makes the following statement:

> I have read and listened, and I think now that I can convincingly crystallize the thoughts chasing about in the minds of, first, those whose concern with AIDS vic- tims is based primarily on a concern for them, and for the maintenance of the most rigid standards of civil liberties and personal privacy, and, second, those whose anxiety to protect the public impels them to give subordinate attention to the civil amenities of those who suffer from AIDS and primary attention to the safety of those who do not.

In style, Buckley's passage is more like Condorcet's than the medical newsletter: It is eloquent, syntactically sophisticated, and literate. Still, it is challenging. Here is another lengthy sentence, perhaps a bit too stylistically ornate for your purposes in quoting it. For your paper on AIDS, you decide to paraphrase Buckley. You might draft something like this:

> ```
> Buckley finds two opposing sides in the AIDS debate:
> those concerned primarily with the civil liberties and
> the privacy of AIDS victims, and those concerned pri-
> marily with the safety of the public.
> ```

Our paraphrases have been somewhat shorter than the original, but this is not always the case. For example, suppose you wanted to paraphrase this statement by Sigmund Freud:

> We have found out that the distortion in dreams which hinders our understanding of them is due to the activities of a censorship, directed against the unacceptable, unconscious wish-impulses.

If you were to paraphrase this statement (the first sentence in the Tenth Lecture of his *General Introduction to Psychoanalysis*), you might come up with something like this:

> ```
> It is difficult to understand dreams because they con-
> tain distortions. Freud believed that these distor-
> tions arise from our internal censor, which attempts
> to suppress unconscious and forbidden desires.
> ```

Essentially, this paraphrase does little more than break up one sentence into two and somewhat rearrange the sentence structure for clarity.

## WHEN TO SUMMARIZE/WHEN TO PARAPHRASE

Like summaries, then, *paraphrases* are useful devices, both in helping you to understand source material and in enabling you to convey the essence of this source material to your readers. When would you choose to write a summary instead of a paraphrase (or vice versa)? The answer to this question depends on your purpose in presenting your source material. As we've said, summaries are generally based on articles (or sections of articles) or books. Paraphrases are generally based on particularly difficult (or important) paragraphs or sentences. You would seldom paraphrase a long passage, or summarize a short one, unless there were particularly good reasons for doing so. (For example, a lawyer might want to paraphrase several pages of legal language so that his or her client, who is not a lawyer, could understand it.) The purpose of a summary is generally to save your reader time by presenting him or her with a brief and quickly readable version of a lengthy source. The purpose of a paraphrase is generally to clarify a short passage that might otherwise be unclear, or to integrate a writer's point into your own essay without shifting voice. Whether you summarize or paraphrase may also depend on the importance of your source. A particularly important source—if it is not too long—may rate a paraphrase. If it is less important, or peripheral to your central argument, you may choose to write a summary instead. And, of course, you may choose to summarize or paraphrase only part of your source—the part that is most relevant to the point you are making.

## Quotations

A *quotation* records the exact language used by someone in speech or in writing. A *summary,* in contrast, is a brief restatement in your own words of what someone else has said or written. And a *paraphrase* also is a restatement, although one that is often as long as the original source. Any paper in which you draw upon sources will rely heavily on quotation, summary, and paraphrase. How do you choose among the three?

Remember that the papers you write should be your own—for the most part: your own language and certainly your own thesis, your own inferences, and your own conclusion. It follows that references to your source materials should be written primarily as summaries and paraphrases, both of which are built on restatement, not quotation. You will use summaries when you need a *brief* restatement, and paraphrases, which provide more explicit detail than summaries, when you need to follow the development of a source closely. When you quote too much, you risk losing ownership of your work: More easily than you might think, your voice can be drowned out by the voices of those you've quoted.

Nevertheless, quoting just the right source at the right time can significantly improve your papers. The trick is to know when and how to use quotations.

## Choosing Quotations

You'll find that using quotations can be particularly helpful in several situations.

### WHEN TO QUOTE

- Use quotations when another writer's language is particularly memorable and will add interest and liveliness to your paper.
- Use quotations when another writer's language is so clear and economical that to make the same point in your own words would, by comparison, be ineffective.
- Use quotations when you want the solid reputation of a source to lend authority and credibility to your own writing.
- Note: Literary analysis, such as an essay on a poem or play, calls for much more frequent use of direct quotations—from the poem or play, *not* from critics of the poem or play.

## QUOTING MEMORABLE LANGUAGE

Assume you're writing a paper on Napoleon Bonaparte's relationship with the celebrated Josephine. Through research you learn that two days after their marriage Napoleon, given command of an army, left his bride for what was to be a brilliant military campaign in Italy. How did the young general respond to leaving his wife so soon after their wedding? You come across the following, written from the field of battle by Napoleon on April 3, 1796:

> I have received all your letters, but none has such an impact on me as the last. Do you have any idea, darling, what you are doing, writing to me in those terms? Do you not think my situation cruel enough without intensifying my longing for you, overwhelming my soul? What a style! What emotions you evoke! Written in fire, they burn my poor heart![3]

A summary of this passage might read as follows:

> On April 3, 1796, Napoleon wrote to Josephine, expressing how sorely he missed her and how passionately he responded to her letters.

You might write the following as a paraphrase of the passage:

> On April 3, 1796, Napoleon wrote to Josephine that he had received her letters and that one among all others had had a special impact, overwhelming his soul with fiery emotions and longing.

How feeble this summary and paraphrase are when compared with the original! Use the vivid language that your sources give you. In this case, quote Napoleon in your paper to make your subject come alive with memorable detail:

> On April 3, 1796, a passionate, lovesick Napoleon responded to a letter from Josephine; she had written longingly to her husband, who, on a military campaign, acutely felt her absence. "Do you have any idea, darling, what you are doing, writing to me in those terms? . . . What emotions you evoke!" he said of her letters. "Written in fire, they burn my poor heart!"

*You must credit your sources for all quotations*, naming them either in (or at the end of) the sentence that includes the quotation or in a footnote.

## QUOTING CLEAR AND CONCISE LANGUAGE

You should quote a source when its language is particularly clear and economical—when your language, by contrast, would be wordy. Read this passage from a text on biology by Patricia Curtis:

> The honeybee colony, which usually has a population of 30,000 to 40,000 workers, differs from that of the bumblebee and many other social bees or wasps in that it survives the winter. This means that the bees must stay warm despite the cold. Like other bees, the isolated honeybee cannot fly if the temperature falls below 10°C (50°F) and cannot walk if the temperature is below 7°C (45°F). Within the

---

[3] Francis Mossiker, trans., *Napoleon and Josephine.* New York: Simon and Schuster, 1964.

wintering hive, bees maintain their temperature by clustering together in a dense ball; the lower the temperature, the denser the cluster. The clustered bees produce heat by constant muscular movements of their wings, legs, and abdomens. In very cold weather, the bees on the outside of the cluster keep moving toward the center, while those in the core of the cluster move to the colder outside periphery. The entire cluster moves slowly about on the combs, eating the stored honey from the combs as it moves.[4]

A summary of this paragraph might read as follows:

Honeybees, unlike many other varieties of bee, are able to live through the winter by "clustering together in a dense ball" for body warmth. (Curtis 822–23)

A paraphrase of the same passage would be considerably more detailed:

According to Patricia Curtis, honeybees, unlike many other varieties of bee (such as bumblebees), are able to live through the winter. The 30 000 to 40 000 bees within a honeybee hive could not, individually, move about in cold winter temperatures. But when "clustering together in a dense ball," the bees generate heat by constantly moving their body parts. The cluster also moves slowly about the hive, eating honey stored in the combs. This nutrition, in addition to the heat generated by the cluster, enables the honeybee to survive the cold winter months (822–23). (To clarify the extent of the paraphrased material, Curtis's name is moved from the citation to the beginning, and the page numbers are given at the end, outside the punctuation of the last sentence.)

In both the summary and the paraphrase we've quoted Curtis's "clustering together in a dense ball," a phrase that lies at the heart of her description of wintering honeybees. For us to describe this clustering in any language other than Curtis's would be pointless since her description is admirably brief and precise.

## QUOTING AUTHORITATIVE LANGUAGE

You will also want to use quotations that lend authority to your work. When quoting an expert or some prominent political, artistic, or historical figure, you elevate your own work by placing it in esteemed company. Quote respected figures to establish background information in a paper, and your readers will tend to perceive that information as reliable. Quote the opinions of respected figures to endorse some statement that you've made, and your statement becomes more credible to your readers. For example, in an essay on the importance of reading well, you could make use of a passage from Thoreau's *Walden:*

Reading well is hard work and requires great skill and training. It "is a noble exercise," writes Henry David Thoreau in *Walden,* "and one that will task the reader more than any exercise which the customs of the day esteem. It requires a training such as the athletes underwent. . . . Books must be read as deliberately and reservedly as they were written" (72).

[4] "Winter Organization" in Patricia Curtis, *Biology,* 2nd ed. New York: Worth, 1976, pp. 822–823.

By quoting a famous philosopher and essayist on the subject of reading, you add legitimacy to your discussion. Not only do *you* regard reading to be a skill that is both difficult and important; so too does Henry David Thoreau, a highly influential thinker. In essays as in the larger world, you are known by the company you keep.

Here is a discussion of space flight. Author David Chandler refers to a physicist and a physicist-astronaut:

> A few scientists—notably James Van Allen, discoverer of the Earth's radiation belts—have decried the expense of the manned space program and called for an almost exclusive concentration on unmanned scientific exploration instead, saying this would be far more cost-effective.
>
> Other space scientists dispute that idea. Joseph Allen, physicist and former shuttle astronaut, says, "It seems to be argued that one takes away from the other. But before there was a manned space program, the funding on space science was zero. Now it's about $500 million a year."

When quoting less famous but impressively qualified sources, you can provide a little biographical data in an appositive phrase right after naming the source:

> Roberta Bondar, the *Canadian scientist, professor, and shuttle astronaut* . . .

The function of appositives is to rename the nouns they follow by providing explicit, identifying detail. Any information about a person that can be expressed in the following sentence pattern can be made into an appositive phrase:

> Roberta Bondar is a Canadian scientist, professor, and shuttle astronaut. She argues that space research is a good investment.

> Roberta Bondar, *the Canadian scientist, professor, and shuttle astronaut,* argues that space research is a good investment.

## Incorporating Quotations Into Your Sentences

### Quoting Only the Part of a Sentence or Paragraph That You Need

We've said that a writer selects passages for quotation that are especially *vivid and memorable, concise,* or *authoritative.* Now put these principles into practice. Suppose that while conducting research on college sports you've come across the following, written by Robert Hutchins, former president of the University of Chicago:

> If athleticism is bad for students, players, alumni and the public, it is even worse for the colleges and universities themselves. They want to be educational institutions, but they can't. The story of the famous halfback whose only regret, when he bade his coach farewell, was that he hadn't learned to read and write is prob-

ably exaggerated. But we must admit that pressure from trustees, graduates, "friends," presidents and even professors has tended to relax academic standards. These gentry often overlook the fact that a college should not be interested in a fullback who is a half-wit. Recruiting, subsidizing and the double educational standard cannot exist without the knowledge and the tacit approval, at least, of the colleges and universities themselves. Certain institutions encourage susceptible professors to be nice to athletes now admitted by paying them for serving as "faculty representatives" on the college athletic board.[5]

Suppose that in this entire paragraph you find a gem, a sentence with quotable words that will enliven your discussion. You may want to quote part of the following sentence:

These gentry often overlook the fact that a college should not be interested in a fullback who is a half-wit.

### INCORPORATING THE QUOTATION INTO THE FLOW OF YOUR OWN SENTENCE

Once you've selected the passage you want to quote, work the material into your paper in as natural and fluid a manner as possible. Here's how we would quote Hutchins:

Robert Hutchins, a former president of the University of Chicago, asserts that "a college should not be interested in a fullback who is a half-wit."

Note that we've used an appositive to identify Hutchins. And we've used only the part of the paragraph—a single clause—that we thought memorable enough to quote directly.

### AVOIDING FREESTANDING QUOTATIONS

A quoted sentence should never stand by itself—as in the following example:

Various people associated with the university admit that the pressures of athleticism have caused a relaxation of standards. "These gentry often overlook the fact that a college should not be interested in a fullback who is a half-wit." But this kind of thinking is bad for the university and even worse for the athletes.

Even if it includes a parenthetical citation, a freestanding quotation would have the problem of being jarring to the reader. Introduce the quotation with a "signal phrase" that attributes the source not in a parenthetical citation, but in some other part of the sentence—beginning, middle, or end. Thus, you could write:

According to Robert Hutchins, "These gentry often overlook the fact that a college should not be interested in a fullback who is a half-wit."

[5] Robert Hutchins, "Gate Receipts and Glory," *The Saturday Evening Post,* December 3, 1983.

A variation with the signal phrase in the middle:

"These gentry," asserts Robert Hutchins, "often overlook the fact that a college should not be interested in a fullback who is a half-wit."

Another alternative is to introduce a sentence-long quotation with a colon:

But Robert Hutchins disagrees: "These gentry often overlook the fact that a college should not be interested in a fullback who is a half-wit."

Use colons also to introduce block (indented) quotations (as in the examples above).

When attributing sources, try to vary the standard "states," "writes," "says," and so on. Other, stronger verbs you might consider: "asserts," "argues," "maintains," "insists," "asks," and even "wonders." Your writing will be more dynamic if you are as precise in your choice of verbs to denote speech acts as you are in choosing verbs to denote physical acts.

## USING ELLIPSIS MARKS

Using quotations is made somewhat complicated when you want to quote the beginning and end of a passage but not its middle—as was the case when we quoted Henry David Thoreau. Here's part of the paragraph in *Walden* from which we quoted a few sentences:

> To read well, that is to read true books in a true spirit, is a noble exercise, and one that will task the reader more than any exercise which the customs of the day esteem. It requires a training such as the athletes underwent, the steady intention almost of the whole life to this object. Books must be read as deliberately and reservedly as they were written.[6]

And here was how we used this material:

> Reading well is hard work and requires great skill and training. It "is a noble exercise," writes Henry David Thoreau in *Walden,* "and one that will task the reader more than any exercise which the customs of the day esteem. It requires a training such as the athletes underwent. . . . Books must be read as deliberately and reservedly as they were written." (72)

Whenever you quote a sentence but delete words from it, as we have done, indicate this deletion to the reader by placing an ellipsis mark, three spaced periods, in the sentence at the point of deletion. The rationale for using an ellipsis mark is that a direct quotation must be reproduced exactly as it was written or spoken. When writers delete or change any part of the quoted material, readers must be alerted so they don't think the changes were part of the original. Ellipsis marks and brackets serve this purpose.

If you are deleting the middle of a single sentence, use an ellipsis in place of the deleted words:

---

[6] Henry David Thoreau. "Reading" in *Walden.* New York: Signet Classic, 1960.

> "To read well . . . is a noble exercise, and one that will task the reader more than any exercise which the customs of the day esteem" (72).

If you are deleting the end of a quoted sentence, or if you are deleting entire sentences of a paragraph before continuing a quotation, add a period before the ellipsis:

> "It requires a training such as the athletes underwent. . . . Books must be read as deliberately and reservedly as they were written." (72)

You should not use ellipses to indicate deleted words at the beginning or end of a quotation, only in the middle.

## USING BRACKETS

Use square brackets whenever you need to add or substitute words in a quoted sentence. The brackets indicate to the reader a word or phrase that does not appear in the original passage but that you have inserted to avoid confusion. For example, when a pronoun's antecedent would be unclear to readers, delete the pronoun from the sentences and substitute an identifying word or phrase in brackets. When you make such a substitution, no ellipsis marks are needed. Assume that you wish to quote the underlined sentence in the following passage:

> Golden Press's *Walt Disney's Cinderella* set the new pattern for America's Cinderella. This book's text is coy and condescending. (Sample: "And her best friends of all were—guess who—the mice!") The illustrations are poor cartoons. And Cinderella herself is a disaster. She cowers as her sisters rip her homemade ball gown to shreds. (Not even homemade by Cinderella, but by the mice and birds.) She answers her stepmother with whines and pleadings. <u>She is a sorry excuse for a heroine, pitiable and useless</u>. She cannot perform even a simple action to save herself, though she is warned by her friends, the mice. She does not hear them because she is "off in a world of dreams." Cinderella begs, she whimpers, and at last has to be rescued by—guess who—the mice![7]

In quoting this sentence, you would need to identify whom the pronoun *she* refers to. You can do this inside the quotation by using brackets:

> Jane Yolen believes that "[Cinderella] is a sorry excuse for a heroine, pitiable and useless."

If the pronoun begins the sentence to be quoted, as it does in this example, you can identify the pronoun outside the quotation and simply begin quoting your source one word later:

> Jane Yolen believes that Cinderella "is a sorry excuse for a heroine, pitiable and useless."

---

[7] Jane Yolen, "America's 'Cinderella,'" APS Publications, Inc. in *Children's Literature in Education* 8, 1977, pp. 21–29.

If the pronoun you want to identify occurs in the middle of the sentence to be quoted, then you'll need to use brackets. Newspaper reporters do this frequently when quoting sources, who in interviews might say something like the following:

> After the fire they did not return to the police station for three hours.

If the reporter wants to use this sentence in an article, he or she needs to identify the pronoun:

> An official from City Hall, speaking on the condition that he not be identified, said, "After the fire [the officers] did not return to the police station for three hours."

You also will need to add bracketed information to a quoted sentence when a reference essential to the sentence's meaning is implied but not stated directly. Read the following paragraphs from Robert Jastrow's "Toward an Intelligence Beyond Man's":

> These are amiable qualities for the computer; it imitates life like an electronic monkey. As computers get more complex, the imitation gets better. Finally, the line between the original and the copy becomes blurred. In another 15 years or so—two more generations of computer evolution, in the jargon of the technologists—we will see the computer as an emergent form of life.
>
> The proposition seems ridiculous because, for one thing, computers lack the drives and emotions of living creatures. But when drives are useful, they can be programmed into the computer's brain, just as nature programmed them into our ancestors' brains as a part of the equipment for survival. For example, computers, like people, work better and learn faster when they are motivated. Arthur Samuel made this discovery when he taught two IBM computers how to play checkers. They polished their game by playing each other, but they learned slowly. Finally, Dr. Samuel programmed in the will to win by forcing the computers to try harder—and to think out more moves in advance—when they were losing. Then the computers learned very quickly. One of them beat Samuel and went on to defeat a champion player who had not lost a game to a human opponent in eight years.[8]

If you wanted to quote only the underlined sentence, you would need to provide readers with a bracketed explanation; otherwise, the words "the proposition" would be unclear. Here is how you would manage the quotation:

> According to Robert Jastrow, a physicist and former official at NASA's Goddard Institute, "The proposition [that computers will emerge as a form of life] seems ridiculous because, for one thing, computers lack the drives and emotions of living creatures."

Remember that when you quote the work of another, you are obligated to credit—or cite—the author's work properly; otherwise, you may be guilty of plagiarism. See Chapter 4 for guidance on citing sources.

---

[8] Excerpt from "Toward an Intelligence Beyond Man's" from *Time,* February 20, 1978. Copyright © 1978 Time Inc. Reprinted by permission.

## WHEN TO SUMMARIZE, PARAPHRASE, AND QUOTE

**Summarize:**
- To present main points of a lengthy passage (article or book)
- To condense peripheral points necessary to discussion

**Paraphrase:**
- To clarify a short passage
- To emphasize main points

**Quote:**
- To capture another writer's particularly memorable language
- To capture another writer's clearly and economically stated language
- To lend authority and credibility to your own writing
- To support a textual analysis with excerpts from the work under discussion

## ▨ EXERCISE

Read "Body Body Double: Cloning Infants a Distant Fantasy," which appeared in the *Focus* section of *The Boston Sunday Globe,* January 11, 1998. Write a "short" summary of the article, following the directions in this chapter for dividing the article into sections, for writing a one-sentence summary of each section, and then for joining section summaries with a thesis. Prepare for the summary by making notes in the margins. Your finished product should be the result of two or more drafts.

# Body Body Double: Cloning Infants a Distant Fantasy

ALEXANDER M. CAPRON

San Francisco—Barely 10 months after researchers at Scotland's Roslin 　1
Institute amazed the world by cloning a sheep, Chicago physicist Richard Seed created a stir when he announced he was establishing the Human Clone Clinic and would use the Roslin technique to make human babies.

　　Are last week's headlines just one more instance of the breathtaking 　2
speed with which science can advance? Not at all.

Seed had no scientific breakthrough to announce. He doesn't have the credibility that might come from having run a fertility center. That, at least, would provide him with state-of-the-art experience in using the techniques of embryo cultivation and transplantation necessary for any realistic attempt at human cloning.    3

Maybe the attention Seed has managed to generate will help him raise the $2 million he claims he needs, but his planned clinic has more in common with Barnum & Bailey's Circus than with Brigham and Women's Hospital. Indeed, the only result he has produced so far is to spark a call from President Clinton yesterday to ban human cloning experiments.    4

Last February, the announcement that scientists had cloned Dolly the sheep was met with a nearly unanimous chorus of concern. The prospect that the techniques used to produce the first copy of an adult mammal could be used to create human genetic replicas struck scientists and politicians alike as dangerous.    5

Concerned about the "serious ethical questions" presented by the "possible use of the technology to clone human embryos," Clinton at the time asked the National Bioethics Advisory Commission to report within 90 days on how the government should respond. He quickly banned the use of federal money for cloning.    6

At subsequent congressional hearings, medical scientists took a skeptical view of the prospect of using the Roslin technique to create humans. Harold Varmus, director of the National Institutes of Health, labeled human cloning "repugnant." Ian Wilmut, the creator of Dolly, told senators that cloning people would be "quite inhuman."    7

Some of the concerns first expressed turned out to be overblown or wrongheaded. For example, two people having the same genetic makeup hardly negates the basic dignity of each individual, as the birth of identical twins makes clear. Furthermore, just as twins differ in many ways as they grow and develop, a genetic clone would exist in a different environment and have different experiences from his or her progenitor.    8

Anyone who made a clone of Michael Jordan expecting to get a great basketball player 20 years later would likely be disappointed, and Mozart's clone wouldn't be a brilliant composer simply because of his genes.    9

But the advisory commission concluded that other concerns about human cloning deserved to be taken very seriously. First, the process of creating Dolly made it clear that the technique used is much too risky to use with humans at this time. Roslin scientists tried 276 times to clone a sheep before they succeeded with Dolly. Many tries did not result in viable embryos or did not produce successful pregnancies once transferred to surrogate mothers. And, before Dolly, all the lambs that went to term had such severe problems that they were stillborn or died shortly after birth. This is not a circumstance in which any responsible person would consider moving the technique to human use.    10

Nor has anything occurred over the past year to alter that conclusion.    11

Safety concerns were the first reason the advisory commission con- 12
cluded that it would be unethical to proceed with cloning a human at this
time. The second reason was that the potential psychological harm to children and the adverse moral and cultural effects of cloning merit further
reflection and deliberation.

Many reasons have been advanced for why people might want to have a 13
cloned child: To replace a child who dies young. To provide a genetic copy
who could donate a kidney, bone marrow, or other life-saving organ. To
allow infertile couples to have a child who is genetically connected to at least
one of them, or to allow a person without a mate of the opposite sex to have
a child. To give a child a "good start in life" by using genes from people
regarded as particularly outstanding according to such criteria as intelligence,
artistic creativity, or athletic prowess.

Some of the ideas are mere fantasy, especially when they reflect a strong 14
streak of genetic determinism, the notion that genes control the people we
become. The fact that they are fantasy does not mean that they won't be acted
on. The chance to have a cloned child may tempt parents to seek excessive
control over their children's characteristics and to value them for how well
they meet such overly detailed parental expectations.

Moreover, if cloning were used, arguments would soon be heard that it 15
was actually a superior way to produce children since it would aim to avoid
the disappointments that now result from the "genetic lottery" inherent in
sexual reproduction. Responsible parenthood in the 21st century might come
to include using "ideal types" as the bases for our children, and perhaps even
doing some "genetic enhancement" of the clones to provide what would now
be regarded as super-human capabilities. Whether such developments arose
voluntarily, as a result of social pressure, or through eventual legislation,
they would amount to a form of eugenics more chilling than those contemplated by the Nazis, more akin to Aldous Huxley's "Brave New World."

These are serious worries, though whether they are compelling enough to 16
justify permanently forbidding cloning needs further debate. If some reasons
for using cloning were accepted, could the procedure be limited to those
uses? Designing a system of regulation that is ethically defensible and practically enforceable would not be easy, but it might be necessary if we concluded that the proper balance between ethical risks and personal liberties meant
that society must allow human cloning under some circumstances.

Thus, the advisory commission concluded that while safety concerns are 17
being addressed, deliberations should go forward to allow an informed public
consensus to develop.

Meanwhile, the president has urged Congress to enact an immediate fed- 18
eral ban on human cloning experiments. While Seed is likely to remain a
sideshow in the ultimate development of this technology, his announcement
ought to prompt Congress to take action now.

■ ■ ■

■ EXERCISES

1. Working in groups, identify the form and extent of representation of outside sources in three scholarly journals, one from the humanities (such as English literature, history, or philosophy), one from the social sciences (such as psychology, sociology, or anthropology), and one from the natural sciences (such as biology, chemistry, or physics). How do the writers in these journals differ in their use of sources? What kinds of sources do they use?

2. Summarize the article "Group Minds" by Doris Lessing (pp. 270–272) using the shorter method of summary—that is, your summary should capture the thesis statement and the main points of the article, but not the details (see pp. 96–97). Remember to "frame" the summary so that the author and title of the article are acknowledged early on and it remains clear that Lessing, not you, is the author of the material being summarized—don't leave it "raw." Your summary should be one paragraph about 150 words long.

3. Summarize and properly frame Shirley Jackson's famous short story, "The Lottery" (338–345). This summary should be one paragraph about 150 words long that captures the main story line and refrains from interpretation.

4. Write a short (one or two paragraph) essay about Lessing's article *and/or* Jackson's story in which you use all the different techniques of paraphrasing and quoting presented in this chapter. Do not worry about making profound comments: In this exercise, what counts is the accuracy of representation only. Specifically, your little essay should include the following elements:
   • two paraphrased sentences
   • a long quotation in block form
   • a sentence-length quotation
   • a short snippet-sized quotation

   Use each of the following techniques at least once:
   • square brackets to signify an alteration of the original
   • ellipsis marks to omit unnecessary words

   Make sure that you do the following for *each* paraphrase and/or quotation:
   • Provide a citation in either MLA or APA form.
   • Punctuate it correctly.

   Finally,
   • Make sure that each quotation is somehow embedded into your own prose—never leave a quotation free-standing (see pp. 119–120).
   • Provide a numbered footnote at the bottom of the page for each of the two paraphrases. In the footnotes, give the original version of the paraphrased material.

# 6

# Critiquing Others: Textual Analysis and Response

## CRITICAL READING

When writing papers in university, you are often called on to respond critically to source materials. Critical reading requires the abilities to both summarize and evaluate a presentation. As you have seen, a *summary* is a brief restatement in your own words of the content of a passage. An *evaluation* is a more difficult matter, however. In your university work, you read to gain and *use* new information; but as sources are not equally valid or equally useful, you must learn to distinguish critically among sources by evaluating them.

There is no ready-made formula for determining validity. Critical reading and its written analogue—the *critique*—require discernment, sensitivity, imagination, and, above all, a willingness to become involved in what you read. These skills cannot be taken for granted and are developed only through repeated practice. You must begin somewhere, though, and we recommend that you start by posing two broad categories of questions about passages, articles, and books that you read: (1) What is the author's purpose in writing? Does he or she succeed in this purpose? (2) To what extent do you agree with the author?

## Question Category 1: What Is the Author's Purpose in Writing? Does He or She Succeed in This Purpose?

All critical reading *begins with an accurate summary*. Before attempting an evaluation, you must be able to locate an author's thesis and identify the selection's content and structure. You must understand the author's *purpose*. Authors write to inform, to persuade, and to entertain. A given piece may be *primarily informative* (a summary of the research on cloning), *primarily persuasive* (an argument on why the government must do something to alleviate homelessness), or *primarily entertaining* (a play about the frustrations of young lovers), or it may be all three (as in Timothy Findley's *The Wars*, about Canadian soldiers in World War I). Sometimes authors are not fully conscious of their purposes. Sometimes their purposes change as they write. But if the finished piece is coherent, it will have a primary reason for having been written, and it should be apparent that the author is attempting primarily to inform, persuade, or entertain a particular audience. To identify this primary reason, this purpose, is your first job as a critical reader. Your next job is to determine how successful the author has been. As a critical reader, you bring different criteria, or standards of judgment, to bear when you read pieces intended to inform or persuade.

## Informative Writing

A piece intended to inform will provide definitions, describe or report on a process, recount a story, give historical background, and/or provide facts and figures. An informational piece responds to questions such as the following:

> What (or who) is _____ ?
> How does _____ work?
> What is the controversy or problem about?
> What happened?
> How and why did it happen?
> What were the results?
> What are the arguments for and against _____ ?

To the extent that an author answers these and related questions and the answers are a matter of verifiable record (you could check for accuracy if you had the time and inclination), the selection is intended to inform. Having determined this, you can organize your response by considering three other criteria: accuracy, significance, and fair interpretation of information.

**Accuracy of Information.** If you are going to use any of the information presented, you must be satisfied that it is trustworthy. One of your responsibilities as a critical reader is to find out if it is accurate.

**Significance of Information.** One useful question that you can put to a reading is "So what?" In the case of selections that attempt to inform, you may reasonably wonder whether the information makes a difference. What can the person who is reading gain from this information? How is knowledge advanced by the publication of this material? Is the information of importance to you or to others in a particular audience? Why or why not?

**Fair Interpretation of Information.** At times you will read reports, the sole function of which is to relate raw data or information. In these cases, you will build your response on the two questions in question category 1: What is the author's purpose? Does she or he succeed in this purpose? More frequently, once an author has presented information, she or he will attempt to evaluate or interpret it—which is only reasonable, since information that has not been evaluated or interpreted is of little use. One of your tasks as a critical reader is to make a distinction between the author's presentation of facts and figures and his or her attempts to evaluate them. You may find that the information is valuable but the interpretation is not. Perhaps the author's conclusions are not justified. Could you offer a contrary explanation for the same facts? Does more information need to be gathered before conclusions can be drawn? Why?

## Persuasive Writing

Writing is frequently intended to persuade—that is, to influence the reader's thinking. To make a persuasive case, the writer must begin with an assertion that is arguable, some statement about which reasonable people could disagree. Such an assertion, when it serves as the essential organizing principle of the article or book, is called a *thesis*. Examples:

> Because they do not speak English, many children in this affluent land are being denied their fundamental right to equal educational opportunity.

> Bilingual education, which has been stridently promoted by a small group of activists with their own agenda, is detrimental to the very students it is supposed to serve.

Thesis statements such as these—and the subsidiary assertions used to help support them—represent conclusions that authors have drawn as a result of researching and thinking about the issue. You go through the same process yourself when you write persuasive papers or critiques. And just as you are entitled to critically evaluate the assertions of authors you read, so your professors—and other students—are entitled to evaluate *your* assertions, whether they are encountered as written arguments or as comments made in class discussion.

Keep in mind that writers organize arguments by arranging evidence to support one conclusion and oppose (or dismiss) another. You can assess the validity of the argument and the conclusion by determining whether the author has (1) clearly defined key terms, (2) used information fairly, (3) argued logically, and not fallaciously.

We will illustrate our discussion on defining terms, using information fairly, and arguing logically by referring to two articles: Glastonbury and LaMendola's "The Nature of Meaning and Data" is reproduced below, and Virginia Postrel's "Fatalist Attraction: The Dubious Case Against Fooling Mother Nature" appears in the biotechnology chapter, pp. 541–544. The student-written example critiques that appear at the end of this chapter will provide two responses to Postrel's article.

## The Nature and Meaning of Data

BRYAN GLASTONBURY AND WALTER LAMENDOLA

### COLLECTING DATA ABOUT YOU

Have you purchased a new home appliance lately? Let's pretend that what you really need is a new vacuum cleaner. You buy one. As you unpack your new appliance, you carefully put aside the enclosed product information and warranty registration. The machine works well the next morning, so you have extra time to fill out and return your product registration card. It asks for your name, address, and telephone number. It asks where you made the purchase—their name, address, and telephone number. It probably goes on to ask for your age, gender, income group, number of members in household, and whether or not you own your own home. How much a year do you spend on appliances? What prompted you to buy the cleaner? Where will it be used? Why did you purchase this brand? Was it purchased for a specific member of your family? Was the decision to buy this cleaner made by a man, woman, or jointly? Have you ever owned a similar product? What was it? What brand? Do you own another cleaner? What model? Such questions are always posed with courtesy, without any sense of compulsion, and with an explanation that your answers will help the company to a better understanding of its customers' needs.

When you fill out and return your card, perhaps wondering what it has    2
to do with your purchase of the cleaner, you might be surprised to know that it usually goes to a company that has paid the manufacturer for the rights to the data. In due course the data will be computerized and resold to other companies, and you have unwittingly become a participant in a wide network, without your knowledge and outside your control. For example, your data may turn up being sold to a firm which markets carpets. As a result, you may start receiving any number of unwanted mailings and telephone calls. In one case reported in a national news service, a data company sold material obtained from a national weight loss association to a chocolate company, which reported a rise in sales as a consequence of using it.

Most of us probably consider the mailing label as the type of data that is    3
commonly bought and sold in the marketplace. That is just the tip of the iceberg, but we can start there. A typical mailing label will contain a name and address. Some of the data companies (also called list brokers) may also want your telephone number. It may be that they can buy a list of names and telephone numbers already on computer, or they have to go through the directory. It is also possible to obtain lists of names linked to job, place of employment and business phone number. By using a computer program these separate sources of data can be merged to build up a comprehensive route for contacting families, at home and work. The computer can cross-reference and link in any other material that is available, like court records of debts or criminal convictions, or the age and income profile you provided with your vacuum cleaner registration.

This type of collection and work with data represents the fastest growing    4
use of computerized data today, and list selling between businesses and industries has become a major activity. For example, credit bureau income from selling data lists to marketing firms or list brokers, presently at about one third of total revenue, may exceed their income from providing credit references within the next few years. Data is a big business for everyone. But what type of data is collected? Is it just the basic factual background material that we have considered so far, or is it more involved?

If we start with the example of a high school student, age 15, in the    5
U.S.A., we may be able to trace some of the major sources of data collection.

As high school students enter their second year their names will start to find a place on computerized lists, especially if they have been selected for any specific recognition or honours. A student of high academic accomplishments will begin to receive mailings from colleges and universities, encouraging the student to consider them. A little later the student may fill out an application for automobile insurance, and this data will be entered into a database and matched with criminal and credit files before the insurance application will be considered for approval. The student will not know the results of the application check or whether due data is bought and sold in the marketplace.

The student may now want a vacation job, and when applying may be asked questions about medical history, brushes with the police, home life, what parents do, and performance in school. If the company is large, the job application will be stored on computer and another check of the applicant will occur. The check may include credit and criminal checks as well as checks of driving record and personal references. Again none of the outcomes will be known to the student. Our student passes the checks and is employed. On receiving the first pay cheque, he or she goes to the bank and opens an account. Here is another application form to fill in, and if the student wants an overdraft facility, some material about the parents' financial viability may be requested.   6

While the student is working, playing, studying, and becoming a productive citizen, the marketing of personal data is leading to mailings about subscriptions to periodicals, cassette tape and compact disc buying clubs, and hosts of other consumers items aimed at teenagers. At the point of leaving school the mailings increase. Depending upon social and economic status, the contents of databases, and some further screening by a credit reporting bureau, the mail could bring an invitation to apply for a credit card. Our student still has not left the family home or gone to college, but look at the data already gathered. The computerized files have material on:   7

Insurance
Driving record
Criminal record
Employment
Medical history and condition
Educational record
Credit
Banking
Home life
Family relationships
Own and family finances
Lifestyle
Preferences and ideologies
Leisure activities
Shopping and consumption patterns
Travel and communications

So far we have shown how personal profiles are established as part of      8
massive data systems. How else can we use the material? To return to vacuum
cleaners, as well as using those questionnaires to assemble personal profiles,
we can use them compositely to build a model of the way groups of people act
to purchase such appliances. We might analyze the data statistically, and
find that people with medium family incomes say they spend the most money
on appliances, and that in those families the woman makes the buying decision for herself, usually at Acme Hardware Stores. The commercial value of
this information is significant.

But what if we take it a step further. As a data company, I have product      9
registration data for vacuum cleaners, but I have also bought hundreds of
other such databases. By performing operations upon the data, such as matching, selecting, relating, and modelling, I am now able to offer a comprehensive
marketing tool to others. One such tool, developed by Lotus and Equifax, is
a piece of personal computer based marketing software called MarketPlace
which, using a compact disc that contains data on about 120 million people
in 80 million households in the U.S., allows the user to type in consumer profiles and print out mailing labels for the people who match the profile. The
data about each person includes name, address, age, gender, estimated annual
income, marital status, and shopping habits.

Such types of data collection, facilitated by computing and communica-      10
tion systems, are commonplace in a modern industrialized society, though the
public presentation of MarketPlace led to opposition and its temporary withdrawal in 1990. It is certainly true that many of the valued services that we
receive depend upon the systematic and orderly collection of data about us.
What this example begins to outline is the pervasiveness of the data collection
and the underlying ability to match and model pieces of data for the purpose
of creating information which can be used to influence our decision making.
Even more to the point, these data are the basis for others to make decisions
about us and therefore control and manipulate our everyday life. And yet, as
large and wide scale as these data systems are, they must be considered *personal* information systems because they hold data which relates to specific,
identifiable individuals.


## THE PERSONAL IN DATA SYSTEMS

Laws in different countries generally hold that storing data which relates to      11
specific, identifiable individuals constitutes a personal database, but they often
do not go a stage further, to distinguish between differing types of data. While
a computer system that collects your buying habits may be intrusive, for example, by sending you mail you do not want, a system which contains data about
your mental health or political activities may be used in ways that can cause
you serious harm, for example, by releasing your past history of depression to
a potential employer. There is some data which people consider to be more
personal than others, or that we consider to be intimate and do not want to be

shared. Alternatively, there is data which we share, but only in confidence. In some situations, not limited to conversations with a lawyer or doctor, people expect that what is shared will be protected in some way by confidentiality. But how do we know that other people share our view of what is personal?

In a most interesting demonstration of defining personal data, Wacks (1989, pp. 226–238) created an index. This is based upon the extent to which the exposure of data could potentially cause harm to a person. The data is rated by the degrees of sensitivity, low, medium or high. He defines *low sensitivity* as biographical data, and puts in this category basic facts about home, job and educational record. *Medium sensitivity* he describes as judgmental, including reports on us (school, employment) and matters involving a judgment or opinion of another person. Data which is *high sensitivity* is intimate, like our mental health record, where "there is a persuasive case for maintaining that at least some . . . should not be collected at all" (p. 229).[1]

Generally, people are highly sensitive to health, ideological, criminal justice, and sexual data. It is true that sensitivity is difficult to define, and may change not only from culture to culture, but from time to time. However, the combination of the ability to identify a particular individual, the potential to cause that individual harm, and the sensitivity of the data being collected are personal considerations which surely need to be, in almost all cases, under the control of the individual.

It is true that many of the services we need, such as health or social security services, rely on us to furnish accurate and truthful data to them. One might also argue that much of this data could be seen as trivial, as opposed to private or sensitive. Indeed, in some countries (all of Scandinavia, for example), data has been categorized to account for differences in sensitivity. It is also possible to argue that some data is of such import to society, and perhaps being HIV positive presently fits this description, that it must not only be collected but also related to specific individuals. Despite these arguments, the ultimate concern needs to be framed within the context of protecting the individual in everyday life. We can do this by honouring the right of the individual to advise and consent. Not only should consent be the cornerstone of all approaches, but also people need to have the right to be informed when and where data about them is collected or stored. They need to give their specific consent to any activity which accesses, operates upon and uses this data. They need to be able to access and correct data without risking vulnerability or expense.

The location and correction of data is not as simple as it may sound. It is easiest to understand if we assume that the data is stored in one computer, but of course it is not. The fact that it is traded means that it has passed to many computers, possibly linked in a network, but just as possibly quite separate. Leaving aside the complex practicalities, what is the value of a fight to view, correct and sanction the use of our personal data, without a parallel right to be informed of all computers on which it is held?

12

13

14

15

---

[1] Wacks, R. (1989). *Personal Information*. Clarendon Press, Oxford.

In order to illustrate these difficulties we can continue the example of our    16
student, who is now a high achieving university student nearing graduation,
but needing support, advice, and counselling about moving into a career.
Though a hard worker, the student has got involved in other activities, and is
worried about a number of matters. Can a campus counsellor help? The
counsellor, a psychologist, administers a number of tests which hint at a
rather unbalanced character. Consequently, in their discussions, they cover
the student's uncertainty about sexuality, disgust with war and government,
experimentation with alcohol and drugs, and concerns about the future of the
world. These discussions are very helpful to the student. They not only relieve
anxiety, but they contribute to a number of healthy decisions to change living
patterns. Things feel a lot more balanced, and, as the lifestyle changes, so
uncertainties disappear.

The future our student desires is a good beginning position in a large firm    17
of stockbrokers. After interviews for a number of positions, none of the
applications succeeds. The student's father has a close friend in one of the
firms, so makes a discreet enquiry. The friend reveals the reasons why no job
was offered. Apparently, there are some damaging psychological test results
which come up in the employment check. In addition, there is a psychological report which describes the student as confused, possibly sexually malad-
justed, with occasional depression, marginally psychotic, and a potential
non-conformist who may be addicted to drugs and alcohol. After calming
down, the student recalls talks with the university counsellor, and also remem-
bers in the first job application agreeing to a recruitment firm seeking a report
from that source.

The student is able to find out that the firm is a subsidiary of Greater    18
Data. They admit to having the files in their main computer in Taiwan and
agree to a formal request to review them for errors and corrections. In talking to a supervisor at Greater Data, the student finds that they have sold the
files to others, and probably those have sent them to others again. In addition,
the supervisor explains that while the student has the right to correct erroneous or incorrect data, the incorrect data will not be removed.

The student has now encountered a number of the major problems we    19
can expect in data collection and retention. The counsellor may have professional values about confidentiality, but does not ensure that they are
extended to the computer system. Old data has been retained, with subjective interpretations which, while useful at the time of counselling, were later
damaging to the interests of the student. No one, least of all the student, had
been given the opportunity to assess whether old test results and notes were
relevant to the present search for employment. Most critically, the student
had no knowledge that the data was being kept, no knowledge of the use to
which the data would be put, and had not been asked to consent to the use
of the data.

■ ■ ■

**Clearly Defined Terms.** The validity of an argument depends to some degree on how carefully key terms have been defined. Take the assertion, for example, that North American society must be grounded in "family values." Just what do people who use this phrase mean by it? The validity of their argument depends on whether they and their readers agree on a definition of "family values"—as well as what it means to be "grounded in" family values. So, in responding to an argument, be sure you (and the author) are clear on what exactly is being argued. Only then can you respond to the logic of the argument, to the author's use of evidence, and to the author's conclusions.

In the article by Glastonbury and LaMendola, "personal data" is a key concept. Not only do they define what they mean by giving examples, but in paragraph 12 they round out their definition by exploring how Wacks created an index "based upon the extent to which the exposure of data could potentially cause harm to a person." By contrast, in her article that argues against those who want to slow down the process of developing and marketing of biomedical advances, Virginia Postrel never defines the key term "biomedicine." Nor does she explain the people who might make up the "set of experts" whose interference she warns against; in the question section following her article (Discussion and Writing Suggestions, #6), the editors begin to do this work when they talk about "genetic intervention being made *not* by individuals but by broader cultural authorities—governments, say, or international bodies of scientists." Because several of her key terms remain unspecified and unclear, it is sometimes difficult to be certain of her argument and thus to respond with confidence to all its parts.

**Fair Use of Information.** Information is used as evidence in support of arguments. When presented with such evidence, ask yourself two questions: The *first*: "Is the information accurate and up-to-date?" At least a portion of an argument is rendered invalid if the information used to support it is inaccurate or out-of-date. The *second*: "Has the author cited *representative* information?" The evidence used in an argument must be presented in a spirit of fair play. An author is less than ethical who presents only evidence favouring his views when he is well aware that contrary evidence exists. For instance, it would be dishonest to argue that an economic recession is imminent and to cite as evidence only those indicators of economic well-being that have taken a decided turn for the worse while ignoring and failing to cite contrary (positive) evidence.

Virginia Postrel's essay provides several examples of unfair use of information. In paragraph 11, for example, she refers to philosopher John Gray's reminder that death is natural as the fatalism of a "biotechnophobe." She also quotes his reference to "macabre high-tech medicine involving organ transplantation," without providing a sense of context that might help us to understand the highly invasive and experimental procedures he may be discussing. Instead, Postrel follows up this brief quote with painting Gray as one opposed to helping suffering humanity ease its pain: "Suffering is the human condition, he suggested: We should just lie back and accept it."

**Logical Argumentation; Avoiding Logical Fallacies.** At some point, you will need to respond to the logic of the argument itself. To be convincing, an argument should be governed by principles of logic—clear and orderly thinking. This does *not* mean that an argument should not be biased. A biased argument—that is, an argument weighted toward one point of view and against others—may be valid as long as it is logically sound.

Here are several examples of faulty thinking and logical fallacies to watch for:

*Emotionally Loaded Terms.* Writers sometimes will attempt to sway readers by using emotionally charged words: words with positive connotations to sway readers to their own point of view; words with negative connotations to sway readers away from the opposing point of view. The fact that an author uses emotionally loaded terms does not necessarily invalidate the argument. Emotional appeals are perfectly legitimate and time-honoured modes of persuasion. But in academic writing, which is grounded in logical argumentation, they should not be the *only* means of persuasion. You should be sensitive to *how* emotionally loaded terms are being used. In particular, are they being used deceptively or to hide the essential facts?

When we looked over the issue of using information unfairly and examined a passage from Postrel above, we might also have pointed out that in using the phrase "lie back and accept it" she is using an emotionally weighted phrase that is often used to taint victims as participants in their suffering. Thus, some readers might object not only that she is unfair in presenting Gray's position shorn of its original context, but also that she uses emotionally-laden terms under the pretense of providing an accurate gloss.

**Ad Hominem** *Argument.* In an *ad hominem* argument, the writer rejects opposing views by attacking the person who holds them. By calling opponents names, an author avoids the issue:

> I could more easily accept my opponent's plan to increase revenues by collecting on delinquent tax bills if he had paid more than a hundred dollars in state taxes in each of the past three years. But the fact is, he's a millionaire with a millionaire's tax shelters. This man hasn't paid a wooden nickel for the state services he and his family depend on. So I ask you: Is *he* the one to be talking about taxes to *us*?

It could well be that the opponent has paid virtually no state taxes for three years; but this fact has nothing to do with, and is a ploy to divert attention from, the merits of a specific proposal for increasing revenues. The proposal is lost in the attack against the man himself, an attack that violates the principles of logic. Writers (and speakers) must make their points by citing evidence in support of their views and by challenging contrary evidence.

Postrel uses an ad hominem argument against German Research Minister Juergen Ruettgers toward the end of her essay to make her point that we should be free to choose our own medicine. First, she quotes a statement of his opposing cloning: "The cloned human would be an attack on the dignity and integrity of every single person on this earth." She goes on to deride him for taking this stance by saying that he is "wildly overreacting" before finally attacking his character: "We should not let the arrogant likes of Ruettgers block . . . future hopes."

*Faulty Cause and Effect.* The fact that one event precedes another in time does not mean that the first event has caused the second. An example: Fish begin dying by the thousands in a lake near your hometown. An environmental group immediately cites chemical dumping by several manufacturing plants as the cause. But other causes are possible: A disease might have affected the fish; the growth of algae might have contributed to the deaths; or acid rain might be a factor. The origins of an event are usually complex and are not always traceable to a single cause. So you must carefully examine cause-and-effect reasoning when you find a writer using it. In Latin, this fallacy is known as *post hoc, ergo propter hoc* ("after this, therefore because of this").

*Either/Or Reasoning.* Either/or reasoning also results from an unwillingness to recognize complexity. If an author analyzes a problem and offers only two explanations, one of which he or she refutes, then you are entitled to object that the other is not thereby true. For usually, several other explanations (at the very least) are possible. For whatever reason, the author has chosen to overlook them. As an example, suppose you are reading a selection on genetic engineering and the author builds an argument on the basis of the following:

> Research in gene splicing is at a crossroads: Either scientists will be carefully monitored by civil authorities and their efforts limited to acceptable applications, such as disease control; or, lacking regulatory guidelines, scientists will set their own ethical standards and begin programs in embryonic manipulation that, however well intended, exceed the proper limits of human knowledge.

Certainly, other possibilities for genetic engineering exist beyond the two mentioned here. But the author limits debate by establishing an either/or choice. Such limitation is artificial and does not allow for complexity. As a critical reader, be on the alert for either/or reasoning.

*Hasty Generalization.* Writers are guilty of hasty generalization when they draw their conclusions from too little evidence or from unrepresentative evidence. To argue that scientists should not proceed with the human genome project because a recent editorial urged that the project be abandoned is to make a hasty generalization. This lone editorial may be unrepresentative of the views of most people—both scientists and laypeople—who have studied and written about the matter. To argue that one should never obey authority because the Milgram experiment shows the dangers of obeying authority is to ignore the fact that Milgram's experiment was concerned primarily with obedience to *immoral* authority. Thus, the experimental situation was unrepresentative of most routine demands for obedience—for example, to obey a parental rule or to comply with a summons for jury duty—and a conclusion about the malevolence of all authority would be a hasty generalization.

In "The Nature and Meaning of Data," Glastonbury and LaMendola rely on an extended example that depicts the plight of a hypothetical individual who falls prey to out-of-control data collection operations. This may encourage some readers to object that a single example is not convincing. Moreover, in this case the fact that the example is hypothetical further weakens its ability to serve as evidence.

*False Analogy.* Comparing one person, event, or issue to another may be illuminating, but it also may be confusing or misleading. The differences between the two may be more significant than the similarities, and the conclusions drawn from the one may not necessarily apply to the other. A writer who argues that it is reasonable to quarantine people with AIDS because quarantine has been effective in preventing the spread of smallpox is assuming an analogy between AIDS and smallpox that (because of the differences between the two diseases) is not valid.

*Begging the Question.* To beg the question is to assume as a proven fact the very thesis being argued. To assert, for example, that Canada is not in decline because it is as strong and prosperous as ever is not to prove anything: It is merely to repeat the claim in different words. This fallacy also is known as circular reasoning.

There is an example of question-begging in paragraph 14 of "The Nature and Meaning of Data." After arguing that individuals should be able to have control over their personal data, the authors cite several areas that might be exempt from such a rule of privacy. Rather than considering the implications for breaches of privacy arising from the creation of these exemptions, the authors return directly to their point that protecting individual rights should be the ultimate goal.

*Non Sequitur.* "Non sequitur" is Latin for "it does not follow"; the term is used to describe a conclusion that does not logically follow from a premise. "Since minorities have made such great strides in the last few decades," a writer may argue, "we no longer need affirmative action programs." Aside from the fact that the premise itself is arguable (*have* minorities made such great strides?), it does not follow that because minorities *may* have made great strides, there is no further need for affirmative action programs.

*Oversimplification.* Be alert for writers who offer easy solutions to complicated problems. "Canada's economy will be strong again if we all 'buy Canadian,'" a politician may argue. But the problems of our economy are complex and cannot be solved by a slogan or a simple change in buying habits. Likewise, a writer who argues that we should ban genetic engineering assumes that simple solutions ("just say 'no'") will be sufficient to deal with the complex moral dilemmas raised by this new technology.

It can be said that Glastonbury and LaMendola's argument partakes of similar oversimplification. After making the case that we are often unaware of how our personal data is being stored and moved through data banks, they recommend that individuals should control the dissemination of personal information, which seems an expression of hope for something that can no longer be.

## Writing That Entertains

Authors write not only to inform and persuade but also to entertain. One response to entertainment is a hearty laugh; but it is possible to entertain without laughter: A good book or play or poem may prompt you to ruminate, grow wistful, elated, angry. Laughter is only one of many possible reactions. You read a piece (or view a work) and react with sadness, surprise, exhilaration, disbelief, horror, boredom, whatever. As with a response to an informative piece or an argument, your response to an essay, poem, story, play, novel, or film should be precisely stated and carefully developed. Ask yourself some of the following questions (you won't have space to explore all of them, but try to consider some of the most important): Did I care for the portrayal of a certain character? Did that character seem too sentimentalized, for example, or heroic? Did his adversaries seem too villainous or stupid? Were the situations believable? Was the action interesting or merely formulaic? Was the theme developed subtly, powerfully, or did the work come across as preachy or shrill? Did the action at the end of the work follow plausibly from what had come before? Was the language fresh and incisive or stale and predictable? Explain as specifically as possible what elements of the work seemed effective or ineffective and why. Offer an overall assessment, elaborating on your views.

## Question Category 2: To What Extent Do You Agree With the Author?

When formulating a critical response to a source, try to distinguish your evaluation of the author's purpose and success at achieving that purpose from your agreement or disagreement with the author's views. The distinction allows you to respond to a piece of writing on its merits. As an unbiased, evenhanded critic, you evaluate an author's clarity of presentation, use of evidence, and adherence to principles of logic. To what extent has the author succeeded in achieving his or her purpose? Still withholding judgment, offer your assessment and give the author (in effect) a grade. Significantly, your assessment of the presentation may not coincide with your views of the author's conclusions: You may agree with an author entirely but feel that the presentation is superficial; you may find the author's logic and use of evidence to be rock solid but at the same time may resist certain conclusions. A critical evaluation works well when it is conducted in two parts. After evaluating the author's purpose and design for achieving that purpose, respond to the author's main assertions. In doing so, you'll want to identify points of agreement and disagreement and also evaluate assumptions.

## IDENTIFY POINTS OF AGREEMENT AND DISAGREEMENT

Be precise in identifying points of agreement and disagreement with an author. You should state as clearly as possible what *you* believe, and an effective way of doing this is to define your position in relation to that presented in the piece. Whether you agree enthusiastically, disagree, or agree with reservations, you can organize your reactions in two parts: First, summarize the author's position; second, state your own position and elaborate on your reasons for holding it. The elaboration, in effect, becomes an argument itself, and this is true regardless of the position you take. An opinion is effective when you support it by supplying evidence. Without such evidence, opinions cannot be authoritative. "I thought the article on inflation was lousy." Why? "I just thought so, that's all." This opinion is worthless because the criticism is imprecise: The critic has taken neither the time to read the article carefully nor the time to explore his own reactions carefully.

## EXPLORE THE REASONS FOR AGREEMENT AND DISAGREEMENT: EVALUATE ASSUMPTIONS

One way of elaborating your reactions to a reading is to explore the underlying *reasons* for agreement and disagreement. Your reactions are based largely on assumptions that you hold and how these assumptions compare with the author's. An *assumption* is a fundamental statement about the world and its operations that you take to be true. A writer's assumptions may be explicitly stated; but just as often assumptions are implicit and you will have to "ferret them out"—that is, to infer them. Consider an example:

> *In vitro* fertilization and embryo transfer are brought about outside the bodies of the couple through actions of third parties whose competence and technical activity determine the success of the procedure. Such fertilization entrusts the life and identity of the embryo into the power of doctors and biologists and establishes the domination of technology over the origin and destiny of the human person. Such a relationship of domination is in itself contrary to the dignity and equality that must be common to parents and children.[1]

This paragraph is quoted from the February 1987 Vatican document on artificial procreation. Cardinal Joseph Ratzinger, principal author of the document, makes an implicit assumption in this paragraph: that no good can come of the domination of technology over conception. The use of technology to bring about conception is morally wrong. Yet there are thousands of childless couples, Roman Catholics included, who reject this assumption in favour of its opposite: that conception technology is an aid to the barren couple; far from

---

[1] From the Vatican document *Instruction on Respect for Human Life in Its Origin and on the Dignity of Procreation*, given at Rome, from the Congregation for the Doctrine of the Faith, February 22, 1987, as presented in *Origins: N.C. Documentary Service* 16 (40), March 19, 1987, p. 707.

creating a relationship of unequals, the technology brings children into the world who will be welcomed with joy and love.

Assumptions provide the foundation on which entire presentations are built. If you find an author's assumptions invalid, you may well disagree with conclusions that follow from these assumptions. The author of a book on developing nations may include a section outlining the resources and time that will be required to industrialize a particular country and so upgrade its general welfare. His assumption—that industrialization in that particular country will ensure or even affect the general welfare—may or may not be valid. If you do not share the assumption, in your eyes the rationale for the entire book may be undermined.

How do you determine the validity of assumptions once you have identified them? In the absence of more scientific criteria, validity may mean how well the author's assumptions stack up against your own experience, observations, and reading. A caution, however: The overall value of an article or book may depend only to a small degree on the validity of the author's assumptions. For instance, a sociologist may do a fine job of gathering statistical data about the incidence of crime in urban areas along the eastern seaboard. The sociologist also might be a Marxist, and you may disagree with her subsequent analysis of the data. Yet you may find the data extremely valuable for your own work.

## CRITIQUE

A *critique* is a *formalized, critical reading of a passage*. It also is a personal response; but writing a critique is considerably more rigorous than saying that a movie is "great," or a book is "fascinating," or "I didn't like it." These are all responses, and, as such, they're a valid, even essential, part of your understanding of what you see and read. But such responses don't help illuminate the subject for anyone—even you—if you haven't explained how you arrived at your conclusions.

Your task in writing a critique is to turn your critical reading of a passage into a systematic evaluation in order to deepen your reader's (and your own) understanding of that passage. Among other things, you're interested in determining what an author says, how well the points are made, what assumptions underlie the argument, what issues are overlooked, and what implications can be drawn from such an analysis. Critiques, positive or negative, should include a fair and accurate summary of the passage; they also should include a statement of your own assumptions. It is important to remember that you bring to bear an entire set of assumptions about the world. Stated or not, these assumptions underlie every evaluative comment you make; you therefore have an obligation, both to the reader and to yourself, to clarify your standards. Not only do your readers stand to gain by your forthrightness, but you do as well: In the process of writing a critical assessment, you are forced to examine your own knowledge, beliefs, and assumptions. Ultimately, the critique is a way of learning about yourself.

# How to Write Critiques

You may find it useful to organize your critiques in five sections: introduction, summary, analysis of the presentation, your response to the presentation, and conclusion.

The box below contains some guidelines for writing critiques. Note that they are guidelines, not a rigid formula. Thousands of authors write critiques that do not follow the structure outlined here. Until you are more confident and practised in writing critiques, however, we suggest you follow these guide-

---

## HOW TO WRITE CRITIQUES

- *Introduction.* Introduce both the passage under analysis and the author. State the author's main argument and the point(s) you intend to make about it.

    Provide background material to help your readers understand the relevance or appeal of the passage. This background material might include one or more of the following: an explanation of why the subject is of current interest; a reference to a possible controversy surrounding the subject of the passage or the passage itself; biographical information about the author; an account of the circumstances under which the passage was written; or a reference to the intended audience of the passage.

- *Summary.* Summarize the author's main points, making sure to state the author's purpose for writing.

- *Analysis of the presentation.* Evaluate the validity of the author's presentation, as distinct from your points of agreement or disagreement. Comment on the author's success in achieving his or her purpose by reviewing three or four specific points. You might base your review on one (or more) of the following criteria:

    Is the information accurate?
    Is the information significant?
    Has the author defined terms clearly?
    Has the author used and interpreted information fairly?
    Has the author argued logically?

- *Your response to the presentation.* Now it is your turn to respond to the author's views. With which views do you agree? With which do you disagree? Discuss your reasons for agreement and disagreement, when possible, tying these reasons to assumptions—both the author's and your own.

- *Conclusion.* State your conclusions about the overall validity of the piece—your assessment of the author's success at achieving his or her aims and your reactions to the author's views. Remind the reader of the weaknesses and strengths of the passage.

lines. They are meant not to restrict you, but rather to provide you with a workable method of writing critical analyses that incorporates a logical sequence of development.

When you write a critique based on an essay in this text, you'll find it helpful to first read the Discussion and Writing Suggestions following that essay. These suggestions will lead you to some of the more fruitful areas of inquiry. Beware of simply responding mechanically to them, however, or your essay could degenerate into a series of short, disjointed responses. You need to organize your reactions into a coherent whole: The critique should be informed by a consistent point of view.

## Demonstration: Critique

The selections you will likely be inclined to critique are those that argue a specific position. Indeed, every argument you read is an invitation to agreement or disagreement. It remains only for you to speak up and justify your position.

In the following sample critiques of Virginia Postrel's "Fatalist Attraction" the writers agree with some of Postrel's claims, but do not accept her argument that the availability of biotechnology should be governed by consumer demands. As you read these two critiques of the one article, notice how each writer pursues somewhat different issues in providing a detailed response to Postrel's text. You might also note how the first writer, Tamara King, summarizes Postrel's position in the opening paragraph of her critique before providing her own response in the second, whereas the other writer, Tom Dorey, begins his critique by giving his negative reaction to Postrel's call for increased consumer access to biotechnology.

In her article "Fatalist Attraction: The Dubious    1
Case Against Fooling Mother Nature," Virginia Postrel,
editor of the liberal and capitalistic magazine
*Reason*, defends biotechnological engineering, claiming
that most potential clients are ordinary people struggling with extraordinary problems. Postrel argues that
scientists and bioethicists conduct their arguments in
the abstract on the topic of bioethicism, and she
implies that society would be better served if the
decision-makers would pay more attention to "ordinary"
people who need biotech engineering. Those against
biotechnology are "pious conservatives" who would
simply "lie back and accept it [the suffering],"
Postrel claims, labelling these conservatives
"biotechnophobes," or "green romantics." According to
these "green romantics," the direction and funding of

biotechnological engineering should not be in the hands of the market, but in the green hands of Mother Nature.

Postrel's relaxed approach to the language made the text easy to read. For example, she uses unique terms such as "biotechnophobe" to refer to those whose concerns about the dangers of biotechnology run counter to her own view that advances in the field are welcome. As the editor of *Reason* magazine, writing for readers who subscribe to her views required little empirical data to prove the argument for biotechnology. Her libertarian perspective on making biotechnology available to meet marketplace demand was probably quite welcome in the magazine, *Reason*. Needless to say, Postrel blended enough fact with opinion to make the article interesting, if not controversial to those unfamiliar with the libertarian platform. Overall, while I agree with the general premise that members of society should be free to make personal decisions, I am opposed to most medical uses of biotechnology on the grounds that Nature knows best.

In Postrel's libertarian opinion, the people who need biotech surgery should also be the ones to decide whether such operations are available. Her attitude is that the "market" will decide the fate of people. Postrel claims that the decision-makers (scientists, "experts," and bioethicists) have made "abstract" arguments about the technology, forgetting about the people who are truly suffering. As a solution, Postrel suggests that the moral questions regarding bioengineering should be left to the free market. A libertarian, capitalist notion pervades our society, and serves some of its members very well, yet 40 000 children die every day due to hunger-related illnesses. If capitalism promotes problems like starvation, why should we, as consumers, add another potential problem to the pile? Postrel claims that hers is a truly humanitarian perspective, yet letting those with wealth make decisions to determine how society works has so far resulted in

creating a world of haves and have-nots. To make a
whole new category of medical interventions available
only to those who can afford them would be to perpetuate this kind of dual-track citizenship. When people
are desperate enough, they will try anything to save
the ones they love. This makes a few members of society
eternally grateful, but if everyone on Earth could save
one person, we soon would not be able to fit on this
Earth. As of October 12, 1999, the world's population
count reached over 6 billion people, and is expected to
double by the year 2020. Although Postrel mocks John
Gray's saying that death is "a friend to be welcomed,"
with the world's population exceeding 12 billion by the
year 2020, death will be inevitable when the world's
water supply runs out. Disease works as a natural form
of population control; if biotechnology became available to the masses and extended life expectancy, how
would everyone find the necessities of life?

Postrel sees healing a disease as not so much of          4
a cure, but as a change—like a genetic alteration.
Genetic operations are seen as changes in the genetic
makeup. For Postrel, death and disease are as natural
as life. Yet, for many people, an alternative definition equates "natural ways" with health. Many people
who promote a natural, healthy lifestyle are not
opposed to using medicines and having operations. Many
of these same people who would be against biotechnology
are not against kidney transplants. This is not necessarily a contradiction because, unlike the very permanent state of genetic alterations, medicine is more
temporary. If medicine does not work, the patient can
simply stop taking the medicine. Sure, medicine can
temporarily "change" our bodies, but permanently altering them with genetic therapy could also permanently
change the human race, in ways that may prove to be
damaging. Mother Nature has been caring for humankind
for over two thousand years, and so we need to ask, why
should we start changing things now?

Postrel is right when she claims that a small,                    5
select group of "experts" cannot make a fair decision
for the rest of society. In my estimation, however,
Postrel is foolish to want to hand this decision over
to consumers who may desperately need gene therapy.
Desperate people will try anything to reach a solution,
and will not consider the societal implications. A representative sample of our population, lawyers, labourers, "experts," mothers and scientists alike should
make up a committee to investigate both the scientific
and moral implications of the genetic engineering. As
the results make the implications more visible, the
general population will be informed, through the various media, and a subsequent referendum could be held.
One small group cannot determine what is just; people
will need to work together for a reasonable solution.

A Critique of "Fatalist Attraction:
The Dubious Case Against Fooling Mother Nature"

Virginia Postrel, the editor of *Reason* magazine, is          1
an advocate for the free market control of the use of
new medical biotechnology. In an editorial that she
wrote for the July issue of *Reason* she makes her
point clear: that the availability and use of new
biotechnological methods should be determined by the
researchers who discover the techniques and the
"ordinary" and "down to earth" people who would make
use of them, and definitely not in the hands of the
"biotechnophobes" in government and the field of medical ethics. Postrel is correct in supporting medical
biotechnology that can cure disease or ease suffering,
but she is wrong when she links this form of helpful
intervention with cloning. Moreover, while Postrel is
correct that decisions about the availability of this
technology should not be solely up to the government
bureaucrats and medical ethicists, she is wrong in her
belief that the decision should be up to the researchers

and the public. For everyone to get the best of the
new biotechnological techniques, decisions should be
made by an organization of people educated in relevant
fields, including medical ethics, and people who could
make use of the technologies. Without this type of
broad-based decision-making body governing the availability of biotechnology, the rich might gain unfair
access and cause a further imbalance to the way power
is structured.

In my opinion, Postrel is right to the degree that
she believes the public should have a say in determining which treatments become available. For the most
part, the people who could use these technologies are
"middle class, traditional families" who are "ordinary"
and "down to earth" and who only want to save their
loved ones from a life of unnecessary physical pain.

2

While almost none of the users of biotech medical
interventions to cure disease or improve health would
be maniacs with a plan of creating a master race,
there are real concerns about the dark motives of
those interested in cloning people. Yet to Postrel,
the "technophobic fulminations of the anti-cloning
pundits" that were heard after it was announced that a
sheep had been cloned were absurd. To her, the possibility of cloning humans only holds good things.
Postrel describes the public debate about the future
uses of biotechnology as "loud and impassioned but,
most of all, abstract." She does not see the points of
her opposition as having any validity. Her belief is
that her opponents view some medical advances as "evil"
creations devised by "scheming scientists." Do they
really think that or is Postrel just altering the
wording of their views to make them sound supersti-
tious and paranoid in order to discredit them? As
editor, she knows the audience of *Reason* magazine, so
she can assume that many of her readers will accept
her representation of what her opponents think without
question. Thus, she appears to play fast and loose

3

with her opponents, subverting their views so that they seem to support her own, or so that they sound foolish and selfish. Yet those who do not share her philosophy can recognize, for example, that some opponents of cloning are trying to prevent it because they fear someone may abuse it to further their own fanatical beliefs. Does anyone want a repeat of the Nazis' experimentations from World War II and their quest for a "racially pure" nation?

Postrel makes a sound point when she argues that all forms of medical intervention are unnatural, from taking an aspirin to having tonsils removed, so that it is hypocritical to support conventional medical practices while opposing even the mildest biotechnological innovation. Many "biotechnophobes" no doubt support the practice of organ transplanting or giving insulin injections for diabetes, or even in vitro fertilization for couples who have the bad luck to be unable to conceive naturally. If they are for any of these treatments, how can they then oppose the treatment of gene therapy to cure someone of cystic fibrosis? One treatment is just as unnatural as the other. Postrel quotes John Gray to good effect here to discredit her opponents by using one of their own to show their ideological contradiction. Postrel then points out how, hundreds of years ago, people suffered through things like headaches, allergies, and menstrual pains without the aid of the medicine we use now. It is then logical with this example that gene therapy and the like may be the next evolution in our treatment of pain. 4

But Postrel does have a fault in her thinking. The decision of whether or not, as well as how, to tamper with peoples' genes is one of magnitude and should not be left up to the public and the free market. Members of the general public, especially in their role as consumers' are often swayed too much by their emotions and not enough by research. Postrel's placement of trust in a money-based providence is irresponsible. The technol- 5 ogy would not be cheap, so only the wealthy classes could afford it. Is it fair to say that a child whose parents have money deserves a life free of constant pain while a child born to poor parents doesn't? Also, who would be able to stop a rich person with a maniacal design to abuse cloning and gene therapy for personal gain? There would have to be a government group to make sure that treatments are available on a fair basis and used with the best intentions.

It would be nice to live in a world where everybody    6
has the noblest intentions. Unfortunately, we do not live in such a world. While Postrel is right that the government should not completely restrict the use of new medical technologies, she is wrong to think that the uses should be completely controlled by the free market and the researchers. Without some sort of government guidance, there is no way to know whether or not the technology will be used to the benefit of mankind.

## ■ EXERCISE

Read the following article that argues that there are advantages to electronic data collection and storage, because it can sometimes be useful to have our personal information and activities on record. The author of this piece is editor of *The Next City*, a magazine that describes itself in its signature phrase as "a solutions-oriented magazine that tackles issues confronting our new urban society."

The argument in this article responds to concerns expressed by Glastonbury and LaMendola in "The Nature and Meaning of Data," the article that appears earlier in this chapter. Read both, and then select one on which to write a critique, using the techniques introduced in this chapter. We provide two arguments from which to choose because each identifies core assumptions of the other and will help you to think critically about the issues. Use (and give credit to) one author in critiquing the other. Your critique should be the result of several drafts.

Note that it is possible for you to tackle this exercise using the authors Postrel and Rifkin, whose opposing views on biotechnology appear side by side later in this volume, in the chapter that features the disciplinary interests of biology and genetics.

# Too Much Privacy Can Be Hazardous to the Person

LAWRENCE SOLOMON

With vast computer network data bases storing detailed information about 1
our private lives, many of us are becoming uneasy about invasions of privacy.
Already, computers track our daily activities, time-stamping every credit and
debit card transaction, monitoring who we call on the telephone or visit over
the World Wide Web. Many businesses snoop on their employees; many
municipalities film activities on city streets to cut down on red-light runners
and other violators. Soon, every highway will be tolled, recording our comings and goings; and so will every neighbourhood road—satellite technology
today tracks the movement of London cabbies, the better to dispatch them;
tomorrow these satellites will economically track private automobiles, the
better to bill their owners.

Some privacy concerns revolve around bothersome junk mail and 2
unwanted telemarketing calls: Air mile and other cards let marketers analyze
your personal shopping habits, opening you up to an avalanche of targeted
offers. Other concerns—particularly access to your genetic code, which contains intimate details about you and your likely future life—are anything but
frivolous. A recent study by the Federal Bureau of Investigation and the
Computer Security Institute found that "most organizations are woefully
unprepared . . . [making] it easier for perpetrators to steal, spy, or sabotage
without being noticed and with little culpability if they are." After sampling
400 sites, the study found 42 per cent had experienced an intrusion or unau-
thorized use over the past year. Even sophisticated agencies are vulnerable.
Pentagon computers suffered 250 000 attacks by intruders in 1995, 65 per
cent of whom gained entry to a computer network. That same year, the
London *Sunday Times* reported that the contents of anyone's electronic health
record could be purchased on the street for £150.

Because the dangers—ranging from financial exploitation to, in the worst 3
case, a police state—can be profound, legislation of various types is being proposed. Some argue that all personal information should be our own private
property, to prevent marketers from storing and exchanging information
about us without our consent; others would severely restrict or even prohib-
it the collection of sensitive personal data. These approaches miss the mark.
The collection of data—the accumulation of knowledge—is almost always
desirable. The relevant question is, when does the information belong in the
public sphere and when in the private?

The claim that we somehow have property rights to our personal infor- 4
mation does not stand up to scrutiny. We all exchange information about
others—"Did you see Andrea's new car?"; "I hear Jim got a promotion"—in
our daily routines without requiring their consent, and a democratic society
that respects free speech could not do otherwise. Even if we did enact laws to

restrict or ban data banks from collecting information about us, it would generally backfire. Junk mail is unwanted precisely because it is indiscriminate and useless. If marketing succeeds in sending us useful, targeted information, many of us would have our goal of restricting unwanted mail. In one survey, 7 per cent of 18- to 20-year-olds wanted mail on products that interested them; in another, 52 per cent of consumers wanted to be profiled if that would lead to special offers. Those who don't want the mail or the offers will only need to make their views heard: Few companies would defy their customers by selling their names.

Valid restrictions governing free speech—such as slandering others or violating their copyright on personal works—are properly limited. But we should add one other restriction—control over the use of our genetic code, where privacy should take precedence over free speech.   5

The field of genetic information promises to be the greatest boon to science and medicine in human history. We suffer from at least 4000 genetic diseases and conditions—everything from Huntington's disease to depression—that may one day be treated or cured as science unravels the mysteries of the human genome. Even today, reading our genes can guide us in making decisions about our future, revealing whether we have predispositions for cancers or alcoholism, medical conditions that preventative measures could ameliorate. The information in your genetic code amounts to a probabilistic future diary that describes an important part of a unique and personal character—not just about your physical and mental health but also about your family, especially your parents, siblings, and children.   6

Yet this field also promises to lead to invasions of privacy unprecedented in their nature and scale. Unlike your personal diary, in which you might reveal your innermost secrets, the information in your genetic code may become known to strangers but not to you. From our own experiences, we know that there are no shortages of people with motives to acquire such information. Insurers and employers would value this information for business purposes. Political operatives might want to discredit opponents, as might combatives in divorces or other domestic disputes. Even where stakes aren't high, people may have malicious curiosities about their friends, neighbours, co-workers, or romantic rivals.   7

Until the turn of the century, our privacy was recognized as a property right and consequently given great legal weight. Our diaries and our secrets, particularly our medical secrets, were our own, in the United Kingdom as in North America. The genetic code, the epitome of that which is personal, is both a present document and a future diary. Giving each of us clear rights to our genetic code and requiring those who would use it to first obtain our consent would provide a necessary and indispensable ingredient to protecting our privacy.   8

Most day-to-day concerns that people have about privacy will evaporate. Those who don't want consumer data collected on them can avoid air miles-type marketing. Those seeking anonymity in making a phone call or a toll road trip can purchase prepaid cards; other technologies will foil telemarketers and e-mail snoops. Those who value record keeping—primarily businesspeople   9 who bill their time or track it for other purposes—will see this data collection as an added-value service. Most of us won't care much one way or the other.

In private spaces—banks, convenience stores, office buildings—we have　10 accepted cameras, taking little notice of them and worrying about their misuse— even less. We understand the proprietor's motives—to protect his property and the security of those who use it—and accept them as valid. Though we want similar protection in our public spaces, we are less trusting here, not because we value public property and security less but because we know the proprietor—the state—may have mixed motives. Too often government officials have used privileged information—whether medical data or income tax files—for self-serving ends. We do need safeguards governing surveillance in public spaces to allay legitimate public fears over the advent of the police state. Less privacy, ironically, would be one such safeguard.

Many criminal lawyers believe the police state arrived some time ago, that　11 law enforcement authorities effectively frame individuals whom they believe to be guilty. Guy Paul Morin is a case in point: Convinced of his guilt, police fudged the facts. When conflicting evidence frustrated their efforts—Morin left work too late to have travelled the 30 miles home in time to have murdered 9-year-old Christine Jessop—police ingenuity overcame this shortcoming.

Morin has plenty of company—Donald Marshall, David Milgaard, and　12 countless others have been convicted of murder and lesser offences because they could not establish where they were at some fateful time. Put another way, they were victims of their privacy. The vacuum of reliable information about their whereabouts created the opening for overzealous or overlazy police officers and prosecutors. Overzealous and overlazy authorities will always be with us, but vacuums of reliable information are increasingly becoming scarce. Had Jessop been murdered today, and had Morin travelled along an electronically tolled road such as Ontario's Highway 407, a record of when he got on and where he got off the highway would have established his whereabouts. The injustices perpetrated by the criminal justice system on this young man would never have occurred. Highway 407 was built too late to help Morin, but not for future travellers, whose record of their comings and goings—unbeknownst to them—adds a touch of security to their lives. So do new advances in DNA analysis, which eventually proved Morin innocent, as they are now doing for others around the world who were also falsely imprisoned.

A world in which we can verify our daily movements—the very world　13 that has been unfolding for decades—diminishes the number of miscarriages of justice that can occur. To fill a void with false information has always been easy; to rewrite data showing that someone drove 30 miles at a particular time along a particular electronic toll road involves reconstructing an alternate route and time, which involves alternate billing, which involves replacing the old invoice with a new one, and on and on. The effort required to spin a web of false information and then overlay it upon an existing factual network without getting tangled up would be so daunting as to virtually never occur. The very data base networks that some fear will usher in the police state, in the end, are really the best protection against it.

# 7

# Synthesizing Self and Others: Research Essays

## WHAT IS A SYNTHESIS?

A *synthesis* is a written discussion that draws on two or more sources. It follows that your ability to write syntheses depends on your ability to infer relationships among sources—essays, articles, fiction, and also non-written sources, such as lectures, interviews, and observations. This process is nothing new for you, since you infer relationships all the time—say, between something you've read in the newspaper and something you've seen for yourself, or between the teaching styles of your favourite and least favourite instructors. In fact, if you've written research papers, you've already written syntheses. In an *academic synthesis*, you make explicit the relationships that you have inferred among separate sources.

The skills you've already learned and practised from the previous six chapters will be vital in writing syntheses. Clearly, before you're in a position to draw relationships between two or more sources, you must understand what those sources say; in other words, you must be able to *summarize* these sources. It will frequently be helpful for your readers if you provide at least partial summaries of sources in your synthesis essays. At the same time, you must go beyond summary to make judgments—judgments based, of course, on your *critical reading* of your sources. You should already have drawn some conclusions about the quality and validity of these sources; and you should know how much you agree or disagree with the points made in your sources and the reasons for your agreement or disagreement.

Further, you must go beyond the critique of individual sources to determine the relationship among them. Is the information in source B, for example, an extended illustration of the generalizations in source A? Would it be useful to compare and contrast source C with source B? Having read and considered sources A, B, and C, can you infer something else—D (not a source, but your own idea)?

Because a synthesis is based on two or more sources, you will need to be selective when choosing information from each. It would be neither possible nor desirable, for instance, to discuss in a 10-page paper on the slide of the Canadian dollar every point that the authors of two books make about their subject. What you as a writer must do is select from each source the ideas and information that best allow you to achieve your purpose.

## PURPOSE

Your purpose in reading source materials and then in drawing on them to write your own material is often reflected in the wording of an assignment. For instance, consider the following assignments on Atlantic Coast hunting and fishing issues:

*Canadian History*: Evaluate your text author's treatment of the origins of the East Coast seal hunt.

*Economics*: Argue the following proposition, in light of your readings: "The East Coast seal hunt was stopped not for reasons of moral principle but for reasons of economic necessity."

*Government*: Prepare a report on the effects of the seal hunt moratorium on Atlantic politics.

*Mass Communications*: Discuss how the use of film and photography of the hunt may have affected the perceptions of wealthy consumers living in industrial cities.

*Literature*: Select two 20th-century writers whose work you believe was influenced by the Greenpeace protests. Discuss the ways this influence is apparent in a novel or a group of short stories written by each author. The works should not be *about* actual protest episodes.

*Applied Technology*: Compare and contrast the technology of the modern seal hunt with the technology available a century earlier.

Each of these assignments creates for you a particular purpose for writing. Having located sources relevant to your topic, you would select, for possible use in a paper, only those parts that helped you in fulfilling this purpose. And how you used those parts, how you related them to other material from other sources, would also depend on your purpose. For instance, if you were working on the government assignment, you might possibly draw on the same source as another student working on the literature assignment by referring to well-known author Farley Mowat's *A Whale for the Killing*, which puts pressure on the animal harvest industry. But because the purposes of these assignments are different, you and the other student would make different uses of this source. Parts or aspects of the novel that you find worthy of detailed analysis might be mentioned only in passing by the other student.

## USING YOUR SOURCES

Your purpose determines not only what parts of your sources you will use but also how you will relate them to one another. Since the very essence of synthesis is the combining of information and ideas, you must have some basis on which to combine them. *Some relationships among the material in your sources must make them worth synthesizing.* It follows that the better able you are to discover such relationships, the better able you will be to use your sources in writing syntheses. Notice that the mass communications assignment requires you to draw a *cause-and-effect* relationship between films and photographs and perceptions of seal hunt cruelty. The applied technology assignment requires you to *compare and contrast* recent to early seal hunt technology. The economics assignment requires you to *argue* a proposition. In each case, *your purpose will determine how you relate your source materials to one another.*

Consider some other examples. You may be asked on an exam question or in instructions for a paper to *describe* two or three approaches to prison reform during the past decade. You may be asked to *compare and contrast* one country's approach to imprisonment with another's. You may be asked to develop an *argument* of your own on this subject, based on your reading. Sometimes (when you are not given a specific assignment) you determine your own purpose: You are interested in exploring a particular subject; you are interested in making a case for one approach or another. In any event, your purpose shapes your essay. Your purpose determines which sources you research, which ones you use, which parts of them you use, at which points in your essay you use them, and in what manner you relate them to one another.

## HOW TO WRITE SYNTHESES

Although writing syntheses can't be reduced to a lockstep method, it should help you to follow the guidelines listed in the box below.

For clarity's sake, we'll emphasize the *argument* synthesis. We'll also consider developing your essays using *explanatory* or *comparison-contrast* techniques.

---

**HOW TO WRITE SYNTHESES**

- **Consider your purpose in writing.** What are you trying to accomplish in your essay? How will this purpose shape the way you approach your sources?
- **Select and carefully read your sources,** according to your purpose. Then reread the passages, mentally summarizing each. Identify those aspects or parts of your sources that will help you in fulfilling your purpose. When rereading, *label* or *underline* the sources for main ideas, key terms, and any details you want to use in the synthesis.
- **Formulate a thesis.** Your thesis is the main idea that you want to present in your synthesis. It should be expressed as a complete sentence. Sometimes the thesis is the first sentence, but more often it is *the final*

*sentence of the first paragraph.* If you are writing an *inductively arranged* synthesis (see p. 184), the thesis sentence may not appear until the final paragraphs. (See Chapter 1 for more information on writing an effective thesis.)

- **Decide how you will use your source material.** How will the information and the ideas in the passages help you to fulfill your purpose?

- **Develop an organizational plan,** according to your thesis. How will you arrange your material? It is not necessary to prepare a formal outline. But you should have some plan that will indicate the order in which you will present your material and that will indicate the relationships among your sources. As an optional step, draft the topic sentences for main sections. This can be a helpful transition from organizational plan to first draft.

- **Write the first draft** of your synthesis, following your organizational plan. Be flexible with your plan, however. Frequently, you will use an outline to get started. As you write, you may discover new ideas and make room for them by adjusting the outline. When this happens, reread your work frequently, making sure that your thesis still accounts for what follows and that what follows still logically supports your thesis.

- **Document your sources.** You may do this by crediting them within the body of the synthesis or by having a list of "Works Cited" at the end. (See Chapter 4 for more information on documenting sources.)

- **Revise your synthesis,** inserting transitional words and phrases where necessary. Make sure that the synthesis reads smoothly, logically, and clearly from beginning to end. Check for grammatical correctness, punctuation, spelling.

*Note: The writing of syntheses is a recursive process, and you should accept a certain amount of backtracking and reformulating as inevitable. For instance, in developing an organizational plan (step 5 of the procedure), you may discover a gap in your presentation that will send you scrambling for another source—back to step 2. You may find that formulating a thesis and making inferences among sources occur simultaneously; indeed, inferences often are made before a thesis is formulated. Our recommendations for writing syntheses will give you a structure; they will get you started. But be flexible in your approach; expect discontinuity and, if possible, be comforted that through backtracking and reformulating you will eventually produce a coherent, well-crafted essay.*

# THE ARGUMENT SYNTHESIS

An argumentative thesis is *persuasive in purpose*. Writers working with the same source materials might conceive of and support other, opposite theses. So the thesis for an argument synthesis is a claim about which reasonable people could disagree. It is a claim about which—given the right arguments—your audience might be persuaded to agree with your position. The strategy of your argument synthesis is therefore to find and use convincing *support* for your *claim*.

## The Elements of Argument: Claim, Support, Assumption

Let's consider the terminology we've just used. One way of looking at an argument is to see it as an interplay of three essential elements: claim, support, and assumption. A *claim* is a proposition or conclusion that you are trying to prove. You prove this claim by using *support* in the form of fact or expert opinion. Linking your supporting evidence to your claim is your *assumption* about the subject. This assumption, also called a *warrant*, is an underlying belief or principle about some aspect of the world and how it operates. By nature, assumptions (which are often unstated) tend to be more general than either claims or supporting evidence. What we do when we *analyze* is to apply the principles and generalizations that underlie our assumptions to the specific evidence that we will use as support for our claims.

For example, here are the essential elements of an argument advocating parental restriction of television viewing for their high school children:

*Claim*

High school students should be restricted to no more than two hours of TV viewing per day.

*Support*

An important new study, as well as the testimony of educational specialists, reveals that students who watch more than two hours of TV a night have, on average, lower marks than those who watch less TV.

*Assumption*

Excessive TV viewing is linked to poor academic performance.

Here are the essential elements of an argument advocating that reopening the fisheries would rejuvenate the Atlantic economy.

```
Claim
```
We must strive to reopen the East-Coast fisheries
to avert plunging the region into further economic
disaster.

Here are the other elements of this argument:

```
Support
```
Because a number of natural resource industries like
mining and trapping have undergone recent closure, the
fisheries need to be reopened as soon as the stocks
are renewed and a plan for sustainable development is
in place.

```
Assumption
```
The fisheries are a mainstay of the Atlantic economy.

For the most part, arguments should be constructed logically, or rational-ly, so that claims are supported by evidence in the form of facts or expert opin-ions. As we'll see, however, logic is only one component of effective arguments.

## The Three Appeals of Argument: *Logos, Ethos, Pathos*

Speakers and writers have never relied upon logic alone in advancing and sup-porting their claims. Over 2000 years ago, the Athenian philosopher and rhetorician Aristotle explained how speakers attempting to persuade others to their point of view could achieve their purpose primarily by relying on one or more *appeals*, which he called *logos, ethos,* and *pathos*.

Since we frequently find these three appeals employed in political argu-ment, we'll use many political examples in the following discussion. But keep in mind that these appeals are also used extensively in advertising, in legal cases, in business plans, and in many other types of argument.

### Logos

*Logos* is the rational appeal, the appeal to reason. If they expect to persuade their audiences, speakers must argue logically and must supply appropriate evidence to support their case. Logical arguments are commonly of two types (often combined). The *deductive* argument begins with a generalization, then cites a specific case related to that generalization, from which follows a con-clusion. A familiar example of deductive reasoning, used by Aristotle himself, is the following:

> All men are mortal. (*generalization*)
> Socrates is a man. (*specific case*)
> Socrates is mortal. (*conclusion about the specific case*)

In the terms we've just been discussing, this deduction may be restated as follows:

Socrates is mortal. (*claim*)
Socrates is a man. (*support*)
All men are mortal. (*assumption*)

An example of a more contemporary deductive argument may be seen in President John F. Kennedy's address to the American nation in June 1963 on the need for sweeping civil rights legislation. Kennedy begins with the generalizations that it "ought to be possible . . . for American students of any color to attend any public institution they select without having to be backed up by troops" . . . and that "it ought to be possible for American citizens of any color to register and vote in a free election without interference or fear of reprisal." Kennedy then provides several specific examples (primarily recent events in Birmingham, Alabama) and statistics to show that this was not the case. He concludes:

> We face, therefore, a moral crisis as a country and a people. It cannot be met by repressive police action. It cannot be left to increased demonstrations in the streets. It cannot be quieted by token moves or talk. It is time to act in the Congress, in your state and local legislative body, and, above all, in all of our daily lives.

Underlying Kennedy's argument is the following reasoning:

All Americans should enjoy certain rights.
Some Americans do not enjoy these rights.
We must take action to ensure that all Americans enjoy these rights.

Another form of logical argumentation is *inductive* reasoning. A speaker or writer who argues inductively begins not with a generalization, but with several pieces of specific evidence. The speaker then draws a conclusion from this evidence. For example, during the Confederation debates back in the 1860s, D'Arcy McGee of Lower Canada supported Canadian union and cautioned his countrymen to recognize the threat of American takeover. He begins this passage by citing situations in which the Americans have asserted their dominance and builds to his conclusion that in its current divided state, Canada is completely dependent on Britain for protection against American aggression:

> The United States have frightful numbers of soldiers and guns. They wanted Florida and seized it. They wanted Louisiana and purchased it. They wanted Texas and stole it. Then they picked a quarrel with Mexico and got California. If we had not had the strong arm of England over us, we too would be a part of the States.

*Statistical evidence* was used by U.S. Senator Edward M. Kennedy (Democrat, Massachusetts) in arguing for passage of the *Racial Justice Act* of 1990, designed to ensure that minorities were not disproportionately singled out for the death penalty. Kennedy points out that 17 defendants in Fulton County, Georgia, between 1973 and 1980, were charged with killing police officers but the only defendant who received the death sentence was a black man. Kennedy also cites statistics to show that "those who killed whites were 4.3 times more likely to receive the death penalty than were killers of blacks," and that "in Georgia, blacks who killed whites received the death penalty 16.7

percent of the time, while whites who killed received the death penalty only 4.2 percent of the time."

Of course, the mere piling up of evidence does not in itself make the speaker's case. Statistics can be selected and manipulated to prove anything, as demonstrated in Darrell Huff's landmark book *How to Lie with Statistics* (1954). Moreover, what appears to be a logical argument may, in fact, be fundamentally flawed. (See Chapter 6 for a discussion of logical fallacies and faulty reasoning strategies.) On the other hand, the fact that evidence can be distorted, statistics misused, and logic fractured does not mean that these tools of reason can be dispensed with or should be dismissed. It means only that audiences have to listen and read critically—perceptively, knowledgeably, and skeptically (though not necessarily cynically).

## ETHOS

*Ethos*, or the ethical appeal, is an appeal based not on the ethical rationale for the subject under discussion, but rather on the ethical nature of the person making the appeal. A person making an argument must have a certain degree of credibility: That person must be of good character, be of sound sense, and be qualified to hold the office or recommend policy.

For example, in attempting to appeal to the public as a man of the people whose common sense and family values equip him to serve as Canadian Prime Minister, Jean Chrétien has often referred to growing up in a big family in small-town Quebec. To draw this self-portrait, he has even described himself as "the little guy from Shawinigan," making an appeal to ethos that suggests that a "regular guy," rather than somebody larger than life, is best suited to lead our country.

L. A. Kauffman is not running for office but rather writing an article arguing against socialism as a viable ideology for the future ("Socialism: No." *Progressive*, April 1, 1993). To defuse objections that he is simply a tool of capitalism, Kauffman begins with an appeal to *ethos*: "Until recently, I was executive editor of the journal *Socialist Review*. Before that I worked for the Marxist magazine, *Monthly Review*. My bookshelves are filled with books of Marxist theory, and I even have a picture of Karl Marx up on my wall." Thus, Kauffman establishes his credentials to argue knowledgeably about Marxist ideology.

## PATHOS

Finally, speakers and writers appeal to their audiences by the use of *pathos*, the appeal to the emotions. There is nothing inherently wrong with using an emotional appeal. Indeed, since emotions often move people far more powerfully than reason alone, speakers and writers would be foolish not to use emotion. And it would be a drab, humourless world if human beings were not subject to the sway of feeling, as well as reason. The emotional appeal becomes problematic only if it is the *sole or primary* basis of the argument. This is the kind of situation that led, for example, to the internment of Japanese Canadians during World War II or that leads to periodic calls for the return of the national anthem and "God Save the Queen" in schools.

U.S. President Ronald Reagan was a master of emotional appeal. He closed his first inaugural address with a reference to the view from the Capitol of Arlington National Cemetery, where lie thousands of markers of "heroes":

> Under one such marker lies a young man, Martin Treptow, who left his job in a small-town barbershop in 1917 to go to France with the famed Rainbow Division. There, on the western front, he was killed trying to carry a message between battalions under heavy artillery fire. We're told that on his body was found a diary. On the flyleaf under the heading, "My Pledge," he had written these words: "America must win this war. Therefore, I will work, I will save, I will sacrifice, I will endure, I will fight cheerfully and do my utmost, as if the issue of the whole struggle depended on me alone." The crisis we are facing today does not require of us the kind of sacrifice that Martin Treptow and so many thousands of others were called upon to make. It does require, however, our best effort and our willingness to believe in ourselves and to believe in our capacity to perform great deeds, to believe that together with God's help we can and will resolve the problems which now confront us.

Surely, Reagan implies, if Martin Treptow can act so courageously and so selflessly, we can do the same. The logic is somewhat unclear, since the connection between Martin Treptow and ordinary Americans of 1981 is rather tenuous (as Reagan concedes); but the emotional power of Martin Treptow, whom reporters were sent scurrying to research, carries the argument.

A more recent American president, Bill Clinton, also used *pathos*. Addressing an audience of the nation's governors on his welfare plan, Clinton closed his remarks by referring to a conversation he had held with a welfare mother who had gone through the kind of training program Clinton was advocating. Asked by Clinton whether she thought that such training programs should be mandatory, the mother said, "I sure do." When Clinton asked her why, she said:

> "Well, because if it wasn't, there would be a lot of people like me home watching the soaps because we don't believe we can make anything of ourselves anymore. So you've got to make it mandatory." And I said, "What's the best thing about having a job?" She said, "When my boy goes to school, and they say, 'What does your mama do for a living?' he can give an answer."

Clinton uses the emotional power he counts on in that anecdote to set up his conclusion: "We must end poverty for Americans who want to work. And we must do it on terms that dignify all of the rest of us, as well as help our country to work better. I need your help, and I think we can do it."

In a speech at his trial for treason in 1885, Louis Riel made a poetic appeal to the emotions of jurors and listeners when he compared his country to his mother and claimed to expect equal protection from harm at the hands of both:

> The day of my birth I was helpless and my mother took care of me. Today I am a man, but I am as helpless before this court in the Dominion of Canada as I was the day of my birth. The Northwest is also my mother; it is my mother country. Although my mother country is sick, some people have come from Lower Canada to help her take care of me. I am sure my mother country will not kill me any more than my mother did.

In a sense, this passage also constitutes an appeal to *ethos*, since in it Riel claims to be rooted in the soil of the Northwest and motivated by his desire to serve and protect it.

## Developing an Argument Synthesis

### THE WAL-MART CONTROVERSY

To demonstrate how to plan and draft an argument synthesis, let's consider the subject of controversies surrounding the development of Wal-Mart. If you were taking an economics or business economics course, you would probably at some point consider the functioning of the market economy. For consumers, one of the most striking trends in this economy in recent times has been the rise of superstores such as Wal-Mart, Home Depot, Costco, and Staples. Most consumers find these vast shopping outlets convenient and economical. Others find them an abomination, contending that these ugly and predatory outlets drive out of business the mom-and-pop stores that were the staple of small-town life.

Suppose, in preparing to write a short paper on Wal-Mart, you came up with the following sources. Read them carefully, noting as you do the kinds of information and ideas you could draw upon to develop an *argument synthesis*.

*Note:* To save space and for the purpose of demonstration, the following passages are brief excerpts only. In preparing your paper, naturally you would draw upon entire articles from which these extracts were made.

# Ban the Bargains

### BOB ORTEGA

#### "ULTIMATE PREDATOR"

To denizens of the counterculture, Wal-Mart stands for everything they dislike about American society—mindless consumerism, paved landscapes and homogenization of community identity. 1

"We've lost a sense of taste, of refinement—we're destroying our culture and replacing it with . . . Wal-Mart," says Allan B. Wolf, a Kent State University alumnus now trying to keep Wal-Mart out of Cleveland Heights, Ohio, where he is a high-school teacher. 2

"We'd never have fought another business as hard as we've fought Wal-Mart," says Alice Doyle, of Cottage Grove, Ore., who calls the giant discounter "the ultimate predator." 3

At Wal-Mart headquarters in Bentonville, Ark., company officials characterize all opponents, ex-hippie and otherwise, as "a vocal minority." They deny that their store has become, for some activists, a kind of successor to Vietnam. 4

Don Shinkle, a Wal-Mart vice president, says "there are maybe eight to 10 sites where there is opposition." However, there are at least 40 organized groups actively opposing proposed or anticipated Wal-Mart stores in communities such as Oceanside, Calif.; Gaithersburg, Md.; Quincy, Mass.; East Lampeter, Penn.; Lake Placid, N.Y.; and Gallatin, Tenn. 5

Local opposition has delayed some stores and led the company to drop its   6
plans in Greenfield, Mass., and two other towns in that state; as well as in
Bath, Maine; Simi Valley, Calif.; and Ross and West Hempfield, Pa.

## PROTEST MARCH

The residents of Cleveland Heights hope to join that list. On a recent Monday   7
there, a large crowd, including some people who had been tear-gassed at
Kent State 24 years ago for protesting the war, led a march on city hall and
chanted, "One, two, three, four—we don't want your Wal-Mart store." Says
Jordan Yin, a leader of the anti–Wal-Mart coalition, "Old hippies describes
the whole town."

In Fort Collins, Colo., Shelby Robinson, a former Vietnam War protest-   8
er and member of the George McGovern campaign, has little success these
days persuading her old companions to join her lobbying for solar power,
animal rights or vegetarianism. But when Wal-Mart proposed coming to
town, the activist impulses of her old friends came alive, and many joined her
in fighting the store.

"I really hate Wal-Mart," says Ms. Robinson, a self-employed clothing   9
designer. "Everything's starting to look the same, everybody buys all the
same things—a lot of small-town character is being lost. They disrupt local
communities, they hurt small businesses, they add to our sprawl and pollution
because everybody drives farther, they don't pay a living wage—and visually,
they're atrocious."

In Boulder, Colo., Wal-Mart real-estate manager Steven P. Lane tried   10
appeasing the city's ex-hippies by proposing a "green store" that he said would
be environmentally friendly, right up to the solar-powered sign out front. But
when city council member Spencer Havlick, who helped organize the first
Earth Day in 1970, suggested that the whole store be solar-powered, Mr. Lane
fell silent. Dr. Havlick, professor of environmental design at the University of
Colorado, says, "Their proposal wasn't as green as they thought it was."

These activists have hardly slowed Wal-Mart's overall expansion—it   11
expects to add 125 stores next year to its existing 2,504. But even so, some
Wal-Mart sympathizers find them irritating. William W. Whyte, who bid
good riddance to hippies when he graduated from Kent State in 1970, now
finds himself annoyed by them again, as an analyst following Wal-Mart for
Stephens Inc.

"The same types of people demonstrating then are demonstrating now,"   12
grumbles Mr. Whyte. "If they had to worry about putting food on the table,
they'd probably be working for Wal-Mart instead of protesting them."

Some Wal-Mart supporters call the protesters elitists for opposing a pur-   13
veyor of low-priced goods. But Tim Allen, who at age 26 has been active in the
development of a "green" housing co-op and an organizer of the Wal-Mart
protest movement in Ithaca, replies that "people aren't poor because they're
paying 15 cents more for a pair of underwear."

# Eight Ways to Stop the Store

ALBERT NORMAN

Last week I received another red-white-and-blue invitation to a Wal-Mart    1
grand opening in Rindge, New Hampshire. I say "another" because Wal-
Mart has already invited me to its new store in Hinsdale, New Hampshire,
just twenty miles away. With over $67 billion in annual sales, and more than
2,000 stores, Wal-Mart holds a grand opening somewhere in America almost
every other day. But it will never invite me to its new store in Greenfield,
Massachusetts, my home town, because Greenfield voters recently rejected
Wal-Mart at the ballot box.

The Arkansas mega-retailer has emerged as the main threat to Main    2
Street, U.S.A. Economic impact studies in Iowa, Massachusetts, and elsewhere suggest that Wal-Mart's gains are largely captured from other merchants. Within two years of a grand opening, Wal-Mart stores in an
average-size Iowa town generated $10 million in annual sales—by "stealing"
$8.3 million from other businesses.

Since our victory in Greenfield, we have received dozens of letters from    3
"Stop the WAL" activists in towns like East Aurora, New York; Palatine,
Illinois; Mountville, Pennsylvania; Williston, Vermont; Branford,
Connecticut—small communities fighting the battle of Jericho. If these towns
follow a few simple rules of engagement, they will find that the WAL *will*
come tumbling down:

*Quote scripture:* Wal-Mart founder Sam Walton said it best in his auto-    4
biography: "If some community, for whatever reason, doesn't want us in
there, we aren't interested in going in and creating a fuss." Or, as one company V.P. stated, "We have so many opportunities for building in communities that want Wal-Marts, it would be foolish of us to pursue construction in
communities that don't want us." The greater the fuss raised by local citizens,
the more foolish Wal-Mart becomes.

*Learn Wal-Math:* Wal-Mathematicians only know how to add. They    5
never talk about the jobs they destroy, the vacant retail space they create or
their impact on commercial property values. In our town, the company agreed
to pay for an impact study that gave enough data to kill three Wal-Marts.
Dollars merely shifted from cash registers on one side of town to Wal-Mart
registers on the other side of town. Except for one high school scholarship per
year, Wal-Mart gives very little back to the community.

*Exploit their errors:* Wal-Mart always makes plenty of mistakes. In our    6
community, the company tried to push its way onto industrially zoned land.
It needed a variance not only to rezone land to commercial use but also to
permit buildings larger than 40,000 square feet. This was the "hook" we
needed to trip the company up. Rezoning required a Town Council vote
(which it won), but our town charter allowed voters to seek reconsideration

of the vote, and ultimately, a referendum. All we needed was the opportunity to bring this to the general public—and we won. Wal-Mart also violated state law by mailing an anonymous flier to voters.

*Fight capital with capital:* In our town (pop. 20,000) Wal-Mart spent          7
more than $30,000 trying to influence the outcome of a general referendum. It even created a citizen group as a front. But Greenfield residents raised $17,000 to stop the store—roughly half of which came from local businesses. A media campaign and grass-roots organizing costs money. If Wal-Mart is willing to spend liberally to get into your town, its competitors should be willing to come forward with cash also.

*Beat them at the grass roots:* Wal-Mart can buy public relations firms and      8
telemarketers but it can't find bodies willing to leaflet at supermarkets, write dozens of letters to the editor, organize a press conference or make calls in the precincts. Local coalitions can draw opinion-makers from the business community (department, hardware and grocery stores, pharmacies, sporting goods stores), environmentalists, political activists and homeowners. Treat this effort like a political campaign: The Citizens versus the WAL.

*Get out your vote:* Our largest expenditure was on a local telemarketing        9
company that polled 4,000 voters to identify their leanings on Wal-Mart. Our volunteers then called those voters leaning against the WAL two days before the election. On election day, we had poll-watchers at all nine precincts. If our voters weren't at the polls by 5 P.M., we reminded them to get up from the dinner table and stop the mega-store.

*Appeal to the heart as well as the head:* One theme the Wal-Mart culture        10
has a hard time responding to is the loss of small-town quality of life. You can't buy rural life style on any Wal-Mart shelf—once you lose it, Wal-Mart can't sell it back to you. Wal-Mart's impact on small-town ethos is enormous. We had graphs and bar charts on job loss and retail growth—but we also communicated with people on an emotional level. Wal-Mart became the WAL—an unwanted shove into urbanization, with all the negatives that threaten small-town folks.

*Hire a professional:* The greatest mistake most citizen groups make is          11
trying to fight the world's largest retailer with a mimeo-machine mentality. Most communities have a political consultant nearby, someone who can develop a media campaign and understand how to get a floppy disk of town voters with phone numbers. Wal-Mart uses hired guns; so should anti–Wal-Mart forces.

"Your real mission," a Wal-Mart executive recently wrote to a commu-           12
nity activist, "is to be blindly obstructionist." On the contrary, we found it was Wal-Mart that would blindly say anything and do anything to bulldoze its way toward another grand opening in America. But if community coalitions organize early, bring their case directly to the public and trumpet the downside of mega-store development, the WALs will fall in Jericho.

# Wal-Mart's War on Main Street

SARAH ANDERSON

Across the country, thousands of rural people are battling to save their local          1
downtowns. Many of these fights have taken the form of anti–Wal-Mart campaigns. In Vermont, citizens' groups allowed Wal-Mart to enter the state only
after the company agreed to a long list of demands regarding the size and operation of the stores. Three Massachusetts towns and another in Maine have
defeated bids by Wal-Mart to build in their communities. In Arkansas, three
independent drugstore owners won a suit charging that Wal-Mart had used
"predatory pricing," or selling below cost, to drive out competitors. Canadian
citizens are asking Wal-Mart to sign a "Pledge of Corporate Responsibility"
before opening in their towns. In at least a dozen other U.S. communities,
groups have fought to keep Wal-Mart out or to restrict the firm's activities.

By attacking Wal-Mart, these campaigns have helped raise awareness of          2
the value of locally owned independent stores on Main Street. Their concerns
generally fall in five areas:

- *Sprawl Mart*—Wal-Mart nearly always builds along a highway outside          3
  town to take advantage of cheap, often unzoned land. This usually attracts
  additional commercial development, forcing the community to extend services (telephone and power lines, water and sewage services, and so forth)
  to that area, despite sufficient existing infrastructure downtown.
- *Wal-Mart channels resources out of a community*—studies have shown          4
  that a dollar spent on a local business has four or five times the economic spin-off of a dollar spent at a Wal-Mart, since a large share of Wal-
  Mart's profit returns to its Arkansas headquarters or is pumped into
  national advertising campaigns.
- *Wal-Mart destroys jobs in locally owned stores*—a Wal-Mart–funded          5
  community impact study debunked the retailer's claim that it would create
  a lot of jobs in Greenfield, Massachusetts. Although Wal-Mart planned to
  hire 274 people at its Greenfield store, the community could expect to
  gain only eight net jobs, because of projected losses at other businesses
  that would have to compete with Wal-Mart.
- *Citizen Wal-Mart?*—in at least one town—Hearne, Texas—Wal-Mart          6
  destroyed its Main Street competitors and then deserted the town in
  search of higher returns elsewhere. Unable to attract new businesses to the
  devastated Main Street, local residents have no choice but to drive long
  distances to buy basic goods.
- *One-stop shopping culture*—in Greenfield, where citizens voted to keep          7
  Wal-Mart out, anti–Wal-Mart campaign manager Al Norman said he
  saw a resurgence of appreciation for Main Street. "People realized there's
  one thing you can't buy at Wal-Mart, and that's small-town quality of
  life," Norman explains. "This community decided it was not ready to die
  for a cheap pair of underwear."

Small towns cannot return to the past, when families did all their shopping and socializing in their hometown. Rural life is changing and there's no use denying it. The most important question is, who will define the future? Will it be Wal-Mart, whose narrow corporate interests have little to do with building healthy communities? Will it be the department of transportation, whose purpose is to move cars faster? Will it be the banks and suppliers primarily interested in doing business with the big guys? Or will it be the people who live in small towns, whose hard work and support are essential to any effort to revitalize Main Street? 8

# Why Is There a Wal-Mart in My Backyard, and How Did It Get There?

CHRISTOPHER LEO

Following the process of city planning can be like watching a film with excellent special effects. It all seems so real, and yet we know it is not. Often there is a big gap between the bureaucratic and legal theory, of planning, and the reality on the street. 1

## WHAT IS CITY PLANNING?

Planning begins with a map of the city, with different colours used to show what kind of development will be allowed in each area. Since about the end of World War II, the standard method in Canadian and American cities has been to designate areas, called zones, as exclusively residential, commercial, industrial or agricultural, with the different types of land use clearly separated from each other. As well, larger commercial buildings are typically separated from smaller ones, single-family homes from townhouses and apartment buildings, and so forth. 2

Such zoning maps are a standard feature of official city plans. They promote by far the most popular style of development in Canada and the United States—but they also effectively cast it in bronze and put barriers in the way of alternatives. 3

## HOW DO DEVELOPMENT PROPOSALS WORK?

With an official plan in place, actual development is initiated by a development proposal. Typically, a developer buys a piece of land and proposes to build something on it. The proposal sets out, usually in considerable detail, what will be included, what revenues the city can expect to gain from property taxes on the development once it is completed, and what will be needed to make the development work. The needs may include connections to the city 4 road, sewer and water systems, or alterations in the official plan, for example environmental safeguards. The proposal is taken to the city planning or development office and a negotiation between the developer and a professional planner ensues.

In this negotiation, many factors must be taken into consideration but it     5
is protection of property values that tends to override other concerns. For developers, even more than for most people, time is money, and lost time in completing a planned development can be extremely costly. Developers are also very aware that the properties in a development, once built, must be sold or leased. The safest thing for them to do is usually just to stick with what is well established—in other words, to choose conventional planning, in which land is divided according to how it will be used.

At the end of the day financial concerns override all others. It is therefore     6
the question of how much the development will cost, compared with the revenue it is expected to produce, that carries the most weight in the city negotiators' minds.

In Winnipeg, three items are taken into consideration when making this     7
calculation. If the developer is prepared to cover the costs of road connections, underground municipal services and parks needed for the new subdivision, the city counts on future tax revenues from these things as a "net gain."

Unfortunately, things are not always as they seem.     8


## OVERLOOKED

Overlooked is the fact that new development at the city's fringe influences not     9
just the costs of these three items, but costs of the full range of municipal services. Once the new, allegedly no-cost, subdivision is in place, the new residents rightly argue that, as residents and taxpayers of Winnipeg, they deserve services comparable to those that other residents enjoy. City politicians have no valid answer when they ask: Why is there no conveniently located library branch and community centre? Why are police and fire response times here slower than in other subdivisions? Why do we not have a neighbourhood school? City council and school boards have no politically realistic alternative but to spend money to meet the demands.

One such subdivision follows another. Each time, the city does not make     10
a rational calculation of what will be required to sustain the overall city network of services and infrastructure, but simply to a limited calculation that treats each subdivision as a self-contained unit requiring only minimal services. Eventually, as costs mount, the city gradually loses its ability to pay its bills.

Meanwhile, people start to move outward to the artificially cheap hous-     11
ing that results from unrealistically priced development. Downtown residential neighbourhoods become depopulated. Perfectly useful downtown schools are closed, while new ones are built in the suburbs. Subdivisions too thinly populated to support public transit nevertheless get subsidized bus service, downtown streets and sewers deteriorate while new roads are built to serve the latest subdivisions, and so forth. This is suburban sprawl.

What is the effect of this tightening of resources? In 1998, a meticulous     12
survey was conducted of the state of Winnipeg's infrastructure. It found a massive disparity between the amount of money needed to maintain existing infrastructure and the amount actually being spent. Regional streets, for example,
were found to be $10.2 million a year short of the required amount. Even more
drastic was the situation of residential streets, which were found to have
received an average of $2.5 million each year, when what was required to keep
them in good condition was closer to $30 million—a huge gap. In 2000, the
total deficit in the maintenance budget for residential streets alone—not including regional streets, back lanes or sidewalks—was $200 million.

Not all cities are as hard-hit by this course of events as Winnipeg has     13
been, but it seems safe to say that all North American cities have paid a price
for it and many have been at least as seriously affected as Winnipeg.


## CULT OF CIVIC IMPOTENCE

As I have noted, it is a private developer who assembles a tract of land, puts     14
together a proposal for its development, and takes it to the city for approval.
In theory, the city government is still in control. It has drawn the zoning map,
it has authority to alter or not alter it, and it has the clear and undisputed legal
right to decide where development takes place, what can be developed there
and to regulate the details of how it will look and how it will be constructed.

However, city governments rarely exercise this authority fully, for a     15
number of interrelated reasons. One of them is competition between cities. In
the dawn of the new century, this competition has become fiercer than ever as
it increasingly takes on global dimensions. Cutbacks in the size of government, and deregulation in many areas where governments previously exercised control, have had the effect of removing limits that once existed upon
many companies. The development of transportation networks and new communications technologies has freed money, ideas and people to move around
the world as never before. Such free trade arrangements as the North
American Free Trade Agreement, the European Union, and numerous others
have removed barriers to the movement of goods, investment dollars and
companies themselves to wherever they can do business most profitably.

This has had the practical effect of reducing the bargaining power of     16
cities in many of their dealings with developers. Often, mobile developers who
are planning a development a city wants can, in effect, dictate the terms of the
development, and force the city to rewrite its bylaws or regulations.

In short, companies often call the tune in their dealings with local gov-     17
ernments, and, in the process, they can, in practice, cancel development plans,
zoning rules, building code regulations, and even the taxes that are levied to
support the city's services. It is important to note that this kind of bargaining
power applies only to mobile firms. Large-scale commercial operations and
manufacturing plants often find themselves in this fortunate position, but
firms that serve a local market, for example developers of housing and local
retail establishments, are not similarly placed. In practice, however, small

companies are often able to win substantial concessions as well, in part because of the psychology of slow growth.

Winnipeg is a case in point. The city has, for a long time, been growing      18
at less than one per cent a year. It is a well-established idea in Canada and the United States that slow growth is a pathology, and that belief is implicit in the way Winnipeg is promoted. When economic development efforts are under discussion, the tone and the words carry a mixed message of assertiveness and self-deprecation that makes it clear that Winnipeggers do not feel happy about their home. An undercurrent of desperation is palpable in advertising campaigns on such themes as "Winnipeg: 100 reasons to love it" or "Love me, love my Winnipeg." What comes through most clearly are two contradictory messages, often asserted at the same time: 1) since Winnipeg is not growing as rapidly as Toronto, or Calgary, there must be something wrong with it and 2) there is absolutely nothing wrong with Winnipeg.

Economic development efforts in slowly growing cities often reflect that      19
same mood of ambivalence with a hint of desperation. Predictions of economic changes tend to take the form either of pessimistic warnings of a clouded future or of declarations that "the big break" is just around the corner: If the Jets leave Winnipeg, $50 million a year will be lost to the economy; if the Canadian Wheat Board is abolished or relocated, 5 000 jobs will be lost; Winnipeg is about to become a major North American transportation hub, thousands of jobs will be created and millions added to the economy. These recent examples of speculations trumpeted in the local media are just samples of what amounts to a steady stream of journalistic manic-depression. Economic development efforts are undertaken in a mood akin to that of an addicted gambler, simultaneously desperate and hopeful.

City councils of slowly growing cities tend to be desperate, and are typ-      20
ically all too eager to make concessions to developers, even when the projects they propose cannot be relocated. A good example of this can be found in the curious calculations, explained in the previous section of this article, that are used in deciding whether a proposal for a new subdivision will make a net contribution to the local economy, and to the city coffers.

## PAYING THE PIPER

In Winnipeg, the uncontrolled deterioration of infrastructure and services,      21
and the costs of trying to keep things patched together, have driven up residential property tax levels. Now competition is an issue, not only between Winnipeg and other, comparable cities across Canada and around the world, but within Winnipeg's own orbit. For some time, residents of the area have been voting with their feet, and accepting property tax reductions they can achieve simply by moving beyond the boundaries of the city. Businesses are beginning to follow.

Indeed, the problem is now largely out of the hands of City Council. With      22
migration out of the city underway, City Council has lost much of the control it might once have exercised over new development. Developers now have

alternatives: if the city is not sufficiently generous with them, it is becoming increasingly easy for them to find a parcel of land for a similar development nearby, in an adjacent municipality.

Planning the growth of the city is no longer an option, at least for city    23
council and its officials. Only a higher authority, or a city with expanded boundaries, could implement a meaningful plan now.

What can be done? What are the alternatives to a planning process that    24
places the convenience of land developers ahead of the needs of the community? There is no question that the planning process can work differently—because it works very differently in many other places.

## GREATER CENTRALIZATION OF POWER

It may seem paradoxical, but one way of making planning more genuinely    25
responsive to the problems of the local community is to give more of the responsibility for planning to a higher level of government. I have noted that cities, such as Winnipeg, that are surrounded by other municipalities that are becoming urbanized are subject to competition for new development.

The competition is not on a level playing-field. The urbanizing munici-    26
pality's property tax payers are typically responsible only for a relatively minimal set of services: roads; possibly sewerage and water service (unless they have septic tanks and wells); education; a low level of policing, at least in the early stages of urbanization; possibly some parks, and not a great deal else.

Major cities inevitably have a range of responsibilities that urbanizing    27
municipalities stand a good chance of avoiding, for example: social services; much more intensive policing; community centres and recreation programs to serve the needs of low-income neighbourhoods; roads that must accommodate regional traffic and through traffic, not just the traffic generated in the immediate area; and so forth.

People who live just outside the city are in a position to enjoy the bene-    28
fits of living near a major city—big-city jobs, ethnic and gourmet restaurants, major league sports, night clubs, symphony and chamber music, theatre and more—but typically they do not share in the property taxes that city residents have to pay to enjoy these facilities. They get the benefits of city life without having to pay the full cost, and this gives them an advantage over the city in the competition for new development.

Provincial governments anxious to avoid being drawn into a potential    29
morass of contention often instruct municipalities to solve their differences by negotiation, but that is usually no solution at all. Once a situation has been set up in which fringe municipalities enjoy large cost advantages, it is unreasonable to expect the local politicians involved to come to terms. If the reeves and mayors do not take advantage of their competitive position, or if they agree to help pay for the costs of city services, they are not serving the best interests of their constituents. If the big-city politicians agree to accept the state of affairs desired by their neighbours, it is *their* constituents that are ill-served. This problem is not likely to be brought under control unless the provincial government steps in.

This is in fact quite feasible. In Europe, it is common for national gov-    30
ernments to exercise substantial control over city planning and major development decisions. The practical result is that developers lose a lot of their
bargaining power. Typically, they are not able to dictate development terms
to local governments, as developers in Winnipeg have done.

There are North American models as well. In a growing number of    31
American jurisdictions, the problems of sprawl development are beginning to be
addressed seriously. In most jurisdictions, the starting point for achieving this
control is a public participation process at the state level, in which citizens
from around the state become involved in the setting of goals for urban growth,
including such things as improvement in water and air quality, increases in average density of development, provision of affordable housing, clear definition of
the boundaries between urban and agricultural land, and so forth.

In Oregon, where this system has been in place the longest, and where it    32
has been quite successful, state legislation requires local governments to meet
state goals in their official development plans, and a state-appointed board
has the power to rule on whether the plans meet the objectives. This allows
local municipalities a great deal of latitude in how they apply the principles,
but it seeks to remove the possibility of influence being used as a means of
overriding the principles.

Such a system would actually be easier to implement in Canada than in    33
the United States. In Canada, provinces have a clear, constitutional responsibility for municipal government. Already such bodies as the Manitoba
Municipal Board have the authority to reject local planning measures. What
would be needed would be a provincially supervised public participation
process to set goals, legislation mandating them, and a little bit of provincial
political will to accept responsibility for problems only the provincial government can solve, instead of letting local municipalities carry the freight.

Oregon has shown that it is possible to bring planning principles to bear    34
on growth without inhibiting growth, and a rapidly growing list of other
American jurisdictions are following suit, or at least trying to.

In Canada, we have an old habit of priding ourselves on the superiority    35
of our cities over American ones, and we can probably afford that luxury for
a while longer yet. However, if provincial governments continue to refuse to
mandate some planning measures to gain control of urban growth, we may
yet find the United States has stolen our "urban livability" crown.

## Who's Really the Villain?

JO-ANN JOHNSTON

Cheap underwear. That's all Wal-Mart Corp. contributes as it squeezes the    1
life out of a community's downtown, according to Albert Norman, an out-
spoken Wal-Mart critic. His sentiment—and talent for rousing support—led
folks in rural Greenfield, Massachusetts, to block the company's plans to

build a store there. It also established the political consultant as one of the best known opponents to "Sprawl-mart" in the country. But fighting off Wal-Mart hasn't done much for the 18,845 residents of Greenfield.

As in numerous other communities during the past ten years, Wal-Mart    2
simply found a site just a short distance away from its original target. In this case, it's in Orange, a smaller town located up the road about twenty-five minutes from downtown Greenfield. Meanwhile, this area ranks as the state's second poorest in per capita income. And in January, it posted an unemployment rate of 6.1 percent—attributable partly to the recent closings of a paper plant, a container factory, and a large store that sold liquidated merchandise. Wal-Mart would have brought to Greenfield 240 tax-paying jobs and increased retail traffic.

Set to open later this year, the store in Orange will be yet another exam-    3
ple of how saying "go away" to the likes of Wal-Mart overlooks a much deeper problem facing small-town America: the need to change a way of doing business while maintaining, or improving, a deeply valued way of life. An increasing number of people are beginning to realize that small-town merchants need to adapt to changes in their communities, the economy, and their industries instead of chastising an outside company. That means accepting the fact that a Wal-Mart, or a similar retailer, may become a neighbor.

Such thinking is hogwash as far as anti–Wal-Marters are concerned.    4
Consumerism has run amok if a town figures it needs a Wal-Mart, says Norman [see "Eight Ways to Stop the Store"], who today works with people in Illinois, Ohio, New England, and other regions to stop Wal-Marts and other large discount retailers from setting up shop. His list of reasons to fight such chain stores is lengthy, with perhaps one of the most popular being the potential loss of small-town quality of life. People move to small towns from urban or suburban America in part to escape from mall and shopping strip development, he says, not to see it duplicated.

That emotional argument carries weight, especially in New England,    5
where twelve cities and one state, Vermont, have fought Wal-Mart. A current battle is taking place in Sturbridge, a historic town in eastern Massachusetts where community activists are fighting to keep Wal-Mart out. The town draws 60 percent of its general business from tourism-related trade, says local Wal-Mart opponent Carol Goodwin. "We market history," she says. The town and its re-creation of an early American village are the state's second largest tourist attraction. A big cookie-cutter mart off the freeway could obscure this town of eight thousand's special appeal, she says.

Sturbridge may want to take a lesson from its neighbor to the northwest,    6
however. Merchants in Greenfield face the possible loss of business due to the fact that Wal-Mart found a location "just over the hill" from where it was first looking to build. Kenneth Stone, an economist at Iowa State University and the country's leading researcher on the economic impacts of Wal-Marts, found that towns in the Midwest and East suffered a "retail leakage" of shoppers who instead drove to the closest regional shopping center with a discount store.

Does that mean Greenfield shoppers will now drive to Orange? Well, several of the town's shoppers complained during the Wal-Mart battle that area merchants could use competition because of their poor selection, high prices, limited hours, and lackluster service. Meanwhile, Wal-Mart has a good reputation for service. A *Consumer Reports* reader poll in late 1994 found that fifty thousand people rated Wal-Mart the highest in customer satisfaction of "value-oriented chains." 7

In many ways, what is happening to small-town retail corridors is similar to how mom-and-pop corporations were caught off guard during the takeover frenzy of the 1980s. Survivors became more efficient to avoid being picked off by raiders looking to maximize shareholder profits. With Wal-Mart, it's a matter of maximizing retailing opportunities for consumers. 8

By the time a community knows the demographically astute Wal-Mart has its eye on an area, it's virtually too late to stop *somebody* from coming into town, says Bill Sakelarios, president of the Concord-based Retail Merchants Association of New Hampshire. In Greenfield, for instance, the threat of competition to that town's small retailers didn't disappear with the Wal-Mart vote. BJ's Wholesale club is considering the town for a store. 9

Wal-Mart is viewed as a threat, though, because it uses bulk buying, discount pricing, and tight inventory and distribution management that smaller retailers can't keep up with. It also has the competitive advantage of size: The company's sales surged 22 percent to more than $82 billion, while net income climbed 15 percent to more than $2.6 billion in the year ended January 31, 1995, compared with year-earlier results. 10

Because it's so huge, the best defense against Wal-Mart for small-town retailers is to adapt, evolve, and create some stronghold that will make them viable and worth keeping, even in the face of new competition, says Robert Kahn, a Lafayette, California, management consultant who has worked with the chain and publishes a newsletter called *Retailing Today*. All kinds of stores have found ways to survive in the shadow of Wal-Mart, he says. Grocery stores have maintained check cashing, hardware stores and nurseries have offered classes, women's clothing retailers have filled in the gaps in the Wal-Mart line. Others point to pharmacies that have been able to compete with Wal-Marts. Stone met one druggist who kept a loyal clientele of shut-ins who spent $200 to $300 a month individually on prescriptions by offering home delivery, something Wal-Mart didn't do in his market. 11

The argument that self-improvement and change for small retailers may be the answer is definitely scorned in some circles. But stores that balk at such notions may not get much sympathy from customers who have had to change jobs or learn new skills—all because of shifts in the structure of the economies in the fields in which they work. 12

"You read stories about how towns don't want Wal-Mart, but in many cases that's a very few people getting a lot of publicity. And I may have on my desk a petition signed by fifteen thousand people saying, 'Please come, ignore the one hundred people who are trying to block the store,'" Wal-Mart President and CEO David Glass told a press gathering in December. "In 13 retailing, you have a very simple answer to all that. Any community that didn't want a Wal-Mart store—all they've got to do is not shop there. And I guarantee a store, even if it's [just] built, won't be there long."

Another thing to consider is what happens if Wal-Mart, or a store like it, comes into town, stays for ten years, and then leaves. Where that's happened, retailers who found ways to adapt to Wal-Mart's presence still believe they're much better as a result. In Nowata, Oklahoma, Wal-Mart pulled up stakes last year and deserted a town of 3,900 people who had come to depend on it as their second largest tax payer, as well as their major retailing center. But several local merchants survived Wal-Mart's stay of fourteen years because they learned to adjust their business practices. Wayne Clark, whose father opened Clark's Sentry Hardware in 1938, says he survived Wal-Mart's presence by providing better service and a more specialized inventory.

Nowata also brings up another interesting question on the Wal-Mart controversy: Could it be that old-time downtowns simply are obsolete and an impediment to efficient retailing? Many retailers have probably been in a precarious position for a long time, for a number of reasons, and then place the blame for problems or eventual demise on the highly visible Wal-Mart, says Sakelarios. "Wal-Mart is being singled out. Small-town business districts brought a lot of this on themselves," agrees Iowa State's Stone.

As cars have drawn shopping to other locales, downtown districts haven't worked hard enough to remain competitive and efficient, data suggest. "Small retailers often believe that the community *owes them* rather than *they owe* the community," Kahn wrote in his December newsletter.

He cites as evidence a recent survey of more than 1,500 Illinois retailers conducted by the state's merchant association. Kahn found it stunning that 54 percent reorder inventory for their stores only when they're already out of stock. That translates into poor selection and service, Kahn says, because small retailers often can't get priority shipments from vendors and most often wait for five to fifteen days to get fresh stock in, leaving customers without that selection in the interim. "That's not providing any service. If it's not in stock, eventually the customer is going to go somewhere else," Kahn points out.

Kahn also criticized the 63 percent of the retailers surveyed who claimed to know what their customers want, even though they didn't track customer purchases.

Apart from self-inflicted injuries, retailers are also pressured on other fronts, says John Donnellan, a member of the Consumer Studies faculty at the University of Massachusetts in Ames. The growth of the mail-order catalogs, cable TV shopping networks, specialized category stores such as Toys 'R' Us, and now, possibly, shopping via on-line computer services, all present more competition for small merchants that draw from local markets.

The only difference with Wal-Mart is that it's the biggest, most identifiable source of that new and increasing competition. As a result, it has become a lightning rod for all the angst and anxiety of struggling shop keepers— deserved or not.

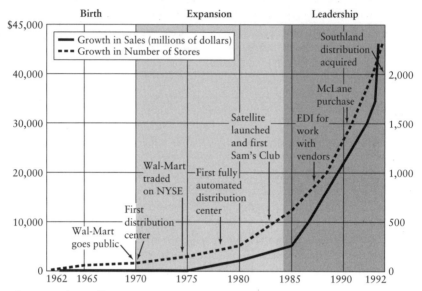

**Wal-Mart Takes Off**

Source: James F. Moore. Chart: "Wal-Mart Takes Off" in "Predators and Prey," *Harvard Business Review*, May–June 1993, p. 82.

# WAL-MART STORES, INC.*

## OVERVIEW

Wal-Mart is a way of life. Bentonville, Arkansas-based Wal-Mart Stores is the world's largest retailer, operating more than 3,400 Wal-Mart discount stores, Sam's Club members-only warehouse stores (#2 in the US, behind Costco), and Wal-Mart Supercenters in all 50 states and in a handful of foreign countries. With the help of its friendly People Greeters, the mammoth chain emphasizes quality service and low prices. Aside from temp firms, Wal-Mart is the nation's largest private employer.

The company doesn't just compete in the discount arena—its stores are also considered a competitor in many category-killer retailing operations. Most of its approximately 500 Supercenters are open 24 hours a day, and they have made the company the #2 grocer in the country (behind Kroger).

About 450 Sam's Club stores worldwide serve small-business and individual customers.

With fewer expansion opportunities for its superstores in the US, the company plans to build a chain of smaller (40,000-sq.-ft.) outlets to take on local grocery stores. Wal-Mart, which wants to be a global brand like Coca-Cola and McDonald's, has opened stores in China; bought a majority interest in Cifra, Mexico's largest retailer; and entered the European and Korean markets (about one-fifth of its stores are outside of the US). Wal-Mart has also ventured into a new frontier—the Internet—with its Sam's Club Online site.

The heirs of the late founder Sam Walton, whose fortune is the second-largest in the US (behind Bill Gates'), own about 38% of the company.

## WHEN

Sam Walton begin his retail career as a J. C. Penney management trainee and later leased a Ben Franklin-franchised dime store in Newport, Arkansas, in 1945. In 1950 he relocated to Bentonville, Arkansas, and opened a Walton 5. By 1962 Walton owned 15 Ben Franklin stores under the Walton 5 name.

After Ben Franklin management rejected his suggestion to open discount stores in small towns, Walton, with his brother James "Bud" Walton, opened the first Wal-Mart Discount City in Rogers, Arkansas, in 1962. Growth was slow at first, but Wal-Mart Stores went public in 1970 with 18 stores and sales of $44 million.

*From Hoover's *Handbook of American Business* 1999. Hoover's Business Press, pages 1508–1509. Reprinted by permission.

Growth accelerated in the 1970s because of two key developments: Wal-Mart's highly automated distribution centers, which cut shipping costs and time, and its computerized inventory system, which sped up checkout and reordering. By 1980 the 276 stores had sales of $1.2 billion. The company bought and sold several operations in those years (including selling off its Ben Franklin stores in 1976).

Wall-Mart opened Sam's Wholesale Club in 1983. Modeled on the successful cash-and-carry, membership-only warehouse format pioneered by the Price Company of California, Sam's lured both small-business owners in metropolitan areas and ordinary consumers paying annual membership fees.

The company started Hypermart*USA in 1987, originally as a joint venture with Cullum Companies, a Dallas-based supermarket chain (Wal-mart bought out Cullum's interest in 1989). The hypermarket, a discount store/supermarket hybrid sprawled out over 200,000 sq. ft., featured ancillary businesses such as branch banks, fast-food outlets, photo developers, and playrooms for shoppers' children. The concept was later retooled as Wal-Mart Supercenters. In 1990 Wal-Mart acquired McLane

Company, a grocery and retail distributor, and launched deep-discounter Bud's Discount City.

In 1992, the year Sam died, the company expanded into Mexico by beginning a joint venture to open Sam's Clubs with Cifra, that country's largest retailer. Wal-Mart acquired 122 former Woolco stores in Canada in 1994. Co-founder Bud died a year later.

The Windsor, Ontario, Wal-Mart became the first in the chain to negotiate under a union labor contract, in 1997. Also that year the company acquired control of its Mexican investment, Cifra, the first direct investment by Wal-Mart in a foreign partner. Wal-Mart decided in 1997 to close most of its 61 low-performing Bud's stores. The company also acquired Wertkauf, a German chain of 21 hypermarkets, in 1997.

In 1998 Wal-Mart bought out the 40% interest Brazilian retail discount chain Lojas Americanas owned in the two companies' joint venture. Wal-Mart expanded in Asia in 1998, buying four stores and additional sites in Korea from Korea Makro. Also the company announced it would create a chain of half-sized stores under the name Wal-Mart Neighborhood Market to give other grocery chains a run for their milk money.

## WHEN

**Chairman:** S. Robson Walton, age 53
**VC and COO:** Donald G. Soderquist, age 64, $1,661,700 pay
**President and CEO:** David D. Glass, age 62, $2,265,846 pay
**EVP and CFO:** John B. Menzer, age 47
**EVP; President and CEO, Wal Mart International:** Bob L. Martin, age 49, $1,044,827 pay
**EVP; President, Wal-Mart Stores Division:** H. Lee Scott Jr., age 49, $943,365 pay
**EVP; President, Wal-Mart Realty:** Paul R. Carter, age 57
**EVP Merchandising:** Bob Connolly, age 54
**EVP, Specialty Divisions:** David Bible, age 50
**EVP, Food Division:** Nicholas J. White, age 53
**SVP and COO, Wal-Mart International:** Carlos Criado-Perez
**SVP and Controller:** James A. Walker Jr., age 51
**President and CEO, McLane:** William G. Rosier, age 49
**EVP and COO, Wal-Mart Stores Division:** Thomas M. Coughlin, age 49, $941,673 pay
**VP Personnel and Administration:** Coleman Petersen
**Auditors:** Ernst & Young LLP

## WHERE

**HQ:** 702 SW 8th St., Bentonville, AR 72716-8611
**Phone:** 501-273-4000          **FAX:** 501-273-1917
**Web site:** http://wal-mart.com

## WHAT

**1998 Stores**

|  | No. |
|---|---|
| Discount stores | 2,421 |
| Supercenters | 502 |
| Sam's Club | 483 |
| **Total** | **3,406** |

**1998 Sales**

|  | % of total |
|---|---|
| Hard goods (hardware, housewares, auto supplies, small appliances) | 23 |
| Soft goods/domestics | 21 |
| Grocery, candy & tobacco | 14 |
| Pharmaceuticals | 9 |
| Records & electronics | 9 |
| Sporting goods & toys | 8 |
| Health & beauty aids | 7 |
| Stationery | 5 |
| Jewelry | 2 |
| Shoes | 2 |
| **Total** | **100** |

**Selected Divisions**

McLane Distribution Centers (19 regional wholesale distribution centers supplying convenience stores and Sam's Clubs, Supercenters, and Wal-Marts)
Sam's Clubs (members-only warehouse clubs)
Supercenters (large, combination general merchandise and food stores)
Wal-Mart Distribution Centers (38 regional centers)
Wal-Mart International Divisions (foreign operations)
Wal-Mart Stores (general merchandise)

## KEY COMPETITORS

| | | |
|---|---|---|
| Albertson's | Fred Meyer | Service |
| AutoZone | Home Depot | Merchandise |
| Best Buy | Hudson's Bay | Staples |
| Circuit City | J. C. Penney | Tandy |
| CompUSA | Kmart | Target Stores |
| Consolidated | Kroger | TJX |
| Stores | Lowe's | Toys 'R' Us |
| Costco | METRO Holding | TruServ |
| Companies | Office Depot | Venator Group |
| CVS | Safeway | Walgreen |
| Dollar General | Sears | |

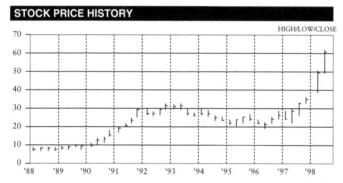

## HOW MUCH

| NYSE symbol: WMT<br>FYE: January 31 | Annual<br>Growth | 1989 | 1990 | 1991 | 1992 | 1993 | 1994 | 1995 | 1996 | 1997 | 1998 |
|---|---|---|---|---|---|---|---|---|---|---|---|
| Sales ($ mil.) | 21.4% | 20,649 | 25,811 | 32,602 | 43,887 | 55,484 | 67,345 | 82,494 | 93,627 | 104,859 | 117,959 |
| Net Income ($ mil.) | 17.3% | 837 | 1,076 | 1,291 | 1,609 | 1,995 | 2,333 | 2,681 | 2,740 | 3,056 | 3,526 |
| Income as % of sales | — | 4.1% | 4.2% | 4.0% | 3.7% | 3.6% | 3.5% | 3.2% | 2.9% | 2.9% | 3.0% |
| Earnings per share ($) | 17.3% | 0.37 | 0.48 | 0.57 | 0.70 | 0.87 | 1.02 | 1.17 | 1.19 | 1.33 | 1.56 |
| Stock price - FY high ($) | — | 8.47 | 11.84 | 18.38 | 29.94 | 32.94 | 34.13 | 29.25 | 27.63 | 28.25 | 41.94 |
| Stock price - FY low($) | — | 6.28 | 7.84 | 10.09 | 16.38 | 25.06 | 23.00 | 20.63 | 19.09 | 20.13 | 23.00 |
| Stock price - FY close ($) | 18.8% | 8.44 | 10.66 | 16.50 | 26.94 | 32.56 | 26.50 | 22.88 | 20.38 | 23.75 | 39.81 |
| P/E - high | — | 23 | 25 | 32 | 43 | 38 | 33 | 25 | 23 | 21 | 27 |
| P/E - low | — | 17 | 16 | 18 | 23 | 29 | 23 | 18 | 16 | 15 | 15 |
| Dividends per share ($) | 23.6% | 0.04 | 0.06 | 0.07 | 0.09 | 0.11 | 0.13 | 0.17 | 0.20 | 0.21 | 0.27 |
| Book value per share ($) | 22.5% | 1.33 | 1.75 | 2.35 | 3.04 | 3.81 | 4.68 | 5.54 | 6.44 | 7.50 | 8.26 |
| Employees | 15.6% | 223,000 | 271,000 | 328,000 | 371,000 | 434,000 | 528,000 | 622,000 | 675,000 | 728,000 | 825,000 |

## STOCK PRICE HISTORY

HIGH/LOW/CLOSE

**1998 FISCAL YEAR-END**

Debt ratio: 34.3%
Return on equity: 19.1%
Cash (mil.): $1,447
Current ratio: 1.34
Long-term debt (mil.): $9,674
No. of shares (mil.): 2,241
Dividends
 Yields: 0.7%
 Payout: 17.3%
Market value (mil.): $89,214

# Sprawl-Busters

## Sprawl-Busting Victories

58 Communities where megastores have been
rejected (at least once) or have withdrawn:

| | | |
|---|---|---|
| Plymouth, MA | Lebanon, NH | Manalapan, NJ |
| Reading, MA | Peterborough, NH | Rehobeth, DE |
| Yarmouth, MA | Buffalo, NY | Mt. Joy, PA |
| Gaithersburg, MD | East Aurora, NY | Warwick, PA |
| Plainville, CT | Hyde Park, NY | West Hempfield, PA |
| Orange, CT | New Paltz, NY | Middletown, RI |
| New Milford, CT | Hornell, NY | Accomac, VA |
| Old Saybrook, CT | Ithaca, NY | Warrenton, VA |
| Tolland, CT | Leeds, NY | Williamsburg, VA |
| St. Albans, VT | Utica, NY | Durham, NC |
| St. Johnsbury, VT | Lake Placid, NY | Hickory, NC |
| Claremont, NH | N Greenbush, NY | Temple Terrace, FL |
| Henniker, NH | Hamilton, NJ | Hallandale, FL |

New Albany, IN
Decorah, IO
Fenton, MI
Warsaw, MO
Broadview Heights, OH
Highland Heights, OH
Lorain, OH
Cleveland Heights, OH
Westlake, OH
North Olmsted, OH
Chardon, OH
Ottawa, OH
Strongsville, OH
Burnsville, MN
West Bend, WI

Waukesha, WI
Brookfield, WI
Wichita, KS
Jefferson County, CO
Silverthorne, CO
Lincoln, NB
Taylorsville, UT
Layton, UT
    (Home Depot)
Hailey, ID
North Auburn, CA
Simi Valley, CA
Santa Rosa, CA
    (Home Depot)

San Francisco, CA
    (Home Depot)
Santa Maria, CA
Grass Valley, CA
Gig Harbor, WA
Waterloo, Ontario,
    Canada
View Royal, BC,
    Canada
Guelph, Ontario,
    Canada
Utuado, P.R.
Barranquitas, P.R.

---

Source: Albert Norman, Sprawl-Busters. 23 Nov. 1998.
<www.sprawl-busters.com/victoryz.htm>.

List updated as of November, 1998.

# Shopping With the Enemy

*This unsigned article first appeared in* The Economist *on October 14, 1995.*

"Something there is that doesn't love a wall," wrote Robert Frost. "Or a Wal-    1
Mart," he might add, were he to rise from his grave behind the Old First
Church and look at the newly opened store just down the hill. Vermont is no
longer the only state without a Wal-Mart, despite a five-year struggle by the
company's opponents to keep it out.

Yet instead of protesting, the locals are pushing and shoving to get in.    2
"The reaction has been tremendous," says Russ Walker, the manager. Mr.
Walker recorded 23,000 transactions in his first week, and this in a town of
16,000 people. Drawn by such locally appealing bargains as red flannel shirts
for $6.56, Vermonters are opening their hearts and their wallets to Wal-Mart.

Does that mean doom for downtown merchants? Not necessarily. Wal-    3
Marts are usually huge, charmless boxes built on the outskirts of towns,
where highways are handy and parking plentiful. But to crack the Vermont
market and avoid the restrictions of the state's tough development-control
law, Wal-Mart put a less-imposing, 50,000-square-foot store into an old
Woolworth's building near the centre of town.

Bennington's downtown merchants seem to be adjusting to Wal-Mart;    4
they are used to competing with other big discount chains such as Kmart,
already established in the local market. "I'm not really worried," says
Catherine Mack, proprietor of the artsy-craftsy Pea Pod gift shop on Main

Street. "I think we're building our own little niche as a specialty store." But not all Wal-Mart patrons are willing to venture downtown, despite a recent effort to spiff up the district. "I think the downtown in Bennington is doomed anyway, because of the lack of parking," Mary Lou Morris said firmly. "I go to malls."

Mall-going Vermonters have little patience with Wal-Mart's opponents.      5
Mr. Walker, the store manager, blames the controversy on "a handful of non-natives" who care more about prettiness than economic development. But if they are a minority in blue-collar Bennington, the company's enemies are more influential elsewhere in the state. In Burlington, the state's biggest city, anxious officials are fighting a 115,000-square-foot Wal-Mart and a 132,000-square-foot Sam's Club planned for a largely undeveloped area outside the city.

Their battle appears lost, however. So far Vermont has largely avoided      6
the suburban sprawl that blights so much of the American landscape. But too many people crave the low prices, large selection and convenient parking offered by the big discount chains. "Progress—can't stand in the way," said Wal-Mart shopper Jack Hodgeman, trundling several new refuse bins out to his pickup truck.

■  ■  ■

The following pair of articles from the *Winnipeg Free Press* (June, 2000) about Wal-Mart's decision to relocate several stores indicates some of the problems that can arise when the retail giant makes decisions that change the pattern of retail in a community.

## Wal-Mart to Build, Abandon City Malls

ALDO SANTIN

The Wal-Mart invasion of Winnipeg is about to produce its first casualties.      1

The owner of Grant Park Shopping Centre and Garden City Square said      2
it expects the retailing giant to close both stores within the year while it opens two new locations in power centres—clusters of big-box retailers sharing the same parking lot—that are under construction or on the drawing board.

"They're the big boys on the block and they can do whatever they want,"      3
said Robert Akman, president of Creswin Properties, which owns both malls.

Akman said Wal-Mart has decided not to renew its lease on its Grant      4
Park store, adding he expects it will close when the retailer's new store at Empress Street and Ellice Avenue is completed.

In addition, Akman said he has been unable to dissuade Wal-Mart from      5
pursuing its plans to open a new store on McPhillips Street, about 1.6 kilo-metres north of its Garden City Square store.

The Grant Park and Garden City stores were part of the Woolco empire   6
that Wal-Mart bought in 1994, which included five stores in Winnipeg.

Since then, Wal-Mart has opened a new store at a power centre complex   7
at Kenaston and McGillivray boulevards and a seventh store is under construction at the power centre complex at Empress and Ellice.

A new store is part of the reconfiguration of the Unicity Mall into a   8
power centre, and it's also building a replacement store for the Crossroads
Shopping Centre in Transcona. Also during the last six years, Wal-Mart had
redeveloped two existing stores.

Wal-Mart's closest discount competitor, Zellers, has seven smaller stores   9
throughout the city.

Wal-Mart's latest moves are more typical of its expansion patterns in the   10
United States. Instead of renovating or expanding its existing locations, Wal-
Mart has increasingly abandoned older buildings.

Municipalities are struggling to find new uses for these empty buildings.   11
Estimates place the number of abandoned Wal-Mart locations across the
United States at about 300.

Akman said he expects to find a replacement tenant at Grant Park, but   12
added market conditions in Garden City will make it impossible to do the
same there.

Akman said an Urbanics study revealed there are at least 200 000 square   13
feet of empty retail space in the McPhillips Street–Leola Avenue area, including a Canadian Tire Store closed when that chain built a new store.

Akman said Wal-Mart's store at Garden City Square would be the same   14
size as a proposed new store, but has a different floor plan. He said he's willing to rebuild the store to meet Wal-Mart's needs, but said the company
doesn't want to deal with the inconvenience that would cause.

A Wal-Mart spokesman could not be reached for comment.   15

However, a Toronto-based retail consultant said Wal-Mart is following   16
a successful business plan that has benefited the city since it came here.

"What they're doing is showing a vote of confidence in Winnipeg,"   17
said Len Kubas of Kubas Consultants. "They're not shutting down and
moving away."

## Mall Owners Vent Anger at Wal-Mart

DAVID O'BRIEN

A plan by Wal-Mart to abandon two Winnipeg shopping centres has sparked   1
a mud-slinging feud between the retail empire and two prominent businessmen.

David Asper and Bob Akman, partners in a company that owns the   2
affected malls, accused Wal-Mart of being a poor corporate citizen and a
major cause of urban sprawl.

"Wal-Mart does nothing for our community," Bob Akman, president of  3
Creswin Properties Ltd., told a public hearing at city hall. "We need to send
a message to Wal-Mart that instead of exporting its profits, the quid pro quo
for doing business here is to be a good corporate citizen at a level commen-
surate with its ability to give."

A spokesman for Wal-Mart's Canadian operations called the remarks  4
"absurd and completely untrue."

"I feel sorry for them," said Andrew Pelletier, Wal-Mart's director of  5
public affairs. "They're using our good name as a political platform (and)
that's outrageous."

Creswin owns several properties in Winnipeg, including Garden City  6
Square, which Wal-Mart is planning to abandon for undeveloped land further
north. The company also has an interest in Grant Park Shopping Centre,
which Wal-Mart also plans to quit.

Asper, a partner in Creswin and son of media mogul Izzy Asper, also  7
expressed disappointment that Wal-Mart wasn't pulling its weight in the
community.

"They're not doing a whole lot for the city," Asper said.  8

Added Akman: "As one peruses the programs of the symphony, ballet,  9
theatre centre, Theatre for Young People, folk festival, Folklorama, West
End Cultural Centre, Assiniboine Park Pavilion and so on, there is a deafen-
ing silence from Wal-Mart." Wal-Mart earns about $350 million in sales
from its six Winnipeg stores, he said.

Akman's comments were made at a public hearing on proposed amend-  10
ments to Plan Winnipeg, the city's development blueprint.

Wal-Mart wants to vacate its 130 000-square-foot location in Garden  11
City Square and build a new store about two kilometres to the north.

However, the land is designated rural and Wal-Mart's developer has  12
asked the city to change it to a classification that permits residential and
commercial development.

Akman and Asper said if Wal-Mart is allowed to open a store in an  13
undeveloped part of Winnipeg, it will fuel urban sprawl and increase the
city's costs for transit, schools and maintenance of streets, sewer and water.

And if Wal-Mart moves from Garden City Square, they said, it will  14
weaken the remaining businesses.

The two businessmen conceded in interviews they had an obvious self-  15
interest in opposing Wal-Mart's relocation.

Meanwhile, Pelletier said Wal-Mart is a generous and responsible cor-  16
porate citizen. Since opening in Canada six years ago, Pelletier said, Wal-Mart
has raised and donated $8 million to local charities.

He said he couldn't say how much the chain contributes to charities in  17
Manitoba, but each store in the chain is responsible for identifying local
causes and raising money to support them.

The retailer was a major contributor to flood relief in Manitoba following  18
the 1997 flood of the century and it has donated 7 000 bottles of water to
Walkerton, Ont., following the tainted-water scandal that devastated the town.

Pelletier also dismissed the idea that Wal-Mart contributes to urban 19
sprawl, calling it "a fear tactic that won't work any more."

The issue is expected to generate fierce debate in council, where the new 20
Plan Winnipeg document must be approved June 21.

■ ■ ■

## Consider Your Purpose

Determining your specific purpose in writing an argument synthesis is crucial.
What, exactly, you want to do will affect your claim, the evidence you select
to support your claim, and the way you organize the evidence. Your purpose
may be clear to you before you begin research, may emerge during the course
of research, or may not emerge until after you have completed your research.
(Of course, the sooner your purpose is clear to you, the fewer wasted motions
you will make. On the other hand, the more you approach research as an
exploratory process, the likelier that your conclusions will emerge from the
sources themselves, rather than from preconceived ideas. For a discussion on
the process of research, see Chapter 3.)

Let's say that while reading these sources, your own encounters with
Wal-Mart influence your thinking on the subject and you find yourself
agreeing more with the supporters than with the detractors of Wal-Mart.
Perhaps you didn't grow up in a small town, so you don't have much experience with or knowledge of the kind of retail stores that the megastores have
been displacing.

On the one hand, you can understand and even sympathize with the
viewpoints of critics such as Norman and Anderson. (You may have shopped
in the smaller stores in towns you have visited, or seen them portrayed in
movies, or perhaps even visited reconstructed small-town stores in heritage
museums.) On the other hand, it seems to you unrealistic in this day and age
to expect that stores like Wal-Mart can be stopped or should be. For you, the
prices and the convenience are a big plus. Your purpose, then, is formed from
this kind of response to the source material.

## Making a Claim: Formulate a Thesis

As we indicated in the introduction to argument synthesis, one useful way of
approaching an argument is to see it as making a *claim*. A claim is a proposition, a conclusion that you are trying to prove or demonstrate. If your purpose
is to demonstrate that it is neither possible nor desirable to stop the spread of
Wal-Mart, then that is the claim at the heart of your argument. The claim is
generally expressed in one-sentence form as a *thesis*. Your thesis usually reflects
the view you have come to adopt on the basis of reading and thinking about an
issue or topic. To develop a "working" or provisional thesis about Y, it is often
useful to complete a "starter" phrase like this: About topic Y, I believe that
_____. If you want to position your view in the context of opposing

claims, you might try a "starter" phrase like this: Although some people believe _____ (and others think _____), I believe that _____. These phrases can initiate the drafting process by nudging you into expressing a position that you have come to hold on the basis of reading and reflecting. As you continue the drafting process, you will of course refine your views and the way you state your claim.

You may not want to divulge your thesis until the end of the paper, to draw the reader along toward your conclusion, allowing the thesis to flow naturally out of the argument and the evidence on which it is based. If you do this, you are working *inductively*. Or, you may wish to be more direct and *begin* with your thesis in your opening paragraph, following the thesis statement with evidence to support it. If you do this, you are working *deductively*. In academic papers, deductive arguments are far more common than inductive arguments.

Based on your reactions to reading the sources, you decide to concede that the case against Wal-Mart has some merit and certainly some homespun appeal, but that opponents of such megastores are being unrealistic in expecting most people to sacrifice convenience and economy for the sake of retaining a vanishing way of life. After a few tries, you arrive at the following provisional thesis:

```
Opponents of the giant discount chains have made pow-
erful arguments against them, and it's too bad that
these megastores are helping to make a way of life
extinct; but opponents should realize that stores such
as Wal-Mart are so successful because most people
prefer bargains and convenience to tradition and
small-town charm.
```

## Decide How You Will Use Your Source Material

To support your claim, you use information found in sources. You can also use appeals to *ethos* and *pathos* in these sources. Of course, not every piece of information in a source is useful for supporting a claim. By the same token, you may draw support for your own claim from sources that make entirely different claims. For example, you may use as support for your own claim—that Wal-Mart is growing at an alarming rate—data from the store's website annual report, which claims the exact opposite: that Wal-Mart's growth is good for both customers and stockholders.

Similarly, you might use one source as part of a counter-argument—an argument opposite to your own—so that you can demonstrate its weaknesses and, in the process, strengthen your own claim. On the other hand, the author of one of your sources may be so convincing in supporting a claim that you adopt it yourself, either partially or entirely. The point is that the argument is in your hands; you must devise it yourself and must use your sources in ways that will support the claim expressed in your thesis.

Your claim commits you to (1) recognize the arguments made by opponents of Wal-Mart, and (2) argue that Wal-Marts will prevail because they offer people advantages that the traditional retail shops can't match. The sources provide plenty of information and ideas—that is, evidence—that will allow you to support your claim. Norman and Anderson sum up the anti–Wal-Mart case, one that is also described more objectively by Ortega and the anonymous author of the *Economist* article. Johnston offers the primary argument for Wal-Mart, and other data showing the growth of the chain are provided by Wal-Mart itself (in its website) and by the chart following Moore's article.

## Develop an Organizational Plan

Having established your overall purpose and your claim, having developed a provisional thesis, and having decided how to use your source materials, how do you logically organize your essay? In many cases, including this one, a well-written thesis will suggest an overall organization. Thus, the first part of your synthesis will address the powerful arguments made by opponents of Wal-Mart. The second part will cover the even more powerful case (in your judgment) to be made on the other side. Sorting through your material and categorizing it by topic and subtopic, you might arrive at the following outline:

A. Introduction. The emotional anti–Wal-Mart case; conflict of values: consumerism vs. small-town America. *Thesis.*
B. Spectacular growth of Wal-Mart.
C. The case against Wal-Mart.
   1. Arguments against Wal-Mart.
   2. Al Norman's crusade.
D. Transition: the case for Wal-Mart.
E. Concession: charm of small-town stores. But—problems with small-town stores.
F. Changes in American economy and lifestyle and their effect on Main Street.
G. How traditionalists and store owners can deal with Wal-Mart.
   1. Fight it.
   2. Adjust by competing in ways that Wal-Mart can't.
H. Conclusion. Wal-Mart is not a "villain" because it offers what people want.

## Argument Strategy

The argument represented by this outline deals with a claim of *value*, rather than a claim of *fact*. In other words, this is not an argument over whether Wal-Marts *are* better, according to some objective standard, than Main Street variety stores, since there is no such standard about which most people would agree. (Of course, if "better" were defined as more profitable, then this argument *would* become one of fact and would, in fact, be easily disposed of, since numbers would provide sufficient support for the claim.) Rather, it is an argument that turns on those values which for different people take priority—convenience and economy versus charm and traditional small-town life. Your *claim,* therefore, is based not only upon the *supporting evidence,* but also upon your *assumptions* about the relative value of convenience and economy, on the one hand, and charm and traditional small-town life, on the other. Accordingly, while some of the arguments are based upon an appeal to *logos,* most are based upon the appeal to *pathos.* Some are even based upon *ethos,* since the writer will occasionally imply that her view is representative of that of most people.

To *support* her *claim,* the writer will rely upon a combination of summary, paraphrase, and quotation—much of it *testimony* from either "average" customers or from proponents of one side or the other of the debate. Note that despite her own essentially pro–Wal-Mart position, the writer provides *counter-arguments* and *concessions,* indicating that she is not afraid to fairly represent the views of the other side, and even to give them some credit (the concession) before she responds and reinforces her own argument.

## Draft and Revise Your Synthesis

The final draft of a completed synthesis, based upon the above outline, follows. Thesis, transitional, and topic sentences are highlighted; Modern Language Association (MLA) documentation style, explained in Chapter 4, is used throughout. Note that for the sake of clarity, references in the following essay are to pages in *Writing and Reading Across the Curriculum.*

A Vote for Wal-Mart

According to one critic, Wal-Mart is waging a "War on Main Street." Anti-Wal-Mart activists think that we should "Ban the Bargains." A pro-Wal-Mart writer asks "Who's Really the Villain?" Obviously, the ever-expanding Wal-Mart brings some people's emotions to the boiling point. This seems strange. After all, Wal-Mart doesn't seem one of those hot-button issues like abortion or capital punishment. But for many, this is not just about discount department stores; it's about conflicting values: the values of small-town North America versus the values of "mindless consumerism" (Ortega 162). I don't consider myself a mindless consumerist, but I happen to like Wal-Marts. Opponents of the giant discount chains have made powerful arguments against them, and it's too bad that these megastores are helping to make a way of life extinct; but opponents should realize that stores like Wal-Mart are so successful because most people prefer bargains and convenience to tradition and small-town charm.

Wal-Mart's growth has been spectacular. Launched in 1962, by 1997 Wal-Mart had over 2900 stores, including 502 "Supercenters" ("Wal-Mart" 177). Al Norman, one of Wal-Mart's most vocal critics, reported that in 1994 Wal-Mart had over $67 billion in sales (164). Four years later, Wal-Mart's annual sales climbed to almost $118 billion ("Wal-Mart" 178). Wal-Mart also owns Sam's Club, another discount chain, which opened in early 1983 (chart: "Wal-Mart Takes Off"), and now numbers 483 stores ("Wal-Mart" 177).

To its critics, Wal-Mart seems to represent everything that's wrong with modern North American society. Sarah Anderson, an economist and the daughter of a small-town retailer, argues that Wal-Mart encourages urban sprawl, drains money from local economies, kills downtowns and local jobs, and destroys the quality of small-town life (166–167). Others blame Wal-Mart for the "homogenization of community identity" (Ortega 162). One local resident complains, "Everything's starting to look the same, everybody buys all the same things--a lot of small-town character is being lost." She adds, "Visually, [Wal-Marts] are atrocious" (qtd. in Ortega 163). Wal-Marts's ugliness is a common theme: the stores have been described as "huge, charmless boxes" ("Shopping" 179).

Activist Al Norman has helped organize local communities to fight the spread of Wal-Mart. His website, "Sprawl-Busters," proudly lists 58 communities that have succeeded in beating back Wal-Mart's advance on their town. (He also lists communities that have rejected other large discounters like Home Depot, Costco, and Kmart.) Norman argues that "Wal-Mart's

gains are largely captured from other merchants"
("Eight Ways" 164). His rallying cry is that communities are "not ready to die for a cheap pair of underwear" (qtd. in Anderson 166).

But rhetoric like this is overkill. Norman might as
well blame computer makers for the death of typewriters or automakers for the death of horse-and-buggy
rigs. Horses and buggies may be more picturesque and
romantic than cars, but most North Americans drive
cars these days because they're a lot faster and more
convenient. If customers choose to buy underwear at
Wal-Mart instead of the mom-and-pop store downtown,
that's because it's easier to get to Wal-Mart--and to
park there--and because cheapness is a quality that
matters to them.

I agree that Wal-Marts are unattractive and "charmless." They just don't have the warmth or individuality of some of the small shops you find in downtown
areas, especially if they've been in business for generations. But like most people, I'm willing to sacrifice warmth and individuality if I can get just what
I want at a price I can afford. As Jo-Ann Johnston
points out, mom-and-pop stores have brought on a lot
of their own problems by not being sufficiently
responsive to what their customers need. She notes,
"several of the town's shoppers complained during the
Wal-Mart battle that area merchants could use competition because of their poor selection, high prices,
limited hours, and lackluster service" (174). Johnston
points out that if customers can't find what they want
at the price they want at local stores, it's not surprising that they go to Wal-Mart. Even residents of
Vermont, one of the areas most likely to resist the
intrusion of Wal-Mart, come flocking to Wal-Mart for
the bargains and the selection ("Shopping" 179). Russ
Walker, store manager of the Bennington Wal-Mart, dis-

misses opposition to the discount chain as "'a handful of non-natives' who care more about prettiness than economic development" ("Shopping" 180).

As even opponents of Wal-Mart admit, North American downtowns were in trouble long before Wal-Mart arrived on the scene. Changes in the economy and in the North American lifestyle have contributed to the end of a traditional way of life. In other words, stores such as Wal-Mart are a symptom rather than a cause of the changes in Main Street. Blaming Wal-Mart "overlooks a much deeper problem facing small-town America," writes Jo-Ann Johnston: "the need to change a way of business while maintaining, or improving, a deeply valued way of life" (173). As Sarah Anderson admits, "Small towns cannot return to the past, when families did all their shopping and socializing in their hometown. Rural life is changing and there's no use denying it" (167).

In "Eight Ways to Stop the Store," Norman provides tips for community activists on how to fight Wal-Mart. I agree that if most people don't want Wal-Mart in their community, they should campaign against it and keep it out. I even think that the community might be a more pleasant place to live without the huge discount chains. But I also believe that residents of these communities should be aware of the price they will pay, both financially and in convenience, for maintaining their traditional way of doing business. Even without Wal-Mart, local downtowns will have trouble holding on to their customers. A better plan than keeping the big discounters out would be for local retailers to adapt to the changing times and to the competition. Some store owners have found ways of offering their customers what Wal-Mart can't provide: personalized services, such as home delivery or special orders, along with merchandise not available in the chain stores (Johnston 174).

Wal-Mart did not become the huge success it is by
forcing its products on an unwilling public. People
shop there because they want to. They want to save
money and they want to find what they're looking for.
Who can blame them? Wal-Mart may not be pretty, but
it's also not "the villain."

Works Cited

Anderson, Sarah. "Wal-Mart's War on Main Street."
    Progressive Nov. 1994: 19–21.

Johnston, Jo-Ann. "Who's Really the Villain?" Business
    Ethics May–June 1995: 16–18.
Moore, James F. Chart: "Wal-Mart Takes Off." "Predators
    and Prey." Harvard Business Review May–June 1993: 82.
Norman, Albert "Eight Ways to Stop the Store." The Nation
    28 Mar. 1994: 418.

---. "Sprawl-Busting Victories." Sprawl-Busters Mar.
    1997. 17 Sept. 1997 <http://www.sprawl-busters.com/
    victoryz.html>.

Ortega, Bob. "Ban the Bargains." The Wall Street Journal
    11 Oct. 1994: 1+.

"Shopping with the Enemy." Economist 14 Oct. 1995: 33.

"Wal-Mart Stores, Inc." Hoover's Handbook of American
    Business. Austin, TX: Business Press, 1998.

## Discussion

The writer of this argument synthesis on Wal-Mart attempts to support a *claim*—
one that essentially favours Wal-Mart—by offering *support* in the form of facts
(examples and statistics) and opinions (testimony of experts and "average" customers). However, since the writer's claim is one of *value*, as opposed to fact, its
effectiveness depends partially upon the extent to which we, as readers, agree
with the *assumptions* underlying the argument. An assumption (sometimes
called a *warrant*) is a generalization or principle about how the world works or
should work—a fundamental statement of belief about facts or values. In this
particular case, the underlying assumption is that the values of cheapness and
convenience are preferable, as a rule, to the values of charm and small-town tradition. Assumptions often are deeply rooted in people's psyches, sometimes
deriving from lifelong experiences and observations, and are not easily changed,
even by the most logical arguments. People who grew up in small-town America
and remember it fondly are therefore far less likely to be persuaded by the support offered for this writer's claim than those who have lived in urban and suburban areas.

- In the *introductory paragraph*, the writer summarizes some of the most heated arguments against Wal-Mart by citing some of the titles of recent articles about the store. The writer goes on to explain the intensity of emotion generated by stores such as Wal-Mart by linking it to a larger conflict of values: the values of small-town North America vs. the values of consumerism. The writer then states her own preference for Wal-Mart, which leads to her *claim* (represented in the *thesis* at the end of the first paragraph).

  **Argument strategy:** The writer sets up the argument as one of con-flicting *values*, relying here upon summary and quotations that sup-port an appeal to *pathos* (emotions of the reader). The writer also provides the beginning of an appeal to *ethos* (establishing herself as credible) by stating her own views as a consumer in the sentence before the thesis.

- In the *second paragraph*, the writer discusses the spectacular growth of Wal-Mart. This growth is indirectly, rather than directly, relevant to the debate itself, since it is this apparently unstoppable growth that has caused Wal-Mart to be perceived as such a threat by opponents.

  **Argument strategy:** This paragraph relies primarily upon the appeal to *logos* (logic) since its main purpose is to establish Wal-Mart's spectacular success. The argument here is supported primarily with statistics.

- In the *third and fourth paragraphs*, the writer discusses the case against Wal-Mart. The third paragraph covers the objections most commonly advanced by Wal-Mart critics. Three sources (Anderson, Ortega, and "Shopping with the Enemy") provide the source material for this paragraph. In the next paragraph, the writer focuses on Al Norman, one of the most prominent anti–Wal-Mart activists, who has helped localities organize campaigns against new Wal-Marts, some of them successful.

  **Argument strategy:** The third paragraph, part of the *counter-argument*, attempts to support claims of value (that is, *pathos*) with a combination of summary (topic sentence), paraphrase (second sentence), and quotation (following sentences). The fourth paragraph, a continuation of the counter-argument, relies on a combination of appeals to *logos* (the numbers of communities that, according to Norman, have rejected Wal-Mart) and *pathos* (the quotation in the final sentence of the paragraph).

- The *fifth paragraph* begins the transition to the opposite side. The writer begins advancing her own claim—that people aren't willing to sacrifice convenience and price to charm and tradition. She also suggests that the small-town North American Main Street that Wal-Mart is replacing was dying anyway.

  **Argument strategy:** This paragraph makes a transition from the counter-argument to the writer's own argument. Initially, the appeal is to *logos*: She draws an analogy between the passing of traditional

Main Street stores and the passing of typewriters and horses and buggies. This is followed by another appeal to *pathos*—the importance of efficiency, convenience, and cheapness.

- In the *sixth paragraph*, the writer admits that Wal-Marts are not pretty, charming, or unique, but argues that the mom-and-pop stores have their own problems: small selection, non-responsiveness to customer needs, indifferent service, and relatively high prices.
  **Argument strategy:** In this paragraph, the writer makes an important *concession* (part of the counter-argument) that charm is important; but she continues to use the appeal to *pathos* to support the primary claim. Note that in the middle of the paragraph, the writer makes an appeal to *ethos* (" . . . like most people, I'm willing to sacrifice warmth and individuality if I can get just what I want at a price I can afford"). This statement aligns the writer with what most people want from their shopping experiences. After all, the writer implies, this is a matter of good sense—a quality the reader is likely to think valuable, a quality that she or he appears to share with the writer.

- *Paragraph seven* deals more explicitly than the fifth paragraph with the passing away of traditional small-town North America, owing to changes in the economy and in lifestyle.
  **Argument strategy:** In this paragraph the writer follows through with her strategy of relying upon a combination of *logos* and *pathos* to support her claim. Beginning by summarizing the reasons for the decline of Main Street, she concludes the paragraph with quotations focusing on the sad but inevitable passing of a way of life.

- In *paragraph eight*, the writer concedes that people are free to fight Wal-Mart coming to their town if they don't want the giant store; but a better course of action might be for local merchants to adjust to Wal-Mart by offering goods and services that the giant store is unwilling or unable to, such as home delivery and specialty merchandise.
  **Argument strategy:** At this point, the writer focuses almost all her attention on the appeal to logic: She summarizes both the essential nature of the conflict and suggestions offered by one source for counteracting the Wal-Mart threat.

- In *paragraph nine*, the writer concludes by reemphasizing her claim: Wal-Mart is successful because it gives customers what they want.
  **Argument strategy:** The writer wraps up her argument by reemphasizing the reasons offered for Wal-Mart's success. She rounds off her discussion by repeating, in quotation marks, the "villain" epithet with which the paper begins. The final sentence again combines the appeal to *pathos* (we admittedly cannot call Wal-Mart "pretty") and *logos* (in view of the evidence offered as support, it makes no sense to label Wal-Mart a "villain").

Of course, many other approaches to an argument synthesis would be possible based on the sources provided here. One, obviously, would be the opposite argument: that in embracing Wal-Marts and other giant chains, North America is losing part of its soul—or, at a less profound level, small towns are losing part of their charm and distinctive character. Another might be to assess the quality of the various positions according, for example, to the nature of the evidence provided or the type of logic employed. Another might be to de-emphasize the more concrete issue of stores such as Wal-Mart and to focus on the broader issue of changes in small-town life. Whatever your approach to the subject, in first *analyzing* the various sources and then *synthesizing* them to support your argument, you are engaging in the kind of critical thinking that is essential to success in a good deal of academic and professional work.

## DEVELOPING AND ORGANIZING THE SUPPORT FOR YOUR ARGUMENTS

Experienced writers seem to have an intuitive sense of how to develop and present the supporting evidence for their claims. Less experienced writers wonder what to say first, and having decided on that, wonder what to say next. There is no single method of presentation. But the techniques of even the most experienced writers often boil down to a few tried and tested arrangements.

As we've seen in the model syntheses in this chapter, the key to devising effective arguments is to find and use those kinds of support that most persuasively strengthen your claim. Some writers categorize support into two broad types: *evidence* and *motivational appeals*. Evidence, in the form of facts, statistics, and expert testimony, helps make the appeal to *logos* or reason. Motivational appeals—appeals to *pathos* and to *ethos*—are employed to get people to change their minds, to agree with the writer or speaker, or to decide upon a plan of activity.

Following are some of the most common principles for using and organizing support for your claims.

### Summarize, Paraphrase, and Quote Supporting Evidence

In most of the papers and reports you will write in college and the professional world, evidence and motivational appeals derive from summarizing, paraphrasing, and quoting material in the sources that either have been provided to you or that you have independently researched. (See Chapter 5, on when to summarize, paraphrase, and quote material from sources.) As we noted above, the third paragraph of the Wal-Mart synthesis offers all three treatments of evidence: In the first sentence, the writer *summarizes* anti–Wal-Mart sentiment in the sources; in the second sentence, she *paraphrases* Sarah Anderson; in the third sentence, she *quotes* Bob Ortega.

## Provide Various Types of Evidence and Motivational Appeals

Keep in mind the appeals to both *logos* and *pathos*. As we've discussed, the appeal to *logos* is based on evidence that consists of a combination of *facts, statistics*, and *expert testimony*. In the Wal-Mart synthesis, the writer uses all of these varieties of evidence: facts (the economic decline of small-town North America, as discussed in paragraph 7, statistics (the growth of Wal-Mart, as documented in paragraph 2), and testimony (the quotations in paragraph 3). The appeal to *pathos* is based on the appeal to the needs and values of the audience. In the Wal-Mart synthesis, this appeal is exemplified in the use of support (for example, the quotations in paragraph 6 about the limitations of mom-and-pop stores) that are likely to make readers upset or dissatisfied because they feel that they need greater selection, efficiency, and economy than the smaller stores can offer them.

## Use Climactic Order

Organize by climactic order when you plan to offer a number of different categories or elements of support for your claim. Recognize, however, that some are more important—that is, are likely to be more persuasive—than others. The basic principle here is that you should *save the most important evidence for the end*, since whatever you have said last is what readers are likely to most remember. A secondary principle is that whatever you say first is what they are *next* most likely to remember. Therefore, when you have several reasons to support your claim, an effective argument strategy is to present the second most important, then one or more additional reasons, and finally, the most important reason.

## Use Logical or Conventional Order

Using logical or conventional order means that you use as a template a preestablished pattern or plan for arguing your case.

- One common pattern is describing or arguing a *problem/solution.* Using this pattern, you begin with an introduction in which you typically define the problem, then perhaps explain its origins, then offer one or more solutions, then conclude. The article in Chapter 6, "The Nature and Meaning of Data," followed this pattern: First the writers provide an extended example of the problem, then they define it and establish its significance and forms, and then toward the conclusion they offer several recommendations for change (if not all-out solutions).

- Another common pattern is presenting *two sides of a controversy.* Using this pattern, you introduce the controversy and (if an argument synthesis) your own point of view or claim, then explain each side's arguments, providing reasons that your point of view should prevail. This was the pattern of our argument synthesis: After an introduction to the controversy, the writer defined the problem by establishing the spectacular growth of Wal-Mart, then presented both sides of the controversy—taking care, because of the principle of climactic order, to present the pro–Wal-Mart side last.

- Another common pattern is *comparison-contrast*. In fact, this pattern is so important that we will discuss it separately in the next section.

- The order in which you present elements of an argument is sometimes dictated by the conventions of the discipline in which you are writing. For example, lab reports and experiments in the sciences and social sciences often follow this pattern: *Opening* or *Introduction, Methods and Materials* [of the experiment], *Results, Discussion*. Legal arguments often follow the IRAC format: *Issue, Rule, Application, Conclusion*.

## Present and Respond to Counter-Arguments

As we have seen in the Wal-Mart synthesis, people who develop arguments on a controversial topic can effectively use *counter-argument* to help support their claims. When you use counter-argument, you present an argument *against* your claim, but then show that this argument is weak or flawed. The advantage of this technique is that you demonstrate that you are aware of the other side of the argument and that you are prepared to answer it.

Here is how a counter-argument typically is developed:

A. Introduction and claim
B. Main opposing argument
C. Refutation of opposing argument
D. Main positive argument

In the Wal-Mart synthesis, the writer gives a fair representation—using summary, paraphrase, and quotation—of the anti–Wal-Mart case for the purpose of showing that it is weaker than the pro–Wal-Mart case.

## Use Concession

*Concession* is a variation of counter-argument. As in counter-argument, you present the opposing viewpoint, but instead of demolishing that argument, you concede that it does have some validity and even some appeal, although your own argument is the stronger one. This bolsters your own standing—your own *ethos*—as a fair-minded person who is not blind to the virtues of the other side.

Here is an outline for a concession argument:

A. Introduction and claim
B. Important opposing argument
C. Concession that this argument has some validity
D. Positive argument(s)

Sometimes, when you are developing a *counter-argument* or *concession argument*, you may become convinced of the validity of the opposing point of view and change your own views. Don't be afraid of this happening. Writing is a tool for learning. To change your mind because of new evidence is a sign of flexibility and maturity, and your writing can only be the better for it.

## Avoid Common Fallacies in Developing and Using Support

In Chapter 6, in the section on "Critical Reading," we considered some of the criteria that, as a reader, you may use for evaluating informative and persuasive writing. We discussed how you can assess the accuracy, the significance, and the author's interpretation of the information presented. We also considered the importance in good argument of clearly defined key terms and the pitfalls of emotionally loaded language. Finally, we saw how to recognize such logical fallacies as either/or reasoning, faulty cause-and-effect reasoning, hasty generalization, and false analogy. As a writer, no less than as a critical reader, be aware of these common problems and try to avoid them.

## THE EXPLANATORY SYNTHESIS

Your job in writing an explanatory paper—or in writing the explanatory portion of an argumentative paper—is not to argue a particular point, but rather to *present the facts in a reasonably objective manner*. Of course, explanatory papers, like other academic papers, should be based on a thesis. But the purpose of a thesis in an explanatory paper is less to advance a particular opinion than to focus the various facts contained in the paper.

The explanatory synthesis is fairly modest in purpose. It emphasizes the materials in the sources themselves, not your own interpretation. Since your reader is not always in a position to read your sources, this kind of synthesis, if well done, can be very informative. But the main characteristic of the explanatory synthesis is that it is designed more to *inform* than to *persuade*. The thesis in the explanatory synthesis is less a device for arguing a particular point than a device for providing focus and direction to an objective presentation of facts or opinions. As the writer of an explanatory synthesis, you remain, for the most part, a detached observer.

You may disagree with this, contending that a thesis for an explanatory synthesis still represents a particular point of view. For example, the following explanatory thesis on the Wal-Mart problem might be seen as taking a position: "In debating the economic, social, and cultural impact of Wal-Mart, writers on both sides raise compelling arguments grounded in concerns about quality of life." By acknowledging that the debate is significant rather than trivial and claiming that the writers are concerned with the quality of our lives, even this balanced and mostly informative thesis represents a particular point of view. Note, however, that the explanatory synthesis does NOT focus on advancing a particular claim, and that it is unlikely that either the sources or discussion included in the essay will encourage the reader to draw conclusions. In this sense, this version of the Wal-Mart thesis is not debatable; it serves to focus and organize the discussion that follows rather than to advance an argument.

Many of the papers you write in class will be more or less explanatory in nature. An explanation helps readers to understand a topic. Writers explain when they divide a subject into its component parts and present them to the reader in a clear and orderly fashion. Explanations may entail descriptions that recreate in words some object, place, emotion, event, sequence of events, or state of affairs. As a student reporter, you may need to explain an event—to relate when, where, and how it took place. In a science lab, you would observe the conditions and results of an experiment and record them for review by others. In a political science course, you might review research on a particular subject—say, the complexities underlying the debate over welfare—and then present the results of your research to your professor.

## CONSIDER YOUR PURPOSE

First remember that before considering the *how*, you must consider the *why*. In other words, what is your *purpose* in synthesizing your sources? You might use them for a paper dealing with a broad issue, such as, for example, the dangers of relying too heavily upon computers. If this were your purpose, your sources would be used to advance an *argument* for a particular viewpoint about the dangers of technology. Or, for a course dealing with the social impact of technology, you might be studying how the development of new programming languages and the decline of old ones can create unforeseen trouble in the years to come. Or, moving out of the academic world and into the commercial one, you might be a computer consultant preparing a brochure for potential clients who, you hope, will hire you to fix problems with their computers. In this brochure, you want to spell out the nature of the problems that can occur and how serious each is.

## FORMULATE A THESIS

The difference between a purpose and a thesis is a difference primarily of focus. Your purpose provides direction to your research and focus to your paper. Your thesis sharpens this focus by narrowing it and formulating it in words of a declarative statement.

When writing an explanatory thesis with the simple purpose of presenting source material with little or no comment, the thesis would be the most obvious statement you could make about the relationship among the passages. By "obvious," we mean a statement based on an idea that is clearly supported in all the passages. Using the Wal-Mart sources, for example, an explanatory thesis could emphasize the fact that there are different ways to look at the store.

*Draft:* Those who write about Wal-Mart are divided in their assessment of whether its impact is positive or negative.

This thesis could be focused more narrowly (for example, which group of writers will be examined?). It can use more specific diction (its impact on what?).

*Redrafted:* Those who report on consumer trends and habits are divided on their assessment of Wal-Mart's economic impact and social influence.

## DECIDE HOW YOU WILL USE YOUR SOURCE MATERIAL

The easiest way to deal with sources is to summarize them. But because you are synthesizing *ideas* rather than sources, you will have to be more selective than if you were writing a simple summary. You don't have to treat *all* the ideas in your sources, just the ones related to your thesis. Some sources might be summarized in their entirety; others, only in part. Using the techniques of summary, determine section by section the main topics of each source, focusing only on those topics related to your thesis. Write brief phrases in the margin, underline key phrases or sentences, or take notes on a separate sheet of paper or in a word processing file or electronic data filing program. Decide how your sources can help you achieve your purpose and support your thesis.

## DEVELOP AN ORGANIZATIONAL PLAN

An organizational plan is your plan for presenting material to the reader. What material will you present? To find out, examine your thesis. Do the content and structure of the thesis (that is, the number and order of assertions) suggest an organizational plan for the paper? Expect to devote at least one paragraph of your paper to developing each section of this plan. Having identified likely sections, think through the possibilities of arrangement. Ask yourself: What information does the reader need to understand first? How do I build on this first section—what block of information will follow? Think of each section in relation to others until you have placed them all and have worked your way through to a plan for the whole paper.

Study your thesis, and let it help suggest an organization. Bear in mind that any one paper can be written—successfully—according to a variety of plans. Your job before beginning your first draft is to explore possibilities. Sketch a series of rough outlines: Arrange and rearrange your paper's likely sections until you sketch a plan that both facilitates the reader's understanding and achieves your objectives as writer. Your final paper may well deviate from your final sketch, since in the act of writing you may discover the need to explore new material, to omit planned material, or to refocus your entire presentation. Just the same, a well-conceived organizational plan will encourage you to begin writing a draft.

Based on the working thesis developed above—about the range of views Wal-Mart elicits from commentators—we could develop a six-point plan, including introduction and conclusion:

A. Introduction: explanation of the two divergent views about Wal-Mart's economic and social impact and identification of those who tend to hold these views.

B. Social Impact: jobs:
   Costs—too many "McJobs" (low pay, low security).
   Advantages—availability of "on-the-job" training jobs.
C. Social Impact: neighbourhoods:
   Costs—rushing through concrete exteriors and landscapes.
   Advantages—all-in-one store and mall shopping.
D. Social Impact: aesthetics:
   Costs—interior as "box."
   Advantages—pressure on small business to become more competitive.
E. Economic Impact:
   Costs—loss of small Canadian-owned business.
   Advantages—pressure on small business to become more competitive.
F. Conclusion—summing up.

As an optional step to strengthen your sense of how to arrange main points, you may want to write draft versions of topic sentences; these will get you started on each main section of your synthesis and will help give you the sense of direction you need to proceed. When read in a sequence following the thesis, topic sentences, even in draft form, can give an idea of the logical progression of the essay as a whole.

# THE COMPARISON-AND-CONTRAST SYNTHESIS

Comparison-and-contrast techniques enable you to examine two subjects (or sources) in terms of one another. When you compare, you consider *similarities*. When you contrast, you consider *differences*. By comparing and contrasting, you perform a multifaceted analysis that often suggests subtleties that otherwise might not have come to your (or the reader's) attention.

Comparison and contrast can serve several purposes. You may want to show differences and similarities, or to place emphasis on one of these. Or you might compare and contrast to recommend a choice, moving into the territory of argument by making the claim that A is better than B.

To organize a comparison-and-contrast argument, you must carefully read sources in order to discover *significant criteria for analysis*. A *criterion* is a specific point to which both of your authors refer and about which they may agree or disagree. (For example, in a comparative report on compact cars, criteria for *comparison and contrast* might be road handling, fuel economy, and comfort of ride.) The best criteria are those that allow you not only to account for obvious similarities and differences between sources but also to plumb deeper, to more subtle and significant similarities and differences.

There are two basic approaches to organizing a comparison-and-contrast analysis: organization by *subject* or *source* and organization by *criteria*.

1. *Organizing by subject or by source.* You can organize a comparative synthesis as two separate presentations or summaries of your subjects, followed by a discussion in which you point out significant similarities

and differences. If you are working with two sources, for example, you would summarize each, and then follow on these summaries by discussing both the obvious and subtle contrasts, focusing on the most significant.

Organization by source is best saved for passages that are briefly summarized. If the summary of your source becomes too long, your audience might forget the remarks you made in the first summary as they are reading the second. A comparison-and-contrast synthesis organized by source might proceed like this:

I. Introduce the essay; lead to thesis.
II. Summarize passage A by discussing its significant features.
III. Summarize passage B by discussing its significant features.
IV. Write a paragraph (or two) in which you discuss the significant points of comparison and contrast between passages A and B.

End with a conclusion in which you summarize you points and, perhaps, raise and respond to pertinent questions.

Using examples from the Wal-Mart sources included in this chapter, we might set out to compare Norman's position against the store to Johnston's defence of it:

I. Introduce the two writers and their ideas; point out that they are different.
II. Summarize Norman's views.
III. Summarize Johnston's views.
IV. Write a paragraph (or two) in which you discuss the significant points of comparison and contrast between Norman and Johnston.
V. End with a conclusion to summarize the main points and, perhaps, to raise and respond to pertinent questions.

2. *Organizing by criteria.* Instead of summarizing entire passages one at a time with the intention of comparing them later, you could discuss two passages simultaneously, examining the views of each author point by point (criterion by criterion), comparing and contrasting these views in the process. The criterion approach is best used when you have a number of points to discuss or when passages are long and/or complex. A comparison-and-contrast synthesis organized by criteria might look like this:

I. Introduce the essay; lead to thesis.
II. Criterion 1
   A. Discuss what author A says about this point.
   B. Discuss what author B says about this point, comparing and contrasting B's treatment of the point with A's.

    III.  Criterion 2
        A.  Discuss what author A says about this point.
        B.  Discuss what author B says about this point, comparing and contrasting B's treatment of the point with A's.

And so on. Proceed criterion by criterion until you have completed your discussion. Be sure to arrange criteria with a clear method; knowing how the discussion of one criterion leads to the next will ensure smooth transitions throughout your paper. End with a conclusion in which you summarize your points and, perhaps, raise and respond to pertinent questions.

Here is an example of a criterion-based outline that compares Norman's and Johnston's views on Wal-Mart:

    I.  Introduce the two writers and their views on the economic and cultural effects of the store and the way the store influences consumers.
    II.  Criterion 1: economic results
        A.  Discuss what Norman says about economic troubles.
        B.  Discuss what Johnston says about economic gains, comparing and contrasting her treatment of the point to Norman's.
    III.  Criterion 2: cultural results
        A.  Discuss what Norman says about the way Wal-Mart destroys North-American culture.
        B.  Discuss what Johnston says about cultural advantages, comparing and contrasting her treatment of the point to Norman's.
    IV.  Criterion 3: influence on consumers
        A.  Discuss what Norman says about cultivating greed and need.
        B.  Discuss what Johnston says about providing service and meeting needs, comparing and contrasting her treatment of the point to Norman's.

## ■ EXERCISE

Read the following two articles that address the issue of how gender difference influences the experiences of boys and girls in Canada. Donna Laframboise argues that boys have been disadvantaged by the recent efforts to improve the treatment and expectations of girls. Stevie Cameron's article points out that the problem for girls and women goes beyond legislating gender equity and resides in changing ingrained and dangerous misogynistic attitudes.

Write a comparison-contrast essay, organized either by source or by criteria. Try to develop an outline to map out points of similarity and difference before you begin.

# Roll Back the Red Carpet for Boys

DONNA LAFRAMBOISE

Every now and again, in random bits and pieces, we run up against the fact    1
that being male isn't the red-carpet experience much of recent feminism would
have us believe. Young males are more likely to be physically abused by their
parents, to drop out of school, and to face unemployment than their female
counterparts. Between the ages of 15 and 24, they take their own lives five
times as often. As adults, males are more likely to be homeless, more prone to
alcohol and gambling addictions, twice as likely to be robbed or murdered,
nine times more likely to be killed in an occupational accident, and [on average, they] go to their graves six years earlier than their sisters.

Yet, so attached are we to the view that the patriarchy has designed the    2
world for the benefit of males that these truths fail to sink in. Although headlines would scream and alarm bells would ring if the opposite were the case,
inequality isn't an important social issue when males are being shortchanged.
Talk about youth suicide, for instance, and you'll be informed that what
really deserves attention is not the appalling number of dead male bodies, but
the fact that girls say they *attempt* suicide more often than do boys.

The latest examples of this "who cares, they're only guys" mentality are    3
reports that girls are outperforming boys in school. In 1996, six out of ten
high-school honours graduates in Ontario and British Columbia were female.
Even though girls were besting boys a decade earlier (in 1986, 53 per cent of
Ontario honours grads and 57 per cent of . . . B.C. [graduates] were girls), the
1990s have been replete with media commentary telling us it's girls who
merit our concern. In 1994, Myra and David Sadker's book *Failing at
Fairness: How Our Schools Cheat Girls* appeared. A year later, Michele
Landsberg wrote a column in *The Toronto Star* [headed] "School sexism so
routine it's almost invisible." A news story, also in *The Star,* about the higher-
than-average Montreal dropout rate implied we should be concerned about
this phenomenon partly because "45 per cent of dropouts are young women."
Despite being in the majority, the boys weren't worth mentioning.

When girls do worse in math and science, when they don't sign up for    4
skilled trades or engineering, it's the system's fault. Their parents aren't
encouraging them; the schools are male-oriented and unwelcoming; the boys
are harassing them; and society is sending them traditional-role-model messages, but when the boys do poorly, it's their own fault. Even though they're
children, the responsibility gets loaded directly onto their meagre shoulders.
In a recent *Globe* article, "Where the Boys Aren't: At the Top of the Class,"
educators tell the media that "too many boys don't seem to be even trying,"
and blame "a boy culture that celebrates bravado, lassitude, and stupidity."
Rather than ask boys for their input, the reporter interviewed girls who criticized the boys' study habits.

The fact that masculinity and intellectualism have always been an uneasy    5
fit (football players get dates, bookworms don't) doesn't even make it into the
conversation. The idea that boys may be confused about whether or not they

should excel, since feminism has drawn a straight line between female oppression and male achievement, isn't discussed. The fact that elementary schools are dominated by female teachers who scold and punish boys more frequently than they do girls, and that boys suffer from more learning disabilities, isn't mentioned. The notion that educators, parents, and governments have spent the past 15 years ignoring boys, so it's little wonder that they themselves have become complacent about their performance, isn't considered.

Girls are victims of circumstance and boys are masters of their own fate. 6 Girls are moulded and manipulated by social pressures; boys make conscious choices. Girls get to blame everyone but themselves; everyone gets to blame boys. Wasn't feminism supposed to be about abolishing double standards?

## Our Daughters, Ourselves

STEVIE CAMERON

They are so precious to us, our daughters. When they are born we see their 1 futures as unlimited, and as they grow and learn we try so hard to protect them: This is how we cross the street, hold my hand, wear your boots, don't talk to strangers, run to the neighbors if a man tries to get you in his car.

We tell our bright, shining girls that they can be anything: firefighters, 2 doctors, policewomen, lawyers, scientists, soldiers, athletes, artists. What we don't tell them, yet, is how hard it will be. Maybe, we say to ourselves, by the time they're older it will be easier for them than it was for us.

But as they grow and learn, with aching hearts we have to start dealing 3 with their bewilderment about injustice. Why do the boys get the best gyms, the best equipment and the best times on the field? Most of the school sports budget? Why does football matter more than gymnastics? Why are most of the teachers women and most of the principals men? Why do the boys make more money at their part-time jobs than we do?

And as they grow and learn we have to go on trying to protect them: 4 We'll pick you up at the subway, we'll fetch you from the movie, stay with the group, make sure the parents drive you home from baby-sitting, don't walk across the park alone, lock the house if we're not there.

It's not fair, they say. Boys can walk where they want, come in when they 5 want, work where they want. Not really, we say; boys get attacked too. But boys are not targets for men the way girls are, so girls have to be more careful.

Sometimes our girls don't make it. Sometimes, despite our best efforts and 6 all our love, they go on drugs, drop out, screw up. On the whole, however, our daughters turn into interesting, delightful people. They plan for college and university, and with wonder and pride we see them competing with the boys for spaces in engineering schools, medical schools, law schools, business schools. For them we dream of Rhodes scholarships, Harvard graduate school, gold medals; sometimes, we even dare to say these words out loud and our daughters reward us with indulgent hugs. Our message is that anything is possible.

We bite back the cautions that we feel we should give them; maybe by the    7
time they've graduated, things will have changed, we say to ourselves.
Probably by the time they're out, they will make partner when the men do, be
asked to join the same clubs, run for political office. Perhaps they'll even be
able to tee off at the same time men do at the golf club.

But we still warn them: park close to the movie, get a deadbolt for your    8
apartment, check your windows, tell your roommates where you are. Call me.
Call me.

And then with aching hearts we take our precious daughters to lunch and    9
listen to them talk about their friends: the one who was beaten by her boy
friend and then shunned by his friends when she asked for help from the dean;
the one who was attacked in the parking lot; the one who gets obscene and
threatening calls from a boy in her residence; the one who gets raped on a
date; the one who was mocked by the male students in the public meeting.

They tell us about the sexism they're discovering in the adult world at    10
university. Women professors who can't get jobs, who can't get tenure. Male
professors who cannot comprehend women's stony silence after sexist jokes.
An administration that only pays lip service to women's issues and refuses to
accept the reality of physical danger to women on campus.

They tell us they're talking among themselves about how men are    11
demanding rights over unborn children; it's not old dinosaurs who go to
court to prevent a woman's abortion, it's young men. It's young men, they say
with disbelief, their own generation, their own buddies with good education,
from "nice" families, who are abusive.

What can we say to our bright and shining daughters? How can we tell    12
them how much we hurt to see them developing the same scars we've carried?
How much we wanted it to be different for them? It's all about power, we say
to them. Sharing power is not easy for anyone and men do not find it easy to
share among themselves, much less with a group of equally talented, able
women. So men make all those stupid cracks about needing a sex-change
operation to get a job or a promotion and they wind up believing it.

Now our daughters have been shocked to the core, as we all have, by the    13
violence in Montreal. They hear the women were separated from the men and
meticulously slaughtered by a man who blamed feminists for his troubles.
They ask themselves why nobody was able to help the terrified women, to
somehow stop the hunter as he roamed the engineering building.

So now our daughters are truly frightened and it makes their mothers    14
furious that they are frightened. They survived all the childhood dangers, they
were careful as we trained them to be, they worked hard. Anything was possible and our daughters proved it. And now they are more scared than they
were when they were little girls.

Fourteen of our bright and shining daughters won places in engineering    15
schools, doing things we, their mothers, only dreamed of. That we lost them
has broken our hearts; what is worse is that we are not surprised.

■ ■ ■

# SUMMARY

In this chapter, we've considered three main types of synthesis: the *argument synthesis*, the *explanatory synthesis*, and the *comparison-contrast synthesis*. Although for ease of comprehension we've placed them into separate categories, these types are not, of course, mutually exclusive. Both argument syntheses and explanatory syntheses often involve elements of one another, and comparison-contrast syntheses can fall into either of the previous categories. Which format you choose will depend upon your *purpose*, and the method you decide is best suited to achieve this purpose.

If your main purpose is to persuade your audience to agree with your viewpoint on a subject, or to change their minds, or to decide upon a particular course of action, then you will be composing an argument synthesis. If your main purpose, on the other hand, is to help your audience understand a particular subject, and in particular to help them understand the essential elements or significance of this subject, then you will be composing an explanatory synthesis. If one effective technique of making your case is to establish similarities or differences between your subject and another one, then you will compose a comparison-contrast synthesis—which may well be just *part* of a larger synthesis.

In planning and drafting these syntheses, you can draw upon a variety of strategies: supporting your claims by summarizing, paraphrasing, and quoting from your sources; using appeal to *logos*, *pathos*, and *ethos*; choosing from among formats such as climactic or conventional order, counter-argument, and concession, that will best help you to achieve your purpose.

# PART III

## An Anthology of Readings

# 8

# Homeless in the "Just Society"

If it is true that "the poor are always with us," it is also true that people have different ideas about the causes of poverty and about the ways we might solve or respond to it. Conservative thinkers usually want to minimize the role of government in economic and social life and tend to hold the view that the poor should take care of themselves. In his article "The Origin of Conservatism," John McGinnis defines the components of a conservative political perspective.

Liberal thinkers who advocate social responsibility think that government should care for and attempt to empower the economically disadvantaged within society. Part of the enduring legacy of Liberal Prime Minister Pierre Trudeau is the *Canadian Charter of Rights and Freedoms,* which attempts to enshrine conditions for citizenry in a "just society." As he imagined it, this society would ensure equal opportunities for advancement by providing those in need with the means to prosper: "The Just Society will be one in which all of our people will have the means and motivation to participate. . . . The just society will be one in which those regions and groups which have not fully shared in the country's affluence will be given a better opportunity. The just society will be one in which such urban problems as housing and pollution will be attacked through the application of new knowledge and new techniques."[1]

Despite Trudeau's efforts to organize a just society of equal opportunity, the number of homeless in Canada continues to grow. In current Canadian politics, it is not always easy to distinguish Liberal from Conservative policy on social issues like dealing with poverty, because political parties often seek middle ground in an effort to court voters. Thus, in defining the political spectrum in Canada, Mark Dickerson and Thomas Flanagan map out the three positions of "Left, Right, and Centre" as those that define our political scene.

On the question of what causes poverty, those with liberal views protest that individuals can become trapped in a cycle of economic disadvantage, while conservatives counter that individuals who are struggling have chosen this way of life. Adopting a version of this latter perspective, John Stackhouse could be identified as a conservative, for he interprets the experience of homelessness as one that individuals choose. On the other hand, Jack Layton espouses liberal views when he points out that the homeless are often trapped by a series of circumstances, and cannot find alternatives to improve their situation.

[1] Pierre Elliott Trudeau, "The Just Society," in *The Essential Trudeau,* Ed. Ron Graham. Toronto: McClelland and Stewart, 1998, pp. 18–19.

Leaving aside political questions about the cause and cure of poverty and homelessness, the final articles describe the situation of people struggling on the street. In "Life on the Streets," a chapter excerpted from a well-researched academic study, the author describes some of the realities facing the homeless, drawing a specific picture through a case study approach. In "No Room of Her Own," the authors investigate how being female can influence one's experience of being poor and homeless.

## The Origin of Conservatism

JOHN O. McGINNIS

*Liberals have often attacked conservatives for advocating "social Darwinism"—that is, applying Charles Darwin's theories of natural selection and the survival of the fittest to the social order. Viewed through the prism of social Darwinism, for example, people on welfare have shown themselves to be ill-adapted to their environment and therefore not suited to "survival." In fact, helping the poor should actually be discouraged, since it violates the natural order and evolutionary progress. Liberals contend that social Darwinism is invalid (because the laws governing biological evolution are not analogous to the principles governing human society) as well as cruel and inhumane.*

*Such liberal arguments are rejected by John McGinnis, a professor at Cardoza Law School, Yeshiva University, in New York City. In his article "The Origin of Conservatism," McGinnis, citing recent research in psychology, economics, anthropology, and linguistics, reaffirms the applicability of evolutionary biology to both human nature and human culture. This article first appeared in the* National Review, *December 22, 1997.*

Today a revolution is remaking the social sciences. For the last two decades, 1
theorists in psychology, economics, anthropology, and linguistics have begun
to discard the traditional social-science model in which man creates the social
world through his culture. They have instead turned to evolutionary biology
to draw an ever more precise and powerful description of the human nature
that generates all cultures. The results of their discoveries are now seeping into
the popular consciousness as the media report through a biological prism such
fundamental topics as the relations between the sexes. Because evolutionary
biology provides an informative picture of man and because citizens are
rapidly assimilating that image, any political movement that hopes to be successful must come to terms with the second rise of Darwinism.

Conservatism will certainly be easier than liberalism to integrate with 2
evolutionary biology. The constraints of our biological nature explode the
most persistent delusion of the Left: that man is so malleable that he can be
reshaped or transformed through political actions. In contrast, the depiction

of our species that is emerging from Darwinism—as composed of individuals who are basically self-interested yet capable of altruism toward family and friends; who are unequal in their abilities yet remarkably similar in their aspirations—comports with fundamental premises of conservative thought.

Thus the new biological learning holds the potential for providing stronger support for conservatism than any other new body of knowledge has done. Yet it may also raise questions about some intellectual traditions of the Right, such as pure libertarianism, and its methodology may disturb religious conservatives. These tensions must be resolved if the conservative coalition is to thrive in the intellectual soil of the coming century.    3

There are seven concepts that are essential to understanding the Darwinian picture of man. The logic of each concept applied to human affairs turns out to bolster major tenets of mainstream conservatism.    4

1. *Self-Interest and Politics.* Like all other animals, our species has been shaped by millions of years of natural selection. Natural selection works through genetic inheritance and variation.[1] Genes for many physical and behavioral traits are inheritable; such genes may also be variable within the population of animals of the same species. Because of recombination and mutation, animals within the same species differ in their genetic makeup. Some inherited traits will enable some individual animals to leave more offspring than others. Genes for such traits then increase in the population of the species.    5

Thus, as Robert Wright has nicely observed, it follows directly from natural selection that any individual animal will have behavioral adaptations designed to favor its own interests over those of others. The single exception is that they may favor other animals who can aid in disseminating their distinctive genes. Thus each human individual has strong innate behavioral tendencies to favor his own interests, those of the comparatively few relatives who share a large proportion of his genes, and the potential mates who are necessary to reproduce his genes. We are not closely and equally related to many other individuals of our species, like ants and some other social insects, who routinely sacrifice themselves for their colony.    6

One interest all human beings share is seeking resources and status. In all past societies surveyed, those who had more relative status and resources left more progeny than those who had less status and fewer resources. (It is possible that this finding would not be true of some present-day societies, but evolution in humans works so slowly that any such counter-trend would    7

---

[1] *Natural Selection:* Charles Darwin's theory, as propounded in *On the Origin of Species* (1859), that through a process of nature those varieties of a species that are best adapted to their environment—an environment of limited resources—are selected for survival and reproduction. (Thus, the doctrine of "survival of the fittest.") Future generations of the species will therefore be dominated by those varieties that are genetically best adapted to the environment. Those varieties that are less well adapted will either perish or dwindle in number. It did not take long for philosophers to adapt Darwin's biological theories to the workings of human society. William Graham Sumner and Herbert Spencer were only two of the "Social Darwinists" of the nineteenth century.

take thousands of years to be reflected in our genetic make-up.) Thus human beings are emotionally and cognitively wired to be resource and status seekers. We also confirm from studies of other primates that we innately view exchange and hierarchy as alternative strategies for gaining resources. For instance, chimpanzees exchange food, but they also make coalitions among themselves to simply take food and sexual access.

The universal affinity for property and status has serious political implications. In any society large or heterogeneous enough for members to sense that they are unrelated, they will seek to turn resources held in common to their own personal advantage. To a biological anthropologist it was thus wholly predictable that individuals under Communism would spend less of their time in productive exchange and more of their time manipulating the state so as to become more equal than others. Similarly, in social democracies individuals will organize themselves into coalitions for the purpose of gaining access to the state treasury. Such political systems lead to a lack of productivity, social conflict, and instability because there is simply a mismatch between collectivism on any large and enduring scale and our evolved nature. As Edward O. Wilson, the world's foremost expert on ants, remarked about Marxism: "Wonderful theory. Wrong species." 8

2. *Kin Selection*. We have evolved an emotional life in which we have a tendency to take an abiding interest in the welfare of our kin, because they share a substantial proportion of our genes. Because children represent a parent's genetic future, the parent-child bond has the potential to be particularly close. Thus, as conservatives have argued for centuries, the family is a natural unit of society, and family affections are not mere social constructs but are deeply rooted in our behavior and psyche. Policies that strengthen the family provide a reliable and lasting form of social insurance. 9

3. *Sexual Differences*. A government that is careful to preserve rather than dissolve family ties is important for other biological reasons. Evolutionary biology predicts that men and women will have different degrees of attachment to their family. Because women are limited in the potential number of their offspring, they are naturally more child-centered in their affections. Men by contrast can have a huge number of children, and thus their relations with any particular child tend to be inherently less secure. Men do provide more care for their progeny than males in most other mammalian species because human infants face a lengthy period of helplessness and fare much better with substantial paternal investment of time and effort in their upbringing. Yet fathers are more likely than mothers to resent and avoid obligations that may deprive them of other mating opportunities. Men are innately more aggressive and obsessed with status than women for similar reasons: because of their low-cost role in sexual reproduction they have far more scope for converting resources and status into the creation of children. 10

Family obligations in some measure counteract the more roving nature of the male by enmeshing men in networks that both provide children with needed paternal affection and prevent socially destructive male aggression. 11

Thus the greatest cost of modern welfare programs may not have been the tax dollars wasted but the paternal investment squandered, because, as Charles Murray has demonstrated, welfare discourages the social norms that anchored men to the women with whom they had children. This has led to generations of children who have had less male nurturing than they need—and generations of men who are excessively aggressive because they have not been restrained by family obligations. The imposition of no-fault divorce has also made it easier for men to shirk parental care. Thus, the new biological learning provides direct support for conservative initiatives such as welfare reform and the introduction in Louisiana of "covenant marriage," which allows women to negotiate for greater permanence for their pair bond.

4. *Reciprocal Altruism and Civil Society.* Our species has also evolved a   12
host of behaviors that facilitate "reciprocal altruism"—a willingness to perform acts beneficial to another unrelated person in the expectation that the person on the receiving end will reciprocate. The bundles of qualities that make us reciprocal altruists are very useful in overcoming "prisoner's dilemmas"—situations in which a cooperative act would lead to benefits for both parties, but only if reciprocity could be assured. In primitive societies, where centralized enforcement of legal obligations was quite imperfect, psychological mechanisms that resulted in cooperation would have been naturally selected. For instance, individuals who did not renege on deals and who repaid a good turn with another increased their wealth compared to those who did not. As reciprocating individuals gained resources and therefore left more children, genes for traits promoting reciprocal altruism spread through the population.

Altruistic behavior, however, tends to be limited by the need for reci-   13
procity. Although individuals are disposed to cooperate, they tend to withdraw their cooperation if no long-term benefits are received. Genes encouraging behavior that did not ultimately redound to the concrete benefit of an actor or his kin did not spread through the population. Much of the emotional life of our species—gratitude, sympathy, moral outrage—is therefore designed to regulate the relations of reciprocal altruism. Cognitively too, we keep a mental account of what other individuals have done for us and to us—a fact nicely captured by Tom Wolfe's concept, in *The Bonfire of the Vanities*, of a "favor bank," in which lawyers and court personnel kept careful track of the favors they had performed.

Because of innate reciprocal altruism, exchange is thus as natural to man   14
as song is to a songbird. The market is not a mere artifact created by the state but a force of nature. Indeed, reciprocal altruism generates not only trade but also civil society as a whole. Organizations spring forth that facilitate all kinds of social exchange, including the trading of information and of affection. Such spontaneous orders differ from one society to the next because of differences in knowledge and circumstances, but the social world everywhere is bound together by the vines of informal cooperation. These are so vibrant that the concrete which states try to lay down over this growth is in perpetual danger of cracking.

The same bonding mechanisms that facilitate this spontaneous order, 15 however, also make political factions more intractable and divisive. As David Hume recognized, "when men are once enlisted on opposite sides they contract an affection to the persons with whom they are united and an animosity against their antagonists: And these passions they often transmit to their posterity." Modern psychological studies confirm that when individuals acquire a group identity, they will act with more solidarity as a group against other groups than individual calculation warrants. By bonding together in numbers, such factions can better control hierarchies, like the state, and thus no longer have to rely on exchange as the primary method to increase their resources.

Therefore, while reciprocity has beneficial effects in the market and in 16 civil society, the factions it facilitates make it more likely that the state will be used to distribute resources from one group to another. Liberal identity politics, whether of class, race, or sex, exacerbate this danger. Conservative political theorists like James Madison, in contrast, have focused on tempering and restraining factions. Factions can be tempered if the individual can be made to identify in some measure with a community that encompasses a wide range of interests. Factions can be restrained if the power of the government can be limited so that it cannot as easily be used for redistribution. One important conservative notion—federalism, or subsidiarity—has in the past simultaneously accomplished both of the political objectives required by our evolutionary nature. By making government local, it makes it easier for individuals to identify with a community; and by putting governments in competition with one another, it restrains the powers of factions.

5. *Deception and Self-Deception.* Deception is pandemic in nature. 17 Camouflage and mimicry are just two of its typical forms. Paradoxically, our tendencies to reciprocal altruism increase the potential gains from deception in our species, because exploiting reciprocators may lead to gaining benefits without having to give any in return. In our species the opportunities for deception are improved by language, which simultaneously provides a valuable medium of exchange—information—and the ability to counterfeit that good.

Of course, it is in the interest of those potentially deceived to discover 18 deception, and it is not surprising that human beings are natural, if imperfect, lie detectors. (That is the reason why we want jurors to hear testimony live rather than read a transcript.) This detection ability encourages selection for behavior that will avoid detection, setting up an arms race between deceptive behavior and mechanisms for detecting deception. Biologists have suggested that this arms race is, in turn, the origin of pervasive self-deception in man. By deceiving himself, an individual may suppress the cues that allow others to detect deception. Hence self-deception is most likely when there is an intense need to deceive others.

The fact that human beings have innate tendencies toward deception and 19 self-deception buttresses the conservative defense of civil society and skepticism about state power. Civil society develops norms to combat deception in private life. In the market, individuals have strong incentives to maintain a reputation for honesty so that others will deal with them. Fraternal and religious organizations arise in part to vouch for the good behavior of their members.

In contrast, it is much harder to root deception out of large-scale politics.   20
For instance, in a democracy citizens are rationally ignorant of most political issues; that is, they know perhaps subconsciously, that their individual votes are so unlikely to influence elections that it simply does not pay to follow the twists and turns of public debate. Politicians have a scope for deception proportionate to this ignorance. A commanding presence, a compassionate demeanor, and rhetorical virtuosity are evolutionarily designed mechanisms that fool the inattentive.

The ingrained susceptibility to self-deception also undermines the cele-   21
bration of sincerity and authenticity that has been at the heart of the Left's project since Rousseau. Evolution suggests that individuals may project the most sincerity and feel the greatest measure of authenticity precisely when they are offering proposals that are deceptive—ideas that benefit themselves and their group at the expense of others.

6.  *Natural Inequality.* Darwinism confirms the view that individuals have   22
inherently unequal abilities and that these inequalities are likely to be greatest in the personality traits, such as intelligence and ambition, that are related to acquiring property. In *On the Origin of Species* Darwin himself formulated this law about natural variation: "A part developed in any extraordinary degree or manner, in comparison with the same part in allied species, tends to be highly variable." When a species breaks into a part of the design space of the world previously unexploited, enormous selective pressure develops in the genes of that species to make ever more effective use of this virgin territory. For instance, the beaks of Darwin's species of finches are highly variable since these finches were able to exploit a large variety of previously inaccessible seeds on the Galapagos Islands. Likewise, since human beings have brains whose cognitive aspects are developed to an extraordinary degree compared to those of other animals, one would expect the human brain's inheritable capacity to be highly variable. This theory is confirmed by recent studies suggesting that measurable personality traits are to a large degree inherited rather than shaped by the environment—and that intelligence is the trait most conserved through generations.

Natural inequality has implications for both the ideological and the struc-   23
tural content of politics. On the level of political philosophy, it undermines the basic premise of liberal egalitarianism: that it is possible to equalize outcomes by eliminating inequality in social circumstances. The engine of inequality is buried so deep in human nature that it is impossible to eradicate. Indeed, as Richard Herrnstein showed, equalizing social circumstances will mean that the inequality in outcomes will become dictated in greater measure by generic inheritance.

In contrast, conservatives are correct in understanding that, because of nat-   24
ural inequality, structures must be fashioned to prevent harmful schemes aimed at the delusive goal of eliminating it. Indeed, in *Federalist* 10, the most cele-

brated document of political philosophy in American history, James Madison observed that the greatest problem for any political structure is how to protect "the unequal faculties for acquiring property" from government interference. Over the long run, such protection assures greater prosperity for all by sustaining the incentives for the talented and productive to exercise their genius through invention and innovation. In the West over the past hundred years, this has allowed a vast array of individuals to enjoy a degree of good health and leisure that was previously available only to a select few.

Nevertheless, as Madison recognized, the very inequality that makes this  25 prosperity possible also makes the protection of the different abilities to acquire property more difficult because it exacerbates the danger that the government will be used as a mechanism for redistribution from one faction to another. Inequality means that there will always be a large pool of individuals with less talent than others for acquiring property. Given the human capacity for self-deception, these citizens are less likely to make a dispassionate assessment of their own abilities than to believe that some prosperous group is holding them back. Skilled demagogues and dissemblers can always be found to provide justifications for redistributing property because individuals are primed to seek status—and nowhere can greater status be acquired than from political leadership.

This natural dynamic of inequality in politics vindicates conservative  26 attempts to establish constitutional structures that limit the power of demagogues and the potential for expropriation of wealth. The original American Constitution—with a complex system of federalism, separation of powers, and national representative democracy—is the most justly venerated of these attempts. While conservatives are right to object to the judicial usurpations that have vitiated this system over time, a Darwinian understanding of politics suggests that simple democracy is no substitute for constructing a system to guard against the passions and self-deceptions of individuals with disparate abilities.

7. *The Fragile and Divided Self*—The final natural fact for politics is  27 also the most personal. The self, like all essential aspects of man, is an adaptation to selective pressures over millions of years and thus is jury-rigged from different mechanisms from our evolutionary past. It is a mistake, for example, to think of the sexual self as completely continuous with the more obviously rational acquisitive self that evolved somewhat later to take advantage of resources and status opportunities. These selves evolved for different purposes and are not fully connected—hence the frequently observed imprudence of sexual passion.

Evolution's understanding of the self is thus an implicit challenge to the  28 modern liberal project of protecting the sphere of sexual autonomy from regulation while heavily regulating exchange of resources. An order that is rational and self-correcting in historical time is much more likely to spring from more calculating modules devoted to reciprocal altruism than the more impulsive modules of sexuality.

After canvassing the social understanding provided by the new biologi-     29
cal learning, we may fairly conclude that a Darwinian politics is a largely
conservative politics. This is not surprising, because conservatives have
always prided themselves on dealing with man as he is, not as we might wish
to imagine him. Despite the congruence of modern Darwinism and conservative thought, some might foresee substantial pitfalls for practical conservative
politics. First is the simple fact that some religious conservatives do not believe
in evolution and have made their antipathy to it a part of their political creed.
But their hostility is not fatal to the future of the conservative coalition. The
description of man that emerges from evolution resembles in many respects
the fallen man posited by Christian theology—a being self-interested and
absorbed in status seeking. Members of political coalitions may have to agree
broadly on human nature, but they do not have to agree on the methodology
that brings them to that understanding. For instance, the Framers of the
American Constitution comprised both deists whose religion was inspired by
the Newtonian science of their day and Christians with far more traditional
religious attachments.

A variation on this concern is the idea that acceptance of Darwinian     30
thinking will undermine religious belief, which is itself a bulwark of social stability. This also seems implausible. There is no logical incompatibility between
belief in evolution and faith in God; the Catholic Church has long understood
that crediting natural selection as the proximate cause of man does not threat-
en God's standing as his ultimate Creator. Moreover, given the universality of
religion across all cultures, religious feeling almost certainly has natural roots
in our emotional psyche and will not be dissolved by scientific discovery.

Another unwarranted concern is that a focus on biology will lead     31
inevitably to a discussion of racial differences and therefore to an increase in
racial tensions. While Darwinism offers strong reason to assume that men
and women differ on average in their emotional affects and aspirations
because women have naturally been more bound up with their children, it
offers no reason to assume the existence of substantial racial differences in the
personality traits important to acquiring property. Of course, it does not
deny the possibility of such differences either. But evolutionary biology and
anthropology do stress the universal nature of man: we are all members of one
species, and through kin selection and reciprocal altruism we tend to have
common aspirations and similar affects for satisfying those aspirations. Thus
a multiracial society can be sustained so long as it is centered on the family
and the market—the loci of our commonality.

On the other hand, evolutionary biology may present a serious challenge     32
to pure libertarianism. This may surprise some people who confuse the rise
of Darwinism in the social sciences with the nineteenth-century tenets of
Social Darwinism. There is no connection. Natural selection leads to the survival of the most reproductively fit; however, it is a classic example of the nat-
uralistic fallacy to infer from this scientific fact the moral conclusion that the
goal of society is to aid the most reproductively fit. Instead, by describing

human nature more precisely, evolutionary biology offers an improved map for the political economy in our age. It shows what are the natural tendencies of man and what are the possible ways human political actions can both release and constrain these tendencies to increase human happiness.

Moreover, the fragile and divided self that evolution describes may not be     33
entirely consonant with the more integrated self at the heart of libertarianism. For instance, the younger self is so weakly connected to the imagination of the older self (primarily because most individuals did not live to old age in hunter-gatherer societies) that most people cannot be expected to save sufficiently for old age. A large group of aging and propertyless individuals would be a source of social instability. Therefore there may be justification for state intervention to force individuals to save for their own retirement. Similarly, the sexual self is so weakly linked to the long-term rational calculating self that simply requiring individuals to live with the consequences of their sexual acts may not be enough to restrain socially destructive activity. Society may need to create institutions to channel and restrain sexual activity.

Evolutionary biology also undermines what might be termed utopian con-     34
servatism: the notion that there is some social structure in which all the possible human goods—family values, patriotism, entrepreneurship—will be fully and equally realized. Evolution shines a somewhat tragic light on the desire for perfection in human affairs: the different adaptations around which emotions are structured are inevitably in conflict, particularly as the environment changes. For instance, as the rule of law in society perfects the axis of reciprocal altruism and makes it easy to gain resources through trade with unrelated individuals, the family becomes less necessary as a source of protection and as an axis of commerce for its members. Western civilization, in fact, has been marked by the continuous shrinking of the extended family, so that "family values" today are generally a reference to the nuclear family—a shadow of the "clan values" that dominated hunter-gatherer societies. One can go to a society with a less rule-oriented regime than ours (like Italy) and get some sense of the encompassing warmth of family life that is lost with the progress of law. A Darwinian conservatism recognizes the fundamental trade-offs in social life and works to conserve what is possible rather than seeking to resurrect what is dead. Darwinian conservatism is thus the conservatism of those, like Edmund Burke, who offer political reforms to meet changing conditions.

Evolutionary biology necessarily underscores the impermanence of all     35
human arrangements. Like any scientific understanding, it echoes the Heraclitean maxim: Everything not supernatural is in flux. When a biologist looks at the behavior of animals, he recognizes that this behavior is an interaction of genes and the environment. As the environment changes, so will the behavior. An evolutionary science of politics thus has nothing in common with genetic determinism.

Because our discoveries and inventions change the human environment     36
faster than that of any other animal, there is always a temptation—to which today's techno-conservatives, like Newt Gingrich, often fall prey—to think

that such changes may usher in an age of harmony and plenty that will solve the dilemmas of politics. Evolutionary biology shows that this is simply a pipe dream. Our nature assures that we will simultaneously be obsessed with our relative status in society and possess unequal abilities for acquiring higher status. Thus individuals will always seek to use the government as a means to rearrange their relative positions. No matter how much wealth free trade produces, no matter how much information the Internet transmits, the central problem of politics will remain: how to empower the government for safe-guarding life and property, and yet simultaneously constrain it from eviscer-ating civil society and expropriating property.

Such changes in information transmission and technology require inno-    37
vative structures to achieve this perennial goal of human politics. For instance, it may be that the federalism of the Framing is no longer an effective structure for containing centralized governmental power. The ease of transportation and the dominance of mass communication have loosened citizens' attach-ments to their states. We simply cannot share the feelings of Robert E. Lee, who in refusing the command of the Union armies stated that he must fight for his "native state" rather than the United States. Some other political devices that are better rooted in current attachments may have to be found for restraining government in our time.

Accordingly, the most important lesson of Darwinism for conservatives    38
today is to remind them that their task is to respond to the ingrained tenden-cies of human nature in a world in flux. Its unique contribution is to provide a powerful scientific framework to describe that nature more precisely than ever before. Thus it should inspire the Right to act in the tradition of the greatest conservatives of past generations, like Madison and Burke, who also used the best science of their day to create political structures that would enable men to flourish in the intersection of their particular circumstances and their enduring nature.

■  ■  ■

## Review Questions

1. Write a two-page summary of this article. Cover each of McGinnis's seven major sections, along with the introductory and concluding sections.
2. What are the innate behavioural tendencies of all individuals, according to McGinnis?
3. Why, according to the author, are communism and socialism doomed to fail?
4. How does evolutionary biology support conservatives' support of family values, according to McGinnis?
5. In light of the natural inequalities of individuals, why do conservatives distrust powerful governments?

6. Why might Christians, on the one hand, and libertarians, on the other, oppose the concept of a Darwinian politics? How does McGinnis respond to their concerns?

## Discussion and Writing Suggestions

1. Accepting McGinnis's claim that evolutionary biology supports the conservative, rather than the liberal, approach to human society and politics depends upon accepting a number of his assumptions. For example, we must accept (a) that all human beings seek resources and status; (b) that such behavioural traits are genetic and are therefore passed down from one generation to the next; (c) that it is valid to draw connections between our biological nature and our social nature; and (d) that these connections ought to determine our public policy regarding such matters as the family, sexual behaviour, and government regulation of business. Examine and evaluate McGinnis's arguments, taking such factors into consideration.

2. Early in his article McGinnis asserts that "one of the most persistent delusions of the left [is that] man is so malleable that he can be reshaped or transformed through political actions." To what extent do you agree that such a belief is a delusion? To what extent do you believe that this belief is valid? Provide examples to support your conclusions.

3. Under the first heading, "Self-Interest and Politics," McGinnis argues that self-interest is a biological imperative, one that impels people toward "seeking resources and status." Many people would argue instead that self-interest and the seeking of resources (or property) and status are dependent upon cultural influences. What do you believe is the role of biology and culture in the human urge to favour one's own interests? What evidence can you cite to support your beliefs?

4. According to McGinnis, altruism, or the desire to help others, will survive genetically only if it is reciprocal—that is, if one gets benefits for giving benefits. Conversely, selflessness, or the giving of oneself without expectation of return, is an unnatural form of behaviour. Extending this biological reality to the realm of politics, the market economy, which is based on exchange, is a more natural economy than a socialist economy, which is based upon the equal distribution of wealth. The market economy, in fact, is "a force of nature." To what extent do you accept such a theory?

5. Conservatives, says McGinnis, "have always prided themselves on dealing with man as he is, not as we might wish to imagine him." Presumably, according to the author, liberals deal with humans as we might wish to imagine them. To what extent do you agree with this characterization of conservatives and liberals and the essential difference between them? Allowing that these generalizations have some degree of truth, where do you place yourself on the conservative-liberal spectrum? Explain your position in terms of McGinnis's ideas.

# Left, Right, and Centre

## MARK O. DICKERSON AND THOMAS FLANAGAN

*Mark Dickerson and Tom Flanagan teach at the University of Calgary in the Department of Political Science. In addition to co-authoring the widely popular textbook from which the following chapter excerpt is drawn, both have extensive experience as authors and editors of books on politics.*

*"Left, Right, and Centre" provides an overview of the political perspectives that dominate the Canadian scene.*

Are ideologies related to each other in a sufficiently systematic way that we     1
can array them along a single dimension? The answer is a qualified yes as far as conservatism, liberalism, and socialism are concerned; this becomes much more complicated when nationalism, feminism, and environmentalism are considered.

Conservatism, liberalism, and socialism are often depicted as lying along a spectrum whose ends are designated *left* and *right*. Many observers would agree more or less on the following construction:

| Left | | Centre | | Right | |
|---|---|---|---|---|---|
| | Social | Reform | Classical | | |
| Communism | Democracy | Liberalism | Liberalism | Conservatism | Fascism |

Although this spectrum corresponds to common perception, it is not     2
easy to say precisely what it means. Is the left for, and the right against, change? That simplistic explanation will hardly do, for everything depends on who is in power. In a communist state, classical liberalism is an ideology of radical change. In constitutional democracies, both communism and fascism represent radical change. As a yardstick, freedom is not much help either. All ideologies, even fascism, claim to be for freedom, but they define it in different ways. Nor does using democracy as a measure solve the problem, because the democratic centralism of Marxism-Leninism is in reality just as antithetical to popular government as fascism is.

Considering the circumstances in which the words left and right first     3
began to be used as political labels sheds some light on the subject. The custom arose shortly after 1789 in the French National Assembly. Those factions that favoured retaining substantial powers for the monarchy, such as the right to appoint judges and to veto legislation, sat to the right of the chairman of the Assembly. Those that favoured reducing the monarch to a purely symbolic figure and letting the elected representatives of the people exercise all political power sat to the left of the chairman. The basic issue was popular sovereignty. The extreme left held that all political power emanated from the people; the extreme right believed that political power was conferred by God on the king through inheritance, and the centre sought a compromise or balance of these two principles.

This political difference between left and right soon took on an economic dimension as socialism assumed a prominent role in European politics. The term "left" was applied to those who favoured equalization of property through political action. Socialists proposed to replace the market process, which is not under the control of any identifiable individual or group, with a system of state planning. Socialism thus extended popular sovereignty from the political to the economic sphere.    4

Many ambiguities of the left–right terminology arise from this double origin. Advocates of popular sovereignty do not inevitably favour socialist planning; they may be sincerely convinced that the market principle will in the long run be of more benefit to ordinary working people. It is also not inevitable that advocates of socialist planning will support popular sovereignty with equal warmth, for the desires of the real, existing people (as opposed to the hypothetical, reformed people) may obstruct the plan. In short, the political and the economic left often but do not necessarily coincide.    5

In contemporary usage, the economic factor predominates, though not entirely. Going back to our commonsense listing of ideologies on the left–right spectrum, we can now give an approximate interpretation in terms of the meanings of equality that have been discussed. Let us now redraw the spectrum, adding the various forms of equality and inequality that the ideologies claim as their own:    6

| Left | | Centre | Right | |
|---|---|---|---|---|
| Equality of Condition | Equality of Opportunity | Equality of Right | Aristocracy | Hierarchy |
| Communism | Social Democracy | Reform Liberalism | Classical Liberalism | Conservatism | Fascism |

This picture could be seriously misleading without appropriate qualifications. Communists advocate long-run equality of result in the sense of the equality of happiness that would be produced by implementing the motto, "From each according to his ability, to each according to his needs." In the short run, they claim to equalize conditions somewhat but not absolutely. Social democrats and reform liberals are not exclusively wedded to equality of opportunity. Their use of the progressive income tax as a levelling measure is also an approach to equality of result. The classical liberal commitment to equality of right is not especially problematic in this context, but the conservative position easily causes confusion. Early conservatives such as Edmund Burke saw hereditary aristocracy as a socially useful institution. Twentieth-century conservatives no longer defend the hereditary principle but may argue that the wealthy will perform some of the same useful functions as a hereditary aristocracy—philanthropy, public service, and so on. Obviously, this position shades into classical liberalism; the difference is only a matter of whether we emphasize the equality of universal rules or the unequal results    7

arising from them. Finally, fascists tended to think of hierarchy not as social       8
transmission through legal inheritance, but as biological transmission of racial
qualities. For Hitler, Germans were the master race (*Herrenvolk*), while Jews
and Slavs were subhuman (*Untermenschen*). This is the most absolute type of
inequality that can be imagined, because there is no conceivable way of altering it. Fascists also completely rejected the constitutional principle of rule of
law, which is another formulation of equality of right.

This underlying dimension of egalitarianism is not an absolute scale of mea-       9
surement that allows us to assign a precise value to an ideology flora any time
or place. "Leftness" is not a measurable attitude like height or weight. However,
it does make a limited amount of sense to say of two ideologies at a certain place
and time that one is to the left or right of the other. The same applies to the
adherents of ideologies. Thus, it is reasonable to say that in recent Canadian
politics, the NDP, as a party of social democracy, is usually to the left of the
Liberal Party. Yet the difference is chiefly one of degree. Prime Minister Louis
St. Laurent said of the CCF, the predecessor of the NDP, that they were only
"Liberals in a hurry." That numerous quasi-socialist measures, such as national health insurance and a publicly owned oil company, were proposed by the
CCF/NDP and ultimately legislated by the Liberal Party shows the kinship
between the two parties. Similarly, the Liberals, as a reformist party, are generally to the left of the Progressive Conservatives. But again there is much overlapping. In the federal election campaign of 1984, the Conservative leader,
Brian Mulroney, proclaimed that medicare was a "sacred trust," even though
it had been created by a Liberal government. The Conservatives may have been
less enthusiastic in the first instance about the various programs of the welfare
state, but they seem reluctant to dismantle them. Finally, the new Reform Party
is generally considered to be ideologically to the right of the Conservatives; but
most of its main policies (a balanced budget, privatization and deregulation,
opposition to official bilingualism and multiculturalism) have also been
espoused by many within the Conservative Party, so that Reformers have sometimes been called "Tories in a hurry." It is, therefore, best to think of parties as
occupying overlapping positions on the ideological spectrum:

       NDP
——————————————
              Liberals
    ——————————————
                         Progressive Conservatives
         ——————————————
                                      Reform
                ——————————————

Note that, except for fascism, we have not attempted to place national-       10
ism on the left–right scale. As explained earlier, nationalism has at different
times been allied with liberalism, conservatism, and socialism. Commitment
to the nation-state does not automatically dictate a position on issues of
equality. It is worth noting here that in times of war, normal political differences are suspended. Parties of the left and right often come together in a

coalition government of national unity to carry out the war effort. This shows that support for the nation is on a different level than other political issues. When the threat to the nation is past, the distinction between left and right reasserts itself, and governments of national unity soon fall apart (as happened in France and Italy after World War II).

The Bloc Québécois furnishes another example of how nationalism does not fit onto the standard left–right spectrum. The Bloc, formed in 1989 by the former Progressive Conservative Lucien Bouchard as a protest against delays in ratifying the Meech Lake Accord, is essentially a single-issue movement devoted to the goal of turning Quebec into a sovereign state. The MPs who joined the Bloc defected from both the Conservative and the Liberal Parties; and they were joined in the 1993 election by candidates who had previously worked for other parties in Quebec, such as the NDP. The present leader, Gilles Duceppe, was a communist in his youth. Although the party takes positions from time to time on various issues, it really has no program except the independence of Quebec and thus cannot be placed on the same dimension as other Canadian federal parties.

The varieties of feminism can be aligned partially, though not completely, with the left–right spectrum. Liberal feminists and socialist feminists can without too much distortion be seen as liberals and socialists who happen to be particularly concerned with a certain set of problems. Overall, their thinking fits into familiar liberal and socialist categories. Radical feminism, however, is much more difficult to place. As a transformation of Marxism, it seems to belong on the left; and when radical feminists get involved in electoral politics, they usually do so with parties of the left. But their overriding concern with patriarchy is fundamentally different from the concerns with popular sovereignty and economic equality that characterize positions on the left–right spectrum, so that we might think of radical feminism as belonging on a dimension that cuts perpendicularly across the left–right dimension. This helps to explain what otherwise might be seen as some strange political coalitions. For example, radical feminists have frequently worked together with conservatives in law-enforcement agencies on issues such as pornography, sexual abuse, and violence against women. The two groups conceptualize the issues in totally different ways, but they agree on the desirability of harsher criminal penalties. Liberals who are thought of as quite left-wing—for example, members of the Canadian Civil Liberties Association—can find themselves on the opposite side on these issues even though they may think of themselves as quite favourable to feminism.

The situation with environmentalism is similar. Generally, we can comfortably sort out environmentalists by examining the means they advocate to achieve their ends. Free-market environmentalists clearly belong with the classical liberals, while many advocates of human welfare ecology just as clearly prefer the more interventionist tools of reform liberalism and social democracy. But deep ecology, like radical feminism, is really on a different dimension because it rejects the materialist goals of the other ideologies.

The left–right spectrum, though often useful, is unidimensional. Real-    14
world ideologies are multidimensional—that is, they are concerned not only
with inequality and equality but with many other political values. For example, it would be possible to map ideologies on a continuum according to
their views on the scope of state control of society:

**Maximum** ⟶ **Minimum**

| Communism | Social Democracy | Classical Liberalism | |
| Fascism | Reform Liberalism | Conservatism | Anarchism |

Communists and fascists favour the total identification of state and soci-    15
ety. Social democrats and reform liberals favour active government regulation
and intervention but do not wish to subject all of society to state control.
Conservatives and classical liberals desire a very limited state to carry out certain restricted functions; otherwise, they want society to evolve according to
its own laws. Anarchists believe that society can exist without any government at all.

The above is as valid as the conventional left–right approach, but it    16
expresses another aspect of the reality of ideologies, and thus does not coincide with the left–right spectrum. To speak of left and right is a useful shorthand way of referring to ideologies as long as the limitations of this approach
are kept in mind. Left and right are only convenient labels; they are no substitute for a detailed understanding of a point of view. Difficulties quickly
become apparent when we try to apply the notion of a left–right continuum
to concrete issues. To illustrate, let us look at several issues from the realms
of economics, politics, and society.

Among economic issues, the left–right spectrum fits very well the debate    17
about progressive taxation. Those furthest to the left are the most vociferous
in their desire to "make the rich pay," as the Communist Party of Canada
used to put it. Those in the centre accept the principle of progressive taxation
but may worry that the marginal rate is so high as to interfere with productivity; they wish the state to act in a redistributive way, but not to "kill the
goose that lays the golden eggs." Those on the right reject progressive taxation in favour of a flat tax, that is, one whose rate is the same for all. The issue
of taxation can be readily mapped onto the left–right continuum because the
underlying question is one of egalitarianism.

On social issues, the left seems to favour a position of individual liber-    18
tarianism—abortion on demand, legalization of marijuana, abolition of movie
censorship—and the right seems to uphold traditional standards of morality.
But this seeming unidimensionality exists only in liberal democracies where
the extreme left is weak, as in North America. Communists and other revolutionary leftists are in fact rather puritanical in their outlook on many moral
questions. Marijuana and other mind-altering drags are rigorously forbidden
in communist countries, as are many mildly obscene books and movies that

would hardly raise an eyebrow in the Western world. Freedom of individual choice is not a high priority for the revolutionary left.

Even with all these nuances and exceptions, the terms left and right are 19 convenient for categorizing ideological tendencies. Most of the inconsistencies disappear if we restrict the application of the terms to stable constitutional democracies in which the extreme right and extreme left are weak or non-existent. Under these conditions, left and right stand for relatively coherent ideological positions—reform liberalism and social democracy on the one side, classical liberalism and conservatism on the other. The more moderate forms of feminism and environmentalism can be fitted into this tableau without too much strain; but if radical feminism and deep ecology ever become dominant ideologies, left and right will have to be either redefined or abandoned altogether as practical labels.

■ ■ ■

## *Discussion and Writing Suggestions*

1. Make some comparisons. Are our left and right clearly divided? Judging from McGinnis's article, do our conservatives share the same philosophy of American conservatives?
2. Why does the analysis of Dickerson and Flanagan give an incomplete account for the rise, and non-stop struggle, of the right-wing Alliance party?
3. Who's in the centre now? In the Canadian political scene, is one's position on the spectrum strictly a matter of party affiliation, or do we think of some of our politicians as individuals?

## CANADIAN CHARTER OF RIGHTS AND FREEDOMS

*The* Charter of Rights and Freedoms *was part of the* Constitution Act *of 1982, which was a modernization of the original* British North America Act *of 1867. Passing this Act required the British Parliament to act on a joint address from the Canadian Senate and the House of Commons. As Dickerson and Flanagan point out in their book* An Introduction to Canadian Politics, *the Act "not only lists and confirms the pre-existing parts of the written constitution but also introduces important new substance, particularly in the first thirty-four sections, known as the Canadian Charter of Rights and Freedoms" (p. 70).*[1]

The sections that we have reproduced are those that speak to civil liberties and to issues of equality rights.

[1] Dickerson, Mark O. and Thomas Flanagan. *An Introduction to Canadian Politics: A Conceptual Approach*. Toronto: Nelson, 1998.

Whereas Canada is founded upon principles that recognize the supremacy of God and the rule of law:

**Guarantee of Rights and Freedoms**

*Rights and freedoms in Canada*

1. The *Canadian Charter of Rights and Freedoms* guarantees the rights and freedoms set out in it subject only to such reasonable limits prescribed by law as can be demonstrably justified in a free and democratic society.

*Fundamental freedoms*

**Fundamental Freedoms**

2. Everyone has the following fundamental freedoms:

*a)* freedom of conscience and religion;

*b)* freedom of thought, belief, opinion and expression, including freedom of the press and other media of communication;

*c)* freedom of peaceful assembly; and

*d)* freedom of association.

*Mobility of citizens*

**Mobility Rights**

6. (1) Every citizen of Canada has the right to enter, remain in and leave Canada.

*Rights to move and gain livelihood*

(2) Every citizen of Canada and every person who has the status of a permanent resident of Canada has the right

*a)* to move to and take up residence in any province; and

*b)* to pursue the gaining of a livelihood in any province.

*Limitation*

(3) The rights specified in subsection (2) are subject to

*a)* any laws or practices of general application in force in a province other than those that discriminate among persons primarily on the basis of province of present or previous residence; and

*b)* any laws providing for reasonable residency requirements as a qualification for the receipt of publicly provided social services.

*Affirmative action programs*

(4) Subsections (2) and (3) do not preclude any law, program or activity that has as its object the amelioration in a province of conditions of individuals in that province who are socially or economically disadvantaged if the rate of employment in that province is below the rate of employment in Canada.

## Legal Rights

*Life, liberty and security of person*

7. Everyone has the right to life, liberty and security of the person and the right not to be deprived thereof except in accordance with the principles of fundamental justice.

*Search or seizure*

8. Everyone has the right to be secure against unreasonable search or seizure.

*Detention or imprisonment*

9. Everyone has the right not to be arbitrarily detained or imprisoned.

*Arrest or detention*

10. Everyone has the right on arrest or detention
    *a*) to be informed promptly of the reasons therefor;
    *b*) to retain and instruct counsel without delay and to be informed of that right; and
    *c*) to have the validity of the detention determined by way of *habeas corpus* and to be released if the detention is not lawful.

*Proceedings in criminal and penal matters*

11. Any person charged with an offence has the right
    *a*) to be informed without unreasonable delay of the specific offence;
    *b*) to be tried within a reasonable time;
    *c*) not to be compelled to be a witness in proceedings against that person in respect of the offence;
    *d*) to be presumed innocent until proven guilty according to law in a fair and public hearing by an independent and impartial tribunal;
    *e*) not to be denied reasonable bail without just cause;
    *f*) except in the case of an offence under military law tried before a military tribunal, to the benefit of trial by jury where the maximum punishment for the offence is imprisonment for five years or a more severe punishment;
    *g*) not to be found guilty on account of any act or omission unless, at the time of the act or omission, it constituted an offence under Canadian or international law or was criminal according to the general principles of law recognized by the community of nations;

*h*) if finally acquitted of the offence, not to be tried for it again and, if finally found guilty and punished for the offence, not to be tried or punished for it again; and

*i*) if found guilty of the offence and if the punishment for the offence has been varied between the time of commission and the time of sentencing, to the benefit of the lesser punishment.

*Treatment or punishment*

**12.** Everyone has the right not to be subjected to any cruel and unusual treatment or punishment.

*Self-crimination*

**13.** A witness who testifies in any proceedings has the right not to have any incriminating evidence so given used to incriminate that witness in any other proceedings, except in a prosecution for perjury or for the giving of contradictory evidence.

*Interpreter*

**14.** A party or witness in any proceedings who does not understand or speak the language in which the proceedings are conducted or who is deaf has the right to the assistance of an interpreter.

**Equality Rights**

*Equality before and under law and equal protection and benefit of law*

**15.** (1) Every individual is equal before and under the law and has the right to the equal protection and equal benefit of the law without discrimination and, in particular, without discrimination based on race, national or ethnic origin, colour, religion, sex, age or mental or physical disability.

*Affirmative action programs*

(2) Subsection (1) does not preclude any law, program or activity that has as its object the amelioration of conditions of disadvantaged individuals or groups including those that are disadvantaged because of race, national or ethnic origin, colour, religion, sex, age or mental or physical disability.

■  ■  ■

## Discussion and Writing Suggestions

1. Do these points guarantee that Canadian citizens have the right to expect a degree of economic security, or is the Charter vague about this?
2. Can you find arguments that use the Charter to defend the point that everyone deserves a basic level of comfort and safety in our society?

# *"I'm Tired of Being a Slave to the Church Floor"*

JOHN STACKHOUSE

*John Stackhouse is now foreign editor of* The Globe and Mail. *Previously, he was the newspaper's correspondent-at-large, based in Toronto, and for seven years its Third World correspondent based in New Delhi. He has also worked as a senior writer for* Report on Business Magazine, *and a reporter for the* Financial Times, London Free Press *and* Toronto Star. *He was educated at Queen's University in Kingston, Ontario, and lives in Toronto.*

*He has won five National Newspaper Awards, a National Magazine Award and an Amnesty International Award for human rights reporting. Understood in this context, his article can be regarded as his attempt to take a sympathetic view of the homeless as individuals making choices. As the response by Jack Layton (in the article that follows this one) brings to light, however, Stackhouse's article had an incendiary effect on those who argue for social and political action to bring an end to suffering caused by inequality.*

## IN TORONTO—DAY 6
## BILLY JACK: A FOOT IN BOTH WORLDS

The wind is still whipping across Toronto's Nathan Phillips Square when a    1
clock tower strikes six and I wake up to find that most of my cardboard shelter has blown away in the night. Someone has also come by and laid an extra sleeping bag on top of me.

The others sleeping in the square, huddled in cardboard boxes, under-    2
neath walkways like me, are also slowly rising, stooped, shivering, searching for the Sally Ann coffee truck that does not come for another hour.

All the money I made the day before—$223 panhandling on Toronto's    3
streets—provides little comfort to my numb joints and sore back, and it won't get me into a toilet within blocks of here. I join a few others behind a wall, the only place downtown at this hour where we can go.

Across the square, however, one man seems to stand above it all. Alone,    4
he looks as though he has lived this way for a thousand years, which, as Billy Jack tells it, is what he's done.

B. J. has just come down from the walkway above me, where he slept with    5
no blanket and two bottles of wine in his system. It was, he says, a fairly restrained night. It was also so cold he tried to stay awake all night, wandering from one coffee shop to the next before he eventually found a windbreak.

I give B. J. my extra sleeping bag and suggest he hide it between a pillar    6
and the wall. He gives me a cigarette as thanks. It's been only weeks since he got out of Collins Bay penitentiary near Kingston, Ont.—five years this time for busting up a couple of guys in a bar—and he's forgotten some of the details of street life.

At 58, with 20 years of jail time behind him, B. J. is still a big bear of a    7
man who looks and sounds like Wolfman Jack. In many ways he is from
another age. He likes to call himself one of the originals, one of the grand old
native drunks who has been on Toronto streets since the sixties.

For years, he and his wife worked part of the year, in Toronto and out-    8
side the city. Sometimes they had their own home, or they stayed in shelters.
They had two kids. And they drank, right up till the days when his wife was
dying, in his arms, from bone cancer.

That was 12 years ago.    9

Street life now is not what it used to be, not with all the drugs, tough new    10
laws and the politics of homelessness. B. J.'s daughter, a nurse at a major
Toronto hospital, keeps pleading with him to come off the street and live with
her and her husband and family. His grandchildren need him, she says. They
need his epic Mi'kmaq tales, his big, thick chest to rest on, and his baritone
voice to lull them to sleep.

They need a hero, which is what B. J. tries to be every now and then,    11
when he's not in prison and shows up at his daughter's house for a night. He
chokes up as he speaks of what she's done with her life. But he can't stay, not
with his pride and sense of place.

B. J.'s voice perks up when he talks of his other home, the one out here.    12
Last night, a complete stranger gave him a pack of cigarettes when he asked
for only one. A man who passes him every day gave him two bottles of wine.

"I drink to forget my troubles," B. J. says. "But you know, every morn-    13
ing I wake up and they're still there."

He could go back to his two-room house in the bush in western    14
Newfoundland, where he was born. A salmon river runs through the property, he says, and the fish jump so high you can almost catch them with your
hands. But the Newfoundland coast is a lonely place, with few jobs and no
one to throw toonies your way.

We both cough from the cold, prompting B. J. to pull out a bottle of    15
mouthwash. He takes a gulp for a morning kick and buckles over to keep
from regurgitating it.

"The loneliness is the hardest part out here," he says.    16

So why does he stay?    17

"I believe God has put me here for a reason. I have no idea what that    18
reason is. I could have walked by it a thousand times. But I gotta keep lookin'.
One day, God will show me His reason."

When the Sally Ann truck finally pulls up on Queen Street, shortly after    19
7 a.m., we join the lineup at its open window. A man in the truck offers coffee
and porridge with brown sugar, as well as new underwear, tuques and gloves
to a half-dozen people waiting, stamping their feet to stay warm.

B. J. does not remember so many people on the street a decade ago, or a    20
decade before that. "It was never like this," he says. "I don't know what's
happened to this city."

He thanks me again for the sleeping bag and goes to find a spot to pan-    21
handle and then a place to drink.

I take a streetcar west, to the Parkdale recreation centre, a smoky store-   22
front room that looks like an old pool hall. I hope to find people who might
be more needful than the panhandlers who get so much public attention
when poverty is the subject.

On a Saturday afternoon, with a light snow starting to swirl in the wind,   23
the centre is filled with people, at least 50 of them who have homes, big needs
and little attention. Packaged up here, a half hour's haul from Yonge Street,
they are not seen as the "homeless" are.

I sit down at a card table with a group of men who are smoking cigarettes   24
and drinking 30-cent cups of coffee. At the end of the table, a man stands and
waves to no one in particular. Another keeps saying, "motherfucker," gur-
gling in between. After a free lunch is served, a third man talks to his plate of
chicken-fried rice, telling each forkful: "You are from Mars."

The confusion does not faze Jim, a middle-aged man who works at a   25
bakery for below minimum wage, to supplement his disability insurance. The
company he gets at the centre is important but not as important as his job, an
occupation that he says is more valuable than a roof or free meal.

"In a constitutional democracy, employment is a fundamental right, but   26
that's not working here," he says earnestly.

He thinks Canada should tie all social assistance to employment. When   27
I mention workfare, he cringes. "'Make them work for it' is the old capitalist idea," he says.

His idea is no different in the end, only justified differently. "I take the   28
view of medical science. According to medical science, working makes people
healthier."

"It's much better than sitting around watching TV and drinking coffee.   29
Look at all the money we would save on health care. In other countries, you
have to take a job. It may not be the right job but you have to take the one the
government gives you or finds for you, if you want assistance."

When the recreation centre closes and I return to Yonge Street, I find   30
myself begging again. I don't need the money any more, or the added experience, but the desire has become insatiable—a desire, as Jim said, to be occupied.

Waiting at a streetcar stop, I sit down on the pavement and hold out my   31
cap. Two dollars, thank you.

Before I buy myself dinner, I feel a need to work for it, so I take a spot in   32
a subway station. I set my target at $5, enough for a McDonald's Value
Meal, but when I reach that in a few minutes, I can't resist shooting for $10
and then $15. As I'm packing up, an elderly woman stops and hands me a
$10 bill. I have to tell myself again to stop, to concede my space to another
panhandler who is sitting beyond the doors. Only when I'm walking upstairs
to the street do I realize that I'm telling myself to do this out loud.

Two Saturdays before Christmas, Yonge Street is jammed with people,   33
festive music and a neon rainbow of lights on every corner. In the middle of
the crush, I spot B. J. on the sidewalk, sorting through coins in his palm to
give to another panhandler, beggar to beggar, on the pavement.

"I can't do business if you're just standin' there," the panhandler com-    34
plains to B. J.

"Fuck off," B. J. says.                                                     35

"No, you fuck off," the other man says, and so B. J. leaves with his fist-   36
ful of change.

As we walk down the crowded street together, I notice after a few steps     37
how drunk he is. He has been in bars all day and can barely keep himself from
falling into the traffic.

I say goodbye to B. J. in front of the Eaton Centre and head inside,        38
watching him one more time through the glass, holding his hand out in the
night, as though he were reaching for salmon in a big-city river of shoppers.

## DAY 7
## A SHELTER AMID AFFLUENCE

On the coldest night so far in December, every downtown shelter was beyond   39
capacity, so I took a subway token from Out of the Cold, plus a plate of stir-
fried chicken, and headed uptown to my last resort, a shelter in Blythwood
Road Baptist Church in affluent north Toronto.

Set on a tony street between three-storey detached houses, each festooned    40
with Christmas lights, the church and its Saturday-night shelter are at the high
end of the homeless universe. When I find the basement, the mattresses are
already laid out, and they're not the slit and stained ones I had at the
Salvation Army. These are firm, thick foam, covered with clean plastic.

Lying on the floor, against the far wall, a squeegee girl gives her boyfriend   41
a back rub, his shoulder tattoos exposed to the gym air. Next to them, a cat
sleeps, chained to a backpack. There are the usual people with troubles, talking to the night, and the regular natives whom I dined with a few nights
before at another church, already passed out on their mats.

Before I can find my own place, a woman says I'm still in time for dinner    42
and suggests I take a plate of shepherd's pie and vegetables, or some hot soup.
I say I'm stuffed, though I can't resist the dessert table, laced with cakes, a gin-
gerbread house and freshly brewed coffee, which the staff made when a
woman complained the old pot was watery.

I take a mug of coffee outside to sit on the front steps with Gary, a big,   43
bearded man I had met at another shelter. Up and down the street there are
Christmas lights to stare at, and above us a sky full of stars not visible
downtown. Gary points to some of the intricate brick design in a neigh-
bouring house.

"This is a real traditional neighbourhood," he says, comparing it with his   44
own life now sleeping in a different place every night. "I bet these people
never have to go anywhere."

Gary has driven taxis and worked in the building trade as a draftsman,      45
but lately he hasn't been able to sit still, not since he "met a witch," a woman
who fleeced him of his money, he says. He's been on the move for three
years now, from shelter to shelter, saving what he can to get back on his feet.

"I'm tired of being a slave to the church floor," he says as we head     46
inside. He plans to have his own place by New Year's.

I nod appreciatively. There are the B. J.s, the people who will always live     47
on the street because of its freedoms. And then there are the Garys, who quietly have a plan to get off the street, if only they can manage their addictions
and illnesses.

In the morning, we're served fried eggs, hash browns, toast, Danish pas-     48
tries, cold cereal, orange juice and coffee as the church volunteers pick up our
mats and wash the floors. I realize that in the past week of free beds and free
meals, I have not once been asked to do a thing, not even clean the dishes.

At 7:30 in the morning, we're thrown back on the street, where a van     49
waits to ferry people downtown. One of the overnight guests walks instead to
the church parking lot to warm up his car. He's off for another day hauling
scrap metal to dumps, a business that earns him $600 to $700 a week.

"I know I shouldn't be here," he says, stamping out his cigarette before     50
heading off for the day. "I shouldn't be in a shelter, but whenever I get
money, I spend it all partying with the ladies."

As soon as we're off church property, just before 8 a.m., a couple of the     51
guys I'm with pull out bottles of Labatt Ice stowed in their jackets. A third pours
whiskey from a flask into a plastic jug, mixing it with orange juice he took from
the church basement in one of their ceramic mugs, which he chucks in a hedge.

This is my last day on the street, and I say goodbye to the others on the     52
bus, which we have pretty much to ourselves since a couple of middle-aged
women moved to sit next to the driver, driven away by our noise. One of the
men tells me to go to Blessed Sacrament Church tonight, up Yonge Street. The
food is always good.

"Hey, man," he says, as I head for the door. "Have a good day."     53

## EPILOGUE

When I had set out a week earlier to live homeless, I did not expect to be     54
eating pancakes and sausage for breakfast and pastries before bed, or to earn
$20 an hour simply by sitting on the ground with a cardboard sign in front of
me. Nor did I expect to see so much crack flowing through the shelters whose
very names have, for years, been the representation of public goodwill.

When I stepped into the shadows of homelessness, for admittedly a fleet-     55
ing moment, I also did not expect to find the isolation and belittlement that
make the street so much more a psychological challenge than a physical one.

I was surprised by the enormous public compassion and desire to see that     56
no one in our society live this way. And I was taken by the large social infrastructure for the homeless, at least to get them through the night—the shelters,
meal centres and emergency vans—as much as it needs to better weed out the
freeloaders.

But what struck me most when I headed home (a luxury I always knew     57
I had), was the large public desire to find a "solution," as though homelessness was a disease and a cure could be discovered.

I could only think of how diverse were the people I met—from Dexter,   58
the hard-working ex-con, to Peter, the dry-waller and inveterate gambler, to
Dwight, the crack-head guitarist—and how each has problems, often unrelated to shelter, that are far different from the other.

Perhaps when we stop talking about the "homeless" as though theirs   59
were a separate world, when we start seeing people such as Dexter, Peter and
Dwight as integral pieces of our society, maybe then we can do more than just
get them through the night.

■ ■ ■

## Discussion and Writing Suggestions

1. If you could ask the author a question about his experience living the life
   of a homeless person, what would it be? In doing this sort of research or
   journalism there are ethical concerns. How long does one need to adopt
   a role in order to begin to "fit in" and gain insight into a way of life? Can
   such "impersonation" be ethical?
2. How would you characterize the tone of this article? Does Stackhouse
   seem to like or respect the homeless people he describes? Does he seem to
   be fair-minded in presenting the evidence?
3. Compare the way in which Stackhouse presents the experience of being
   homeless to the way in which it is treated by Thomas O'Reilly Fleming.
   Consider how the conventions of journalism and academic writing are
   apparent, respectively, in each writer's approach.

# The Homeless: Are We Part of the Problem?

JACK LAYTON

*Jack Layton is the president of the Federation of Canadian Municipalities and
chairs its National Housing Policy Options team. His work at the Federation
has led to the creation of a coalition of municipalities from across Canada that
are working together for a renewed federal housing policy. On Toronto's
council he co-chairs the Homeless Advisory Committee, which provides a
vital policy link to front-line workers and people who have experienced homelessness. He is the author of* Homelessness: The Making and Unmaking of a
Crisis. *Layton has taught urban studies at all of Toronto's universities and is
now adjunct professor in the planning program of the geography department
at the University of Toronto.*

*In "Don't Blame the Victims," an article that appeared in* The Globe and
Mail *in December of 1999, written specifically to rebut John Stackhouse's
article "'I'm Tired of Being a Slave to the Church Floor,'" Layton calls for*

*action to solve the "looming housing crisis" in Canada. He is critical of Stackhouse's field-research approach to homelessness, saying that trying to understand the problem by spending seven days on the street requires "ignoring years of research in favour of a week outdoors."*

It couldn't have been worse timed.　　　　　　　　　　　　　　　　　1

　　Just when we thought we had broken through the Canadian conscious-　2
ness and begun to forge a national consensus on the problem of homelessness, along came *Globe and Mail* reporter John Stackhouse and his pretense of life on the street.

　　The day after Claudette Bradshaw, the federal co-ordinator for home-　3
lessness, announced in Toronto that the government would contribute $753-million to build housing and shelters, Mr. Stackhouse, ignoring years of research in favour of a week outdoors, told us that public resources are used by crack dealers, that beggars earn professional wages and that "there is more free food than the homeless can eat."

　　Most people I know have been reading and talking about the series ever　4
since, but for many of the wrong reasons. I could hear the cynical "I told you so" reverberating over morning coffee.

　　Mr. Stackhouse's seven-day masquerade among the thousands of legiti-　5
mately homeless on Toronto's streets has done a great disservice to these people.

　　This is not to say that there was nothing valuable in the three-part series.　6
Reading all the diaries allowed us to reach the conclusions where Mr. Stackhouse offers wisdom. He suggests that simply expanding emergency services month after month will not solve the problems that the homeless face. More government money, he says, will solve the problem only if it gets to the root of the high cost of urban housing and addresses crack and alcohol abuse. In these solid conclusions, the author is repeating fragments of the comprehensive plans developed by those who devoted years to the study of the issue.

　　The problem is that, in getting to these conclusions, he fans the flames of　7
the "blame the victim" psychology that motivates those who deny any social responsibility for the homeless crisis.

　　Now, anyone who spent eight years reporting on the affairs of countries　8
with average per-capita incomes measured in hundreds of dollars would have a unique perspective on homelessness in Toronto. To someone who watched as meagre grains of rice were distributed to outstretched hands in wartorn refugee camps, a church basement breakfast served up by volunteers complete with eggs, fruit and hot coffee would seem luxurious.

　　But does that warrant calling people who go to these breakfasts "free-　9
loaders"?

　　In a way, still, the series had the surreal feel of a report from the front　10
lines by a journalist dropped into a foreign land by parachute. This journalist was, fortunately, secure in knowing he'd be brought back to home base after the seven-day assignment. His security made his situation fundamentally different than the people he was trying to mimic.

And therein lies the problem. Pretending not to have a home can never be    11
the same as not having one at all.

Knowing you have a home means you are not without hope. Many on the    12
street are, literally, without hope or home. The bravado we saw some homeless people express to the newcomer on the streets is only one expression of
that hopelessness—carving out an identity, masking the reality with display.

When the entrepreneurship that beggars illustrated as they ganged up to    13
protect their turf forced small fry such as Mr. Stackhouse out of the subway
station, the actions were implicitly criticized. Yet the same entrepreneurship
exercised upstairs in the bank towers is celebrated. The more takeovers,
mergers and market share, the better! Panhandlers were merely replicating the
titans of business.

The reportage was best in its accounts of how ordinary Torontonians    14
reacted to the homeless: "I've seen women give money and kind words 10
times more often than men."

Mr. Stackhouse's successful days of panhandling suggests that    15
Torontonians are generous people and do not blame others for the conditions
in which they find themselves.

Let's suppose that the series about seven days in the lives of a city's    16
homeless had been written by people who had been homeless themselves but
had found a way out. How would it have been different?

The daily struggles to find housing would have played a more prominent    17
part in the narrative. Thousands of people calling the homelessness hotline
trying desperately to find a place. Those who have escaped from the cycle of
homelessness invariably focus on the importance of having their own safe and
affordable place. A home has often been the starting point for recovery.

In Toronto, a homeless addict finishing a treatment program is tossed    18
back out into the street and emergency environment. There's no home in
which to carry out a long-term recovery. A person struggling with a mental-
health challenge, complete with a medication regime, is left on the streets with
no secure place to be well. A convict is released from prison, again to the
streets, only to be recycled through the system once again. Emergency wards
and hospitals discharge people to the streets and hostels when what they really
need is a healthy house and some personal support so they can recuperate.

The diary of the truly homeless would also see the simple desire to be    19
treated with respect rising powerfully to the surface. Whatever the pathway to
homelessness might have been, support and respect have to characterize the
way out.

Success stories can be found amongst the emergency programs. These are    20
the ones that have been founded on these three key principles: The housing
must be secure so you do not have to line up night after night in the cold for
a mat or cot; respect, encouragement and careful support for the wounds and
personal challenges faced by each homeless individual must be present; and,
in the best programs, homeless people themselves actually have some say
about what happens to them.

Emergency shelters alone are not the answer, that's for sure. The old    21
slogan "homes not hostels" still applies. Besides, shelters are terribly expensive compared to permanent housing. At $25 000 to $40 000 a shelter bed a year, we could house five people in long-term housing for the same price. The taxpayer would win and so would those facing homelessness. Do we really want more hostels when we could have positive supportive programs such as Homes First, an operation in the city centre? Homes First focuses on providing permanent housing while addressing the individual needs of each resident. It's all done in a climate of respect.

Mr. Stackhouse acknowledges the effects of the loss of respect he felt as    22
a homeless person on our streets. Even though his homelessness was temporary, he knew in his gut what could happen to his humanity, stripped of an identity, of his own place in our city. Re-establishing his place, and the place of all those facing the looming housing crisis, requires housing, respect and support, all of which will take dollars. But they will be well spent.

■ ■ ■

## Discussion and Writing Suggestions

1. If you could interview this author about his response to Stackhouse, what would you ask him?
2. Layton addresses the issue of the homeless in Toronto. For those of us who live outside Toronto, do you think any of his observations are still pertinent?

# Life on the Streets

THOMAS O'REILLY FLEMING

*People on the street need a place to go,*
*People on the street need a place to go,*
*Walkin' through the night up and down the avenue,*
*Lookin' for a place, a place to go, a place to go,*
*There's a muffled scream from the alley scene,*
*From the alley scene comes a muffled scream,*
*And the siren wails while the system fails,*
*In the steaming heat people walk in the street,*
*People can't run and hide,*
*If you want to feel good then you gotta feel good inside.*

Neil Young[1]

One of the central problems of our attempts to understand the homeless    1
resides in explaining why they have been cast off by the mainstream of soci-

ety. When I interviewed homeless people throughout this country two questions were the focus of much of the discussion that took place. First, why do people become trapped within the cycles of homelessness for months or even years? Secondly, what is it about the life course of this individual that has locked them into a cycle of despair? The answers to both these questions were neither simple nor easily explored with homeless people. In a sense one is asking how a person constructs reality, and to reflect more deeply upon the forces, both personal and structural, that have brought them to this position as a social pariah. While it is not possible in the constraints of a book such as this to record every life story of homeless persons it is possible to provide accounts of lives that reflect broader themes in the construction of a homeless identity in Canadian society. From these accounts it has been possible to construct images of the process of being homeless and the role played by the homeless and various social service agencies in either ameliorating and/or perpetuating the homeless condition.

While no single explanation of either the causes or the realities of home-    2
less existence would be fair to the variety of individual life courses developed by homeless people, there are commonalities which link their experiences. Further, this chapter will proceed first to present the experience of homelessness from the viewpoint of various homeless "groups" and social service personnel and then move on to an analysis of the core problems that predominate in relegating, and keeping, homeless people in the position of societal misfits. Finally, the lifeworks of the homeless will be put into perspective by a critical examination of the various forms of legal control that regulate their lives, from municipal by-laws through to welfare regulations.

## JUST GETTING BY

To the average observer Joe is a typical 24-year-old. He is well groomed and    3
dressed in neat blue jeans, a striped clean shirt, running shoes and a pale blue windbreaker. He has a pleasant personality and a direct manner of speaking. He talks in an animated style, is intelligent and able to contemplate his life with insight and directness. Joe is homeless. Joe has not always been homeless. Neither is he a victim of a child welfare system that cannot cope with its all too many charges. He does not have a problem with alcohol or drugs, although he has used "coke." His behaviour is not pathological. Joe's story is one that tells us much about the series of contingencies that can move one from full status in our society to its farthest margins. As we begin our interview I tell him what we will be exploring. He immediately blurted out the following summary of his life, "I left home at 16, got myself a job working for a cleaner, pretty soon I had my own contacts and started a company. I got married at 18, had two kids, and had a house and a mortgage. My wife left me and after that I couldn't take it and started using cocaine. Pretty soon I couldn't pay the bills and I didn't care anymore. I lost everything and now I'm here."

Joe is used to telling his story to social workers and has developed a one    4
minute travelogue to guide them through his life. It is a symptom that is prevalent amongst the homeless, tired of talking about the same "sad" story to

worker after worker who is either looking for the root cause of their home-lessness or simply going through the motions of filling out the forms. Front line workers and those that do intakes with the homeless at shelters and hostels often explain the behaviour of the homeless in terms of one overriding prob-lem. For teens this is most often abuse whether physical or sexual; for men it is frequently a problem with booze or drugs; for families the problem is one characterized by social dependency handed down from generation to genera-tion. The real dimensions of the problems of the homeless like Joe may lie hidden in much more complex contingencies that affect their life, but are less amenable to quick diagnoses and quick fixes. In this workers fall prey to the process of labelling people, an approach that sociologists have long explored. Labels, while they may simplify the world, are often constructed at the expense of some loss to those labelled. Howard Becker, a well known sociologist, instructs us that, "Deviance is behavior that is so labelled." In other words, the labelling of a person as "someone with a booze problem" or "the product of an abused home" has the effect of transforming them into a deviant individual. In this characterization their current position in society as a homeless person reflects some personal failing, inadequacy or lack of effort.[2] Persons in our society who are so labelled are therefore seen as being the authors of their own problems. Although on one level we may have some sympathy for the home-less person, the refusal to look more deeply into the roots of homelessness as a structural problem in society has had immediate consequences for both the treatment of the homeless person as a dependent in the social welfare network, and in their view of themselves. One feature of labelling is that persons may, after countless interactions in which this label is reaffirmed, begin to self-label themselves as having a problem that is largely beyond their control.[3] At the same time they are constantly confronted with it by social workers and other agency staff. The homeless person develops what has been termed a **master status**, which means that once one learns about their problem one knows all one needs to in order to interact with the individual.

Joe is viewed as a young man with intelligence and potential by the staff. 5 In his own words, "I can do the job of the staff when you come right down to it. They all know it. I had my own business for several years, so this is noth-ing." Joe is also seen as a man whose homelessness is related to his "drug problem." A further analysis of Joe's story is instructive in terms of both the factors that lead to homelessness and the reasons that persons often remain stuck in a homeless situation for long periods of time.

During his marriage, relations with his wife were good according to Joe. 6 He and his wife were well off financially and enjoyed each other's company. Joe enjoyed drinking occasionally at a local bar, and there a young woman, a friend of his brother's, became infatuated with him. She often joined him, his brother and his brother's girlfriend for a drink. She asked Joe to have sex with her on several occasions but he refused telling her he was happily married with children. One evening Joe returned to his home to find that his wife was extremely upset and was packing to leave with the children. Apparently, the young woman who desired his sexual attention had gone to his home and told his wife that she had been having an affair with her husband, "and went into all of the details of having sex and how I didn't love her anymore." His wife did not believe his story regarding the other woman despite the support of others who had seen him interact with her. His wife left him and soon after he "slumped into a deep, deep depression." As Joe describes it, "Nothing meant anything to me anymore. I loved my wife and children and it just didn't make any sense. I hadn't done anything and here I was being punished." Soon Joe was drinking constantly and began to take cocaine to dull the pain of the loss of his family. "I just didn't care about anything anymore, like if the world can be that cruel when you're a good guy, work hard, give your family a good life, what's the point?" In the end Joe lost his business, then his house, and within a few months of his wife's departure he was homeless.

Now after almost a year in various homeless shelters in several cities he   7
is able to reflect on his fall from "normalcy." "A lot of the staff think my problem is cocaine, but I haven't done any since I became homeless. My problem is I get overwhelmed by thinking about starting out again. I guess I've earned some time off to think and get a new start. I don't want to get back into the mainstream of society right away, I've got to get my head straight. I can do it again easily, that's not the hard part (getting a job) it's knowing that I've found out what I need, then I'll be outta here." So for Joe, homelessness presents somewhat of a resting place from some of the pressures of society. What he is as a person cannot be taken away from him; he is one of the small number of homeless who can understand the label accorded them, but has the personal resources to reject this label and remain optimistic about the future. Joe observes, "Look, just because a guy loses some money that doesn't mean he's stupid. Look at Donald Trump. He lost millions. Do you hear anyone saying he's stupid, that he won't climb back again. It's all relative to where you are in society and how much you can afford to lose without sinking into a hole. I'll be back, but when it's right for me." Far from being simple bragging, Joe's comments are based in his belief in his own abilities and his assessment of his current state of mind. Like many homeless interviewed Joe had lost his connections or bonds to society when, as a good citizen doing what he felt were the right things, his world was wrongfully demolished. This was a world, then, that he could no longer simply continue to invest in. His adaptations through alcohol and cocaine resulted in his demise as a person with a stake in society, but it was precisely because he did not want a stake in a society that he saw as having betrayed him.

## GOING DOWN SLOW

Jake is a native Canadian who is 26 years of age. Born on a Saskatchewan farm   8
he is currently living in a men's shelter in Vancouver. He is immaculately dressed in clean deep blue jogging shorts, running shoes and a crisp white shirt. He does not have a dishevelled appearance traditionally, and mistakenly today, accorded to the homeless. Jake has short neat black hair that is clean. He is well groomed and could easily be mistaken for one of the social workers in the local shelter. He is pleasant and his perceptions of his own situation are clear

and unwashed. Jake left the family farm when he was 16 years old. He had been adopted from the reserve into a white farm family, and completed a high school education. "After that I met my wife. I married her when she was 16; I was 19 at the time. That was the bad thing, at that time coming off of the farm and I guess the stress of a new child in the family. I guess if I looked hard enough . . . it was wham, bam thank you ma'am and you find yourself in a predicament that you totally don't need to." He describes his adoptive parents as "the most supportive people I know. See, in Saskatchewan they distinguish between the Indian and white people whatever." Jake loved school and said in the interview, "I'd loved to go back to school."

Jake finally got work just before birth of his first child. He feels that his    9
daughter "changed his life quite a bit." He was employed as a farm labourer, and had a natural knack with engines. "I could run anything, I still can run any tractor and combine, you name it I can run it. I know how to weld . . ."

What happened in Jake's life to bring him to the margins of existence?    10
"Everything was going great like before I came out here in February of last year I was incarcerated for 18 months. At that time I was drinking and it was a violent crime you know. Took a baseball bat, fought with a guy over a hundred dollars, took his knees out, it's just as simple as that, and obviously the courts didn't think too much of it." Previously he had spent five years in prison in Saskatchewan for committing an armed robbery. "I guess, I don't know maybe I wanted to prove something. I don't know what it was. I could see that upsetting the marriage, I mean, wouldn't you?"

Jake spent the time after prison working in a well-known restaurant bar.    11
"It's great. The thing that happened to me I got burnt out, burn out syndrome . . . like six days a week and when you're on a management team and you're working on salary it doesn't matter how many hours you put in." Jake made $500 a week at the job take home pay and had an apartment that cost $460 a month. "I just don't know what went wrong really." Jake had no savings when he quit his job in July of 1991. "I don't know, I bought a lot of things. I don't know, I'm a material person. I like to buy a t.v., everything, you see, you know that you may want later . . . like I've still got all of this in storage." Jake had worked for almost 18 months full time six days a week in a progressively more responsible position, finally achieving the status of kitchen manager. He suddenly found one day that his will to work had left him. For him, homelessness was an oasis away from the responsibilities he was being asked to perform to survive. "It's not that I'm lazy or anything. I just want to get my head clear. I've only been off work for a couple of months." Although he is entitled to unemployment he does not collect it, a view of welfare support that is widely espoused by homeless people. Welfare of any kind places a person in a position of perceived dependency. As psychopaths I researched in a hospital in Britain put it, "Don't give me a gift, then I'm in debt to you." The homeless do not want to accumulate any more social debts than possible and often view various forms of welfare above the minimum required to survive with a jaundiced eye. As Jake put it, "Yes, I'm entitled to it but if I wanted to abuse the system I could go ahead and abuse the system up and down and left

and centre and without paying anything but I don't want to do it. That's not what I'm after. I just want to get my head cleared."

## THE LONER

Dave is 27 years old and comes from a foster parent background. He left   12
home at 16 and has been living in the shelter system and on the street ever since. He displays the signs of complete dependence on the system and has resigned himself to shelter life. He rarely breaks the cycle of dependency:

I'll meet somebody like a friend or a girl. I may stay there for a couple of   13
weeks just for the hell of it depending on the situation. I'm basically here though because I don't like livin' with other people . . . it's not right, I'm not used to it. Well, it's a matter of pride and dignity you know, you feel weird you know like, I'm just not used to it. I don't like the idea, I'm uh, like a loner.

Dave is indeed an outcast from society. He has no friends and his only   14
forms of social communication come with social workers and drinking buddies in the parks. He lives hedonistically enjoying the moment since the future is unreal for him:

Some people have their own style of living, my style just happens to be   15
have a good time . . . you're limited to the amount of friends you have (in the shelter). The hostel's full of all kinds of people, grubby people, ignorant people, people who have no brains, ignorant people, people who have no ambition, people who drink and they can't do anything like they're idiots so I meet the odd person I can get along with.

While he accepts his own limitations as a fully functioning human being   16
he does not place blame for the predicament which besets homeless people on the system. He voices a common view that the homeless are the source of their own problems:

Yah either drugs or they just screwed up . . . (Is it the system that screwed   17
up?) No, no I don't believe that for one minute. Well okay, it's hard to get work but there's a lot of people here that complain about work but they don't even try get up and look. They don't even know how to comb their hair. They don't even know how to present themselves so how are they gonna get a job? They stay out all night drinkin', they wake up with a hangover, it's just that they're abusing the system.

For Dave his current homeless condition is explained as a temporary   18
state of affairs though it has lasted over six months now:

I'm not rushin nothin'. I'm just gonna reconstruct my life slowly. I'm not   19
gonna rush nothin' cause I've got enough grey hair. I'm just gonna do it, but do it slowly and casually, and be happy that's all. I wanna take care of the mind. No stress, no nothin'.

While Dave portrays his homelessness as being relatively free of stress, in   20
actual fact he is constantly under pressure by the front line workers to seek employment, is constantly searching for a place to stay, and is subject to the rigours of street life. While being interviewed he sported deep healing cuts on his face, the result of a brawl in a local bar. Such wounds are common in the sample interviewed for this book, as violence in many forms is endemic to homeless life.

Dave in concert with many of his fellow homeless views his current state    21
of affairs as a form of relative freedom, having exchanged the pressures of the
workplace for the problems of the street. He sees himself as having:

Lots of freedom . . . in respect of somebody telling me where to go, how    22
to do it, or you know, what to do.

## FIGHTING DOCILITY: SOCIAL CONTROL AGENCIES VERSUS THE HOMELESS

For homeless Canadians, social service, welfare, and helping agencies are    23
often viewed in a negative context as more likely to hurt them than help them.
Despite the best and worst intentions of each of these types of agencies,
homeless people have instinctively and through numerous encounters with the
therapeutic enterprise come to realize that they are often better off with a minimum of recourse to the state for assistance. Sociologists, like Stan Cohen,
have described the "net" of control that extends throughout society.[4] He
argues that all social service functions are either implicitly themselves, or are
tied to institutions that control the behaviour of those considered "different"
in society. Canadian civil rights activist Alan Borovoy has written about our
society's limited ability to tolerate behaviour of others that we find even
mildly irritating.[5] Whether it is a group of picketers trying to protest to protect their jobs, or a homeless person asking for assistance, we often expect
someone to remove them from view, in essence, to control them.

The homeless do not have a single identity in the world of helping agen-    24
cies. As I argued earlier, homeless persons are often assigned a master status
that helps social service personnel to "get a fix" on them, and explain their
present and previous behaviours. Various agencies assign the homeless to
differing categories to fit the mandate of their organization. A homeless
person may be an alcohol abuser for one agency, an unemployable person for
another group, and a person with mental problems at another facility.
Although these may form either significant or minor facets of their personality the point is that they face a constant stripping down of self and categorization into multiple deviant selves as they move from agency to agency. The
homeless also become "known" on their trek through various shelters and
hostels. Their thick accumulating files become less of an aid to assisting them
and more of a means of denigrating their lack of success in altering their life
circumstances, and of providing material for cutting personal criticisms. At
the same time, the homeless represent fodder for the various agencies' struggle to assert "ownership" over the homeless problem. The homeless, like
other marginalized groups, such as criminals, make possible the existence of
a wide variety of "helping" agencies, who besides assisting the homeless,
"help" themselves to substantial salaries.

The homeless sense, and are the victims of, this interconnectedness of    25
agencies. The homeless are reduced to a state of childlike dependency. Critics
of the welfare system have long been aware of the inadequacies of a system of
assistance that is characterized by over-bureaucratization, inhumanity and
mistrust. Ben Carniol, a professor and social worker at Ryerson Polytechnic,
has written scathingly of this system. He writes what we commonly under-

stand but is often disputed: "It has become commonplace for people in need to desperately try to avoid getting into the welfare system in the first place."[6] Tied in with this concept of attempting to remain above the dark and forbidding waters of the welfare ocean is the recurring myth of capitalist culture, "the belief that each individual has both the responsibility and the opportunity to 'make it.'" Echoing the words of persons interviewed across Canada for this book Carniol's sample of welfare recipients found that there was "most often a debilitating sense of dehumanization in being on welfare."[7] In fact, most homeless persons, as with the overwhelming majority of welfare recipients, go to great lengths to avoid being on welfare. Being "on the pogey" even for the homeless means that one has hit bottom, has sunk to a state of total dependency with no resources left to draw upon. Many contemplating the status of welfare recipients will starve themselves, commit petty crimes, beg, take the most menial of underpaid jobs or even prostitute themselves, to stay off the dole.

The medicalization of the problems of the homeless is a common 26 approach taken by social agencies in Canada. Although all homeless are subject to categorization as somehow being slightly less than whole, women are far more commonly the brunt of such approaches. While viewing the homeless problem as emanating most centrally from some form of "sickness" in the form of depression or some other form of mental malady has a certain appeal in that ill health may be attacked by medical intervention, a more sinister interpretation is that the illness is chronic. Again, by shifting the blame onto the victim, in this case often of family violence, oppressed by a male partner, and in the wider realms of society, as well as by asserting that the problem is largely psychological, the burden for recovery lands once again in the lap of the downtrodden. These strategic interventions put social workers in the position of reinforcing and adding to the negative images of their supposed clients. The woman is now not only homeless, but suffering from some form of mental illness! How reassuring to be a single mother thrust out from the security of one's home only to be declared essentially insane by a helpful social worker! One woman interviewed in Vancouver put it this way, "My husband left and it was a couple of months until everything fell apart. No one could help me anymore or they didn't want to, and so I had to go on welfare. Jesus, the first thing they told me was that I was sick and needed help, as if I didn't have enough worries. So I told the worker, 'Who the fuck wouldn't be depressed, no husband, no money, no place to live, no job and now I have to listen to this.'" Helen Levine wrote compellingly about the impotency of women in modern social relations who are encouraged to be the authors of their own destruction. Levine wrote it "is an insidious tool used to contain women's rage and despair to invalidate our experience of the world." Eventually, usually sooner than later, it results in "guilt, anxiety and depression" keeping women "docile and fearful, unable to act on our own behalf."[8] More destructive than this process, Levine argues, and more damnable, is the collusion that is exercised by the so-called helping professions who "in practice as in theory, collude with and reinforce the self-destruct mechanism in women."[9]

Through 20 years of reports on welfare by federal and provincial gov-     27
ernments, two constant themes have emerged. One is that of alienation of the
recipients within the process who feel lessened by the treatment they receive
attempting to collect what is essentially a social right. Secondly, those who
look after the welfare system, and its many manifestations through the shelters and hostels of the country, are disenchanted with the system and its
recipients. Throughout the system of social services across this country
humanity is in short supply as recipients of any form of benefit are forced to
act as beggars in order to receive their due, supplicating at the altar of the welfare agent. Doyle and Visano's report on social welfare services underscores
the constant barrage of intimidation and humiliation that awaits those who
must queue in the lengthening welfare lines in this country, the longest now
in history.[10] The very position that the homeless find themselves in, asking for
assistance, provides reinforcement that these are people who are not part of
the "deserving poor," that is, those who are not personally responsible for
their own sorrows. The systematic inferiorization of the homeless, the constant reminding of this status, and its continual reaffirmation in consultations
between agents and agencies informs the homeless person that they are brand-
ed and stigmatized wherever they turn.

Little wonder that in a few months the homeless person has often slid     28
into a state of dependency unable to see any means of altering their station in
life. Workers that are in a position to assist them are also in an equal position
to withhold services, finances, shelter, and advice. My overwhelming impression of the interviews between social workers and the homeless during some
four years of research was that the worker has certain ideas about the character and problems of the individual. The worker ideally is supposed to work
with the client on strategies for achieving certain goals, most generally,
obtaining employment. However, the worker generally winds up lecturing the
client on his/her inadequacies and lack of personal effort. The exchange is not
one of equals working to solve a problem but is more accurately characterized
as an exercise in control on the part of the worker. Workers often do not consciously realize that they are engaged in this process. Many genuinely wish to
help their clients. A greater number, however, have grown tired of "the whin-
ing" and "laziness" of their charges. With staggering caseloads and the
demand for shelter space constant, and growing, they are faced with an
unending stream of anxious would-be shelter residents throughout the day. As
a young female worker at one shelter put it, "I see 15 or more every day here
wanting to get in. They've usually got files several inches thick and they're
hopeless. You go through the same routine you did last time and they still
don't do a thing to help themselves. I'm leaving this job in two months and
going to . . . . After two years in welfare and two years here I've had it. You
tell these people, 'Yes there's welfare, but you've got to do something for
yourself.' They have no idea, no idea at all." The homeless person is not in a
position to seek other alternatives if they don't like the service they are receiving. The immediate concerns of getting a place to stay are paramount and
realistically they understand that they are without the power to complain.

Who would listen to a complaint by a homeless person? The homeless made their complaints over and over again to the writer in the course of interviews and conversations, but they remain secret and whispered for fear of losing even the little they have managed to wrangle from the welfare system.

Few homeless people will admit to ever being physically ill, ill enough that      29
is to require medical treatment. Few of the homeless trust doctors or hospitals to treat them without some other obligation on their part being involved. Many fear that seeking treatment for an illness or injury will result in them being institutionalized as mentally ill. As one 25-year-old put it, "If you go to an emergency room looking this bad they'll think you've lost your marbles and try to lock you up as crazy." Medical personnel are also viewed as having links to the police and other social agencies, which they certainly do. Many of the homeless do not want any involvement with the police and so avoid doctors. Going to a physician also requires that a person give their name, address if available, and a health insurance number. There are many homeless who do not want to make this kind of information available to others, whether they are inmates on parole seeking to avoid possible trouble, persons who do not want to be found for a variety of reasons, or simply those who harbour unfounded fears. Some shelters have developed a relationship with a local doctor and/or nurse to provide on-site treatment on a weekly basis without the necessity of patients divulging information they would not be comfortable giving. In Toronto, two nurses run a drop-in clinic where homeless men and women can have their afflictions tended to without giving any information on themselves. Most commonly they are treated for ailments related to their feet or hands— exposure, hypothermia and breathing disorders. Their clinic has been operating successfully for over two years and has been able to avoid the intrusion of the medical establishment and the paraphernalia of paranoia that over-formalization seems to bring in the minds of the homeless.

## "LAWS ARE FOR RICH PEOPLE"

Laws have particular functions in our society. The homeless being both with-      30
out accommodation and hence visible on the street are subject to an inordinate amount of attention on the part of the police and other agents of control in our society. Previously in this chapter it was argued that society organizes its control institutions into a form of network. The social analyst Michel Foucault referred to the ability of these institutions to exert power over the lives of individuals in society, to make them into docile citizens, as the "micropolitics of control."[11] Of any group in Canada, the homeless are most subject to the ministrations of these control measures and their lives are largely circumscribed by both formal and informal regulation by welfare rules, by-laws and criminal laws. In this section the impact of these various legal sanctions on the lives of homeless people will be explored.

## WELFARE REGULATION: THE POLITICS OF EXCLUSION

While social assistance is intended as a safety net for those who become most      31
vulnerable in society, the rules surrounding the acquisition of entitlement to

welfare are questionable at best.[12] It may reasonably be argued that the current welfare system does much to perpetuate the problems of the homeless by short-circuiting their attempts to re-establish themselves in the mainstream of society. The first and most significant problem with the welfare system is the ridiculous requirement that persons must have a place of residence in order to receive a welfare cheque. Without a place to stay that has an identifiable address, a homeless person is not permitted any form of assistance. Many of the homeless do not, and will perhaps never, have any address other than an abandoned car, a neglected dumpster, or a park bench. Are they any less deserving of help? Obviously, it is these individuals who are most in need of sustenance, but are rendered ineligible because they do not have a place to stay. It is the great Catch-22 of homelessness; in order to get welfare you have to have a home, if you don't have a home you can't collect welfare. Although some jurisdictions, most notably in Montreal, have developed innovative schemes to counter this inequity in our welfare system, few homeless people in this country can collect assistance without first getting enmeshed in the social control system. In other words, most homeless have to seek residence at a shelter or hostel, which then becomes their address for the purposes of welfare.

In many provinces persons are entitled to "emergency" welfare cheques 32 when they first present themselves to a shelter. In Ontario, they may collect slightly more than $300 under this scheme. However, one of the further problems with the residence requirements is the transient nature of the homeless population. There are, again, a not insignificant number of homeless persons who leave the shelter before a cheque can arrive. While this behaviour strikes the uninformed as incredible, one must put it in the context of life in degrading, threatening, and sometimes violent lodgings. Whether one is threatened, gets fed up with being treated badly or simply wanders off because of a lack of investment in life, cheques are often undeliverable because the intended recipient has left the address given.

While there are many critics of public assistance for the needy, few would 33 want to change places with the homeless despite their criticisms of them as lazy and shiftless. This attitude was expressed by Mike Harris, the leader of the Ontario Progressive Conservative party. Harris argued before a business luncheon at The Canadian Club that welfare recipients abuse the system. He stated, "I'm suggesting that we should not be paying out all that money to stay home and do nothing."[13] While Harris argues that the majority on welfare can be trained or educated for jobs, and suggests timing welfare payments to compliance with these initiatives he demonstrated a complete ignorance of the plight of homeless Canadians. If one considers a single mother of one child as a homeless person who will collect social assistance then how will she accomplish retraining? If she has a preschool child it is expected that somehow she will arrange for the care of the child during her retraining. While this may seem a practical idea any cursory examination of child care in this country leads one to the simple conclusion that it is in short supply and high demand. Even if the mother were to be able to secure a place in a childcare setting for her child it is unlikely she will be able to afford it while retraining herself for employment that is going to yield a wage insufficient to meet her childcare expenses. The alternative is to leave her child in suspect care, spending her working days worrying constantly about her child's welfare. Women with children suffer more greatly than any other group amongst our homeless population for there is little societal comprehension of the impossibilities associated with trying to provide a decent life on a meagre allowance while juggling several disparate roles. Welfare remains for the most part as a form of indentured pauperism.

■ ■ ■

## Discussion and Writing Suggestions

1. Compare the experience of homelessness as it is depicted in two or more case study situations.
2. On the basis of O'Reilly Fleming's presentation, is it possible to say if he has a liberal or conservative orientation in relation to the problem of homelessness?
3. Compare this writer's tone to that of Stackhouse and Layton. Does he strike a more objective stance?

## Endnotes

[1] Neil Young, "People on the Street" 1986, Silver Fiddle Music, ASCAP.

[2] See Howard S. Becker, *Outsiders*. New York: Free Press, 1963. Ostensibly the argument is that no behaviour is deviant until it is so labelled by society. The use of LSD, for example, was not illegal in the U.S.A. until the late 1960s when its use became criminalized. Before that point it was one of the "tolerable" deviances in our society, as Robert Stebbins pointed out in his work *Deviance: Tolerable Differences*. Toronto: Prentice-Hall, 1988. This process is referred to as labelling. While some labels have little effect on those to whom they are applied, others may carry significant weight in terms of evoking negative societal reactions. The label "ex-criminal" has moral, legal and social implications, while the label "lazy" carries with it more limited sanctions.

[3] Richard Ericson's early study of released delinquents in Britain, *Young Offenders and Their Social Work*. Farnborough: Gower, 1975 is one of the finest examples of field research on a group that engaged in self-labelling. For an exhaustive analysis of labelling theory see R. Ericson, *Criminal Reactions: The Labelling Perspective*. Farnborough: Gower, 1975.

[4] Stan Cohen, "The Punitive City: Notes on the Dispersal of Social Control," *Contemporary Crises*, Vol. 3, 1979: 339–363, and Stan Cohen, *Visions of Social Control: Crime, Punishment and Classification*. Cambridge: Polity Press, 1985. According to Cohen, the net of control is growing progressively wider in contemporary society and the mesh is becoming increasingly smaller, trapping persons who were formerly of no interest to social control agencies in its web. This is, in essence, an outgrowth of the increasing size of control agencies like the police and

the progress in technological invasion into privacy. This argument is very similar to that produced by Emile Durkheim on the boundary maintenance functions of deviance, that is, as the system of control swallows up all of the most visible and severe forms of deviance, new more marginal types of deviance will be scanned for infractions and be subject to criminalization. See my earlier article, "The Bawdy House Boys: Some Notes on Media, Sporadic Moral Crusades and Selective Law Enforcement," *Canadian Criminology Forum,* Vol. 3, No. 3, 1981.

[5] Borovoy, *ibid.*

[6] Ben Carniol, *Case Critical: Challenging Social Work in Canada.* Second Edition. Toronto: Between the Lines, 1990–91.

[7] *Ibid.,* at 92.

[8] Helen Levine, "The Personal is Political: Feminism and the Helping Professions," in A. Miles and G. Finn (eds.) *Feminism in Canada: From Pressure to Politics.* Montreal: Black Rose, 1982.

[9] *Ibid.,* 91.

[10] Robert Doyle and L. Visano, *A Time for Action!—Access to Health and Social Services for Members of Diverse Cultural and Racial Groups in Metropolitan Toronto* (Report 1). Toronto: Social Planning Council of Metropolitan Toronto, 1987.

[11] M. Foucault, *ibid.*

[12] For a feminist analysis see J. Dale and P. Foster, *Feminists and State Welfare,* London: RKP, 1986. See also *The General Welfare Assistance Act,* Sec 1 (i) (i) Chapter 188, R.S.C. Statutes of Canada; The Special Senate Subcommittee on Poverty, Poverty in Canada, Ottawa: Information Canada, 1971: 83 found that the welfare process was degrading to all parties involved in it: "It repels both the people who depend on the hand-outs and those who administer them. Alienation on the part of welfare recipients and disenchantment on the part of welfare administrators was evident . . ." In Ontario, short-term benefits known as general welfare assistance typically are allocated to the jobless and those with temporary illnesses. Family benefits is a longer term form of aid and goes mainly to sole-support parents and disabled people. See also Richard Titmuss, *Commitment to Welfare,* London: Unwin, 1970.

[13] *The Windsor Star,* April 1990.

# No Room of Her Own

## CMHC, SYLVIA NOVAC, J. BROWN, AND C. BOURBONNAIS

*The following excerpt appeared under the section heading of "Discourse and Homelessness" in a November 1996 softcover publication whose full title was* No Room of Her Own: A Literature Review of Women and Homelessness. *The authors all have academic credentials—Sylvia Novac, Ph.D., Joyce Brown, M.S.W., M.E.S., and Carmen Bourbonnais, B.A.—and were commissioned by the Canada Mortgage and Housing Corporation to prepare this document. The front page of the document gives as a note that "One of the ways CMHC contributes to the improvement of housing and living conditions in Canada is by communicating the results of its research."*

Based on archival documents and early social scientific research, Rossi (1989)          1
conducted an historic review of homelessness in the United States during the 20th century in which he outlined several distinctions between the "old" and "new" homeless. The decline in homelessness that serves as the historic point of change occurred during the 1960s, by which time there were fewer traditional urban missions, and those that existed provided fewer beds but bolstered services (O'Flaherty 1996: 48). Demographic distinctions between the old and new homeless are based on a shift from a fairly homogeneous profile of older white males to a diverse profile with variances of age, gender, and ethno-racial status.

Rossi's summation of the changed form of homelessness outlines why it          2
has now become defined as a social problem, with advocate groups and organizations.

> [M]ore Americans are exposed to the sight of homelessness because homeless persons are *less spatially concentrated* today. Second, homelessness has shifted in meaning: the old homeless were sheltered in inadequate accommodations, but they were not sleeping out on the streets and in public places in great numbers. *Literal homelessness has increased* from virtually negligible proportions to more than half of the homeless population. Third, homelessness now means *greater deprivation*. The homeless men living on Skid Row were surely poor, but their average income from casual and intermittent work was three to four times that of the current homeless. The emergency shelter housing now available is at best only marginally better than the cubicle rooms of the past. Finally, the composition of the homeless has changed dramatically. Thirty years ago old men were the majority among the homeless, with only a handful of women in that condition and virtually no families. The current homeless are younger and include a significant proportion of women [emphasis in original]. (Rossi 1989: 43–4)

Harris and Pratt (1993) state that the composition of working class house-          3
holds in Canada has altered significantly during this century. While boarders were common in such households until the end of the Depression, the vast majority of families currently live without a boarder or another family. And by 1991, almost a quarter of households were comprised of a single person (Novac 1995). Given the regressive effects of federal housing policy, Harris and Pratt suggest that we may be "returning to the housing arrangements typical of the early twentieth century" (Harris and Pratt 1993: 296). They note that while major public redevelopments that threaten neighbourhoods have been effectively challenged, gentrification processes continue unabated, and tenant rights are being lost. They also argue that government policy threatens one of the meanings attached to home—security and personal control.

> [F]or many Canadians, the home as place of security and personal control is intermingled with stress, related to lack of affordability and insecurity of tenure. Growing homelessness in many large urban centres represents the extreme experience of such insecurity; ethnographic reports suggest that it touches and transforms the core of personal identity. (*Ibid.*: 297)

## MEANINGS OF HOME AND HOMELESSNESS

Due to the shift of paid employment away from the house, the meaning of home has changed over the last century, and with this increased separation between home and work, the home has taken on new meanings (Harris and Pratt 1993). [4]

> It has become a haven for a family life protected from the stimulation and threat of the city. For the adult, it has become a refuge from an alienating and exhausting world of work, a place of security, privacy, and personal control. Third, it has become an important status symbol, a measure and symbol of personal success. (*Ibid.*: 281)

Women attach a variety of meanings to the concept "home," which include decent material conditions and standards, emotional and physical well-being, loving and caring social relations, control and privacy, and simply living/sleeping space. Consequently, homelessness is defined by the absence or inadequacy of these same qualities. This mixture of emotional, psychological, social and material aspects far surpasses the standard definitions of homelessness that focus on lack of physical shelter (Watson and Austerberry 1986). [5]

In their exploration of the meaning of home, Tomas and Dittmar (1995) argue that while current formulations suggest that the homelessness of women is a problem, and housing the solution, their findings suggest that housing is the problem, to which homelessness may well be a solution. Compared to securely housed working class women, the majority of moves in the housing history of homeless women had been made to avoid abuse and social service relocations. While all of the securely housed women could confidently define a difference in meaning between a "house" and a "home," most of the homeless women did not. They equated "home" with safety and security, the same terms used in the literature to define what housing means, and the two most salient features largely absent in homeless women's experience of housing. Residential instability per se did not sufficiently distinguish their experiences from that of the securely housed women, rather it was the pattern of abuse and relocation that marked the experience of homeless women. For homeless women, a house is someone else's house where other people live with you (dependence). The relationship between 'housing' as a place of safety and security and home as psychologically meaningful had been severed completely for these women. Physical and sexual abuse were particularly common when women depended on men for housing. Thus, the homeless women did not consider themselves homeless—they just lacked a place of safety and security. Their housing histories were marked by a dependence on others to provide [6] housing, coupled with residential instability arising from both abusive and disruptive episodes which began in childhood and continued into the present.

## REPRESENTATION AND DISCOURSE

It is probable that women have always been among the homeless, but the        7
gender pattern has varied. For example, among those who lacked designated settlement rights in 17th-century New England, and least likely to obtain public assistance, were "widows and children as well as disabled or aged adults, [who] were often 'warned' to leave town" (Rossi 1989: 17). In the 19th century, transient homelessness became masculinized, as well as institutionalized and segregated in cities in the form of "skid row" concentrations of businesses and services that catered to the basic needs of poor, "familyless workingmen" (*Ibid*.: 20–1). Skid row areas reached their peak during the early decades of the 20th century when the men living there provided a necessary pool of day workers who carried out heavy work, much of it in the shipping yards. Since the decline in homelessness during the 1960s, the gender and racial balance changed dramatically among the growing numbers of new homeless, and there was an absolute and proportional rise in the number who were female or racial minority. By the end of the 1980s, the North American public was familiar with the term "shopping bag ladies" as a reflection of urban life (O'Flaherty 1996), and homeless women were subjectified in various ways, not only through the popular media, but in expert, discourse as well (Fraser 1990).

According to Hoch (1986), homelessness discourse has incorporated        8
varied social meanings from the past that portray the homeless as vagrant, deviant, sick, or victim, all grounded in a cultural framework of the work ethic that remains intact. All of these interpretations are reflected in contemporary studies of the homeless, but most of the new homeless are defined as victims of the economy or sick. Certainly, there is a great deal of literature on mental illness and substance abuse among the homeless. Allen (1994) suggests that in the current developing discourse of homelessness, these people are viewed not only as victims but also as perpetrators of their circumstances.

Harris (1991) has explored several images of homeless women: as victim,        9
exile, predator, and rebel. She argues that the extreme dissonance aroused by the sight of homeless women "hunched over and clinging to the sides of city buildings" in contrast to the American dream image of a modern wife in the suburbs contributes to a definition of the homeless women as "other." Alienation and disaffiliation from the dominant culture, as well as self, mark the state of homelessness.

Susser (1993) interprets the New York City shelter system in terms of its        10
imposition of a female-headed household as the model for poor people who receive government subsidies, contrasting means-tested welfare provision with universal social security welfare programs that are based on a nuclear family model and designed to provide financial assistance to higher income households. She notes that access to the shelter system is largely determined by sex, age, mental status, and family structure, with separate barracks for

men and women. Susser argues that by separating fathers from mothers and their children, shelters are depriving mothers of their company and assistance with child care, which men are sometimes able to provide in the privately run "homeless" hotels.

> In spite of their official absence from statistics and measures of households among the poor, men were certainly present among the families of the homeless. As soon as the women with whom we worked were relocated to apartments, men appeared in their homes. But within the institutions, both hotels and transitional housing, men and young boys were relegated to the status of criminals and reduced to sneaking in illegally (in the hotels) or shut out altogether (in the transitional housing). . . . Thus, the overall impact of the shelter system was to separate households and undermine whatever co-operation or mutual responsibilities might have been developed among men, women and children. (Susser 1993: 278)

Allen (1994) similarly argues that such municipal shelter policies have a diverse effect on couples and undermine the stated goal of helping families. [11]

> Even when men are the mates or legal husbands of the women admitted to the shelter and the fathers of the children, men are separated from homeless women and children and are required to live somewhere else, in facilities for single men. If the main component of a home may be considered to be the family and the basic unit of the family, a couple, to separate a couple is to damage the integrity of families and homes. (*Ibid.*: 181)

And Passaro (1996) argues that men are "being written out of the picture of home" (*Ibid.*: 90), although her analysis stresses the preferential treatment given to homeless women within a context of favouring family formation and protection. [12]

There is no research on these aspects of shelter policies in Canada, however, one case has been reported of an immigrant woman who resisted the separation of her oldest son when she and two children were homeless (Nova 1996: 72). She was told that he would have to go to another shelter. The majority of shelters in Toronto do separate men and older male youth, except for the municipal family shelter which is obligated to house entire families, placing them in motels if necessary. [13]

## VICTIM OR AGENT

The literature on homelessness is divided on whether its causes are the result of personal failings or a combination of impersonal forces (Bentley 1996). While the former approach risks pathologizing homeless people, the latter may also be problematic in this regard. [14]

Ruddick argues that presentations of the homeless as victims of a host of interrelated structural causes have effectively countered the image of "homeless by choice, a vision which characterized the homeless as intractable or even happy in their situation" (1996: 166). While successful in this regard, she points out there is a problem with portraying the homeless as victims since "we confuse notions of structural victimization with those of personal, and by [15]

extension, political incapacities," which leads to the "conflation of the homeless with social pathologies" (*Ibid.*: 168). Ruddick contrasts the portrayal of
homeless as victims with homeless as agents, stating that the latter is accomplished by advocacy researchers,

> often working within a post modern or post structuralist framework, that has
> attempted to establish the role of the homeless as agents, by examining the
> way that the homeless, through their own acts, have attempted to confront
> their victimization, the ways they challenge received notions about who they
> are. (*Ibid.*)

This approach, however, has garnered concerns that homelessness would
thus be portrayed as an acceptable condition, normalized, possibly feeding
political inaction.

By referring to a critique of the women's shelter movement over the past       16
20 years, Ruddick suggests that there is an inherent tension between focusing
on broad political analysis or action and specific ameliorative work.

> [T]he response of women's shelters has moved away from wider political con-
> nection with the feminist movement, away from linking the need for women's
> shelters with wider systemic structures of sexism and patriarchy, and confin-
> ing the shelter industry—not with the intent to blame the victim, but rather
> with the intent of treating the victim, rehabilitating her to be able to return to
> what is considered a "normal and functioning (read homed) society."
> (Ruddick 1996: 169)

Her proposed solution to the dilemma of portraying the homeless as victims or
agents is to erase the division by addressing the homeless as active, creative and
thinking political agents, "to build a new vision of the homeless not as people
we must organize for, but as people we might organize with" (*Ibid.*: 170).

Baxter's (1991) discussions with a group of squatters in Vancouver            17
emphasizes the significance to them of being viewed as "radicals" challenging
the authority of private property, rather than "victims" or "helpless homeless" who are non-threatening. This distinction frames their agency and
involvement in a progressive political critique.

On the other hand, Farge (1989) has addressed the question of homeless       18
women's "freedom of choice," advising caution in the application of this concept. She notes that within extreme constraints, homeless women do have elements of choice, including that of avoiding hostels and remaining on the streets.

> To the women who "choose" to use hostels as a primary vehicle of housing,
> the pay-offs of safety, secure (if temporary) food and shelter, and the concern
> of other women for their welfare, outweigh the punitive aspects of hostel life.
> This fact is less a comment on the value of the hostels themselves than it is a
> statement about the impoverishment which our society is content to leave at
> the core of the lives of marginalized women. (*Ibid.*: 143)

Liggett suggests that the homeless experience a "social death" because         19
they are penniless and alienated from normal community and support systems; they are dishonoured, being difficult to look at; and common identifi-

cation of "the homeless with substance abuse, the deinstitutionalised mentally ill, minority groups, dirt and bad smells" are distancing mechanisms (Liggett 1991: 206). The homeless are not needed within an advanced capitalist structure. They form a "surplus population outside of the generative structures of society" (Ruddick 1996), however, they may serve an ideological function.

Liggett speculates that there is a social control element to homelessness in  20 postmodern society that operates in the interests of capital, with a powerful message especially for the working class.

> Productive activity in society can only continue if the orderly continuation of reproductive relations is assured (a hard working labor pool, the urban professional slave, for example). In pre-industrial society people were kept in their place by an ideology of natural order, which they helped to represent. In industrial society people are kept in their place by the promise that they could leave it. In postmodern society there is some basis for arguing that people are kept in their place by the fear that they might lose it (*Ibid.*).

Certainly there is a powerful stigma associated with being homeless.

> [A]ssigning the adjective 'homeless' to a given segment of the population is seen to suggest that they are persons *without a home*, persons who lack something essential in the sphere of human relations . . . Homeless families represent a social step down from families receiving welfare who have stable, albeit publicly subsidized housing. Several homeless mothers told me that this stigma is the worst part of being homeless. (Allen 1994: 179)

Drawing on Foucault's work on the particular importance of the fields of  21 medicine and the social sciences to the creation of contemporary Western discourse, Allen comments on the "enormous, recent attention to homelessness paid by medical and social scientists . . . virtually all of the work is written by medical professionals, psychologists, and psychiatrists, the 'experts' in this new field" (*Ibid.*: 183).

State-funded and directed agencies play a dominant role in determining  22 who falls outside the bounds of normal society, with an emphasis on "restoring docility" by a complex web of institutional responses that primarily regulates a particular segment of society (Farge 1987). While observing the public inquiry that followed the death of a homeless woman in Toronto, Farge described how the "picture of Drina which emerged from this process was not of a once-living, breathing woman, but of someone who had fallen 'under the jurisdiction' of various agencies of the state and whose life and death were now defined by these institutional relationships" (*Ibid.*: 22).

■  ■  ■

## Discussion and Writing Suggestions

1. While these passages investigate the situation of homeless women, can you think of other groups whose situation might be better understood if examined in isolation? (For example, looking at homeless people using

age or race as criteria.) Why is it sometimes useful to look at subgroups rather than the group as a whole?

2. Write a short summary of the piece.
3. Why are the authors concerned with defining the term "homelessness" both in relation to what it has meant and to how it is currently applied?

## NEWS READINGS: A "FINAL EXAM" ASSIGNMENT

In the final section of the chapter we present seven short pieces that look at issues of poverty and homelessness from different ideological perspectives. Try to relate the ideas expressed by any or all of these authors to what you have read earlier in the chapter, and then explain where they stand on the political spectrum, and why you think so.

# Who Makes the Clothes We Wear?
## The Price for Our Fashion Is Often Paid by Workers Laboring in Intolerable Conditions.

JESSE JACKSON

Would you spend $20 for a stylish Gap T-shirt if you knew it was made by       1
teen-age girls in El Salvador forced to work 18 hours a day in a sweatshop for about 16 cents a shirt?

Would you pay top dollar for designer fashions at Neiman Marcus that        2
were made by immigrant Thai women imprisoned behind barbed wire in forced-labor conditions?

Would you give Nike $80 for a pair of athletic shoes if you knew they       3
were made by teen-age girls in Indonesia working 60-hour weeks for less than Indonesia's miserable minimum wage? Would you buy them if you knew that one young woman who organized a strike to demand that Nike pay the statutory minimum wage in Indonesia was abducted, raped and murdered?

Across the world—including in the United States, the sweatshop is back       4
in the press. High-profit, high-profile, high-priced retailers have grown callous and uncaring about the inhuman working conditions of the desperate—here and abroad—who make their products. Private companies turn their backs as their subcontractors routinely trample the basic rights of their workers— speech, association, the right to organize, the right to a living wage, the right to a bathroom break, to healthy and safe work conditions, to overtime, the prohibition of child and slave labor. Desperate workers have been too weak to resist.

Look, for instance, at the conditions in El Monte, Calif. On Aug. 2,       5
government officials raided a sweatshop filled with immigrant Thai women

laboring for as little as 59 cents per hour for 16 to 22 hours a day. Discipline was enforced by threats of rape and beatings. The women were locked up day and night as they produced garments for Neiman Marcus, J.C. Penney and other U.S. retailers and manufacturers.

As these outrages have gained public attention, manufacturers and retailers are getting nervous. The $200 million or so that Nike spends each year to paste its symbol on everything from Pete Sampras at the U.S. Open to the Dallas Cowboy uniforms can be wasted by one powerful scandal that ignites consumers' moral sensibilities. "Just do it" is Nike's multimillion-dollar slogan. But many Americans, if informed of these sweatshop realities, just might not do it; and that has major clothing and shoe manufacturers terrified. A consumer time bomb has begun to tick.    6

Republicans are out of step with this growing popular concern. They are busy gutting what few government protections exist for working people. The budget to enforce U.S. labor laws and workplace health and safety is being slashed. Republicans are blocking efforts to codify minimal labor and environmental standards in global trade treaties and develop international investigation and reporting.    7

Their opposition isn't just about trimming "big government." They also oppose legislation that would empower workers to elect their own representatives to monitor workplace safety. Even House Speaker Newt Gingrich—self-styled Third Wave revolutionary—has had little to say about the growing consumer reaction.    8

Unions, consumer groups and human-rights organizations are expanding their monitoring of labor conditions here and abroad. Many citizens would happily join a groundswell to hold one of these global corporate behemoths accountable for how they treat the least of their workers. If consumers spurn just one popular brand name, the other companies will rush to clean up their act.    9

Then the companies will push for government regulation and policing as insulation against independent consumer movements. Gingrich will scurry to get in front of the parade. Conservatives will shelve opposition to big government and line up to pass the laws and codes of conduct that businesses want.    10

Practices like those in El Monte aren't about reasonable profit; they are about greed. These companies have grown arrogant in their global reach. Like true cynics, they know the price of everything and the value of nothing. In 1993, the labor cost to Nike for a pair of $80 sneakers was 12 cents; in 1994, the company had more than $4.3 billion in sales. Nike paid more to give shoes away in promotions than to pay 12,000 women in Indonesia who make them. Organizers estimate that 1% of the Nike advertising budget could double the wages paid to the women and lift them above the poverty line.    11

Nike and other global companies can afford minimal rights for their workers. Now informed consumers may begin to make the trampling of basic decency a whole lot more expensive than the cost of respecting it.    12

# The Criminalization of Homelessness

CELINE-MARIE PASCALE

In a misguided effort to deal with homelessness, an increasing number of U.S.      1
cities are criminalizing non-criminal behavior such as loitering and sleeping in
public. At least 50 cities are considering or already have adopted ordinances
that specifically target the behavior of homeless people, according to Michael
Stoops of the National Coalition for the Homeless.

Nowhere is this spate of new legislation more noticeable than in      2
California, where the homeless population is now estimated to include a million people. This estimate, made by the California Homeless and Housing
Coalition, is based on an extrapolation of AFDC assistance to homeless families. Within 15 recent months, eight municipalities in Southern California
passed anti-sleeping ordinances, according to an op-ed piece in the
Washington edition of the *Los Angeles Times* (Dec. 16, 1993). This desire to
legislate noncriminal behavior is evident in Northern California as well.

San Francisco, famous for its Matrix laws (a whole set of city ordinances      3
targeting the homeless), spent 450 police hours and $11,000 to arrest 15
people for begging in 1993, according to *The Progressive* (May 1994). This
past June, the city approved Proposition J, making it illegal to linger for more
than 60 seconds within 30 feet of an automatic teller in use. Although this
ordinance is said to protect residents from robberies, radio station KPFA
(June 9, 1994) reported that only 20 robberies were committed at ATMs in
San Francisco last year. Washington, D.C., passed a similar ordinance last
year, and copycat ones are pending in New York City and Berkeley.

Berkeley has been using trespassing laws to keep its sidewalks clear. The      4
San Francisco alternative weekly *Bay Guardian* (Dec. 29, 1993) quoted a
police spokesperson as saying that "the city considers the sidewalks in front
of stores to belong to the store owners." Berkeley's new anti-loitering law
applies to a one-block radius around laundromats, parks, recreation centers,
and other property; it's based on an individual's *intent* to buy, sell, exchange,
or use drugs. A person who refuses to leave the area when requested to do so
by police can be arrested and charged with a misdemeanor.

Santa Cruz has a reputation for progressive politics; the current mayor is      5
a war tax resister. Like other cities, however, Santa Cruz now arrests people
who sit on the sidewalk. Riot police in full gear were called out on May 11,
1994, to arrest a group of people for sitting on the sidewalk while they ate
free soup. Santa Cruz, which has about 250 shelter beds to serve a homeless
population almost ten times that size, also has a law that makes it illegal to
sleep out of doors or inside a vehicle.

Across the country, ordinances like these have been proposed and      6
advanced by merchants. So it isn't surprising to find that many businesses that
donate to nonprofits serving the homeless have made their continued support
contingent upon the nonprofits' speaking out against those who challenge the
ordinances. Five donors pressured a single agency in Santa Cruz.

In New York City, businesses have taken another tack. Katherine Gordy     7
writes in *In These Times* (April 4, 1994): "New York has launched ad campaigns that portray the housed, clad, and fed citizens whom panhandlers ask for help as victims who have every right to be selfish and annoyed." The number of homeless people in New York City is hard to comprehend; during *one month* of 1992, 14,000 *families* applied for public shelter, according to Jennifer Toth, author of *Mole People* (Chicago Review Press, 1993), a recent book about the people who live in the subways and other tunnels beneath New York City.

City governments tell us we need Matrix-type anti-homeless ordinances     8
because laws against harassment, assault, battery, theft, vandalism, and obstructing traffic do not protect businesses adequately. Why is that? The answer is that visible poverty, not criminal behavior, may be the greatest threat to business in the 1990s—or so many merchants believe.

Visible poverty does discourage shoppers—especially those out to spend     9
discretionary dollars that they could just as easily spend elsewhere. No one wants to run a gauntlet of panhandlers to get to a boutique or step over people sleeping on the sidewalk to buy a cappuccino. But neither do people want to live in the kind of poverty that leads to panhandling or sleeping on the sidewalk.

Henry Cisneros, secretary of housing and urban development, said on the     10
*MacNeil/Lehrer NewsHour* (May 16, 1994) that between 1985 and 1990, 7 million Americans experienced homelessness. Yet as a culture, we still want to believe that poverty is the fault of the individual rather than society.

Anti-sleeping, anti-sitting, and anti-panhandling ordinances reflect con-     11
cerns for the civil liberties of the fortunate rather than for the human rights of the destitute. People often defend their right to walk through a bus station without confronting beggars, but what about the basic human right to food and shelter?

The city of Berkeley is now considering an ordinance that would limit to     12
one shopping bag the number of belongings people can carry with them. Imagine having to discard half of your possessions because people with houses find it offensive that you need two shopping bags to contain your worldly goods.

## Now, They're Killing the Homeless

KATHY HARDILL

In the wee hours of June 5, Adrian Fillmore was found in the bus shelter he     1
called home, his throat cut. On May 28, a homeless woman about my age was shot in the head near a downtown apartment building. Casey Smith was only 40 years old. A few days before that, John Currie was found beaten to death at another downtown intersection.

These acts startle us in their brutality, perhaps make us shudder if we    2
think about them in too much detail. They should not, however, surprise us.
We know, for example, that young homeless men in Toronto are seven to
nine times more likely to be murdered than their housed counterparts, according to recent research conducted by Dr. Stephen Hwang.

These murders—ugly and brutal and stark—are only the most glaring    3
manifestations of a pervasive climate of hatred toward poor people generally, and homeless people quite specifically. Such carefully orchestrated perceptions are spun by politicians and bureaucratic "opinion makers," and
eagerly accepted by those of us who wish to believe that poor and homeless
people are some strange "other," fundamentally different from the rest of us,
and either responsible for their sorry lots or, better yet, deserving of their
tragic fates.

If you don't believe this, consider for a moment the following:    4

The city has refused to open enough shelters, leaving an estimated 1000    5
to 2000 people with no choice but to scramble for shelter wherever they can
find it—parks, ravines, garages, abandoned buildings. In a perverse Catch-22,
the city then says, "But remember, it's against the law to sleep outside."

Police have been directed to ensure that homeless people are removed    6
from public view. Presumably to drive that point home, a group of homeless
people were recently burned out of their site at Spadina Ave. and Lake Shore
Blvd. Imagine seeing everything you own in this world wilfully ignited and—
poof—gone.

Last summer, I met a homeless man whose sleeping bags were pepper-    7
sprayed by police during the much heralded Community Action Policing program. Does this sound like crime fighting activity to you? If that act was not
purely about harassment and intimidation, I don't know what is.

People who are unable to get into shelters then lose the meals that may go    8
with that and the few dollars a week they may get as a small allowance. Then
the city says (with the handy legislative help of the province), "But remember,
you can't beg for money or earn it by cleaning car windshields, and if you do,
the police will give you a fine."

To the general public, we hear the politicians say, "We will not toler-    9
ate people living in 'our' parks. We will not tolerate the use of parks as toilets"—at the same time as public washrooms in parks are locked after
hours. As if homeless people, these frightening "others," are so patently
uncivilized that they wander around wantonly despoiling the parks, choosing or, perhaps, even preferring to carry out the most basic private human
functions in public.

Urban planners design public spaces which are deliberately "unfriendly"    10
to homeless users. Perhaps you have noticed, for example, park benches with
those metal bars in the middle to prevent anyone from lying down on them.

The provincial government cancelled 17 000 units of affordable housing    11
under the guise of stamping out the so-called public housing "boondoggle."

It cut social assistance rates to force people off the so-called "free-ride" of welfare nirvana. It has made it easier to evict low-income tenants and created the misnamed "Safe Streets Act" which outlaws "aggressive panhandling and squeegeeing"—in effect, allowing municipalities to characterize survival at its most desperate level as a criminal act.

Federal homelessness minister Claudette Bradshaw recently breezed back    12
into town for another instalment of her government's funding shell game, re-announcing insufficient dollars which still have not flowed since they were first announced in December. The feds have an enormous budget surplus but are so caught up in ideological posturing about governments needing to get out of the housing business, that we still have no hint of the national housing strategy we so desperately need.

And so we watch the systematic inertia created by each level of govern-    13
ment comfortably pointing fingers at each other ad infinitum, keeping the media on a perpetual tail chase and advocates lobbying and demanding and pleading until we are hoarse.

Homeless people are being killed, because homelessness is an extremely    14
dangerous circumstance to be in. Whether one is murdered or not, it kills people at an alarming rate.

Stuart Mitchell died in February, 19 days after he had claimed he was    15
assaulted by police in St. Jamestown. Jennifer Caldwell died in March at the tender age of 20—20 years old—when her makeshift shelter burned in the Don River Valley. The body of one of my clients was pulled from Lake Ontario in early April. It is unknown whether he put himself in that cold water or was put there—but either way, he died a grim death.

The homeless people I know are frightened. They are frightened of stay-    16
ing outside, for fear of being harassed, arrested, ticketed, beaten. They are now frightened of being murdered or attacked while they sleep. They are afraid of crowded, disease ridden shelters.

One woman I know has multiple chronic health problems. She rightly    17
understands that she would be at risk of contracting infectious diseases inside shelters—so she prefers her odds on the street.

She will not tell anyone her real name because if she dies homeless, as she    18
is quite convinced she will, she does not want to bring shame to her family and friends by having her real name flashed through the media.

A newly homeless woman I spoke with after Fillmore's death told me that    19
in her worst, most paranoid moments, she can envision these recent murders as a campaign of terror to drive homeless people out of Toronto in order to secure the Olympic Games. She said, "I wouldn't put it past them. It's just unbelievable what they are doing to homeless people now. You know, one day all these homeless people are going to rise up, and fight back. And I want to be there when it happens."

Well, I told her, so do I. Because someone is killing homeless people, and    20
the killers deserve to pay for their crimes.

# The Stones Missed the Real Target

PAT CAPPONI

What's so terribly upsetting about the Queen's Park riot is that, as word of it   1
spreads across Canada, it will be greeted with relief and excitement by the
country's growing underclass. My own reaction, as a longtime activist with
anti-poverty and psychiatric-survivor groups, is more troubled. If people
think this is the way to go, there's more tragedy ahead.

Last Thursday I was at home and chanced to catch live coverage of the   2
riot on television. (Although mine is not much of a home—I've lived at what
Statistics Canada defines as "below the poverty level" off and on for most of
my adult life—at least I have a roof, a chair and a TV.)

At first, I admit, I too felt excitement. I recognized that someone felt the   3
urgency, someone cared to act. Governments refuse to take responsibility,
agencies and institutions are preoccupied with their own survival, and the
middle class clamours for attention to its own rights: the right to walk down
city sidewalks unmolested by the poor with their dirty hands thrust out; the
right to enjoy public parks without having to step in puddles of urine or
worse; the right to not be hounded by those who make lifestyle choices of
indigence or addiction.

But I also know that no one understands desperation until they have lost   4
their job, car, possessions and home: after they've found themselves on the
street, getting more beaten down and more exhausted every day, wandering
from agency to agency, talking to workers even more demoralized than they
are. What are their rights? They've lost those along with everything else. There
is a violence here and its impact is more shattering than stone-throwing.

Yet I think there is a difference between fighting for your rights and bar-   5
barously attacking people, even if they are armed and in uniform.

As I watched TV, a police officer caught my eye. He was out of shape, his   6
belly kind of hung over his belt, and he was scared. I'm not enough of a radical not to have empathized with him. Then I saw some jerk lob a chunk of
concrete right into the midst of the police. Good God, I thought, what if
someone were killed?

And then I saw a woman, in her 20s, her hands cuffed, about to be   7
pushed into a police car. There was an intensity on her face, a look that
showed that she had fought for what she believed in. Are people entitled to
fight for their lives? For the right to shelter and safety, for the right to work
and opportunity? Are people entitled to fight for self-respect?

Much of Canada has failed to come to grips with the need for affordable   8
housing, jobs and community development. In Ontario, the Harris government
has compounded this with punishingly heavy-handed cutbacks, workfare,
and increasingly tight welfare-eligibility requirements, combined with legislation to decrease the visibility of those afflicted. And Queen's Park asks
people to believe that these moves are good for the poor. It's the Big Lie.

Once being on welfare didn't mean you had nothing to offer. Now the 9
poor are rapidly becoming a different species from the rest of society. And
they know it. When people living on Toronto's streets die each winter it creates no public demand for action. It's easy to conclude that the Harris government is deliberately not taking action—perhaps hoping that, through
attrition, the problem will solve itself.

Into this vacuum comes the increasingly militant Ontario Coalition 10
Against Poverty and its ideology-bound leader, John Clarke. Those people in
the front lines at Queen's Park were prepared for battle, with mattresses and
rocks. Their deliberate and calculated baiting of police was reckless and disturbing. Targeting and dehumanizing the police is no more just or fair than
targeting and dehumanizing the poor. Violence is never an answer.

The really sad thing is, though I and others like me choose to work 11
within the system—and though we try to maintain discourse—we have not
been permitted to be any more effective than the stone-throwers.

## Children of Poverty

MARK NICHOLS with BRIAN BERGMAN,
SUSAN McCLELLAND, and JOHN DEMONT

Candace Warner, a jobless single parent, lives with her sons—two-month-old 1
Keo and 1-1/2-year-old Skai—in Winnipeg's run-down Wolseley district. The
product of an impoverished background, Candace, 24, struggles to pay the
apartment rent and feed and care for her children on about $1000 a month in
social assistance. "My sons need new clothes and things that I can't buy," she
says, "because I don't have the money." With Canada's once sturdy social
safety net badly frayed, the plight of Candace and her kids is not unusual.
According to a study released last week by the United Nations Children's
Fund—UNICEF (the organization long ago changed its name, but kept the old
acronym)—15.5 per cent of Canadians under 18 live in poverty. That relegated
Canada to 17th place in a ranking of 23 industrialized nations and prompted
demands for action. "Politicians talk about eradicating child poverty," said
Jean-Marie Nadeau, executive assistant at the New Brunswick Federation of
Labour. "Then they shut their big doors and the young are forgotten."

As it happened, publication of the UN study coincided with a Statistics 2
Canada report showing that a buoyant economy finally pushed 1998 family
incomes past levels recorded before the recession of the early 1990s, with
after-tax family incomes averaging $49 626. The numbers also showed the
gap between low-income and affluent Canadians steadily widening, leaving
3.7 million Canadians in straitened circumstances.

Income disparities figured prominently in the UNICEF study, which esti- 3
mated that 47 million impoverished children live in the world's 23 richest
countries. The report found the lowest rates of child poverty among northern

European countries with strong traditions of wealth redistribution. Sweden—with only 2.6 per cent of its children living in poverty—had the lowest rate, while Canada ranked behind France, Germany, Hungary, and Japan, but ahead of Britain, Italy, the United States and Mexico, in last place with a 26.2-per-cent child poverty rate.

The sometimes surprising findings were partly due to methodology—the    4 rankings were based on "relative poverty," defined as household income that is less than half of the national median. That meant nations like the Czech Republic and Poland, with high overall poverty rates, came out ahead of Canada, Britain and the United States, where higher average incomes and income disparities make more people relatively poor. "Canada reflects poorly in a relative measurement," said Marta Morgan, director of children's policy at Human Resources Development Canada, "because middle incomes in this country are quite high." Even so, when social advocacy groups use StatsCan's low-income cutoff as a measure of poverty, they generally estimate there were about 1.4 million poor children in Canada in 1997—a child poverty rate of 19.8 per cent that is well above UNICEF's.

The study's authors argued that even when children from families with    5 limited resources have the necessities of life, they suffer by being excluded from normal childhood activities. Linda Rowe, a single Halifax mother who stretches aid of about $1400 a month to support herself and two young sons, knows they are feeling that pinch. "Right now, I'm trying to borrow $20 so my kids can go on a school trip," she says.

With the years of stringent budget-cutting behind them, Ottawa and    6 some provinces have started to rebuild social supports that benefit low-income families. Finance Minister Paul Martin's February budget reduced taxes for families with children and earmarked $2.5 billion in additional funding for Ottawa's child tax benefit, which currently pays up to about $160 a month for children in low-income families. And after nearly three years of wrangling, federal-provincial talks on a proposed National Children's Agenda—that could usher in early childhood development and child-care programs—appeared to be moving ahead, with ministers agreeing to draft a policy framework by the fall. Even so, some provinces still insist that Ottawa will have to restore billions of dollars in lost health and social funding before the agenda becomes a reality—a stumbling block that could hold up long-overdue measures to help Canada's children.

## ■ SYNTHESIS ACTIVITIES

1. Write an article for a newsmagazine about the current political land-scape in Canada. Focus on the difference between Liberals and Conservatives, but include other political ideologies, such as those of the NDP, the Alliance, or the Bloc, indicating where ideological boundaries sometimes seem to blur. Don't take sides, but do your best to give an objective account of some of the key political debates and the kinds of arguments they have generated.

Draw upon Dickerson and Flanagan to begin defining the boundaries between the Liberals and Conservatives, but from there consult newsmagazines and journals for more up-to-the-minute and detailed descriptions of our current political landscape.

2. Write either (1) an objective newsmagazine article or (2) an editorial or argumentative article, drawing upon some of the selections included in the News Readings at the end of the chapter. You might want to begin this question as you did the first, by consulting Dickerson and Flanagan to develop a basic definition of the political spectrum in Canada; then use this as a yardstick to determine where along the political spectrum the various views expressed appear to be located, explaining your reasons for categorizing particular viewpoints under more general ideological headings.

   If you choose the first option for this assignment, your paper should be relatively objective. If you choose the second, explain why you advocate one set of positions and oppose the other. In developing your argument, you must do more than simply express your opinion; try to support your opinion with solid evidence and logical reasoning.

3. Select two or three authors represented in this chapter and compare and contrast their use of argument. Compare selections that have some common denominator—for example, subject matter, or position on the political spectrum, or type of argument, or use of language. For instance, you might look at articles that draw on outside sources (O'Reilly Fleming and the CMHC document) or the two on homelessness by Stackhouse and Layton. You might compare and contrast the kinds of evidence and logic used by Stackhouse and Layton to support their arguments and the types of language they use. Discuss the strategies that the authors use in advancing their cases and the effectiveness of their arguments.

4. Write a speech, either for the Prime Minister or a provincial premier, advocating a position and a recommended course of action on an aspect of the poverty issue addressed in this chapter. Draw upon the relevant selections in the chapter to obtain evidence and also to determine key points of ideological contention on the issue. Use a "concession" format to acknowledge and then respond to opposing points of view. (See outline, p. 195.)

5. You are a public relations consultant for either the Liberal, Conservative, Alliance, Bloc, or NDP party. Write a campaign or fund-raising letter designed for mass mailing to prospective voters that outlines your party's assessment of what causes poverty and an action plan for stopping these causes and ending poverty. (You may focus on the more specific issue of homelessness if you wish.) Draw upon other selections in the chapter, as appropriate, for evidence and talking points. Focus on why your programs and proposals deserve voter backing and why competing programs or proposals deserve rejection.

6. Some have observed of the media in Canada that they are generally soft on liberals and harder on conservatives. Journalists are often stereotyped as

ex-protesters—bleeding hearts who have championed left-wing causes—who use their writing to salve their own consciences and, perhaps, do some social good. Do the articles we have selected contain this sort of left-wing slant? If so, is it obvious or covert, and what forms of evidence can you cite to demonstrate your point? If you want to evaluate another source, you might look instead at your local paper(s) over a period of time (say a full week), to see if you can identify the presence—subtle or obvious—of a political perspective in the articles. Alternatively, with the same question in mind, you might consider whether a newsmagazine like *Maclean's* can be identified with a particular political perspective.

## ■ RESEARCH ACTIVITIES

1. Write an article of five pages for a newsmagazine on the ideological debate surrounding poverty and homelessness, representing views across the political spectrum. Try to be as objective as possible. Your job is to inform your readers of the nature of the debate, not to argue one side or another on any particular issue.

2. Prepare an *annotated bibliography* of sources, drawn from across the political spectrum, that address the issue of poverty. Write at least eight bibliographical entries: Include at least one magazine or newspaper article or editorial and one book or monograph report from left-wing publishers; include one article or editorial or book report from right-wing publishers. Use *APA* or *MLA format* for citations. Instead of arranging these citations alphabetically, however, arrange them into a political spectrum going from far right to far left—or vice versa. Thus, your bibliography could provide a detailed plan—in terms of both content and organization—for an actual paper dealing with the range of political positions and political rhetoric. Each entry should be one-half page to one page long.

   Identify each author's political position, using clues from affiliation with a particular research institute, book publisher, journal of opinion, party, or organization, as well as the discussions of political ideology in Dickerson and Flanagan. Give enough quotations to support your identification. In cases for which the author is not arguing from an identifiable position but only reporting facts, indicate which position the reported facts support, and explain how. (*Note:* Some newspapers or magazines have an identifiable political viewpoint in general, in their news and op-ed orientation, but also attempt to present other views at least some of the time. For example, *The Globe and Mail* is predominantly liberal, but often carries conservative op-ed columns, letters, etc. So you shouldn't assume that any article appearing in such a periodical will automatically have its predominant viewpoint; look for other identifying clues.)

3. As a member of a group of three or four, select one of the following scenarios:

- You are a member of an election (or re-election) campaign staff for a political candidate.
- You are a member of a citizen's action group that is working for the passage of a voter referendum.
- Some other comparable scenario of your own choosing.

Focus your efforts on the interaction of poverty with a particular controversial *domestic issue*—for example, affirmative action, immigration policy, abortion, education, law and order, health care, or drug policy. (If you are working for a political candidate, recognize that there may be other issues in the campaign, but imagine that this particular issue is the crucial one at this particular time.)

Produce *three reports* for the benefit of your candidate or your group:

- A background survey of the issue. What is the history of this issue, both in a social context and as it has affected recent political events and campaigns? (4–5 pp.)
- A survey and analysis of the *pro* and *con* arguments on the issue, as they have been articulated by recent commentators and political figures. Organize your discussion of these arguments and positions *along a political spectrum*, ranging from *extreme left* (or *right*) to *moderate* to *extreme right* (or *left*). If you have already prepared the annotated bibliography called for in the previous assignment, you may wish to use it as a basis for this section. (6–7 pp.)
- A set of *recommendations for strategy* based on your assignment of the most effective ways to proceed and for your side to prevail. Suggest effective *rhetorical* ways of promoting your side and attacking the other side. Suggest ways of using *language* for maximum effect. At the same time, suggest ways to avoid coming across as extreme in your position, ways by which your position might be perceived as the most reasonable one. (4–5 pp.)

4. Select one of the non-mainstream federal political parties—*Bloc, NDP,* or *Alliance*—and write a report on its philosophy and political activities in the past decade or so. Or research the Canadian Communist party. Check major newspaper and magazine indexes; check government documents; write to the parties themselves, asking for information. Who have been some of their candidates? What were their programs? How well have they done at election time? Has their popularity been increasing or decreasing?

5. Examine two or three successive issues of a magazine or journal at the left or right ends of the political spectrum and write an analysis of the kinds of positions authors of articles in these periodicals take on various issues, as well as the type of rhetorical devices they use to persuade their readers.

# 9

# Obedience to Authority

Would you obey an order to inflict pain on another person? Most of us, if confronted with this question, would probably be quick to answer: "Never!" Yet if the conclusions of researchers are to be trusted, it is not psychopaths who kill non-combatant civilians in wartime and torture victims in prisons around the world but rather ordinary people following orders. People obey. This is a basic, necessary fact of human society. As an author in this chapter has put it, "Obedience is as basic an element in the structure of social life as one can point to. Some system of authority is a requirement of all communal living."

The question, then, is not, "Should we obey the orders of an authority figure?" but rather, "To what *extent* should we obey?" Each generation seems to give new meaning to these questions. When senior Nazi officers were charged at Nuremberg with responsibility for crimes committed under their charge in concentration camps, they offered the defence that they were only following orders. During the Vietnam War, a number of American soldiers followed a commander's orders and murdered civilians in the hamlet of My Lai. In the 1990s the world was horrified by genocidal violence in Rwanda and in the former nation of Yugoslavia. These were civil wars, in which people who had been living for generations as neighbours suddenly, upon the instigation and orders of their leaders, turned upon and slaughtered one another.

Sadly, this phenomenon of brutal behaviour associated with group mentality is not only seen in wartime. In less dramatic ways, conflicts over the extent to which we obey orders surface in everyday life. How often have you read of people who claim they were just going along with the gang when they assaulted a teenager or terrorized an elderly person in the course of a home invasion? Perhaps you have found yourself going against your own better judgment in your school years to tease or bully a classmate because everyone else in your group of friends was doing it; if not, you almost certainly observed such behaviour. There may not have been any explicit order; the group may not even have a leader—but it had sufficient authority nonetheless to command obedience. At one point or another, you may face a moral dilemma at work. Perhaps it will take this form: The boss tells you to overlook File X in preparing a report for a certain client. But you're sure that File X pertains directly to the report and contains information that will alarm the client. What should you do? The dilemmas of obedience also emerge on some campuses with the rite of fraternity hazing. Psychologists Janice Gibson and Mika Haritos-Fatouros have made the startling observation that whether the obedience in question involves a pledge's joining a fraternity or a torturer's joining an elite military corps, the *process* by which one acquiesces to a superior's order (and thereby becomes a member of the group) is remarkably the same:

> There are several ways to teach people to do the unthinkable, and we have developed a model to explain how they are used. We have also found that college fraternities, although they are far removed from the grim world of torture and violent combat, use similar methods for initiating new members, to ensure their faithfulness to the fraternity's rules and values. However, this unthinking loyalty can sometimes lead to dangerous actions: Over the past 10 years, there have been countless injuries during fraternity initiations and 39 deaths. These training techniques are designed to instill obedience in people, but they can easily be a guide for an intensive course in torture.
>
> 1. *Screening to find the best prospects:* Normal, well-adjusted people with the physical, intellectual and, in some cases, political attributes necessary for the task.
> 2. *Techniques to increase binding among these prospects:* Initiation rites to isolate people from society and introduce them to a new social order, with different rules and values.
>
>     Elitist attitudes and "in-group" language, which highlight the differences between the group and the rest of society.
> 3. *Techniques to reduce the strain of obedience:* Blaming and dehumanizing the victims, so it is less disturbing to harm them.
>
>     Harassment, the constant physical and psychological intimidation that prevents logical thinking and promotes the instinctive responses needed for acts of inhuman cruelty.
>
>     Rewards for obedience and punishments for not cooperating.
>
>     Social modelling by watching other group members commit violent acts and then receive rewards.
>
>     Systematic desensitization to repugnant acts by gradual exposure to them, so they appear routine and normal despite conflicts with previous moral standards.[1]

In this chapter, you will explore the dilemmas inherent in obeying the orders of an authority. First, in a brief essay adapted from a lecture, British novelist Doris Lessing helps set a context for the discussion by questioning the manner in which we call ourselves individualists yet fail to understand how groups define and exert influence over us. Next, psychologist Solomon Asch describes an experiment he devised to demonstrate the powerful influence of group pressure upon individual judgment. Psychologist Stanley Milgram then reports on his own landmark study in which he set out to determine the extent to which ordinary individuals would obey the clearly immoral orders of an authority figure. The results were shocking, not only to the psychiatrists who predicted that few people would follow such orders but also to many other social scientists and laypeople—some of whom applauded Milgram for his fiendishly ingenious design, some of whom bitterly attacked him for uneth-

---

[1] "The Education of a Torturer" by Janice T. Gibson and Mika Haritos-Fatouros from *Psychology Today*, November 1986. Reprinted with permission from *Psychology Today* Magazine. Copyright 1986 Sussex Publishers, Inc.

ical procedures. We include one of these attacks, a scathing review by psychologist Diana Baumrind. Karen Messing then takes up another aspect of the motive for obedience demonstrated by Milgram's work: the unquestioning respect that people have for science and scientists. Next Philip Zimbardo reports on his famous (and controversial) Stanford Prison Experiment, in which volunteers exhibited astonishingly convincing authoritarian and obedient attitudes as they play acted at being prisoners and guards. An essay and two pieces of chillingly realistic fiction follow. In "Disobedience as a Psychological and Moral Problem," psychoanalyst and philosopher Erich Fromm discusses the comforts of obedient behaviour. In a passage from *The Handmaid's Tale*, Margaret Atwood shows how individual behaviour can be controlled by group participation in ritualized violence. In "The Lottery," Shirley Jackson tells the story of a community that faithfully meets its yearly obligation.

# Group Minds

## DORIS LESSING

*Doris Lessing sets a context for the discussion on obedience by illuminating a fundamental conflict: We in the Western world celebrate our individualism, but we're naive in understanding the ways that groups largely undercut our individuality. "We are group animals still," says Lessing, "and there is nothing wrong with that. But what is dangerous is . . . not understanding the social laws that govern groups and govern us." This chapter is largely devoted to an exploration of these tendencies. As you read selections by Milgram and the other authors here, bear in mind Lessing's troubling question: If we know that individuals will violate their own good common sense and moral codes in order to become accepted members of a group, why then can't we put this knowledge to use and teach people to be wary of group pressures?*

*Doris Lessing, the daughter of farmers, was born in Persia, now Iran, in 1919. She attended a Roman Catholic convent and a girls' high school in southern Rhodesia (now Zimbabwe). From 1959 through to the present, Lessing has written more than 20 works of fiction and has been called "the best woman novelist" of the postwar era. Her work has received a great deal of scholarly attention. She is, perhaps, best known for her* Five Short Novels *(1954),* The Golden Notebook *(1962), and* Briefing for a Descent into Hell *(1971). The jury that awarded her the Asturias Prize for literature in 2001 described her as "an impassioned freedom fighter, who has spared no effort in her commitment to Third World causes, through literature and the personal experience of a hazardous biography."[1]*

---

[1] Associated Press, "Top Literary Prize for 'Freedom Fighter' Lessing," *Winnipeg Free Press* B7, 9 June 2001.

People living in the West, in societies that we describe as Western, or as the       1
free world, may be educated in many different ways, but they will all emerge
with an idea about themselves that goes something like this: I am a citizen of
a free society, and that means I am an individual, making individual choices.
My mind is my own, my opinions are chosen by me, I am free to do as I will,
and at the worst the pressures on me are economic, that is, I may be too poor
to do as I want.

This set of ideas may sound something like a caricature, but it is not so       2
far off how we see ourselves. It is a portrait that may not have been acquired
consciously, but is part of a general atmosphere or set of assumptions that
influence our ideas about ourselves.

People in the West therefore may go through their entire lives never       3
thinking to analyze this very flattering picture, and as a result are helpless
against all kinds of pressures on them to conform in many kinds of ways.

The fact is that we all live our lives in groups—the family, work groups,       4
social, religious and political groups. Very few people indeed are happy as
solitaries, and they tend to be seen by their neighbors as peculiar or selfish or
worse. Most people cannot stand being alone for long. They are always seeking groups to belong to, and if one group dissolves, they look for another. We
are group animals still, and there is nothing wrong with that. But what is dangerous is not the belonging to a group, or groups, but not understanding the
social laws that govern groups and govern us.

When we're in a group, we tend to think as that group does: we may even       5
have joined the group to find "like-minded" people. But we also find our
thinking changing because we belong to a group. It is the hardest thing in the
world to maintain an individual dissident opinion, as a member of a group.

It seems to me that this is something we have all experienced—something       6
we take for granted, may never have thought about it. But a great deal of
experiment has gone on among psychologists and sociologists on this very
theme. If I describe an experiment or two, then anyone listening who may be
a sociologist or psychologist will groan, oh God not *again*—for they will
have heard of these classic experiments far too often. My guess is that the rest
of the people will never have heard of these experiments, never have had these
ideas presented to them. If my guess is true, then it aptly illustrates my general
thesis, and the general idea behind these talks, that we (the human race) are
now in possession of a great deal of hard information about ourselves, but we
do not use it to improve our institutions and therefore our lives.

A typical test, or experiment, on this theme goes like this. A group of       7
people are taken into the researcher's confidence. A minority of one or two
are left in the dark. Some situation demanding measurement or assessment is
chosen. For instance, comparing lengths of wood that differ only a little from
each other, but enough to be perceptible, or shapes that are almost the same
size. The majority in the group—according to instruction—will assert stubbornly that these two shapes or lengths are the same length, or size, while the
solitary individual, or the couple, who have not been so instructed will assert

that the pieces of wood or whatever are different. But the majority will continue to insist—speaking metaphorically—that black is white, and after a
period of exasperation, irritation, even anger, certainly incomprehension, the
minority will fall into line. Not always, but nearly always. There are indeed
glorious individuals who stubbornly insist on telling the truth as they see it,
but most give in to the majority opinion, obey the atmosphere.

When put as badly, as unflatteringly, as this, reactions tend to be incred-    8
ulous: "I certainly wouldn't give in, I speak my mind. . . ." But would you?

People who have experienced a lot of groups, who perhaps have observed    9
their own behavior, may agree that the hardest thing in the world is to stand
out against one's group, a group of one's peers. Many agree that among our
most shameful memories is this, how often we said black was white because
other people were saying it.

In other words, we know that this is true of human behavior, but how do    10
we know it? It is one thing to admit it, in a vague uncomfortable sort of way
(which probably includes the hope that one will never again be in such a testing situation) but quite another to make that cool step into a kind of objectivity, where one may say, "Right, if that's what human beings are like,
myself included, then let's admit it, examine and organize our attitudes
accordingly."

This mechanism, of obedience to the group, does not only mean obedi-    11
ence or submission to a small group, or one that is sharply determined, like a
religion or political party. It means, too, conforming to those large, vague, ill-
defined collections of people who may never think of themselves as having a
collective mind because they are aware of differences of opinion—but which,
to people from outside, from another culture, seem very minor. The underlying assumptions and assertions that govern the group are never discussed,
never challenged, probably never noticed, the main one being precisely this:
that it *is* a group mind, intensely resistant to change, equipped with sacred
assumptions about which there can be no discussion.

But suppose this kind of thing were taught in schools?    12

Let us just suppose it, for a moment. . . . But at once the nub of the prob-    13
lem is laid bare.

Imagine us saying to children, "In the last fifty or so years, the human    14
race has become aware of a great deal of information about its mechanisms;
how it behaves, how it must behave under certain circumstances. If this is to
be useful, you must learn to contemplate these rules calmly, dispassionately,
disinterestedly, without emotion. It is information that will set people free
from blind loyalties, obedience to slogans, rhetoric, leaders, group emotions."
Well, there it is.

■  ■  ■

## Review Questions

1. What is the flattering portrait Lessing paints of people living in the
   West?

2. Lessing believes that individuals in the West are "helpless against all kinds of pressures on them to conform in many kinds of ways." Why?

3. Lessing refers to a class of experiments on obedience. Summarize the "typical" experiment.

## Discussion and Writing Suggestions

1. Lessing writes that "what is dangerous is not the belonging to a group, or groups, but not understanding the social laws that govern groups and govern us." What is the danger Lessing is speaking of here?

2. Lessing states that "we (the human race) are now in possession of a great deal of hard information about ourselves, but we do not use it to improve our institutions and therefore our lives." First, do you agree with Lessing? Can you cite other examples (aside from information on obedience to authority) in which we do not use our knowledge to better humankind?

3. Explore some of the difficulties in applying this "hard information" about humankind that Lessing speaks of. Assume she's correct in claiming that we don't incorporate our knowledge of human nature into the running of our institutions. Why don't we? What are the difficulties of *acting* on information?

4. Lessing speaks of "people who remember how they acted in school" and of their guilt in recalling how they succumbed to group pressures. Can you recall such an event? What feelings do you have about it now?

# Opinions and Social Pressure

SOLOMON E. ASCH

*In the early 1950s, Solomon Asch (b. 1907), a social psychologist at Rutgers University in New Brunswick, New Jersey, conducted a series of simple but ingenious experiments on the influence of group pressure upon the individual. Essentially, he discovered, individuals can be influenced by groups to deny the evidence of their own senses. Together with the Milgram experiments of the following decade (see the following selections), these studies provide powerful evidence of the degree to which individuals can surrender their own judgment to others, even when those others are clearly in the wrong. The results of these experiments have implications far beyond the laboratory: They can explain a good deal of the normal human behaviour we see every day—at school, at work, at home.*

That social influences shape every person's practices, judgments and beliefs is    1
a truism to which anyone will readily assent. A child masters his "native" dialect down to the finest nuances; a member of a tribe of cannibals accepts cannibalism as altogether fitting and proper. All the social sciences take their

departure from the observation of the profound effects that groups exert on their members. For psychologists, group pressure upon the minds of individuals raises a host of questions they would like to investigate in detail.

How, and to what extent, do social forces constrain people's opinions and     2
attitudes? This question is especially pertinent in our day. The same epoch that has witnessed the unprecedented technical extension of communication has also brought into existence the deliberate manipulation of opinion and the "engineering of consent." There are many good reasons why, as citizens and as scientists, we should be concerned with studying the ways in which human beings form their opinions and the role that social conditions play.

Studies of these questions began with the interest in hypnosis aroused by     3
the French physician Jean Martin Charcot (a teacher of Sigmund Freud) toward the end of the 19th century. Charcot believed that only hysterical patients could be fully hypnotized, but this view was soon challenged by two other physicians, Hyppolyte Bernheim and A. A. Liébault, who demonstrated that they could put most people under the hypnotic spell. Bernheim proposed that hypnosis was but an extreme form of a normal psychological process which became known as "suggestibility." It was shown that monotonous reiteration of instructions could induce in normal persons in the waking state involuntary bodily changes such as swaying or rigidity of the arms, and sensations such as warmth and odor.

It was not long before social thinkers seized upon these discoveries as a     4
basis for explaining numerous social phenomena, from the spread of opinion to the formation of crowds and the following of leaders. The sociologist Gabriel Tarde summed it all up in the aphorism: "Social man is a somnambulist."

When the new discipline of social psychology was born at the beginning of     5
this century, its first experiments were essentially adaptations of the suggestion demonstration. The technique generally followed a simple plan. The subjects, usually college students, were asked to give their opinions or preferences concerning various matters; some time later they were again asked to state their choices, but now they were also informed of the opinions held by authorities or large groups of their peers on the same matters. (Often the alleged consensus was fictitious.) Most of these studies had substantially the same result: confronted with opinions contrary to their own, many subjects apparently shifted their judgments in the direction of the views of the majorities or the experts. The late psychologist Edward L. Thorndike reported that he had succeeded in modifying the esthetic preferences of adults by this procedure. Other psychologists reported that people's evaluations of the merit of a literary passage could be raised or lowered by ascribing the passage to different authors. Apparently the sheer weight of numbers or authority sufficed to change opinions, even when no arguments for the opinions themselves were provided.

Now the very ease of success in these experiments arouses suspicion.     6
Did the subjects actually change their opinions, or were the experimental victories scored only on paper? On grounds of common sense, one must question whether opinions are generally as watery as these studies indicate. There is some reason to wonder whether it was not the investigators who, in

their enthusiasm for a theory, were suggestible, and whether the ostensibly gullible subjects were not providing answers which they thought good subjects were expected to give.

The investigations were guided by certain underlying assumptions, which 7 today are common currency and account for much that is thought and said about the operations of propaganda and public opinion. The assumptions are that people submit uncritically and painlessly to external manipulation by suggestion or prestige, and that any given idea or value can be "sold" or "unsold" without reference to its merits. We should be skeptical, however, of the supposition that the power of social pressure necessarily implies uncritical submission to it: independence and the capacity to rise above group passion are also open to human beings. Further, one may question on psychological grounds whether it is possible as a rule to change a person's judgment of a situation or an object without first changing his knowledge or assumptions about it.

In what follows I shall describe some experiments in an investigation of the 8 effects of group pressure which was carried out recently with the help of a number of my associates. The tests not only demonstrate the operations of group pressure upon individuals but also illustrate a new kind of attack on the problem and some of the more subtle questions that it raises.

A group of seven to nine young men, all college students, are assembled 9 in a classroom for a "psychological experiment" in visual judgment. The experimenter informs them that they will be comparing the lengths of lines. He shows two large white cards [see Figure 1]. On one is a single vertical black line—the standard whose length is to be matched. On the other card are three vertical lines of various lengths. The subjects are to choose the one that is of the same length as the line on the other card. One of the three actually is of the same length; the other two are substantially different, the difference ranging from three quarters of an inch to an inch and three quarters.

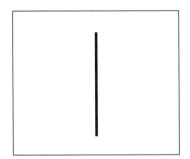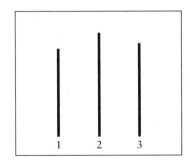

**FIGURE 1**

Subjects were shown two cards. One bore a standard line. The other bore three lines, one of which was the same length as the standard. The subjects were asked to choose this line.

The experiment opens uneventfully. The subjects announce their answers    10
in the order in which they have been seated in the room, and on the first
round every person chooses the same matching line. Then a second set of
cards is exposed; again the group is unanimous. The members appear ready
to endure politely another boring experiment. On the third trial there is an
unexpected disturbance. One person near the end of the group disagrees with
all the others in his selection of the matching line. He looks surprised, indeed
incredulous, about the disagreement. On the following trial he disagrees
again, while the others remain unanimous in their choice. The dissenter
becomes more and more worried and hesitant as the disagreement continues
in succeeding trials; he may pause before announcing his answer and speak in
a low voice, or he may smile in an embarrassed way.

What the dissenter does not know is that all the other members of the    11
group were instructed by the experimenter beforehand to give incorrect
answers in unanimity at certain points. The single individual who is not a
party to this prearrangement is the focal subject of our experiment. He is
placed in a position in which, while he is actually giving the correct answers,
he finds himself unexpectedly in a minority of one, opposed by a unanimous
and arbitrary majority with respect to a clear and simple fact. Upon him we
have brought to bear two opposed forces: the evidence of his senses and the
unanimous opinion of a group of his peers. Also, he must declare his judgments in public, before a majority which has also stated its position publicly.

The instructed majority occasionally reports correctly in order to reduce    12
the possibility that the naive subject will suspect collusion against him. (In only
a few cases did the subject actually show suspicion; when this happened, the
experiment was stopped and the results were not counted.) There are 18 trials
in each series, and on 12 of these the majority responds erroneously.

How do people respond to group pressure in this situation? I shall report    13
first the statistical results of a series in which a total of 123 subjects from three
institutions of higher learning (not including my own Swarthmore College)
were placed in the minority situation described above.

Two alternatives were open to the subject: he could act independently,    14
repudiating the majority, or he could go along with the majority, repudiating
the evidence of his senses. Of the 123 put to the test, a considerable percentage yielded to the majority. Whereas in ordinary circumstances individuals
matching the lines will make mistakes less than 1 per cent of the time, under
group pressure the minority subjects swung to acceptance of the misleading
majority's wrong judgments in 36.8 per cent of the selections.

Of course individuals differed in response. At one extreme, about one    15
quarter of the subjects were completely independent and never agreed with
the erroneous judgments of the majority. At the other extreme, some individuals went with the majority nearly all the time. The performances of individuals in this experiment tend to be highly consistent. Those who strike out
on the path of independence do not, as a rule, succumb to the majority even
over an extended series of trials, while those who choose the path of compliance are unable to free themselves as the ordeal is prolonged.

The reasons for the startling individual differences have not yet been    16
investigated in detail. At this point we can only report some tentative generalizations from talks with the subjects, each of whom was interviewed at the
end of the experiment. Among the independent individuals were many who
held fast because of staunch confidence in their own judgment. The most significant fact about them was not absence of responsiveness to the majority but
a capacity to recover from doubt and to reestablish their equilibrium. Others
who acted independently came to believe that the majority was correct in its
answers, but they continued their dissent on the simple ground that it was
their obligation to call the play as they saw it.

Among the extremely yielding persons we found a group who quickly    17
reached the conclusion: "I am wrong, they are right." Others yielded in order
"not to spoil your results." Many of the individuals who went along suspected that the majority were "sheep" following the first responder, or that
the majority were victims of an optical illusion; nevertheless, these suspicions
failed to free them at the moment of decision. More disquieting were the reactions of subjects who construed their difference from the majority as a sign of
some general deficiency in themselves, which at all costs they must hide. On
this basis they desperately tried to merge with the majority, not realizing the
longer-range consequences to themselves. All the yielding subjects underestimated the frequency with which they conformed.

Which aspect of the influence of a majority is more important—the size    18
of the majority or its unanimity? The experiment was modified to examine
this question. In one series the size of the opposition was varied from one to
15 persons. The results showed a clear trend. When a subject was confronted with only a single individual who contradicted his answers, he was swayed
little: he continued to answer independently and correctly in nearly all trials.
When the opposition was increased to two, the pressure became substantial:
minority subjects now accepted the wrong answer 13.6 per cent of the time.
Under the pressure of a majority of three, the subjects' errors jumped to 31.8
per cent. But further increases in the size of the majority apparently did not
increase the weight of the pressure substantially. Clearly the size of the opposition is important only up to a point.

Disturbance of the majority's unanimity had a striking effect. In this    19
experiment the subject was given the support of a truthful partner—either
another individual who did not know of the prearranged agreement among
the rest of the group, or a person who was instructed to give correct answers
throughout.

The presence of a supporting partner depleted the majority of much of its    20
power. Its pressure on the dissenting individual was reduced to one fourth:
that is, subjects answered incorrectly only one fourth as often as under the
pressure of a unanimous majority. The weakest persons did not yield as readily. Most interesting were the reactions to the partner. Generally the feeling
toward him was one of warmth and closeness; he was credited with inspiring
confidence. However, the subjects repudiated the suggestion that the partner
decided them to be independent.

Was the partner's effect a consequence of his dissent, or was it related to    21
his accuracy? We now introduced into the experimental group a person who
was instructed to dissent from the majority but also to disagree with the subject. In some experiments the majority was always to choose the worst of the
comparison lines and the instructed dissenter to pick the line that was closer
to the length of the standard one; in others the majority was consistently intermediate and the dissenter most in error. In this manner we were able to study
the relative influence of "compromising" and "extremist" dissenters.

Again the results are clear. When a moderate dissenter is present the    22
effect of the majority on the subject decreases by approximately one third, and
extremes of yielding disappear. Moreover, most of the errors the subjects do
make are moderate, rather than flagrant. In short, the dissenter largely controls the choice of errors. To this extent the subjects broke away from the
majority even while bending to it.

On the other hand, when the dissenter always chose the line that was    23
more flagrantly different from the standard, the results were of quite a different kind. The extremist dissenter produced a remarkable freeing of the subjects; their errors dropped to only 9 per cent. Furthermore, all the errors
were of the moderate variety. We were able to conclude that dissents *per se*
increased independence and moderated the errors that occurred, and that the
direction of dissent exerted consistent effects.

In all the foregoing experiments each subject was observed only in a    24
single setting. We now turned to studying the effects upon a given individual
of a change in the situation to which he was exposed. The first experiment
examined the consequences of losing or gaining a partner. The instructed
partner began by answering correctly on the first six trials. With his support
the subject usually resisted pressure from the majority: 18 of 27 subjects
were completely independent. But after six trials the partner joined the majority. As soon as he did so, there was an abrupt rise in the subjects' errors. Their
submission to the majority was just about as frequent as when the minority
subject was opposed by a unanimous majority throughout.

It was surprising to find that the experience of having had a partner and    25
of having braved the majority opposition with him had failed to strengthen
the individuals' independence. Questioning at the conclusion of the experiment suggested that we had overlooked an important circumstance; namely,
the strong specific effect of "desertion" by the partner to the other side. We
therefore changed the conditions so that the partner would simply leave the
group at the proper point. (To allay suspicion it was announced in advance
that he had an appointment with the dean.) In this form of the experiment,
the partner's effect outlasted his presence. The errors increased after his
departure, but less markedly than after a partner switched to the majority.

In a variant of this procedure the trials began with the majority unani-    26
mously giving correct answers. Then they gradually broke away until on the
sixth trial the naive subject was alone and the group unanimously against him.
As long as the subject had anyone on his side, he was almost invariably inde-

pendent, but as soon as he found himself alone, the tendency to conform to the majority rose abruptly.

As might be expected, an individual's resistance to group pressure in 27 these experiments depends to a considerable degree on how wrong the majority is. We varied the discrepancy between the standard line and the other lines systematically, with the hope of reaching a point where the error of the majority would be so glaring that every subject would repudiate it and choose independently. In this we regretfully did not succeed. Even when the difference between the lines was seven inches, there were still some who yielded to the error of the majority.

The study provides clear answers to a few relatively simple questions, and 28 it raises many others that await investigation. We would like to know the degree of consistency of persons in situations which differ in content and structure. If consistency of independence or conformity in behavior is shown to be a fact, how is it functionally related to qualities of character and personality? In what ways is independence related to sociological or cultural conditions? Are leaders more independent than other people, or are they adept at following their followers? These and many other questions may perhaps be answerable by investigations of the type described here.

Life in society requires consensus as an indispensable condition. But con- 29 sensus, to be productive, requires that each individual contribute independently out of his experience and insight. When consensus comes under the dominance of conformity, the social process is polluted and the individual at the same time surrenders the powers on which his functioning as a feeling and thinking being depends. That we have found the tendency to conformity in our society so strong that reasonably intelligent and well-meaning young people are willing to call white black is a matter of concern. It raises questions about our ways of education and about the values that guide our conduct.

Yet anyone inclined to draw too pessimistic conclusions from this report 30 would do well to remind himself that the capacities for independence are not to be underestimated. He may also draw some consolation from a further observation: those who participated in this challenging experiment agreed nearly without exception that independence was preferable to conformity.

■  ■  ■

## Review Questions

1. What is "suggestibility"? How is this phenomenon related to social pressure?
2. Summarize the procedure and results of the Asch experiment. What conclusions does Asch draw from these results?
3. To what extent did varying the size of the majority and its unanimity affect the experimental results?
4. What distinction does Asch draw between consensus and conformity?

## Discussion and Writing Suggestions

1. Before discussing the experiment, Asch considers how easily people's opinions or attitudes may be shaped by social pressure. To what extent do you agree with this conclusion? Write a short paper on this subject, drawing upon examples from your own experience or observation or from your reading.

2. Do the results of this experiment surprise you? Or do they confirm facts about human behaviour that you had already suspected, observed, or experienced? Explain, in two or three paragraphs. Provide examples, relating these examples to features of the Asch experiment.

3. Frequently, the conclusions drawn from a researcher's experimental results are challenged on the basis that laboratory conditions do not accurately reflect the complexity of human behaviour. Asch draws certain conclusions about the degree to which individuals are affected by group pressures based on an experiment involving subjects choosing matching line lengths. To what extent, if any, do you believe that these conclusions lack validity because the behaviour at the heart of the experiment is too dissimilar to real-life situations of group pressure on the individual? Support your opinions with examples.

4. We are all familiar with the phenomenon of "peer pressure." To what extent do Asch's experiments demonstrate the power of peer pressure? To what extent do you think that other factors may be at work? Explain, providing examples.

5. Asch's experiments, conducted in the early 1950s, involved groups of "seven to nine young men, all college students." To what extent do you believe that the results of a similar experiment would be different today? To what extent might they be different if the subjects had included women, as well, and subjects of various ages, from children, to middle-aged people, to older people? To what extent do you believe that the social class or culture of the subjects might have an impact upon the experimental results? Support your opinions with examples and logical reasoning. (Beware, however, of overgeneralizing, based upon insufficient evidence.)

## The Perils of Obedience

STANLEY MILGRAM

*In 1963, a Yale psychologist conducted one of the classic studies on obedience that Doris Lessing refers to in "Group Minds." Stanley Milgram designed an experiment that forced participants either to violate their conscience by obeying the immoral demands of an authority figure or to refuse those demands. Surprisingly, Milgram found that few participants could resist the authority's orders, even when the participants knew that following these orders would result in another person's pain. Were the participants in these experiments incipient mass murderers? No, said Milgram. They were "ordinary people, simply doing their jobs." The implications of Milgram's conclusions are immense.*

*Consider: Where does evil reside? What sort of people were responsible for the Holocaust, and for the long list of other atrocities that seem to blight the human record in every generation? Is it a lunatic fringe, a few sick but powerful people who are responsible for atrocities? If so, then we decent folk needn't ever look inside ourselves to understand evil since (by our definition) evil lurks out there, in "those sick ones." Milgram's study suggested otherwise: that under a special set of circumstances the obedience we naturally show authority figures can transform us into agents of terror.*

*The article that follows is one of the longest in this text, and it may help you to know in advance the author's organization. In paragraphs 1–11, Milgram discusses the larger significance and the history of dilemmas involving obedience to authority; he then summarizes his basic experimental design and follows with a report of one experiment. Milgram organizes the remainder of his article into sections, which he has subtitled "An Unexpected Outcome," "Peculiar Reactions," "The Etiquette of Submission," and "Duty Without Conflict." He begins his conclusion in paragraph 108. If you find the article too long to complete in a single sitting, then plan to read sections at a time, taking notes on each until you're done. Anticipate the article immediately following Milgram's: It reviews his work and largely concerns the ethics of his experimental design. Consider these ethics as you read so that you, in turn, can respond to Milgram's critics.*

*Stanley Milgram (1933–1984) taught and conducted research at Yale and Harvard universities and at the Graduate Center, City University of New York. He was named Guggenheim Fellow in 1972–1973 and a year later was nominated for the National Book Award for* Obedience to Authority. *His other books include* Television and Antisocial Behavior *(1973),* The City and the Self *(1974),* Human Aggression *(1976), and* The Individual in the Social World *(1977).*

Obedience is as basic an element in the structure of social life as one can point     1
to. Some system of authority is a requirement of all communal living, and it
is only the person dwelling in isolation who is not forced to respond, with
defiance or submission, to the commands of others. For many people, obedience is a deeply ingrained behavior tendency, indeed a potent impulse overriding training in ethics, sympathy, and moral conduct.

The dilemma inherent in submission to authority is ancient, as old as the     2
story of Abraham, and the question of whether one should obey when commands conflict with conscience has been argued by Plato, dramatized in
*Antigone,* and treated to philosophic analysis in almost every historical epoch.
Conservative philosophers argue that the very fabric of society is threatened by
disobedience, while humanists stress the primacy of the individual conscience.

The legal and philosophic aspects of obedience are of enormous import,     3
but they say very little about how most people behave in concrete situations.

I set up a simple experiment at Yale University to test how much pain an ordinary citizen would inflict on another person simply because he was ordered to by an experimental scientist. Stark authority was pitted against the subjects' strongest moral imperatives against hurting others, and, with the subjects' ears ringing with the screams of the victims, authority won more often than not. The extreme willingness of adults to go to almost any lengths on the command of an authority constitutes the chief finding of the study and the fact most urgently demanding explanation.

In the basic experimental design, two people come to a psychology laboratory to take part in a study of memory and learning. One of them is designated as a "teacher" and the other a "learner." The experimenter explains that the study is concerned with the effects of punishment on learning. The learner is conducted into a room, seated in a kind of miniature electric chair; his arms are strapped to prevent excessive movement, and an electrode is attached to his wrist. He is told that he will be read lists of simple word pairs, and that he will then be tested on his ability to remember the second word of a pair when he hears the first one again. Whenever he makes an error, he will receive electric shocks of increasing intensity.                                   4

The real focus of the experiment is the teacher. After watching the learner being strapped into place, he is seated before an impressive shock generator. The instrument panel consists of thirty level switches set in a horizontal line. Each switch is clearly labeled with a voltage designation ranging from 15 to 450 volts. The following designations are clearly indicated for groups of four switches, going from left to right: Slight Shock, Moderate Shock, Strong Shock, Very Strong Shock, Intense Shock, Extreme Intensity Shock, Danger: Severe Shock. (Two switches after this last designation are simply marked XXX.)          5

When a switch is depressed, a pilot light corresponding to each switch is illuminated in bright red; an electric buzzing is heard; a blue light, labeled "voltage energizer," flashes; the dial on the voltage meter swings to the right; and various relay clicks sound off.                                          6

The upper left-hand corner of the generator is labeled SHOCK GENERATOR, TYPE ZLB, DYSON INSTRUMENT COMPANY, WALTHAM, MASS. OUTPUT 15 VOLTS–450 VOLTS.                                                               7

Each subject is given a sample 45-volt shock from the generator before his run as teacher, and the jolt strengthens his belief in the authenticity of the machine.                                                              8

The teacher is a genuinely naïve subject who has come to the laboratory for the experiment. The learner, or victim, is actually an actor who receives no shock at all. The point of the experiment is to see how far a person will proceed in a concrete and measurable situation in which he is ordered to inflict increasing pain on a protesting victim.                                       9

Conflict arises when the man receiving the shock begins to show that he is experiencing discomfort. At 75 volts, he grunts; at 120 volts, he complains loudly; at 150, he demands to be released from the experiment. As the voltage increases, his protests become more vehement and emotional. At 285          10 volts, his response can be described only as an agonized scream. Soon thereafter, he makes no sound at all.

For the teacher, the situation quickly becomes one of gripping tension. It is not a game for him; conflict is intense and obvious. The manifest suffering of the learner presses him to quit; but each time he hesitates to administer a shock, the experimenter orders him to continue. To extricate himself from this plight, the subject must make a clear break with authority.[1]    11

The subject, Gretchen Brandt,[2] is an attractive thirty-one-year-old medical technician who works at the Yale Medical School. She had emigrated from Germany five years before.    12

On several occasions when the learner complains, she turns to the experimenter coolly and inquires, "Shall I continue?" She promptly returns to her task when the experimenter asks her to do so. At the administration of 210 volts, she turns to the experimenter, remarking firmly, "Well, I'm sorry, I don't think we should continue."    13

EXPERIMENTER: The experiment requires that you go on until he has learned all the word pairs correctly.    14

BRANDT: He has a heart condition. I'm sorry. He told you that before.    15

EXPERIMENTER: The shocks may be painful but they are not dangerous.    16

BRANDT: Well, I'm sorry, I think when shocks continue like this, they *are* dangerous. You ask him if he wants to get out. It's his free will.    17

EXPERIMENTER: It is absolutely essential that we continue. . . .    18

BRANDT: I'd like you to ask him. We came here of our free will. If he wants to continue I'll go ahead. He told you he had a heart condition. I'm sorry. I don't want to be responsible for anything happening to him. I wouldn't like it for me either.    19

EXPERIMENTER: You have no other choice.    20

BRANDT: I think we are here on our own free will. I don't want to be responsible if anything happens to him. Please understand that.    21

She refuses to go further and the experiment is terminated.    22

The woman is firm and resolute throughout. She indicates in the interview that she was in no way tense or nervous, and this corresponds to her controlled appearance during the experiment. She feels that the last shock she administered to the learner was extremely painful and reiterates that she "did not want to be responsible for any harm to him."    23

The woman's straightforward, courteous behavior in the experiment, lack of tension, and total control of her own action seem to make disobedience a simple and rational deed. Her behavior is the very embodiment of what I envisioned would be true for almost all subjects.    24

---

[1] The ethical problems of carrying out an experiment of this sort are too complex to be dealt with here, but they receive extended treatment in the book from which this article is adapted.

[2] Names of subjects described in this piece have been changed.

## AN UNEXPECTED OUTCOME

Before the experiments, I sought predictions about the outcome from various    25
kinds of people—psychiatrists, college sophomores, middle-class adults, graduate students and faculty in the behavioral sciences. With remarkable similarity, they predicted that virtually all subjects would refuse to obey the
experimenter. The psychiatrists, specifically, predicted that most subjects
would not go beyond 150 volts, when the victim makes his first explicit
demand to be freed. They expected that only 4 percent would reach 300
volts, and that only a pathological fringe of about one in a thousand would
administer the highest shock on the board.

These predictions were unequivocally wrong. Of the forty subjects in the    26
first experiment, twenty-five obeyed the orders of the experimenter to the end,
punishing the victim until they reached the most potent shock available on the
generator. After 450 volts were administered three times, the experimenter called
a halt to the session. Many obedient subjects then heaved sighs of relief, mopped
their brows, rubbed their fingers over their eyes, or nervously fumbled cigarettes.
Others displayed only minimal signs of tension from beginning to end.

When the very first experiments were carried out, Yale undergraduates    27
were used as subjects, and about 60 percent of them were fully obedient. A
colleague of mine immediately dismissed these findings as having no relevance
to "ordinary" people, asserting that Yale undergraduates are a highly aggressive, competitive bunch who step on each other's necks on the slightest provocation. He assured me that when "ordinary" people were tested, the results
would be quite different. As we moved from the pilot studies to the regular
experimental series, people drawn from every stratum of New Haven life
came to be employed in the experiment: professionals, white-collar workers,
unemployed persons, and industrial workers. *The experiment's total outcome was the same as we had observed among the students.*

Moreover, when the experiments were repeated in Princeton, Munich,    28
Rome, South Africa, and Australia, the level of obedience was invariably
somewhat *higher* than found in the investigation reported in this article. Thus
one scientist in Munich found 85 percent of his subjects to be obedient.

Fred Prozi's reactions, if more dramatic than most, illuminate the con-    29
flicts experienced by others in less visible form. About fifty years old and
unemployed at the time of the experiment, he has a good-natured, if slightly
dissolute, appearance, and he strikes people as a rather ordinary fellow. He
begins the session calmly but becomes tense as it proceeds. After delivering the
180-volt shock, he pivots around in his chair and, shaking his head, addresses the experimenter in agitated tones:

PROZI: I can't stand it. I'm not going to kill that man in there. You hear him    30
    hollering?
EXPERIMENTER: As I told you before, the shocks may be painful, but . . .    31
PROZI: But he's hollering. He can't stand it. What's going to happen to him?    32

EXPERIMENTER (*his voice is patient, matter-of-fact*): The experiment requires    33
that you continue, Teacher.

PROZI: Aaah, but unh, I'm not going to get that man sick in there—know    34
what I mean?

EXPERIMENTER: Whether the learner likes it or not, we must go on, through all    35
the word pairs.

PROZI: I refuse to take the responsibility. He's in there hollering!    36

EXPERIMENTER: It's absolutely essential that you continue, Prozi.    37

PROZI (*indicating the unused questions*): There's too many left here. I mean,    38
Jeez, if he gets them wrong, there's too many of them left. I mean, who's
going to take the responsibility if anything happens to that gentleman?

EXPERIMENTER: I'm responsible for anything that happens to him. Continue,    39
please.

PROZI: All right. (*Consults list of words.*) The next one's "Slow—walk, truck,    40
dance, music." Answer, please. (*A buzzing sound indicates the learner has
signaled his answer.*) Wrong. A hundred and ninety-five volts. "Dance."
(*Zzumph!*)

LEARNER (*yelling*): Let me out of here! My heart's bothering me! (*Teacher    41
looks at experimenter.*)

EXPERIMENTER: Continue, please.    42

LEARNER (*screaming*): Let me out of here! You have no right to keep me    43
here! Let me out of here, my heart's bothering me, let me out!

PROZI (*shakes head, pats the table nervously*): You see, he's hollering. Hear    44
that? Gee, I don't know.

EXPERIMENTER: The experiment requires . . .    45

PROZI (*interrupting*): I know it does, sir, but I mean—hunh! He don't know    46
what he's getting in for. He's up to 195 volts! (*Experiment continues,
through 210 volts, 225 volts, 240 volts, 255 volts, 270 volts, at which
point Prozi, with evident relief, runs out of word-pair questions.*)

EXPERIMENTER: You'll have to go back to the beginning of that page and go    47
through them again until he's learned them all correctly.

PROZI: Aw, no. I'm not going to kill that man. You mean I've got to keep    48
going up with the scale? No sir. He's hollering in there. I'm not going to
give him 450 volts.

EXPERIMENTER: The experiment requires that you go on.    49

LEARNER: Ohhh. I absolutely refuse to answer anymore. (*Shouting urgently    50
now.*) Let me out of here! You can't hold me here! Get me out. Get-me-
out-of-here!

EXPERIMENTER: Continue. The next word is "Green," please.    51

PROZI: "Green—grass, hat, ink, apple." (*Nothing happens. No answering    52
buzz. Just gloomy silence.*)

PROZI: I don't think he is going to answer.    53

EXPERIMENTER: If the learner doesn't answer in a reasonable time, about four    54
or five seconds, consider the answer wrong. And follow the same procedures you have been doing for wrong answers. Say, "Wrong," tell him the

number of volts, give him the punishment, read him the correct answer. Continue, please.

PROZI: "Green—grass, hat, ink, apple." Answer, please. (*More silence. Subject*    55
*just sits there.*)

EXPERIMENTER: Go on with the procedure, please.    56

PROZI: Three hundred and fifteen volts. The answer is "ink." (*Zzumph!*)    57

LEARNER: Ohh. Ooohh.    58

PROZI (*relieved to hear response*): Next one . . .    59

LEARNER: I absolutely refuse to answer.    60

PROZI: You got to. You get a shock if you don't answer. (*Experiment con-*    61
*tinues with learner refusing to answer, and finally, failing even to grunt or*
*groan. At 375 volts, the subject stands up.*)

PROZI: I think something's happened to that fellow in there. I don't get no    62
answer. He was hollering at less voltage. Can't you check in and see if he's
all right, please?

EXPERIMENTER: (*with same detached calm*): Not once we've started. Please    63
continue, Teacher.

PROZI (*sits down, sighs deeply*): "Cool—day, shade, water, paint." Answer,    64
please. Are you all right in there? Are you all right?

EXPERIMENTER: Please continue, Teacher. Continue, please. (*Subject pushes*    65
*lever. Zzumph!*)

PROZI (*swiveling around in his chair*): Something's happened to that man in    66
there. (*Swiveling back.*) Next one. "Low—dollar, necklace, moon, paint."
(*Turning around again.*) Something's happened to that man in there. You
better check in on him, sir. He won't answer or nothing.

EXPERIMENTER: Continue. Go on, please.    67

PROZI: You accept all responsibility?    68

EXPERIMENTER: The responsibility is mine. Correct. Please go on. (*Subject*    69
*returns to his list, starts running through words as rapidly as he can read*
*them, works through to 450 volts.*)

PROZI: That's that.    70

EXPERIMENTER: Continue using the 450 switch for each wrong answer.    71
Continue, please.

PROZI: But I don't get anything!    72

EXPERIMENTER: Please continue. The next word is "white."    73

PROZI: Don't you think you should look in on him, please?    74

EXPERIMENTER: Not once we've started the experiment.    75

PROZI: What if he's dead in there? (*Gestures toward the room with the elec-*    76
*tric chair.*) I mean, he told me he can't stand the shock, sir. I don't mean to
be rude, but I think you should look in on him. All you have to do is look
in on him. All you have to do is look in the door. I don't get no answer, no
noise. Something might have happened to the gentleman in there, sir.

EXPERIMENTER: We must continue. Go on, please.    77

PROZI: You mean keep giving him what? Four-hundred-fifty volts, what he's    78
got now?

EXPERIMENTER: That's correct. Continue. The next word is "white."  79

PROZI: (*now at a furious pace*): "White—cloud, horse, rock, house." Answer,  80
please. The answer is "horse." Four hundred and fifty volts. (*Zzumph!*)
Next word, "Bag—paint, music, clown, girl." The answer is "paint." Four
hundred and fifty volts. (*Zzumph!*) Next word is "Short—sentence,
movie . . ."

EXPERIMENTER: Excuse me, Teacher. We'll have to discontinue the experiment.  81

## PECULIAR REACTIONS

Morris Braverman, another subject, is a thirty-nine-year-old social worker. He  82
looks older than his years because of his bald head and serious demeanor. His
brow is furrowed, as if all the world's burdens were carried on his face. He
appears intelligent and concerned.

When the learner refuses to answer and the experimenter instructs  83
Braverman to treat the absence of an answer as equivalent to a wrong answer,
he takes his instruction to heart. Before administering 300 volts he asserts offi-
ciously to the victim, "Mr. Wallace, your silence has to be considered as a
wrong answer." Then he administers the shock. He offers half-heartedly to
change places with the learner, then asks the experimenter, "Do I have to
follow these instructions literally?" He is satisfied with the experimenter's
answer that he does. His very refined and authoritative manner of speaking is
increasingly broken up by wheezing laughter.

The experimenter's notes on Mr. Braverman at the last few shocks are:  84

> Almost breaking up now each time gives shock. Rubbing face to hide laugh-
> ter. Squinting, trying to hide face with hand, still laughing. Cannot control
> his laughter at this point no matter what he does. Clenching fist, pushing it
> onto table.

In an interview after the session, Mr. Braverman summarizes the exper-  85
iment with impressive fluency and intelligence. He feels the experiment may
have been designed also to "test the effects on the teacher of being in an
essentially sadistic role, as well as the reactions of a student to a learning situation that was authoritative and punitive." When asked how painful the
last few shocks administered to the learner were, he indicates that the most
extreme category on the scale is not adequate (it read EXTREMELY PAINFUL)
and places his mark at the edge of the scale with an arrow carrying it beyond
the scale.

It is almost impossible to convey the greatly relaxed, sedate quality of his  86
conversation in the interview. In the most relaxed terms, he speaks about his
severe inner tension.

EXPERIMENTER: At what point were you most tense or nervous?  87

MR. BRAVERMAN: Well, when he first began to cry out in pain, and I realized  88
this was hurting him. This got worse when he just blocked and refused to
answer. There was I. I'm a nice person, I think, hurting somebody, and

caught up in what seemed a mad situation . . . and in the interest of science, one goes through with it.

When the interviewer pursues the general question of tension, Mr.      89
Braverman spontaneously mentions his laughter.

"My reactions were awfully peculiar. I don't know if you were watching      90
me, but my reactions were giggly, and trying to stifle laughter. This isn't the way I usually am. This was a sheer reaction to a totally impossible situation. And my reaction was to the situation of having to hurt somebody. And being totally helpless and caught up in a set of circumstances where I just couldn't deviate and I couldn't try to help. This is what got me."

Mr. Braverman, like all subjects, was told the actual nature and purpose      91
of the experiment, and a year later he affirmed in a questionnaire that he had learned something of personal importance: "What appalled me was that I could possess this capacity for obedience and compliance to a central idea, i.e., the value of a memory experiment, even after it became clear that continued adherence to this value was at the expense of violation of another value, i.e., don't hurt someone who is helpless and not hurting you. As my wife said, 'You can call yourself Eichmann.'[3] I hope I deal more effectively with any future conflicts of values I encounter."

## THE ETIQUETTE OF SUBMISSION

One theoretical interpretation of this behavior holds that all people harbor      92
deeply aggressive instincts continually pressing for expression, and that the experiment provides institutional justification for the release of these impulses. According to this view, if a person is placed in a situation in which he has complete power over another individual, whom he may punish as much as he likes, all that is sadistic and bestial in man comes to the fore. The impulse to shock the victim is seen to flow from the potent aggressive tendencies, which are part of the motivational life of the individual, and the experiment, because it provides social legitimacy, simply opens the door to their expression.

It becomes vital, therefore, to compare the subject's performance when he      93
is under orders and when he is allowed to choose the shock level.

The procedure was identical to our standard experiment, except that the      94
teacher was told that he was free to select any shock level on any of the trials. (The experimenter took pains to point out that the teacher could use the highest levels on the generator, the lowest, any in between, or any combination of levels.) Each subject proceeded for thirty critical trials. The learner's protests were coordinated to standard shock levels, his first grunt coming at 75 volts, his first vehement protest at 150 volts.

---

[3] *Adolf Eichmann* (1906–1962), the Nazi official responsible for implementing Hitler's "Final Solution" to exterminate the Jews, escaped to Argentina after World War II. In 1960, Israeli agents captured him and brought him to Israel, where he was tried as a war criminal and sentenced to death. At his trial, Eichmann maintained that he was merely following orders in arranging murders of his victims.

The average shock used during the thirty critical trials was less than 60    95
volts—lower than the point at which the victim showed the first signs of discomfort. Three of the forty subjects did not go beyond the very lowest level
on the board, twenty-eight went no higher than 75 volts, and thirty-eight did
not go beyond the first loud protest at 150 volts. Two subjects provided the
exception, administering up to 325 and 450 volts, but the overall result was
that the great majority of people delivered very low, usually painless, shocks
when the choice was explicitly up to them.

This condition of the experiment undermines another commonly offered    96
explanation of the subjects' behavior—that those who shocked the victim at
the most severe levels came only from the sadistic fringe of society. If one considers that almost two-thirds of the participants fall into the category of
"obedient" subjects, and that they represented ordinary people drawn from
working, managerial, and professional classes, the argument becomes very
shaky. Indeed, it is highly reminiscent of the issue that arose in connection
with Hannah Arendt's 1963 book, *Eichmann in Jerusalem*. Arendt contend-
ed that the prosecution's effort to depict Eichmann as a sadistic monster was
fundamentally wrong, that he came closer to being an uninspired bureaucrat
who simply sat at his desk and did his job. For asserting her views, Arendt
became the object of considerable scorn, even calumny. Somehow, it was felt
that the monstrous deeds carried out by Eichmann required a brutal, twisted
personality, evil incarnate. After witnessing hundreds of ordinary persons
submit to the authority in our own experiments, I must conclude that Arendt's
conception of the banality of evil comes closer to the truth than one might
dare imagine. The ordinary person who shocked the victim did so out of a
sense of obligation—an impression of his duties as a subject—and not from
any peculiarly aggressive tendencies.

This is, perhaps, the most fundamental lesson of our study: ordinary    97
people, simply doing their jobs, and without any particular hostility on their
part, can become agents in a terrible destructive process. Moreover, even
when the destructive effects of their work become patently clear, and they are
asked to carry out actions incompatible with fundamental standards of morality, relatively few people have the resources needed to resist authority.

Many of the people were in some sense against what they did to the    98
learner, and many protested even while they obeyed. Some were totally convinced of the wrongness of their actions but could not bring themselves to
make an open break with authority. They often derived satisfaction from their
thoughts and felt that—within themselves, at least—they had been on the side
of the angels. They tried to reduce strain by obeying the experimenter but
"only slightly," encouraging the learner, touching the generator switches gin-
gerly. When interviewed, such a subject would stress that he had "asserted my
humanity" by administering the briefest shock possible. Handling the conflict
in this manner was easier than defiance.

The situation is constructed so that there is no way the subject can stop    99
shocking the learner without violating the experimenter's definitions of his
own competence. The subject fears that he will appear arrogant, untoward,
and rude if he breaks off. Although these inhibiting emotions appear small in

scope alongside the violence being done to the learner, they suffuse the mind and feelings of the subject, who is miserable at the prospect of having to repudiate the authority to his face. (When the experiment was altered so that the experimenter gave his instructions by telephone instead of in person, only a third as many people were fully obedient through 450 volts.) It is a curious thing that a measure of compassion on the part of the subject—an unwillingness to "hurt" the experimenter's feelings—is part of those binding forces inhibiting his disobedience. The withdrawal of such deference may be as painful to the subject as to the authority he defies.

## DUTY WITHOUT CONFLICT

The subjects do not derive satisfaction from inflicting pain, but they often like   100
the feeling they get from pleasing the experimenter. They are proud of doing a good job, obeying the experimenter under difficult circumstances. While the subjects administered only mild shocks on their own initiative, one experimental variation showed that, under orders, 30 percent of them were willing to deliver 450 volts even when they had to forcibly push the learner's hand down on the electrode.

Bruno Batta is a thirty-seven-year-old welder who took part in the vari-   101
ation requiring the use of force. He was born in New Haven, his parents in Italy. He has a rough-hewn face that conveys a conspicuous lack of alertness. He has some difficulty in mastering the experimental procedure and needs to be corrected by the experimenter several times. He shows appreciation for the help and willingness to do what is required. After the 150-volt level, Batta has to force the learner's hand down on the shock plate, since the learner himself refuses to touch it.

When the learner first complains, Mr. Batta pays no attention to him. His   102
face remains impassive, as if to dissociate himself from the learner's disruptive behavior. When the experimenter instructs him to force the learner's hand down, he adopts a rigid, mechanical procedure. He tests the generator switch. When it fails to function, he immediately forces the learner's hand onto the shock plate. All the while he maintains the same rigid mask. The learner, seated alongside him, begs him to stop, but with robotic impassivity he continues the procedure.

What is extraordinary is his apparent total indifference to the learner; he   103
hardly takes cognizance of him as a human being. Meanwhile, he relates to the experimenter in a submissive and courteous fashion.

At the 330-volt level, the learner refuses not only to touch the shock plate   104
but also to provide any answers. Annoyed, Batta turns to him, and chastises him: "You better answer and get it over with. We can't stay here all night." These are the only words he directs to the learner in the course of an hour. Never again does he speak to him. The scene is brutal and depressing, his hard, impassive face showing total indifference as he subdues the screaming learner and gives him shocks. He seems to derive no pleasure from the act itself, only quiet satisfaction at doing his job properly.

When he administers 450 volts, he turns to the experimenter and asks, 105 "Where do we go from here, Professor?" His tone is deferential and expresses his willingness to be a cooperative subject, in contrast to the learner's obstinacy.

At the end of the session he tells the experimenter how honored he has 106 been to help him, and in a moment of contrition, remarks, "Sir, sorry it couldn't have been a full experiment."

He has done his honest best. It is only the deficient behavior of the learn- 107 er that has denied the experimenter full satisfaction.

The essence of obedience is that a person comes to view himself as the 108 instrument for carrying out another person's wishes, and he therefore no longer regards himself as responsible for his actions. Once this critical shift of viewpoint has occurred, all of the essential features of obedience follow. The most far-reaching consequence is that the person feels responsible *to* the authority directing him but feels no responsibility *for* the content of the actions that the authority prescribes. Morality does not disappear—it acquires a radically different focus: the subordinate person feels shame or pride depending on how adequately he has performed the actions called for by authority.

Language provides numerous terms to pinpoint this type of morality: *loy-* 109 *alty, duty, discipline* all are terms heavily saturated with moral meaning and refer to the degree to which a person fulfills his obligations to authority. They refer not to the "goodness" of the person per se but to the adequacy with which a subordinate fulfills his socially defined role. The most frequent defense of the individual who has performed a heinous act under command of authority is that he has simply done his duty. In asserting this defense, the individual is not introducing an alibi concocted for the moment but is reporting honestly on the psychological attitude induced by submission to authority.

For a person to feel responsible for his actions, he must sense that the 110 behavior has flowed from "the self." In the situation we have studied, subjects have precisely the opposite view of their actions—namely, they see them as originating in the motives of some other person. Subjects in the experiment frequently said, "If it were up to me, I would not have administered shocks to the learner."

Once authority has been isolated as the cause of the subject's behavior, it 111 is legitimate to inquire into the necessary elements of authority and how it must be perceived in order to gain his compliance. We conducted some investigations into the kinds of changes that would cause the experimenter to lose his power and to be disobeyed by the subject. Some of the variations revealed that:

- *The experimenter's physical presence has a marked impact on his author-* 112 *ity.* As cited earlier, obedience dropped off sharply when orders were given by telephone. The experimenter could often induce a disobedient subject to go on by returning to the laboratory.
- *Conflicting authority severely paralyzes action.* When two experimenters 113 of equal status, both seated at the command desk, gave incompatible orders, no shocks were delivered past the point of their disagreement.

- *The rebellious action of others severely undermines authority.* In one   114
  variation, three teachers (two actors and a real subject) administered a test
  and shocks. When the two actors disobeyed the experimenter and refused
  to go beyond a certain shock level, thirty-six of forty subjects joined their
  disobedient peers and refused as well.

Although the experimenter's authority was fragile in some respects, it is   115
also true that he had almost none of the tools used in ordinary command
structures. For example, the experimenter did not threaten the subjects with
punishment—such as loss of income, community ostracism, or jail—for failure to obey. Neither could he offer incentives. Indeed, we should expect the
experimenter's authority to be much less than that of someone like a general,
since the experimenter has no power to enforce his imperatives, and since participation in a psychological experiment scarcely evokes the sense of urgency
and dedication found in warfare. Despite these limitations, he still managed
to command a dismaying degree of obedience.

I will cite one final variation of the experiment that depicts a dilemma   116
that is more common in everyday life. The subject was not ordered to pull
the lever that shocked the victim, but merely to perform a subsidiary task
(administering the word-pair test) while another person administered the
shock. In this situation, thirty-seven of forty adults continued to the highest
level on the shock generator. Predictably, they excused their behavior by
saying that the responsibility belonged to the man who actually pulled the
switch. This may illustrate a dangerously typical arrangement in a complex
society: it is easy to ignore responsibility when one is only an intermediate
link in a chain of action.

The problem of obedience is not wholly psychological. The form and   117
shape of society and the way it is developing have much to do with it. There
was a time, perhaps, when people were able to give a fully human response to
any situation because they were fully absorbed in it as human beings. But as
soon as there was a division of labor things changed. Beyond a certain point,
the breaking up of society into people carrying out narrow and very special
jobs takes away from the human quality of work and life. A person does not
get to see the whole situation but only a small part of it, and is thus unable to
act without some kind of overall direction. He yields to authority but in
doing so is alienated from his own actions.

Even Eichmann was sickened when he toured the concentration camps,   118
but he had only to sit at a desk and shuffle papers. At the same time the man
in the camp who actually dropped Cyclon-b into the gas chambers was able
to justify *his* behavior on the ground that he was only following orders from
above. Thus there is a fragmentation of the total human act; no one is confronted with the consequences of his decision to carry out the evil act. The
person who assumes responsibility has evaporated. Perhaps this is the most
common characteristic of socially organized evil in modern society.

■   ■   ■

## Review Questions

1. Milgram states that obedience is a basic element in the structure of social life. How so?
2. What is the dilemma inherent in obedience to authority?
3. Summarize the obedience experiments.
4. What predictions did experts and laypeople make about the experiments before they were conducted? How did these predictions compare with the experimental results?
5. What are Milgram's views regarding the two assumptions bearing on his experiment that (1) people are naturally aggressive and (2) a lunatic, sadistic fringe is responsible for shocking learners to the maximum limit?
6. How do Milgram's findings corroborate Hannah Arendt's thesis about the "banality of evil"?
7. What, according to Milgram, is the "essence of obedience"?
8. How did being an intermediate link in a chain of action affect a subject's willingness to continue with the experiment?
9. In the article's final two paragraphs, Milgram speaks of a "fragmentation of the total human act." To what is he referring?

## Discussion and Writing Suggestions

1. "Conservative philosophers argue that the very fabric of society is threatened by disobedience, while humanists stress the primacy of the individual conscience." Develop the arguments of both the conservative and the humanist regarding obedience to authority. Be prepared to debate the ethics of obedience by defending one position or the other.
2. Would you have been glad to have participated in the Milgram experiments? Why or why not?
3. The ethics of Milgram's experimental design came under sharp attack. Diana Baumrind's review of the experiment typifies the criticism; but before you read her work, try to anticipate the objections she raises.
4. Given the general outcome of the experiments, why do you suppose Milgram gives as his first example of a subject's response the German émigré's refusal to continue the electrical shocks?
5. Does the outcome of the experiment upset you in any way? Do you feel the experiment teaches us anything new about human nature?
6. Comment on Milgram's skill as a writer of description. How effectively does he portray his subjects when introducing them? When recreating their tension in the experiment?
7. Mrs. Braverman said to her husband: "You can call yourself Eichmann." Do you agree with Mrs. Braverman? Explain.
8. Reread paragraphs 29 through 81, the transcript of the experiment in which Mr. Prozi participated. Appreciating that Prozi was debriefed— that is, was assured that no harm came to the learner—imagine what

Prozi might have been thinking as he drove home after the experiment. Develop your thoughts into a monologue, written in the first person, with Prozi at the wheel of his car.

## Review of Stanley Milgram's Experiments on Obedience

DIANA BAUMRIND

*Many of Milgram's colleagues saluted him for providing that "hard information" about human nature that Doris Lessing speaks of. Others attacked him for violating the rights of his subjects. Still others faulted his experimental design and claimed he could not, with any validity, speculate on life outside the laboratory based on the behaviour of his subjects within.*

*In the following review, psychologist Diana Baumrind excoriates Milgram for "entrapping" his subjects and potentially harming their "self-image or ability to trust adult authorities in the future." In a footnote (p. 298), we summarize Milgram's response to Baumrind's critique.*

*Diana Baumrind is a psychologist who, when writing this review, worked at the Institute of Human Development, University of California, Berkeley. The review appeared in* American Psychologist *shortly after Milgram published the results of his first experiments in 1963.*

. . . The dependent, obedient attitude assumed by most subjects in the exper-    1
imental setting is appropriate to that situation. The "game" is defined by the experimenter and he makes the rules. By volunteering, the subject agrees implicitly to assume a posture of trust and obedience. While the experimental conditions leave him exposed, the subject has the right to assume that his security and self-esteem will be protected.

There are other professional situations in which one member—the patient    2
or client—expects help and protection from the other—the physician or psychologist. But the interpersonal relationship between experimenter and subject additionally has unique features which are likely to provoke initial anxiety in the subject. The laboratory is unfamiliar as a setting and the rules of behavior ambiguous compared to a clinician's office. Because of the anxiety and passivity generated by the setting, the subject is more prone to behave in an obedient, suggestible manner in the laboratory than elsewhere. Therefore, the laboratory is not the place to study degree of obedience or suggestibility, as a function of a particular experimental condition, since the base line for these phenomena as found in the laboratory is probably much higher than in most other settings. Thus experiments in which the relationship to the experimenter as an authority is used as an independent condition are imperfectly designed for the same reason that they are prone to injure the subjects involved. They disregard the special quality of trust and obedience with which the subject appropriately regards the experimenter.

Other phenomena which present ethical decisions, unlike those mentioned    3
above, *can* be reproduced successfully in the laboratory. Failure experience, conformity to peer judgment, and isolation are among such phenomena. In these
cases we can expect the experimenter to take whatever measures are necessary
to prevent the subject from leaving the laboratory more humiliated, insecure,
alienated, or hostile than when he arrived. To guarantee that an especially sensitive subject leaves a stressful experimental experience in the proper state sometimes requires special clinical training. But usually an attitude of compassion,
respect, gratitude, and common sense will suffice, and no amount of clinical
training will substitute. The subject has the right to expect that the psychologist
with whom he is interacting has some concern for his welfare, and the personal attributes and professional skill to express his good will effectively.

Unfortunately, the subject is not always treated with the respect he    4
deserves. It has become more commonplace in sociopsychological laboratory
studies to manipulate, embarrass, and discomfort subjects. At times the insult
to the subject's sensibilities extends to the journal reader when the results are
reported. Milgram's (1963) study is a case in point. The following is
Milgram's abstract of his experiment:

> This article describes a procedure for the study of destructive obedience in the
> laboratory. It consists of ordering a naive S to administer increasingly more
> severe punishment to a victim in the context of a learning experiment.[1]
> Punishment is administered by means of a shock generator with 30 graded
> switches ranging from Slight Shock to Danger: Severe Shock. The victim is a
> confederate of E. The primary dependent variable is the maximum shock the
> S is willing to administer before he refuses to continue further.[2] 26 Ss obeyed
> the experimental commands fully, and administered the highest shock on the
> generator. 14 Ss broke off the experiment at some point after the victim
> protested and refused to provide further answers. The procedure created
> extreme levels of nervous tension in some Ss. Profuse sweating, trembling,
> and stuttering were typical expressions of this emotional disturbance. One
> unexpected sign of tension—yet to be explained—was the regular occur-
> rence of nervous laughter, which in some Ss developed into uncontrollable
> seizures. The variety of interesting behavioral dynamics observed in the
> experiment, the reality of the situation for the S, and the possibility of para-
> metric variation[3] within the framework of the procedure point to the fruit-
> fulness of further study [p. 371].

The detached, objective manner in which Milgram reports the emotion-    5
al disturbance suffered by his subjects contrasts sharply with his graphic
account of that disturbance. Following are two other quotes describing the
effects on his subjects of the experimental conditions:

---

[1] In psychological experiments, *S* is an abbreviation for *subject; E* is an abbreviation for
*experimenter.*

[2] In the context of a psychological experiment, a *dependent variable* is a behavior that is
expected to change as a result of changes in the experimental procedure.

[3] *Parametric variation* is a statistical term that describes the degree to which information
based on data for one experiment can be applied to data for a slightly different experiment.

I observed a mature and initially poised businessman enter the laboratory smiling and confident. Within 20 minutes he was reduced to a twitching, stuttering wreck, who was rapidly approaching a point of nervous collapse. He constantly pulled on his earlobe, and twisted his hands. At one point he pushed his fist into his forehead and muttered: "Oh God, let's stop it." And yet he continued to respond to every word of the experimenter, and obeyed to the end [p. 377].

In a large number of cases the degree of tension reached extremes that are rarely seen in sociopsychological laboratory studies. Subjects were observed to sweat, tremble, stutter, bite their lips, groan, and dig their fingernails into their flesh. These were characteristic rather than exceptional responses to the experiment.

One sign of tension was the regular occurrence of nervous laughing fits. Fourteen of the 40 subjects showed definite signs of nervous laughter and smiling. The laughter seemed entirely out of place, even bizarre. Full-blown, uncontrollable seizures were observed for 3 subjects. On one occasion we observed a seizure so violently convulsive that it was necessary to call a halt to the experiment . . . [p. 375].

Milgram does state that,

After the interview, procedures were undertaken to assure that the subject would leave the laboratory in a state of well being. A friendly reconciliation was arranged between the subject and the victim, and an effort was made to reduce any tensions that arose as a result of the experiment [p. 374].

It would be interesting to know what sort of procedures could dissipate the type of emotional disturbance just described. In view of the effects on subjects, traumatic to a degree which Milgram himself considers nearly unprecedented in sociopsychological experiments, his casual assurance that these tensions were dissipated before the subject left the laboratory is unconvincing.

What could be the rational basis for such a posture of indifference?   6
Perhaps Milgram supplies the answer himself when he partially explains the subject's destructive obedience as follows, "Thus they assume that the discomfort caused the victim is momentary, while the scientific gains resulting from the experiment are enduring [p. 378]." Indeed such a rationale might suffice to justify the means used to achieve his end if that end were of inestimable value to humanity or were not itself transformed by the means by which it was attained.

The behavioral psychologist is not in as good a position to objectify his   7
faith in the significance of his work as medical colleagues at points of breakthrough. His experimental situations are not sufficiently accurate models of real-life experience; his sampling techniques are seldom of a scope which would justify the meaning with which he would like to endow his results; and these results are hard to reproduce by colleagues with opposing theoretical views. Unlike the Sabin vaccine,[4] for example, the concrete benefit to humanity of his particular piece of work, no matter how competently han-

---

[4] The Sabin vaccine provides immunization against polio.

dled, cannot justify the risk that real harm will be done to the subject. I am not speaking of physical discomfort, inconvenience, or experimental deception per se, but of permanent harm, however slight. I do regard the emotional disturbance described by Milgram as potentially harmful because it could easily effect an alteration in the subject's self-image or ability to trust adult authorities in the future. It is potentially harmful to a subject to commit, in the course of an experiment, acts which he himself considers unworthy, particularly when he has been entrapped into committing such acts by an individual he has reason to trust. The subject's personal responsibility for his actions is not erased because the experimenter reveals to him the means which he used to stimulate these actions. The subject realizes that he would have hurt the victim if the current were on. The realization that he also made a fool of himself by accepting the experimental set results in additional loss of self-esteem. Moreover, the subject finds it difficult to express his anger outwardly after the experimenter in a self-acceptant but friendly manner reveals the hoax.

A fairly intense corrective interpersonal experience is indicated wherein the subject admits and accepts his responsibility for his own actions, and at the same time gives vent to his hurt and anger at being fooled. Perhaps an experience as distressing as the one described by Milgram can be integrated by the subject, provided that careful thought is given to the matter. The propriety of such experimentation is still in question even if such a reparational experience were forthcoming. Without it I would expect a naive, sensitive subject to remain deeply hurt and anxious for some time, and a sophisticated, cynical subject to become even more alienated and distrustful.      **8**

In addition the experimental procedure used by Milgram does not appear suited to the objectives of the study because it does not take into account the special quality of the set which the subject has in the experimental situation. Milgram is concerned with a very important problem, namely, the social consequences of destructive obedience. He says,      **9**

> Gas chambers were built, death camps were guarded, daily quotas of corpses were produced with the same efficiency as the manufacture of appliances. These inhumane policies may have originated in the mind of a single person, but they could only be carried out on a massive scale if a very large number of persons obeyed orders [p. 371].

But the parallel between authority-subordinate relationships in Hitler's Germany and in Milgram's laboratory is unclear. In the former situation the SS man or member of the German Officer Corps, when obeying orders to slaughter, had no reason to think of his superior officer as benignly disposed towards himself or their victims. The victims were perceived as subhuman and not worthy of consideration. The subordinate officer was an agent in a great cause. He did not need to feel guilt or conflict because within his frame of reference he was acting rightly.      **10**

It is obvious from Milgram's own descriptions that most of his subjects were concerned about their victims and did trust the experimenter, and that their distressful conflict was generated in part by the consequences of these      **11** two disparate but appropriate attitudes. Their distress may have resulted from shock at what the experimenter was doing to them as well as from what they thought they were doing to their victims. In any case there is not a convincing parallel between the phenomena studied by Milgram and destructive obedience as the concept would apply to the subordinate-authority relationship demonstrated in Hitler's Germany. If the experiments were conducted "outside of New Haven and without any visible ties to the university," I would still question their validity on similar although not identical grounds. In addition, I would question the representativeness of a sample of subjects who would voluntarily participate within a noninstitutional setting.

In summary, the experimental objectives of the psychologist are seldom incompatible with the subject's ongoing state of well being, provided that the experimenter is willing to take the subject's motives and interests into consideration when planning his methods and correctives. Section 4b in *Ethical Standards of Psychologists* (APA, undated) reads in part:     12

> Only when a problem is significant and can be investigated in no other way is the psychologist justified in exposing human subjects to emotional stress or other possible harm. In conducting such research, the psychologist must seriously consider the possibility of harmful aftereffects, and should be prepared to remove them as soon as permitted by the design of the experiment. Where the danger of serious aftereffects exists, research should be conducted only when the subjects or their responsible agents are fully informed of this possibility and volunteer nevertheless [p. 12].

From the subject's point of view procedures which involve loss of dignity, self-esteem and trust in rational authority are probably most harmful in the long run and require the most thoughtfully planned reparations, if engaged in at all. The public image of psychology as a profession is highly related to our own actions, and some of these actions are changeworthy. It is important that as research psychologists we protect our ethical sensibilities rather than adapt our personal standards to include as appropriate the kind of indignities to which Milgram's subjects were exposed. I would not like to see experiments such as Milgram's proceed unless the subjects were fully informed of the dangers of serious aftereffects and his correctives were clearly shown to be effective in restoring their state of well being.[5]

---

[5] Stanley Milgram replied to Baumrind's critique in a lengthy critique of his own [From Stanley Milgram, "Issues in the Study of Obedience: A Reply to Baumrind," *American Psychologist* 19, 1964, pp. 848–851]. Following are his principal points:

- Milgram believed that the experimental findings were in large part responsible for Baumrind's criticism. He writes:

> Is not Baumrind's criticism based as much on the unanticipated findings as on the method? The findings were that some subjects performed in what appeared to be a shockingly immoral way. If, instead, every one of the subjects had broken off at "slight shock," or at the first sign of the learner's discomfort, the results would have been pleasant, and reassuring, and who would protest?

- Milgram objected to Baumrind's assertion that those who participated in the experiment would have trouble justifying their behavior. Milgram conducted follow-up questionnaires. The results, summarized in Table 1, indicate that 84 percent of the subjects claimed they were pleased to have been a part of the experiment.

**TABLE 1 Excerpt from Questionnaire Used in a Follow-up Study of the Obedience Research**

| NOW THAT I HAVE READ THE REPORT, AND ALL THINGS CONSIDERED . . . | DEFIANT | OBEDIENT | ALL |
|---|---|---|---|
| 1. I am very glad to have been in the experiment | 40.0% | 47.8% | 43.5% |
| 2. I am glad to have been in the experiment | 43.8% | 35.7% | 40.2% |
| 3. I am neither sorry nor glad to have been in the experiment | 15.3% | 14.8% | 15.1% |
| 4. I am sorry to have been in the experiment | 0.8% | 0.7% | 0.8% |
| 5. I am very sorry to have been in the experiment | 0.0% | 1.0% | 0.5% |

*Note*—Ninety-two percent of the subjects returned the questionnaire. The characteristics of the nonrespondents were checked against the respondents. They differed from the respondents only with regard to age; younger people were overrepresented in the nonresponding group.

- Baumrind objected that studies of obedience cannot meaningfully be carried out in a laboratory setting, since the obedience occurred in a context where it was appropriate. Milgram's response: "I reject Baumrind's argument that the observed obedience does not count because it occurred where it is appropriate. That is precisely why it *does* count. A soldier's obedience is no less meaningful because it occurs in a pertinent military context."
- Milgram concludes his critique in this way: "If there is a moral to be learned from the obedience study, it is that every man must be responsible for his own actions. This author accepts full responsibility for the design and execution of the study. Some people may feel it should not have been done. I disagree and accept the burden of their judgment."

## REFERENCES

American Psychological Association. Ethical standards of psychologists: A summary of ethical principles. Washington, D.C.: APA, undated.

Milgram, S. Behavioral study of obedience. *Journal of Abnormal and Social Psychology* 67, 1963, pp. 371–378.

■  ■  ■

## Review Questions

1. Why might a subject volunteer for an experiment? Why do subjects typically assume a dependent, obedient attitude?
2. Why is a laboratory not a suitable setting for a study of obedience?
3. For what reasons does Baumrind feel that the Milgram experiment was potentially harmful?
4. For what reasons does Baumrind question the relationship between Milgram's findings and the obedient behaviour of subordinates in Nazi Germany?

## Discussion and Writing Suggestions

1. Baumrind contends that the Milgram experiment is imperfectly designed for two reasons: (1) The laboratory is not the place to test obedience; (2) Milgram disregarded the trust that subjects usually show an experimenter. Do you agree with Baumrind's objections? Do you find them equally valid?

2. Baumrind states that the ethical procedures of the experiment keep it from having significant value. Do you agree?

3. Do you agree with Baumrind that the subjects were "entrapped" into committing unworthy acts?

4. Assume the identity of a participant in Milgram's experiment who obeyed the experimenter by shocking the learner with the maximum voltage. You have just returned from the lab, and your spouse asks you about your day. Compose the conversation that follows.

## The Scientific Mystique: Can a White Lab Coat Guarantee Purity in the Search for Knowledge About the Nature of Women?

KAREN MESSING

*Karen Messing is the director of Centre d'études des interactions biologiques santé/environnement (CINBOISE) and professor of Biological Sciences at the University of Quebec in Montreal. In this article, the author brings the issue of "blind obedience" into the realm of medical research, where, she argues, highly specialized scientists with a vested interest in pursuing their own research have inappropriate influence over other researchers and the general public.*

In the 1950s and 1960s, Yale professor Stanley Milgram reported results    1
from a series of experiments that shocked many academics.[1] In these experiments he asked his subjects to press a button which they believed delivered painful electric shocks to people, in an ostensible attempt to find out how much electricity the human body could stand. The "victims" were confederates of the experimenter and simulated increasing pain and anguish as the subjects thought they were intensifying the shocks. To Milgram's surprise, 20 per cent of the subjects could be induced to administer "shocks" that they believed were lethal, when told by the experimenter that the study required it. And if the investigator wore a lab coat, the percentage of "killer" subjects who would do this increased to 65 per cent. These experiments were commonly interpreted as showing that people are very obedient to authority. It is clear that they also demonstrate the tremendous respect lay people have for the authority of scientists and for scientific experiments.

Part of this scientific mystique comes from the image of science as the    2
search for objective truth, a pursuit of knowledge carried out in neutral sur-

roundings by disinterested observers. This view is based on a romanticism that most scientists do not actively discourage, but which has, as all of us engaged in science know, very little to do with reality.

In the present chapter I will show that the scientific community is in fact moulded by the society of which it is a part. Scientists, and the data we produce, are not and cannot be free from the prejudices, ideologies, or interests of the larger society. This lack of objectivity is manifested in the ways scientists are selected and in the scientific results themselves. The examples I use will relate primarily to the treatment of women[2] by the scientific community, but similar mechanisms affect working-class people, blacks, or other groups that are under-represented in the scientific establishment.

3

It will be useful to look at several components of the scientific process; they can be divided roughly into those relating to the scientists themselves and those pertaining to the process.

4

### The scientist
1. The selection of scientists
2. Their access to facilities for scientific work.

I will show that research scientists are a highly selected group whose interests are not typical of a cross section of society. This situation has a strong influence on the scientific process.

### The process
3. The choice of research topic
4. The wording of the hypothesis
5. The choice of experimental subjects
6. The choice of appropriate controls
7. The method of observation
8. Data analysis
9. The interpretation of data
10. The publication of results
11. The popularization of results

For each of these components, I will give examples of how the ideology and background of the researcher can influence the results, and how these results then become accepted scientific truth.

## THE SELECTION OF THE SCIENTIST

Many articles have been written lately on the difficulties facing women who want to be scientists. These barriers have been of various kinds: exploitation of women scientists,[3] undervaluing of their contributions,[4] and exclusion of them from "old-boy" communication networks.[5]

5

In addition, many women are cut off at the start by the forced choice between child bearing and graduate studies.[6] It usually takes eight to nine years of post-secondary education to get a PhD in the sciences. For a person to get through this, he or she must have a great deal of persistence and con-

6

fidence and either a good supply of money or the time to earn it. Financial needs go up and available time, of course, goes down when child care is involved. The demands of research can produce major conflicts for those of us with children. Chemical reactions, physical phenomena, and cell behaviour do not fit neatly into an eight-hour day. Therefore, the laboratory scientist must be available at all hours and often on weekends. The same is true of field work in ecology or geology, for example.

For this reason, conciliation of research schedules with child bearing and     7
child raising is nearly impossible to do well. At 5 p.m. just as one has finally got conditions for an experiment right, it is time to pick up the children. One has the unacceptable choices of rushing off to the day-care centre, thereby wasting the day's work, or making the phone calls to the day-care centre, arranging a sitter, changing the arrangements for supper, and staying to do the experiment, afterward facing one's own guilt and the eventual revenge of children and mate. The total exhaustion associated with this period is not conducive to creative work of any kind.[7] One of my graduate students supports her two children, aged 1 and 2, by taking part-time jobs. By the time she gets to the lab in the morning, she feels she has already put in a full work day,

The scientific community does not tolerate the temporary lowering of     8
productivity associated with child raising, although the years of graduate studies are also those in which most people have children. The Canadian NSERC fellowships for gifted students have an absolute limit of two years in which to obtain the Master of Sciences degree. While maternity leave (unpaid) is granted, no provision is made for a slower rhythm of work once the mother returns to the laboratory or field. If she takes longer than two years for the MSc, she can get no PhD support.

These conditions make it equally difficult for anyone to hold a part-time     9
job, so that the student who must earn money in order to stay in school faces the same problem as someone with family responsibilities.

## ACCESS TO FACILITIES FOR SCIENTIFIC WORK

Doing science requires space, equipment, and infrastructure. While some     10
world-shaking results have been obtained using minimal facilities, most modern biological endeavours, for example, are facilitated by the latest models of spectrophotometers, computer-assisted chromatography, scintillation counters, ultracentrifuges, and so on. Plenty of these machines are found in the top-rated universities, where up-and-coming scientists are hired to tenure track positions if they have been superstars in graduate school. Less successful scientists are found in underequipped universities and in less secure jobs, where even access to a laboratory may be a problem.

In the United States, female PhDs are more than four times as likely as     11
males to be unemployed and constitute only 6.6% of tenured PhD faculty in the sciences. Most of the scientific community is now white and male.[8] This is not to say that blacks or females necessarily would do neutral, non-sexist

research, but that science is done primarily by only certain people, who seek recognition from peers who are similar to them.

## THE CHOICE OF RESEARCH TOPIC

The choice of topic is influenced by several factors: the interest of the scientist, that of his or her present and future employers, and the ability to get funding for the work. Because of their sex and class, the large majority of scientists are less likely than the general population to be interested in such topics as the occupational exposures that present a risk to the nursing mother, alternate (non-hormonal) treatments for the discomforts of menopause, how a woman can give herself a safe (and, where necessary, secret) abortion, what work postures increase the likelihood of menstrual cramps, and how a low-income family can provide itself with nutritious meals. On the other hand, there is plenty of research, supported by drug companies, on drug therapy for menopausal women,[9] by government on what racial and income groups have the most abortions,[10] by employers on the relationship between women's physiological cycles and productivity,[11] and by private charity on how to prevent a rich, fat-laden diet from causing heart disease.[12]

12

## THE WORDING OF THE RESEARCH HYPOTHESIS

Articulating the hypothesis is crucial to the scientific method. Research is done in order to find an answer to a specific question, and the way the question is posed often determines the way the research will be carried out and how the eventual data will be interpreted. John Money and Anke Ehrhardt, for example, have done a good deal of research on whether prenatal hormone exposures explain sex-specific behaviours. In one study[13] they looked at children who have only one sex chromosome, an $x$, rather than the usual two ($xx$ for girls, $xy$ for boys), a condition that is called Turner's syndrome and is symbolized $xo$. Money and Ehrhardt hypothesized that since $xo$ children, like normal girls, are less exposed than males to prenatal androgens (so-called male hormones) they should be "feminine," just as normal $xx$ girls are. They defined "femininity" as not being a tomboy, preferring "girls' toys," wearing dresses rather than pants, being marriage-oriented rather than career-oriented in early adolescence, and so forth. By these criteria, their $xo$ subjects were indeed found to be even more feminine than normal $xx$ girls. It is unlikely that an investigator who was less accepting of present-day sex role stereotypes would have shaped the hypothesis this way, since she or he would consider "femininity" an inappropriate variable on which to study individuals with Turner's syndrome, who, though they have a vulva and not a penis, in fact lack most primary and all secondary female sexual characteristics. They are further distinguished by being unusually short, and many have a webbed neck and are mentally retarded. Hence, they probably have quite different social and biological experiences than

13

most ordinary girls. A more critical investigator might also question the criteria of "femininity" chosen by these authors.

The controversy surrounding *xyy* males a few years ago is a similar exam-    14
ple of a hypothesis that was based on a socially-defined point of view, this time
involving prejudice about males. Early investigators, finding a large number of
men with an extra male (*y*) chromosome in prisons, formulated the hypothesis that people who have an extra *y* chromosome (*xyy*) must be "supermales,"
which they took to mean that these people would be especially prone to violence. They failed to consider the fact that *xyy* males are unusually large,
slow, and somewhat retarded. Thus, it was only after much money and time
had been wasted that another hypothesis, that *xyy* males had the same chance
as other retarded males of being in prison, was tested and confirmed.[14]

## THE CHOICE OF EXPERIMENTAL SUBJECTS

The clearest example of bias in the choice of a study population is the simple    15
and extremely common exclusion of *women* from studies in which one wishes
to obtain information about *people*. In a study of occupational cancers in the
lead industry, all 950 women (but not blacks or short people) were excluded
in order to keep the sample uniform.[15] In another study, as reported by
Jeanne Stellman, 370 599 males were studied by the National Institutes of
Health, in order to identify risk factors for heart disease.[16] Heart disease is
also the leading cause of death in women, but women's risk factors were not
studied. In reporting the results of such studies, authors rarely state clearly
that they apply only to men.

Another way that a poor image of women (especially poor Third World    16
women) conditions research strategies is by a callous disregard for the welfare
of female subjects. For example, the birth control pill, though developed in
Massachusetts, was first tested in Puerto Rico. And in 1971, long after its efficacy had been established, Dr. Joseph Goldzieher decided to test the Pill once
more at his clinic. *Without their knowledge,* eighty of his 398 patients were
given placebos (pills that looked and tasted like the Pill but were ineffective)
instead of the Pill. All of the women chosen for this study had proven themselves fertile by having at least three previous children. Within a few months,
10 of the women who were receiving the fake pills had become pregnant with
unwanted fetuses.[17] Legal abortion was not available for these women.

## THE CHOICE OF APPROPRIATE CONTROLS

The choice of controls is probably the factor that has the most influence on    17
research results. Our research group was recently confronted with this issue
when trying to determine whether rates of congenital malformations were
higher than usual among the offspring of men occupationally exposed to a
radioactive dust. These men lived near the factory, which discharged its
untreated effluent into the air. If we used neighbours as controls, we would
underestimate the effects of *factory*-caused exposures, since both groups

would have some exposure to the dust. If we used as controls people who lived elsewhere, the measured effect might be greater, but we would be unable to identify the proportion due to specifically occupational exposures. Yet the usefulness of the results in bargaining with employers might be enhanced, because of the greater difference between the workers and the unexposed control population.

A glaring example of a poor choice of control group comes from a study of the effects of occupational exposure to radium.[18] Sharpe examined the incidence of stillbirths and miscarriages among female workers exposed to radium and compared them to pregnancy outcomes of the wives of their male co-workers, calling this "a not unreasonable control group." Not unreasonable, that is, if one forgets that males can also suffer genetic damage from radium exposure and pass it on to their children. The common idea that child bearing is an exclusively female province may account for Sharpe's forgetfulness.

Another example of the selection of a control group by sex-biased assumptions occurred at a seminar given in 1977 at the Université du Québec by an ethologist from the Université de Rennes in France. The speaker described a study of the mating behaviour of large mammals, in which three female goats, sheep, or cows were tethered in separate stalls and offered serially to 100 males. The subsequent pawing, sniffing, and copulatory behaviour of the males was recorded. When asked why 100 males were necessary, the speaker replied that it was necessary to observe the full range of behaviour. When asked why, in that case, there were only three females, he answered, "To keep the conditions standard." In studying the most bilateral of behaviours, sexual intercourse, a feminist would find it less reasonable to select females to represent "standard conditions" and males to study the "range of behaviour." She would assume that results would be as skewed by the choice of a limited number of individuals of one sex as of the other.

## THE METHOD OF OBSERVATION

The data an investigator collects are affected by the choice of tools (questionnaires, interview schedules, observations, biochemical tests) and the data that are considered valid and relevant. Ideology can affect all of these.

For example, in their study of the prevalence of warts among poultry slaughter-house workers, Mergler, Vezina and Beauvais[19] recorded the incidence by asking workers on a questionnaire how many warts they had. The study showed that workers who reported that they worked with saws, that their workplace was humid, and/or that their protective gloves did not fit correctly had a significantly higher incidence of warts. During a presentation of these results at a scientific meeting, the study was criticized on the basis that the workers were incompetent to count their warts and that counting should be done by a qualified medical practitioner. This criticism ignored the fact that doctors are in general less familiar with these warts than are the affected workers, some of whom had upwards of a hundred warts on their hands.

Crucial data can also be ignored because of ideological bias. In a 1963    22
study of the effect of work on pregnancy outcome by the U.S. Public Health
Service, the worker's *husband's* occupation was recorded, but that of the
pregnant worker herself was not.[20] This expensive study was thus useless for
identifying working conditions that pose a risk to pregnant women and their
fetuses, and the absence of such data has rendered protection very difficult.[21]
Nevertheless, a recent (1980) study of the causes of premature delivery did not
even include in its parameters the question of *whether* the mother was
employed, let alone her particular occupation.[22] The bias that blinds investigators to the fact that many married women work outside the home prevents
research results from helping employed women.

A methodological weakness found in many studies of sex-specific behav-    23
iour is the reliance on a single observer who is aware of the hypothesis being
tested, and who may therefore be biased. The Money and Ehrhardt studies,[23]
for example, compared girls of various hormonal statuses with respect to
"femininity" on the basis of an interview with a single counsellor who knew
the girl's history. Another example of a single-observer study comes from
sociobiology. David Barash formulated the hypothesis that male ducks rape
females because the males need to ensure a maximal number of descendants
to maximize their own "reproductive success." Based on this, he predicted
that a female who had been raped by a strange male would be re-raped as
soon as possible by her usual consort (ducks live in couples). To test this complex hypothesis, Barash (alone) observed mallards for 558 hours, decided
(alone) which male ducks were "husbands" and which were "strangers,"
and also which copulations were rape and which were mutually desired, he
found, unsurprisingly, that his observations squared with his hypothesis.[24]

Even when experiments are performed under controlled laboratory con-    24
ditions, observers may be biased by their political or social interests. A technical study of the chromosomes (hereditary material) of people exposed to
industrial pollutants ran into this problem. For many years, the Hooker
Chemical company discharged waste products into Love Canal, New York.
Residents noticed a high rate of congenital malformations and illness among
their children and pets and asked the Environmental Protection Agency to do
a study. Eleven of 37 residents were found to have abnormal-looking chromosomes. When the residents demanded to be evaluated, a review panel was
set up to look at the chromosomes. The panel did not see the same abnormalities as the EPA.[25] Thus started a long exchange in the pages of scientific
journals. Each side has its scientists, but the scientists on the two sides did not
perceive the chromosomes on the microscope slides in the same way.

## DATA ANALYSIS

There is a large literature on "demand characteristics" of experimental situ-    25
ations; that is, the tendency of experimenters, their subjects, and their research
assistants to produce by unconscious manipulations the data desired by the
investigator.[26] Steven Gould has illustrated this point in his re-analysis of

data on cranial capacity of different races, showing how a distinguished 19th century investigator manipulated his data to prove (incorrectly) that blacks had smaller brains than whites.[27] Another study of experimenter bias showed that research assistants made three times as many errors in arithmetic that favoured the chief's hypothesis as errors that went against it.[28]

Few non-scientists are aware of how many simple errors can be found in the scientific literature and in well-known, respected journals. For instance, the previously cited Money and Ehrhardt article used a statistical (chi-square) test under conditions where the use of this test is forbidden by elementary statistics texts (too many expected values were less than five). The Barash study contained an arithmetic error that rendered results statistically significant, in that the probability of the situation occurring by chance is given as less than .001, when the data in fact yield a probability of its occurring through chance alone as greater than .05.

There are also instances of intentional mis-analyses of data. A case that has recently come to light is that of Sir Cyril Burt, a prominent British psychologist and educational planner, who is now known to have manipulated data supposedly collected from twins reared apart so as to demonstrate a strong genetic component in IQ.[29] The fact that it took nearly 50 years for Burt's deceptions to be revealed is perhaps evidence that his conclusions, used for many years to argue for racial and class differences in intelligence, agreed so closely with widely held prejudices that a critical eye was never cast on the data.

## THE INTERPRETATION OF DATA

One of the major questions in the occupational health and safety field, as well as in the anti-nuclear movement, is the degree of genetic damage induced by low levels of ionizing radiation. In Quebec, a case is under arbitration in which a radiodiagnostic technician applied for leave with pay during her pregnancy in accordance with a contract clause that provides for such leave if working conditions endanger a fetus. The employer argued that radiation below a certain threshold level poses no problem for the fetus; the union argued that there is no threshold, and that any exposure is associated with some probability of damage.[30] Scientists were found to testify on both sides, since the argument turns on the extrapolation of a particular dose-responsive curve, for which it is prohibitively time-consuming and expensive to obtain complete data to the lowest possible doses.[31,32] Scientists testifying on behalf of the union or the employer interpreted the same data in opposite ways; each found that the data supported the contention of her or his side.

There are many such cases where interpretation of data depends on one's point of view; the controversies about race and IQ,[33] about male "genes" for mathematical ability,[34] and about the effectiveness of chemical spraying in insect control[35] are examples of areas where all intensive research effort has not succeeded in settling a scientific question, owing to the involvement of opposing groups with a vested economic or social interest in opposite conclusions.

## THE PUBLICATION OF RESULTS

After writing up the research results, the scientist submits a paper to a jour-    30
nal, which sends it to a few people working in the same field for review. This
process is meant to guarantee that no slipshod work is published, that errors
will be corrected, and that worthy articles find an audience. In practice the
system is far from ideal. Once a scientist has made a name, he or she (though,
of course, usually he) can often get an article published quickly after only perfunctory review. Less well-known scientists can have considerably more difficulty, especially if their results depart from accepted dogma.

Results that reinforce prevalent biases are often accepted without ques-    31
tion. For example, recently, the anthropologist C. O. Lovejoy published an
article in *Science* with the ambitious title "The Origin of Man."[36] Some weeks
later, he informed the journalists that he had played a little joke. He had
stated in his discussion that "the human female is continually sexually recep-
tive." As authority for this statement he cited not research results, but "D. C.
Johannsen, personal communication." This is the learned equivalent of
saying, "My buddy told me in the locker room." Presumably because the original statement did not seem unreasonable to the reviewers, none of them
picked up the faulty citation. A feminist reviewer might have, of course.

## THE POPULARIZATION OF RESULTS

Many research papers have been published on the cause of superior male per-    32
formance on mathematics tests in high school.[37] Some papers support the
hypothesis that males have superior genes, others that they have an environmentally conferred advantage. Therefore, it is hard to find a scientific basis for
the fuss and furor that followed the publication of a recent study by Benbow
and Stanley showing that one proposed environmental determinant—number
of mathematics courses taken—could be eliminated from consideration.[38]
There was no attempt by the authors to eliminate all environmental influences, and no evidence for genetic determination was offered. Yet the paper
elicited editorial comment in the issue of *Science* magazine in which it
appeared, and within a few weeks of publication *Time, Newsweek,* and local
newspapers were publishing articles with titles like "Sex differences in
achievement in and attitudes toward mathematics result from superior mathematical ability."[39] No similar publicity had accompanied Elizabeth
Fennema's article of a few years earlier,[40] in which, based on the same data,
she had argued for an environmental determination. The ideology of the
media greatly influences which scientific results enter into the popular culture.

Some results lend themselves to use in political and social battles. Money    33
and Ehrhardt's research on hormonal determination of sex-typical behaviour has slipped into the givens of popular science. They are quoted extensively in the sexology courses at the Université du Québec and in popular
magazine articles.[41]

And David Barash, after studying rape in birds, wrote a widely read    34
*Psychology Today* article in which he suggested that the double standard of

sexual behaviour among humans follows the bird pattern, owing to men's biologically based need to inject their sperm into as many women as possible.[42] This view was also quickly picked up and published by *Playboy* under the title, "Do Men Need to Cheat on Their Women? A New Science Says Yes."[43]

On the other hand, ideology and special interests may prevent some   35
research results from becoming publicized. In 1979, Dr. David Horrobin was fired from the Clinical Research Institute of Montreal for having "prematurely" publicized research results suggesting that the tranquilizer Valium may promote cancer of the breast in women. These results, subsequently confirmed by other investigators, were certainly of immediate practical value for women since one woman in eleven gets breast cancer and Valium is the most commonly used prescription drug on the market.[44] No such censorship has been practised on Benbow's and Stanley's results or interpretations, which are prejudicial to women's education, on those of Barash, which justify rape, or on those of Burt, which support racism, although Horrobin's studies were based on much more data than any of these.

In fact, as we have seen in the preceding examples, scientists, protected by   36
their image as zealous seekers after truth, have been allowed to say the most outrageous things about women with impunity. Such statements have been used to limit women's access to educational and occupational opportunities and have damaged our health. And, of course, scientists have also done damage to minority and working-class men. The problem of scientific objectivity is therefore not simply an academic one.

It is about time that scientists be regarded with the same skepticism as other   37
members of the establishment. If and when we achieve an egalitarian society, we may hope for a science more in touch with people's needs. Industrial hygienists will listen to workers when they look for risks associated with working conditions. Biologists will consult with, rather than experiment on, women who want contraceptive devices, and psychologists will search for the basis of cooperative rather than aggressive behaviour. Until that time, since we still have a long struggle ahead of us, we would be wise to examine closely, even belligerently, what scientists have to say about the nature of women.

## REFERENCES

*Acknowledgements*—I would like to thank Lesley Lee for bringing the methodological issues in the mathematics and sex research to my attention, and Jean-Pierre Reveret and Luc Desnovers for reading the manuscript.

1. Stanley Milgram, *Obedience to Authority* (New York: Harper & Row, 1973).

2. The treatment of women is more specifically covered in Ruth Hubbard, Mary Sue Henifin and Barbara Fried, eds., *Biological Woman—The Convenient Myth* (Cambridge, MA: Schenkman Publishing Co., 1982). This book contains an extensive bibliography.

3. Naomi Weisstein, "Adventures of a Woman in Science," *Fed. Proc. 35* (1976): 2226–2231.

4. Anne Sayre, *Rosalind Franklin and DNA: A Vivid View of What It Is Like to Be a Gifted Woman in an Especially Male Profession* (New York: W. W. Norton and Co., 1975).

5. Nancy Hopkins, "The High Price of Success in Science," *Radcliffe Quarterly* 62 (June 1976): 16–18.

6. Liliane Stehelin, "Science, Women and Ideology," in *Ideology of / in the National Science,* H. Rose and S. Rose, eds. (Cambridge, MA: Schenkman Publishing Co., 1979).

7. I speak from my own experience and that of my graduate students.

8. Betty Vetter, "Degree Completion by Women and Minorities in Science Increases," *Science* 214 (1982): 1313–1321; Betty M. Vetter and Elinor L. Babco, "New Data Show Slow Changes in Science Labour Force," *Science* 216 (1982): 1094–1095.

9. M. Whitehead et al., "Synthetic Absorption from Premarin Vaginal Cream" in I. D. Cooke, ed., *The Role of Estrogen / Progesterone in the Management of the Menopause* (Baltimore, MD: University Park Press, 1978).

10. Centre for Disease Control, *Abortion Surveillance,* 1978. (Issued November 1980. U.S. Department of Health and Human Services.)

11. F. S. Preston et al., "Effects of Flying and of Time Changes on Menstrual Cycle Length and on Performance in Airline Stewardesses," *Aerospace Medicine* 44 (1973): 438–443.

12. A. Kurkis et al., "Effect of Saturated and Unsaturated Fat Diets on Lipid Profiles of Plasma Lipoproteins," *Atherosclerosis* 41 (1982): 221–241.

13. Anke Ehrhardt, Nancy Greenberg, and John Money, "Female Gender Identity and Absence of Fetal Gonadal Hormones: Turner's Syndrome," *Johns Hopkins Medical Journal* 126 (1970): 237–248.

14. Herman A. Witkin et al., "Criminality in XYY and XXY Men," *Science* 193 (1976): 547–555.

15. W. Clarke Cooker, "Cancer Mortality Patterns in the Lead Industry," *Annals N. Y. Acad. Sci.* 271 (1976): 2250–2259.

16. Jeanne M. Stellman, *Women's Work, Women's Health: Myths and Realities* (New York: Pantheon Books, 1977), pp. 32–33.

17. Gena Corea, *The Hidden Malpractice* (New York: HBJ. Books, 1977), p. 16.

18. William D. Sharpe, "Chronic Radium Intoxication: Clinical and Autopsy Findings in Long-term New Jersey Survivors," *Environmental Research* 8 (1974): 243–383, 310.

19. Donna Mergler, Nicole Vezina, and Annette Beauvais, "Warts Amongst Workers in Poultry Slaughter-houses," *Scand. J. of Work, Envi. and Health* 8, suppl. 1 (1982): 180-184.

20. U.S. Department of Health, Education and Welfare, *Employment During Pregnancy: Legitimate Live Births 1963* (Washington, D.C: U.S. Government Printing Office, 1963).

21. Karen Messing, "Est-ce que la travailleuse enceinte est protegée au Quebec?" *Union Médicale* (February, 1982).

22. Gertrud S. Berkowitz, "All Epidemiologic Study of Preterm Delivery," *Am. J. Epidemiol.* 113 (1981): 81–92.

23. Anke A. Ehrhardt, Ralph Epstein, and John Money, "Fetal Androgens and Female Gender Identity in the Early-treated Androgenital Syndrome," *Johns Hopkins Med. Journal* 122 (1968): 160–168; see also study in note 13.

24. David Barash, "Sociobiology of Rape in Mallards (*Arias platyrynchos*): Responses of the Mated Male," *Science* 197 (1977): 788–789.

25. Gina B. Kolata, "Love Canal: False Alarm Caused by Botched Study," *Science* 208 (1980): 1239–1240.

26. Robert Rosenthal, *Experimenter Effects in Behavioural Research* (New York: Appleton-Century-Crofts, 1966).

27. Steven J. Gould, "Morton's Ranking of Races by Cranial Capacity," *Science* 200 (1978): 503–509.

28. J. L. Kennedy and H. P. Uhoff, Experiments on the Nature of Extrasensory Perception, III. Recording Error Criticizer of Extra-chance Scores," *J. Parapsychol.* 3 (1939): 226–245.

29. D. D. Dorfman, "The Cyril Burt Question: New Findings," *Science* 201 (1978): 1177–1180.

30. Arbitration hearing on the case of Mme. Adrienne Robichaud, before Judge Jean-Jacques Turcotte, Quebec, 1980–82.

31. Charles E. Land, "Estimating Cancer Risks from Low Doses of Ionizing Radiation," *Science* 209 (1980): 1197–1203.

32. John W. Gofman, *Radiation and Human Health* (San Francisco: Sierra Club Books, 1981).

33. Joanna J. Ryan, "I.Q.—The Illusion of Objectivity," in Ken Richardson and David Spears, eds., *Race and Intelligence* (Baltimore, MD: Penguin Books, 1972): 36–55.

34. Jon Beckwith and John Durkin, "Girls, Boys and Math," *Science for the People* 13, No. 5 (Sept./Oct. 1981): 6–9; 32–35.

35. Robert Van den Bosch, *The Pesticide Conspiracy* (New York: Doubleday, 1978).

36. C. Owen Lovejoy, "The Origin of Man," *Science* 211 (1981): 341–350.

37. Lynn H. Fox et al., eds., *Women and the Mathematical Mystique* (Baltimore, MD: Johns Hopkins University Press, 1980).

38. Camilla P. Benbow and Julian C. Stanley, "Sex Differences in Math Ability: Fact or Artifact," *Science* 210 (1980): 1262–1264.

39. D. A. Williams and P. King, "Sex Differences in Achievement in and Attitudes toward Mathematics Result from Superior Mathematical Ability," *Newsweek* December 15, 1980): 73.

40. Elizabeth Fennema, "Sex-Related Differences in Mathematical Achievement: Where and Why?" in L. H. Fox et al., eds., *Women and the Mathematical Mystique* (Baltimore, MD: Johns Hopkins University Press, 1980).

41. For example, Pierre Sormany, "Le cerveau a-t-il un sexe?" *L'Actualité* (November 1980): 35 ff.

42. David Barash, "Sexual Selection in Birdland," *Psychology Today* (March 1978): 81–86.

43. Scot Morris, "Do Men *Need* to Cheat on Their Women? A New Science Says Yes: Darwin and the Double Standard," *Playboy* (May 1978): 109 ff.

44. Francie F. Pelletier, "La belle au bois dormant se meurt: le valium et le cancer du sein," *La Vie en Rose* (Juin, Juillet, Août 1981): 33–37.

■ ■ ■

## Discussion and Writing Suggestions

1. Do you agree with Messing's basic point that science is not objective? Do you think it is possible to achieve a completely unbiased scientific method to ensure that the kinds of biases Messing identifies are filtered out of science?

2. Even if there is scientific bias against women and other non-dominant cultural groups, does it do any real harm? Or is Messing overdramatizing the case? Should we be worried or not? What kinds of harm might be done by the unquestioning acceptance of biased science?

3. Messing refers to science as having a "mystique" that protects it from public scrutiny. Are the sciences alone among academic disciplines in cultivating this aura of untouchable authority? Thinking about your experience of college or university so far, can you identify any ways in which academics present their knowledge as unquestionable? Or is it your experience that critical scrutiny is encouraged?

# The Stanford Prison Experiment

PHILIP K. ZIMBARDO

*As well known—and as controversial—as the Milgram obedience experiments, the Stanford Prison Experiment (1973) raises troubling questions about the ability of individuals to resist authoritarian or obedient roles, if the social setting requires these roles. Philip K. Zimbardo, professor of psychology at Stanford University, set out to study the process by which prisoners and guards "learn" to become compliant and authoritarian, respectively. To find subjects for the experiment, Zimbardo placed an advertisement in a local newspaper:*

> Male college students needed for psychological study of prison life. $15 per day for 1–2 weeks beginning Aug. 14. For further information & applications, come to Room 248, Jordan Hall, Stanford U.

*The ad drew 75 responses. From these Zimbardo and his colleagues selected 21 university-age men, half of whom would become "prisoners" in the experiment, the other half "guards." The elaborate role-playing scenario, planned for two weeks, had to be cut short due to the intensity of subjects' responses. This article first appeared in the* New York Times Magazine *(April 8, 1973).*

> *In prison, those things withheld from and denied to the prisoner become precisely what he wants most of all.*
> —Eldridge Cleaver, "Soul on Ice"

> *Our sense of power is more vivid when we break a man's spirit than when we win his heart.*
> —Eric Hoffer, "The Passionate State of Mind"

> *Every prison that men build is built with bricks of shame, / and bound with bars lest Christ should see how men their brothers maim.*
> —Oscar Wilde, "The Ballad of Reading Gaol"

> *Wherever anyone is against his will that is to him a prison.*
> —Epictetus, "Discourses"

The quiet of a summer morning in Palo Alto, Calif., was shattered by a     1
screeching squad car siren as police swept through the city picking up college students in a surprise mass arrest. Each suspect was charged with a felony, warned of his constitutional rights, spread-eagled against the car, searched, handcuffed and carted off in the back seat of the squad car to the police station for booking.

After fingerprinting and the preparation of identification forms for his     2
"jacket" (central information file), each prisoner was left isolated in a detention cell to wonder what he had done to get himself into this mess. After a while, he was blindfolded and transported to the "Stanford County Prison." Here he began the process of becoming a prisoner—stripped naked, skin-searched, deloused and issued a uniform, bedding, soup and towel.

The warden offered an impromptu welcome:     3

"As you probably know, I'm your warden. All of you have shown that     4
you are unable to function outside in the real world for one reason or another—that somehow you lack the responsibility of good citizens of this great country. We of this prison, your correctional staff, are going to help you learn what your responsibilities as citizens of this country are. Here are the rules. Sometime in the near future there will be a copy of the rules posted in each of the cells. We expect you to know them and to be able to recite them by number. If you follow all of these rules and keep your hands clean, repent for your misdeeds and show a proper attitude of penitence, you and I will get along just fine."

There followed a reading of the 16 basic rules of prisoner conduct,     5
"Rule Number One: Prisoners must remain silent during rest periods, after lights are out, during meals and whenever they are outside the prison yard. Two: Prisoners must eat at mealtimes and only at mealtimes. Three:

Prisoners must not move, tamper, deface or damage walls, ceilings, windows, doors, or other prison property. . . . Seven: Prisoners must address each other by their ID number only. Eight: Prisoners must address the guards as 'Mr. Correctional Officer.' . . . Sixteen: Failure to obey any of the above rules may result in punishment."

By late afternoon these youthful "first offenders" sat in dazed silence on   6
the cots in their barren cells trying to make sense of the events that had transformed their lives so dramatically.

If the police arrests and processing were executed with customary detach-   7
ment, however, there were some things that didn't fit. For these men were
now part of a very unusual kind of prison, an experimental mock prison, created by social psychologists to study the effects of imprisonment upon volunteer research subjects. When we planned our two-week-long simulation of
prison life, we sought to understand more about the process by which people
called "prisoners" lose their liberty, civil rights, independence and privacy,
while those called "guards" gain social power by accepting the responsibility for controlling and managing the lives of their dependent charges.

Why didn't we pursue this research in a real prison? First, prison systems   8
are fortresses of secrecy, closed to impartial observation, and thereby immune
to critical analysis from anyone not already part of the correctional authority. Second, in any real prison, it is impossible to separate what each individual brings into the prison from what the prison brings out in each person.

We populated our mock prison with a homogeneous group of people   9
who could be considered "normal-average" on the basis of clinical interviews and personality tests. Our participants (10 prisoners and 11 guards)
were selected from more than 75 volunteers recruited through ads in the city
and campus newspapers. The applicants were mostly college students from all
over the United States and Canada who happened to be in the Stanford area
during the summer and were attracted by the lure of earning $15 a day for
participating in a study of prison life. We selected only those judged to be
emotionally stable, physically healthy, mature, law-abiding citizens.

The sample of average, middle-class, Caucasian, college-age males (plus one   10
Oriental student) was arbitrarily divided by the flip of a coin. Half were randomly assigned to play the role of guards, the others of prisoners. There were
no measurable differences between the guards and the prisoners at the start of
the experiment. Although initially warned that as prisoners their privacy and
other civil rights would be violated and that they might be subjected to harassment, every subject was completely confident of his ability to endure whatever
the prison had to offer for the full two-week experimental period. Each subject
unhesitatingly agreed to give his "informed consent" to participate.

The prison was constructed in the basement of Stanford University's psy-   11
chology building, which was deserted after the end of the summer-school session. A long corridor was converted into the prison "yard" by partitioning off
both ends. Three small laboratory rooms opening onto this corridor were
made into cells by installing metal barred doors and replacing existing furni-
ture with cots, three to a cell. Adjacent offices were refurnished as guards'

quarters, interview-testing rooms and bedrooms for the "warden" (Jaffe) and the "superintendent" (Zimbardo). A concealed video camera and hidden microphones recorded much of the activity and conversation of guards and prisoners. The physical environment was one in which prisoners could always be observed by the staff, the only exception being when they were secluded in solitary confinement (a small, dark storage closet, labeled "The Hole").

Our mock prison represented an attempt to simulate the psychological   12
state of imprisonment in certain ways. We based our experiment on an in-depth analysis of the prison situation, developed after hundreds of hours of discussion with Carlo Prescott (our ex-con consultant), parole officers and correctional personnel, and after reviewing much of the existing literature on prisons and concentration camps.

"Real" prisoners typically report feeling powerless, arbitrarily controlled,   13
dependent, frustrated, hopeless, anonymous, dehumanized and emasculated. It was not possible, pragmatically or ethically, to create such chronic states in volunteer subjects who realize that they are in an experiment for only a short time. Racism, physical brutality, indefinite confinement and enforced homosexuality were not features of our mock prison. But we did try to reproduce those elements of the prison experience that seemed most fundamental.

We promoted anonymity by seeking to minimize each prisoner's sense of   14
uniqueness and prior identity. The prisoners wore smocks and nylon stocking caps; they had to use their ID numbers; their personal effects were removed and they were housed in barren cells. All of this made them appear similar to each other and indistinguishable to observers. Their smocks, which were like dresses, were worn without undergarments, causing the prisoners to be restrained in their physical actions and to move in ways that were more feminine than masculine. The prisoners were forced to obtain permission from the guard for routine and simple activities such as writing letters, smoking a cigarette or even going to the toilet; this elicited from them a childlike dependency.

Their quarters, though clean and neat, were small, stark and without   15
esthetic appeal. The lack of windows resulted in poor air circulation, and persistent odors arose from the unwashed bodies of the prisoners. After 10 P.M. lockup, toilet privileges were denied, so prisoners who had to relieve themselves would have to urinate and defecate in buckets provided by the guards. Sometimes the guards refused permission to have them cleaned out, and this made the prison smell.

Above all, "real" prisons are machines for playing tricks with the human   16
conception of time. In our windowless prison, the prisoners often did not even know whether it was day or night. A few hours after falling asleep, they were roused by shrill whistles for their "count." The ostensible purpose of the count was to provide a public test of the prisoners' knowledge of the rules and of their ID numbers. But more important, the count, which occurred at least once on each of the three different guard shifts, provided a regular occasion for the guards to relate to the prisoners. Over the course of the study, the duration of the counts was spontaneously increased by the guards from their initial perfunctory 10 minutes to a seemingly interminable several hours.

During these confrontations, guards who were bored could find ways to amuse themselves, ridiculing recalcitrant prisoners, enforcing arbitrary rules and openly exaggerating any dissension among the prisoners.

The guards were also "deindividualized": They wore identical khaki uni-    17
forms and silver reflector sunglasses that made eye contact with them impossible. Their symbols of power were billy clubs, whistles, handcuffs and the keys to the cells and the "main gate." Although our guards received no formal training from us in how to be guards, for the most part they moved with apparent ease into their roles. The media had already provided them with ample models of prison guards to emulate.

Because we were as interested in the guards' behavior as in the prisoners',    18
they were given considerable latitude to improvise and to develop strategies and tactics of prisoner management. Our guards were told that they must maintain "law and order" in this prison, that they were responsible for handling any trouble that might break out, and they were cautioned about the seriousness and potential dangers of the situation they were about to enter. Surprisingly, in most prison systems, "real" guards are not given much more psychological preparation or adequate training than this for what is one of the most complex, demanding and dangerous jobs our society has to offer. They are expected to learn how to adjust to their new employment mostly from on-the-job experience, and from contacts with the "old bulls" during a survival-of-the-fittest orientation period. According to an orientation manual for correctional officers at San Quentin, "the only way you really get to know San Quentin is through experience and time. Some of us take more time and must go through more experiences than others to accomplish this; some really never do get there."

You cannot be a prisoner if no one will be your guard, and you cannot    19
be a prison guard if no one takes you or your prison seriously. Therefore, over time a perverted symbiotic relationship developed. As the guards became more aggressive, prisoners became more passive; assertion by the guards led to dependency in the prisoners; self-aggrandizement was met with self-deprecation, authority with helplessness, and the counterpart of the guards' sense of mastery and control was the depression and hopelessness witnessed in the prisoners. As these differences in behavior, mood and perception became more evident to all, the need for the now "righteously" powerful guards to rule the obviously inferior and powerless inmates became a sufficient reason to support almost any further indignity of man against man:

Guard K: "During the inspection, I went to cell 2 to mess up a bed which    20
the prisoner had made and he grabbed me, screaming that he had just made it, and he wasn't going to let me mess it up. He grabbed my throat, and although he was laughing I was pretty scared. . . . I lashed out with my stick and hit him in the chin (although not very hard), and when I freed myself I became angry. I wanted to get back in the cell and have a go with him, since he attacked me when I was not ready."

Guard M: "I was surprised at myself . . . I made them call each other    21
names and clean the toilets out with their bare hands. I practically considered

the prisoners cattle, and I kept thinking: 'I have to watch out for them in case they try something.'"

Guard A: "I was tired of seeing the prisoners in their rags and smelling the strong odors of their bodies that filled the cells. I watched them tear at each other on orders given by us. They didn't see it as an experiment. It was real and they were fighting to keep their identity. But we were always there to show them who was boss." 22

Because the first day passed without incident, we were surprised and totally unprepared for the rebellion that broke out on the morning of the second day. The prisoners removed their stocking caps, ripped off their numbers and barricaded themselves inside the cells by putting their beds against the doors. What should we do? The guards were very much upset because the prisoners also began to taunt and curse them to their faces. When the morning shift of guards came on, they were upset at the night shift who, they felt, must have been too permissive and too lenient. The guards had to handle the rebellion themselves, and what they did was startling to behold. 23

At first they insisted that reinforcements be called in. The two guards who were waiting on stand-by call at home came in, and the night shift of guards voluntarily remained on duty (without extra pay) to bolster the morning shift. The guards met and decided to treat force with force. They got a fire extinguisher that shot a stream of skin-chilling carbon dioxide and forced the prisoners away from the doors; they broke into each cell, stripped the prisoners naked, took the beds out, forced the prisoners who were the ringleaders into solitary confinement and generally began to harass and intimidate the prisoners. 24

After crushing the riot, the guards decided to head off further unrest by creating a privileged cell for those who were "good prisoners" and then, without explanation, switching some of the troublemakers into it and some of the good prisoners out into the other cells. The prisoner ringleaders could not trust these new cellmates because they had not joined in the riot and might even be "snitches." The prisoners never again acted in unity against the system. One of the leaders of the prisoner revolt later confided: 25

"If we had gotten together then, I think we could have taken over the place. But when I saw the revolt wasn't working, I decided to toe the line. Everyone settled into the same pattern. From then on, we were really controlled by the guards." 26

It was after this episode that the guards really began to demonstrate their inventiveness in the application of arbitrary power. They made the prisoners obey petty, meaningless and often inconsistent rules, forced them to engage in tedious, useless work, such as moving cartons back and forth between closets and picking thorns out of their blankets for hours on end. (The guards had previously dragged the blankets through thorny bushes to create this disagreeable task.) Not only did the prisoners have to sing songs or laugh or refrain from smiling on command; they were also encouraged to curse and vilify each other publicly during some of the counts. They sounded off their numbers endlessly and were repeatedly made to do pushups, on occasion with a guard stepping on them or a prisoner sitting on them. 27

Slowly the prisoners became resigned to their fate and even behaved in     28
ways that actually helped to justify their dehumanizing treatment at the hands
of the guards. Analysis of the tape-recorded private conversations between
prisoners and of remarks made by them to interviewers revealed that fully half
could be classified as nonsupportive of other prisoners. More dramatic, 85
percent of the evaluative statements by prisoners about their fellow prisoners
were uncomplimentary and deprecating.

This should be taken in the context of an even more surprising result.     29
What do you imagine the prisoners talked about when they were alone in
their cells with each other, given a temporary respite from the continual
harassment and surveillance by the guards? Girl friends, career plans, hobbies
or politics?

No, their concerns were almost exclusively riveted to prison topics. Their     30
monitored conversations revealed that only 10 percent of the time was devoted to "outside" topics, while 90 percent of the time they discussed escape
plans, the awful food, grievances or ingratiating tactics to use with specific
guards in order to get a cigarette, permission to go to the toilet or some other
favor. Their obsession with these immediate survival concerns made talk
about the past and future an idle luxury.

And this was not a minor point. So long as the prisoners did not get to     31
know each other as people, they only extended the oppressiveness and reality of their life as prisoners. For the most part, each prisoner observed his
fellow prisoners allowing the guards to humiliate them, acting like compliant
sheep, carrying out mindless orders with total obedience and even being
cursed by fellow prisoners (at a guard's command). Under such circumstances, how could a prisoner have respect for his fellows, or any self-respect
for what *he* obviously was becoming in the eyes of all those evaluating him?

The combination of realism and symbolism in this experiment had fused     32
to create a vivid illusion of imprisonment. The illusion merged inextricably
with reality for at least some of the time for every individual in the situation.
It was remarkable how readily we all slipped into our roles, temporarily gave
up our identities and allowed these assigned roles and the social forces in the
situation to guide, shape and eventually to control our freedom of thought
and action.

But precisely where does one's "identity" end and one's "role" begin?     33
When the private self and the public role behavior clash, what direction will
attempts to impose consistency take? Consider the reactions of the parents,
relatives and friends of the prisoners who visited their forlorn sons, brothers
and lovers during two scheduled visitors' hours. They were taught in short
order that they were our guests, allowed the privilege of visiting only by
complying with the regulations of the institution. They had to register, were
made to wait half an hour, were told that only two visitors could see any one
prisoner; the total visiting time was cut from an hour to only 10 minutes, they
had to be under the surveillance of a guard, and before any parents could
enter the visiting area, they had to discuss their son's case with the warden. Of
course they complained about these arbitrary rules, but their conditioned,

middle-class reaction was to work within the system to appeal privately to the superintendent to make conditions better for their prisoners.

In less than 36 hours, we were forced to release prisoner 8612 because of extreme depression, disorganized thinking, uncontrollable crying and fits of rage. We did so reluctantly because we believed he was trying to "con" us— it was unimaginable that a volunteer prisoner in a mock prison could legitimately be suffering and disturbed to that extent. But then on each of the next three days another prisoner reacted with similar anxiety symptoms, and we were forced to terminate them, too. In a fifth case, a prisoner was released after developing a psychosomatic rash over his entire body (triggered by rejection of his parole appeal by the mock parole board). These men were simply unable to make an adequate adjustment to prison life. Those who endured the prison experience to the end could be distinguished from those who broke down and were released early in only one dimension—authoritarianism. On a psychological test designed to reveal a person's authoritarianism, those prisoners who had the highest scores were best able to function in this authoritarian prison environment. 34

If the authoritarian situation became a serious matter for the prisoners, it became even more serious—and sinister—for the guards. Typically, the guards insulted the prisoners, threatened them, were physically aggressive, used instruments (night sticks, fire extinguishers, etc.) to keep the prisoners in line and referred to them in impersonal, anonymous, deprecating ways: "Hey, you," or "You [obscenity], 5401, come here." From the first to the last day, there was a significant increase in the guards' use of most of these domineering, abusive tactics. 35

Everyone and everything in the prison was defined by power. To be a guard who did not take advantage of this institutionally sanctioned use of power was to appear "weak," "out of it," "wired up by the prisoners," or simply a deviant from the established norms of appropriate guard behavior. Using Erich Fromm's definition of sadism, as "the wish for absolute control over another living being," all of the mock guards at one time or another during this study behaved sadistically toward the prisoners. Many of them reported—in their diaries, on critical-incident report forms and during post-experimental interviews—being delighted in the new-found power and control they exercised and sorry to see it relinquished at the end of the study. 36

Some of the guards reacted to the situation in the extreme and behaved with great hostility and cruelty in the forms of degradation they invented for the prisoners. But others were kinder; they occasionally did little favors for the prisoners, were reluctant to punish them, and avoided situations where prisoners were being harassed. The torment experienced by one of these good guards is obvious in his perceptive analysis of what it felt like to be responded to as a "guard": 37

"What made the experience most depressing for me was the fact that we were continually called upon to act in a way that just was contrary to what I really feel inside. I don't feel like I'm the type of person that would be a guard, just constantly giving out [orders] . . . and forcing people to do things, and 38 pushing and lying—it just didn't seem like me, and to continually keep up and put on a face like that is just really one of the most oppressive things you can do. It's almost like a prison that you create yourself—you get into it, and it becomes almost the definition you make of yourself, it almost becomes like walls, and you want to break out and you want just to be able to tell everyone that 'this isn't really me at all, and I'm not the person that's confined in there—I'm a person who wants to get out and show you that I am free, and I do have my own will, and I'm not the sadistic type of person that enjoys this kind of thing.'"

Still, the behavior of these good guards seemed more motivated by a    39
desire to be liked by everyone in the system than by a concern for the inmates' welfare. No guard ever intervened in any direct way on behalf of the prisoners, ever interfered with the orders of the cruelest guards or ever openly complained about the subhuman quality of life that characterized this prison.

Perhaps the most devastating impact of the more hostile guards was their    40
creation of a capricious, arbitrary environment. Over time the prisoners began to react passively. When our mock prisoners asked questions, they got answers about half the time, but the rest of the time they were insulted and punished—and it was not possible for them to predict which would be the outcome. As they began to "toe the line," they stopped resisting, questioning and, indeed, almost ceased responding altogether. There was a general decrease in all categories of response as they learned the safest strategy to use in an unpredictable, threatening environment from which there is no physical escape—do nothing, except what is required. Act not, want not, feel not and you will not get into trouble in prisonlike situations.

Can it really be, you wonder, that intelligent, educated volunteers could    41
have lost sight of the reality that they were merely acting a part in an elaborate game that would eventually end? There are many indications not only that they did, but that, in addition, so did we and so did other apparently sensible, responsible adults.

Prisoner 819, who had gone into an uncontrollable crying fit, was about to    42
be prematurely released from the prison when a guard lined up the prisoners and had them chant in unison, "819 is a bad prisoner. Because of what 819 did to prison property we all must suffer. 819 is a bad prisoner." Over and over again. When we realized 819 might be overhearing this, we rushed into the room where 819 was supposed to be resting, only to find him in tears, prepared to go back into the prison because he could not leave as long as the others thought he was a "bad prisoner." Sick as he felt, he had to prove to them he was not a "bad" prisoner. He had to be persuaded that he was not a prisoner at all, that the others were also just students, that this was just an experiment and not a prison and the prison staff were only research psychologists. A report from the warden notes, "While I believe that it was necessary for *staff* [me] to enact the warden role, at least some of the time, I am startled by the ease with which I could turn off my sensitivity and concern for others for 'a good cause.'"

Consider our overreaction to the rumor of a mass escape plot that one of    43
the guards claimed to have overheard. It went as follows: Prisoner 8612,

previously released for emotional disturbance, was only faking. He was going to round up a bunch of his friends, and they would storm the prison right after visiting hours. Instead of collecting data on the pattern of rumor transmission, we made plans to maintain the security of our institution. After putting a confederate informer into the cell 8612 had occupied to get specific information about the escape plans, the superintendent went back to the Palo Alto Police Department to request transfer of our prisoners to the old city jail. His impassioned plea was only turned down at the last minute when the problem of insurance and city liability for our prisoners was raised by a city official. Angered at this lack of cooperation, the staff formulated another plan. Our jail was dismantled, the prisoners, chained and blindfolded, were carted off to a remote storage room. When the conspirators arrived, they would be told the study was over, their friends had been sent home, there was nothing left to liberate. After they left, we would redouble the security features of our prison making any future escape attempts futile. We even planned to lure ex-prisoner 8612 back on some pretext and imprison him again, because he had been released on false pretenses! The rumor turned out to be just that—a full day had passed in which we collected little or no data, worked incredibly hard to tear down and then rebuild our prison. Our reaction, however, was as much one of relief and joy as of exhaustion and frustration.

When a former prison chaplain was invited to talk with the prisoners (the    44
grievance committee had requested church services), he puzzled everyone by disparaging each inmate for not having taken any constructive action in order to get released. "Don't you know you must have a lawyer in order to get bail, or to appeal the charges against you?" Several of them accepted his invitation to contact their parents in order to secure the services of an attorney. The next night one of the parents stopped at the superintendent's office before visiting time and handed him the name and phone number of her cousin who was a public defender. She said that a priest had called her and suggested the need for a lawyer's services! We called the lawyer. He came, interviewed the prisoners, discussed sources of bail money and promised to return again after the weekend.

But perhaps the most telling account of the insidious development of this    45
new reality, of the gradual Kafkaesque metamorphosis of good into evil, appears in excerpts from the diary of one of the guards, Guard A:

*Prior to start of experiment:* "As I am a pacifist and nonaggressive indi-    46
vidual I cannot see a time when I might guard and/or maltreat other living things."

*After an orientation meeting:* "Buying uniforms at the end of the meeting    47
confirms the gamelike atmosphere of this thing. I doubt whether many of us share the expectations of 'seriousness' that the experimenters seem to have."

*First Day:* "Feel sure that the prisoners will make fun of my appearance    48
and I evolve my first basic strategy—mainly not to smile at anything they say or do which would be admitting it's all only a game. . . . At cell 3 I stop and setting my voice hard and low say to 5486, 'What are you smiling at?' 'Nothing, Mr. Correctional Officer.' 'Well, see that you don't.' (As I walk off I feel stupid.)"

*Second Day:* "5704 asked for a cigarette and I ignored him—because I am a non-smoker and could not empathize. . . . Meanwhile since I was feeling empathetic towards 1037, I determined not to talk with him . . . after we had count and lights out [Guard D] and I held a loud conversation about going home to our girl friends and what we were going to do to them." 49

*Third Day (preparing for the first visitors' night):* "After warning the prisoners not to make any complaints unless they wanted the visit terminated fast, we finally brought in the first parents. I made sure I was one of the guards on the yard, because this was my first chance for the type of manipulative power that I really like—being a very noticed figure with almost complete control over what is said or not. While the parents and prisoners sat in chairs, I sat on the end of the table dangling my feet and contradicting anything I felt like. This was the first part of the experiment I was really enjoying. . . . 817 is being obnoxious and bears watching." 50

*Fourth Day:* ". . . The psychologist rebukes me for handcuffing and blindfolding a prisoner before leaving the [counseling] office, and I resentfully reply that it is both necessary security and my business anyway." 51

*Fifth Day:* "I harass 'Sarge' who continues to stubbornly overrespond to all commands. I have singled him out for special abuse both because he begs for it and because I simply don't like him. The real trouble starts at dinner. The new prisoner (416) refuses to eat his sausage . . . we throw him into the Hole ordering him to hold sausages in each hand. We have a crisis of authority; this rebellious conduct potentially undermines the complete control we have over the others. We decide to play upon prisoner solidarity and tell the new one that all the others will be deprived of visitors if he does not eat his dinner. . . . I walk by and slam my stick into the Hole door. . . . I am very angry at this prisoner for causing discomfort and trouble for the others. I decided to force-feed him, but he wouldn't eat. I let the food slide down his face. I didn't believe it was me doing it. I hated myself for making him eat but I hated him more for not eating." 52

*Sixth Day:* "The experiment is over. I feel elated but am shocked to find some other guards disappointed somewhat because of the loss of money and some because they are enjoying themselves." 53

We were no longer dealing with an intellectual exercise in which a hypothesis was being evaluated in the dispassionate manner dictated by the canons of the scientific method. We were caught up in the passion of the present, the suffering, the need to control people, not variables, the escalation of power and all of the unexpected things that were erupting around and within us. We had to end this experiment: So our planned two-week simulation was aborted after only six (was it only six?) days and nights. 54

Was it worth all the suffering just to prove what everybody knows—that some people are sadistic, others weak and prisons are not beds of roses? If that is all we demonstrated in this research, then it was certainly not worth the anguish. We believe there are many significant implications to be derived from this experience, only a few of which can be suggested here. 55

The potential social value of this study derives precisely from the fact that   56
normal, healthy, educated young men could be so radically transformed
under the institutional pressures of a "prison environment." If this could
happen in so short a time, without the excesses that are possible in real prisons, and if it could happen to the "cream-of-the-crop of American youth,"
then one can only shudder to imagine what society is doing both to the actual
guards and prisoners who are at this very moment participating in that unnatural "social experiment."

The pathology observed in this study cannot be reasonably attributed in   57
pre-existing personality differences of the subjects, that option being eliminated by our selection procedures and random assignment. Rather, the subjects' abnormal social and personal reactions are best seen as a product of
their transaction with an environment that supported the behavior that would
be pathological in other settings, but was "appropriate" in this prison. Had
we observed comparable reactions in a real prison, the psychiatrist undoubtedly would have been able to attribute any prisoner's behavior to character
defects or personality maladjustment, while critics of the prison system would
have been quick to label the guards as "psychopathic." This tendency to
locate the source of behavior disorders inside a particular person or group
underestimates the power of situational forces.

Our colleague, David Rosenhan, has very convincingly shown that once   58
a sane person (pretending to be insane) gets labeled as insane and committed
to a mental hospital, it is the label that is the reality which is treated and not
the person. This dehumanizing tendency to respond to other people according to socially determined labels and often arbitrarily assigned roles is also
apparent in a recent "mock hospital" study designed by Norma Jean Orlando
to extend the ideas in our research.

Personnel from the staff of Elgin State Hospital in Illinois role-played   59
either mental patients or staff in a weekend simulation on a ward in the hospital. The mock mental patients soon displayed behavior indistinguishable
from that we usually associate with the chronic pathological syndromes of
acute mental patients: Incessant pacing, uncontrollable weeping, depression,
hostility, fights, stealing from each other, complaining. Many of the "mock
staff" took advantage of their power to act in ways comparable to our mock
guards by dehumanizing their powerless victims.

During a series of encounter debriefing sessions immediately after our   60
experiment, we all had an opportunity to vent our strong feelings and to
reflect upon the moral and ethical issues each of us faced, and we considered
how we might react more morally in future "real-life" analogues to this situation. Year-long follow-ups with our subjects via questionnaires, personal
interviews and group reunions indicate that their mental anguish was transient and situationally specific, but the self-knowledge gained has persisted.

By far the most disturbing implication of our research comes from the   61
parallels between what occurred in that basement mock prison and daily
experiences in our own lives—and we presume yours. The physical institution

of prison is but a concrete and steel metaphor for the existence of more pervasive, albeit less obvious, prisons of the mind that all of us daily create, populate and perpetuate. We speak here of the prisons of racism, sexism, despair, shyness, "neurotic hang-ups" and the like. The social convention of marriage, as one example, becomes for many couples a state of imprisonment in which one partner agrees to be prisoner or guard, forcing or allowing the other to play the reciprocal role—invariably without making the contract explicit.

To what extent do we allow ourselves to become imprisoned by docilely    62
accepting the roles others assign us or, indeed, choose to remain prisoners because being passive and dependent frees us from the need to act and be responsible for our actions? The prison of fear constructed in the delusions of the paranoid is no less confining or less real than the cell that every shy person erects to limit his own freedom in anxious anticipation of being ridiculed and rejected by his guards—often guards of his own making.

■ ■ ■

## Review Questions

1. What was Zimbardo's primary goal in undertaking the prison experiment?
2. What was the profile of subjects in the experiments? Why is this profile significant?
3. Zimbardo claims that there is a "process" (paragraphs 2, 7) of becoming a prisoner. What is this process?
4. What inverse psychological relationships developed between prisoners and guards?
5. What was the result of the prison "riot"?
6. Why did prisoners have no respect for each other or for themselves?
7. How does the journal of Guard A illustrate what Zimbardo calls the "gradual Kafkaesque metamorphosis of good into evil"? See paragraphs 45–54.
8. What are the reasons people would voluntarily become prisoners?
9. How can the mind keep people in jail?

## Discussion and Writing Suggestions

1. Reread the four epigraphs to this article. Write a paragraph of response to any one of them, in light of Zimbardo's discussion of the prison experiment.
2. You may have thought, before reading this article, that being a prisoner is a physical fact, not a psychological state. What are the differences between these two views?
3. In paragraph 8, Zimbardo explains his reasons for not pursuing his research in a real prison. He writes that "it is impossible to separate what each individual brings into the prison from what the prison brings

out in each person." What does he mean? And how does this distinction prove important later in the article (see paragraph 57)?

4. Zimbardo reports that at the beginning of the experiment each of the "prisoner" subjects "was completely confident of his ability to endure whatever the prison had to offer for the full two-week experimental period" (paragraph 10). Had you been a subject, would you have been so confident, prior to the experiment? Given what you've learned of the experiment, do you think you would have psychologically "become" a prisoner or guard if you had been selected for these roles? (And if not, what makes you so sure?)

5. Identify two passages in this article: one that surprised you relating to the prisoners; and one that surprised you relating to the guards. Write a paragraph explaining your response to each. Now read the two passages in light of each other. Do you see any patterns underlying your responses?

6. Zimbardo claims that the implications of his research matter deeply— that the mock prison he created is a metaphor for prisons of the mind "that all of us daily create, populate and perpetuate" (paragraph 61). Zimbardo mentions the prisons of "racism, sexism, despair, [and] shyness." Choose any one of these and discuss how it is a mental prison.

7. Reread paragraphs 61 and 62. Zimbardo makes a metaphorical jump from his experiment to the psychological realities of your daily life. Prisons—the artificial one he created and actual prisons—stand for something: social systems in which there are those who give orders and those who obey. All metaphors break down at some point. Where does this one break down?

8. Zimbardo suggests that we might "choose to remain prisoners because being passive and dependent frees us from the need to act and be responsible for our actions" (paragraph 62). Do you agree? What are the burdens of being disobedient?

# Disobedience as a Psychological and Moral Problem

ERICH FROMM

*Erich Fromm (1900–1980) was one of this century's distinguished writers and thinkers. Psychoanalyst and philosopher, historian and sociologist, he ranged widely in his interests and defied easy characterization. Fromm studied the works of Freud and Marx closely, and published on them both, but he was not aligned strictly with either. In much of his voluminous writing, he struggled to articulate a view that could help bridge ideological and personal conflicts and bring dignity to those who struggled with isolation in the industrial world. Author of more than 30 books and contributor to numerous edited collections and journals, Fromm is best known for* Escape from Freedom *(1941),* The Art of Loving *(1956), and* To Have or to Be? *(1976).*

*In the essay that follows, first published in 1963, Fromm discusses the seductive comforts of obedience and he makes distinctions among varieties of obedience, some of which he believes are destructive, and others, life affirming. His thoughts on nuclear annihilation may seem dated in these days of post–cold war cooperation, but it is worth remembering that Fromm wrote his essay just after the Cuban missile crisis, when fears of a third world war ran high. (We might note that despite the welcomed reductions of nuclear stockpiles, the United States and Russia still possess, and retain battle plans for, thousands of warheads; many other countries have since developed nuclear missiles.) On the major points of his essay, concerning the psychological and moral problems of obedience, Fromm remains as pertinent today as when he wrote 40 years ago.*

For centuries kings, priests, feudal lords, industrial bosses and parents have insisted that *obedience is a virtue* and that *disobedience is a vice.* In order to introduce another point of view, let us set against this position the following statement: *human history began with an act of disobedience, and it is not unlikely that it will be terminated by an act of obedience.*     1

Human history was ushered in by an act of disobedience according to the Hebrew and Greek myths. Adam and Eve, living in the Garden of Eden, were part of nature; they were in harmony with it, yet did not transcend it. They were in nature as the fetus is in the womb of the mother. They were human, and at the same time not yet human. All this changed when they disobeyed an order. By breaking the ties with earth and mother, by cutting the umbilical cord, man emerged from a prehuman harmony and was able to take the first step into independence and freedom. The act of disobedience set Adam and Eve free and opened their eyes. They recognized each other as strangers and the world outside them as strange and even hostile. Their act of disobedience broke the primary bond with nature and made them individuals. "Original sin," far from corrupting man, set him free; it was the beginning of history. Man had to leave the Garden of Eden in order to learn to rely on his own powers and to become fully human.     2

The prophets, in their messianic concept, confirmed the idea that man had been right in disobeying; that he had not been corrupted by his "sin," but freed from the fetters of pre-human harmony. For the prophets, *history* is the place where man becomes human; during its unfolding he develops his powers of reason and of love until he creates a new harmony between himself, his fellow man and nature. This new harmony is described as "the end of days," that period of history in which there is peace between man and man, between man and nature. It is a "new" paradise created by man himself, and one which he alone could create because he was forced to leave the "old" paradise as a result of his disobedience.     3

Just as the Hebrew myth of Adam and Eve, so the Greek myth of Prometheus sees all of human civilization based on an act of disobedience. Prometheus, in stealing the fire from the gods, lays the foundation for the evolution of man.     4

There would be no human history were it not for Prometheus' "crime." He, like Adam and Eve, is punished for his disobedience. But he does not repent and ask for forgiveness. On the contrary, he proudly says: "I would rather be chained to this rock than be the obedient servant of the gods."

Man has continued to evolve by acts of disobedience. Not only was his spiritual development possible only because there were men who dared to say no to the powers that be in the name of their conscience or their faith, but also his intellectual development was dependent on the capacity for being disobedient—disobedient to authorities who tried to muzzle new thoughts and to the authority of long-established opinions which declared a change to be nonsense.

If the capacity for disobedience constituted the beginning of human history, obedience might very well, as I have said, cause the end of human history. I am not speaking symbolically or poetically. There is the possibility, or even the probability, that the human race will destroy civilization and even all life upon earth within the next five to ten years. There is no rationality or sense in it. But the fact is that, while we are living technically in the Atomic Age, the majority of men—including most of those who are in power—still live emotionally in the Stone Age; that while our mathematics, astronomy, and the natural sciences are of the twentieth century, most of our ideas about politics, the state, and society lag far behind the age of science. If mankind commits suicide it will be because people will obey those who command them to push the deadly buttons; because they will obey the archaic passions of fear, hate, and greed; because they will obey obsolete clichés of State sovereignty and national honor. The Soviet leaders talk much about revolutions, and we in the "free world" talk much about freedom. Yet they and we discourage disobedience—in the Soviet Union explicitly and by force, in the free world implicitly and by the more subtle methods of persuasion.

But I do not mean to say that all disobedience is a virtue and all obedience a vice. Such a view would ignore the dialectical relationship between obedience and disobedience. Whenever the principles which are obeyed and those which are disobeyed are irreconcilable, an act of obedience to one principle is necessarily an act of disobedience to its counterpart and vice versa. Antigone is the classic example of this dichotomy. By obeying the inhuman laws of the State, Antigone necessarily would disobey the laws of humanity. By obeying the latter, she must disobey the former. All martyrs of religious faiths, of freedom and of science have had to disobey those who wanted to muzzle them in order to obey their own consciences, the laws of humanity and of reason. If a man can only obey and not disobey, he is a slave; if he can only disobey and not obey, he is a rebel (not a revolutionary); he acts out of anger, disappointment, resentment, yet not in the name of a conviction or a principle.

However, in order to prevent a confusion of terms an important qualification must be made. Obedience to a person, institution or power (heteronomous obedience) is submission; it implies the abdication of my autonomy and the acceptance of a foreign will or judgment in place of my own. Obedience to my own reason or conviction (autonomous obedience) is not an act of submission but one of affirmation. My conviction and my judgment, if authentically mine, are part of me. If I follow them rather than the judgment of others, I am being myself; hence the word *obey* can be applied only in a metaphorical sense and with a meaning which is fundamentally different from the one in the case of "heteronomous obedience."

But this distinction still needs two further qualifications, one with regard to the concept of conscience and the other with regard to the concept of authority.    9

The word *conscience* is used to express two phenomena which are quite distinct from each other. One is the "authoritarian conscience" which is the internalized voice of an authority whom we are eager to please and afraid of displeasing. This authoritarian conscience is what most people experience when they obey their conscience. It is also the conscience which Freud speaks of, and which he called "Super-Ego." This Super-Ego represents the internalized commands and prohibitions of father, accepted by the son out of fear. Different from the authoritarian conscience is the "humanistic conscience"; this is the voice present in every human being and independent from external sanctions and rewards. Humanistic conscience is based on the fact that as human beings we have an intuitive knowledge of what is human and inhuman, what is conducive of life and what is destructive of life. This conscience serves our functioning as human beings. It is the voice which calls us back to ourselves, to our humanity.    10

Authoritarian conscience (Super-Ego) is still obedience to a power outside of myself, even though this power has been internalized. Consciously I believe that I am following *my* conscience; in effect, however, I have swallowed the principles of *power*; just because of the illusion that humanistic conscience and Super-Ego are identical, internalized authority is so much more effective than the authority which is clearly experienced as not being part of me. Obedience to the "authoritarian conscience," like all obedience to outside thoughts and power, tends to debilitate "humanistic conscience," the ability to be and to judge oneself.    11

The statement, on the other hand, that obedience to another person is *ipso facto* submission needs also to be qualified by distinguishing "irrational" from "rational" authority. An example of rational authority is to be found in the relationship between student and teacher; one of irrational authority in the relationship between slave and master. Both relationships are based on the fact that the authority of the person in command is accepted. Dynamically, however, they are of a different nature. The interests of the teacher and the student, in the ideal case, lie in the same direction. The teacher is satisfied if he succeeds in furthering the student; if he has failed to do so, the failure is his and the student's. The slave owner, on the other hand, wants to exploit the slave as much as possible. The more he gets out of him the more satisfied he is. At the same time, the slave tries to defend as best he can his claims for a minimum of happiness. The interests of slave and master are antagonistic, because what is advantageous to the one is detrimental to the other. The superiority of the one over the other has a different function in each case; in the    12 first it is the condition for the furtherance of the person subjected to the authority, and in the second it is the condition for his exploitation. Another distinction runs parallel to this: rational authority is rational because the authority, whether it is held by a teacher or a captain of a ship giving orders in an emergency, acts in the name of reason which, being universal, I can accept without submitting. Irrational authority has to use force or suggestion, because no one would let himself be exploited if he were free to prevent it.

Why is man so prone to obey and why is it so difficult for him to dis-    13
obey? As long as I am obedient to the power of the State, the Church, or public opinion, I feel safe and protected. In fact it makes little difference what power it is that I am obedient to. It is always an institution, or men, who use force in one form or another and who fraudulently claim omniscience and omnipotence. My obedience makes me part of the power I worship, and hence I feel strong. I can make no error, since it decides for me; I cannot be alone, because it watches over me; I cannot commit a sin, because it does not let me do so, and even if I do sin, the punishment is only the way of returning to the almighty power.

In order to disobey, one must have the courage to be alone, to err and to    14
sin. But courage is not enough. The capacity for courage depends on a person's state of development. Only if a person has emerged from mother's lap and father's commands, only if he has emerged as a fully developed individual and thus has acquired the capacity to think and feel for himself, only then can he have the courage to say "no" to power, to disobey.

A person can become free through acts of disobedience by learning to say    15
no to power. But not only is the capacity for disobedience the condition for freedom; freedom is also the condition for disobedience. If I am afraid of freedom, I cannot dare to say "no," I cannot have the courage to be disobedient. Indeed, freedom and the capacity for disobedience are inseparable; hence any social, political, and religious system which proclaims freedom, yet stamps out disobedience, cannot speak the truth.

There is another reason why it is so difficult to dare to disobey, to say    16
"no" to power. During most of human history obedience has been identified with virtue and disobedience with sin. The reason is simple: thus far throughout most of history a minority has ruled over the majority. This rule was made necessary by the fact that there was only enough of the good things of life for the few, and only the crumbs remained for the many. If the few wanted to enjoy the good things and, beyond that, to have the many serve them and work for them, one condition was necessary: the many had to learn obedience. To be sure, obedience can be established by sheer force. But this method has many disadvantages. It constitutes a constant threat that one day the many might have the means to overthrow the few by force; furthermore there are many kinds of work which cannot be done properly if nothing but fear is behind the obedience. Hence the obedience which is only rooted in the fear of force must be transformed into one rooted in man's heart. Man must want and even need to obey, instead of only fearing to dis-

obey. If this is to be achieved, power must assume the qualities of the All Good, of the All Wise; it must become All Knowing. If this happens, power can proclaim that disobedience is sin and obedience virtue; and once this has been proclaimed, the many can accept obedience because it is good and detest disobedience because it is bad, rather than to detest themselves for being cowards. From Luther to the nineteenth century one was concerned with overt and explicit authorities. Luther, the pope, the princes, wanted to uphold it; the middle class, the workers, the philosophers, tried to uproot it. The fight against authority in the State as well as in the family was often the very basis for the development of an independent and daring person. The fight against authority was inseparable from the intellectual mood which characterized the philosophers of the enlightenment and the scientists. This "critical mood" was one of faith in reason, and at the same time of doubt in everything which is said or thought, inasmuch as it is based on tradition, superstition, custom, power. The principles *sapere aude* and *de omnibus est dubitandum*—"dare to be wise" and "of all one must doubt"—were characteristic of the attitude which permitted and furthered the capacity to say "no."

The case of Adolf Eichmann is symbolic of our situation and has a sig-    17
nificance far beyond the one in which his accusers in the courtroom in Jerusalem were concerned with. Eichmann is a symbol of the organization man, of the alienated bureaucrat for whom men, women and children have become numbers. He is a symbol of all of us. We can see ourselves in Eichmann. But the most frightening thing about him is that after the entire story was told in terms of his own admissions, he was able in perfect good faith to plead his innocence. It is clear that if he were once more in the same situation he would do it again. And so would we—and so do we.

The organization man has lost the capacity to disobey, he is not even    18
aware of the fact that he obeys. At this point in history the capacity to doubt, to criticize and to disobey may be all that stands between a future for mankind and the end of civilization.

■ ■ ■

## Review Questions

1. What does Fromm mean when he writes that disobedience is "the first step into independence and freedom"?
2. Fromm writes that history began with an act of disobedience and will likely end with an act of obedience. What does he mean?
3. What is the difference between "heteronomous obedience" and "autonomous obedience"?
4. How does Fromm distinguish between "authoritarian conscience" and "humanistic conscience"?
5. When is obedience to another person *not* submission?
6. What are the psychological comforts of obedience, and why would authorities rather have people obey out of love than out of fear?

## Discussion and Writing Suggestions

1. Fromm suggests that scientifically we live in the 20th century but that politically and emotionally we live in the Stone Age. As you observe events in the world, both near and far, would you agree? Why?

2. Fromm writes: "If a man can only obey and not disobey, he is a slave; if he can only disobey and not obey, he is a rebel (not a revolutionary)." Explain Fromm's meaning here. Explain, as well, the implication that to be fully human one must have the freedom to both obey and disobey.

3. Fromm writes that "obedience makes me part of the power I worship, and hence I feel strong." Does this statement ring true for you? Discuss, in writing, an occasion in which you felt powerful because you obeyed a group norm.

4. In paragraph 16, Fromm equates obedience with cowardice. Can you identify a situation in which you were obedient but, now that you reflect on it, also were cowardly? That is, can you recall a time when you caved in to a group but now wish you hadn't? Explain.

5. Fromm says that we can see ourselves in Adolf Eichmann—that as an organization man he "has lost the capacity to disobey, he is not even aware of the fact that he obeys." To what extent do you recognize yourself in this portrait?

# *The Handmaid's Tale*

MARGARET ATWOOD

*In* The Handmaid's Tale, *Canada's most prolific novelist tells the story of a not-too-distant future society where a patriarchal form of fundamentalist Christianity has taken over political power in the United States, totally controlling the lives of everyone in the society. Women are acutely oppressed, having been stripped of their freedoms practically overnight—even their ATM cards were invalidated to cut off access to money—with nary a word of protest from men. As extreme as the depiction is, the roots of Atwood's sexist society can perhaps be found not only in the history of Puritan theocracy in New England, but in contemporary Canada as well, and many readers of this novel have found it a frighteningly imaginable forecast of the future, should the country become swept up in right-wing religious political trends. In the chapters excerpted here, people have gathered to participate in the public executions of several people who have violated the laws of Gilead. As you read these chapters, think about how the authorities win assent for punishing political dissidents under the guise of protecting the population.*

*Atwood is an internationally renowned writer of poetry, essays, literary criticism, children's books, short stories, and most famously, novels. Among the most noted are* The Edible Woman, Surfacing, The Journals of Susannah

Moodie, Cat's Eye, The Robber Bride, Alias Grace, The Blind Assassin, *and* The Handmaid's Tale. *She has won numerous literary awards for her works, among them the Governor General's Award, the* Ms Magazine's *Woman of the Year, the Ida Nudel Humanitarian Award from the Canadian Jewish Congress, the American Humanist of the Year Award, the Commonwealth Writers Prize, and the* Sunday Times *Prize, the Booker Prize, the Giller Prize, the* Sunday Times *Award for Literary Excellence, and Le Chevalier dans l'Ordre des Arts et des Lettres in France. Born in Ottawa in 1939, she has lived in many cities in Canada, Europe, and the United States and has resided in Toronto since 1992, where she maintains an active presence as a writer and social activist. She is a Companion of the Order of Canada.*

## CHAPTER FORTY-TWO

The bell is tolling; we can hear it from a long way off. It's morning, and today   1
we've had no breakfast. When we reach the main gate we file through it, two by two. There's a heavy contingent of guards, special-detail Angels, with riot gear—the helmets with the bulging dark plexiglass visors that make them look like beetles, the long clubs, the gas-canister guns—in cordon around the outside of the Wall. That's in case of hysteria. The hooks on the Wall are empty.

This is a district Salvaging, for women only. Salvagings are always seg-   2
regated. It was announced yesterday. They tell you only the day before. It's not enough time, to get used to it.

To the tolling of the bell we walk along the paths once used by students,   3
past buildings that were once lecture halls and dormitories. It's very strange to be in here again. From the outside you can't tell that anything's changed, except that the blinds on most of the windows are drawn down. These build-ings belong to the Eyes now.

We file onto the wide lawn in front of what used to be the library. The   4
white steps going up are still the same, the main entrance is unaltered. There's a wooden stage erected on the lawn, something like the one they used every spring, for Commencement, in the time before. I think of hats, pastel hats worn by some of the mothers, and of the black gowns the students would put on, and the red ones. But this stage is not the same after all, because of the three wooden posts that stand on it, with the loops of rope.

At the front of the stage there is a microphone; the television camera is   5
discreetly off to the side.

I've only been to one of these before, two years ago. Women's Salvagings   6
are not frequent. There is less need for them. These days we are so well behaved.

I don't want to be telling this story.   7

We take our places in the standard order: Wives and daughters on the   8
folding wooden chairs placed towards the back, Econo-wives and Marthas around the edges and on the library steps, and Handmaids at the front, where everyone can keep an eye on us. We don't sit on chairs, but kneel, and this time we have cushions, small red velvet ones with nothing written on them, not even *Faith*.

Luckily the weather is all right: not too hot, cloudy-bright. It would be miserable kneeling here in the rain. Maybe that's why they leave it so late to tell us: so they'll know what the weather will be like. That's as good a reason as any. 9

I kneel on my red velvet cushion. I try to think about tonight, about making love, in the dark, in the light reflected off the white walls. I remember being held. 10

There's a long piece of rope which winds like a snake in front of the first row of cushions, along the second, and back through the lines of chairs, bending like a very old, very slow river viewed from the air, down to the back. The rope is thick and brown and smells of tar. The front end of the rope runs up onto the stage. It's like a fuse, or the string of a balloon. 11

On stage, to the left, are those who are to be salvaged: two Handmaids, one Wife. Wives are unusual, and despite myself I look at this one with interest. I want to know what she has done. 12

They have been placed here before the gates were opened. All of them sit on folding wooden chairs, like graduating students who are about to be given prizes. Their hands rest in their laps, looking as if they are folded sedately. They sway a little, they've probably been given injections or pills, so they won't make a fuss. It's better if things go smoothly. Are they attached to their chairs? Impossible to say, under all that drapery. 13

Now the official procession is approaching the stage, mounting the steps at the right: three women, one Aunt in front, two Salvagers in their black hoods and cloaks a pace behind her. Behind them are the other Aunts. The whisperings among us hush. The three arrange themselves, turn towards us, the Aunt flanked by the two black-robed Salvagers. 14

It's Aunt Lydia. How many years since I've seen her? I'd begun to think she existed only in my head, but here she is, a little older. I have a good view, I can see the deepening furrows to either side of her nose, the engraved frown. Her eyes blink, she smiles nervously, peering to left and right, checking out the audience, and lifts a hand to fidget with her headdress. An odd strangling sound comes over the P.A. system: she is clearing her throat. 15

I've begun to shiver. Hatred fills my mouth like spit. 16

The sun comes out, and the stage and its occupants light up like a Christmas crèche. I can see the wrinkles under Aunt Lydia's eyes, the pallor of the seated women, the hairs on the rope in front of me on the grass, the blades of grass. There is a dandelion, right in front of me, the colour of egg yolk. I feel hungry. The bell stops tolling. 17

Aunt Lydia stands up, smooths down her skirt with both hands, and steps forward to the mike. "Good afternoon, ladies," she says, and there is an instant and ear-splitting feedback whine from the P.A. system. From among us, incredibly, there is laughter. It's hard not to laugh, it's the tension, and the look of irritation on Aunt Lydia's face as she adjusts the sound. This is supposed to be dignified. 18

"Good afternoon, ladies," she says again, her voice now tinny and flattened. It's *ladies* instead of *girls* because of the Wives. "I'm sure we are all aware of the unfortunate circumstances that bring us all here together on this beautiful 19 morning, when I am certain we would all rather be doing something else, at least I speak for myself, but duty is a hard taskmaster, or may I say on this occasion taskmistress, and it is in the name of duty that we are here today."

She goes on like this for some minutes, but I don't listen. I've heard this   20
speech, or one like it, often enough before: the same platitudes, the same slogans, the same phrases: the torch of the future, the cradle of the race, the task before us. It's hard to believe there will not be polite clapping after this speech, and tea and cookies served on the lawn.

That was the prologue, I think. Now she'll get down to it.   21

Aunt Lydia rummages in her pocket, produces a crumpled piece of   22
paper. This she takes an undue length of time to unfold and scan. She's rubbing our noses in it, letting us know exactly who she is, making us watch her as she silently reads, flaunting her prerogative. Obscene, I think. Let's get this over with.

"In the past," says Aunt Lydia, "it has been the custom to precede the   23
actual Salvagings with a detailed account of the crimes of which the prisoners stand convicted. However, we have found that such a public account, especially when televised, is invariably followed by a rash, if I may call it that, an outbreak I should say, of exactly similar crimes. So we have decided in the best interests of all to discontinue this practice. The Salvagings will proceed without further ado."

A collective murmur goes up from us. The crimes of others are a secret   24
language among us. Through them we show ourselves what we might be capable of, after all. This is not a popular announcement. But you would never know it from Aunt Lydia, who smiles and blinks as if washed in applause. Now we are left to our own devices, our own speculations. The first one, the one they're now raising from her chair, black-gloved hands on her upper arms: reading? No, that's only a hand cut off, on the third conviction. Unchastity, or an attempt on the life of her Commander? Or the Commander's Wife, more likely? That's what we're thinking. As for the Wife, there's mostly just one thing they get salvaged for. They can do almost anything to us, but they aren't allowed to kill us, not legally. Not with knitting needles or garden shears, or knives purloined from the kitchen, and especially not when we are pregnant. It could be adultery, of course. It could always be that.

Or attempted escape.   25

"Ofcharles," Aunt Lydia announces. No one I know. The woman is   26
brought forward; she walks as if she's really concentrating on it, one foot, the other foot, she's definitely drugged. There's a groggy off-centre smile on her mouth. One side of her face contracts, an uncoordinated wink, aimed at the camera. They'll never show it, of course, this isn't live. The two Salvagers tie her hands, behind her back.

From behind me there's a sound of retching.   27

That's why we don't get breakfast.   28

"Janine, most likely," Ofglen whispers.   29

I've seen it before, the white bag placed over the head, the woman helped   30
up onto the high stool as if she's being helped up the steps of a bus, steadied there, the noose adjusted delicately around the neck, like a vestment, the

stool kicked away. I've heard the long sigh go up, from around me, the sigh like air coming out of an air mattress, I've seen Aunt Lydia place her hand over the mike, to stifle the other sounds coming from behind her, I've leaned forward to touch the rope in front of me, in time with the others, both hands on it, the rope hairy, sticky with tar in the hot sun, then placed my hand on my heart to show my unity with the Salvagers and my consent, and my complicity in the death of this woman. I have seen the kicking feet and the two in black who now seize hold of them and drag downwards with all their weight. I don't want to see it any more. I look at the grass instead. I describe the rope.

## CHAPTER FORTY-THREE

The three bodies hang there, even with the white sacks over their heads looking curiously stretched, like chickens strung up by the necks in a meatshop window; like birds with their wings clipped, like flightless birds, wrecked angels. It's hard to take your eyes off them. Beneath the hems of the dresses the feet dangle, two pairs of red shoes, one pair of blue. If it weren't for the ropes and the sacks it could be a kind of dance, a ballet, caught by flashcamera: mid-air. They look arranged. They look like showbiz. It must have been Aunt Lydia who put the blue one in the middle.

"Today's Salvaging is now concluded," Aunt Lydia announces into the mike. "But . . ."

We turn to her, listen to her, watch her. She has always known how to space her pauses. A ripple runs over us, a stir. Something else, perhaps, is going to happen.

"But you may stand up, and form a circle." She smiles down upon us, generous, munificent. She is about to give us something. *Bestow.* "Orderly, now."

She is talking to us, to the Handmaids. Some of the Wives are leaving now, some of the daughters. Most of them stay, but they stay behind, out of the way, they watch merely. They are not part of the circle.

Two Guardians have moved forward and are coiling up the thick rope, getting it out of the way. Others move the cushions. We are milling around now, on the grass space in front of the stage, some jockeying for position at the front, next to the centre, many pushing just as hard to work their way to the middle where they will be shielded. It's a mistake to hang back too obviously in any group like this; it stamps you as lukewarm, lacking in zeal. There's an energy building here, a murmur, a tremor of readiness and anger. The bodies tense, the eyes are brighter, as if aiming.

I don't want to be at the front, or at the back either. I'm not sure what's coming, though I sense it won't be anything I want to see up close. But Ofglen has hold of my arm, she tugs me with her, and now we're in the second line, with only a thin hedge of bodies in front of us. I don't want to see, yet I don't pull back either. I've heard rumours, which I only half believed. Despite everything I already know, I say to myself: they wouldn't go that far.

"You know the rules for a Particicution," Aunt Lydia says. "You will wait until I blow the whistle. After that, what you do is up to you, until I blow the whistle again. Understood?"

A noise comes from among us, a formless assent.　　39

"Well then," says Aunt Lydia. She nods. Two Guardians, not the same　40
ones that have taken away the rope, come forward now from behind the
stage. Between them they half-carry, half-drag a third man. He too is in a
Guardian's uniform, but he has no hat on and the uniform is dirty and torn.
His face is cut and bruised, deep reddish-brown bruises; the flesh is swollen
and knobby, stubbled with unshaven beard. This doesn't look like a face
but like an unknown vegetable, a mangled bulb or tuber, something that's
grown wrong. Even from where I'm standing I can smell him: he smells of
shit and vomit. His hair is blond and falls over his face, spiky with what?
Dried sweat?

I stare at him with revulsion. He looks drunk. He looks like a drunk　41
that's been in a fight. Why have they brought a drunk in here?

"This man," says Aunt Lydia, "has been convicted of rape." Her voice　42
trembles with rage, and a kind of triumph. "He was once a Guardian. He has
disgraced his uniform. He has abused his position of trust. His partner in
viciousness has already been shot. The penalty for rape, as you know, is death.
Deuteronomy 22:23–29. I might add that this crime involved two of you and
took place at gunpoint. It was also brutal. I will not offend your ears with any
details, except to say that one woman was pregnant and the baby died."

A sigh goes up from us; despite myself I feel my hands clench. It is too　43
much, this violation. The baby too, after what we go through. It's true, there
is a bloodlust; I want to tear, gouge, rend.

We jostle forward, our heads turn from side to side, our nostrils flare,　44
sniffing death, we look at one another, seeing the hatred. Shooting was too
good. The man's head swivels groggily around: has he even heard her?

Aunt Lydia waits a moment; then she gives a little smile and raises her　45
whistle to her lips. We hear it, shrill and silver, an echo from a volleyball game
of long ago.

The two Guardians let go of the third man's arms and step back. He stag-　46
gers—is he drugged?—and falls to his knees. His eyes are shrivelled up inside
the puffy flesh of his face, as if the light is too bright for him. They've kept
him in darkness. He raises one hand to his cheek, as though to feel if he is still
there. All of this happens quickly, but it seems to be slowly.

Nobody moves forward. The women are looking at him with horror; as　47
if he's a half-dead rat dragging itself across a kitchen floor. He's squinting
around at us, the circle of red women. One corner of his mouth moves up,
incredible—a smile?

I try to look inside him, inside the trashed face, see what he must really　48
look like. I think he's about thirty. It isn't Luke.

But it could have been, I know that. It could be Nick. I know that what-　49
ever he's done I can't touch him.

He says something. It comes out thick, as if his throat is bruised, his　50
tongue huge in his mouth, but I hear it anyway. He says, "I didn't . . ."

There's a surge forward, like a crowd at a rock concert in the former　51
time, when the doors opened, that urgency coming like a wave through us.

The air is bright with adrenalin, we are permitted anything and this is freedom, in my body also, I'm reeling, red spreads everywhere, but before that tide of cloth and bodies hits him Ofglen is shoving through the women in front of us, propelling herself with her elbows, left, right, and running towards him. She pushes him down, sideways, then kicks his head viciously, one, two, three times, sharp painful jabs with the foot, well-aimed. Now there are sounds, gasps, a low noise like growling, yells, and the red bodies tumble forward and I can no longer see, he's obscured by arms, fists, feet. A high scream comes from somewhere, like a horse in terror.

I keep back, try to stay on my feet. Something hits me from behind. I 52 stagger. When I regain my balance and look around, I see the Wives and daughters leaning forward in their chairs, the Aunts on the platform gazing down with interest. They must have a better view from up there.

He has become an *it*. 53

Ofglen is back beside me. Her face is tight, expressionless. 54

"I saw what you did," I say to her. Now I'm beginning to feel again: shock, 55 outrage, nausea. Barbarism. "Why did you do that? You! I thought you . . ."

"Don't look at me," she says. "They're watching." 56

"I don't care," I say. My voice is rising, I can't help it. 57

"Get control of yourself," she says. She pretends to brush me off, my arm 58 and shoulder, bringing her face close to my ear. "Don't be stupid. He wasn't a rapist at all, he was a political. He was one of ours. I knocked him out. Put him out of his misery. Don't you know what they're doing to him?"

One of ours, I think. A Guardian. It seems impossible. 59

Aunt Lydia blows her whistle again, but they don't stop at once. The two 60 Guardians move in, pulling them off, from what's left. Some lie on the grass where they've been hit or kicked by accident. Some have fainted. They straggle away, in twos and threes or by themselves. They seem dazed.

"You will find your partners and re-form your line," Aunt Lydia says 61 into the mike. Few pay attention to her. A woman comes towards us, walking as if she's feeling her way with her feet, in the dark: Janine. There's a smear of blood across her cheek, and more of it on the white of her headdress. She's smiling, a bright diminutive smile. Her eyes have come loose.

"Hi there," she says. "How are you doing?" She's holding something, 62 tightly, in her right hand. It's a clump of blond hair. She gives a small giggle.

"Janine," I say. But she's let go, totally now, she's in free fall, she's in 63 withdrawal.

"You have a nice day," she says, and walks on past us, towards the gate. 64

I look after her. Easy out, is what I think. I don't even feel sorry for her, 65 although I should. I feel angry. I'm not proud of myself for this, or for any of it. But then, that's the point.

My hands smell of warm tar. I want to go back to the house and up to 66 the bathroom and scrub and scrub, with the harsh soap and the pumice, to get every trace of this smell off my skin. The smell makes me feel sick.

But also I'm hungry. This is monstrous, but nevertheless it's true. Death 67 makes me hungry. Maybe it's because I've been emptied; or maybe it's the body's way of seeing to it that I remain alive, continue to repeat its bedrock prayer: *I am, I am.* I am, still.

I want to go to bed, make love, right now.                                        68

I think of the word *relish*.                                                     69

I could eat a horse.                                                              70

■  ■  ■

## Discussion and Writing Suggestions

1. As we noted when introducing Atwood's story, many readers have found the events depicted chillingly realistic, just "certain tendencies now in existence carried to their logical conclusion," as the hardcover dustjacket notes. What is your response to Atwood's story? Is it totally farfetched? Or do you, too, find the society she depicts all too easy to imagine? Why or why not?

2. Some of the women have joined enthusiastically in the "particicution" of the tortured Guardian, but the narrator reveals a very conflicted set of emotions and motivations as she watches the executions. In what ways does she find herself drawn into participating, outwardly and inwardly, despite her distaste for the proceedings?

3. How does it serve the interests of the Gilead authorities to have the women believe the executed man was a rapist?

4. Most Canadian women have had the right to vote for at least 50 years (status Indians did not win the right to vote until 1960), depending on their province of residence, and there has been significant progress achieved in the struggle for women's equality before the law. But at current rates, it will be another 500 years before women are equally represented in influential sectors such as government, academia, business management, and the professions. What insights does Atwood offer into the psychological impact of authority that might account for women's resigned attitude to this extremely slow progress?

5. Do you think that you and an equally talented, determined, educated, prosperous female classmate (if you are a man, or male, if you are a woman) have the same chance of becoming Prime Minister of Canada? How would group mentality affect your ambitions and your chances?

## The Lottery

SHIRLEY JACKSON

On the morning of June 28, 1948, I walked down to the post office in our little Vermont town to pick up the mail. I was quite casual about it, as I recall—I opened the box, took out a couple of bills and a letter or two, talked to the postmaster for a few minutes, and left, never supposing that it was the last time for months that I was to pick up the mail without an active feeling of panic. By the next week I had to change my mailbox to the largest one in the post office, and casual conversation with the postmaster was out of the question, because he wasn't speaking to me. June 28, 1948, was the day *The New Yorker* came out with a story of mine in it. It was not my first published story, nor my last, but I have been assured over and over that if it had been the only story I ever wrote or published, there would be people who would not forget my name.[1]

*So begins Shirley Jackson's "biography" of her short story "The Lottery." The New Yorker published the story in the summer of 1948 and some months later, having been besieged with letters, acknowledged that the piece had generated "more mail than any . . . fiction they had ever published"—the great majority of it negative. In 1960, Jackson wrote that "millions of people, and my mother, had taken a pronounced dislike to me" for having written the story—which, over the years, proved to be Jackson's most widely anthologized one. If you've read "The Lottery," you will have some idea of why it was so controversial. If you haven't, we don't want to spoil the effect by discussing what happens.*

*Shirley Jackson (1919–1965), short-story writer and novelist, was born in San Francisco and was raised in California and New York. She began her post-secondary education at the University of Rochester and completed it at Syracuse University. She married Stanley Edgar Hyman (writer and teacher) and with him had four children. In her brief career, Jackson wrote six novels and two works of non-fiction. She won the Edgar Allen Poe Award (1961) as well as a Syracuse University Arents Pioneer Medal for Outstanding Achievement (1965).*

The morning of June 27th was clear and sunny, with the fresh warmth of a full-summer day; the flowers were blossoming profusely and the grass was richly green. The people of the village began to gather in the square, between the post office and the bank, around ten o'clock; in some towns there were so many people that the lottery took two days and had to be started on June 26th, but in this village, where there were only about three hundred people, the whole lottery took less than two hours, so it could begin at ten o'clock in the morning and still be through in time to allow the villagers to get home for noon dinner.     1

The children assembled first, of course. School was recently over for the summer, and the feeling of liberty sat uneasily on most of them; they tended to gather together quietly for a while before they broke into boisterous play, and their talk was still of the classroom and the teacher, of books and reprimands. Bobby Martin had already stuffed his pockets full of stones, and the other boys soon followed his example, selecting the smoothest and roundest stones; Bobby and Harry Jones and Dickie Delacroix—the villagers pronounced this "Dellacroy"—eventually made a great pile of stones in one     2

---

corner of the square and guarded it against the raids of the other boys. The girls stood aside, talking among themselves, looking over their shoulders at the boys, and the very small children rolled in the dust or clung to the hands of their older brothers or sisters.

Soon the men began to gather, surveying their own children, speaking of 3 planting and rain, tractors and taxes. They stood together, away from the pile of stones in the corner, and their jokes were quiet and they smiled rather than laughed. The women, wearing faded house dresses and sweaters, came short-ly after their menfolk. They greeted one another and exchanged bits of gossip as they went to join their husbands. Soon the women, standing by their hus-bands, began to call to their children, and the children came reluctantly, having to be called four or five times. Bobby Martin ducked under his mother's grasping hand and ran, laughing, back to the pile of stones. His father spoke up sharply, and Bobby came quickly and took his place between his father and his oldest brother.

The lottery was conducted—as were the square dances, the teenage club, 4 the Halloween program—by Mr. Summers, who had time and energy to devote to civic activities. He was a round-faced, jovial man and he ran the coal business, and people were sorry for him, because he had no children and his wife was a scold. When he arrived in the square, carrying the wooden black box, there was a murmur of conversation among the villagers, and he waved and called, "Little late today, folks." The postmaster, Mr. Graves, fol-lowed him, carrying a three-legged stool, and the stool was put in the center of the square and Mr. Summers set the black box down on it. The villagers kept their distance, leaving a space between themselves and the stool, and when Mr. Summers said, "Some of you fellows want to give me a hand?" there was a hesitation before two men, Mr. Martin and his oldest son, Baxter, came forward to hold the box steady on the stool while Mr. Summers stirred up the papers inside it.

The original paraphernalia for the lottery had been lost long ago, and the 5 black box now resting on the stool had been put into use even before Old Man Warner, the oldest man in town, was born. Mr. Summers spoke fre-quently to the villagers about making a new box, but no one liked to upset even as much tradition as was represented by the black box. There was a story that the present box had been made with some pieces of the box that had pre-ceded it, the one that had been constructed when the first people settled down to make a village here. Every year, after the lottery, Mr. Summers began talking again about a new box, but every year the subject was allowed to fade off without anything's being done. The black box grew shabbier each year; by now it was no longer completely black but splintered badly along one side to show the original wood color, and in some places faded or stained.

Mr. Martin and his oldest son, Baxter, held the black box securely on the 6 stool until Mr. Summers had stirred the papers thoroughly with his hand. Because so much of the ritual had been forgotten or discarded, Mr. Summers had been successful in having slips of paper substituted for the chips of wood that had been used for generations. Chips of wood, Mr. Summers had argued, had been all very well when the village was tiny, but now that the population was more than three hundred and likely to keep on growing, it was necessary to use something that would fit more easily into the black box. The night before the lottery, Mr. Summers and Mr. Graves made up the slips of paper and put them in the box, and it was then taken to the safe of Mr. Summers' coal company and locked up until Mr. Summers was ready to take it to the square next morning. The rest of the year, the box was put away, sometimes one place, sometimes another; it had spent one year in Mr. Graves's barn and another year underfoot in the post office, and sometimes it was set on a shelf in the Martin grocery and left there.

There was a great deal of fussing to be done before Mr. Summers declared 7 the lottery open. There were the lists to make up—of heads of families, heads of households in each family, members of each household in each family. There was the proper swearing-in of Mr. Summers by the postmaster, as the official of the lottery; at one time, some people remembered, there had been a recital of some sort, performed by the official of the lottery, a perfunctory, tuneless chant that had been rattled off duly each year; some people believed that the official of the lottery used to stand just so when he said or sang it, others believed that he was supposed to walk among the people, but years and years ago this part of the ritual had been allowed to lapse. There had been, also, a ritual salute, which the official of the lottery had had to use in addressing each person who came up to draw from the box, but this also had changed with time, until now, it was felt necessary only for the official to speak to each person approaching. Mr. Summers was very good at all this; in his clean white shirt and blue jeans, with one hand resting carelessly on the black box, he seemed very proper and important as he talked interminably to Mr. Graves and the Martins.

Just as Mr. Summers finally left off talking and turned to the assembled 8 villagers, Mrs. Hutchinson came hurriedly along the path to the square, her sweater thrown over her shoulders, and slid into place in the back of the crowd. "Clean forgot what day it was," she said to Mrs. Delacroix, who stood next to her, and they both laughed softly. "Thought my old man was out back stacking wood," Mrs. Hutchinson went on, "and then I looked out the window and the kids was gone, and then I remembered it was the twenty-seventh and came a-running." She dried her hands on her apron, and Mrs. Delacroix said, "You're in time, though. They're still talking away up there."

Mrs. Hutchinson craned her neck to see through the crowd and found 9 her husband and children standing near the front. She tapped Mrs. Delacroix on the arm as a farewell and began to make her way through the crowd. The people separated good-humoredly to let her through; two or three people said, in voices just loud enough to be heard across the crowd, "Here comes your Missus, Hutchinson," and "Bill, she made it after all." Mrs. Hutchinson reached her husband, and Mr. Summers, who had been waiting, said cheerfully, "Thought we were going to have to get on without you, Tessie." Mrs. Hutchinson said, grinning, "Wouldn't have me leave m'dishes in the sink, now, would you, Joe?," and soft laughter ran through the crowd as the people stirred back into position after Mrs. Hutchinson's arrival.

"Well, now," Mr. Summers said soberly, "guess we better get started, get      10
this over with, so's we can go back to work. Anybody ain't here?"

"Dunbar," several people said. "Dunbar, Dunbar."                              11

Mr. Summers consulted his list. "Clyde Dunbar," he said. "That's right.       12
He's broke his leg, hasn't he? Who's drawing for him?"

"Me, I guess," a woman said, and Mr. Summers turned to look at her.           13
"Wife draws for her husband," Mr. Summers said. "Don't you have a grown
boy to do it for you, Janey?" Although Mr. Summers and everyone else in the
village knew the answer perfectly well, it was the business of the official of the
lottery to ask such questions formally. Mr. Summers waited with an expression of polite interest while Mrs. Dunbar answered.

"Horace's not but sixteen yet," Mrs. Dunbar said regretfully. "Guess I        14
gotta fill in for the old man this year."

"Right," Mr. Summers said. He made a note on the list he was holding.        15
Then he asked, "Watson boy drawing this year?"

A tall boy in the crowd raised his hand. "Here," he said. "I'm drawing       16
for m'mother and me." He blinked his eyes nervously and ducked his head as
several voices in the crowd said things like "Good fellow, Jack," and "Glad
to see your mother's got a man to do it."

"Well," Mr. Summers said, "guess that's everyone. Old Man Warner             17
make it?"

"Here," a voice said, and Mr. Summers nodded.                               18

A sudden hush fell on the crowd as Mr. Summers cleared his throat and        19
looked at the list. "All ready?" he called. "Now, I'll read the names—heads
of families first—and the men come up and take a paper out of the box. Keep
the paper folded in your hand without looking at it until everyone has had a
turn. Everything clear?"

The people had done it so many times that they only half listened to the     20
directions; most of them were quiet, wetting their lips, not looking around.
Then Mr. Summers raised one hand high and said, "Adams." A man disengaged himself from the crowd and came forward. "Hi, Steve," Mr. Summers
said, and Mr. Adams said, "Hi, Joe." They grinned at one another humor-
ously and nervously. Then Mr. Adams reached into the black box and took
out a folded paper. He held it firmly by one corner as he turned and went
hastily back to his place in the crowd, where he stood a little apart from his
family, not looking down at his hand.

"Allen," Mr. Summers said. "Anderson. . . . Bentham."                        21

"Seems like there's no time at all between lotteries any more," Mrs.         22
Delacroix said to Mrs. Graves in the back row. "Seems like we got through
with the last one only last week."

"Time sure goes fast," Mrs. Graves said.                                     23

"Clark. . . . Delacroix."                                                    24

"There goes my old man," Mrs. Delacroix said. She held her breath           25
while her husband went forward.

"Dunbar," Mr. Summers said, and Mrs. Dunbar went steadily to the            26
box while one of the women said, "Go on, Janey," and another said, "There
she goes."

"We're next," Mrs. Graves said. She watched while Mr. Graves came   27
around from the side of the box, greeted Mr. Summers gravely, and selected
a slip of paper from the box. By now, all through the crowd there were men
holding the small folded papers in their large hands, turning them over and
over nervously. Mrs. Dunbar and her two sons stood together, Mrs. Dunbar
holding the slip of paper.

"Harburt. . . . Hutchinson."                                          28

"Get up there, Bill," Mrs. Hutchinson said, and the people near her   29
laughed.

"Jones."                                                             30

"They do say," Mr. Adams said to Old Man Warner, who stood next to    31
him, "that over in the north village they're talking of giving up the lottery."

Old Man Warner snorted. "Pack of crazy fools," he said. "Listening to   32
the young folks, nothing's good enough for *them*. Next thing you know,
they'll be wanting to go back to living in caves, nobody work any more, live
*that* way for a while. Used to be a saying about 'Lottery in June, corn be
heavy soon.' First thing you know, we'd all be eating stewed chickweed and
acorns. There's *always* been a lottery," he added petulantly. "Bad enough to
see young Joe Summers up there joking with everybody."

"Some places have already quit lotteries," Mrs. Adams said.           33

"Nothing but trouble in *that*," Old Man Warner said stoutly. "Pack of   34
young fools."

"Martin." And Bobby Martin watched his father go forward.            35
"Overdyke. . . . Percy."

"I wish they'd hurry," Mrs. Dunbar said to her older son. "I wish they'd   36
hurry."

"They're almost through," her son said.                               37

"You get ready to run tell Dad," Mrs. Dunbar said.                    38

Mr. Summers called his own name and then stepped forward precisely    39
and selected a slip from the box. Then he called, "Warner."

"Seventy-seventh year I been in the lottery," Old Man Warner said as he   40
went through the crowd. "Seventy-seventh time."

"Watson." The tall boy came awkwardly through the crowd. Someone      41
said, "Don't be nervous, Jack," and Mr. Summers said, "Take your time,
son."

"Zanini."                                                             42

After that, there was a long pause, a breathless pause, until Mr. Summers,   43
holding his slip of paper in the air, said, "All right, fellows." For a minute, no
one moved, and then all the slips of paper were opened. Suddenly, all the
women began to speak at once, saying, "Who is it?," "Who's got it?," "Is it
the Dunbars?," "Is it the Watsons?" Then the voices began to say, "It's
Hutchinson. It's Bill," "Bill Hutchinson's got it."

"Go tell your father," Mrs. Dunbar said to her older son.             44

People began to look around to see the Hutchinsons. Bill Hutchinson was   45
standing quiet, staring down at the paper in his hand. Suddenly, Tessie
Hutchinson shouted to Mr. Summers, "You didn't give him time enough to
take any paper he wanted. I saw you. It wasn't fair!"

"Be a good sport, Tessie," Mrs. Delacroix called, and Mrs. Graves said,    46
"All of us took the same chance."

"Shut up, Tessie," Bill Hutchinson said.                                   47

"Well, everyone," Mr. Summers said, "that was done pretty fast, and        48
now we've got to be hurrying a little more to get done in time." He consulted his next list. "Bill," he said, "you draw for the Hutchinson family. You got
any other households in the Hutchinsons?"

"There's Don and Eva," Mrs. Hutchinson yelled. "Make *them* take their     49
chance!"

"Daughters draw with their husbands' families, Tessie," Mr. Summers        50
said gently. "You know that as well as anyone else."

"It wasn't *fair*," Tessie said.                                           51

"I guess not, Joe," Bill Hutchinson said regretfully. "My daughter draws   52
with her husband's family, that's only fair. And I've got no other family
except the kids."

"Then, as far as drawing for families is concerned, it's you," Mr.         53
Summers said in explanation, "and as far as drawing for households is concerned, that's you, too. Right?"

"Right," Bill Hutchinson said.                                             54

"How many kids, Bill?" Mr. Summers asked formally.                         55

"Three," Bill Hutchinson said. "There's Bill, Jr., and Nancy, and little   56
Dave. And Tessie and me."

"All right, then," Mr. Summers said. "Harry, you got their tickets back?"  57

Mr. Graves nodded and held up the slips of paper. "Put them in the box,    58
then," Mr. Summers directed. "Take Bill's and put it in."

"I think we ought to start over," Mrs. Hutchinson said, as quietly as she  59
could. "I tell you it wasn't *fair*. You didn't give him enough time to choose.
*Everybody* saw that."

Mr. Graves had selected the five slips and put them in the box, and he     60
dropped all the papers but those onto the ground, where the breeze caught
them and lifted them off.

"Listen, everybody," Mrs. Hutchinson was saying to the people around       61
her.

"Ready, Bill?" Mr. Summers asked, and Bill Hutchinson, with one quick      62
glance around at his wife and children, nodded.

"Remember," Mr. Summers said, "take the slips and keep them folded        63
until each person has taken one. Harry, you help little Dave." Mr. Graves
took the hand of the little boy, who came willingly with him up to the box.
"Take a paper out of the box, Davy," Mr. Summers said. Davy put his hand
into the box and laughed. "Take just *one* paper," Mrs. Summers said.
"Harry, you hold it for him." Mr. Graves took the child's hand and removed
the folded paper from the tight fist and held it while little Dave stood next to
him and looked up at him wonderingly.

"Nancy next," Mr. Summers said. Nancy was twelve and her school          64
friends breathed heavily as she went forward, switching her skirt, and took a
slip daintily from the box. "Bill, Jr.," Mr. Summers said, and Billy, his face

red and his feet overlarge, nearly knocked the box over as he got a paper out. "Tessie," Mr. Summers said. She hesitated for a minute, looking around defiantly, and then set her lips and went up to the box. She snatched a paper out and held it behind her.

"Bill," Mr. Summers said, and Bill Hutchinson reached into the box and felt around, bringing his hand out at last with the slip of paper in it.    65

The crowd was quiet. A girl whispered, "I hope it's not Nancy," and the sound of the whisper reached the edges of the crowd.    66

"It's not the way it used to be," Old Man Warner said clearly. "People ain't the way they used to be."    67

"All right," Mr. Summers said. "Open the papers, Harry, you open little Dave's."    68

Mr. Graves opened the slip of paper and there was a general sigh through the crowd as he held it up and everyone could see that it was blank. Nancy and Bill, Jr., opened theirs at the same time, and both beamed and laughed, turning around to the crowd and holding their slips of paper above their heads.    69

"Tessie," Mr. Summers said. There was a pause, and then Mr. Summers looked at Bill Hutchinson, and Bill unfolded his paper and showed it. It was blank.    70

"It's Tessie," Mr. Summers said, and his voice was hushed. "Show us her paper, Bill."    71

Bill Hutchinson went over to his wife and forced the slip of paper out of her hand. It had a black spot on it, the black spot Mr. Summers had made the night before with the heavy pencil in the coal-company office. Bill Hutchinson held it up, and there was a stir in the crowd.    72

"All right, folks," Mr. Summers said. "Let's finish quickly."    73

Although the villagers had forgotten the ritual and lost the original black box, they still remembered to use stones. The pile of stones the boys had made earlier was ready; there were stones on the ground with the blowing scraps of paper that had come out of the box. Mrs. Delacroix selected a stone so large she had to pick it up with both hands and turned to Mrs. Dunbar. "Come on," she said. "Hurry up."    74

Mrs. Dunbar had small stones in both hands, and she said, gasping for breath, "I can't run at all. You'll have to go ahead and I'll catch up with you."    75

The children had stones already, and someone gave little Davy Hutchinson a few pebbles.

Tessie Hutchinson was in the center of a cleared space by now, and she held her hands out desperately as the villagers moved in on her. "It isn't fair," she said. A stone hit her on the side of the head.    76

Old Man Warner was saying, "Come on, come on, everyone." Steve Adams was in front of the crowd of villagers, with Mrs. Graves beside him.    77

"It isn't fair, it isn't right," Mrs. Hutchinson screamed, and then they were upon her.    78

■  ■  ■

## Discussion and Writing Suggestions

1. Many readers believed that the events depicted in "the Lottery" actually happened. A sampling of the letters that Jackson received in response to the story:

   > (Kansas) Will you please tell me the locale and the year of that custom?
   > (Oregon) Where in heaven's name does there exist such barbarity as described in the story?
   > (New York) Do such tribunal rituals still exist and if so where?
   > (New York) To a reader who has only a fleeting knowledge of traditional rites in various parts of the country (I presume the plot was laid in the United States) I found the cruelty of the ceremony outrageous, if not unbelievable. It may be just a custom or ritual which I am not familiar with.
   > (New York) Would you please explain whether such improbable rituals occur in our Middle Western states, and what their origin and purpose are?
   > (Nevada) Although we recognize the story to be fiction is it possible that it is based on fact?

   What is your response to comments such as these that suggest surprise, certainly, but also acceptance of the violence committed in the story?

2. One reader of "The Lottery," from Missouri, wrote to the *New Yorker* and accused it of "publishing a story that reached a new low in human viciousness." Do you feel that Jackson has reached this "new low"? Explain your answer.

3. Several more letter writers attempted to get at the meaning of the story:

   > (Illinois) If it is simply a fictitious example of man's innate cruelty, it isn't a very good one. Man, stupid and cruel as he is, has always had sense enough to imagine or invent a charge against the objects of his persecution: the Christian martyrs, the New England witches, the Jews and Negroes. But nobody had anything against Mrs. Hutchinson, and they only wanted to get through quickly so they could go home for lunch.
   > (California) I missed something here. Perhaps there was some facet of the victim's character which made her unpopular with the other villagers. I expected the people to evince a feeling of dread and terror, or else sadistic pleasure, but perhaps they were laconic, unemotional New Englanders.
   > (Indiana) When I first read the story in my issue, I felt that there was no moral significance present, that the story was just terrifying, and that was all. However, there has to be a reason why it is so alarming to so many people. I feel that the only solution, the only reason it bothered so many people is that it shows the power of society over the individual. We saw the ease with which society can crush any single

one of us. At the same time, we saw that society need have no rational reason for crushing the one, or the few, or sometimes the many.

Take any one of these readings of the story and respond to it by writing a brief essay or, perhaps, a letter.

4. What does the story suggest to you about authority and obedience to authority? Who—or what—holds authority in the village? Why do people continue with the annual killing, despite the fact that "some places have already quit lotteries"?

## ■ SYNTHESIS ACTIVITIES

1. Compare and contrast the Asch and the Milgram experiments, considering their separate (1) objectives, (2) experimental designs and procedures, (3) results, and (4) conclusions. To what extent do the findings of these two experiments reinforce one another? To what extent do they highlight different, if related, social phenomena? To what extent do their results reinforce those of Zimbardo's prison experiment?

2. Assume for the moment you agree with Doris Lessing: Children need to be taught how to disobey so they can recognize and avoid situations that give rise to harmful obedience. If you were the curriculum coordinator for your local school system, how would you teach children to disobey? What would be your curriculum? What homework would you assign? What class projects? What field trips? One complicated part of your job would be to train children to understand the difference between *responsible* disobedience and anarchy. What is the difference?

   Take up these questions in an essay that draws on both your experiences as a student and your understanding of the selections in this chapter. Points that you might want to consider in developing the essay: defining overly obedient children; appropriate classroom behaviour for responsibly disobedient children (as opposed to inappropriate behaviour); reading lists (would "The Lottery" and *The Handmaid's Tale* be included?); homework assignments; field trips; class projects.

3. A certain amount of obedience is a given in society, observe Stanley Milgram and others. Social order, civilization itself, would not be possible unless individuals were willing to surrender a portion of their autonomy to the state. Allowing that we all are obedient (we must be), define the point at which obedience to a figure of authority becomes dangerous.

   As you develop your definition, consider the ways you might use the work of authors in this chapter and their definitions of acceptable and unacceptable levels of obedience. Do you agree with the ways in which others have drawn the line between reasonable and dangerous obedience? What examples from current stories in the news or from your own experience can you draw on to test various definitions?

4. Describe a situation in which you were faced with a moral dilemma of whether to obey a figure of authority. After describing the situation and the action you took (or didn't take), discuss your behaviour in light of any two readings in this chapter. You might consider a straightforward, four-part structure for your essay: (1) your description; (2) your discussion, in light of source A; (3) your discussion, in light of source B; and (4) your conclusion—an overall appraisal of your behaviour.

5. At one point in his essay (paragraph 16), Erich Fromm equates obedience with cowardice. Earlier in the chapter, Doris Lessing (paragraph 9) observes that "among our most shameful memories is this, how often we said black was white because other people were saying it." Using the work of these authors as a point of departure, reconsider an act of obedience or disobedience in your own life. Describe pertinent circumstances for your reader. Based on what you have learned in this chapter, reassess your behaviour. Would you behave similarly if given a second chance in the same situation?

6. Reread "The Lottery" and/or our excerpt from *The Handmaid's Tale* and analyze the patterns of and reasons for obedience in the story(s). Base your analysis on two sources in this chapter: Erich Fromm's essay, especially paragraphs 13–16 on the psychological comforts of obedience; and Doris Lessing's speech on the dangers of "not understanding the social laws that govern groups."

7. In his response to Diana Baumrind, Stanley Milgram makes a point of insisting that follow-up interviews with subjects in his experiments show that a large majority were pleased, in the long run, to have participated. (See Table 1 in the footnote to Baumrind, page 299.) Writing on his own post-experiment surveys and interviews, Philip Zimbardo writes that his subjects believed their "mental anguish was transient and situationally specific, but the self-knowledge gained has persisted" (paragraph 60). Why might they *and* the experimenters nonetheless have been eager to accept a positive, final judgment of the experiments? Develop an essay in response to this question, drawing on the selections by Milgram, Zimbardo, and Baumrind.

8. Develop a synthesis in which you extend Baumrind's critique of Milgram to the Stanford prison experiment. This assignment requires that you understand the core elements of Baumrind's critique; that you have a clear understanding of Zimbardo's experiment; and that you systematically apply elements of the critiques, as you see fit, to Zimbardo's work. In your conclusion, offer your overall assessment of the Stanford Prison Experiment. To do this, you might answer Zimbardo's own question in paragraph 55: "Was [the experiment] worth all the suffering?" Or you might respond to another question: Do you agree that Zimbardo is warranted in extending the conclusions of his experiment to the general population?

9. In response to the question "Why is man so prone to obey and why is it so difficult for him to disobey?" Erich Fromm suggests that obedience

lets people identify with the powerful and invites feelings of safety. Disobedience is psychologically more difficult and requires an act of courage. (See paragraphs 13 and 14.) Solomon Asch notes that the tendency to conformity is generally stronger than the tendency to independence. And in his final paragraph, Philip Zimbardo writes that a "prison of fear" keeps people compliant and frees them of the need to take responsibility for their own actions. In a synthesis that draws on these three sources, explore the interplay of *fear* and its opposite, *courage*, in relation to obedience. To prevent the essay from becoming too abstract, direct your attention repeatedly to a single case, the details of which will help to keep your focus. "The Lottery" could serve nicely as this case, as could a particular event from your own life.

## ■ RESEARCH ACTIVITIES

1. When Milgram's results were first published in book form in 1974, they generated heated controversy. The reaction reprinted here (by Baumrind) represents only a very small portion of that controversy. Research other reactions to the Milgram experiments and discuss your findings. Begin with the reviews listed and excerpted in the *Book Review Digest*; also use the *Social Science Index*, the *Readers' Guide to Periodical Literature*, and newspaper indexes to locate articles, editorials, and letters to the editor on the experiments (and any other general or social science periodical indexes in print or electronic form that cover material written as far back as 1974). (Note that editorials and letters are not always indexed. Letters appear within two to four weeks of the weekly magazine articles to which they refer, and within one to two weeks of newspaper articles.) What were the chief types of reactions? To what extent were the reactions favourable?

2. Milgram begins his article "Obedience to Authority" with a reference to Nazi Germany. The purpose of his experiment, in fact, was to help throw light on how the Nazi atrocities could have happened. Research the Nuremberg war crimes tribunals following World War II. Drawing specifically on the statements of those who testified at Nuremberg, as well as those who have written about it, show how Milgram's experiments do help explain the Holocaust and other Nazi crimes. In addition to relevant articles, see Telford Taylor, *Nuremberg and Vietnam: An American Tragedy* (1970); Hannah Arendt, *Eichmann in Jerusalem: A Report on the Banality of Evil* (1963); Richard A. Falk, Gabriel Kolko, and Robert J. Lifton (eds.), *Crimes of War* (1971).

3. Obtain a copy of the transcript of the trial of Adolf Eichmann—the Nazi official who carried out Hitler's "final solution" for the extermination of the Jews. Read also Hannah Arendt's *Eichmann in Jerusalem: A Report on the Banality of Evil*, along with the reviews of this book. Write a critique both of Arendt's book and of the reviews it received.

4. The My Lai massacre in Vietnam in 1969 was a particularly egregious case of overobedience to military authority in wartime. Show the connections between this event and Milgram's experiments. Note that Milgram himself treated the My Lai massacre in the epilogue to his *Obedience to Authority: An Experimental View* (1974).

5. Since feminism re-emerged as a strong activist movement in the early 1970s, it has been passionately resisted by social conservatives who argue that women are better off under a patriarchal system. Among them are the R.E.A.L. Women of Canada ("Realistic Equal Active for Life"), an anti-feminist group largely composed of middle-class Catholic and Protestant fundamentalist women over the age of 40[1]; the group was originally connected with Conservative backbenchers in the House of Commons who opposed the extension of women's legal rights and protections. Use general and social science periodical indexes to find articles about R.E.A.L. Women and other instances of women fighting to preserve social structures that feminists oppose as sexist. Also search your library catalogue for related books on the backlash against feminism, including Andrea Dworkin's *Right Wing Women*. Using these books and articles as sources of insight, write an essay that accounts for the political phenomenon of women who advocate obedience to patriarchal authority.

6. At the outset of his article, Stanley Milgram refers to imaginative works revolving around the issue of obedience to authority: the story of Abraham and Isaac; three of Plato's dialogues, "Apology," "Crito," and "Phaedo;" and the story of Antigone (dramatized by both the fifth-century B.C. Athenian Sophocles and the 20th-century Frenchman Jean Anouilh). In this chapter, we have reprinted Shirley Jackson's "The Lottery," and an excerpt from Margaret Atwood's *The Handmaid's Tale*, which also can be read as stories about obedience to authority. And many other fictional works deal with obedience to authority—for example, Herman Wouk's novel *The Caine Mutiny* (and his subsequent play *The Caine Mutiny Court Martial*). Check with your instructor, with a librarian, and with such sources as the *Short Story Index* to locate other imaginative works on this theme. Write a paper discussing the various ways in which the subject has been treated in fiction and drama. To ensure coherence, draw comparisons and contrasts among works showing the connections and the variations on the theme of obedience to authority.

---

[1] L. K. Erwin, "REAL Women, Anti-Feminism, and the Welfare State," *Resources for Feminist Research/Documentation sur la Recherche Feministe* 17. 3 (1988): 147–49.

# 10

# The Book of Job

When tidal waves devastate coastal communities, when bridges fail, when wars consume a countryside: In man-made and natural disasters alike, innocent people suffer. On the television and in newspapers we witness the tragedies in far-flung places such as Bangladesh and Rwanda, and we ache from a distance. All too often, though, we learn the lessons of suffering close to home—when, for example, cancer strikes a family member in the prime of life. Why should one person be stricken and not another? How do we understand the deaths of the three high-school students in Kentucky who had just bowed their heads at a prayer meeting when a fellow student burst into the room firing a gun? How do we justify the hardships of the child born on one side of town while, on the other, a child is born to the security of good schools and abundant food?

Blameless people *do* suffer, and we have long struggled to understand why. As children many of us are taught to believe that a strict moral logic governs this world: People who obey biblical law (and its secular equivalents) enjoy good fortune while those who disobey do not. When the world contradicts this logic and brings suffering to good people, we feel betrayed. No work of literature gives voice to this sense of betrayal more beautifully or hauntingly than the Book of Job. Written by an anonymous author 2500 years ago and installed later as a book in the *Old Testament*, Job raises questions about faith and justice that are as vexing for us as they were for the ancients. When we ask *Where was God* in the face of a calamity, we are posing what philosophers and theologians call a Job*an* question. It was the question of Jews who survived the Holocaust. It is the question of a father who sees his happiness shattered by an accident (a car skidding into his car in a snowstorm): "I was one of those guys who thought tragedy always happened to the other person," he writes. "You just never know. One day you're a happy guy with . . . two beautiful children, a nice home, a nice job and enough income to meet the mortgage payments and a few extras."[1] And the next day, he observes, you're disabled, dependent on the state for financial assistance. Why?

If you have never read or heard of Job, you will nonetheless recognize the story of the virtuous person who strives to do right but is struck down just the same. The sufferer cries: *Why me?* Well-intentioned friends offer consolation, but they cannot understand the sufferer's despair and dismay. Inevitably,

[1] James Calogero. "Auto accident leaves husband disabled, family devastated." *Boston Globe*, 4 December 1997, p. B10.

someone claiming to understand the grand Order of the Universe will suggest that truly blameless people do not suffer (it is not God's way) and that, therefore, this particular suffering must be deserved.

If you can allow that students killed at a prayer meeting, a cancer victim, or victims of ethnic cleansing in Rwanda did *not* deserve misfortune, and that disasters and sickness can strike randomly, then read on: for it is just this awareness that lies both at the heart of Job and in the hearts of every person who has been assaulted by life.

In its earliest form, Job existed as an oral tale with variants that date to the ancient Babylonians. Around the year 500 BCE,[2] the anonymous writer of the Job we read in the *Old Testament* borrowed from the original oral story and used it as a frame—or as the opening and closing sections—of a new *written* version. In the original, Job is the pious servant of God who in quick succession loses his children, his wealth, and his health—but endures patiently. He believes that whether God gives or takes, God must be blessed, never doubted. The writer of the biblical story made a radical break with the original oral version by adding an extended middle section, in verse, on Job's *im*patient reply to his sufferings. This reinvented Job challenges God to justify why calamities should strike down a faithful servant. Job believes himself blameless and ill-treated, and he will not be silent. He complains bitterly, until God appears in a whirlwind with a thunderous answer.

Not surprisingly for a text that poses fundamental questions about faith and divine justice, a rich history of commentary has grown around Job. Among the earliest were commentaries in the third and fourth centuries CE, composed by rabbis who were assembling a multi-volumed study of the *Old Testament*. In the year 600, Pope Gregory the Great concluded a 34-volume exegesis (or close reading) of Job. A scholar researching that work characterizes Gregory's position on Job and quotes him this way:

> Reflecting on the adversities of saintly men such as Job . . . Gregory concludes that God strikes those whom he loves because "he knows how to reward them. . . . He casts them down outwardly to something despicable in order to lead them on inwardly to the height of things incomprehensible."[3]

Gregory's argument that "suffering actually is necessary to *cure*"[4] a person's deluded view of reality became a bedrock of Church teachings that lasted well over a thousand years. According to Gregory, suffering led Job to greater awareness of God; hence, suffering, however painful, was a useful tool in Job's spiritual development and, by extension, can be understood as a useful tool in ours. How satisfying for you is the view that suffering can serve as a reward?

---

[2] BCE is an abbreviation for *Before the Common Era*, another way of writing before the birth of Christ. CE refers to the *Common Era*, or the years after the birth of Christ.

[3] Susan Schreiner, *Where Shall Wisdom Be Found: Calvin's Exegesis of Job from Medieval and Modern Perspectives* (Chicago: University of Chicago Press, 1994), 34.

[4] Schreiner, 31.

Writing in the early 12th century, the medieval Jewish philosopher Moses Maimonides discussed Job at some length in his *Guide to the Perplexed*. Maimonides wrote that people labour under a confusion if they expect rewards from God to be measured in anything but spiritual gain:

> Man's task is to approach to God as close as humanly possible. . . . The evil are punished not by the withholding of material rewards but by their alienation from God, their debarment from human perfection. The good are rewarded not by worldly success but by the possibility of enlightenment, knowledge of God, which virtue opens to the truly wise.[5]

Job complained because his children had died, his wealth was stolen, and his body was devastated by disease. According to Maimonides, Job mistakenly expected the wrong sort of reward (children, money, and health) as acknowledgment of pious behaviour. Eight hundred years ago, Maimonides believed that personal suffering and personal happiness are not the currency in which God administers justice.

That we can with interest read an ancient text and the comments of thinkers centuries removed and then be drawn into an opinion ourselves is a remarkable achievement, suggesting both the enduring value of Job and of the very qualities that make us human. Consider: Why has Job's complaint always been understood by readers as a *contemporary* complaint—whether "contemporary" is defined as the year 400, 600, 1200, or 2000? The Book of Job is timeless: Through it we find connection to those who lived 2500 years ago and to all who followed and also read. Through it, others will find connection to us.

Whether you read Job as a sacred text (sacred in the sense that it appears in the Bible) or as a classic of world literature valuable not because of its origins but because of what it says—however you read, realize that you do so in a tradition of interpretation. In addition to Pope Gregory and Moses Maimonides, many religious figures have written on Job, including Thomas Aquinas and John Calvin. As secular text, Job has received equal attention from philosophers, literary critics, poets, and essayists. Which is to say, you have licence to read and interpret. As Peter Gomes, Minister in The Memorial Church and Plummer Professor of Christian Morals at Harvard University observes,

> Interpretation is the fuel that drives understanding. The making of meaning is what scripture is all about, the effort by every possible device to make sense of the divine in search of the human, and the human in search of the divine, the joy of discovery, the sorrow of loss. If scripture is about anything in all of its splendid diversity, it is about this, and so it is not really about whether there is or is not interpretation in the reading of scripture. Of course there is interpretation. The question is, what kind of interpretation?[6]

---

[5] Moses Maimonides, "From *Moreh Nevukhim* III:22," in *Rambam: Readings in the Philosophy of Moses Maimonides*, ed. Lenn Evan Goodman (New York: Schocken, 1976), 356n.

[6] Peter Gomes, *The Good Book: Reading the Bible With Mind and Heart* (New York: Morrow, 1996), 33.

What kind of interpretation is a matter for you to decide. What we have done is to provide an occasion to interpret, with five selections that bear directly, and indirectly, on the Book of Job. We begin with an excerpt from *The Good Book: Reading the Bible With Mind and Heart* by Peter Gomes. In this selection, Gomes does not refer directly to the Book of Job; rather, he discusses the larger human context of human suffering in which Job is situated. You can read "The Bible and Suffering" as an introduction to the *idea* of this chapter. Next comes an excerpt from Job. The unabridged text is too long for inclusion; but since its lengthy middle section consists of three largely repetitive cycles of debate between Job and his friends, we believe that an extended excerpt captures the spirit of the work. (In any event, a complete version is as close as the nearest Bible.) The headnote to Job will detail which verses have been excerpted, as well as offer a note on translation.

Job is followed by three selections. The first is Harold Kushner, a rabbi and author of *When Bad Things Happen to Good People*. Kushner wrote his book in response to the loss of his son to a rare disease. Rather than deny God's existence or accept a God who would knowingly let the innocent suffer, Kushner prefers to believe in a God who is *not* all powerful (who could not, for instance, prevent a child from contracting a fatal illness).

In "The Myth of Justice," the late novelist and essayist Michael Dorris writes a bitter essay rejecting the idea of justice, both in this world and in the next. Justice here, writes Dorris, does not exist. As for eternal justice, that's an illusion (a "palliative myth"). Dianne Bergant, Professor of Biblical Studies at Catholic Theological Union (Chicago), sees in Job a tragic temptation to deny meaning in life. Job, she writes, resists that temptation and deepens his faith.

The Book of Job jolts us into reexamining core beliefs, among them: *Why should any of us struggle to be virtuous when the good suffer along with the wicked?* Beset by calamities, Job posed troubling questions. The fact that neither he nor we find easy answers defines, in large measure, the human predicament.

## The Bible and Suffering

PETER GOMES

*Peter Gomes (b. 1942) is Minister at The Memorial Church at Harvard University. In his responsibilities as a professor of theology, and more particularly as a spiritual guide for a large and varied community, he has often had occasion to address the subject of innocent suffering. The selection that follows, "The Bible and Suffering," appears in* The Good Book: Reading the Bible With Mind and Heart *and grows out of his years of ministering and the obligation it placed upon him to offer meaningful consolation in times of tragedy. While Gomes, an African American and a Baptist preacher, does not refer directly to the Book of Job, he prepares us for reading Joban themes.*

The church was crowded with the young and the good, those filled with    1
promise and the first flush of achievement. Many of them were in the "industry," the almost oxymoronic euphemism that describes what people in
Hollywood do to entertain and divert us, and to make enormous sums of
money while doing so. Some observers of Harvard graduates have noted that
the three cities to which our brightest and best gravitate are New York,
Washington, D.C., and Hollywood. In New York they make money, in
Washington they make policy, and in Hollywood they make not only films
but fantasy for the whole world. Those who go there in some sense never
grow up. They are Peter Pans, and they are in the business of catering to the
Peter Pan and Wendy in all of us.

   This was such a crowd. I had last seen many of them on Commencement    2
morning fewer than five years before when they were also in church, and
among a large crowd; and on that morning the world was bright with promise
and waiting for them, the sober black of academic dress neither concealing
nor checking their exuberance and expectations. Few if any of them on that
glad day had expected to return to Harvard or to The Memorial Church quite
so soon, or for the sad and solemn purpose of burying one of their own who
had been killed in a senseless, irrational car accident in the prime of life. Here
they were, however, black-suited, still fair of face, and looking younger and
indeed more vulnerable than when last we had all been together. Death had
intruded, and with it a monstrous assault on the human claim to immortali-
ty. They wept, and they raged at the loss of their friend. Death was an abstraction about which movies were made, and death happened to grandparents, to
the occasional victim of terrible crime, or to participants in war. Death in
theory would come to them eventually, but so far down the road of reality
that it was hardly real at all. How does one deal with unscripted death? How
do the worldly-wise, the hip, the interpreters of life in the fast, or at least in
the interesting, lane deal with it? How do they deal with the irrational and
immutable judgments of death unprepared, unexpected, unwelcome?

   The Victorians, we are told, loved death and feared sex, and hence their    3
culture embraced a culture of death and mourning, and constructed strong
taboos against sex. We, on the other hand, love sex and fear death, and our
taboos are of a different sort. We delight in sexuality, we pander to the sen-
sual, and we have made Calvin Klein a very wealthy man. Death is not something we want to understand or to know; death is somehow unfair, and in this
country it is culturally unconstitutional, violating our right to life, liberty, and
the pursuit of happiness. Thus, when death intrudes, particularly among the
young, we respond in terror, anger, and fear.

   As I listened to the heartrending eulogies of the young for their young, I    4
heard anger and fear. I heard their love as well, and their pained, pathetic
desire to make sense of it all. "What does it mean?" asked one tearful young
woman. "We must make it mean something," said another. "It doesn't make
sense," said a third. "Will it get easier to understand this as we get older?" a
bright young man asked me as the white wine flowed at the reception. "Will

I wake up some day and understand why Willie had to die in this way, at this time?" It was not a question that required an answer, at least not then, for he was baying at the moon, not making a theological inquiry.

I think I said most of the right things. One hopes, in my calling, that one does on occasions like this. Clichés become truths when they are applied to one's own situation, I have discovered, and I reminded these young people that while funeral-going was perhaps a new experience for most of them, it was an all too familiar habit for the rest of us. I reminded them that the context of life is not living, but death, and that it is out of death that life comes. Death is the rule to which life is the exception. It is not how long you live, but how well you live with what you have, and I quoted that lovely and relatively unfamiliar passage from the Apocrypha, which says of early death: "He, being made perfect in a short time, fulfilled a long time; for his soul pleased the Lord: therefore hasted he to take him away from among the wicked." (Wisdom 4:8–14)

I always end memorial services and funerals with the prayer long associated with Cardinal Newman, and I did so on this day. Many were familiar with it, and many more were not, but were interested in it:

> O Lord, support us all the day long of this troublous life, until the shadows lengthen and the evening comes, and the fever of life is over, and our work is done. Then, in thy great mercy, grant us a safe lodging, a holy rest, and peace at the last.

We scattered again, as we always do, back to the demands and diversions of this troublous life, pondering the meaning of suffering, the purpose of life, and trying to make sense of it all as in the making of a living we try to make a life as well. It is for moments such as these that religion was made, and when we confront the unconfrontable, or more to the point, when it confronts us, we are at a religious moment, and for a moment at least we are religious. Contrary to the popular misconception, religion is not an escape from reality but rather a genuine effort to make sense of what passes for reality and all that surrounds it. Religious people are not escape artists; they are not practitioners of evasion or of self-deception. Religion is not the answer to the unknowable or the unfaceable or the unendurable; religion is what we do and what we are in the face of the unknowable, the unfaceable, and the unendurable. It is a constant exercise in the making of sense first, and then of meaning.

"I'm not very religious, but I had to come to this service," said one of my secular young mourners. He was more religious than he thought, not because he professed certain doctrines or behaved in a particular way or performed certain rites and rituals and believed in what they said and did. He was religious because he wanted to make sense of what he was experiencing, pain and all, and on his own and by himself he could not. Legal, medical, physiological, even psychological answers, themselves definitive and helpful, were not sufficient of themselves; somehow something else was wanted and needed.

## THE THIN PLACES

That something else wanted and needed is what religion is about. "Religion    9
in its simplest terms," says John Habgood,[1] the recently retired Archbishop of
York, "is about making sense of life, of this life first of all, and particularly of
those aspects of it which challenge and disturb us. This is why suffering and
ways of responding to it have always been so central to religion." Not only do
we have a need to try to make sense of suffering, Dr. Habgood tells us, but we
also want to make sense where we can of joy—"undeserved happiness," he
calls it—or "blessings," as the devout and pious call it; and of mystery, those
close encounters of the transcendent kind that suggest relationships beyond
the power of our experience to reckon, but which we know in some fundamental way to be true. Suffering, joy, and mystery are those points where the
human and the divine come into the most intimate and profound of proxim-
ities. They unite all human experience in all ages and beyond all particulars of
place and of circumstance. All religions of the world are and always have been
concerned with their substance. It is the common ambition of our common
humanity to make sense and meaning of these encounters wherever we can.
Religion is the attempt to give some formal record of what we may learn from
these experiences, and, for Christians, the Bible is the authoritative record of
the human encounter with God at these points.

There is in Celtic mythology the notion of "thin places" in the universe,    10
where the visible and the invisible world come into their closest proximity. To
seek such places is the vocation of the wise and the good, and those who find
them find the clearest communication between the temporal and the eternal.
Monasteries and holy places were meant to be founded at such spots to
increase the likelihood of a transcendental communication. These thin places
were threshold places, from the Latin *limen*, which can mean a border or
frontier place where two worlds meet and where one has the possibility of
communicating with the other. In Celtic studies the phrase can refer to places
that stand at the border between the spiritual and temporal realms, and
between people gifted with supernatural gifts in the mundane world and
those living on the border.

Perhaps we can adapt the concept of such thin places to the experience    11
that people are likely to have as they encounter suffering, joy, and mystery,
and seek in some fashion to make sense of that encounter. If we think of these
encounters as the ultimate thin places of human experience, and of religion as
a way of talking and thinking about the encounters, we might do very well to
think of the Bible as our guide through the thin places, and as providing us
with a record of how our ancestors coped with their encounters, and guidance
beyond their particular situation which may be useful in ours. Contrary to the
efforts and assumptions of many, the Bible is not a systematic book. It is not
a doctrinal handbook or a systematic theology, nor is it a comprehensive history or a compendium of morals and ethics. To argue that it is any of these is
to make the Bible conform to an extra-biblical set of convictions and assump-

tions, and to make it pass a test of theological orthodoxy of which it is not capable. Doctrines of inerrancy and infallibility are merely modern human efforts to impose order both on scripture and on those who read it. These are what John Huxtable[2] once called "dogmatic vested interest," designed to preserve as the word of God a particularly partisan way of looking at scripture. Such a way of reading the Bible is designed to support those interests, and they are "found" in the Bible because they are brought to the Bible.

There are principles and ideas that develop over time through the pages    12
of scripture that make it possible for us to detect truths that transcend the contexts in which they are found, principles that go beyond captivity to a given situation, and which stand out like the mountains on the moon. Indeed, it is such normative teaching and such developing ideas and ideals that enable us to judge scriptural situation by scriptural principle, and thus, in order to be biblical, we are able to read scripture freed of the expectation that we must reproduce its every detail and circumstance. . . .

If we are to think of scripture not so much as we would a book of histo-    13
ry, theology, or philosophy, but as the human experience of the divine at the thin places of encounter, then perhaps we may enter into a book that is perhaps less elusive and more accessible than we might have at first been led to believe. If the Bible is understood to be the place where not only others long dead but we ourselves encounter those thin places of suffering, joy, and mystery, and the efforts to make sense and meaning of those encounters, then perhaps we have rescued it from the clutches of the experts and the specialists and placed it where it rightly belongs, namely in the hands of those who find themselves more religious than they thought.

## WHAT DARE WE MAKE OF SUFFERING?

I recall reading some years ago of the death of the young son of William Sloan    14
Coffin, in a horrible automobile accident in Boston. At some point, perhaps at the funeral, perhaps later in a sermon, the anguished father discussed his reaction to this terrible experience, saying that frequently people would attempt to comfort him with the Christian cliché, "It is God's will." Coffin thundered, "The hell it is. When my boy was killed, God was the first who cried." If God can be sympathetic and empathetic, why can't God prevent the source of those troubles that require human and divine sympathy? Suffering makes us ask hard questions of God, i.e., where were you when I needed you? Suffering also makes us ask hard questions of ourselves: What have I done to deserve this?

If suffering is, as I suggest that it is, a thin place, indeed a place of prox-    15
imity to the divine, such proximity has served to alienate many from God rather than draw them nearer. If God is indifferent to suffering—for example, if God really does not care about the manifest human sufferings in Bosnia, or in Rwanda, or in the AIDS wards of the local hospitals, or in the galloping Alzheimer's disease of an old and once-bright friend or spouse—who cares for that kind of God?

If God is merely sympathetic but impotent in the face of such difficulties, 16
then again, of what value is the idea? Sympathy is cheap, and hence abundant.
Divine sympathy is no more or less helpful than any other kind.

If God is the source or cause of the suffering, and the suffering is an 17
expression of God's will, then is this not a malevolent, vengeful, even perverse
God, who exercises ultimate power in a capricious, or even immoral, way?

Indifferent, sympathetic, arbitrary—somehow God is usually called into 18
our conversations about suffering, for the ultimate suffering is that suffering
itself is meaningless and must be endured alone. Misery loves company, we
are told. Well, there is more to it than that, for misery actually requires company. Just as it is really not possible to be happy alone, "the sound of one
hand clapping" and all of that, so too it is not really possible to suffer alone.
That is why we invoke God, even the godless among us, and that is why we
are constantly looking for companionship in suffering, either to share or to
blame or at times to do both.

Suffering, we are taught very early on, is a part of life. As the Yankee 19
adage has it, "What can't be cured must be endured," and most of us were
brought up with an understanding of that concept. We were taught as well
that suffering was redemptive or, at the very least, instructive. When we
suffer, we are more apt to learn. Our mothers used to say that suffering was
God's way of getting our attention, and that there were lessons to be learned
from suffering. We would be the better for it.

Redemptive—dare we even say therapeutic?—suffering is that of which 20
Paul speaks with a beguiling candor when, in writing his second letter to the
Corinthians, he speaks of his "thorn in the flesh": "And to keep me from
being too elated by the abundance of revelations, a thorn was given me in the
flesh, a messenger of Satan, to harass me, to keep me from being too elated."

Paul was not a masochist delighting in this object lesson in humility 21
and suffering, for he asked not once but three times to be rid of this trouble:
"Three times I besought the Lord about this, that it should leave me; but
he said to me, 'My grace is sufficient for you, for my power is made perfect
in weakness.'"

Paul's sufferings were not relieved, and he understood his weakness to be 22
an opportunity to manifest the power of God: "I will all the more gladly boast
of my weaknesses, that the power of Christ may rest upon me. For the sake of
Christ, then, I am content with weaknesses, insults, hardships, persecutions,
and calamities; for when I am weak, then I am strong." (II Corinthians
12:7–10)

• • •

Suffering . . . is not an exception to the human condition, it *is* the human 23
condition, and as such it is almost impossible to avoid; and since religion, as
we have said, has to do with the human condition, and indeed with the enormous task of trying to make sense and meaning of it, religion by its very
nature has an intimacy with suffering. That intimacy is the stuff of which our
lives are composed.

Sigmund Freud,[3] no friend of religion, nevertheless gives us a compre-    24
hensive sense of suffering, and thus we are enabled to see the scope of religion's intimate relations with it. Says Freud:

> We are threatened with suffering from three directions: from our own body,
> which is doomed to decay and dissolution and which cannot even do that
> without pain and anxiety as warning signals; from the external world, which
> may rage against us with overwhelming and merciless forces of destruction;
> and finally, from our relations to other men. The suffering which comes
> from this last source is perhaps more painful than any other.

Morality, conflict, and ethics: These sources of our sufferings have always    25
been the business of religion and of the Bible. How do we deal with the fact
that inevitably we die, that our life before we die is conflicted and besieged,
and that we find it difficult to get along with our fellow creatures? These are
not Freudian categories; this is life itself.

## REFERENCES

1. John Habgood. *Making Sense* (London: SPCK, 1993). As Archbishop of York,
   Habgood was the Primate of England, whereas his brother Archbishop of
   Canterbury was Primate of *All* England, with a seat in the House of Lords as
   one of the Lords Spiritual and a reputation as a thinking bishop. Indeed, David
   L. Edwards in the jacket blurb said of Habgood, "Were there to be an Olympics
   in episcopal theology, Dr. Habgood would win the gold." The tradition of
   "thinking bishops" in the Church of England is an old and lively one, but in this
   managerial and politically correct age, where the lowest point of nonoffense is
   appealed to, the appointment of a thinking bishop who makes others think as
   well is a rarity in the Church of England and nearly nonexistent in the other
   realms of the Anglican Communion. These essays are drawn from his writings
   in his own diocesan magazine, professional and scholarly journals, articles in
   the press, and some of his lectures and sermons. In the essay "Do Pigs Have
   Wings?" he argues, "Religion in its simplest terms is about making sense of life,
   this life, first of all, and particularly those aspects of it which challenge and disturb us." It was from this essay that the third and final section of my own book,
   the pastoral section, took its inspiration.
2. John Huxtable, *The Bible Says* (London: SCM Press, 1962). This is a small but
   very effective essay against the ever-present temptation to make a graven
   image out of the Bible. One of his best lines is "Jesus Christ came into the
   world to be its saviour, not an authority on biblical criticism." (p. 70)
3. Sigmund Freud, *Civilization and Its Discontents* (London: 1930), Chapter 2.
   Richard Webster in *Why Freud Was Wrong: Sin, Science, and Psychoanalysis*
   (New York: Basic Books, 1995), in writing of Freud's low estimate of the
   human condition, quotes from a letter to Lou Andreas-Salome in which he
   says, "In the depths of my heart I can't help being convinced that my dear
   fellow men, with a few exceptions, are worthless." (p. 324)

■ ■ ■

## Review Questions

1. Why, according to Gomes, do we (and particularly young people) "respond in terror, anger, and fear" to death, especially to the death of a young person?
2. What is a "religious moment," according to Gomes?
3. What is the purpose of religion, according to Gomes?
4. How does Gomes adapt the Celtic notion of "thin places" to his discussion of suffering?
5. Why does human suffering eventually cause us to pose difficult questions about God?

## Discussion and Writing Questions

1. Why do you suppose Gomes opens his discussion with an account of a memorial service? What was your response to the comments of the mourners? Have you found yourself in a similar setting? To what extent do you recognize the mourners' responses to the death of their friend?
2. Gomes speaks of a young mourner being "more religious than he [the mourner] thought." What does Gomes mean by this? And why, several paragraphs later, does Gomes suggest it is a good thing that the Bible be placed "in the hands of those who find themselves more religious than they thought"?
3. Gomes discusses the apostle Paul's speaking of a "thorn in the flesh" (paragraph 20). Paul explains the thorn in terms of what the Lord says to him: "'My grace is sufficient for you, for my power is made perfect in weakness.'" What does it mean to you that God's power is made perfect in weakness? How is one made strong in weakness?
4. "Suffering . . . is not an exception to the human condition, it *is* the human condition." Do you agree with this assessment?
5. Describe the effect of this selection on you: Are you calmed, perhaps, by the "voice" of this writer? Perplexed? Are you struck by Gomes's wisdom? Do you find that he has the voice of a minister? What *is* that voice and, again: What is its effect on you? Write your response as a journal entry.

## ▌ *The Book of Job*

*The essay introducing this chapter provides an overview that will help orient your reading of Job. This headnote is devoted to other matters: the complex authorship of the text and the difficulties of translation.*

*Not only do we not know the author of the Book of Job, biblical scholars are confident that more than one author is responsible for the work. Carol Newsom summarizes the speculations concerning authorship in this way:*

In scholarly discussions of the past century, [evidence has emerged] . . . that the book of Job grew by stages, the various parts attributable to different authors working at different times. Although there are many different versions of this hypothesis, it usually includes at least the following claims.

*Stage 1.* The oldest form of the book would have been the prose tale, an ancient story, originally told orally, about Job the pious. This stage is represented by chaps. 1–2 and 42:7–17. The middle part of this form of the story is no longer extant, but would have included some sort of brief dialogue between Job and his friends in which they spoke disparagingly of God, while Job steadfastly refused to curse God.

*Stage 2.* An Israelite author who considered the old story inadequate and in need of critique decided to use it as the framework for a much more ambitious, sophisticated retelling of the story in which the figure of Job does not remain the patiently enduring character of the traditional tale, but challenges God's treatment of him. According to this hypothesis, the author substituted a new poetic dialogue between Job and his friends (3:1–31:37) in place of the discussion in which they engaged in the older story and added a long speech by God as the climax (38:1–42:6). The author used the conclusion of the old story (42:7–17) as the conclusion of his thoroughly transformed new version of the book. The poem on wisdom in chap. 28 may be a composition by this author, who used it as a transition between Job's dialogue with his friends and Job's dialogue with God, or it may be an addition by a later hand.

*Stage 3.* Another author, writing sometime later, considered the new version of the book of Job unsatisfactory, because he perceived that Job had gotten the better of his three friends in their argument, and because he did not find the divine speeches to be an entirely adequate answer to Job. Consequently, he created a new character, Elihu, and inserted his long speech into the book in order to provide what seemed to him a decisive refutation of Job's arguments.

*Stage 4.* Sometime during the transmission of the book, copyists who were shocked by Job's blasphemous words attempted to soften their impact by rearranging the third cycle of speeches, putting some of Bildad's and Zophar's speeches into Job's mouth.

*The Book of Job has posed famously difficult obstacles to translators over the centuries. Read two translations of the same passage and you may be surprised at the differences. Compare, for instance, two translations of Job's first words (3:3–5), spoken after he has lost children and wealth and has been afflicted with a loathsome disease. First, here is the* Revised Standard Version, *the translation you will read in this chapter:*

> Let the day perish wherein I was born, and the night which said,
>     'A man-child is conceived.'
> Let that day be darkness! May God above not seek it, nor light shine
>     upon it.
> Let gloom and deep darkness claim it. Let clouds dwell upon it; let
>     the blackness of the day terrify it.

*And here is a translation of Job's first words by poet Stephen Mitchell:*

God damn the day I was born
    and the night that pushed me from the womb.
On that day—let there be darkness;
    let it never have been created;
    let it sink back into the void.
Let chaos overpower it;
    let black clouds overwhelm it;
    let the sun be plucked from its sky.[1]

*Obscurities in the Hebrew text make translation highly challenging and subject to the interpretive whims of individual translators. Whereas the examples above might seem to indicate poetic or stylistic differences only, there exist key passages in Job that, translated in alternative ways, present entirely conflicting views of Job's character and the extent of his rebelliousness. In* The First Dissident, *William Safire calls attention to the following line (13:15) from the Marvin H. Pope translation* (The Anchor Bible). *Job is speaking and explaining how he would stand before God and present his case as an aggrieved and innocent sufferer:*

He may slay me, I'll not quaver.

*Compare this with the* King James Version:

Though he slay me, yet I will trust in him.

*Compare, again, with the* Revised Standard Version *(the translation you will read):*

Behold, he will slay me; I have no hope; yet I will defend my ways to his
    face.

*There's an enormous distance between obediently trusting in God and not quavering or between not quavering and defending oneself before God. As Safire observes, "Thousands of sermons have been preached on [the* King James'] *serene expression of faith, but the* King James *text on which the sermons were based was a twisting of Job's meaning—from blasphemy to piety—too severe to be attributed to error. The point of this key line, modern translators agree, is not faith, but courage; not submission, but defiance."[2] Safire implies that the King James translators had an agenda—to present Job as a less rebellious figure than he was in the original Hebrew.*

    *This is to say that the translation you read here, the* Revised Standard Version *(RSV, published by American Bible Scholars in 1952), cannot be called definitive—nor can any translation of so difficult a work. We present the RSV translation here because of its general readability and the fact that a great deal of Joban scholarship refers to it.*

---

[1] Stephen Mitchell, *Into the Whirlwind: A Translation of the Book of Job* (New York: Doubleday, 1979), 19.
[2] William Safire, *The First Dissident: The Book of Job in Today's Politics* (New York: Random, 1992), xi.

*As noted in our introduction to the chapter, we provide an extended excerpt from the Book of Job. Immediately below, you will find Carol Newsom's out-line of Job. We have placed a check beside sections included in the excerpt. The notable omissions are the second and third cycles of dialogue between Job and his friends, and the speech of Elihu. Should you have access to an Internet con-nection, point your browser to The Bible Gateway, where you will find the full text in several translations: The URL is* **http://bible.gospelcom.net/.** *Select "RSV" from the pull-down menu at "Version." Enter "Job" in the "Passage" category and click "Lookup."*

Outline of Job[3]

✓   I. Job 1:2–2:13, The Prose Narrative: Introduction

    ✓   A.   1:1–22, The First Test

        1:1–5, Scene 1: Introduction to Job

        1:6–12, Scene 2: A Dialogue About Job

        1:13–22, Scene 3: The Test–Destruction of "All That He Has"

    ✓   B.   2:1–10, The Second Test

        2:1–6, Scene 4, A Second Dialogue About Job

        2:7–10, Scene 5: The Test–Disease

    ✓   C.   2:11–13, Scene 6: The Three Friends

✓   II. Job 3:1–31:40, The Poetic Dialogue Between Job and His Friends

    ✓   A.   3:1–14:22, The First Cycle

        3:1–26, Job Curses the Day of His Birth

        4:1–5:27, Traditional Understandings of Misfortune

        6:1–7:21, Job Defends the Vehemence of His Words

        6:1–30, Anguish Made Worse by the Failure of Friendship

        7:1–21, Job Confronts God

        8:1–22, A Metaphor of Two Plants

        9:1–10:22, Job Imagines a Trial with God

        11:1–20, Zophar Defends God's Wisdom

        12:1–14:22, Job Burlesques the Wisdom of God and Struggles

           with Mortality

        12:1–13:2, Job Parodies Traditional Praise of God

        13:3–19, Job Criticizes Deceitful Speech

        13:20–14:22, Job Experiences the Destruction of Hope

      B.   15:1–21:34, The Second Cycle

        15:1–35, Eliphaz Describes the Fate of the Wicked

        16:1–17:16, Job Complains of God's Criminal Violence

        18:1–21, Bildad Describes the Fate of the Wicked

        19:1–29, Job Denounces God's Injustice

        20:1–29, Zophar Describes the Fate of the Wicked

        21:1–34, The Fate of the Wicked Is Prosperity and Honor

---

[3] From *The New Interpreter's Bible.*

## JOB 1[4]

[1]There was a man in the land of Uz, whose name was Job; and that man was blameless and upright, one who feared God, and turned away from evil. [2]There were born to him seven sons and three daughters. [3]He had seven thousand sheep, three thousand camels, five hundred yoke of oxen, and five hundred she-asses, and very many servants; so that this man was the greatest of all the people of the east. [4]His sons used to go and hold a feast in the house of each on his day; and they would send and invite their three sisters to eat and drink with them. [5]And when the days of the feast had run their course, Job would send and

---

[4] From *The Book of Job. Revised Standard Version.* American Bible Scholars. Numbers before sentences in this section indicate verse numbers.

sanctify them, and he would rise early in the morning and offer burnt offerings according to the number of them all; for Job said, "It may be that my sons have sinned, and cursed God in their hearts." Thus Job did continually.

$^6$Now there was a day when the sons of God came to present themselves before the LORD, and Satan also came among them. $^7$The LORD said to Satan, "Whence have you come?" Satan answered the LORD, "From going to and fro on the earth, and from walking up and down on it." $^8$And the LORD said to Satan, "Have you considered my servant Job, that there is none like him on the earth, a blameless and upright man, who fears God and turns away from evil?" $^9$Then Satan answered the LORD, "Does Job fear God for nought? $^{10}$Hast thou not put a hedge about him and his house and all that he has, on every side? Thou hast blessed the work of his hands, and his possessions have increased in the land. $^{11}$But put forth thy hand now, and touch all that he has, and he will curse thee to thy face." $^{12}$And the LORD said to Satan, "Behold, all that he has is in your power; only upon himself do not put forth your hand." So Satan went forth from the presence of the LORD.

$^{13}$Now there was a day when his sons and daughters were eating and drinking wine in their eldest brother's house; $^{14}$and there came a messenger to Job, and said, "The oxen were plowing and the asses feeding beside them; $^{15}$and the Sabe'ans fell upon them and took them, and slew the servants with the edge of the sword; and I alone have escaped to tell you." $^{16}$While he was yet speaking, there came another, and said, "The fire of God fell from heaven and burned up the sheep and the servants, and consumed them; and I alone have escaped to tell you." $^{17}$While he was yet speaking, there came another, and said, "The Chalde'ans formed three companies, and made a raid upon the camels and took them, and slew the servants with the edge of the sword; and I alone have escaped to tell you." $^{18}$While he was yet speaking, there came another, and said, "Your sons and daughters were eating and drinking wine in their eldest brother's house; $^{19}$and behold, a great wind came across the wilderness, and struck the four corners of the house, and it fell upon the young people, and they are dead; and I alone have escaped to tell you." $^{20}$Then Job arose, and rent his robe, and shaved his head, and fell upon the ground, and worshiped. $^{21}$And he said, "Naked I came from my mother's womb, and naked shall I return; the LORD gave, and the LORD has taken away; blessed be the name of the LORD." $^{22}$In all this Job did not sin or charge God with wrong.

## JOB 2

$^1$Again there was a day when the sons of God came to present themselves before the LORD, and Satan also came among them to present himself before the LORD. $^2$And the LORD said to Satan, "Whence have you come?" Satan answered the LORD, "From going to and fro on the earth, and from walking up and down on it." $^3$And the LORD said to Satan, "Have you considered my servant Job, that there is none like him on the earth, a blameless and upright man, who fears God and turns away from evil? He still holds fast his integrity, although you moved me against him, to destroy him without cause." ⁴Then Satan answered the LORD, "Skin for skin! All that a man has he will give for his life. ⁵But put forth thy hand now, and touch his bone and his flesh, and he will curse thee to thy face." ⁶And the LORD said to Satan, "Behold, he is in your power; only spare his life."

⁷So Satan went forth from the presence of the LORD, and afflicted Job with loathsome sores from the sole of his foot to the crown of his head. ⁸And he took a potsherd with which to scrape himself, and sat among the ashes.

⁹Then his wife said to him, "Do you still hold fast your integrity? Curse God, and die." ¹⁰But he said to her, "You speak as one of the foolish women would speak. Shall we receive good at the hand of God, and shall we not receive evil?" In all this Job did not sin with his lips.

¹¹Now when Job's three friends heard of all this evil that had come upon him, they came each from his own place, Eli'phaz the Te'manite, Bildad the Shuhite, and Zophar the Na'amathite. They made an appointment together to come to condole him and comfort him. ¹²And when they saw him from afar, they did not recognize him; and they raised their voices and wept; and they rent their robes and sprinkled dust upon their heads toward heaven. ¹³And they sat with him on the ground seven days and seven nights, and no one spoke a word to him, for they saw that his suffering was very great.

## JOB 3

¹After this Job opened his mouth and cursed the day of his birth.
²And Job said:
³"Let the day perish wherein I was born, and the night which said, 'A man-child is conceived.'
⁴Let that day be darkness! May God above not seek it, nor light shine upon it.
⁵Let gloom and deep darkness claim it. Let clouds dwell upon it; let the blackness of the day terrify it.
⁶That night—let thick darkness seize it! let it not rejoice among the days of the year, let it not come into the number of the months.
⁷Yea, let that night be barren; let no joyful cry be heard in it.
⁸Let those curse it who curse the day, who are skilled to rouse up Levi'athan.
⁹Let the stars of its dawn be dark; let it hope for light, but have none, nor see the eyelids of the morning;
¹⁰because it did not shut the doors of my mother's womb, nor hide trouble from my eyes.
¹¹"Why did I not die at birth, come forth from the womb and expire?
¹²Why did the knees receive me? Or why the breasts, that I should suck?
¹³For then I should have lain down and been quiet; I should have slept; then I should have been at rest,
¹⁴with the kings and counselors of the earth who rebuilt ruins for themselves,
¹⁵or with princes who had gold, who filled their houses with silver.

¹⁶Or why was I not as a hidden untimely birth, as infants that never see the light?

¹⁷There the wicked cease from troubling, and there the weary are at rest.

¹⁸There the prisoners are at ease together; they hear not the voice of the taskmaster.

¹⁹The small and the great are there, and the slave is free from his master.

²⁰"Why is light given to him that is in misery, and life to the bitter in soul,

²¹who long for death, but it comes not, and dig for it more than for hid treasures;

²²who rejoice exceedingly, and are glad, when they find the grave?

²³Why is light given to a man whose way is hid, whom God has hedged in?

²⁴For my sighing comes as my bread, and my groanings are poured out like water.

²⁵For the thing that I fear comes upon me, and what I dread befalls me.

²⁶I am not at ease, nor am I quiet; I have no rest; but trouble comes."

## JOB 4

¹Then Eli'phaz the Te'manite answered:

²"If one ventures a word with you, will you be offended? Yet who can keep from speaking?

³Behold, you have instructed many, and you have strengthened the weak hands.

⁴Your words have upheld him who was stumbling, and you have made firm the feeble knees.

⁵But now it has come to you, and you are impatient; it touches you, and you are dismayed.

⁶Is not your fear of God your confidence, and the integrity of your ways your hope?

⁷"Think now, who that was innocent ever perished? Or where were the upright cut off?

⁸As I have seen, those who plow iniquity and sow trouble reap the same.

⁹By the breath of God they perish, and by the blast of his anger they are consumed.

¹⁰The roar of the lion, the voice of the fierce lion, the teeth of the young lions, are broken.

¹¹The strong lion perishes for lack of prey, and the whelps of the lioness are scattered.

¹²"Now a word was brought to me stealthily, my ear received the whisper of it.

¹³Amid thoughts from visions of the night, when deep sleep falls on men,

¹⁴dread came upon me, and trembling, which made all my bones shake.

¹⁵A spirit glided past my face; the hair of my flesh stood up.

¹⁶It stood still, but I could not discern its appearance. A form was before my eyes; there was silence, then I heard a voice:

¹⁷'Can mortal man be righteous before God? Can a man be pure before his Maker?

[18]Even in his servants he puts no trust, and his angels he charges with error;

[19]how much more those who dwell in houses of clay, whose foundation is in the dust, who are crushed before the moth.

[20]Between morning and evening they are destroyed; they perish for ever without any regarding it.

[21]If their tent-cord is plucked up within them, do they not die, and that without wisdom?'

## JOB 5

[1]"Call now; is there any one who will answer you? To which of the holy ones will you turn?

[2]Surely vexation kills the fool, and jealousy slays the simple.

[3]I have seen the fool taking root, but suddenly I cursed his dwelling.

[4]His sons are far from safety, they are crushed in the gate, and there is no one to deliver them.

[5]His harvest the hungry eat, and he takes it even out of thorns; and the thirsty pant after his wealth.

[6]For affliction does not come from the dust, nor does trouble sprout from the ground;

[7]but man is born to trouble as the sparks fly upward.

[8]"As for me, I would seek God, and to God would I commit my cause;

[9]who does great things and unsearchable, marvelous things without number:

[10]he gives rain upon the earth and sends waters upon the fields;

[11]he sets on high those who are lowly, and those who mourn are lifted to safety.

[12]He frustrates the devices of the crafty, so that their hands achieve no success.

[13]He takes the wise in their own craftiness; and the schemes of the wily are brought to a quick end.

[14]They meet with darkness in the daytime, and grope at noonday as in the night.

[15]But he saves the fatherless from their mouth, the needy from the hand of the mighty.

[16]So the poor have hope, and injustice shuts her mouth.

[17]"Behold, happy is the man whom God reproves; therefore despise not the chastening of the Almighty.

[18]For he wounds, but he binds up; he smites, but his hands heal.

[19]He will deliver you from six troubles; in seven there shall no evil touch you.

[20]In famine he will redeem you from death, and in war from the power of the sword.

[21]You shall be hid from the scourge of the tongue, and shall not fear destruction when it comes.

[22]At destruction and famine you shall laugh, and shall not fear the beasts of the earth.

[23]For you shall be in league with the stones of the field, and the beasts of the field shall be at peace with you.

[24]You shall know that your tent is safe, and you shall inspect your fold and miss nothing.

[25]You shall know also that your descendants shall be many, and your offspring as the grass of the earth.

[26]You shall come to your grave in ripe old age, as a shock of grain comes up to the threshing floor in its season.

[27]Lo, this we have searched out; it is true. Hear, and know it for your good."


## JOB 6

[1]Then Job answered:

[2]"O that my vexation were weighed, and all my calamity laid in the balances!

[3]For then it would be heavier than the sand of the sea; therefore my words have been rash.

[4]For the arrows of the Almighty are in me; my spirit drinks their poison; the terrors of God are arrayed against me.

[5]Does the wild ass bray when he has grass, or the ox low over his fodder?

[6]Can that which is tasteless be eaten without salt, or is there any taste in the slime of the purslane?

[7]My appetite refuses to touch them; they are as food that is loathsome to me.

[8]"O that I might have my request, and that God would grant my desire;

[9]that it would please God to crush me, that he would let loose his hand and cut me off!

[10]This would be my consolation; I would even exult in pain unsparing; for I have not denied the words of the Holy One.

[11]What is my strength, that I should wait? And what is my end, that I should be patient?

[12]Is my strength the strength of stones, or is my flesh bronze?

[13]In truth I have no help in me, and any resource is driven from me.

[14]"He who withholds kindness from a friend forsakes the fear of the Almighty.

[15]My brethren are treacherous as a torrent-bed, as freshets that pass away,

[16]which are dark with ice, and where the snow hides itself.

[17]In time of heat they disappear; when it is hot, they vanish from their place.

[18]The caravans turn aside from their course; they go up into the waste, and perish.

[19]The caravans of Tema look, the travelers of Sheba hope.

[20]They are disappointed because they were confident; they come thither and are confounded.

[21]Such you have now become to me; you see my calamity, and are afraid.

[22]Have I said, 'Make me a gift'? Or, 'From your wealth offer a bribe for me'?

[23]Or, 'Deliver me from the adversary's hand'? Or, 'Ransom me from the hand of oppressors'?

[24]"Teach me, and I will be silent; make me understand how I have erred.

[25]How forceful are honest words! But what does reproof from you reprove?

[26]Do you think that you can reprove words, when the speech of a despairing man is wind?

[27]You would even cast lots over the fatherless, and bargain over your friend.

<sup>28</sup>"But now, be pleased to look at me; for I will not lie to your face.
<sup>29</sup>Turn, I pray, let no wrong be done. Turn now, my vindication is at stake.
<sup>30</sup>Is there any wrong on my tongue? Cannot my taste discern calamity?

## JOB 7

<sup>1</sup>"Has not man a hard service upon earth, and are not his days like the days of a hireling?
<sup>2</sup>Like a slave who longs for the shadow, and like a hireling who looks for his wages,
<sup>3</sup>so I am allotted months of emptiness, and nights of misery are apportioned to me.
<sup>4</sup>When I lie down I say, 'When shall I arise?' But the night is long, and I am full of tossing till the dawn.
<sup>5</sup>My flesh is clothed with worms and dirt; my skin hardens, then breaks out afresh.
<sup>6</sup>My days are swifter than a weaver's shuttle, and come to their end without hope.
<sup>7</sup>"Remember that my life is a breath; my eye will never again see good.
<sup>8</sup>The eye of him who sees me will behold me no more; while thy eyes are upon me, I shall be gone.
<sup>9</sup>As the cloud fades and vanishes, so he who goes down to Sheol does not come up;
<sup>10</sup>he returns no more to his house, nor does his place know him any more.
<sup>11</sup>"Therefore I will not restrain my mouth; I will speak in the anguish of my spirit; I will complain in the bitterness of my soul.
<sup>12</sup>Am I the sea, or a sea monster, that thou settest a guard over me?
<sup>13</sup>When I say, 'My bed will comfort me, my couch will ease my complaint,'
<sup>14</sup>then thou dost scare me with dreams and terrify me with visions,
<sup>15</sup>so that I would choose strangling and death rather than my bones.
<sup>16</sup>I loathe my life; I would not live for ever. Let me alone, for my days are a breath.
<sup>17</sup>What is man, that thou dost make so much of him, and that thou dost set thy mind upon him,
<sup>18</sup>dost visit him every morning, and test him every moment?
<sup>19</sup>How long wilt thou not look away from me, nor let me alone till I swallow my spittle?
<sup>20</sup>If I sin, what do I do to thee, thou watcher of men? Why hast thou made me thy mark? Why have I become a burden to thee?
<sup>21</sup>Why dost thou not pardon my transgression and take away my iniquity? For now I shall lie in the earth; thou wilt seek me, but I shall not be."

## JOB 8

<sup>1</sup>Then Bildad the Shuhite answered:
<sup>2</sup>"How long will you say these things, and the words of your mouth be a great wind?

³Does God pervert justice? Or does the Almighty pervert the right?

⁴If your children have sinned against him, he has delivered them into the power of their transgression.

⁵If you will seek God and make supplication to the Almighty,

⁶if you are pure and upright, surely then he will rouse himself for you and reward you with a rightful habitation.

⁷And though your beginning was small, your latter days will be very great.

⁸"For inquire, I pray you, of bygone ages, and consider what the fathers have found;

⁹for we are but of yesterday, and know nothing, for our days on earth are a shadow.

¹⁰Will they not teach you, and tell you, and utter words out of their understanding?

¹¹"Can papyrus grow where there is no marsh? Can reeds flourish where there is no water?

¹²While yet in flower and not cut down, they wither before any other plant.

¹³Such are the paths of all who forget God; the hope of the godless man shall perish.

¹⁴His confidence breaks in sunder, and his trust is a spider's web.

¹⁵He leans against his house, but it does not stand; he lays hold of it, but it does not endure.

¹⁶He thrives before the sun, and his shoots spread over his garden.

¹⁷His roots twine about the stoneheap; he lives among the rocks.

¹⁸If he is destroyed from his place, then it will deny him, saying, 'I have never seen you.'

¹⁹Behold, this is the joy of his way; and out of the earth others will spring.

²⁰"Behold, God will not reject a blameless man, nor take the hand of evildoers.

²¹He will yet fill your mouth with laughter, and your lips with shouting.

²²Those who hate you will be clothed with shame, and the tent of the wicked will be no more."


*JOB 9*

¹Then Job answered:

²"Truly I know that it is so: But how can a man be just before God?

³If one wished to contend with him, one could not answer him once in a thousand times.

⁴He is wise in heart, and mighty in strength—who has hardened himself against him, and succeeded?—

⁵he who removes mountains, and they know it not, when he overturns them in his anger,

⁶who shakes the earth out of its place, and its pillars tremble,

⁷who commands the sun, and it does not rise; who seals up the stars;

⁸who alone stretched out the heavens, and trampled the waves of the sea;

⁹who make the Bear and Orion, the Plei'ades and the chambers of the south;
¹⁰who does great things beyond understanding, and marvelous things without number.

¹¹Lo, he passes by me, and I see him not; he moves on, but I do not perceive him.

¹²Behold, he snatches away; who can hinder him? Who will say to him, 'What doest thou'?

¹³"God will not turn back his anger; beneath him bowed the helpers of Rahab.

¹⁴How then can I answer him, choosing my words with him?

¹⁵Though I am innocent, I cannot answer him; I must appeal for mercy to my accuser.

¹⁶If I summoned him and he answered me, I would not believe that he was listening to my voice.

¹⁷For he crushes me with a tempest, and multiplies my wounds without cause,
¹⁸he will not let me get my breath, but fills me with bitterness.

¹⁹If it is a contest of strength, behold him! If it is a matter of justice, who can summon him?

²⁰Though I am innocent, my own mouth would condemn me; though I am blameless, he would prove me perverse.

²¹I am blameless; I regard not myself, I loathe my life.

²²It is all one; therefore I say, he destroys both the blameless and the wicked.

²³When disaster brings sudden death, he mocks at the calamity of the innocent.

²⁴The earth is given into the hand of the wicked; he covers the faces of its judges—if it is not he, who then is it?

²⁵"My days are swifter than a runner; they flee away, they see no good.

²⁶They go by like skiffs of reed, like an eagle swooping on the prey.

²⁷If I say, 'I will forget my complaint, I will put off my sad countenance, and be of good cheer,'
²⁸I become afraid of all my suffering, for I know thou wilt not hold me innocent.

²⁹I shall be condemned, why then do I labor in vain?

³⁰If I wash myself with snow, and cleanse my hands with lye,
³¹yet thou wilt plunge me into a pit, and my own clothes will abhor me.

³²For he is not a man, as I am, that I might answer him, that we should come to trial together.

³³There is no umpire between us, who might lay his hand upon us both.

³⁴Let him take his rod away from me, and let not dread of him terrify me.

³⁵Then I would speak without fear of him, for I am not so in myself.


## JOB 10

¹"I loathe my life; I will give free utterance to my complaint; I will speak in the bitterness of my soul.

²I will say to God, Do not condemn me; let me know why thou dost contend against me.

³Does it seem good to thee to oppress, to despise the work of thy hands and favor the designs of the wicked?

⁴Hast thou eyes of flesh? Dost thou see as man sees?

⁵Are thy days as the days of man, or thy years as man's years,

⁶that thou dost seek out my iniquity and search for my sin,

⁷although thou knowest that I am not guilty, and there is none to deliver out of thy hand?

⁸Thy hands fashioned and made me; and now thou dost turn about and destroy me.

⁹Remember that thou hast made me of clay; and wilt thou turn me to dust again?

¹⁰Didst thou not pour me out like milk and curdle me like cheese?

¹¹Thou didst clothe me with skin and flesh, and knit me together with bones and sinews.

¹²Thou hast granted me life and steadfast love; and thy care has preserved my spirit.

¹³Yet these things thou didst hide in thy heart; I know that this was thy purpose.

¹⁴If I sin, thou dost mark me, and dost not acquit me of my iniquity.

¹⁵If I am wicked, woe to me! If I am righteous, I cannot lift up my head, for I am filled with disgrace and look upon my affliction.

¹⁶And if I lift myself up, thou dost hunt me like a lion, and again work wonders against me;

¹⁷thou dost renew thy witnesses against me, and increase thy vexation toward me; thou dost bring fresh hosts against me.

¹⁸"Why didst thou bring me forth from the womb? Would that I had died before any eye had seen me,

¹⁹and were as though I had not been carried from the womb to the grave.

²⁰Are not the days of my life few? Let me alone, that I may find a little comfort

²¹before I go whence I shall not return, to the land of gloom and deep darkness,

²²the land of gloom and chaos, where light is as darkness."

*JOB 11*

¹Then Zophar the Na'amathite answered:

²"Should a multitude of words go unanswered, and a man full of talk be vindicated?

³Should your babble silence men, and when you mock, shall no one shame you?

⁴For you say, 'My doctrine is pure, and I am clean in God's eyes.'

⁵But oh, that God would speak, and open his lips to you,

⁶and that he would tell you the secrets of wisdom! For he is manifold in understanding. Know then that God exacts of you less than your guilt deserves.

⁷"Can you find out the deep things of God? Can you find out the limit of the Almighty?

⁸It is higher than heaven—what can you do? Deeper than Sheol—what can you know?

⁹Its measure is longer than the earth, and broader than the sea.

¹⁰If he passes through, and imprisons, and calls to judgment, who can hinder him?

¹¹For he knows worthless men; when he sees iniquity, will he not consider it?

¹²But a stupid man will get understanding, when a wild ass's colt is born a man.

¹³"If you set your heart aright, you will stretch out your hands toward him.

¹⁴If iniquity is in your hand, put it far away, and let not wickedness dwell in your tents.

¹⁵Surely then you will lift up your face without blemish; you will be secure, and will not fear.

¹⁶You will forget your misery; you will remember it as waters that have passed away.

¹⁷And your life will be brighter than the noonday; its darkness will be like the morning.

¹⁸And you will have confidence, because there is hope; you will be protected and take your rest in safety.

¹⁹You will lie down, and none will make you afraid; many will entreat your favor.

²⁰But the eyes of the wicked will fail; all the way of escape will be lost to them, and their hope is to breathe their last."

## JOB 12

¹Then Job answered:

²"No doubt you are the people, and wisdom will die with you.

³But I have understanding as well as you; I am not inferior to you. Who does not know such things as these?

⁴I am a laughingstock to my friends; I, who called upon God and he answered me, a just and blameless man, am a laughingstock.

⁵In the thought of one who is at ease there is contempt for misfortune; it is ready for those whose feet slip.

⁶The tents of robbers are at peace, and those who provoke God are secure, who bring their god in their hand.

⁷"But ask the beasts, and they will teach you; the birds of the air, and they will tell you;

⁸or the plants of the earth, and they will teach you; and the fish of the sea will declare to you.

⁹Who among all these does not know that the hand of the LORD has done this?

¹⁰In his hand is the life of every living thing and the breath of all mankind.

¹¹Does not the ear try words as the palate tastes food?

¹²Wisdom is with the aged, and understanding in length of days.

¹³"With God are wisdom and might; he has counsel and understanding.

¹⁴If he tears down, none can rebuild; if he shuts a man in, none can open.

¹⁵If he withholds the waters, they dry up; if he sends them out, they overwhelm the land.

¹⁶With him are strength and wisdom; the deceived and the deceiver are his.

¹⁷He leads counselors away stripped, and judges he makes fools.

¹⁸He looses the bonds of kings, and binds a waistcloth on their loins.

¹⁹He leads priests away stripped, and overthrows the mighty.

²⁰He deprives of speech those who are trusted, and takes away the discernment of the elders.

²¹He pours contempt on princes, and looses the belt of the strong.

²²He uncovers the deeps out of darkness, and brings deep darkness to light.

²³He makes nations great, and he destroys them; he enlarges nations, and leads them away.

²⁴He takes away understanding from the chiefs of the people of the earth, and makes them wander in a pathless waste.

²⁵They grope in the dark without light; and he makes them stagger like a drunken man.

## JOB 13

¹"Lo, my eye has seen all this, my ear has heard and understood it.

²What you know, I also know; I am not inferior to you.

³But I would speak to the Almighty, and I desire to argue my case with God.

⁴As for you, you whitewash with lies; worthless physicians are you all.

⁵Oh that you would keep silent, and it would be your wisdom!

⁶Hear now my reasoning, and listen to the pleadings of my lips.

⁷Will you speak falsely for God, and speak deceitfully for him?

⁸Will you show partiality toward him, will you plead the case for God?

⁹Will it be well with you when he searches you out? Or can you deceive him, as one deceives a man?

¹⁰He will surely rebuke you if in secret you show partiality.

¹¹Will not his majesty terrify you, and the dread of him fall upon you?

¹²Your maxims are proverbs of ashes, your defenses are defenses of clay.

¹³"Let me have silence, and I will speak, and let come on me what may.

¹⁴I will take my flesh in my teeth, and put my life in my hand.

¹⁵Behold, he will slay me; I have no hope; yet I will defend my ways to his face.

¹⁶This will be my salvation, that a godless man shall not come before him.

¹⁷Listen carefully to my words, and let my declaration be in your ears.

¹⁸Behold, I have prepared my case; I know that I shall be vindicated.

¹⁹Who is there that will contend with me? For then I would be silent and die.

²⁰Only grant two things to me, then I will not hide myself from thy face:

²¹withdraw thy hand far from me, and let not dread of thee terrify me.

²²Then call, and I will answer; or let me speak, and do thou reply to me.

²³How many are my iniquities and my sins? Make me know my transgression and my sin.

²⁴Why dost thou hide thy face, and count me as thy enemy?

²⁵Wilt thou frighten a driven leaf and pursue dry chaff?

²⁶For thou writest bitter things against me, and makest me inherit the iniquities of my youth.

²⁷Thou puttest my feet in the stocks, and watchest all my paths; thou settest a bound to the soles of my feet.

²⁸Man wastes away like a rotten thing, like a garment that is moth-eaten.

## JOB 14

¹"Man that is born of a woman is of few days, and full of trouble

²He comes forth like a flower, and withers; he flees like a shadow, and continues not.

³And dost thou open thy eyes upon such a one and bring him into judgment with thee?

⁴Who can bring a clean thing out of an unclean? There is not one.

⁵Since his days are determined, and the number of his months is with thee, and thou hast appointed his bounds that he cannot pass,

⁶look away from him, and desist, that he may enjoy, like a hireling, his day.

⁷"For there is hope for a tree, if it be cut down, that it will sprout again, and that its shoots will not cease.

⁸Though its root grow old in the earth, and its stump die in the ground,

⁹yet at the scent of water it will bud and put forth branches like a young plant.

¹⁰But man dies, and is laid low; man breathes his last, and where is he?

¹¹As waters fail from a lake, and a river wastes away and dries up,

¹²so man lies down and rises not again; till the heavens are no more he will not awake, or be roused out of his sleep.

¹³Oh that thou wouldest hide me in Sheol, that thou wouldest conceal me until thy wrath be past, that thou wouldest appoint me a set time, and remember me!

¹⁴If a man die, shall he live again? All the days of my service I would wait, till my release should come.

¹⁵Thou wouldest call, and I would answer thee; thou wouldest long for the work of thy hands.

¹⁶For then thou wouldest number my steps, thou wouldest not keep watch over my sin;

¹⁷my transgression would be sealed up in a bag, and thou wouldest cover over my iniquity.

¹⁸"But the mountain falls and crumbles away, and the rock is removed from its place;

¹⁹the waters wear away the stones; the torrents wash away the soil of the earth; so thou destroyest the hope of man.

²⁰Thou prevailest for ever against him, and he passes; thou changest his countenance, and sendest him away.

²¹His sons come to honor, and he does not know it; they are brought low, and he perceives it not.

²²He feels only the pain of his own body, and he mourns only for himself."

• • •

## JOB 28

[1]"Surely there is a mine for silver, and a place for gold which they refine.

[2]Iron is taken out of the earth, and copper is smelted from the ore.

[3]Men put an end to darkness, and search out to the farthest bound the ore in gloom and deep darkness.

[4]They open shafts in a valley away from where men live; they are forgotten by travelers, they hang afar from men, they swing to and fro.

[5]As for the earth, out of it comes bread; but underneath it is turned up as by fire.

[6]Its stones are the place of sapphires, and it has dust of gold.

[7]"That path no bird of prey knows, and the falcon's eye has not seen it.

[8]The proud beasts have not trodden it; the lion has not passed over it.

[9]"Man puts his hand to the flinty rock, and overturns mountains by the roots.

[10]He cuts out channels in the rocks, and his eye sees every precious thing.

[11]He binds up the streams so that they do not trickle, and the thing that is hid he brings forth to light.

[12]"But where shall wisdom be found? And where is the place of understanding?

[13]Man does not know the way to it, and it is not found in the land of the living.

[14]The deeps says, 'It is not in me,' and the sea says, 'It is not with me.'

[15]It cannot be gotten for gold, and silver cannot be weighed as its price.

[16]It cannot be valued in the gold of Ophir, in precious onyx or sapphire.

[17]Gold and glass cannot equal it, nor can it be exchanged for jewels of fine gold.

[18]No mention shall be made of coral or of crystal; the price of wisdom is above pearls.

[19]The topaz of Ethiopia cannot compare with it, nor can it be valued in pure gold.

[20]"Whence then comes wisdom? And where is the place of understanding?

[21]It is hid from the eyes of all living, and concealed from the birds of the air.

[22]Abaddon and Death say, 'We have heard a rumor of it with our ears.'

[23]"God understands the way to it, and he knows its place.

[24]For he looks to the ends of the earth, and sees everything under the heavens.

[25]When he gave to the wind its weight, and meted out the waters by measure;

[26]when he made a decree for the rain, and a way for the lightning of the thunder,

[27]then he saw it and declared it; he established it, and searched it out.

[28]And he said to man, 'Behold, the fear of the Lord, that is wisdom; and to depart from evil is understanding.'"

## JOB 29

[1]And Job again took up his discourse, and said:

[2]"Oh, that I were as in the months of old, as in the days when God watched over me;

³when his lamp shone upon my head, and by his light I walked through darkness;

⁴as I was in my autumn days, when the friendship of God was upon my tent;

⁵when the Almighty was yet with me, when my children were about me;

⁶when my steps were washed with milk, and the rock poured out for me streams of oil!

⁷When I went out to the gate of the city, when I prepared my seat in the square,

⁸the young men saw me and withdrew, and the aged rose and stood,

⁹the princes refrained from talking and laid their hand on their mouth;

¹⁰the voice of the nobles was hushed, and their tongue cleaved to the roof of their mouth.

¹¹When the ear heard, it called me blessed, and when the eye saw, it approved;

¹²because I delivered the poor who cried, and the fatherless who had none to help him.

¹³The blessing of him who was about to perish came upon me, and I caused the widow's heart to sing for joy.

¹⁴I put on righteousness, and it clothed me; my justice was like a robe and a turban.

¹⁵I was eyes to the blind, and feet to the lame.

¹⁶I was a father to the poor, and I searched out the cause of him whom I did not know.

¹⁷I broke the fangs of the unrighteous, and made him drop his prey from his teeth.

¹⁸Then I thought, 'I shall die in my nest, and I shall multiply my days as the sand,

¹⁹my roots spread out to the waters, with the dew all night on my branches,

²⁰my glory fresh with me, and my bow ever new in my hand.'

²¹"Men listened to me, and waited, and kept silence for my counsel.

²²After I spoke they did not speak again, and my word dropped upon them.

²³They waited for me as for the rain; and they opened their mouths as for the spring rain.

²⁴I smiled on them when they had no confidence, and the light of my countenance they did not cast down.

²⁵I chose their way, and sat as chief, and I dwelt like a king among his troops, like one who comforts mourners.

## JOB 30

¹"But now they make sport of me, men who are younger than I, whose fathers I would have disdained to set with the dogs of my flock.

²What could I gain from the strength of their hands, men whose vigor is gone?

³Through want and hard hunger they gnaw the dry and desolate ground;

⁴they pick mallow and the leaves of bushes, and to warm themselves the roots of the broom.

⁵They are driven out from among men; they shout after them as after a thief.

[6]In the gullies of the torrents they must dwell, in holes of the earth and of the rocks.

[7]Among the bushes they bray; under the nettles they huddle together.

[8]A senseless, a disreputable brood, they have been whipped out of the land.

[9]"And now I have become their song, I am a byword to them.

[10]They abhor me, they keep aloof from me; they do not hesitate to spit at the sight of me.

[11]Because God has loosed my cord and humbled me, they have cast off restraint in my presence.

[12]On my right hand the rabble rise, they drive me forth, they cast up against me their ways of destruction.

[13]They break up my path, they promote my calamity; no one restrains them.

[14]As through a wide breach they come; amid the crash they roll on.

[15]Terrors are turned upon me; my honor is pursued as by the wind, and my prosperity has passed away like a cloud.

[16]"And now my soul is poured out within me; days of affliction have taken hold of me.

[17]The night racks my bones, and the pain that gnaws me takes no rest.

[18]With violence it seizes my garment; it binds me about like the collar of my tunic.

[19]God has cast me into the mire, and I have become like dust and ashes.

[20]I cry to thee and thou dost not answer me; I stand, and thou dost not heed me.

[21]Thou has turned cruel to me; with the might of thy hand thou dost persecute me.

[22]Thou liftest me up on the wind, thou makest me ride on it, and thou tossest me about in the roar of the storm.

[23]Yea, I know that thou wilt bring me to death, and to the house appointed for all living.

[24]"Yet does not one in a heap of ruins stretch out his hand, and in his disaster cry for help?

[25]Did not I weep for him whose day was hard? Was not my soul grieved for the poor?

[26]But when I looked for good, evil came; and when I waited for light, darkness came.

[27]My heart is in turmoil, and is never still; days of affliction come to meet me.

[28]I go about blackened, but not by the sun; I stand up in the assembly, and cry for help.

[29]I am a brother of jackals, and a companion of ostriches.

[30]My skin turns black and falls from me, and my bones burn with heat.

[31]My lyre is turned to mourning, and my pipe to the voice of those who weep.

## JOB 31

[1]"I have made a covenant with my eyes; how then could I look upon a virgin?

[2]What would be my portion from God above, and my heritage from the Almighty on high?

³Does not calamity befall the unrighteous, and disaster the workers of iniquity?
⁴Does not he see my ways, and number all my steps?
⁵"If I have walked with falsehood, and my foot has hastened to deceit;
⁶(Let me be weighed in a just balance, and let God know my integrity!)
⁷if my step has turned aside from the way, and my heart has gone after my eyes, and if any spot has cleaved to my hands;
⁸then let me sow, and another eat; and let what grows for me be rooted out.
⁹"If my heart has been enticed to a woman, and I have lain in wait at my neighbor's door;
¹⁰then let my wife grind for another, and let others bow down upon her.
¹¹For that would be a heinous crime; that would be an iniquity to be punished by the judges;
¹²for that would be a fire which consumes unto Abaddon, and it would burn to the root all my increase.
¹³"If I have rejected the cause of my manservant or my maidservant, when they brought a complaint against me:
¹⁴what then shall I do when God rises up? When he makes inquiry, what shall I answer him?
¹⁵Did not he who made me in the womb make him? And did not one fashion us in the womb?
¹⁶"If I have withheld anything that the poor desired, or have caused the eyes of the widow to fail,
¹⁷or have eaten my morsel alone, and the fatherless has not eaten of it
¹⁸(for from his youth I reared him as a father, and from his mother's womb I guided him);
¹⁹if I have seen any one perish for lack of clothing, or a poor man without covering;
²⁰if his loins have not blessed me, and if he was not warmed with the fleece of my sheep;
²¹if I have raised my hand against the fatherless, because I saw help in the gate;
²²then let my shoulder blade fall from my shoulder, and let my arm be broken from its socket.
²³For I was in terror of calamity from God, and I could not have faced his majesty.
²⁴"If I have made gold my trust, or called fine gold my confidence;
²⁵if I have rejoiced because my wealth was great, or because my hand had gotten much;
²⁶if I have looked at the sun when it shone, or the moon moving in splendor,
²⁷and my heart has been secretly enticed, and my mouth has kissed my hand;
²⁸this also would be an iniquity to be punished by the judges, for I should have been false to God above.
²⁹"If I have rejoiced at the ruin of him that hated me, or exulted when evil overtook him
³⁰(I have not let my mouth sin by asking for his life with a curse);
³¹if the men of my tent have not said, "'Who is there that has not been filled with his meat?'

[32](the sojourner has not lodged in the street; I have opened my doors to the wayfarer);

[33]if I have concealed my transgressions from men, by hiding my iniquity in my bosom,

[34]because I stood in great fear of the multitude, and the contempt of families terrified me, so that I kept silence, and did not go out of doors—

[35]Oh, that I had one to hear me! (Here is my signature! let the Almighty answer me!) Oh, that I had the indictment written by my adversary!

[36]Surely I would carry it on my shoulder; I would bind it on me as a crown;

[37]I would give him an account of all my steps; like a prince I would approach him.

[38]"If my land has cried out against me, and its furrows have wept together;

[39]if I have eaten its yield without payment, and caused the death of its owners;

[40]let thorns grow instead of wheat, and foul weeds instead of barley." The words of Job are ended.


## JOB 32

[1]So these three men ceased to answer Job, because he was righteous in his own eyes.

•   •   •


## JOB 38

[1]Then the LORD answered Job out of the whirlwind:

[2]"Who is this that darkens counsel by words without knowledge?

[3]Gird up your loins like a man, I will question you, and you shall declare to me.

[4]"Where were you when I laid the foundation of the earth? Tell me, if you have understanding.

[5]Who determined its measurements—surely you know! Or who stretched the line upon it?

[6]On what were its bases sunk, or who laid its cornerstone,

[7]when the morning stars sang together, and all the sons of God shouted for joy?

[8]"Or who shut in the sea with doors, when it burst forth from the womb;

[9]when I made clouds its garment, and thick darkness its swaddling band,

[10]and prescribed bounds for it, and set bars and doors,

[11]and said, 'Thus far shall you come, and no farther, and here shall your proud waves be stayed'?

[12]"Have you commanded the morning since your days began, and caused the dawn to know its place,

[13]that it might take hold of the skirts of the earth, and the wicked be shaken out of it?

[14]It is changed like clay under the seal, and it is dyed like a garment.

¹⁵From the wicked their light is withheld, and their uplifted arm is broken.

¹⁶"Have you entered into the springs of the sea, or walked in the recesses of the deep?

¹⁷Have the gates of death been revealed to you, or have you seen the gates of deep darkness?

¹⁸Have you comprehended the expanse of the earth? Declare, if you know all this.

¹⁹"Where is the way to the dwelling of light, and where is the place of darkness,

²⁰that you may take it to its territory and that you may discern the paths to its home?

²¹You know, for you were born then, and the number of your days is great!

²²"Have you entered the storehouses of the snow, or have you seen the storehouses of the hail,

²³which I have reserved for the time of trouble, for the day of battle and war?

²⁴What is the way to the place where the light is distributed, or where the east wind is scattered upon the earth?

²⁵"Who has cleft a channel for the torrents of rain, and a way for the thunderbolt,

²⁶to bring rain on a land where no man is, on the desert in which there is no man;

²⁷to satisfy the waste and desolate land, and to make the ground put forth grass?

²⁸"Has the rain a father, or who has begotten the drops of dew?

²⁹From whose womb did the ice come forth, and who has given birth to the hoarfrost of heaven?

³⁰The waters become hard like stone, and the face of the deep is frozen.

³¹"Can you bind the chains of the Plei'ades, or loose the cords of Orion?

³²Can you lead forth the Maz'zaroth in their season, or can you guide the Bear with its children?

³³Do you know the ordinances of the heavens? Can you establish their rule on the earth?

³⁴"Can you lift up your voice to the clouds, that a flood of waters may cover you?

³⁵Can you send forth lightnings, that they may go and say to you, 'Here we are'?

³⁶Who has put wisdom in the clouds, or given understanding to the mists?

³⁷Who can number the clouds by wisdom? Or who can tilt the waterskins of the heavens,

³⁸when the dust runs into a mass and the clods cleave fast together?

³⁹"Can you hunt the prey for the lion, or satisfy the appetite of the young lions,

⁴⁰when they crouch in their dens, or lie in wait in their covert?

⁴¹Who provides for the raven its prey, when its young ones cry to God, and wander about for lack of food?

*JOB 39*

¹"Do you know when the mountain goats bring forth? Do you observe the calving of the hinds?

²Can you number the months that they fulfill, and do you know the time when they bring forth,

³when they crouch, bring forth their offspring, and are delivered of their young?

⁴Their young ones become strong, they grow up in the open; they go forth, and do not return to them.

⁵"Who has let the wild ass go free? Who has loosed the bonds of the swift ass,

⁶to whom I have given the steppe for his home, and the salt land for his dwelling place?

⁷He scorns the tumult of the city; he hears not the shouts of the driver.

⁸He ranges the mountains as his pasture, and he searches after every green thing.

⁹"Is the wild ox willing to serve you? Will he spend the night at your crib?

¹⁰Can you bind him in the furrow with ropes, or will he harrow the valleys after you?

¹¹Will you depend on him because his strength is great, and will you leave to him your labor?

¹²Do you have faith in him that he will return, and bring your grain to your threshing floor?

¹³"The wings of the ostrich wave proudly; but are they the pinions and plumage of love?

¹⁴For she leaves her eggs to the earth, and lets them be warmed on the ground,

¹⁵forgetting that a foot may crush them, and that the wild beast may trample them.

¹⁶She deals cruelly with her young, as if they were not hers; though her labor be in vain, yet she has no fear;

¹⁷because God has made her forget wisdom, and given her no share in understanding.

¹⁸When she rouses herself to flee, she laughs at the horse and his rider.

¹⁹"Do you give the horse his might? Do you clothe his neck with strength?

²⁰Do you make him leap like the locust? His majestic snorting is terrible.

²¹He paws in the valley, and exults in his strength; he goes out to meet the weapons.

²²He laughs at fear, and is not dismayed; he does not turn back from the sword.

²³Upon him rattle the quiver, the flashing spear and the javelin.

²⁴With fierceness and rage he swallows the ground; he cannot stand still at the sound of the trumpet.

²⁵When the trumpet sounds, he says 'Aha!' He smells the battle from afar, the thunder of the captains, and the shouting.

<sup>26</sup>"Is it by your wisdom that the hawk soars, and spreads his wings toward the south?

<sup>27</sup>Is it at your command that the eagle mounts up and makes his nest on high?

<sup>28</sup>On the rock he dwells and makes his home in the fastness of the rocky crag.

<sup>29</sup>Thence he spies out the prey; his eyes behold it afar off.

<sup>30</sup>His young ones suck up blood; and where the slain are, there is he."

## JOB 40

<sup>1</sup>And the LORD said to Job:

<sup>2</sup>"Shall a faultfinder contend with the Almighty? He who argues with God, let him answer it."

<sup>3</sup>Then Job answered the LORD:

<sup>4</sup>"Behold, I am of small account; what shall I answer thee? I lay my hand on my mouth.

<sup>5</sup>I have spoken once, and I will not answer; twice, but I will proceed no further."

<sup>6</sup>Then the LORD answered Job out of the whirlwind:

<sup>7</sup>"Gird up your loins like a man; I will question you, and you declare to me.

<sup>8</sup>Will you even put me in the wrong? Will you condemn me that you may be justified?

<sup>9</sup>Have you an arm like God, and can you thunder with a voice like his?

<sup>10</sup>"Deck yourself with majesty and dignity; clothe yourself with glory and splendor.

<sup>11</sup>Pour forth the overflowings of your anger, and look on every one that is proud, and abase him.

<sup>12</sup>Look on every one that is proud, and bring him low; and tread down the wicked where they stand.

<sup>13</sup>Hide them all in the dust together; bind their faces in the world below.

<sup>14</sup>Then will I also acknowledge to you, that your own right hand can give you victory.

<sup>15</sup>"Behold, Be'hemoth, which I made as I made you; he eats grass like an ox.

<sup>16</sup>Behold, his strength in his loins, and his power in the muscles of his belly.

<sup>17</sup>He makes his tail stiff like a cedar; the sinews of his thighs are knit together.

<sup>18</sup>His bones are tubes of bronze, his limbs like bars of iron.

<sup>19</sup>"He is the first of the works of God; let him who made him bring near his sword!

<sup>20</sup>For the mountains yield food for him where all the wild beasts play.

<sup>21</sup>Under the lotus plants he lies, in the covert of the reeds and in the marsh.

<sup>22</sup>For his shade the lotus trees cover him; the willows of the brook surround him.

<sup>23</sup>Behold, if the river is turbulent he is not frightened; he is confident though Jordan rushes against his mouth.

<sup>24</sup>Can one take him with hooks, or pierce his nose with a snare?

## JOB 41

¹"Can you draw out Levi'athan with a fishhook, or press down his tongue with a cord?

²Can you put a rope in his nose, or pierce his jaw with a hook?

³Will he make many supplications to you? Will he speak to you soft words?

⁴Will he make a covenant with you to take him for your servant for ever?

⁵Will you play with him as with a bird, or will you put him on leash for your maidens?

⁶Will traders bargain over him? Will they divide him up among the merchants?

⁷Can you fill his skin with harpoons, or his head with fishing spears?

⁸Lay hands on him; think of the battle, you will not do it again!

⁹Behold, the hope of a man is disappointed; he is laid low even at the sight of him.

¹⁰No one is so fierce that he dares to stir him up. Who then is he that can stand before me?

¹¹Who has given to me, that I should repay him? Whatever is under the whole heaven is mine.

¹²"I will not keep silence concerning his limbs, or his mighty strength, or his goodly frame.

¹³Who can strip off his outer garment? Who can penetrate his double coat of mail?

¹⁴Who can open the doors of his face? Round about his teeth is terror.

¹⁵His back is made of rows of shields, shut up closely as with a seal.

¹⁶One is so near to another that no air can come between them.

¹⁷They are joined one to another; they clasp each other and cannot be separated.

¹⁸His sneezings flash forth light, and his eyes are like the eyelids of the dawn.

¹⁹Out of his mouth go flaming torches; sparks of fire leap forth.

²⁰Out of his nostrils comes forth smoke, as from a boiling pot and burning rushes.

²¹His breath kindles coals, and a flame comes forth from his mouth.

²²In his neck abides strength, and terror dances before him.

²³The folds of his flesh cleave together, firmly cast upon him and immovable.

²⁴His heart is hard as a stone, hard as the nether millstone.

²⁵When he raises himself up the mighty are afraid; at the crashing they are beside themselves.

²⁶Though the sword reaches him, it does not avail; nor the spear, the dart, or the javelin.

²⁷He counts iron as straw, and bronze as rotten wood.

²⁸The arrow cannot make him flee; for him slingstones are turned to stubble.

²⁹Clubs are counted as stubble; he laughs at the rattle of javelins.

³⁰His underparts are like sharp potsherds; he spreads himself like a threshing sledge on the mire.

³¹He makes the deep boil like a pot; he makes the sea like a pot of ointment.

³²Behind him he leaves a shining wake; one would think the deep to be hoary.

³³Upon earth there is not his like, a creature without fear.
³⁴He beholds everything that is high; he is king over all the sons of pride."

## JOB 42

¹Then Job answered the LORD:
²"I know that thou canst do all things, and that no purpose of thine can be thwarted.
³'Who is this that hides counsel without knowledge?' Therefore I have uttered what I did not understand, things too wonderful for me, which I did not know.
⁴'Hear, and I will speak; I will question you, and you declare to me.'
⁵I had heard of thee by the hearing of the ear, but now my eye sees thee;
⁶therefore I despise myself, and repent in dust and ashes."

⁷After the LORD had spoken these words to Job, the LORD said to Eli'phaz the Te'manite: "My wrath is kindled against you and against your two friends; for you have not spoken of me what is right, as my servant Job has. ⁸Now therefore take seven bulls and seven rams, and go to my servant Job, and offer up for yourselves a burnt offering; and my servant Job shall pray for you, for I will accept his prayer not to deal with you according to your folly; for you have not spoken of me what is right, as my servant Job has." ⁹So Eli'phaz the Te'manite and Bildad the Shuhite and Zophar the Na'amathite went and did what the LORD had told them; and the LORD accepted Job's prayer.

¹⁰And the LORD restored the fortunes of Job, when he had prayed for his friends; and the LORD gave Job twice as much as he had before. ¹¹Then came to him all his brothers and sisters and all who had known him before, and ate bread with him in his house; and they showed him sympathy and comforted him for all the evil that the LORD had brought upon him; and each of them gave him a piece of money and a ring of gold. ¹²And the LORD blessed the latter days of Job more than his beginning; and he had fourteen thousand sheep, six thousand camels, a thousand yoke of oxen, and a thousand she-asses. ¹³He had also seven sons and three daughters. ¹⁴And he called the name of the first Jemi'mah; and the name of the second Kezi'ah; and the name of the third Ker'en-hap'puch. ¹⁵And in all the land there were no women so fair as Job's daughters; and their father gave them inheritance among their brothers. ¹⁶And after this Job lived a hundred and forty years, and saw his sons, and his sons' sons, four generations. ¹⁷And Job died an old man, and full of days.

■ ■ ■

## Discussion and Writing Suggestions

1. The Book of Job was written 2500 years ago. What elements of the story make it contemporary? In other words, are its main themes as relevant today as they were in ancient times?

2. In Job 2:11–12, we learn that Job's three friends "come to condole with him and comfort him." Reread their words to Job: the speeches of Eli'phaz (chapters 4–5), Bildad (chapter 8), and Zophar (chapter 11). Describe the tone of these speeches. How comforting do you find them? How appropriate for one who is suffering? In your description, cite examples from the speeches.

3. In Job 1:9, Satan says: "Does Job fear God for nought?" In this famous line, Satan argues that Job's pious behaviour and love of God is cheap because it has never been tested. It is easy for the wealthy person, blessed with health, to claim that God is good. Love for God must be tested through hardship, says Satan. Do you agree? Explain.

4. Many commentators have noted the extreme irony at the end of Job. If God tells Eli'phaz that he and his two friends have "not spoken what is right," then *why*, with what justification, is Job made to suffer if *he* has spoken what is right? Fourteen hundred years ago, Pope Gregory the Great responded to this puzzle as follows: "[God] knows how to reward [saintly people]. . . . He casts them down outwardly to something despicable in order to lead them on inwardly to the height of things incomprehensible."[5] Do you agree with Gregory's view on why innocent people suffer?

5. Subscribing to the same view of cause-and-effect morality as that espoused by Job's three friends, some people believe that if they behave a certain way they will be spared hardship. That is to say, pious behaviour can be counted on to bring certain tangible benefits. Writing 800 years ago, Moses Maimonides argues that the aim of pious behaviour is *not* material gain but knowledge of God:

   > Man's task is to approach to God as close as humanly possible. . . . The evil are punished not by the withholding of material rewards but by their alienation from God, their debarment from human perfection. The good are rewarded not by worldly success but by the possibility of enlightenment, knowledge of God, which virtue opens to the truly wise.[6]

   According to Maimonides, the success of a pious person's behaviour has *nothing* to do with tangible benefits, like wealth, health, or a large family. Which view of piety is the more compelling—that of Maimonides or the view that pious behaviour should bring tangible rewards?

6. Why does God accept the wager with Satan? If God is all-knowing and all powerful, wouldn't God know *exactly* the quality of Job's love? Wouldn't God know how the wager will turn out?

7. Job's comforters argue for what is called "conventional piety": that is, a view of an ordered, moral world in which the good behave and are rewarded, whereas sinners are punished. Based on their certainty the

---

[5] Pope Gregory the Great, qtd. in Susan Schreiner, *Where Shall Wisdom Be Found: Calvin's Exegesis of Job from Medieval and Modern Perspectives* (Chicago: University of Chicago Press, 1994), 34.

[6] Moses Maimonides. "From *Moreh Nevukhim* III:22," in *Rambam: Readings in the Philosophy of Moses Maimonides*, ed. Lenn Evan Goodman (New York: Schocken, 1976), 356n.

world works this way, they conclude that Job's suffering *must* be a sign that he has sinned. At the conclusion of the story, speaking from the whirlwind, God says to Eli'phaz: "My wrath is kindled against you and against your two friends; for you have not spoken of me what is right, as my servant Job has" (42:7). In what ways have the three friends not spoken what was right? What are the flaws with the conventional piety that they preach to Job?

8. Reread God's speeches from the whirlwind: chapters 38–40:2, 40:6–41. What is the meaning of these speeches and of God's display of power? How directly does God answer Job's challenge to justify the torturing of an innocent man? In developing your answer, consider the remarks of psychoanalyst Carl Jung:

> For seventy-one verses [God–Yahweh] proclaims his world-creating power to his miserable victim, who sits in ashes and scratches his sores with potsherds, and who by now has had a bellyful of superhuman violence. Job has absolutely no need of being impressed by further exhibitions of this power. Yahweh, in his omniscience, could have known just how incongruous his attempts at intimidation were in such a situation. He could easily have seen that Job believes in his omnipotence as much as ever and has never doubted it or wavered in his loyalty. Altogether, he pays so little attention to Job's real situation that one suspects him of having an ulterior motive which is more important to him. . . . His thunderings at Job so completely miss the point that one cannot help but see how much he is occupied with himself.[7]

Notice that Jung's attention is drawn to God as a *personality*. (In fact, in his book, Jung goes on to psychoanalyze God!) Why would God behave so violently? Does God have something to prove? Is God insecure? Some authors in this chapter suggest (as have many commentators over the centuries) that the context of Creation is so much vaster than human logic and human principles of justice that God makes displays of grandeur in order to break Job's limited views of the Universe and open him to a more cosmic understanding. How do you respond to God's shows of grandeur and power?

9. What is Job's response to God's speech from the whirlwind? What has Job seen? What has he learned? Why does he lay his hand on his mouth (40:4)? What is *your* response to God's speech from the whirlwind?

10. Reread Job's speeches and make notes on his use of legal language and images. See, for instance, 13:13–18. What pattern emerges? What sense do you make of this pattern?

11. Based on your reading of Job, develop (and write down) two questions for small-group discussion. Base each question on specific lines that confuse you, trouble you, or otherwise pique your interest. Your questions should be such that they invite a variety of answers that reflect the varying points of view of different readers. In small-group discussion, exchange questions and take up each, one at a time.

---

[7] Carl Jung, *Answer to Job*, trans. R.F.C. Hull (London: Routledge & Kegan Paul, 1954), 25.

# *When Bad Things Happen to Good People*

HAROLD S. KUSHNER

*As Rabbi of Temple Israel in Natick, Massachusetts, Harold Kushner (b. 1935) has had many opportunities to console those who have been struck down by tragedy. His perspective on these interactions fundamentally changed when he suffered the loss of his son to a rare childhood disease. Devastated, Kushner questioned God and questioned himself; he raged against the unfairness of a child's death. He needed an explanation, like so many others he had counselled. His questions and doubts led, ultimately, to the writing of a best-seller,* When Bad Things Happen to Good People *(1981). Through his many lectures and writings (Kushner has penned several books, including* When Children Ask About God *and* When All You've Wanted Isn't Enough: The Search for a Life That Matters), *Kushner has appealed to people of many faiths. We reprint his introduction to* When Bad Things Happen *as well as that book's chapter on Job.*

In Memory of Aaron Zev Kushner
1963–1977

And David said: While the child was yet alive, I fasted and wept, for I said,
Who knows whether the Lord will be gracious to me and the child will live.
But now that he is dead, why should I fast? Can I bring him back again?
I shall go to him, but he will not return to me.      (II Samuel 12:22–23)

## WHY I WROTE THIS BOOK

This is not an abstract book about God and theology. It does not try to use       1
big words or clever ways of rephrasing questions in an effort to convince us
that our problems are not really problems, but that we only think they are.
This is a very personal book, written by someone who believes in God and in
the goodness of the world, someone who has spent most of his life trying to
help other people believe, and was compelled by a personal tragedy to rethink
everything he had been taught about God and God's ways.

Our son Aaron had just passed his third birthday when our daughter       2
Ariel was born. Aaron was a bright and happy child, who before the age of
two could identify a dozen different varieties of dinosaur and could patiently explain to an adult that dinosaurs were extinct. My wife and I had been
concerned about his health from the time he stopped gaining weight at the age
of eight months, and from the time his hair started falling out after he turned
one year old. Prominent doctors had seen him, had attached complicated
names to his condition, and had assured us that he would grow to be very
short but would be normal in all other ways. Just before our daughter's birth,
we moved from New York to a suburb of Boston, where I became the rabbi
of the local congregation. We discovered that the local pediatrician was doing
research in problems of children's growth, and we introduced him to Aaron.
Two months later—the day our daughter was born—he visited my wife in the

hospital, and told us that our son's condition was called progeria, "rapid aging." He went on to say that Aaron would never grow much beyond three feet in height, would have no hair on his head or body, would look like a little old man while he was still a child, and would die in his early teens.

How does one handle news like that? I was a young, inexperienced rabbi,    3
not as familiar with the process of grief as I would later come to be, and what I mostly felt that day was a deep, aching sense of unfairness. It didn't make sense. I had been a good person. I had tried to do what was right in the sight of God. More than that, I was living a more religiously committed life than most people I knew, people who had large, healthy families. I believed that I was following God's ways and doing His work. How could this be happening to my family? If God existed, if He was minimally fair, let alone loving and forgiving, how could He do this to me?

And even if I could persuade myself that I deserved this punishment for    4
some sin of neglect or pride that I was not aware of, on what grounds did Aaron have to suffer? He was an innocent child, a happy, outgoing three-year-old. Why should he have to suffer physical and psychological pain every day of his life? Why should he have to be stared at, pointed at, wherever he went? Why should he be condemned to grow into adolescence, see other boys and girls beginning to date, and realize that he would never know marriage or fatherhood? It simply didn't make sense.

Like most people, my wife and I had grown up with an image of God as    5
an all-wise, all-powerful parent figure who would treat us as our earthly parents did, or even better. If we were obedient and deserving, He would reward us. If we got out of line, He would discipline us, reluctantly but firmly. He would protect us from being hurt or from hurting ourselves, and would see to it that we got what we deserved in life.

Like most people, I was aware of the human tragedies that darkened the    6
landscape—the young people who died in car crashes, the cheerful, loving people wasted by crippling diseases, the neighbors and relatives whose retarded or mentally ill children people spoke of in hushed tones. But that awareness never drove me to wonder about God's justice, or to question His fairness. I assumed that He knew more about the world than I did.

Then came that day in the hospital when the doctor told us about Aaron    7
and explained what progeria meant. It contradicted everything I had been taught. I could only repeat over and over again in my mind, "This can't be happening. It is not how the world is supposed to work." Tragedies like this were supposed to happen to selfish, dishonest people whom I, as a rabbi, would then try to comfort by assuring them of God's forgiving love. How could it be happening to me, to my son, if what I believed about the world was true?

I read recently about an Israeli mother who, every year on her son's    8
birthday, would leave the birthday party, go into the privacy of her bedroom, and cry, because her son was now one year closer to military service, one year closer to making her one of the thousands of Israeli parents who would have to stand at the grave of a child fallen in battle. I read that, and I

knew exactly how she felt. Every year, on Aaron's birthday, my wife and I would celebrate. We would rejoice in his growing up and growing in skill. But we would be gripped by the cold foreknowledge that another year's passing brought us closer to the day when he would be taken from us.

I knew then that one day I would write this book. I would write it out of     9
my own need to put into words some of the most important things I have come to believe and know. And I would write it to help other people who might one day find themselves in a similar predicament. I would write it for all those people who wanted to go on believing, but whose anger at God made it hard for them to hold on to their faith and be comforted by religion. And I would write it for all those people whose love for God and devotion to Him led them to blame themselves for their suffering and persuade themselves that they deserved it.

There were not many books, as there were not many people, to help us     10
when Aaron was living and dying. Friends tried, and were helpful, but how much could they really do? And the books I turned to were more concerned with defending God's honor, with logical proof that bad is really good and that evil is necessary to make this a good world, than they were with curing the bewilderment and the anguish of the parent of a dying child. They had answers to all of their own questions, but no answer for mine.

I hope that this book is not like those. I did not set out to write a book that     11
would defend or explain God. There is no need to duplicate the many treatises already on the shelves, and even if there were, I am not a formally trained philosopher. I am fundamentally a religious man who has been hurt by life, and I wanted to write a book that could be given to the person who has been hurt by life—by death, by illness or injury, by rejection or disappointment—and who knows in his heart that if there is justice in the world, he deserved better. What can God mean to such a person? Where can he turn for strength and hope? If you are such a person, if you want to believe in God's goodness and fairness but find it hard because of the things that have happened to you and to people you care about, and if this book helps you do that, then I will have succeeded in distilling some blessing out of Aaron's pain and tears.

If I ever find my book bogging down in technical theological explanations     12
and ignoring the human pain which should be its subject, I hope that the memory of why I set out to write it will pull me back on course. Aaron died two days after his fourteenth birthday. This is his book, because any attempt to make sense of the world's pain and evil will be judged a success or a failure based on whether it offers an acceptable explanation of why he and we had to undergo what we did. And it is his book in another sense as well— because his life made it possible, and because his death made it necessary.

•  •  •

## THE STORY OF A MAN NAMED JOB

About twenty-five hundred years ago, a man lived whose name we will never     13
know, but who has enriched the minds and lives of human beings ever since.

He was a sensitive man who saw good people getting sick and dying around him while proud and selfish people prospered. He heard all the learned, clever, and pious attempts to explain life, and he was as dissatisfied with them as we are today. Because he was a person of rare literary and intellectual gifts, he wrote a long philosophical poem on the subject of why God lets bad things happen to good people. This poem appears in the Bible as the Book of Job.

Thomas Carlyle called the Book of Job "the most wonderful poem of any age and language; our first, oldest statement of the never-ending problem— man's destiny and God's way with him here in this earth. . . . There is nothing written in the Bible or out of it of equal literary merit." I have been fascinated by the Book of Job ever since I learned of its existence, and have studied it, reread it, and taught it any number of times. It has been said that just as every actor yearns to play Hamlet, every Bible student yearns to write a commentary on the Book of Job. It is a hard book to understand, a profound and beautiful book on the most profound of subjects, the question of why God lets good people suffer. Its argument is hard to follow because, through some of the characters, the author presents views he himself probably did not accept, and because he wrote in an elegant Hebrew which, thousands of years later, is often hard to translate. If you compare two English translations of Job, you may wonder if they are both translations of the same book. One of the key verses can be taken to mean either "I will fear God" or "I will not fear God," and there is no way of knowing for sure what the author intended. The familiar statement of faith "I know that my Redeemer lives" may mean instead "I would rather be redeemed while I am still alive." But much of the book is clear and forceful, and we can try our interpretive skills on the rest. **14**

Who was Job, and what is the book that bears his name? A long, long time ago, scholars believe, there must have been a well-known folk story, a kind of morality fable told to reinforce people's religious sentiments, about a pious man named Job. Job was so good, so perfect, that you realize at once that you are not reading about a real-life person. This is a "once-upon-a-time" story about a good man who suffered. **15**

One day, the story goes, Satan appears before God to tell Him about all the sinful things people were doing on earth. God says to Satan, "Did you notice My servant Job? There is no one on earth like him, a thoroughly good man who never sins." Satan answers God, "Of course Job is pious and obedient. You make it worth his while, showering riches and blessings on him. Take away those blessings and see how long he remains Your obedient servant." **16**

God accepts Satan's challenge. Without in any way telling Job what is going on, God destroys Job's house and cattle and kills his children. He afflicts Job with boils all over his body, so that his every moment becomes physical torture. Job's wife urges him to curse God, even if that means God's striking him dead. He can't do anything worse to Job than He already has done. Three friends come to console Job, and they too urge him to give up his piety, if this is the reward it brings him. But Job remains steadfast in his faith. Nothing that happens to him can make him give up his devotion to God. At the end, God appears, scolds the friends for their advice, and rewards Job for his faithfulness. **17**

God gives him a new home, a new fortune, and new children. The moral of the story is: when hard times befall you, don't be tempted to give up your faith in God. He has His reasons for what He is doing, and if you hold on to your faith long enough, He will compensate you for your suffering.

Over the generations, many people must have been told that story. Some, 18 no doubt, were comforted by it. Others were shamed into keeping their doubts and complaints to themselves after hearing Job's example. Our anonymous author was bothered by it. What kind of God would that story have us believe in, who would kill innocent children and visit unbearable anguish on His most devoted follower in order to prove a point, in order, we almost feel, to win a bet with Satan? What kind of religion is the story urging on us, which delights in blind obedience and calls it sinful to protest against injustice? He was so upset with this pious old fable that he took it, turned it inside out, and recast it as a philosophical poem in which the characters' positions are reversed. In the poem, Job *does* complain against God, and now it is the friends who uphold the conventional theology, the idea that "no ills befall the righteous."

In an effort to comfort Job, whose children have died and who is suf-   19 fering from the boils, the three friends say all the traditional, pious things. In essence, they preach the point of view contained in the original Job-fable: Don't lose faith, despite these calamities. We have a loving Father in Heaven, and He will see to it that the good prosper and the wicked are punished.

Job, who has probably spoken these same words innumerable times to   20 other mourners, realizes for the first time how hollow and offensive they are. What do you mean, He will see to it that the good prosper and the wicked are punished?! Are you implying that my children were wicked and that is why they died? Are you saying that I am wicked, and that is why all this is happening to me? Where was I so terrible? What did I do that was so much worse than anything you did, that I should suffer so much worse a fate?

The friends are startled by this outburst. They respond by saying that a   21 person can't expect God to tell him what he is being punished for. (At one point, one of the friends says, in effect, "what do you want from God, an itemized report about every time you told a lie or ignored a beggar? God is too busy running a world to invite you to go over His records with him.") We can only assume that nobody is perfect, and that God knows what He is doing. If we don't assume that, the world becomes chaotic and unlivable.

And so that argument continues. Job doesn't claim to be perfect, but says   22 that he has tried, more than most people, to live a good and decent life. How can God be a loving God if He is constantly spying on people, ready to pounce on any imperfection in an otherwise good record, and use that to justify punishment? And how can God be a just God if so many wicked people are not punished as horribly as Job is?

The dialogue becomes heated, even angry. The friends say: Job, you   23 really had us fooled. You gave us the impression that you were as pious and religious as we are. But now we see how you throw religion overboard the first time something unpleasant happens to you. You are proud, arrogant, impatient, and blasphemous. No wonder God is doing this to you. It just proves our point that human beings can be fooled as to who is a saint and who is a sinner, but you can't fool God.

After three cycles of dialogue in which we alternately witness Job voicing     24
his complaints and the friends defending God, the book comes to its thunderous climax. The author brilliantly has Job make use of a principle of biblical criminal law: if a man is accused of wrongdoing without proof, he may take an oath, swearing to his innocence. At that point, the accuser must either come up with evidence against him or drop the charges. In a long and eloquent statement that takes up chapters 29 and 30 of the biblical book, Job swears to his innocence. He claims that he never neglected the poor, never took anything that did not belong to him, never boasted of his wealth or rejoiced in his enemy's misfortune. He challenges God to appear with evidence, or to admit that Job is right and has suffered wrongly.

And God appears.     25

There comes a terrible windstorm, out of the desert, and God answers     26
Job out of the whirlwind. Job's case is so compelling, his challenge so forceful, that God Himself comes down to earth to answer him. But God's answer is hard to understand. He doesn't talk about Job's case at all, neither to detail Job's sins nor to explain his suffering. Instead, He says to Job, in effect, What do you know about how to run a world?

> Where were you when I planned the earth?
> Tell me, if you are wise.
> Do you know who took its dimensions,
> Measuring its length with a cord? . . .
> Were you there when I stopped the sea . . .
> And set its boundaries, saying, "Here you may come,
> But no further"?
> Have you seen where the snow is stored,
> Or visited the storehouse of the hail? . . .
> Do you tell the antelope when to calve?
> Do you give the horse his strength?
> Do you show the hawk how to fly?     [Job 38, 39]

And now a very different Job answers, saying, "I put my hand to my     27
mouth. I have said too much already; now I will speak no more."

The Book of Job is probably the greatest, fullest, most profound discus-     28
sion of the subject of good people suffering ever written. Part of its greatness lies in the fact that the author was scrupulously fair to all points of view, even those he did not accept. Though his sympathies are clearly with Job, he makes sure that the speeches of the friends are as carefully thought out and as carefully written as are his hero's words. That makes for great literature, but it also makes it hard to understand his message. When God says, "How dare you challenge the way I run my world? What do you know about running a world?", is that supposed to be the last word on the subject, or is that just one more paraphrase of the conventional piety of that time?

To try to understand the book and its answer, let us take note of three    29
statements which everyone in the book, and most of the readers, would like
to be able to believe:

A. God is all-powerful and causes everything that happens in the world.
   Nothing happens without His willing it.
B. God is just and fair, and stands for people getting what they deserve, so
   that the good prosper and the wicked are punished.
C. Job is a good person.

As long as Job is healthy and wealthy, we can believe all three of those    30
statements at the same time with no difficulty. When Job suffers, when he
loses his possessions, his family and his health, we have a problem. We can no
longer make sense of all three propositions together. We can now affirm any
two only by denying the third.

If God is both just and powerful, then Job must be a sinner who deserves    31
what is happening to him. If Job is good but God causes his suffering anyway,
then God is not just. If Job deserved better and God did not send his suffering, then God is not all-powerful. We can see the argument of the Book of Job
as an argument over which of the three statements we are prepared to sacrifice, so that we can keep on believing in the other two.

Job's friends are prepared to stop believing in (C), the assertion that Job    32
is a good person. They want to believe in God as they have been taught to.
They want to believe that God is good and that God is in control of things.
And the only way they can do that is to convince themselves that Job deserves
what is happening to him.

They start out truly wanting to comfort Job and make him feel better.    33
They try to reassure him by quoting all the maxims of faith and confidence on
which they and Job alike were raised. They want to comfort Job by telling
him that the world does in fact make sense, that it is not a chaotic, meaningless place. What they do not realize is that they can only make sense of the
world, and of Job's suffering, by deciding that he deserves what he has gone
through. To say that everything works out in God's world may be comforting to the casual bystander, but it is an insult to the bereaved and the unfortunate. "Cheer up, Job, nobody ever gets anything he doesn't have coming to
him" is not a very cheering message to someone in Job's circumstances.

But it is hard for the friends to say anything else. They believe, and want    34
to continue believing, in God's goodness and power. But if Job is innocent,
then God must be guilty—guilty of making an innocent man suffer. With that
at stake, they find it easier to stop believing in *Job's* goodness than to stop
believing in God's perfection.

It may also be that Job's comforters could not be objective about what    35
had happened to their friend. Their thinking may have been confused by
their own reactions of guilt and relief that these misfortunes had befallen Job
and not them. There is a German psychological term, *Schadenfreude*, which
refers to the embarrassing reaction of relief we feel when something bad hap-

pens to someone else instead of to us. The soldier in combat who sees his friend killed twenty yards away while he himself is unhurt, the pupil who sees another child get into trouble for copying on a test—they don't wish their friends ill, but they can't help feeling an embarrassing spasm of gratitude that it happened to someone else and not to them. . . .

We see this psychology at work elsewhere, blaming the victim so that evil 36 doesn't seem quite so irrational and threatening. If the Jews had behaved differently, Hitler would not have been driven to murder them. If the young woman had not been so provocatively dressed, the man would not have assaulted her. If people worked harder, they would not be poor. If society did not taunt poor people by advertising things they cannot afford, they would not steal. Blaming the victim is a way of reassuring ourselves that the world is not as bad a place as it may seem, and that there are good reasons for people's suffering. It helps fortunate people believe that their good fortune is deserved, rather than being a matter of luck. It makes everyone feel better—except the victim, who now suffers the double abuse of social condemnation on top of his original misfortune. This is the approach of Job's friends, and while it may solve their problem, it does not solve Job's, or ours.

Job, for his part, is unwilling to hold the world together theologically by 37 admitting that he is a villain. He knows a lot of things intellectually, but he knows one thing more deeply. Job is absolutely sure that he is not a bad person. He may not be perfect, but he is not so much worse than others, by any intelligible moral standard, that he should deserve to lose his home, his children, his wealth and health while other people get to keep all those things. And he is not prepared to lie to save God's reputation.

Job's solution is to reject proposition (B), the affirmation of God's good- 38 ness. Job is in fact a good man, but God is so powerful that He is not limited by considerations of fairness and justice.

A philosopher might put it this way: God may *choose* to be fair and give 39 a person what he deserves, punishing the wicked and rewarding the righteous. But can we say logically that an all-powerful God *must* be fair? Would He still be all-powerful if we, by living virtuous lives, could *compel* Him to protect and reward us? Or would He then be reduced to a kind of cosmic vending machine, into which we insert the right number of tokens and from which we get what we want (with the option of kicking and cursing the machine if it doesn't give us what we paid for)? An ancient sage is said to have rejoiced at the world's injustice, saying, "Now I can do God's will out of love for Him and not out of self-interest." That is, he could be a moral, obedient person out of sheer love for God, without the calculation that moral obedient people will be rewarded with good fortune. He could love God even if God did not love him in return. The problem with such an answer is that it tries to promote justice and fairness and at the same time tries to celebrate God for being so great that He is beyond the limitations of justice and fairness.

Job sees God as being above notions of fairness, being so powerful that 40 no moral rules apply to Him. God is seen as resembling an Oriental potentate, with unchallenged power over the life and property of his subjects. And in fact, the old fable of Job does picture God in just that way, as a deity who afflicts Job without any moral qualms in order to test his loyalty, and who feels that He has "made it up" to Job afterward by rewarding him lavishly. The God of the fable, held up as a figure to be worshiped for so many generations, is very much like an (insecure) ancient king, rewarding people not for their goodness but for their loyalty.

So Job constantly wishes that there were an umpire to mediate between     41
himself and God, someone God would have to explain Himself to. But when it comes to God, he ruefully admits, there are no rules. "Behold He snatches away and who can hinder Him? Who can say to Him, What are You doing?" (Job 9:12)

How does Job understand his misery? He says, we live in an unjust     42
world, from which we cannot expect fairness. There is a God, but He is free of the limitations of justice and righteousness.

What about the anonymous author of the book? What is his answer to     43
the riddle of life's unfairness? As indicated, it is hard to know just what he thought and what solution he had in mind when he set out to write his book. It seems clear that he has put his answer into God's mouth in the speech from the whirlwind, coming as it does at the climax of the book. But what does it mean? Is it simply that Job is silenced by finding out that there is a God, that there really is someone in charge up there? But Job never doubted that. It was God's sympathy, accountability, and fairness that were at issue, not His existence. Is the answer that God is so powerful that He doesn't have to explain Himself to Job? But that is precisely what Job has been claiming throughout the book: There is a God, and He is so powerful that He doesn't have to be fair. What new insight does the author bring by having God appear and speak, if that is all He has to say, and why is Job so apologetic if it turns out that God agrees with him?

Is God saying, as some commentators suggest, that He has other consid-     44
erations to worry about, besides the welfare of one individual human being, when He makes decisions that affect our lives? Is He saying that, from our human vantage point, our sicknesses and business failures are the most important things imaginable, but God has more on His mind than that? To say that is to say that the morality of the Bible, with its stress on human virtue and the sanctity of the individual life, is irrelevant to God, and that charity, justice, and the dignity of the individual human being have some source other than God. If that were true, many of us would be tempted to leave God, and seek out and worship that source of charity, justice, and human dignity instead.

Let me suggest that the author of the Book of Job takes the position     45
which neither Job nor his friends take. He believes in God's goodness and in Job's goodness, and is prepared to give up his belief in proposition (A): that God is all-powerful. Bad things do happen to good people in this world, but it is not God who wills it. God would like people to get what they deserve in life, but He cannot always arrange it. Forced to choose between a good God who is not totally powerful, or a powerful God who is not totally good, the author of the Book of Job chooses to believe in God's goodness.

The most important lines in the entire book may be the ones spoken by 46
God in the second half of the speech from the whirlwind, chapter 40, verses
9–14:

> Have you an arm like God?
> Can you thunder with a voice like His?
> *You* tread down the wicked where they stand,
> Bury them in the dust together . . .
> Then will I acknowledge that your own right hand
> Can give you victory.

I take these lines to mean "if you think that it is so easy to keep the world 47
straight and true, to keep unfair things from happening to people, *you* try it."
God wants the righteous to live peaceful, happy lives, but sometimes even He
can't bring that about. It is too difficult even for God to keep cruelty and
chaos from claiming their innocent victims. But could man, without God, do
it better?

The speech goes on, in chapter 41, to describe God's battle with the sea 48
serpent Leviathan. With great effort, God is able to catch him in a net and pin
him with fish hooks, but it is not easy. If the sea serpent is a symbol of chaos
and evil, of all the uncontrollable things in the world (as it traditionally is in
ancient mythology), the author may be saying there too that even God has a
hard time keeping chaos in check and limiting the damage that evil can do.

Innocent people do suffer misfortunes in this life. Things happen to them 49
far worse than they deserve—they lose their jobs, they get sick, their children
suffer or make them suffer. But when it happens, it does not represent God
punishing them for something they did wrong. The misfortunes do not come
from God at all.

There may be a sense of loss at coming to this conclusion. In a way, it 50
was comforting to believe in an all-wise, all-powerful God who guaranteed
fair treatment and happy endings, who reassured us that everything happened for a reason, even as life was easier for us when we could believe that
our parents were wise enough to know what to do and strong enough to
make everything turn out right. But it was comforting the way the religion of
Job's friends was comforting: it worked only as long as we did not take the
problems of innocent victims seriously. When we have met Job, when we
have *been* Job, we cannot believe in that sort of God any longer without
giving up our own right to feel angry, to feel that we have been treated
badly by life.

From that perspective, there ought to be a sense of relief in coming to the 51
conclusion that God is not doing this to us. If God is a God of justice and not
of power, then He can know that we are good and honest people who deserve
better. Our misfortunes are none of His doing, and so we can turn to Him for
help. Our question will not be Job's question "God, why are You doing this
to me?" but rather "God, see what is happening to me. Can You help me?"
We will turn to God, not to be judged or forgiven, not to be rewarded or punished, but to be strengthened and comforted.

If we have grown up, as Job and his friends did, believing in an all-wise, 52
all-powerful, all-knowing God, it will be hard for us, as it was hard for them,
to change our way of thinking about Him (as it was hard for us, when we
were children, to realize that our parents were not all-powerful, that a broken
toy had to be thrown out because they *could not* fix it, not because they did
not want to). But if we can bring ourselves to acknowledge that there are
some things God does not control, many good things become possible.

We will be able to turn to God for things He can do to help us, instead 53
of holding on to unrealistic expectations of Him which will never come about.
The Bible, after all, repeatedly speaks of God as the special protector of the
poor, the widow, and the orphan, without raising the question of how it happened that they became poor, widowed, or orphaned in the first place.

We can maintain our own self-respect and sense of goodness without 54
having to feel that God has judged us and condemned us. We can be angry at
what has happened to us, without feeling that we are angry at God. More
than that, we can recognize our anger at life's unfairness, our instinctive
compassion at seeing people suffer, as coming from God who teaches us to be
angry at injustice and to feel compassion for the afflicted. Instead of feeling
that we are opposed to God, we can feel that our indignation is God's anger
at unfairness working through us, that when we cry out, we are still on God's
side, and He is still on ours.

■ ■ ■

## Review Questions

1. In the introduction to *When Bad Things Happen to Good People*, Kushner
   relates the story of his son's illness and of the tragedy the family faced.
   What questions, what crises, did these experiences prompt in Kushner,
   and how did Aaron's illness and death provide a motivation to Kushner for
   writing his book?
2. In his paraphrase of Job, Kushner states that Job is afflicted and is then
   visited by friends who, in their effort to comfort him, "say all the traditional, pious things." Job realizes, says Kushner, "how hollow and offensive they are" (paragraph 20). Why are the words of the comforters, in
   Job's eyes, hollow and offensive?
3. Why do the three friends find it psychologically convenient to condemn
   Job: to conclude that if he suffers he must therefore have sinned?
4. What are the three propositions that Kushner says that the character of
   Job and most readers want to believe? Why, according to Kushner, does
   the story require us to accept two of these propositions and reject the
   third? Which proposition does Kushner say the Job poet rejects? What
   about Job's friends: which do they reject? What about Job himself?
5. When innocent people suffer misfortune, why do they suffer "double
   abuse" when would-be comforters suggest that God punishes only
   the wicked?

6. What is lost when we accept (what Kushner believes to be) the Joban poet's conclusion about God's power? What is gained? Why is this conclusion significant?

## Discussion and Writing Suggestions

1. What is the effect on you of Kushner's story about his son, Aaron? Do you have a similar story to tell, or have you encountered similar stories among people you know? If yes, are there any senses in which you find people's responses to innocent suffering to be consistent or predictable?
2. What are the ways in which Kushner's loss of his son prepared him to interpret Job in the way that he has? That is, given the story of Aaron's brief life and its effect on Kushner, would you expect him to produce the analysis of Job that he does?
3. In the opening to "The Story of a Man Named Job," Kushner quotes Thomas Carlyle (a 19th-century British author) as writing that Job is "our first, oldest statement of the never-ending problem—man's destiny and God's way with him here in this earth." In a paragraph or two, define in your own words this "never-ending problem."
4. Kushner asserts that one of the three propositions in paragraph 29 must be rejected. Of Kushner's three propositions, which do you reject—and why?
5. Kushner concludes that, by interpreting the story of Job as the Joban author does, we "will turn to God, not to be judged or forgiven, not to be rewarded or punished, but to be strengthened and comforted." We will not be opposed to God, in times of hardship, but allied with God—since we will understand that God is not causing bad things to happen to us. To what extent do you agree with Kushner's reading of the story? Do you think the Job poet takes the position Kushner says he does? What is your evidence for thinking so?

# The Myth of Justice

## MICHAEL DORRIS

*Michael Dorris (1945–1997), anthropologist and novelist, was the much-respected author of* The Broken Cord *and* A Yellow Raft in Blue Water. *With his longtime collaborator (and spouse) Louise Erdrich, he wrote* The Crown of Columbus *and other works of fiction. A winner of numerous prizes, including the National Book Critics Circle award and awards from the Guggenheim and Rockefeller foundations and the National Endowment for the Arts, Dorris was one of the most celebrated Native American writers of his generation. (He traced his ancestry to the Modoc tribe and founded the Native American Studies Department at Dartmouth College.) In the selection that follows, written shortly before he ended his life, Dorris attacks our culture's belief in Justice. With his deep skepticism, he sounds at moments like a Job who has been crushed by life but who will not seek Justice because he has lost faith in a moral system that rights the wrongs of innocent sufferers.*

Where did we ever get the idea that life is ultimately fair? Who promised that there was a balance to things, a yin and yang that perfectly cancels each other out, a divine score sheet that makes sure that all the totals eventually ring even? Who exactly reaps what they sow? Does everything that goes around come around? 1

If that's some people's experience, I haven't met them, and my guess is, if they still believe it, they simply haven't lived long enough to know better. 2

Justice is one of those palliative myths—like afterlife with acquired personality and memory intact—that makes existence bearable. As long as we can think that our experience of being periodically screwed by fate is the exception to the rule we can hope for, as they used to say in commercials, a brighter tomorrow. As long as we can trust in an ultimate squaring of accounts, we can suffer what we assume to be temporary setbacks, transitory stumbles on our path toward redemption through good works and sacrifice. 3

When I was a child we were told of a Golden Ledger in which God (or one of his executive assistants) kept tabs on our every plus and minus, and as long as we wound up in the black we were "in"—as *in* heaven for all eternity. Our journey through the years was a test that was passable, if only we stretched hard enough. We were in control of our destinies. We were, at worst, Job: Hang in there, and you will be paid back with compound interest. 4

Uh huh. In your dreams, sucker. 5

Religion isn't the opiate of the people, the conception of justice is. It's our last bastion of rationality, our logical lighthouse on a stormy sea, our anchor. We extend its parameters beyond death—if we haven't found equity in this life, all the great belief systems assure us, just wait until the next. Or the next, or the next. Someday our prince will come. 6

That may be true, but the paradigm is based on faith, not fact. We can believe in the tooth fairy until the alarm goes off, but unless there's a benevolent parent to value our loss as worth a quarter, we wake up with used calcium, not negotiable currency, under our pillows. 7

Anthropologists and other social scientists make a distinction between contextual and blind justice. In the former archetype, the goddess has her eyes wide open. It matters—boy, does it matter—who does what to whom, when, how much, and why. In contextual-justice-crazy societies like ours, or like the Yurok of precontact California, rich folks get to pay off their victims, either through a dream team of attorneys or via a prearranged valuation in woodpecker scalps—the murder of an aristocrat worth ever so much more than the slaying of a commoner. If you can afford it, you can do it, and that's the way the game is played. You can't even complain, have begrudging thoughts, or retry the case if the price is right and coughed up in full. 8

In the theoretical latter case—and is there any manifest and irrefutable instance, really?—it matters not what your station is or what you intended: The act's the thing. All equal before the law. Don't ask, don't tell. A level field, a blank slate. The verdict is impartial and therefore fair. Gripe and you're a sore loser, short-sighted, an excuser of your own incapacities. Strike out and it's because you wanted to in your heart, you didn't wait through the rain, you didn't expend maximum effort. Because if you had, well, you'd wind up—justified. It's a utopian notion, blind justice, an Eden where expectations are perfectly in tune with possibility. But for each of us there comes an undeniable catch, a flaw in the argument. What any human being not convicted of a capital crime has to one day wonder is: What did I do to deserve the death penalty? Be born?    9

Yet despite the evidence of our private and cultural histories, despite the inevitability of the maximum sentence, when things *don't* work out, we are perpetually surprised. Is this a naiveté carried to an absurd extreme? Wouldn't it be wiser, safer to be shocked at a fleeting *happy* outcome? Wouldn't a pleasant astonishment, however brief, beat bitter disappointment?    10

But that's too dour. It's downright discouraging. We watch our gritty TV dramas with assurance of retribution, of confirmation. Right prevails, if not this week, then next. Good wins out against all odds. When the innocent victim is convicted on *NYPD Blue* or *Law and Order*, we are outraged; and when the perp goes free, we're appalled. It's not supposed to be that way. We recognize injustice when we see it. We're positively Old Testament in our condemnation. We know how things *should* be.    11

Our truth. As if it were happening to us.    12

As it is. All the time.    13

I've talked to underpaid public defenders, idealistic law school top-ten percenters who chose working within the system over six-figure starting salaries. First year, they're motivated, blessed. Second year, they're cynically busting their chops to spring drug dealers. Third year, they're burnt out, ready for corporate, a health plan, into locking up the very bad guys they've been so busy turning loose. Sellouts, but just ask them and they'll tell you why not. They sleep at night now, go to bed with clear conscience, know what's what, and act on it.    14

Are their serial analyses accurate? Unless you're an avower of the innate goodness of human nature at twenty-one you'll never be, so use or loose it. Because at thirty you'll know better, you'll have your own kids to protect, you'll be wise to the ways of the world, clear-eyed, maybe even a Republican. Was Kunstler just an old kid, a guy who wouldn't admit harsh facts when they stared him square in the face? Is a $300 suit a give-up buy-in or the minimum salary for upholding civilization as we know it?    15

Questions, questions, questions. If we knew the answers or were sure of them we wouldn't have to ask. We yearn to be proven wrong, returned to the innocence of righteous hope. We don't want to be our parents. We want to be as we were: true believers. Please.    16

We're every generation with a minimal sense of integrity who came before   17
use and reluctantly, partially conceded the fight. We're us. We're our children
in twenty years. We're wish. We're further disillusionment waiting to happen.

Do I need examples from "real life" to prove my point? Read the news-   18
paper. Look at world history. Examine your own family. People got what
they deserve, right? Oh, really? They didn't?

Okay, call me a downer. There's divine justice, we're assured, a future   19
payday in which everybody knows everything about everybody and rewards
and punishments are meted out in precisely the correct quotients. We all
stand there on judgment day, quivering, humiliated by our secret transgressions, dreading exposure. There's this apocalyptic division point, like at the
Nazi camps: go right, go left. Life, death.

But all that is beside the point, finally. If there's punishment for trans-   20
gression, that means that order does actually prevail—and the alternative is
arguably scarier than hell itself. What if all is chaos and it is simply our own
fear, our own cosmological terror, our own instinct as a species to impose
structure on whatever we behold? There are scientists who specialize in precisely this kind of bubble-popping on a minor scale: Dr. Amos Tversky, a
Stanford University psychologist, working with Dr. Donald Redelmeier, an
internist at the University of Toronto, has neatly disproven the long-held
truism that people with arthritis can anticipate rainy weather and that a chill
brings on a cold; Dr. Albert Kligman, a dermatology professor at the
University of Pennsylvania, roundly disproved the widely held notion that
eating chocolate exacerbates acne in teenagers. According to these and other
researchers, human beings innately desire predictability and so search out
patterns even when there are none. We disregard contrary indications in
order to stick firm to our collective wishful thought that events conform to
knowable design.

This is the basis, after all, of ritual act. If I do X and Y, then Z will nec-   21
essarily follow. If once upon a time when I wanted it to rain I sang a certain
song at a certain time of day, decked out in a particular outfit, having either
eaten or not eaten, had sex or abstained, vocalized or remained silent—and it
rained!—then next drought I'd better replicate all the details as precisely as
possible. Who knows what caused the moisture to arrive: Was it the
sequence? All the ingredients? And if not all, which ones dare I omit? So to be
sure, replay, and if the heavens don't open it must have been *my* fault, *I* must
have messed up on some aspect. We wear ourselves out in pursuit of the right
key to understanding the nature of things, whether we call it physics or witch-
doctoring or philosophy. What other sane option is there? If we are ineffectual, if there isn't any grand scheme to discover and plug into, then we're
simply spinning wheels. When the sun goes down, it might not rise again.
When we go to sleep, we might not wake up. When we die, regardless of
whether we've been a sinner or a saint—yikes!

The good news about this impulse of ours is that it begets common   22
assumptions, which are the next best thing to reality. When we give group credence to the same hypotheses we function as if they're absolute, we allow them

to define us. When a culture is healthy, cohesive, intellectually homogenous and in sync, we agree that our explanations work—and they seem to. But when we're clustered in a society that's atomized, discordant, at odds, psychological clarity explodes like confetti from a firecracker. If truth is relative, if law is haphazard, if what we term justice is nothing more than occasional and statistical circumstance that we utilize bogusly to reenforce our hope for righteousness, then we dwell not just on a shaky foundation but mired in quicksand.

Not all cultures have grounded their sense of reality in cause-effect rela-     23
tionships. While Genesis postulates a planned, intentionally ordered universe and later books of the Bible stipulate the myriad of rules and regulations we must follow in order to placate, if not please, the divinity, the Nootka Tribe of the Pacific Northwest takes a different approach. In their schema the culture hero is a unisex trickster personified as Raven. Their human creation story goes something like this:

Once, Raven was flying around when it spied a bush loaded with lus-     24
cious, purple, irresistible berries. Down swoops Raven and gobbles up every one. Finally its breast feathers are stained with juice and its belly is so bloated that it has to get a running start and jump off a cliff to again become airborne. In no time at all, Raven experiences the worst stomach cramps it has ever known, and shortly thereafter a horrible case of diarrhea. It seems to last forever, but when the attack is over, Raven breathes a sigh of relief and looks down to the earth to see the mess it has made. And there we are!

In the Nootka cosmology, justice, like much else, is chance not ordained.     25
Things simply happen without structure or divine plan. The proper response to the tale—and to the organization of the world that it implies—is laughter rather than smugness or indignation. Don't expect from me, the universe seems to suggest, but don't blame me either. You're on your own.

An interesting notion, but we in the West are programmed to content     26
ourselves with being appalled, insisting that we're stunned when injustice seems to triumph. The *human*-created system has broken down, we persuade ourselves. This is but a temporary aberration. Just hold out for the eventual guaranteed happy ending. Cling to the Beatitudes and the meek *will* inherit the earth. Be like Pascal and choose to behave as if we're sure in our convictions, betting that if, God forbid, we're wrong, we'll never have to find out. Like the ground beneath the circling trickster, we'll never know what hit us.

■  ■  ■

## Review Questions

1. Dorris begins his essay with a question: "Where did we ever get the idea that life is ultimately fair?" In the essay, how does Dorris answer his own question?
2. What is the "Golden Ledger" and its significance?
3. Dorris writes: "Questions, questions, questions. If we knew the answers or were sure of them we wouldn't have to ask. We yearn to be proven

wrong, returned to the innocence of righteous hope." What is the "innocence of righteous hope"?

4. To what use does Dorris put the research finding that eating chocolate does not exacerbate acne in teenagers?

5. Why does Dorris call it "good news" that "we search out patterns even when there are none"?

6. What is the danger of letting our beliefs, whether true or not, define us?

## Discussion and Writing Suggestions

1. In this essay, Dorris rejects the biblical notion of justice and the sense of order and sanity that comes with it. He offers the Nootka creation myth, and the relationship between the cosmos and humankind that it implies, as an alternative to the Bible's tightly ordered universe. If Dorris fully accepted the Nootka creation myth, why do you suppose he sounds so bitter?

2. "We wear ourselves out in pursuit of the right key to understanding the nature of things, whether we call it physics or witch-doctoring or philosophy. What other sane option is there?" Why would Dorris term the alternative *in*sane? And what has the finding of order to do with Dorris's calling the belief in justice a myth?

3. Explain how the Nootka tribe's myth of creation is more in keeping with Dorris's view of justice (and, generally, of expecting life to work out) than the Genesis creation myth is. What is your view of the Nootka myth?

4. Consider this brief poem by Stephen Crane:

> A man said to the universe:
> "Sir, I exist!"
> "However," replied the universe,
> "The fact has not created in me
> A sense of obligation."[1]

To what extent does Crane's poem reflect the point Dorris is making in this essay? You might consider, especially, the Nootka creation myth in light of the poem.

5. Are you "stunned when injustice seems to triumph" (paragraph 26)? To the extent that you are, what does your reaction tell you about your assumptions regarding the orderliness of the universe? That is to say, do you believe more in the biblical sense of justice or in the sense of justice (or lack thereof) implied by the Nootka creation myth?

6. Respond to Dorris's argument that our notion of justice is a myth. Be prepared to articulate and defend your response in a class discussion. A consideration for those who agree with Dorris: How does one agree and *not* become bitter?

---

[1] Stephen Crane, "A Man Said to the Universe." in eds. Sculley Bradley et al., *The American Tradition in Literature*, 5th ed. (New York: Random, 1981), 1241.

# Job: Implications for Today

DIANNE BERGANT

*Dianne Bergant, C.S.A. (Congregation of St. Agnes) is a professor of Biblical Studies at the Catholic Theological Union in Chicago. In this selection, which concludes her book-length study of Job, Bergant argues that Job shows us the importance of interpreting religious traditions so that we can find in them "wisdom for the present and the future." Job's three comforters represented an accepted, conventional wisdom that was utterly inadequate to the task of comforting Job in his suffering. By opposing the comforters—by insisting on his innocence and yet not rejecting his tradition, Job broke through to a new and deepened faith. In our day, writes Bergant, any number of misfortunes can "rip away a false . . . certainty and order and catapult the vulnerable human creature" into a chaos that prompts Joban questions. We can use our questions, as Job used his, to find in established traditions a deepened, contemporary meaning.*

The drama of Job has touched the hearts of women and men down through    1
the ages to the present time. It has never lost its appeal because of the universality of the issues addressed. Although humankind has not basically changed, the world in which it finds itself and which it has helped to create presents new challenges for each generation. If a society's religious tradition is to remain vital and creative, it must be able to speak to the contemporary world in the language of the time. Its message must be capable of being interpreted without being compromised. . . . [I]t is not possible to treat all of the concerns of the book in a commentary of this nature. The following are reflections that flow from those issues that have been considered here.

The underlying motif of the book is ORDER, cosmic and experiential. At    2
the heart of Job's dilemma is the collapse of his world of meaning brought on by the incomprehensible events of his life. This is not a unique experience for Job alone but one that he shares with every thinking human being. The simple process of growth and maturation demands that world views be constructed and revised or changed constantly throughout one's life. This usually occurs gradually and with little or no distress, but there are many normal situations that can result in unusual trauma and there are experiences that can wrench one from the securities of life and terrify one with the prospect of annihilation. A certain amount of understanding seems essential for human stability. When the framework of this understanding crumbles and life ceases to make sense, people often thrash around for some means of survival or, too often, despair of any solution and give up.

No one is protected from personal misfortunes such as sudden and tragic    3
death, human exploitation or betrayal, unexpected collapse of business or career, or from disasters such as flooding or other ravages of nature. The horrors of war, or of ethnic, racial, sexual, or other social discrimination or brutality victimize countless women and men and defy all standards of justice and harmony. Is it any wonder that scores of people attempt to escape the apparent

meaninglessness of existence? The gravity of these situations and the demand to remedy the evils and help bear the burdens of the afflicted are not to be minimized. However, these human miseries often lead to an even greater tragedy—the denial of any meaning to life. This is the great temptation that faces Job and it is to this trial that the book speaks.

When one's authentic and profound life experience and the generally    4 accepted way of understanding life are in conflict, an individual seldom embraces an external standard which opposes one's own practical knowledge. The impasse between the visitors and Job reflects just such a conflict. It is more than foolhardy; it is unconscionable to tell a victim of exploitation or violence that he or she is always in some way responsible for what has happened. Even when there is some degree of culpability, the extent of the evil endured frequently far exceeds the seriousness of the human error. How does one explain crime, social injustice or war from a retributive frame of reference? The author of the Book of Job has done a masterful job of exposing the inadequacy of a rigid theory of retribution. The men who had come to assist Job with their wisdom only compound his hardship with their disregard of his many afflictions, their insensitivity to his intellectual dilemma, and their offensiveness in offering empty counsel and harsh judgment. They would have him deny what he knows to be true and accept the conventional teaching which they espouse rather than listen to his protestations and admit their inability to offer him a more suitable explanation. They are right about one thing, however. The religious tradition need not be scorned nor discarded. The truth contained within it, if it is indeed truth, must be rediscovered, embraced and allowed to speak to the present situation. They err in refusing to admit that the expression of truth is wanting and needs to change and evolve.

A similar situation faces society today. Not only sinfulness and inhu-    5 manity but the pace of life, the burst of technology with its frightening implications, human accomplishments that seem to proliferate by leaps and bounds can all rip away a false security of certainty and order and catapult the vulnerable human creature into a world of rapid change and ambiguity. The theories and answers of the past are frequently inadequate and new structures of meaning must be devised. The guardians of tradition cannot merely perpetuate the perceptions and articulations of the past. In their devotion to truth they must allow the development of its understanding and expression or they will end up as antiquarians collecting treasures of the past rather than sages possessing wisdom for the present and the future.

What message is the author propounding by presenting Job as he does?    6 From the outset Job is an upright man whose virtue is attested to by God. When calamity befalls him it is completely unrelated to his own doing. This initial portrayal of Job as an innocent sufferer either undermines any inflexible belief in retribution or casts doubt on the management and justice of God. These are the options available to Job as the Dialogue opens. There is one thing that Job never doubts and that is his own integrity. Nor will he compromise human dignity and admit to something that he knows is false. It makes no difference that he is opposed by as cherished a treasure as his religious tradition. He will not relinquish his forthrightness nor minimize the veracity of his stand. Such a position is difficult to take when one is assured of understanding and support from others. To assume it alone, in opposition to religious custom and belief, with no buttress but the assurance of one's own life is indeed a courageous act. It also runs the danger of alienating one from the rest of reality.

Men and women of conscience have often been brought to this point of    7
decision. Many have had to stand in opposition to the religious, political or social groups which they love and of which they are a part. Denounced as rebels and apostates, they have chosen to side with reality as experienced rather than as traditionally interpreted and have unwittingly become the real champions of truth.

There is, however, a serious flaw in Job's argument. Immersed in mis-    8
fortune of which he is innocent, Job points an accusing finger at God and falls into the same trap as did his inept counselors. While they uphold strict retribution and thus reject the authenticity of Job's claims, he clings to the same theory and charges God with folly of injustice. It is only through the insights gained from the theophany that Job can see the deficiency of this world view and reconcile his dilemma.

Many times when people are caught in similar predicaments, they too    9
accuse God of injustice. They wonder how a just God could allow the inhumanity that seems to run rampant across the face of the earth. They watch defenseless victims stricken by unbridled evil and feel compelled to deny the existence of a loving God. As in the case of Job, traditional explanations are hollow, familiar advice is flat, and customary devotion is saccharine. The temptation is to declare God a hoax and life absurd or cruel.

In such desperate situations intellectual discussions are seldom effective    10
because the operations of the universe are beyond human comprehension. Anyone who blames God still believes in God's existence and so it is this faith rather than concepts of logic that must be strengthened and developed. Job is a perfect example of a person whose previous religious ideas had to be broken in order that a more vibrant and mature faith could emerge. Unlike the traditionalists who remained imprisoned in their theories, Job availed himself of the new insights received and risked the uncertainties of an evolving world view. It is the combination of honesty, humility and openness that is praised by the Lord.

Several meaningful insights can be drawn from reflection on Yahweh's    11
attitude toward Job. He does not directly defend himself against Job's charge of injustice. Perhaps this is because the accusation is more an erroneous conclusion than an outright rebellion. Since Job was certain of his own guiltlessness and was an adherent of the orthodox world view, he had no other alternative but to be skeptical about God's integrity. Innocent suffering is neither denied nor explained. Instead, the discussion is moved to an entirely different plane and the fundamental issue of cosmic sovereignty is addressed. The force of God's interrogation elicits awe and submission and Job stands quietly before a panorama that has burst the confines of his narrow perspective. Neither prosperity nor affliction matters in the face of such wonders. If this is

true on the cosmic plane, it is all the more so on the human plane. Contrary to a widely held misconception, happiness and success are not demonstrable rewards for righteous living nor are grief and failure concomitant reprisals. Wealth may well be the fruit of wise management, but it can also stem from greed and graft. Likewise, there are too many examples of decent men and women and helpless children suffering indignities. One implication of the Yahweh Speeches clearly illustrates the serious error of an inflexible theory of retribution. Misfortune can indeed befall the righteous. Suffering is not the sure sign of alienation from God.

A second point concerns anthropological presuppositions. Yahweh may    12
have denounced any grandiose notion of human prominence but did not undermine the authentic dignity of Job. In fact, whenever Job is called to a superhuman feat he comes to see his own inadequacy. This is not an affront but an honest appreciation of true human potential. It includes admitting limitations as well as praising abilities.

Confidence in his own integrity was Job's only mainstay throughout his    13
turmoil. When all else seemed to have deserted him or to have turned against him, he continued to trust his human powers of discernment and judgment and he insisted that others accord him the hearing and justice that were his due. Here is a man who will not relinquish his self-respect nor sense of right regardless of the odds against him. He may be crushed by adversity but his spirit is undaunted. The other men read this as insolence and blasphemy, but Yahweh never accused Job of either. He calls upon Job to stand as a man of valor before the divine teacher and there is no trace of insult in God's speech to Job. Job survives his encounter with God without having to demean himself nor disavow his sense of dignity. He admits that his perception has been wrong but that admission is not self-deprecating. Had he succumbed to the pressure of the others and renounced his point of view, there would have been no breakthrough to a new insight. Job would have had to live with mediocre compromise rather than stark honesty, with false humility rather than human dignity, and with empty teaching rather than challenging truth. His vindication by Yahweh affirms him in his stand and justifies his perspective.

Genuine and forthright human accomplishments are to be valued and    14
trusted as long as they are not an act of defiance in the face of God. In the normal course of human life, one cannot always determine whether progress is advantageous or defiant. This was true in the case of Job and it is true today. The only safeguards available are profound commitment to the sovereignty of God, honesty in testing limits, and humble acknowledgment of finite creaturehood.

Several questions were posed at the beginning of this study. "What is the    15
origin of the universe and what holds it together?" "What is the meaning of suffering?" "What role does God play in life as humans experience it?" The biblical tradition, specifically the Book of Job, offers direction and insights for coming to grips with these questions. Ultimately, each person must face them, struggle with them, and somehow resolve them.

■  ■  ■

## Review Questions

1. Why is the word "order" important in Job, according to Bergant?
2. What is the fundamental trial, or struggle, to which Job speaks, according to Bergant?
3. What is a "retributive frame of reference"?
4. Why is it necessary to continually reinterpret religious tradition?
5. What risk does Job run in maintaining his innocence before his friends and before God?
6. What is the flaw in Job's argument, according to Bergant?
7. What does Job discover during the speech with God?

## Discussion and Writing Suggestions

1. A premise of Bergant's essay is that Job is a contemporary story because human nature does not change, while circumstances in which humans find themselves do. Thus, human questions and passions and foibles remain relatively constant over thousands of years, even though technology and political institutions change the world dramatically. Do you agree with Bergant's premise?
2. Bergant believes that Job, though an ancient text, can speak to people in our time. Do you agree?
3. Why is it "unconscionable" to tell a victim of exploitation or abuse that she or he is in some way responsible for what happened?
4. In paragraph 6, Bergant observes that Job will not "compromise human dignity and admit to something that he knows is false. It makes no difference that he is opposed by as cherished a treasure as his religious tradition." In what ways is Job's position, here, a radical or revolutionary position? In developing your answer, consider the roles that individuals and institutions (such as religion) play in human culture.
5. Job trusts his own integrity and sees his position as dignified. His friends, on the other hand, see his insistence on his innocence as blasphemous—as proof of sinfulness. How can we tell when a person in Job's position—someone who insists, "I am right!"—is being principled or merely close-minded? In paragraph 14, Bergant offers a method for making the distinction. Do you agree with her?

## ■ SYNTHESIS ACTIVITIES

1. What are the problems (or central questions) posed by the Book of Job? In an explanatory synthesis that defines these problems, refer to Job itself and one or more of the selections by Kushner, Bergant, and Gomes. (See also an excerpt from an article by Moshe Greenberg, quoted in Synthesis Activity #6.) Write this essay for an audience who has *not* read Job. (For this audience, you will need to summarize the story: see Chapter 5, on summarizing a narrative.)

2.  Develop a synthesis in which you argue that the problem posed by the Book of Job, and the way in which that problem is expressed, warrant our calling Job a timeless work of literature. Beyond defining the problems (as you would need to do in question #1), you will need to discuss the manner in which the problems are expressed and what makes those problems timeless—of concern to people in any age. You might want to refer to the passages from Pope Gregory the Great (600 CE) and Maimonides (1100 CE), quoted in the introduction to this chapter. See also the selection by Dianne Bergant.

3.  In their writings, Peter Gomes, Harold Kushner, and Dianne Bergant react differently toward injustice and suffering than does anthropologist and writer Michael Dorris. Using the Book of Job as a point of reference, develop a comparison-contrast synthesis in which you explore the reasons some people (Gomes, Kushner, and/or Bergant) can salvage meaning from injustice and can continue to live productively while others (Dorris, for example) cannot and are consumed by bitterness.

4.  Among the authors in this chapter are three ministers to congregations: Peter Gomes, Harold Kushner, and Dianne Bergant. What do they share—in tone, point of view, or some other characteristic—that defines them as spiritual leaders? And what sets Gomes, Kushner, and Bergant apart from one another? (Gomes is an American Baptist; Kushner is Jewish; and Bergant is Catholic.) Develop your comparison-contrast synthesis into an argument.

5.  The concepts of "Fairness" and "Justice" are frequently referred to in this chapter. Drawing on Job and two or more of the selections by Gomes, Kushner, Bergant, and Dorris, write an explanatory synthesis defining these concepts in relation to Job's world *or* ours. In developing your essay, you might consider what associations Job (or we) have loaded onto these words and why they are pivotally important words in Job's culture (or ours).

6.  Moshe Greenberg, a biblical scholar and translator, writes as follows on the theology in the Book of Job:

    > Job is a book not so much about God's justice as about the transformation of a man whose piety and view of the world were formed in a setting of wealth and happiness, and into whose life burst calamities that put an end to both. How can piety nurtured in prosperity prove truly deep-rooted and disinterested, and not merely a spiritual adjunct of good fortune ("God has been good to me so I am faithful to Him")? Can a man pious in prosperity remain pious when he is cut down by anarchical events that belie his orderly view of the world? The Book of Job tells how one man suddenly awakened to the anarchy rampant in the world, yet his attachment to God outlived the ruin of his tidy system.[1]

---

[1] Moshe Greenberg, "Reflections on Job's Theology," in *The Book of Job: A New Translation According to the Traditional Hebrew Text* (Philadelphia: Jewish Publication Society of America, 1980), xvii.

Greenberg argues that Job is about a piety that comes too cheaply and must be tested. Do you share this view of Job? Write a critique of Greenberg's analysis, drawing on Job itself and any of the other selections in this chapter. The critique will be an argument in which you carefully explain your reasons for agreement or disagreement with Greenberg (and lay out your own views—also well supported).

7. Choose four or five verses from one of the chapters in Job and write a careful analysis of the passage. To guide your analysis, draw on the main ideas of *one* of these authors: Kushner, Dorris, or Bergant. The resulting essay will be an application of the ideas of your selected author to the specific verses that you have chosen. If possible, select verses from Job that particularly interest or confuse you, and use the ideas of the author you select to help you think about these verses. You might structure your essay as follows: Begin with an overview of Job and its significance. In the context of your overview, present the verses you've selected and explain your reasons for selection. Next, briefly summarize the work of the author you are drawing on. Then systematically apply key points of that author's work to the verses in question and analyze the meaning of those verses. Write a conclusion in which you bring the analysis to a close and explain what you have accomplished.

8. To what extent do you think it an error that Job equates God's governance of the universe with humankind's governance of the world? Job expects the cause-and-effect morality on which humans draw to govern the world, through institutions like courts of law, to be the same morality that governs the universe. Job equates God's justice with human justice. Why should God be expected to operate according to rules of justice that are convenient for and acceptable to us? Develop your answer into an argument synthesis, drawing on the Book of Job as well as on selections by Dorris, Bergant, and others.

9. Read this brief poem by Stephen Crane. Drawing on the selections by Dorris, Kushner, and Gomes, write a synthesis in which you argue that the implications of Crane's poem are comparable to the implications of Job.

> A man said to the universe:
> "Sir, I exist!"
> "However," replied the universe,
> "The fact has not created in me
> A sense of obligation."

10. Where do you see images of Job in our culture? Scan the newspapers and newsmagazines for examples of the "patient sufferer"—the Job of the opening and closing frame (that is, the Job of the oral tale). Look, also, for examples of the Job who protests loudly in the face of injustice. How radical is this Job? In developing your discussion, you may want to draw on the work of Kushner and Bergant.

11. To what extent do you find that the problem of innocent suffering, the problem at the heart of the Book of Job, is a problem in our world?

Read newspapers and magazines and identify a *single* situation that recalls for you Job's struggle: not just his suffering, but his questioning as well. Use some of the sources in this chapter, especially Gomes, in developing your essay.

12. What do we risk by giving up our faith that a universal moral Judge rules the Earth, a judge who distinguishes right from wrong and rewards or punishes people accordingly? Develop your answer into an argument synthesis, drawing on the selections by Gomes, Kushner, and Dorris.

## ■ RESEARCH ACTIVITIES

1. Read selected portions of three translations of Job and compare them. We suggest the King James Version, The Anchor Bible (Marvin H. Pope), and the translation by Stephen Mitchell, *Into the Whirlwind*. It would be too daunting a task to prepare an analysis comparing competing translations of the entire text of Job. Rather, select several verses that you think are important and compare those. Develop your observations into a report.

2. Locate a copy of William Blake's interpretive watercolours and engravings of scenes from the Book of Job and write an essay-length response. Blake was a mystic, poet, and artist who produced these works in 1820 (watercolours) and 1825 (engravings). William Safire makes this observation of Blake's work:

   [The] engravings are more interpretations than illustrations of the biblical book. "Not a line is drawn without intention," he cautioned, inviting the reader into his world of symbols. In the artist's conception, the story is played out inside Job's mind. The sufferer's affliction is not physical, but a disease of his own soul; the pain humbling his pride is not punishment for sin but a stimulus to reject tradition and assert his individual spirit.[2]

3. Read Canadian scholar Northrop Frye's response to Blake's watercolours and engravings, "Blake's Reading of the Book of Job" (in *Spiritus Mundi*, Indiana UP, 1976). Refer to Frye to enrich the essay-length response requested in question 2, above.

4. Read Carl Jung's *Answer to Job* (translated from the German by R.F.C. Hull, London: Routledge & Paul, 1954) in which Jung psychoanalyzes God. Write a critique of Jung's arguments.

5. Read the play inspired by Job: *J. B.* by Archibald MacLeish. Research the reviews of the play and write a review yourself, drawing on your knowledge of Job and of its critical reception.

---

[2] William Safire, *The First Dissident: The Book of Job in Today's Politics* (New York: Random, 1992), xi.

6. Read the long poem inspired by Job: "A Masque of Reason," offered by Robert Frost as the 43rd chapter to Job. Write an analysis of the poem.

7. In university libraries you will likely have access to several exegetical works on Job—that is, books in which authors annotate Job, chapter by chapter. These scholarly glosses to individual lines, and individual words, in the story are often fascinating. Locate a passage of Job that you think is especially significant and compare scholarly comments on this passage. Prepare a report on your findings.

# 11

# Power and Privilege
# in School Culture

Whatever else schools might be, they have always operated as instruments of normalization, servants of the state whose primary responsibility is to take five-year-olds through a 10- or 12-year character-building process that will make them into citizens who share behaviours and values compatible with the smooth functioning of the state: loyalty, obedience, hard work, and self-reliance. Historically, this mission has been visible in such practices as reciting the Lord's Prayer and the national anthem, and most notoriously in the establishment of the residential school system, which was designed to assimilate Aboriginal children into mainstream culture by annihilating their own.

Canadians often think of excesses of citizenship as being a U.S. phenomenon, and it is true that there are comparatively fewer proponents of the "My country, right or wrong" form of patriotism here. But while we may like to think that our school systems are now organized around dedication to all children achieving their potential, there is a large body of scholarship that indicates otherwise. Studies in the sociology of education analyze the many ways (inappropriately standardized testing, greater resources for schools in prosperous neighbourhoods) in which schools effectively serve to reproduce the existing hierarchies of society, where social inequities are manifested along lines of race, gender, class, sexual orientation, and other differences. Ironically, as Doris Lessing argues in her essay "Group Minds,"[1] education does this in part by teaching people that if they are poor, or harshly treated, it is their own fault, and not the result of any injustice in our social arrangements. Given the personal conflicts built into the school system, it should not be surprising, then, that individuals within it can be caught up in their own power struggles.

In this chapter, we bring together readings that approach various issues of power and privilege in school culture. One important perspective is signalled in the opening piece by Karen Mock: There are many teachers now in the school system who conceive good citizenship not as blind loyalty but as critical intelligence and a passion for justice that includes the courage to defy the group. This is followed by two readings about the residential school system in which Aboriginal children were abused by white teachers who participated in the racist group mentality of colonial Canada. Judges Murray Sinclair and A.C. Hamilton and law professor Anne McGillivray analyze both state-sanctioned and systemic abuses of power in residential schools, and the

[1] See her essay in Chapter 9 on Obedience to Authority.

416

traumatic effects of abuse that persist in Aboriginal communities today. A reading by Paul Olson then analyzes how power is still organized unjustly in contemporary school settings.

Perhaps the most pressing issue of power in schools today is bullying. Shocked into rethinking the significance of bullying after a string of high school shootings across North America in which bullying victims retaliated against their tormentors, most of us now agree that it is wrong to dismiss complaints of bullying with a "kids will be kids" attitude. Teachers and school officials who used to reply to the complaints of victimized students with the message that bullying was wrong, but that tattling was even worse, are now trying to learn how to recognize bullying and take responsibility for intervening in it. Some of them are even wondering about how the culture of schools participates in the production of bullying: Are children just showing they've learned their lessons well when they bully those who are somehow different from the norm?

As you read the texts in this chapter, you may find yourself thinking back to Chapter 9, with its focus on the psychological roots and ramifications of obedience to authority and the value we place on it in our society.

# Victims, Perpetrators, Bystanders, Activists: Who Are They? Who Are You?

KAREN R. MOCK

*In this article, Karen Mock claims that if we are to work against the possibility of future holocausts, teachers need to help students develop their own sense of humanity so that when evil forces are at work, they will be prepared to be activists and risk-takers rather than bystanders or perpetrators.*

*Dr. Mock is a registered psychologist and the National Director of the League for Human Rights of B'nai B'rith Canada, an agency committed to the struggle against racism and bigotry. She has worked as a human rights consultant, taught in the Education faculties of the University of Toronto, Ryerson Polytechnical University, and York University, and served on many boards and committees related to race relations and multiculturalism.*

I have just returned from leading the 1996 Holocaust and Hope Educators' Study Tour to Germany, Poland, and Israel. Although it is the fourth time I have conducted the program, I continue to be overwhelmed by images and emotions of the trip, and even more overwhelmed by the challenges of raising a generation to believe that the world can be a better place and that they can acquire the skills and commitment to make it so. By the time you read this, we will be well into another school year, implementing a curriculum that results in our students' being able to rhyme off the names and deeds of evil murderers and perpetrators of wars far more readily than the stories and names of the countless victims. Try it, and you'll see what I mean.

With our emphasis on skills and knowledge for outcomes-based learning, how often do we reflect on the factors that lead to moral behaviour—to acts of bravery, courage and altruism—rather than the more typical behaviours of following the crowd, bullying, or scapegoating others to get our way, or merely being spectators to world events, bystanders to unspeakable evil? As Yehuda Bauer once said: "After the Holocaust, we live in a world where the impossible became possible." How do we begin to understand this? Who were the victims—as people, as individuals and not just as numbers? What was it about the perpetrators that could lead them to commit such inhuman, barbaric acts? How could so many stand by in silence? What differentiated the rescuers, those few who took a stand and risked their lives to save others, from the masses who aided and abetted the murderers? Who were they? What would I have done in the same circumstances? What would I do today? What would you do? And what relevance does all of this have for our lives in Canada in the 1990s? These are the questions that haunt the educators who took this difficult trip. The answers are crucial in shaping their teaching upon their return, and are relevant to all our teaching, no matter what the subject area. Perhaps Haim Ginott, in his open letter to teachers, said it best: 2

> Dear Teacher,
> I am a survivor of a concentration camp. My eyes saw what no man should witness: Gas chambers built by learned engineers. Children poisoned by educated physicians. Infants killed by trained nurses. Women and babies shot and burned by high school and college graduates. So I am suspicious of education. My request is: Help your students become human. Your efforts must never produce learned monsters, skilled psychopaths, educated Eichmanns. Reading, writing, arithmetic are important only if they serve to make our children more humane.
>
> Haim Ginott,
> Teacher and Child, 1972

## VICTIMS—TELLING THEIR STORY IN COLOUR

I want to write first of the victims, because that is so rarely the case. Almost all of our historical accounts over the centuries are told from the point of view of those in power or of the conquerors, rarely of the people or the cultures that were destroyed. The same is true today. We read of victorious Crusaders, not of vanquished communities. We remember Marc Lepine, but how many of his victims, young female engineering students, can we name? We call it the Nerland Inquiry, when Carny Nerland was the white supremacist perpetrator and Leo LaChance was the aboriginal man he murdered. It is as the African proverb says: until the lions learn to speak and to write, tales of bravery and courage will only be told of the hunters. 3

The voices of the victims are silent. It is we who must speak up for them, to tell their stories so that the tremendous void they left is felt in our classrooms, and in the way that they would like to have been remembered—not as emaciated victims or "lambs led to the slaughter" but as human beings who 4 lived colourful, vibrant lives and struggled valiantly to survive with dignity in whatever way possible. As Rachel Maier Korazin (1996), a noted Holocaust educator in Israel, has said:

> The only thing black and white in their lives was the photography of the era. We must put the colour back in their lives, not by showing Nazi photos of their victimization, but by teaching about the life and the culture that was lost. It is OK to visit and to dance in Poland. Jews lived in there for over 800 years; they were murdered there for only six.

Once survivors began to speak about the unspeakable, extensive research and writings indicate that many of the victims proved the human capacity to rise above their horrifying circumstances. In the concentration camps every event conspired to make the prisoner lose hold, but resistance took a variety of forms. As Viktor Frankl (1959) explains: "Hunger, humiliation, fear and deep anger at injustice are rendered tolerable by closely guarded images of beloved persons, by religion, by a grim sense of humour—and glimpses of the healing beauties of nature." But Frankl goes on to point out that these don't establish the will to live unless the victim makes larger sense out of apparently senseless suffering. Quoting Nietzsche, Frankl, who was himself a survivor and near death several times during the war, believes that "he who has a WHY to live can bear with almost any HOW." This, then, for Frankl is the central theme of existentialism: to live is to suffer; to survive is to find meaning in the suffering; if there is a purpose in life at all, there must be a purpose in suffering and in dying. But no one can tell another what this purpose is. Each must find out for the self and must accept the responsibility that the answer prescribes.

Elie Wiesel (1990) describes exactly this phenomenon in the remarkable efforts of several victims who chronicled otherwise unbelievable events. Prompted by the taunts of SS guards that even if some survived, no one would ever believe them, victims such as Zalman Gradowski, Leib Langfuss and Yankel Wiernik wrote testimonies, diaries, chronologies of events, and the personal stories of other victims. Why? Because, according to Wiesel just as the killer was determined to erase Jewish memory, his victims fought to maintain it. Wrote Gradowski: "The purpose of my writing is to make sure that something of the truth reaches the world and moves it to avenge our lives. This is the purpose of my life." In the final analysis, what alone remains is, as Frankl says, "the last of human freedoms—the ability to choose one's attitude in a given set of circumstances."

In the face of evil—of racial hatred, rape, child abuse—or even in the face of senseless, inexplicable accidents or acts of God—one is cast in the role of victim, a powerless and helpless position over which the victim has no control. It is reported that many victims chanted the viddui, the prayer asking forgiveness, on their way to the gas chambers. Rape victims feel a tremendous sense of guilt and shame. Abused children apologize, beg forgiveness, convinced they are to blame for vicious beatings. But such events are never the fault of the victims or of innocent survivors, although overwhelming guilt and self-blame sometimes lead to suicide. The question "Why me?" becomes "Why not me?"—sometimes with tragic answers. There is, of course, another common reaction; that is, for the victim to become the victimizer, the abused become the abuser, the survivor become the perpetrator—leading to self-hatred and sometimes also to suicide. The cycle of victimhood cannot be broken unless there is an intervention—someone to show it is not the fault of the victim, someone to substitute other models of behaviour.

## PERPETRATORS—ORDINARY PEOPLE OR WILLING ACCOMPLICES?

There are those who try to describe the architects and perpetrators of the Holocaust as inhuman sadists who were aberrant, insane, or otherwise marginalized and unusual. Browning describes them as ordinary men, in his book about a Ukrainian police battalion who had rather mundane choices to make as to whether they would take on the railway deportation shifts and other tasks to facilitate the murder of Jews, instead of their regular policing duties. And the choices were often made for rather trivial reasons. On the other hand, Goldhagen describes them as Hitler's "willing executioners," living in a Europe ripe with anti-Semitism such that the majority of the population willingly and knowingly became accomplices to murder. The reality is that then, as now, the origin of the Holocaust—or of rape or hate crime or child abuse—is the story of the perpetrators and what was done to their psyches, not about the victims who were targets no matter what they did. 8

Perpetrators feel themselves to be victims, usually have low self-esteem, and are looking for someone to blame for their problems. They have often been raised in abusive, authoritarian environments. They are easily swayed by propaganda, usually foisted on them by a hatemonger who is looking to increase his own power base by promising his audience more power, opportunity and self-reliance, all the while imposing increasing discipline and control, building on their anger and alienation, and stereotyping and scapegoating others who are less powerful. Perpetrators let themselves be convinced that they are acting for the good of their own people, often believing that they are justified by religion. We should not forget that each SS officer's belt buckle bore the inscription "Gott Mit Uns," God Is With Us. We see the same pattern today in the so-called neo-Nazi movement, skinheads, Holocaust deniers, white supremacist groups, and even in the black Nation of Islam—charismatic leaders gathering adherents with religious and pseudo-religious fervour. Such hatemongers know how to manipulate a following who can be easily bullied into submission under the guise of strict discipline and who rarely think for themselves. Followers get further and further drawn in by the rhetoric until it's too late to get out, for the perpetrators inevitably use the same tactics to control their own ranks as they do to victimize others. 9

Are we all just ordinary people who, under the right circumstances, could become willing accomplices? Could they be us if the right "hot buttons" were pressed? Before we too readily dismiss such a notion, think for a 10 moment of some examples of modern perpetrators—people who put a lesser value on some human lives than others. Soldiers in Somalia who dehumanized a people until murder was the punishment for alleged theft of food. Officials who decided, for whatever reason, not to test blood for HIV, resulting in the deaths of thousands of innocent patients. Politicians who stir up anger and scapegoat immigrants and people of colour to garner votes. And what about those who blame the victims of harassment or even rape; or, worse still, those who turn a blind eye? Are bystanders who might have intervened to stop such inhuman acts not themselves perpetrators?

## BYSTANDERS—PASSIVE ACCOMPLICES

"Bigotry and hatred are not the most urgent problems—the most important 11 and tragic problem is silence." These are the words of Rabbi Joachim Prinz who spoke just before Martin Luther King delivered his "I have a dream" speech at the March on Washington in 1963. Rabbi Prinz had been a rabbi in Berlin at the time of the Third Reich and knew all too well the tragic consequences when good people stand by and do nothing in the face of evil. It remains incomprehensible that the whole world stood by in silence, as in many cases it does today, as innocents continued to be murdered. The transcript of the Evian Conference of 1938 and the Bermuda Conference of 1943, when the nature and extent of the death factories were well documented, exposes the excuses given by the world powers—the Allies and neutral countries—and by major agencies such as the Red Cross and the Vatican for not intervening and for not taking refugees from Nazi-occupied Europe: we're drained by the war effort, poor economy, not enough room, and so on. It was the tiny Dominican Republic who agreed to take the most refugees while other doors remained closed.

　　It will interest readers to note that Canada refused to rescue any doomed 12 souls, and even refused to host the conference, which was originally supposed to be held in Ottawa, lest the local community and desperate relatives might bring too much pressure to bear on our government to do something. Bystanders all.

　　What do you do today when a friend or colleague reveals an incident of 13 abuse or harassment—turn a blind eye? Accuse the victim of being oversensitive? Does your organization or department go into "coverup" mode when a gross injustice or ethical breach is revealed? Does the "whistle blower" get marginalized and accused of not being a team player? Do the needs of the organization get put before the needs and lives of human beings? Do we think of the minor inconvenience to ourselves and families as more important than helping a friend in dire need, or even a stranger in mortal danger? Do we let the bullies abuse others and manipulate us without standing up? Where people are arbitrarily victimized, do we stand up or stand by? There are always choices to be made.

　　When you look at a map of Europe and examine the locations of all the 14 slave labour camps, concentration camps, and death camps (as we did with

Dr. Racelle Weiman at the Ghetto Fighters Holocaust Education Centre near Haifa), you are immediately struck by the fact that while the majority were in Germany, Poland, and other parts of Eastern Europe, such camps existed in almost every country occupied by the Nazis, except for two: Denmark and Bulgaria. There was not one camp in either Denmark or Bulgaria because their populations said no. They would not build such camps nor subject their own citizens to slave labour or death, regardless of their religion. Their leaders, their governments, and their people refused to give up their Jews. They stood up to the Nazis, and the Nazis backed down. And we are faced with the stark realization that it didn't have to happen. The Nazis proceeded to implement the mass murder of innocents, the "final solution," in countries where the leadership and most of the population either stood by or collaborated, where there was no active, organized resistance to the war against the Jews.

But even there, in the darkness, there were some rays of light—the res- 15 cuers, the "righteous gentiles," truly the Righteous Among the Nations, as they are called by the State of Israel—people who saved Jews for absolutely no personal gain. Who are they? Who are those who made the moral choice to take action, to become "participants" as Wiesel calls them, rather than bystanders? What makes a person become an activist, to take a stand, often at great personal risk to themselves and their families? And what can we learn from them to teach others?

## ACTIVISTS, PARTICIPANTS, RISK-TAKERS—RAYS OF LIGHT AND HOPE

Why does a person risk his or her life to save another, and what do such res- 16 cuers, true heroes, have in common? This was exactly what Oliner and Oliner (*The Altruistic Personality*, 1988) set out to discover in their exhaustive study of hundreds of righteous gentiles. Surprisingly, when asked why they risked their lives to save a Jew, most could give no specific reason, it was not that they saved friends—indeed, many rescued absolute strangers and even people they didn't like very much. They did it because it was the only human thing to do. There was no other reason, in Rabbi Joachim's words, again at the March on Washington in 1963: "Neighbour is not a geographic term, it is a moral concept."

In an effort to determine what comprises the altruistic personality, Oliner 17 and Oliner conducted thorough interviews and personality assessments of several hundred rescuers. They found these activists had four factors in common—characteristics that speak volumes to educators about how we might teach to achieve our most important outcome, that of making our students more humane.

1. *Rescuers were and are critical thinkers.* These activists were self- 18 determining individuals who did not have a "follow the crowd" mentality; rather, they evaluated what they heard and saw with a strong sense of independence and autonomy. So they could reject the Nazi ideology and propa-

ganda as irrational and simply not true, and even reject the laws, rather than blindly following along. Personality tests revealed that the ego was well-developed but not self-centred or narcissistic. They were "mavericks" in other aspects of their lives as well, people who marched to their own tune.

2. *Rescuers had role models who taught right from wrong.* Rescuers were 19 and are ordinary people from all walks of life—farmers, teachers, business people, rich, poor, parents, singles, Protestant, Catholic. And most had done nothing very dramatic or exceptional before the war. According to Oliner and Oliner, what most distinguished them were their connections with others in relationships of commitment and care, and their perception of who and what should be obeyed. Their rules and examples of conduct were learned from a parent, peer, teacher or mentor who helped them understand the way of determining right from wrong, and the importance of holding yourself accountable, regardless of what others say or do. The people I am calling activists, then, inevitably had a person who modelled for them a way of behaving differently, morally, and with a strong sense of social justice, regardless of the level of authority in the hierarchy of whoever is giving the orders to behave otherwise.

3. *Rescuers had a strong sense of self-worth.* It has often been said that if 20 you value yourself, you can give something to others. Psychological profiles revealed that rescuers of intended victims during the war had a positive sense of self-esteem. They were much more likely than bystanders, who were also interviewed, to have had the kind of approving, non-punitive early parenting that is associated with low ethnocentrism and high democratic potential. Their parents were described as warm people and models of caring behaviours, often with empathy for the underdog. They taught that one must perceive others as individuals, not as representatives of a type or group. Rescuers generally felt good about what they had done, and reflected on the rescuing experience as one of the high points in their lives, despite the tremendous additional strain and hardship placed on themselves and their families over and above the effects of the war. Bystanders, on the other hand, stressed their own victimization during the war, compared their pain to the victims, blamed others for their situation, claimed they did not know, were angry that the people they turned away didn't appreciate their risk or offer them money or other forms of compensation, and generally described themselves as powerless in the situation.

4. *Rescuers had a sense of optimism and hope.* Almost all of the righteous 21 gentiles interviewed by the Oliners expressed a strong sense of feeling during the war that there had to be something better, that the world could and should be a better place, and that it was possible to achieve it. Rescuers refused to see Jews as guilty or beyond hope, and refused to see themselves as helpless, despite whatever evidence there was to the contrary. They believed that even one person could make a difference, and did not shrink from taking action in the direction of hope. Oliner and Oliner concluded their study as follows:

If we persist in defining ourselves as doomed, human nature as beyond redemption, and social institutions beyond reform, then we shall create a future that will merely confirm this view. Rescuers made a choice that affirmed the value and meaningfulness of each life in the midst of a diabolical social order that denied it. Can we do otherwise?

## WHO ARE YOU? AND WHAT DO WE WANT OUR STUDENTS TO BE?

What are the lessons to be drawn from all of this? The purpose of the 22 Holocaust and Hope Educators' Study Tour, and of my raising these issues, is not to enshrine Holocaust education as a memorial to the victims or as an anthropology or history lesson about a thousand years of European Jewish culture lost. Rather, the issues discussed here must have meaning for our own lives and the lives of our students. What do we want our students to learn? For those who understand oppression and have been hurt by prejudice, racism, sexism or exclusion, one lesson to be learned is never to allow yourself to be victimized again, and to develop skills and defence mechanisms to ensure that does not happen. But what about never allowing yourself to be the perpetrator? Victims must not become victimizers, and must learn to recognize totalitarian thinking and behaviour in themselves as well as in others. We must break the cycle of abuse and victimization, and ensure that the oppressed do not become the oppressors.

Whatever we teach about the Holocaust, we must make it very clear that 23 there was right and there was wrong, and we must not be afraid to set clear parameters. These are not issues of relativity. I do not believe that one person's terrorist is another's freedom fighter. This is not a matter of point of view. The murder of innocents is wrong, no matter what the cause, no matter what political or national side you are on. What is right is the dignity of human life, and the equality and indivisibility of human life. No life is worth less than another. Racelle Weiman captured it best when she warned that we should not be Holocaust educators, but Non-Holocaust educators; that is, we must teach towards creating a world without ethnic cleansing and genocide, without hate, racism, anti-Semitism, or human rights abuses.

We must also reach the point of accepting that we can never understand 24 what it means to be a victim—of the Holocaust, of rape, of abuse, of racism, of gay bashing—unless we were there, in that person's shoes. Who are we, then, to evaluate another's reaction? Or to argue about someone's personal interpretation of a traumatic experience? Or to judge and compare levels of grief or create a hierarchy of pain? As Rachel Maier Korazin so poignantly put it when our minds were still reeling from the images and sensations of the camps: "Say to the survivor, I will never understand the way you do—and, God forbid, you do not want me to. But I need to know. And we can start from here."

And so we have a starting point with our students: for learning about and 25 helping to heal the victim and the survivor; for becoming activists, risk-takers, critical thinkers, role models; for refusing to be perpetrators of, or bystanders to, evil or abuse of any kind. We have a starting point for teaching our students how to become humane, so that they will create a world where the impossible could not be possible again.

■ ■ ■

*Author's Note:* I want to thank two outstanding educators, colleagues and friends, Rachel Maier Korazin and Racelle Weiman, for their continuing contribution to the Holocaust and Hope Program, and for their inspiration for this article. It is dedicated to the memory of Richard Youngman.

## REFERENCES

Frankl, Viktor. *Man's Search for Meaning.* New York: Washington Square Press, 1985.
Ginott, Haim. *Teacher and Child.* New York: Pelican Books, 1972.
Korazin, Rachel. Personal Communication, 1996.
Oliner, S. P. and P. M. Oliner. *The Altruistic Personality.* New York: The Free Press, 1988.
Weiman, Racelle. "True Hero." *Jerusalem Post,* April 27, 1994.
Wiesel, E., L. Dawidowicz, D. Rabinowitz, and R. McAfee Brown. *Dimensions of the Holocaust* (2nd ed.). Evanston, IL: Northwestern University Press, 1990.

■ ■ ■

## Discussion and Writing Suggestions

1. Think about your own knowledge of terrible events in human history. Do you know more about the perpetrators of the events than you do about the victims? What were your sources of information? What would Mock say is missing from your knowledge of these events?
2. Do you agree with Mock that the school curriculum should be changed to place much more emphasis on the production of the courage needed to defy unjust authority? Could this be done only in the context of history courses? Or could such lessons in humanity have a place in other subjects as well?

# The Residential School System

MURRAY SINCLAIR AND A. C. HAMILTON

*Although Aboriginal people have long said that the justice system of Canada was racist, it was not until 1988, in the aftermath of high-profile cases involving the violent deaths of Aboriginal people, that the province of Manitoba instituted the Aboriginal Justice Inquiry (AJI). When the massive report was released in 1991, it included an analysis of the racist mentality behind the development of the residential school system, with its explicit goals of assimilating Aboriginal people by destroying their culture. The system, together with other aspects of European colonization of Canada, had disastrous effects, one of them being the over-representation of Aboriginal people in the courts and prisons. The entire report can be found at www.ajic.mb.ca/.*

*The two authors of the report are the Honourable Murray Sinclair and Associate Chief Justice A. C. Hamilton. Sinclair was appointed a Judge of the Manitoba Court of Queen's Bench in 2001, having served since 1988 as Associate Chief Judge of the Provincial Court of Manitoba, an appointment that made him Manitoba's first Aboriginal Judge, and Canada's second. (At present there are 18 Aboriginal judges in Canada.) Hamilton was appointed to the Manitoba Court of Queen's Bench in 1971, and as Associate Chief Justice of the Family Division (Manitoba's new Unified Family Court) in 1983; he retired from the Bench in 1993 to focus on mediation work and Aboriginal issues.*

Since the time of earliest contact, Aboriginal people and European settlers        1
have seen things from vastly divergent points of view, because their attitudes and philosophies differed. The interaction of the two groups has been characterized as one of "cooperation and conflict but, more importantly, by misconceptions and contradictions."[4] One of the first, and perhaps the most enduring, of these misconceptions was that:

> Europeans assumed the superiority of their culture over that of any Aboriginal peoples. Out of that misconception grew the European conviction that in order for the Indians to survive, they would have to be assimilated into the European social order.[5]

At first, these differences had minimal impact upon most Aboriginal         2
people. The missionaries tried to convert Aboriginal people and to mould them into their religious ideal, often with mixed results.

> The Indians . . . had no more idea of religious authority, as opposed to personal beliefs, than they had of a coercive political hierarchy. The individual freedom that was fundamental to Indian culture ruled out both the idea of heresy and of subordinating one's will to priestly guidance. The concept of authority and the respect for it that was inculcated into all civilized peoples provided the missionary and the civilized non-Christian with a common basis of understanding that was totally lacking between the missionary and the Indians of Eastern Canada. The fundamental problem that the Recollets saw impeding their work was that the Indians were too "primitive" to be converted. From this they drew the devastatingly simple conclusion that if they were to convert the Indians they had first to find ways of "civilizing" them.[6]

This was an impossible task as long as Aboriginal people continued to live      3
in vibrant, self-sufficient communities often far removed from the missionaries' influence. However, this did not prevent the missionaries from forming opinions about the ways Aboriginal people raised and taught their children, or from laying the foundation for future misconceptions of Aboriginal child-rearing methods. In view of current ideas about child-rearing, it is interesting

to reflect that no aspect of behaviour shocked the French more than their refusal to use physical punishment to discipline their children. On general principles, the Huron considered it wrong to coerce or humiliate an individual publicly. To their own way of thinking, a child was an individual with his or her own needs and rights rather than something amorphous that must be molded into shape. The Huron feared a child who was unduly humiliated, like an adult, might be driven to commit suicide.[7]

Aboriginal parents taught their children                                        4

> . . . to assume adult roles in an atmosphere of warmth and affection. Learning emphasized such values as respect for all living things, sharing, self-reliance, individual responsibility, and proper conduct. Children also had to learn how to utilize the environment most effectively for economic survival. Integral to all aspects of the education of the young was the spiritual, and events in the life-cycle from birth to death were marked with ceremonies stressing the individual's link to the spiritual and sacred. Cultural continuity was thus ensured.[8]

The early missionaries also condemned Aboriginal child-rearing methods     5
as being negligent, irresponsible and "uncivilized." This stereotype was to endure even after Aboriginal people had lost much of their independence and "in the point of view of the European, the Indian became irrelevant."[9] From then on, the relationship between Aboriginal people and Europeans became even more one-sided and paternalistic. Aboriginal people were reduced to being "wards of the state."[10] All relevant decision-making power on financial, social or political matters, and even education, came to rest in the hands of the federal government. Eventually, the cause of "civilizing" Aboriginal people to European cultures and values evolved into the government policy of "assimilation," and education became "the primary vehicle in the civilization and advancement of the Indian race."[11]

The federal government had little previous experience in "civilizing"     6
Aboriginal people so it turned to the United States for an example. It sent Nicholas F. Davin to study the Americans' "aggressive civilization policy,"[12] based on sending Indian children to large, racially segregated, industrial schools. Davin was convinced the Americans were correct in their approach and the only way to "civilize" Aboriginal people was to remove them from the disruptive influences of the parents and the community. His final comment in the report to Ottawa was representative of attitudes of the time that ". . . if anything is to be done with the Indian, we must catch him very young."[13]

The federal government delegated the job of "civilizing" and "educating"     7
Aboriginal people in Canada to religious organizations and churches. It encouraged the opening of large, industrial residential schools far from reserves and, later, of boarding schools for younger children nearer to their homes. There, every aspect of European life, from dress and behaviour to religion and language, was impressed upon the Aboriginal children. The belief was that Indians were a vanishing race and their only hope of surviving was to assimilate. Their uncivilized and pagan ways would be replaced by good Christian values.

The residential school system was a conscious, deliberate and often brutal     8
attempt to force Aboriginal people to assimilate into mainstream society,
mostly by forcing the children away from their languages, cultures and societies. In 1920, during debates in the House of Commons on planned changes
to the *Indian Act*, Duncan Campbell Scott, the Deputy Superintendent of
Indian Affairs, left no doubt about the federal government's aims: "Our
object is to continue until there is not a single Indian in Canada that has not
been absorbed into the body politic and there is no Indian question, and no
Indian department, that is the whole object of this Bill."[14]

The experience of residential schools is one shared by many Aboriginal     9
people all across Canada. That experience was marked by emotional, physical and sexual abuse, social and spiritual deprivation, and substandard education. "Even as assimilation was stated as the goal of education for Native
people," one researcher wrote, "the assimilation was to take place under
conditions which would cause no threat to the surrounding business and
farming community."[15] Few Aboriginal people achieved more than a grade
five level of education.

The main goal of residential schools and the assimilation policy, however,     10
was not further education, but, rather, to remove Aboriginal children from
the influences of their parents and communities, and to rid them of their languages and cultures. The methods, as one former residential school student
explained, often were brutally effective:

> The elimination of language has always been a primary stage in a process of
> cultural genocide. This was the primary function of the residential school. My
> father, who attended Alberni Indian Residential School for four years in the
> twenties, was physically tortured by his teachers for speaking Tseshaht: they
> pushed sewing needles through his tongue, a routine punishment for language
> offenders. . . . The needle tortures suffered by my father affected all my family
> (I have six brothers and six sisters). My Dad's attitude became "why teach my
> children Indian if they are going to be punished for speaking it?" so he would
> not allow my mother to speak Indian to us in his presence. I never learned how
> to speak my own language. I am now, therefore, truly a "dumb Indian."[16]

After the Second World War, the federal government began to reconsider     11
its assimilation policy. It wanted a more effective means of accomplishing the
ultimate aims of the policy. This coincided with yet another revamping of the
*Indian Act* and another set of hearings at the House of Commons. This also
allowed another famous Canadian, noted anthropologist Diamond Jenness, to
unveil his "Plan for Liquidating Canada's Indian Problems Within 25 Years."
Jenness proposed abolishing Indian reserves, scrapping the treaties and inte-
grating Indian students into the public school system. For the time being, the
federal government shelved most of Jenness' proposals. It did, however, heed
his suggestion to change the *Indian Act* to allow Indian children to be enrolled
in public schools. This event signalled "the beginning of the end for many residential schools."[17]

The effects upon Aboriginal societies of the federal government's resi-     12
dential school system, and its policy of assimilation, have been astounding.
Residential schools denigrated Aboriginal cultures, customs and religions,
and disrupted the traditional practices of Aboriginal child-rearing and education. They tore apart families and extended families, leaving the children
straddling two worlds, the European one and that of their own Aboriginal
societies, but belonging to neither. These policies have caused a wound to
fester in Aboriginal communities that has left them diminished to this day. In
testimony to our Inquiry, Janet Ross said:

> I'd like to begin at the boarding school. The boarding school is where the
> alienation began. Children were placed there, plucked out of their homes. The
> bond between parents and children was fragmented severely—some lost for-
> ever. Some searched for the love between parent and child endlessly, searching
> for it in other ways, never to be restored. The boarding schools taught us vio-
> lence. Violence was emphasized through physical, corporal punishment, strap-
> pings, beatings, bruising and control. We learned to understand that this was
> power and control. I remember being very confused when someone told me
> that my natural mother had died. Hence growing up for me not knowing
> whether my mother was really mine always created some more confusion. I
> searched for that love in [foster] parents, but that bond had been broken; you
> felt that it just wasn't there. The boarding schools were extremely influential
> towards our poor self-image and low self-esteem, because we were continuously
> put down by the use of text books portraying negative images of Indian people.

The loss of successive generations of children to residential schools, the     13
destruction of Aboriginal economic bases, the decimation of their populations
through diseases and the increasing dependence on government welfare have
led to social chaos. This manifests itself in Aboriginal communities through
staggering poverty rates, high unemployment rates, high suicide rates, lower
education levels, high rates of alcoholism and high rates of crime. In individuals, the legacy of the residential schools has been lowered self-esteem, confusion of self-identity and cultural identity, and a distrust of, and antagonism
toward, authority.

The residential school experience also resulted in a breakdown in tradi-     14
tional Aboriginal methods of teaching child-rearing and parenting. Entire families once took part in the raising of children. Young parents, like young parents
everywhere, learned how to raise their children from their own parents, by
example. Traditionally, they also drew upon the examples and advice of their
extended families, their grandparents, uncles, aunts and siblings. The residential
schools made this impossible. Without that example, many Aboriginal parents
today feel that they have never learned how to raise their own children.

Aboriginal communities have not yet recovered from the damage caused     15
by the residential schools. It is only in recent times that children are again
being taught close to home. For the first time in over 100 years, many families are experiencing a generation of children who live with parents until

their teens. The readjustment to this new situation has been difficult for both the parents and their children. The current generation of parents does not even have its own experiences as children growing up in a unified family upon which to draw.

The damage done by these schools is still evident today, as Aboriginal people struggle to recapture their cultural practices and beliefs. The return of self-identity and self-esteem is a slow process.    16

■  ■  ■

## Notes

4. Jean Barman, Yvonne Hebert and Don McCaskill, eds., *Indian Education in Canada, Vol. I: The Legacy* (Vancouver: University of British Columbia Press, 1986), p. 2.
5. *Ibid.*
6. Bruce G. Trigger, *The Children of Aataentsic: A History of the Huron People to 1660* (Montreal and Kingston: McGill-Queen's University Press, 1976), p. 378.
7. *Ibid.*, p. 47.
8. Barman, Hebert and McCaskill, *Indian Education in Canada*, p. 3.
9. E. P. Patterson, *The Canadian Indian: A History since 1500* (Don Mills: Collier-Macmillan, 1972), p. 72.
10. Kahn-Tineta Miller and George Lerchs, *The Historical Development of the Indian Act* (Ottawa: Treaties and Historical Research Branch, Department of Indian Affairs and Northern Development, 1978), p. 114.
11. Canada, Department of Indian Affairs and Northern Development, *Annual Report* (Ottawa, 1976), p. 6.
12. N. F. Davin, "Report on Industrial Schools for Indians and Halfbreeds" (Ottawa: Public Archives, 14 March 1879), PAC RG 10, Vol. 6001, File 1-1-1, Part 1.
13. *Ibid.*
14. Cited in J. R. Miller, *Skyscrapers Hide the Heavens: A History of Indian-White Relations in Canada* (Toronto: University of Toronto Press, 1989), pp. 206–7.
15. Celia Haig-Brown, *Resistance and Renewal: Surviving the Indian Residential School* (Vancouver: Tillacum Library, 1988), p. 67.
16. Randy Fred, "Introduction," in *Ibid.*, pp. 1–2.
17. Haig-Brown, *Resistance and Renewal*, p. 28.

■  ■  ■

## Discussion and Writing Suggestions

1. What assumptions about the nature of civilization would have served to justify the Canadian government's decision to annihilate "Indian" culture?

2. Has mainstream Canadian society progressed from the clearly racist days in which the residential school system was implemented? Or are there still signs of old beliefs in the superiority of British culture?

3. Do you agree with this thesis statement? "The curriculum of modern-day public schools and private schools continues to serve the interests of dominant culture by marginalizing minority cultures." How could you support (or refute) this thesis based on your own experience?

■ ■ ■

# *Civilizing Childhood* and *Education and Normalization: The Residential School*

ANNE McGILLIVRAY

*In this extract from a much longer work, Anne McGillivray examines the roots of the residential school program in a racist 19th-century concept of adult Indians as children and Indian children as needing to be civilized into Anglo-Canadian culture. McGillivray argues that "the residential schools were maintained far beyond their time, when child welfare policy had moved toward family-centred solutions and interventions were at least overtly based less on class and "race" than apprehension of harm. The project 'failed dismally' due in large part to Indian resistance."*

*Dr. McGillivray is a law professor at the University of Manitoba, and the author of many book chapters and journal articles on a wide range of legal topics. Several of her publications address issues concerning the concepts, status, and treatment of children in the Canadian legal system, including* Governing Childhood *(Aldershot Press, 1997). A complete list of her work can be found on the University website: **www.umanitoba.ca/academic/faculties/law/faculty/mcgillivray.html**.*

## CIVILIZING CHILDHOOD

Eighteenth-century utopian constructs of innocence uncontaminated by civi-    1
lization made the "noble savage" a cognate of childhood. As Sir Hector Langevin observed during the 1876 *Indian Act* debates, "Indians were not in the same position as white men . . . they were like children to a very great extent. They, therefore, required a great deal more protection."[33] Nineteenth-century assimilation policies infantilized the Indian, remaking the adult in the image of childhood. Indians were in law state wards under the *Indian Act,* confined to the reserve, subject to protectionist policies (Indian agents, pass systems, liquor prohibitions),[34] forbidden religious and cultural practices,[35] subjects of projects of improvement, objects of pity, finally welfare-dependent.

The equation of Aboriginal peoples with childhood and dependency in    2
English foreign policy was reflected in two reports: the 1834 *Report from His*

*Majesty's Commission for Inquiring into the Administration and Practical Operation of the Poor Laws* and the 1837 House of Commons *Report of the Select Committee on Aborigines.* The Select Committee was concerned with "Native Inhabitants of Countries where British Settlements are made . . . to promote the spread of civilization among them," while the Commission on the Poor Laws was concerned with problems of the outcast closer to home. Both reports provided for special overseers or protectors, proposed training programs aimed at low-level employment and emphasized assimilation of their respective target groups into the larger society. Both reports stressed childhood and the need to educate, civilize, and bring into Christianity the young pauper or Aborigine. As the Select Committee on Aborigines noted, "True civilization and Christianity are inseparable: the former has never been found, but as a fruit of the latter."

If the adult "Aborigine" was infantilized in the process of assimilation,    3
the child was literally to be pressed into its service. This arose from a series of changes in Anglo-Canadian ideas about the governance of childhood. This chapter introduces these ideas, taking as illustration two childsaving projects which shared the civilizing vision which came to centre on Aboriginal childhood: the English child migration movement and the Winnipeg Home of the Friendless.

Childhood is both focus and creation of civilization, a life stage dedi-    4
cated to the inculcation of a sociospecific citizenship. By the close of the 18th century, childhood had fully emerged as a legally and socially distinct life estate and numerous European constructs of childhood were extant.[36] By the last third of the 19th century, childhood was identified as both social problem and locus of charitable and state projects of citizenship. The health, welfare and rearing of children, as Rose observed, was "linked in thought and practice to the destiny of the nation and the responsibilities of the state,"[37] an association which was to make childhood "the most intensively governed sector of human existence." In the late 19th-century shift from government *of* the family to governance *through* the family,[38] the child became a symptom of relational problems within the family and between family and state, a major point of entry into the family for the new complex of family-oriented tutelary disciplines and agencies empowered to remove children from "abnormal" environments. Intervention and removal primarily affected families of marginal social status, while expert tutelage, being "voluntary," was to have a broader impact. Childhood was, in effect, colonized by the state.

The governance of childhood was aimed at the induction of a docile cit-    5
izenship, the creation of a disciplined soul. What motivated the "great project," Rose argues, was not the "repressive desire for surveillance and control" initially posited by Foucault. It was, rather,

> a profoundly humanistic and egalitarian project, one that searched for the causes of failure of citizenship and sought to provide the knowledge that was to ensure the extension of the benefits of society to all its members.[39]

Where the "members" had no perception of themselves as such, and no desire to join, this humanistic project of reform might well be perceived as "repressive surveillance."

The shift in relations between "childhood" and state was reflected in the massive expansion of child welfare powers and programs in late 19th-century Canada.[40] The province of Manitoba, carved out of the North-West Territories in 1870, based its child welfare legislation on that of Ontario. The Ontario *Humane Societies Act* had been amended to give animal protection groups the power to remove children from the lawful custody of parents and guardians for neglect or mistreatment (*qua* the New York *Mary Ellen* case) but the need for separate societies and legislation became apparent. Canadian child law reformer J. J. Kelso wrote in his diary 10 January, 1890, "The difficulty is cropping up of keeping the animals and children from clashing, the two having their separate and distinct friends."[41] Ontario legislation was appropriately amended and Manitoba followed suit, instituting a system of quasi-charitable Children's Aid Societies in 1891 and enacting its *Child Protection Act* in 1898. (The Children's Aid Society model is extant in Manitoba and Ontario but was never adopted by provinces further west.)

The spate of reform continued in Manitoba, as elsewhere, into the next century. In place of a single statute based on the Tudor Poor Laws (the Manitoba *Apprentices and Minors Act, 1877*), there were by 1913 a multitude of statutory provisions in Manitoba empowering agencies to apprehend children for parental delict (neglect and abuse, immoral conduct) and delict of the child (vagrancy, truancy, expulsion from school, petty crime, exposure to immorality). The apprehended child would be placed in a normalizing environment, at first the industrial school; later, under the Kelso family model, in a foster family. By the 1920s, child welfare philosophy was moving away from child apprehension and institutional regimes, instead favouring family therapy and family-based settings.[42] Professional social workers and university-based experts were replacing the charitable amateur, to become the new "owners" of child welfare. To honour the new therapeutic commitment, "child protection" was renamed "child and family services."

The new childsaving, despite the renaming, shared much with the old.

> Despite the advancement of new ideas and procedures, the ultimate goal . . . remained unchanged from that of earlier generations of middle-class child-savers: to avoid present and future expenditures on public welfare and to guarantee social peace and stability by transforming dependent children into industrious, law-abiding workers.[43]

The new expertise legitimated the middle-class bias of child welfare established by 19th-century moral crusaders and poor and non-anglophone families continued to be singled out. The new agencies and experts defined the normative family according to certain assumptions,

> first, that the natural, inevitable, and highest form of the family is a particular type of household arrangement—a nuclear unity comprising two adults in a monogamous, heterosexual, legal marriage, and their dependent children;

second, that the family is premised on the biological or sexual division of labour that gives each member a different, but complementary, role with attendant obligations; third, the family is a private haven that operates on the basis of consensus as opposed to the public sphere of the marketplace where competition and conflict prevail.[44]

The construct has central implications for Aboriginal child welfare: it omits    10
the childcare networks of kith and kin which function in pre-industrial societies to intervene in times of difficulty and provide alternate caregiving[45] and it ignores the complex extended-family structure of original societies. It is a monolithic construct[46] tailored to justify state intervention in "abnormal" families.

Canadian child welfare philosophy prior to the Second World War was    11
imbricated in a social Darwinism which read into "survival of the fittest" a Canadian imperialism aspiring to equal partnership with England in the Empire.[47] The Canadian social purity movement embraced this vision of citizenship in its therapeutic focus on cleanliness and purity, medical and moral hygiene. The movement evangelicized a nativism which excised Aboriginal peoples from the Canadian landscape and viewed childhood as a blank slate upon which could be inscribed a chosen character. While the child might be irredeemably tainted by parental shortcomings, ethnicity or race, the enterprise, due to much confusion about eugenics and determinism, was nonetheless worth the try. Child welfare in the age of moral hygiene was characterized by an "unabashed" interventionism in which sociology and religion formed a seamless web: "the perfect sociology, perfectly applied, will realize the Kingdom of God on Earth."[48]

The English child migration movement exemplified the imperialist project    12
of citizenship and provides parallels to the "normalization" of Aboriginal children. Beginning in 1618 with a group of "orphaned and destitute" children sent from England to Virginia and lasting 350 years, 150 000 British children aged four to fourteen were exported to the colonies for apprenticeship as farm and household labourers.[49] Two out of three were sent to Canada, the "healthiest" colony, between 1870 and 1925 in the evangelical entrepreneurship of such Victorian childsavers as "Dr." Thomas Barnardo and the infamous Maria Rye. Under banners of Empire and child-saving, health and opportunity, children were exported to save public welfare costs and costs of future delinquency, and to fill colonial needs for cheap labour and English stock. Fear of uncivilized children was also a motive. A contemporary poem urged, perhaps tongue-in-cheek,[50]

> Take them away! Take them away!
> Out of the gutter, the ooze, and the slime,
> Where the little vermin paddle and crawl
> Till they grow and ripen in crime.

The conclusion reflects 19th-century beliefs in the restorative powers of the    13
New World: "The new shall repair the wrongs of the old."

At least two-thirds of child migrants were not orphans, as the public and    14
the publicity supposed, but children placed in institutional care, primarily by

parents and often on a temporary basis, and exported without consent. Many lost all contact with family. Despite sharing a language and "mother" culture with the colonies which received them, the children experienced cultural disorientation, discrimination as the "offal of the most depraved characters in the city of the old country," much physical and sexual abuse, emotional loss and inadequate and sometimes deadly living conditions. Moral panics circled about the child migrants. "Much crime, drunkenness and prostitution was seen as a result," wrote a late 19th-century Winnipeg correspondent, although the *Winnipeg Free Press* observed that most of the "crimes" in question were committed by local children. Labour unions complained that the child migrants were driving the working man out of the workplace.[51] The children were morally and genetically unfit to associate with Canadian children, wrote the prestigious Dr. Kenneth Clarke after sharing a train with a new shipment. "In Canada we are deliberately adding to our population hundreds of children bearing all the stigmata of physical and mental degeneracy" and the government should be held criminally liable. The 1893 "Highways and Hedges" magazine of the English National Children's Homes Society was in accord.

> For some of them are of poor human material; their constitution—physical and mental—is of inferior texture; they are naturally deficient in force of character and moral stamina; their antecedents were once vicious or at least unpromising; the sad entail of hereditary weakness or wickedness makes these unfortunate juveniles peculiarly the objects of our compassionate and continuous care . . . Canada is no place to shoot rubbish. It is a magnificent British colony waiting for development . . .

The majority of children were sent to Ontario and Manitoba and were a   15
common feature of rural life.[52] These provinces not being places "to shoot rubbish," restrictive legislation was enacted in 1897 which prohibited, under penalty of a fine of $100 or 3 months' imprisonment, immigration of any child

> who has been reared or who has resided amongst habitual criminals, or any child whose parents have been habitual criminals, lunatics or idiots, or weak-minded or defective constitutionally or confirmed paupers, or diseased . . .

Canada stopped accepting the children in 1925 due to new and more   16
expensive ideas about child welfare management (vetted placements and follow-up visits, for example) at the onset of the Depression.[53] These new ideas about child welfare were not without their opponents on the homefront.

The Winnipeg Home of the Friendless, an evangelical "Christian refuge   17
of last resort" for "orphaned or destitute" children and unwed mothers, was founded and run by Kansas evangelist Laura Crouch from 1900 to 1929. The Home was exempted from child welfare legislation by certificate of incorporation in 1913, a timely move as provincial powers of investigation and apprehension were reaching a temporary zenith. Empowered to refuse direct access of any "person or agency" (including parents) to child inmates, and to apprentice or adopt out any child without consent of child or parent, the Home was privately funded by a wealthy grocer (Crouch testified she began operation with $5.00 and prayer provided the rest), held impressive rural and

urban properties and operated two farms run on child labour.[54] Sixty-three former inmates testified before a provincial inquiry to beatings with straps, laths and switches—some "for cause," others ritual; to fear and intimidation, inadequate diet, isolation in cellars for up to four weeks at a time, 15 to 20 hour workdays, badly crowded dormitories, forced religious observance (Crouch evangelized a doomsday "holy roller" cult), lack of medical help and inadequate education. All complaints were dismissed.

Those who managed the Home were "extremely earnest Christian 18 people" while "retrospective recollections of happenings in youth are apt to be distorted, unduly favourable or the reverse," wrote Deputy Minister of Education Dr. Robert Fletcher in his 1927 report. The corporal punishment described by witnesses was deserved, exaggerated or fabricated. Fletcher mused on the religious benefits of such punishment.

> Notwithstanding that physical punishment is no remedy at all for the disease of mind and body complained of, we are further impressed with the religious possibilities in the matter. The strictest mentor is he or she who lives by the letter rather than by the spirit . . . The true object of all punishment is to reform the mind of the victim.

Fletcher viewed the conflicting views expressed before his inquiry— 19 "Social investigators claim to have been refused admission to the premises, the Home officials say they have been spied upon"—as conflicts of ideology caused by a "fundamental difference in policy" between the new social work and the religious mandate of the Home.

> Social workers today have as objective the placing of every homeless child with a family in a home with adoptive or foster parents . . . The Home of the Friendless is conducted on diametrically opposed lines. It is not only an institutional home for children but also it endeavours to absorb those children for life as workers . . . and in the religious work [of the Home] . . .

Fletcher was sufficiently impressed by Crouch and her staff that he rec- 20 ommended that the Home continue operation and be given a tax bailout by the province. This was not done. The Home was closed in 1929 for failure to pay taxes. Its huge property holdings—"The farm equipment alone is large even in western conception"—became the object of a series of disputed property grabs by city and province. The children were seized by provincial authorities. Crouch took the remainder of her flock to British Columbia, where her Burnaby operation was shut down 10 years later amid similar controversy.

The history of the Home of the Friendless illustrates the endurance and 21 sanctioning of the 19th-century institutional model well into the Progressive Era of professional childsaving and foster care. It further illustrates inadequacies of the new child welfare legislation and philosophy. Children's Aid Society workers had attempted over a 10-year period, without success, to gain access to Home records and child inmates. Questions were raised in the Manitoba legislature. Affidavits of former inmates were taken by Percy Paget, Chair of the Board of Welfare Supervision and it was these, together with the direct testimony of former inmates, which formed the basis of evidence before the inquiry. Claims of inadequate educational curriculum rather than of child maltreatment may have finally attracted government action, as child welfare and education were a single department at the time. The Fletcher report did recommend that "no new child-caring institution be permitted to commence operation in Manitoba until it shows itself willing to subscribe to . . . lawful Government requirements."

The Home's practices of isolation, corporal punishment, child labour,     22
minimal education, regimentation, evangelicism and cultural devaluation— many of its inmates were the children of immigrants—illustrate strategies for the governance of childhood which disabled distinctions between corporal punishment and abuse, child labour and exploitation, minimal education and inadequate education. These distinctions were unclear even to government policy-makers, as the competing views of Fletcher and Paget demonstrate.

Child migration and the residential schooling exemplified in the Home of     23
the Friendless were designed to normalize childhood by instilling values of Anglo-Canadian Christian citizenship in the children of the poor. The fact that they were challenged by the "new" childsaving of the first decades of the 20th century illustrates competing modes of child management—foster care and family support versus the orphanage, industrial school or reformatory; family model versus institutional model—rather than a fundamental disagreement with earlier technologies of transformation and normalization. The perishing child and the dangerous child were to be reformed by corporal punishment, regimentation and surveillance, isolation from kin and culture, cultural deval- uation, religious indoctrination, education tailored to social status and child labour, whatever the model. These technologies were appropriated for assim- ilating the Aboriginal child. Indian residential schools were closely modelled on mainstream 19th-century institutional regimes for normalizing childhood. Like the Home of the Friendless, Indian residential schools escaped the attentions of the new childsaving by virtue of an insulating legal regime.

## EDUCATION AND NORMALIZATION: THE RESIDENTIAL SCHOOL

Aboriginal parenting practices shocked early observers. The Jesuit missionary     24
Le Jeune spent the winter of 1633–34 with the Montaignais, a Quebec Algonkian people linguistically and culturally related to the Plains Cree. His observations of Aboriginal childhood point to an unusual freedom to exper- iment, inclusion in the adult activities of the community and, worst of all, no corporal punishment but only a single reprimand as a last resort. Le Jeune concluded that removal from family and tribe was essential to the institution of a proper educational regime. In his imagined regime, the children would have a period of complete freedom to accustom them to the pleasures of European food and clothing such that "they will have a horror of Savages and their filth." A disciplinary regime, with appropriate corporal punishments, would then be introduced.[55] Le Jeune's was perhaps the earliest example of a normalization scheme for Aboriginal childhood based on residential school- ing and corporal punishment. This chapter is a brief survey of Indian resi- dential schooling in Canada.

The foundations of a mission school which would board Aboriginal chil-    25
dren at Red River were laid by Hudson's Bay Company chaplain John West
on his arrival at the trading post of York Factory in August 1820.[56] West was
immediately impressed with the need for his services. The "corrupt influence
and barter of spirituous liquors at a Trading Post" made it "peculiarly incumbent upon me to seek to ameliorate their sad condition, as degraded, emaciated, and wandering in ignorance." Further, "some spoke of impossibilities in
the way of teaching them Christianity or the first rudiments of settled and civilized life." West had a ready answer for this problem on his first contact with
the new world and its indigenous inhabitants. The answer was childhood.

> If little hope could be cherished of arresting the adult Indian in his wanderings
> and unsettled habits of life, it appeared to me, that a wide and most extensive
> field, presented itself for cultivation in the instruction of the native children.
> With the aid of an interpreter, I spoke to an Indian called Withawee-capo,
> about taking two of his boys to the Red River Colony with me to educate and
> maintain. He yielded to my request; and I shall never forget the affectionate
> manner in which he brought the eldest in his arms, and placed him in the
> canoe on the morning of my departure . . . I considered that I bore a pledge
> from the Indian that many more children might be found, if an Establishment
> was formed in British Christian sympathy, and British liberality for their edu-
> cation and support (15 August, 1820).

West sought Hudson's Bay Company support for his "Establishment."    26
His argument was not based on Christian sympathy for the noble savage but,
more cleverly, on the threat to social order posed by deserted "Half Caste
children" who must "equally claim the attention of the Christian
Philanthropist with those who are of pure Aboriginal blood."

> I have suggested to the Committee of the H. B. Company the importance of col-
> lecting and educating the numerous Half Breed children, whose parents have
> died or deserted them, and who are found running about the different Factories
> in ignorance and idleness. Neglected as they hitherto have been, they grow up
> in great depravity, and should they be led to "find their grounds" with the
> Indians, it cannot be a matter of surprise, if at any time collectively, or in par-
> ties they should threaten the peace of the country and the safety of the Trading
> Posts (12 August, 1822).

This was an astute appeal to the widespread fears of unmediated childhood
which propelled 19th-century evangelical childsaving.

Parents posed a problem. Like Le Jeune before him, West saw the need to    27
separate child from mother culture and from the mother.

> [T]he last two Indian Saulteaux boys have given us a little trouble in disci-
> plining them to the school, from the mother living constantly about the set-
> tlement, and occasionally visiting them, when they have run off with their
> sisters to the wigwam (20 April, 1823).

This convinced him that "it is far better to obtain the children from a distance,
as those who are in the school and at a distance from their parents soon

become reconciled to the restraint, and happy upon the Establishment."[57] West returned to England disappointed by the failure of the Hudson's Bay Company to support his efforts. His Mission, however, was not lost.

The 1842 Bagot Commission recognized the difficulty of assimilating Aboriginal children who remained in contact with families. The Commission recommended as antidote the establishment of farm-based boarding schools far away from parental influence and interference. Residential schooling was approved by the Upper Canada Chiefs gathered at Orillia in 1846 who agreed to pay one-fourth of their annuities for 25 years in support of the school, although they objected to its assimilationist agenda. The system was extended in Upper Canada in the 1850s and 1860s. The Indian Department sent lawyer-journalist Nicholas Davin to investigate the United States model of "aggressive civilization" which removed Plains Aboriginal youth "from the tribal way of life" for industrial school training. Davin's 1879 *Report on Industrial Schools for Indians and Half-breeds* reflected the Bagot Commission conclusion that the schools worked best when farm-based and church-run. **28**

The Canadian system was designed for Indian Affairs by Egerton Ryerson, Chief Superintendent of Education for Upper Canada. Ryerson led the campaign in the latter half of the 19th century for the establishment of a system of free universal compulsory education which would, he believed, create social cohesion by inculcating a common morality. Ryerson objected in principle to industrial schooling, as it segregated the children of the poor, but conceded it would do for the "worst" children. These presumably included Aboriginal children. His "Indian industrial schools" "were to give [the Indian] a plain English education adapted to the working farmer and mechanic" and would include a strong Christian component because "nothing can be done to improve and elevate [the Indian's] character without the aid of religious feeling." The schools were to be joint undertakings of the federal Indian Department and major Christian denominations, supported by contributory child labour. **29**

Although the precedent system of small mission schools like West's proposed "Establishment" continued, Indian Affairs policy shifted in favour of industrial and boarding schools (a distinction dropped in 1923 for the term "residential school"). Beginning in the 1880s in fulfilment of the Numbered Treaty obligations to educate Indian children, the residential school system expanded throughout the Northwest, the former territory of the Hudson's Bay Company and West's original mission. West's "Half-breed children" had no place in official Indian policy. In total, 80 schools were constructed, most in the Prairie region. Between 1901 and 1961, the percentage of registered Indian children enrolled in residential schools fluctuated between 12 per cent and 37 per cent. In 1936, 42 per cent of Manitoba Indian children were registered in a residential school. This compares with 3 per cent in Quebec, 36 per cent in Ontario, 77 per cent in Saskatchewan, and 98 per cent in Alberta.[58] **30**

The schools were to be located as far as possible from the Indian bands. As a member of Parliament explained in 1883,[59] **31**

[i]f these schools are to succeed, we must not have them too near the bands; in order to educate the children properly we must separate them from their families. Some people may say this is hard, but if we want to civilize them we must do that.

Children between the ages of three or four and 14 were taken from their    32
parents and "villages," by now "reserves," to schools hundreds of kilometres away. Their hair was cut or shaved off, they were separated by age and gender, denied sibling contact and given new names. The curriculum consisted of morning classes, rarely above a grade 3–5 level, with field or house work for the rest of the day. Only English speech was permitted, reflecting conscious assimilation and unconscious racial superiority. The poet Matthew Arnold, then British Inspector of Schools, had written in 1852 of the link between language and empire.[60]

> It must always be the desire of a government to render its dominions, as far as possible, homogenous. Sooner or later the difference of language . . . will probably be effaced . . . an event which is socially and politically desirable.

A similar philosophy underlay residential school policy. Speaking an    33
Aboriginal language was prohibited or severely restricted and punishment for infraction could be severe.[61] The efficacy of a residential school education depended equally on removal from family and culture, and on "precept and example." According to the 1889 Indian Affairs *Annual Report*,[62]

> The boarding school disassociates the Indian child from the deleterious home influences to which he would otherwise be subjected. It reclaims him from the uncivilized state in which he has been brought up. It brings him into contact from day to day with all that tends to effect a change in his views and habits of life. By precept and example he is taught to endeavour to excel in what will be most useful to him.

Removal of children from "the demoralizing and degrading influence of    34
the tepees," as the *Calgary Herald* rather crudely put it in 1892, was necessary to the program. But a Presbyterian missionary wrote home in 1903 that the schools were no more than an attempt "to educate & colonize a people against their will."[63]

Nineteenth-century imperialism was carried into 20th-century Indian    35
Affairs policy under the stewardship of Duncan Campbell Scott, whose service lasted from 1878 to 1932. By 1909, assimilation was becoming less "aggressive" due to cost, tactical resistance and the successful marginalization of Plains Indians. The path of Prairie settlement having been cleared, the path of assimilation was less important and citizenship through protective segregation—a slower assimilation—now became the justification for continuing the Indian Affairs policy of apartheid. Scott, mid-career as Indian Affairs Superintendent of Education, wrote of the change in 1909.[64]

> The government and the churches have abandoned, to a large extent, previous policies which attempted to "Canadianize" the Indians. Through a process of vocational, and to a smaller extent academic training, they are now

attempting to make good Indians, rather than poor mixtures of Indians and whites. While the idea is still Christian citizenship, the government now hopes to move towards this end by continuing to segregate the Indian population, in large measure from the white races.

Despite a gradual relaxation of policy—newer schools were located closer    36
to the bands; language restrictions were eased—resistance to schooling increased. In summer breaks, familial and cultural norms were confusingly reasserted. Some children had lost their Aboriginal language and skills but by summer's end had lost their English. Children resisted by speaking their own languages, playing truant or avoiding the Indian agent who collected children at summer's end. A few engaged in acts of violence or arson. Parents resisted, visiting against the rules (one Saskatchewan school built a sleeping porch for parents, to the consternation of the Bishop), withdrawing children because of corporal punishment practices, removing instructors for physical or sexual abuse, boycotting schools with overt assimilationist policies, fighting for the establishment of schools which would give their children a European education without Christian indoctrination, refusing to enrol their children without assurance of non-conversion. Although an "English" education was sought and valued by Aboriginal peoples who recognized the inevitability of change, assimilation was consistently rejected.

Some children may have been assimilated, depending on how success is    37
here defined. Certainly the schools produced children who had learned enough for effective resistance and who became 20th-century social and political leaders—"the most promising pupils are found to have retrograded and to have become leaders in the pagan life of the reserves," Scott wrote in 1913. Up to one half of all children enrolled prior to 1914 never went home. Indian Affairs medical officer P. H. Bryce reported in 1912 that "It is quite within the mark to say that 50 per cent of the children who passed through these schools did not live to benefit from the education which they received therein."[65] There are rumours of unmarked graves behind residential schools, said to hold the infanticided offspring of nuns.[66] If such graves exist, it is probable that they hold the unclaimed bodies of child victims of tuberculosis. The disease was spread in the stifling conditions of crowded and airless dormitory life during the long harsh Prairie winters and by the English love of brass bands, the instruments being vectors of the disease. "TB" sanitariums still dot the Prairie landscape. These child deaths were an unforeseen example of resolving "the Indian problem" by extermination, not by war, genocide, starvation, ignorance or neglect, but by "doing good."

Other children graduated to a life which did not accommodate their skills    38
and whose skills they had lost. The non-nurturing attentions of instructors, early and prolonged separation from parents and siblings and the experience of institutional life did not teach residential school pupils either Aboriginal or Euro/Anglo–Canadian parenting norms. Corporal punishment, a longstanding feature of European education,[67] was an important part of the regime and came to symbolize the cultural and social destruction of the residential school

experience. Some schools had a "discipline officer" whose rod required a certain number of weekly strokes.[68] William Clarence Thomas, Superintendent, Peguis School Board, told the Kimelman Inquiry in 1985 that[69]

> [o]ne school principal in Brandon used to call us God's children three times on Sundays at the three services and the rest of the week call us dirty little Indians. No one ever told us they loved us. We were mere numbers. Strapping, beatings, hair cut to baldness, being tethered to the flag pole, half day school with unqualified tutors, and slave labour the other half . . .

Janet Ross told the 1991 Manitoba Aboriginal Justice Inquiry that

> [t]he boarding school is where the alienation began. Children were placed there, plucked out of their homes. The bond between parents and children was fragmented severely—some lost forever. . . The boarding schools taught us violence. Violence was emphasized through physical, corporal punishment, strapping, beatings, bruising and control. We learned to understand that this was power and control.

Many children were sexually abused by teachers and clerics or by older children who had been similarly abused; most were controlled through abasement, cultural devaluation, humiliation and corporal punishment. The Aboriginal Justice Inquiry summarized the experience as one "marked by emotional, physical and sexual abuse, social and spiritual deprivation, and substandard education . . . Aboriginal communities have not yet recovered from the damage."[70] Sexual use of children, corporal punishment and damaged parent-child bonds, recognized precursors of abuse, infiltrated reserve childhood. Economic disintegration leading to apathy and substance abuse provided the conditions of neglect and an environment in which child abuse as defined by child welfare policy and legislation could flourish.

The residential schools were maintained far beyond their time, when child welfare policy had moved toward family-centred solutions and interventions were at least overtly based less on class and "race" than apprehension of harm. The project "failed dismally" due in large part to Indian resistance[71] and the last schools (excepting a few which were turned over to First Nations management) were closed in the 1960s. The dream of empire which fuelled the assimilation of Indian childhood, as it fuelled assimilation of the children of poor and the marginalized through child migration and 19th-century child welfare, backfired. The imperialist mission of reconstructing Indian childhood on an Anglo-Canadian model made residential schooling an important symbol of assimilation and cultural destruction. A second system has emerged as an equally powerful symbol of cultural genocide: the 20th-century child protection system.

■ ■ ■

## Notes

33. Miller, 1989, *supra note* 10 at 191.
34. The pass system was instituted to control movements during the summer of 1885 in the wake of the North-West Rebellion and was virtually unen-

forced by 1893 but the petty power it gave federal Indian Agents has long been a sore point. Control over band membership, reserve access and use of alcohol on-reserve are now governed by band by-law.

35. Delegitimation creates resistance. The custom of the potlatch, for example, died out as a cultural practice in Alaska, where it was not prohibited, long before it died out in Canada, where it was illegal.

36. Stone describes four views of the nature of the child which had emerged by the mid-19th century, "the adoption of each of which profoundly affects the way [the child] is treated": born in Original Sin and requiring total subordination of will to adult authority (the "religious" view); born *tabula rasa,* entirely malleable (the "environmental" view); born with character and potential predetermined but somewhat susceptible to improvement through education (the "biological" view); born good and corrupted by society (the "Utopian" view, crystallized in Rousseau's *Emile*). L. Stone, *The Family, Sex and Marriage in England 1500–1800* (Pelican, 1979) 254. These competing visions of childhood are all visible in 19th-century childhood discourse and protection policy.

37. N. Rose, *Governing the Soul: The Shaping of the Private Self* (Routledge, 1989) 257. See R. Dingwall *et al.,* "Childhood as a Social Problem: A Survey of the History of Legal Regulation" (1984) 11 J. *Law and Society;* M. D. A. Freeman, *The Rights and Wrongs of Children* (Pinter, 1983). The difference for late 19th-century child welfare is one of degree.

38. J. Donzelot, *The Policing of Families* (Hutchinson, 1980). Donzelot's observation that the changing governance of childhood improved conditions for children and women is not borne out to any great degree in this study of Aboriginal childhood.

39. Rose, *supra* note 37 at 186.

40. J. Ursel, *Private Lives, Public Policy: 100 Years of State Intervention in the Family* (Women''s Press, 1992). The new interest in the regulation of childhood and the statutory augmentation of state powers is seen in England, France, and the United States, with remarkable similarities in provisions and justifications.

41. Kelso was a key figure in the development of the Canadian foster care system, Children's Aid Societies, statutory powers of apprehension and the juvenile court. See J. Bullen, "J. J. Kelso and the 'New' Child-savers: The Genesis of the Children's Aid Movement in Ontario" (1990) 82 *Ontario History* 107. The need for new legislation was publicized in the New York "Mary Ellen" case, in which a child houseworker was removed from abusive guardians under animal protection legislation, there being no other legal grounds for her apprehension.

42. D. E. Chunn, *From Punishment to Doing Good: Family Courts and Socialized Justice in Ontario 1890–1940* (University of Toronto Press, 1992); Ursel, note 36; L. Gordon, *Heroes of Their Own Lives: The Politics and History of Family Violence, Boston 1880–1960* (Penguin, 1988); C. Hooper, "Child Sexual Abuse and the Regulation of Women: Variations on a Theme" in C. Smart, ed., *Regulating Womanhood: Historical Essays on Marriage, Motherhood and Sexuality* (Routledge, 1992).

43. Bullen, *supra* note 41 at 157–58. Children were placed on farms, given a bare education, subjected to "many obvious injustices" and "condemned to a working-class world that offered few opportunities for personal development and social mobility."

44. Chunn, *supra* note 42 at 36.

45. See J. Korbin, *Child Abuse and Neglect: Cross-Cultural Perspectives* (University of California Press, 1981). The "norm" is also heterosexually biased and omits family formations which do not include children.

46. M. Eichler, *Families in Canada Today: Recent Changes and their Policy Consequences* (Gage, 1983). Eichler calls this the "monolithic bias." Closely linked is the "conservative bias" which includes "a tendency to either ignore children altogether, or to see them merely as objects to be acted upon, rather than as active participants in family life."

47. M. Valverde, *The Age of Light, Soap and Water: Moral Reform in English Canada, 1885–1925* (McClelland & Stewart, 1991). Valverde establishes linkages between hygiene (cleanliness, moral reform, social and racial purity); Canadian nativism (anglo-Protestant patriotism which sought to identify a "native" Canadian identity in the British Empire); and the "unabashed" interventionism of social work. "Nativism" was most strident on the Prairies, "fantastical" in view of the fact that Western Canada was neither administratively nor in its general population "white," until late in the 19th century (107–8).

48. *Ibid.* at 54, citing Canadian Methodist minister Samuel Dwight Chown, one of the first of the proto-professionals to attempt the reconciliation of social science and religious values.

49. An estimated 11 per cent of the Canadian population may be their descendants. The last group left England in 1967. See P. Bean and J. Melville, *Lost Children of the Empire: The Untold Story of Britain's Child Migrants* (Unwin Hyman, 1990). The movement was both "welfarist" and "instrumentalist" according to J. Eekalaar, "The Chief Glory: The Export of Children from the U.K." (1994) 4 J. *Law and Society* 487. For a Canadian perspective, see K. Bagnell, *The Little Immigrants* (Macmillan, 1980).

50. "The Departure of the Innocents" in Bean and Melville, *ibid.* at 59.

51. Untrue, given the children's farm or domestic placement and lack of skills, but effective in the enactment of Canadian child labour laws which tended to benefit adults rather than children.

52. For depictions of Manitoba "Barnardo boys" in fiction, see R.J.C. Stead, *The Bail Jumper* (Briggs, 1914) and E.A.W. Gill, *Love in Manitoba* (Musson, 1911). In both novels, the "Barnardo boys" are ill-treated, of problematic morals and all but nameless. Gill, a cleric with St. John's Cathedral Winnipeg on leave from England, also wrote *A Manitoba Chore Boy: Letters From an Emigrant* (London Religious Tract Society, 1908), a glowing account of a year on a Manitoba farm aimed at juvenile readers and overt propaganda for child migration.

53. The economic value of child labour was vitiated by child labour laws and by political and economic change. Exploitation of the "Home" children was apparent by the turn of the century and lack of follow-up by British child export agencies was strongly criticized by Canadian observers. Imperialism shaped child welfare until the "Great War" changed Canada's relations with England and ended colonialist aspirations. The Depression coincided with "The Dirty Thirties" of Prairie drought and deep poverty.

54. *Home of the Friendless Report of the Investigating Committee, 1926* (Manitoba Sessional Paper No. 47). The Home's purpose, according to its Articles of Incorporation, was "sheltering, relieving, assisting, reclaiming or otherwise dealing with the fallen, helpless, destitute and afflicted, or other person, whether male or female, needing help, protection or assistance including children." Its religious agenda was protected by the provision that "No person shall hold the office of directress or manager unless she shall be an Evangelical Protestant." The Home could contract for an "absolute and uninterrupted custody of and control" of children "which shall be upheld by all courts." Control of girls would cease at 18, of boys at 16. As the 1926 Report noted, the provisions were "in obvious conflict with both the spirit and the letter of general provisions of *The Child Welfare Act*" of 1922; s. 188 of that Act exempted the Home from its general provisions, permitting only a right of inspection. This was a "bare right" according to its Directress. The Articles were based on those of the Winnipeg Children's Home, incorporated in 1887. S. 188 was amended effective 23 April, 1926, in consultation with Crouch, to authorize the public inquiry. The evidence points strongly to a spy on the Fletcher committee, alerting Crouch to "surprise" Home inspections. I am grateful to Dr. Len Kaminski, University of Manitoba, for sharing this important archival research with me and for his helpful discussions on the implications and aftermath of the Report.

55. L.R. Bull, "Indian Residential Schooling: the Native Perspective" (1991) 18 (Supplement) *Canadian Journal of Native Education 3* at 14–15. On residential schools, see also note 10 generally; J.R. Miller, "Owen Glendower, Hotspur, and Canadian Indian Policy" in Miller, 1991, note 10; Aboriginal Justice Inquiry, note 9; N.R. Ing, "The Effects of Residential Schools on Native Child-Rearing Practices" (1991) 18 (Supplement) *Canadian Journal of Native Education 65*; Cariboo Tribal Council and University of Guelph, "Faith Misplaced: Lasting Effects of Abuse in a First Nations Community" (1991) 18 *Canadian Journal of Native Education 161*; J. Gresko, "White "Rites" and Indian "Rites": Indian Education and National Responses in the West, 1870–1910", in D.C. Jones *et al.*, *Shaping the Schools of the Canadian West* (Detselig, 1979) at 84.

56. Reverend John West, First Priest of the Church of England in the Red River Settlement in the Years 1820 to 1823, *The British North West*

*American Indians With Free Thoughts on the Red River Settlement* (type-script copy of the original diary manuscript, St. John College Library, University of Manitoba). "In my appointment as Chaplain to the [Hudson's Bay] Company, my instructions were to reside at the Red River Settlement; and under the encouragement and support of the Church Missionary Society, I was to seek the Instruction and to ameliorate the condition of the native Indians." West embarked 27 May, 1820 at Graves End on the company ship *Eddystone*. His diary records many instances of the care taken by Indian parents of their children "of whom they were passionately fond" (yet "they brutally lend their daughters of tender age, for a few beads, or a little tobacco"). He returned 10 September, 1823 with a disappointing letter from Governor Simpson which elicited the observation that "the resolves of Council in Hudson's Bay relative to the amelioration of the condition of the Indians, and promoting morality and religion in the country, were like the acts of the west Indian legislatures passed professedly with a view to the promoting of religion among the slaves: *worse than nullities.*" Costs of his "Establishment" must fall to Mission charity. I am grateful to Russell Smandych for bringing the manuscript to my attention.

57. The mother, a widow who refused to entrust her daughters to West, secretly took her sons away amid rumours that West would "cut off the ears of one of them for leaving the school without leave." West makes mention of the jealousy of "the Catholics" of his "Native Indian School Establishment," with the inference that this was the source of the rumours: "The attempt is made to prejudice the minds of the Indians against giving their children, insinuating that I wish to collect them, with the intention of taking them to England." The mother's decampment was occasioned by preparations of West's ally Chief Pigewis [Peguis] to make war on her people, the Sioux. West's hopes of addressing Peguis' tribe on educating their children were frustrated: "Oh! what faith, and patience, and perseverance are necessary lest the mind should grow weary in the arduous work of seeking to evangelize the Heathen" (*ibid.*, 30 March, 1823).

58. Based on Armitage, *supra* note 10 at 107 *et seq.*

59. Miller 1989, *supra* note 33 at 196.

60. Arnold referred to the "effacement" of the Welsh language, a unique branch of Gaelic. When English state education was enforced in Wales in 1880, Welsh was outlawed from the schools and children were punished for speaking it, a point of pride for many. The anglicization project backfired, leading to the late–19th-century renaissance of Welsh literature and culture. English schooling for Wales was fuelled by the Commissioners' horror at the lack of religious knowledge of children interviewed, who were probably pulling their collective leg. J. Morris, *The Matter of Wales* (Oxford, 1984) 239. The difference for Aboriginal children is most notably the removal from family and village systems of support and the imposition of a much more alien system. On the "invention" or "redis-

covery" of Welsh culture (with parallels yet to be explored for Aboriginal cultural rediscovery), see P. Morgan, "From a Death to a View: The Hunt for the Welsh Past in the Romantic Period" in E. Hobsbawm and T. Ranger, *The Invention of Tradition* (Cambridge, 1983).

61. These included beating, head-shaving, isolation and ridicule. Restrictions were eventually relaxed. Children in later decades learned rudiments of their own languages from other students and were exposed to other Aboriginal cultures, an experience which later played a strong role in the pan-Indian movement (*supra* note 32) and the strategies of self-government.

62. Miller 1989, *supra* note 33 at 196.

63. J.R. Miller, "Owen Glendower," "Hotspur and Canadian Indian Policy" in J.R. Miller, ed. *Sweet Promises: A Reader on Indian-White Relations in Canada* (University of Toronto Press, 1991) at 332.

64. Bull, *supra* note 55.

65. Miller, 1989, *supra* note 33 at 213.

66. Conversation of the author with a Cree student, April 1994.

67. A. McGillivray, "*R. v. K.(M.)*: Legitimating Brutality" (1993) 16 *Criminal Reports* (4th) 125; Stone, *supra* note 36.

68. Conversation of the author with a former Alberta residential school student, October 1993, who planned to form a victim collective for male survivors of residential school discipline. He is searching for the nun, now in her 80s, who acted as discipline officer, in order to sue the Catholic Church for damages. Officials have confirmed that she is still alive, but will not say where she now lives.

69. The Committee Final Report, *No Quiet Place*. [Kimelman Report] Manitoba Community Services 1985 at 201.

70. Aboriginal Justice Inquiry, *supra* note 5 at 514–515. See Ing, *supra* note 55 for accounts by former pupils. But see Cariboo Tribal Council, *supra* note 55 at 180, suggesting that "The type of school attended by the respondents' mothers did not seem to affect family life, while respondents whose fathers had attended residential school had somewhat different experiences from those whose fathers had attended non-residential school." While perhaps the majority of Indian children did not attend residential school, studies and personal accounts suggest far-reaching effect on the quality of family life and community cohesion where even one family member, especially a father, did so. The picture is complex. Christian corporal punishment values even without the residential school experience have suggested to elders that the birch switch is somehow part of traditional Aboriginal values, while domestic violence and child sexual abuse in "closed" stressed communities can spread rapidly. "Culture" may deny as well as protect.

71. Miller 1989, *supra* note 33 at 199. Miller also cites state parsimony as a cause of the failure of the system.

■  ■  ■

## Discussion and Writing Suggestions

1. McGillivray describes how and why the Canadian government employed two key institutions of society—the school system and organized religion—in its attempt to assimilate Aboriginal people into a British version of civilization. Under pressure of objections that presenting any one religious perspective is problematic in a culturally diverse society, the Church has generally been sidelined in the public school system. Is the school system now ideology-free? Or is it still used for purposes of social engineering?

2. Why would McGillivray see "the reserve, the residential school, the child protection system, young offender facilities and jail" as a "Foucauldian carceral archipelago"? (If you don't know these terms, start by investigating their meanings.)

3. McGillivray makes the claim that strong resistance by Aboriginal people caused the project of residential schooling to fail dismally. What are the implications of her claim for other instances of oppression and resistance in the school system?

# Poverty and Education in Canada

PAUL OLSON

*From a chapter in a text exploring Canadian educational policy, the author argues that poverty is not random, but socially organized along gender, ethnic, regional, and other lines. He also argues that our oppressive social attitudes to people living in poverty are mobilized in classrooms, resulting in an irrelevant curriculum that is destined to fail children from low-income families.*

*Paul Olson teaches in the Department of Sociology and Equity Studies at the Ontario Institute for Studies in Education at the University of Toronto.*

## UNDERSTANDING POVERTY IN CANADA

Poverty is a word most of us believe we understand. But do we? In Canada, poverty has historically been associated with happenings somewhere else—the Third World ghettos, Native reserves, or the streets. Recently, many of us have seen the structural shifts in the economy and wonder if our futures will be poorer than in the past. Still, for many people, especially those in professions or the middle classes, poverty is a remote concern, one more for religious or humanitarian concern than for personal or professional worry. Yet is this the whole story? Encapsulated in a seemingly straightforward word—poverty—are sets of values and subjectivities, mores, and positions about other people in the world. Also involved are economic and social realities that are more than an abstraction to people who must live with poverty. These realities prefigure what one can do with those who are educated in conditions of poverty and how poverty itself can be influenced by education.

What is understood about poverty (and education) often influences outcomes. Poverty is therefore not a passively descriptive condition; it is socially constructed, and is mediated by how people understand, think, and act. It is a multilayered set of perceptions, relations, and actions toward people by people.

## POVERTY, THE STATE, AND INDIVIDUAL AND COLLECTIVE INTEREST

Traditionally, people have had their own explanations for poverty. Many people see the poor as just lazy. Sociologically, however, we know that poverty tends to be neither random nor individual. Rather, it tends to be statistically associated with certain groups. Analyzing the make-up of these groups can help us shed light on the reasons why some groups are poorer than others. Often, we find that how rich or poor an individual is may depend on where (or even when) that individual lives. Most Canadians, for instance, have relative economic wealth because they live in an industrial country. In Canada, per capita family income in 1989 for a family of four was $51 342 (Statistics Canada, 1993a). By contrast, per capita income per person in much of the Third World is little more than several thousand per annum, if that high. The point is that material conditions are often beyond one's control, but can profoundly affect what is possible and what one experiences as "reality." One can be very industrious yet still be very poor. Collective or socioeconomic factors dramatically affect what can be accomplished in such contexts.   3

The relationship of wealth and poverty is also directly affected by government policies. Taxes, social programs, and schools are all forms of social policy. Such policies often create, as well as address, issues.   4

Pockets of poverty are found in every region in every province of Canada, with variations between northern and southern Canada, rural and urban. Generalizations are again dangerous since variations can occur both within communities as well as between them.   5

## INDUSTRIALISM AND THE RISE OF THE WELFARE STATE

While Canada in the 19th century was still labouring under a variety of antiquated laws about poverty, gender, and the like, powerful new formulations associated with social and industrial relations were taking place. The Industrial Revolution was transforming Euro-American society and beginning to influence Canada. By the mid-1800s British liberals made a powerful variant on the theme of poverty as "just rewards." This was the rise of the welfare state spearheaded by the so-called "child-saving movement."   6

The child-savers (Platt, 1969) saw urbanization as destructive to the family. City slums were new "evils" that impacted especially on youth. Children in this new apocalypse were victims of the new social conditions and needed to be "saved." This new doctrine of child-saving, like today's "wars" on drugs, poverty, and social ills, had ardent support in the popular press, which (like today) alternatively portrayed the poor and youth as both villain and victim.   7

In asserting the incompetence of youth to fend off poverty, and therefore the need for the state to act as ward, the state also assigned to itself the right to intervene in poor children's affairs "for their own good." Curriculum the-   8 orist Madeleine Grumet (1985) has argued that curriculum is at its worst when the curriculum is "for other people's children." Grumet suggests that actions are taken on behalf of those who are supposed to be served by a governmental, educational, or service sector for their benefit; however, in fact, the aim of such action is to contain or limit those individuals so that they will not become a problem to society or the agencies that deal with them. Very often these actions take the form of policy decisions that those administering such programs would not allow to happen to their own children.

## HELPING THE CHILDREN AND
## THE POOR OR CONTROLLING THEM?

The idea of saving the poor was (and remains) very much a two-edged sword.    9
On the one hand are the very real needs of the poor and the genuine efforts of many to help them. On the other hand, child-saving and programs for the poor may be seen as forms of containment of social programs.

In this latter thesis, the poor are problematic because of their potential to    10
disrupt or limit a society. A traditional way of handling such problems was direct social control such as policing, prisons, and the like. In the 19th century, as Foucault (1979) and others have argued, the emphasis of social control shifted from regulation of the body by direct constraint (prisons, corporal punishment, expulsion) to control of the mind or of values held.

Socializing and regulating agencies became central to state operations. In    11
this respect two independent theories put forward by American sociologist Amiti Etzioni (1961, 1964) may be useful to review. The first of these is Etzioni's hypothesis that one can tell the degree of social stability in a society by the types and amounts of social control it has to use. The most stable authority, in Etzioni's terms, is that based on normative regulations, wherein individuals conform to social values because they have been socialized to believe in them. Control is *internal*; that is, people believe in social values and therefore accept them. Most control in society, Etzioni reasons, is *utilitarian*. Utilitarian control is represented in the exchange of rewards. The most obvious example is that people work for money. If society offers the poor little opportunity, one way of making sure they are not driven to extreme measures is to establish some form of economic redistribution such as welfare. A cynical comment by a member of the British House of Lords in the era of Lloyd George is telling: Welfare, he reasoned, was the "ransom" the rich paid for peace. Etzioni's third form of social control is "direct coercion," or control through the legal system, the effect of which on society should not be underestimated.

## WHO ARE THE POOR?

The poor in Canada are hardly a random group. Poverty has three general    12
characteristics: it tends to be cyclical; it affects particular social and regional groups more than others; and it tends to be structural. Women and children make up 45 percent of all poor. Other groups are youth, the old, and marginalized groups, like Native Canadians.

Statistics Canada generates a series of reports detailing the income dis-   13
tributions in the country (Statistics Canada, 1993a, 1993b; see also Economic
Council of Canada, 1992; Canadian Parliament, 1991). A brief review of
these data is instructive. Statistics Canada determines that if an individual or
household must spend 58.5 percent or more of total income on food, shelter,
and clothing, they are considered poor (Statistics Canada, 1993a). Statistics
Canada uses 1978 as its base year for constant-dollar comparisons of whether
particular groups are "gaining" or "losing" in real dollars. Our comparisons
in this section are based on these Statistics Canada criteria.

Let us examine our claims that poverty is cyclical, affects particular   14
groups more than others, and is structural in light of the data.

## THE CYCLICAL NATURE OF POVERTY

Statistics Canada estimated that in 1990, 13.2 percent of Canada's population   15
was poor. This figure is 207 000 less than in 1987 and almost 800 000 less
than in 1983 (Statistics Canada, 1988). The first half of the 1980s saw an
actual decline in real wealth measured in constant dollars for most Canadians
(Statistics Canada, 1989). The rate of real income growth for the 1980s as a
whole was small: 0.05 percent, compared with 2.3 percent for the 1971–81
period or 3.9 percent for 1951–61. Within the 1980s there was a marked difference between the pre- and post-1985 periods. In the earlier period, incomes
measured in constant or real dollars (dollars corrected for inflation) actually
fell. The comparative rates of decline were greatest for men, although (as we
will see) it was women who bore the disproportionate brunt of poverty.

The worst year of decline in the 1980s was 1982, when the country was   16
in a recession. Poverty rates increased nationally and, to an even greater
extent, regionally. Not surprisingly, the numbers of poor followed the economic trends and also increased. During the latter part of the 1980s, Canada
was in a comparatively prosperous economic period, and levels of absolute
poverty decreased. Boom times, however, do not account for all of the gains.
As a group, Canadians were getting older, with the mean age reaching the
thirties during the decade. Higher percentages of the population in the workforce also contributed to lessening levels of poverty. Thus poverty tends, in
our current scheme, to mirror economic and demographic trends. With economic downturn, one can expect poverty to increase proportionally.

Much of the support for the poor in Canada has come in the form of   17
social assistance programs devised by the federal government but implemented by the provinces. There was little change in the social support system
of the "liberal welfare state" between the 1960s and 1980s. In fact, much of
the state's handling of poverty was, until recently, characterized by indifference. Rodney Haddow observes:

> Despite the high public profile of poverty issues none of the national politi-
> cal parties gave poverty reform a major place in its program. In general they
> were not strongly motivated to reform policies that were mainly of interest to
> marginal citizens. (Haddow, 1993, p. 166)

Increasing pressures on federal transfer payments to the provinces are    18
likely to mean that future poverty reform may depend on the extent to which
Canadians can support programs already in place. Informally, various indices
show that "social nets" are fraying. In the Christmas weekend of 1993, for
instance, soup kitchens in Montreal fed almost 60 000, while in Toronto all
shelters for displaced families were full and unable to accommodate everyone,
including children.

## HOW POVERTY AFFECTS DIFFERENT GROUPS

Gender, age, family arrangements, region, ethnicity, education, and geogra-    19
phy are key determinants of who is poor. Single-parent families and the unat-
tached elderly experience the highest levels of unemployment. Children
accounted for one-quarter of all the poor in Canada (Canadian Parliament,
1991; Economic Council of Canada, 1992; Statistics Canada, 1993a, 1993b).

- *Age and gender.* One-income families had an average income of less than    20
  half that of double-income families. Young families have the lowest
  incomes of Canadians—55.5 percent of young families have low incomes,
  compared with an average of 36.9 percent for all families. A lower proportion (46 percent) of those 70 years of age or more have low incomes
  (Information Canada, 1994; *Canada Yearbook,* 1994, p. 217). Low
  income is characteristic of certain categories of family status: 47.6 percent
  of lone-parent families headed by a female, compared with 16 percent for
  those headed by a male. Married couples with children or other relatives
  in the household have only 17 percent of the incidence of low incomes
  (Information Canada, 1994; *Canada Yearbook,* 1994, p. 218).
- *Marital status.* Single-parent families were virtually the only group that    21
  experienced no real growth in income. One-earner families had an average income of less than half.
- *Education.* The lowest poverty rates are found in families headed by hold-    22
  ers of university degrees. The poverty rate was 6.8 percent for family
  heads with university degrees but 18.3 percent for family heads with eight
  years of school (National Council of Welfare, 1994).
- *Geography.* Percentages of persons living in poverty in 1990 varied from    23
  region to region. The lowest rates were in Prince Edward Island with 10.3
  percent and Ontario with 10.9 percent, while Newfoundland with 15.8
  percent and Quebec with 16.2 percent had the highest rates nationally.
  Differences within regions of various provinces were even greater, with
  noticeable disparities across the North. These areas are particularly susceptible to cyclical shift because of their dependence on single industries.
- *Ethnicity.* Canadians of European, and particularly Anglo-Saxon, back-    24
  grounds tended to earn several thousand dollars more than other groups.
  Many new Canadian immigrant groups, however, had incomes well above
  the mean.

## POVERTY AND "STRUCTURAL ADJUSTMENT"

Our statistics illustrate that poverty is hardly random. In the 1990s Canada 25 has experienced what many believe to be a global phenomenon: structural adjustment. Structural adjustment means that there are changes in where and how goods and services are made and produced. In general, the twin process- es of technological replacement of labour and shifting of labour from com- paratively high-cost areas (such as Canada) to low-cost areas (such as the Third World) are taking place.

The impacts of such shifts in developed countries like Canada in the 26 early 1990s have been recessionary. This has had twin effects. First, the demands on social and educational programs have increased while resources have diminished. Government programs, such as transfer payments, have been reduced. Second, the "adjustments" do not hit everyone equally. Job losses in manufacturing, mining, and agriculture are borne by particular groups and social classes and sectors. People are either outright unemployed or transferred to where they are underemployed. This makes the so-called "high-risk" groups—youths, single mothers, the uneducated—more vulnera- ble. The process is not random (Gaskell 1985).

## THE FEMINIZATION OF POVERTY

In the last two decades, the feminization of poverty has become a focus of 27 much research (Boyd, 1982; Connell, 1987; Connell, 1992; Eichler, 1986; Scott, 1954; Sidel, 1987). As family forms change, women are especially affect- ed by poverty in a variety of quantitative and qualitative ways. The large number of single mothers with children under 18 (58.4 percent in 1992) means that many women are left to raise children on their own (National Council of Welfare, 1994). This not only leaves them with the expenses of child-rearing, but often limits their own ability to work. While female status in itself tends to be a factor in income distribution, other factors of social class (education levels, social prestige) further limit options to women. Women—particularly working-class women—are further burdened by a double standard: they are expected to carry out both paid work and domestic responsibilities.

Women are also burdened by a variety of other related economic factors. 28 Particularly, there have been, and remain, income gaps between women and men. Jane Gaskell (1984, 1985) argues forcefully that these gaps are not attributable to "skill levels," but result instead from the ability of male- dominated trades to unionize, to restrict access to certification, and in general, to bargain for better conditions. Pat Connelly (1978) shows how, historically, women in Canada have also suffered by functioning as "reserve" labour, which Connelly typifies by the slogan "last hired, first fired." In the past decade, Canadian women have been entering the workforce in greater and greater numbers: today, 60 percent of women are in the workforce (Statistics Canada, 1993). In addition, women make up over one-half of those enrolled in post-secondary institutions: in 1992, women accounted for 54 percent of full-time college enrollments and 52 percent of university enrollments (Statistics Canada, 1993). However, women still tend to work in lower-paying jobs, just as they tend to be grouped into humanities, education, nursing, and other "traditional" areas in the post-secondary stream.

The second related consequence of the feminization of poverty is the increase in youth poverty: children of poor women cannot easily escape the cycle of poverty. Over half of Canada's youth living in independent circumstances qualify as living below the poverty line. (This statistic may, however, be a bit misleading, in that youth have the least access to jobs, are at the beginning of their careers, and are often in educational institutions or going through transitional phases in their lives.) Again, family situation plays no small part in this phenomenon. MacLeod and Homer's (1980) analysis suggests that families improve their economic chances if they remain united and both parents work. Double-income families are in fact a major stratifying variable on available income in Canada. The corollary is that single-income families undergo a decline in comparative income levels. [29]

MacLeod and Homer also found that gains/losses in family income are influenced by the socioeconomic status of the parents. White-collar women benefit the most, in both percentages and absolute terms, from participation in the labour force, compared with their blue-collar counterparts. What all this means is that single, blue-collar women and their children bear a very heavy load in terms of poverty. The feminization of poverty is not only a "women's" issue, it is also very much an issue of marital status, occupational structures, pay rates, and social-class background. The biggest losers in this equation are the children of poor, single women. [30]

## SCHOOLING, SOCIAL CLASS, AND THE QUALITATIVE DATA: NEW EXPLANATIONS

The period since the 1960s saw a greater understanding of the relationship of schools, school curriculum, and education to socioeconomic status and poverty. A variety of studies (Apple, 1982; Bourdieu & Passeron, 1977; Connell et al., 1982; McLaren 1986) have illustrated that schools vary in the way they relate to children of different class backgrounds, and how they represent a systematic preference for middle-class values, language, and views of the world. Bernstein (1977) forcefully argues that the middle-class language/values of schooling represent a "code," or a way of mapping, that is accepted and sanctioned even by those members of society who are excluded by the coding. Bernstein documents how the working class and the poor vary in the form of their language (the working class tend to use nouns or "universal codes"). Despite formal differences in language, values, and world views between middle and working classes, the content of the two speech forms is equivalent. This was radically important, since it meant that in valuing one form as "correct" and the other as unacceptable, education was not measuring differences in "intelligence" or ability, but differences in cultural norms. This work also suggested that the curricular practices of schools actually drove a wedge [31] between values practised in working-class homes and those practised in the school. Therefore it is on the basis of motivation (based partly on the co-operation of home and school) and access to varying degrees of difficulty of curricular material (based on evaluations of "ability" level) that schooling for working classes and middle classes varied.

This finding was noted in a variety of comparative empirical studies showing that forms of curriculum, testing, body regulation, level of material, and instructional techniques vary with the socioeconomic class being taught (Anyon, 1981; Connell et al., 1982). Working-class education tends to be rote learning, drill, and practice. Supervision is authoritarian and, as McLaren (1986) illustrates in his comprehensive study of under-class Portuguese youth in Toronto separate schools, the under-class face a rigid regime of both phys-ical and mental control that contrasts dramatically with their outside lives. 32

## HOW SCHOOLS FAIL THE POOR

We have noted that poverty tends to be structural and associated with various groups over time. Given the high expectation that schooling will attenuate poverty, it is reasonable to ask why education has not served the poor well. 33

Facile answers include variations on older moralist themes—i.e., viewing the poor as lazy, and the makers of their own destiny. Those who believe in genetic theories have their explanations, too (Hernstein, 1973; Jensen, 1973). But newer alternative explanations are evolving from empirical work within the micro level of schooling. Three notable examples of this newer work are studies by three Canadians: Jane Gaskell (1984, 1985), Alison Griffith (1984), and Ann Manicom (1981, 1984). 34

Manicom set out to examine how the teachers' work within classrooms related to the work of women, especially mothers within the home. Implicit was a second question: Why do teachers systematically report that they treat children equally when we know sociologically that outcomes of education are systematically skewed along class lines? 35

Manicom's empirical approach was to look at teachers' relations to stu-dents as "work processes" or material sets of practices. What she illustrated was that the work of teachers, especially in the elementary panels, was highly dependent on the implicit assumption that someone else (the mother at home) had already done some type of prior work. If a parent has done some prior work at home, such as instructing the child to draw or to "place paint brush-es only in similar coloured paint jars," then one can proceed to other more complex levels. If no one has given such instructions at home, the teacher must retard progress in order to reach this level. This is where the problem begins. Middle-class and better-educated parents tend to have the material cir-cumstances and time to undertake such activities. Poorer and single-parent families often do not. The material practices of middle-class parents tend to complement the work of teachers, while the demands for child care, employ-ment, and meeting basic needs of poorer mothers often conflict with the demands of the teachers. 36

In observing differences in "who can draw"—to continue the analogy—    37
the teacher is really seeing differences in experience with drawing and not in
innate talent or ability. Nonetheless, it is extremely easy for teachers (because
of their own work demands) to view such differences not as experience differences (needing a few extra lessons), but as ability differences. What is
insidious about such a judgement is that it quickly leads to tracking and
stratification based on explicit or tacit labelling procedures. Children's access
to knowledge therefore becomes limited.

Manicom's work complements Bernstein's early research on how the    38
middle-class bias of language in schools effectively forced poorer and working-class children to operate in a foreign environment. Empirically, we know
that poorer children are highly streamed in the school stricture (Harris, 1989;
Oakes, 1985). The result is that in 1985, one-third of children dropped out
before finishing high school (Radwanski, 1987). In so-called general streams,
where many of the poor are assigned, the dropout rate is two-thirds, and the
real task of teaching is what might loosely be called "crowd control"
(Jackson, 1968).

One significance of Manicom's work is that it illustrates that the evaluation    39
and sifting taking place in tracking is not, as is often alleged, based on "natural" variation, but is instead based on a systematic reading of behaviour that has
meaning according to the teacher's and the school's own special mandates.
The processes and evaluations of schooling form, as well as mirror, results.

Manicom's work meshes nicely with the work of Griffith (1984), who    40
empirically studied how the idea of "single parent" was treated by school systems in Vancouver and Toronto. In her study, educators claimed that the term
"single parent" was used by schools only nominally. There were indications
that no evaluation was placed on it, and that it was merely descriptive. When
Griffith examined official records and files, a variety of patterns emerged
that led her to question whether or not the use of such terms was strictly nominal. First, certain single parents were almost never referred to as such.
Widows, for instance, were seldom classified as "single parents." More
tellingly, "single parent" was used almost exclusively to describe possible
causes for school failure or delinquency. By contrast it was virtually never
used to explain school achievement, even though numerous such instances
could be cited. Sometimes the same parent would be listed in relation to a
troublesome child as "single parent" and not so with a child doing academi-
cally well. Files often cited single parenthood as the "cause" of a child's
problems; there were no testimonials of a child's doing well due to the excellent single parenting he or she was receiving at home.

Griffith found a further point of interest regarding this pattern. "Single    41
parent" was most often used in official records to describe middle-class mothers. Her analysis of the reasons for this parallelled the notion of Bernstein's
codes. "Code" in this instance means a set of implicit, institutionally understood terms of communication between formal agencies and workers, especially those described earlier as "para-professionals." "Single parent" as a key
term was nested within a hierarchy of value-judgement labels that could super-

sede less powerful ones. In the official records, one did not need to use the term "single parent" as a tacit way of signalling to other professionals "this one is trouble" if one had other, even more powerful, coding labels such as "working class," "poor," "Native," "disadvantaged," "visible minority," "special," or the like. Gender, Griffith argued, was a layer of social convention that worked inside of class and racial hierarchies. If one was poor, or from an under-class ethnic group (Native, Portuguese, etc.), key institutional labelling had been done. "Single parent" only came to the fore as a "blame-the-victim" strategy when gender (and single parenting) were the only aberrations from the social ideal—in this case, the unspoken belief/role/code that children should live in traditional two-parent families like those of 1950s American television.

A third useful empirical analysis of class and gender difference in school-   42
ing comes from Gaskell's work in British Columbia (1984, 1987). Her findings were consistent with data discussed earlier: that the kinds of curriculum knowledge given in schools varies greatly in pedagogical style, context, rigour, and relevance, and is based on social class, economic background, and gender. In being taught to use computers, for instance, academic-stream procedures were obsolete in actual applied business.

Gaskell also illustrated that few girls in such programs had romantic illu-   43
sions that their own training would yield them rewarding careers. The reason, Gaskell showed, why girls stayed with such programs despite the fact that they recognized them to be poor, was that they judged the programs to be comparatively more relevant to their own life expectations than other school choices. One-half of all women employed in British Columbia are office workers. Among working-class women, 75 percent are office workers whose salary levels tend to peak 10 years before those of their male counterparts.

## CONCLUSIONS

As we have seen, poverty tends to be structural, affecting women, children,   44
and those in particular situations—such as the elderly, single parents, minorities, or inhabitants of specific regions. Moreover, poverty is often the result of constructed social policies and situations, and not of moral failings.

We have also seen that since the 1960s, numerous policy actions and pro-   45
grams pointed at ending poverty have been initiated, usually as remedies for "cultural deprivation" or to overcome "disadvantages." Since most of these have not worked, a key question is whether they *could* work and, if so, how?

Manicom, Griffith, and Gaskell suggest that at least part of why schools   46
fail working-class children is that the labour practices of schools, the nature of the curriculum, the labelling and processing of children, and the differentiation of curriculum all make schooling less than relevant. Evaluations and differences are often not the result of "ability" or "cultural deprivation," but instead reflect differences in the amounts of time spent on particular tasks.

We know that programs for the disadvantaged (Connell et al., 1990,   47
1992) and head-start programs do help children. What they require is extensive labour and material commitment, which must attend to where the child

comes from and not solely where the teacher or school would like to take "other people's children." Few would argue with the principle that each child should have access to needed resources; however, in reality, poor children seldom have that access. One reason is that such activity requires very real time and money. Teaching a child to read means someone must sit with that child—be it a parent, a teacher, a helper, or another child—and someone must organize and finance this undertaking. Will it be done?

If history is a guide, the most probable answer is no, because costs are    48 real and those who are poor—women, children, and the marginal—are the least able to lobby for their own interests. Also, it is unlikely to happen because the reality of mass "people processing" is still too often undertaken for reasons of social control or in order to blame rather than to serve clients. What is needed is better support (day care, support, teachers, programs to get people involved with others, alternative curricula, and new evaluation techniques). All of this is costly, and governments give it low priority.

But the cost of ignoring such programs grows. Costs of all social pro-    49 grams escalate when one program fails to address a specific social need. But the potential of moving even a portion of Canada's poor youth to the mean income level would result in literally billions of dollars in increased national wealth and competitiveness. At an individual level, the impact is also great: material rewards and enhanced dignity.

What must be emphasized is that poverty is not a given or natural phe-    50 nomenon. It is constructed (and perpetuated) by things we do both socially and individually. It is easy to shift the blame for poverty. It is even easier (if it does not directly affect us) to ignore it. Yet to do so is to make us all less than we might be.

## REFERENCES

Anyon, J. (1981). Elementary schooling and distinctions of Class. *Interchange*, 12(2/3), 18–32.

Apple, M. (Ed.). (1982). *Cultural and economic reproduction in education.* Boston: Routledge and Kegan Paul.

Bernstein, B. (1972). *Class, codes and control.* (Vol. 3). London: Routledge and Kegan Paul.

Bernstein, B. (1977). Class and pedagogies: Visible and invisible. In J. Karabel & A. H. Halsey (Eds.). *Power and ideology in education.* New York: Oxford University Press.

Bernstein, B. (1982). Codes, modalities and the process of cultural reproduction. In, M. Apple (Ed.). *Cultural and economic reproduction in education.* London: Routledge and Kegan Paul.

Bourdieu, R, & Passeron, J. P. (1977). *Reproduction in education, society and culture.* Beverly Hills: Sage.

Boyd, M. (1982). Sex differences in the Canadian occupational attainment process. *Canadian Review of Sociology and Anthropology,* 19(1), 1–28. *Canada Yearbook.* (1994).

Canadian Parliament. (1991). *House of Commons Sub-committee on Poverty.* Ottawa: Queen's Printer.

Connell, R. W. (1987). *Gender and power.* Palo Alto: Stanford University Press.

Connell, R. W., Ashenden, D. J., Kessler, S., & Dowsett, G. W. (1982). *Making the difference: Schools, families, and social divisions.* Sydney: Allen and Unwin.

Connell, R. W., Ashenden, D. J., Kessler, S., & Dowsen, G. W. (1982). *Teachers' work.* Sydney: Allen and Unwin.

Connell, R. W., White, V., & Johnson, K. (1990). *Poverty, education and the disadvantaged schools program (D.S.P.).* Sydney: Department of Employment and Training at Macquarie University.

Connell, R. W., White, V., & Johnston, K. (1992). An experiment in justice: The disadvantaged schools program and the question of poverty, 1974–1990. *British Journal of Sociology of Education, 13*(4), 447–64.

Connelly, P. (1978). *Last hired, first fired: Women and the Canadian workforce.* Toronto: Women's Educational Press.

Economic Council of Canada. (1992). *The new face of poverty: Income security needs of Canadian families.* Ottawa: Ministry of Supply and Services Canada.

Eichler, M. (1986). *Families in Canada.* Toronto: OISE Press.

Etzioni, A. (1961). *Complex organizations: A sociological reader.* New York: Holt, Rinehart and Winston.

Etzioni, A. (1964). *Modern organizations.* Englewood Cliffs, NJ: Prentice-Hall.

Foucault, M. (1979). *Discipline and punishment.* New York: Vintage Books.

Gaskell, J. (1984). Gender and course choice: The orientations of male and female students. *Journal of Education, 166(1),* 89–102.

Gaskell, J. (1985). Course enrolment in the high school: The perspective of working class females. *Sociology of Education, 58*(1), 48–59.

Griffith, A. I. (1984). *Ideology, education and single-parent families: The normative ordering of families through schooling.* Ph.D. thesis. Toronto: OISE.

Grumet, M. (1985, March). *Other people's children.* Paper presented to OISE.

Haddow, R. (1993). *Poverty reform in Canada: State and class influences on policy making.* Kingston and Montreal: McGill-Queen's University Press.

Harris, P. (1989). *Child poverty, inequality, and social justice.* Melbourne: Brotherhood of St. Lawrence.

Hernstein, R. (1973). *IQ in the meritocracy.* Boston: Little, Brown.

Information Canada. (1994).

Jackson, P. (1968). *The practice of teaching.* New York: Teachers College Press.

Jencks, C., Bartlett, S., Corcoran, M., Crouse, J., Eaglesfield. D., Jackson, G., McClelland, K., Mueser, P., Olneck, M., Swartz, J., Ward, S., & Williams. J. (1979). *Who gets ahead?* New York: Basic Books.

Jencks, C., Smith. M., Acland, H., Bane, M. J., Cohen, D., Gintis. H., Heyns, G., & Stephan, M. (1972). *Inequality: A reassessment of the effect of family and schooling in America.* New York: Harper and Row.

Jenson, A. (1973). *Educability and group difference.* New York: Harper and Row.

McLaren, P. (1986). *Schooling as a ritual performance.* Boston: Routledge and Kegan Paul.

MacLeod, N., & Homer, K. (1980). *Analyzing post-war changes in the Canadian income distribution.* Winnipeg: Economic Council of Canada.

Manicom, A. (1981, *October). Reproduction of class: The relations between two work processes.* Paper presented to the Political Economy of Gender Relations in Education Symposium. Toronto: OISE.

Manicom, A. (1984). Feminist frameworks and teacher education. *Journal of Education, 166(1),* 77–87.

National Council of Welfare. (1994). *Poverty profile 1992.* Ottawa: National Council of Welfare.

Oakes, J. (1985). *Keeping track: How schools structure inequality.* New Haven: Yale University Press.

Platt, A. (1969). *The child savers.* Chicago: University of Chicago Press.

Porter, J. (1965). *The vertical mosaic: An analysis of social class and power in Canada.* Toronto: University of Toronto Press.

Porter, J., Porter, M., & Blishen, B. A. (1982). *Stations and callings: Making it through the school system.* Toronto: Methuen.

Radwanski, G. (1987). *Ontario study of the relevance of education and the issue of dropouts.* Toronto: Ministry of Education.

Scott, H. (1984). *Working your way to the bottom: The feminization of poverty.* London: Pandora Press.

Sidel, R. (1987). *Women and children last: The plight of poor women in affluent America.* New York: Penguin.

Statistics Canada. (1988). *Family incomes, census families.* Ottawa: Government Printing Services.

Statistics Canada. (1989). *Total income: Individuals.* Ottawa: Ministry of Regional Industrial Expansion and the Ministry for Science and Technology, in co-operation with Canadian Government Publishing Centre and Statistics Canada.

Statistics Canada. (1993). *Selected income data.* Ottawa: Statistics Canada.

■ ■ ■

## *Discussion and Writing Suggestions*

1. How could schools be reformed to address the needs of low-income students better, and help to break the cycle of poverty in Canada?

2. Olson reports Lloyd George's view that welfare is the "ransom" the rich pay for peace. What attitudes to poverty are implied in this word "ransom"? Do you agree with the implication that welfare ultimately

serves the rich more than the poor by perpetuating the status quo? Do the "workfare" reforms initiated in some Canadian provinces and American states offer any more promise of eradicating poverty?

3. Olson argues that the school curriculum is usually irrelevant to the needs and interests of children living in poverty. Is it more relevant to middle-class families?

## PERSPECTIVES ON DEALING WITH SCHOOL BULLIES

The following texts are drawn from sources produced for different purposes and a variety of audiences. Using them as your preliminary research base on the issue of school bullies, assess the merits and possible uses of each text for an essay in which you develop an argument about the issue. To do this, you will need not only to assess the scholarly merit of the sources but to consider the merits of the perspectives they articulate. You may want to use some of the sources drawn from the popular press mainly as clues for what to search for in scholarly databases.

## Bullying at School: A Canadian Perspective (scholarly article)

### ALICE CHARACH, DEBRA PEPLER, AND SUZANNE ZIEGLER

Children who terrorize others have been an element of school life for many 1 years. Such aggression in school-aged children has been the subject of wide research in Europe, but bullying in schools has been largely unexplored in North America. Scandinavian researchers have been investigating "mobbing" or bully/victim problems since the early 1970s.[1] More recently, educators and researchers in the United Kingdom have identified bullying as disturbingly common in British schools.[2]

Bullying is generally acknowledged to be a form of childhood aggression 2 imbedded in an ongoing relationship between a bully or bullies and a victim or victims. Olweus defines bullying as occurring when a person is "exposed,

---

[1] D. Olweus, *Aggression in Schools: Bullies and Whipping Boys* (Washington, DC: Hemisphere Publishing, 1978); D. Olweus, "Bully/Victim Problems Among School Children: Basic Facts and Effects of a School-based Intervention Program," in D. Pepler and K. H. Rubin (eds.) *The Development and Treatment of Childhood Aggression* (Hillsdale, NJ: Erlbaum, 1991), pp. 411–448; and E. Roland, "Bullying: Scandinavian Research Tradition," in D. Tattum and D. Lane (eds.) *Bullying in Schools* (London: Trentham Books, 1989).

[2] M. Boulton and K. Underwood, "Bully/Victim Problems Among Middle School Children," *British Journal of Educational Psychology* 62 (1992), pp. 73–87; and C. Yates and P. Smith, "Bullying in Two English Comprehensive Schools" in E. Roland and E. Munthe (eds.) *Bullying: An International Perspective* (London: David Fulton, 1989), pp. 22–34.

repeatedly and over time, to negative actions on the part of one or more persons."[3] Bullies appear intent on causing distress for their own gain or gratification, and the victim or victims are less powerful than the bully or bullies.[4] Bullying can be direct physical or verbal aggression, or indirect, such as threats and intimidation, exclusion or gossip.

Rates of bully-victim problems vary from country to country. In 1983, Olweus and his colleagues used an anonymous self-report survey to study bullying among students aged 8–16 in the Norwegian comprehensive school system. Fifteen per cent of students were involved in bully-victim problems more than once or twice a term: 7% identified themselves as bullies and 9% identified themselves as victims. Five per cent of students reported serious bullying, occurring weekly or more often, of these 2% were bullies and 3% were victims.[5]    3

In Great Britain, a survey of young adolescents using Olweus' self-report questionnaires, with minor changes to suit the British context, revealed higher rates of bullying. Among 234 secondary school students, ages 13 and 15 years, 12% of students indicated they were bullies, and 22% indicated they were victims more than once or twice a term.[6] Fourteen per cent of students reported serious bullying, of these 4% were bullies and 10% were victims. In a similar survey at three middle schools, 296 younger children, ages 8–9 and 11–12, reported similarly high rates of bully-victim problems. Seventeen per cent of students reported bullying others, and 21% of students reported being victimized, more than once or twice a term.[7] Ten per cent of students reported bullying, weekly or more often, nearly 4% as bullies and 6% as victims.    4

To date no one has published a similar survey of bullying among students in North American schools. Perry, Kusel and Perry[8] used a peer nomination scale to examine victimization among children in grades 3 to 6 (ages 8–12). In a survey of 165 students, 10% of children were reported to be severely victimized. Bully-victim problems are a major concern for educators because most bullying occurs on school grounds, rather than on the way to or from school.[9] In the Norwegian study, the prevalence of bullying on the schoolyard was inversely related to the number of teachers on yard duty. Students reported that teachers generally did little to stop bullying at school. The parents of both bullies and victims were generally unaware of bullying incidents at school and rarely discussed it with their children.[10]    5

---

[3] D. Olweus, "Bully/Victim Problems Among School Children," *op. cit.*, p. 413.

[4] V. E. Besag, *Bullies and Victims in Schools* (Milton Keynes, PA: Open University Press, 1989); and D. Olweus, *ibid.*

[5] D. Olweus, *ibid.*

[6] C. Yates and P. Smith, *op. cit.*

[7] M. Boulton and K. Underwood, *op. cit.*

[8] D. G. Perry, S. J. Kusel and L. C. Perry, "Victims of Peer Aggression," *Developmental Psychology* 24:6 (1988), pp. 807–814.

[9] D. Otweus, "Bully/Victim Problems," *op. cit.*

[10] *Ibid.*

Although the child's temperament and family environment are signifi-    6
cant factors in the personality development of individual bullies and victims,[11]
the school environment also plays a role. Stephenson and Smith compared
teacher attitudes in six schools where there were many bullying incidents
with teacher attitudes in six schools where there were few bullying incidents. Teachers in five of the six schools with few bully-victim problems consistently expressed the importance of preventing bullying. In schools with
high levels of bully-victim problems teachers expressed a wide variety of
opinions regarding what to do when students bully others.

In the late 1980s public concern arose in Toronto over the increasing vio-    7
lence seen in various communities. This coincided with the publication of
reports describing the Norwegian bully-victim intervention program that successfully reduced the incidence of self-reported bully-victim problems by 50%
over two years.[12] Educators at the City of Toronto Board of Education
responded by sponsoring the survey reported here. The purpose of the survey
was to investigate the extent of bully-victim problems within the City of
Toronto schools; to inquire about students' ideas, attitudes, and experiences
of bullying and victimization, and to gather information regarding parents'
and teachers' perceptions of bully-victim problems.

## THE SURVEY

## SETTING AND SUBJECTS

This study was conducted in schools in the City of Toronto. The population    8
of the city and of the schools is extremely diverse and heavily immigrant.
Twenty-two classrooms in 16 schools were selected to ensure students from
a wide variety of backgrounds were included in the study. The classrooms
ranged from junior kindergarten (JK) to grade 8 (ages 4–14). Six of the classrooms were for children with special needs. One day before distributing questionnaires, each classroom held a group discussion about bullying problems.
This ensured that all students understood the concept of bullying.

## SELF-REPORT QUESTIONNAIRES

Three anonymous self-report questionnaires were distributed, one to stu-    9
dents, one to school staff, and one to parents. The student questionnaire was
an English translation of the self-report questionnaire developed by Olweus
for use in schools in Scandinavia.[13] It was modified slightly for Canadian
expressions. Similar questionnaires were developed for parents and school
staff. All three surveys were distributed in May of the school year. The refer-

[11] D. Olweus, *Aggression in Schools, op. cit.*; P. Stephenson and D. Smith, "Bullying in the
Junior School," in D. Tattum and D. Lane (eds) *Bullying in Schools* (London: Trentham
Books, 1989); and V. E. Besag, *op. cit.*

[12] D. Olweus, "Bully/Victim Problems," *op. cit.*

[13] D. Olweus, "Questionnaire for Students: Junior," unpublished document, University of
Bergen, Norway, 1989.

ence period for the questionnaire was "since the beginning of the term," and indicated since mid-March, a time of approximately two months.

Six questions, not derived from the Norwegian questionnaire, were also  10
included in the survey: (1) Why do you think that some students bully other students? (2) Where does this happen? (3) What do you think students should do if they are bullied? (4) What do you think teachers can do to help? (5) What do you think parents can do to help? and (6) At your school, how often does it happen that children are bullied because of race?

The student self-report questionnaire was administered by teachers to  11
211 students, 106 females and 105 males in 14 classrooms from grades 4 to 8. Some grade 3 students were included if they were part of a split grade 3/4 classroom. The questionnaire was not suitable for students below grade 3.[14]

The staff survey was given to all teachers of the 22 classrooms involved  12
in the research, and to all the other staff members (teachers, administrators, lunchroom supervisors, caretakers) in the 16 schools. The response rate for staff members completing the questionnaires was 60% (372 staff).

The questionnaire for parents was translated into 16 languages and dis-  13
tributed to parents of the students in the 22 classrooms in the study. It was completed by 172 parents, a response rate of 38%.

## RESULTS AND DISCUSSION

### PREVALENCE OF BULLYING-VICTIM PROBLEMS

Bullying is a frequent occurrence according to students in Toronto: 49%  14
reported having been bullied at least once or twice during the term. Parents appeared to be less aware than students of bullying; only 32% indicated that their children had been bullied at least once or twice during the term. Twenty per cent of students reported being bullied more than once or twice during the term, and 14% of parents reported that their children experienced this level of more frequent bullying. Eight per cent of students reported being bullied regularly, weekly or more often. These rates are similar to rates of bullying in Great Britain.[15] They are approximately twice those reported by students in Norway.[16]

When asked whether they had bullied other students during the term,  15
61% of students indicated they had not bullied other students at all in the present term. Twenty-four per cent said they had done so only once or twice. The remaining 15% of students admitted to more frequent bullying. Only 2% of students admitted to a very high frequency of bullying (once a week or more). This figure, however, may be an underestimate: when asked whether they had bullied anyone in the last five school days, one-quarter of all students and one-third of the self-reported bullies acknowledged that they had done so.

[14] E. Roland, *op. cit.*

[15] C. Yates and P. Smith, *op. cit.*; and M. Boulton and K. Underwood, *op. cit.*

[16] D. Olweus, "Bully/Victim Problems," *op. cit.*

Corroborating evidence on the prevalence of bullying comes from reports    16
of the number of bullies per class. Thirty-eight per cent of students and 36%
of their teachers reported that there were at least three or four bullies in their
class. This represents at least one bully per ten students, suggesting that the
self-report rate of 15% of children involved in frequent bullying is not an
underestimate. Only 16% of students and 29% of teachers indicated that
there were no children in their class who had bullied during the term.

## AGE AND GENDER

The gender and age patterns in the Toronto data were similar to those in the    17
Norwegian and British surveys. The proportions of boys (20%) and girls
(21%) who reported being victimized were essentially the same; however,
three times as many boys (23%) as girls (8%) acknowledged bullying others
more than once or twice per term. Younger children (40% of 9-year-olds)
reported more victimization than did older children (8% of 13-year-olds and
5% of 14-year-olds). The 10-, 11-, and 12-year olds reported similar levels of
victimization (30%, 21% and 30%, respectively).

The highest proportion of children admitting to bullying was in grades 5    18
and 6, ages 11 to 12 years. When students, parents and staff were asked about
the relative ages of bullies and victims, they all indicated that bullies were
most often peers of the victim, the same age and in the same class or grade—
those children who spend the most time together.

## WHY CHILDREN BULLY

All students, and the subset of bullies, cited the desire to feel powerful (68%    19
and 59%) followed by a desire to be "cool" (65% and 56%) as the primary
motives for bullying. Staff and parents also cited the desire for power as the
primary reason for bullying (75% and 71%), but they differed from the students by indicating that bullies were motivated by low-self esteem (55%,
41% and 17%, respectively).

## FACTORS IN VICTIMIZATION

Race appeared to be a factor in victimization. Race-related bullying was    20
reported by 43% of students and 36% of the classroom teachers. Overall, one
in five students reported that race-related bullying happens often in their
school; one in two students from disadvantaged neighbourhoods reported
that race-related bullying happens often.

Compared to the other students, victims were more likely to describe    21
themselves as often alone at recess, often lonely at school, and feeling less
well-liked than others. In particular, students in self-contained classrooms for
children with special needs were more likely to report being victimized than
students in regular classes, 38% and 18%, respectively.

## HOW CHILDREN RESPOND TO BULLYING

The present study documents children's emotional responses and actions in     22
bullying situations. Children were asked how they felt watching bullying incidents, even if they themselves were not the victims. Sixty-one per cent reported feeling that bullying is very unpleasant. Twenty-nine per cent reported that
bullying is somewhat unpleasant and 10% expressed indifference to bullying.
The children who "did not feel much" were more likely to be bullies.

Forty-three per cent of children reported that they try to help when a     23
child is being bullied; 33% reported that they felt they should help but do not;
and 24% reported that bullying was none of their business. This pattern is
similar to that reported among British middle school students.[17] Thirty-two
per cent of the students said that peers frequently try to stop bullying incidents
at school, and 13% reported that peers intervene at least occasionally.

Taken together the data on children's feelings and actions in response to     24
seeing bullying indicate that a majority of students in grades 3 through 8 dislike bullying in their schools and want to help stop it. Only a third of the students (more often boys than girls) indicated they could join a bullying episode.

A major thrust of the Toronto survey was to collect information that     25
would help in customizing an intervention to address bullying and victimization in the schools. Students, school staff and parents were asked what students should do if bullied. With the exception of bullies, a majority of
respondents in all groups advised telling parents and teachers. Bullies were
more likely to suggest fighting back than were either victims or students who
were neither bullies nor victims. Victims' pattern of responses was also
unique. They were more likely to suggest doing nothing if bullied. These
responses suggest that any intervention designed to decrease bullying must
involve adults as well as children.

## THE ROLE OF ADULTS

When asked what teachers can do to help, a majority of each group of respon-     26
dents thought teachers should talk to students. About half of each group
thought a teacher should punish the bully. Students did not agree with school
staff that teachers should get bully and victim to talk with each other.
Students and school staff also suggested that parents talk to the students
about bullying and victimization.

From the above responses, it is clear that most students, parents and     27
school personnel see adults as having a major role to play in addressing bullying in schools. Yet when asked about where bullying occurs and what is
done to stop it, discrepancies appear between the perspectives of children and
adults. For example, students and parents differed on where they thought bullying occurred. Students reported that bullying happened at school in areas
that parents may assume are supervised, such as playgrounds, school hall-
ways, and classrooms.

[17] M. Boulton and K. Underwood, *op. cit.*

Parents and students both indicated that the playground was the most     28
common site for bullying; however, parents cited unsupervised routes on the
way to and from school more frequently than did children. Parents and school
staff were less aware of the bullying that happens in classrooms than were students. Apparently, adults assume that bullying seldom occurs where students
are supervised.

The majority of students who had been victimized had talked to their par-     29
ents and/or their teachers about it. Nevertheless, almost a third of the victims,
many of those who were most frequently bullied, reported that they had not
sought adult help. So even though teachers reported that many students come
to them for help, this apparently does not include some children who are at
highest risk. Many parents and teachers may be unaware that these particular children are being bullied. Boulton and Underwood, after interviewing victims, suggest that many victims do not report bullying incidents because they
fear retaliation by the bully.[18]

The frequency of adult intervention to stop bullying was also seen quite     30
differently by students and by teachers. Whereas nearly three-quarters of the
teachers reported that they usually intervene if they see bullying going on,
only one-quarter of the students reported that teachers typically intervene.
Such a discrepancy may arise because students see a greater number of incidents than teachers, thus accounting for their impression that teachers rarely
intervene. Craig and Pepler[19] observed aggressive children and socially competent children in schoolyards and found that teachers intervened in only 4%
of bullying incidents.

## THE ROLE OF CHILDREN

From the classroom group discussions about bullying, it was clear that younger     31
children, in kindergarten to grade 4, look to adults for protection from bullying. By grade 6, however, students generally feel that bullying cannot be
stopped. As children get older they retain the perception that adult intervention
is both infrequent and ineffective. They develop a more sophisticated understanding of antisocial behaviour as originating in early childhood experiences
in the family. In the classroom discussions, students in grades 5 and 6 openly
acknowledged that bullying is fun, and blamed victims for being "wimps,"
"nerds," "weak" and "afraid to fight back." By contrast, older students, in
grade 8 classrooms, described the bullies as troubled, and developed an image
of a bully as the product of a violent and neglectful home.

How a child's increased understanding of bullying might influence his or     32
her behaviour is not yet clear. The survey data reported here suggest that over
time students relinquish their attempts to stop bullying: One out of two students aged 9–12 reported trying to help children who were being bullied,

[18] *Ibid.*

[19] W. M. Craig and D. J. Pepler, "Contextual Factors in Bullying and Victimization," paper
presented at the Canadian Psychological Association Conference, Quebec City, June 1992.

while only three out of ten students aged 13–14 reported doing so. One important component of an intervention, therefore, is to develop children's understanding of bullying and victimization in conjunction with strategies they can use to curtail the problem.

## INTERVENTION: AN ECOLOGICAL APPROACH

Bullying is best understood using an ecological perspective. The behaviours of the bullies, victims and peers are interrelated and unfold within the wider system of the school. The aggression of bullies is inextricably linked to the passivity of victims in a context where adults are generally unaware of the extent of the problem, and other children are unsure about whether or how to get involved. In fact, students advise each other to avoid bullies and stay with friends. Thus, victims, who described themselves as lonely and socially isolated, may indeed be left alone to fend for themselves against overwhelming odds.    33

The attitudes of parents, teachers, and school administrators may inadvertently perpetuate bully/victim problems. Canadian schools exist within a cultural context where violent acts often go unacknowledged, victims are blamed for their own fates, and a curtain of silence is maintained. Societal attitudes toward bullying in schools are similar to those about racism, family violence and child abuse. There appears to be a lack of understanding about the extent and seriousness of the problem and a feeling that outsiders should not get involved.    34

Numerous interventions to address aggressive behaviour in children have been tried, most at the level of the individual child or family. Many of these have shown only partial success.[20] Interventions for aggressive behaviour problems include social skills, cognitive, and parent training programs, as well as experimental classrooms. Interventions designed to combat bully-victim problems in schools will need to address the complex issues at several different levels.    35

Olweus describes the optimal intervention as one that addresses bullying at the whole school, classroom, and individual levels. The intervention must be a collaborative effort of teachers and parents and students. The first step in the intervention process is the development of a school policy with clearly stated rules against bullying. Classroom discussions are also an essential feature. Such discussions serve to sensitize children to the problem, engage them in establishing rules and consequences for bullying, and in developing strategies for assist-    36

---

[20] For example, see J. D. Coie, M. Underwood, and J. E. Lochman, "Programmatic Intervention with Aggressive Children in the School Setting," in D. J. Pepler and K. H. Rubin (eds.) *The Development and Treatment of Childhood Aggression* (Hillsdale, NJ: Erlbaum, 1991), pp. 389–410; G. R. Patterson, D. Capaldi, and L. Bank, "An Early Starter Model for Predicting Delinquency," in D. J. Pepler and K. H. Rubin, *op. cit.*, pp. 139-168; and D. J. Pepler, G. King, and W. Byrd, "A Social-cognitively Based Social Skills Training Program for Aggressive Children," in D. J. Pepler and K. H. Rubin, *op. cit.*, pp. 361–379.

ing children who are victimized. The optimal intervention also includes increased adult supervision of playgrounds. These components were incorporated in the model intervention used in schools throughout Norway which significantly decreased the incidence of self-reported bully-victim problems.[21]

The current survey provides direction for further development of programs to address bully-victim problems. In particular, a whole school intervention should build on the students' desire for bullying to stop and their attempts to be helpful. Extra effort should be focused in grades 5 and 6 classrooms where students expressed attitudes blaming the victims. It is important to encourage children to continue their attempts to stop bullying and to give them strategies that will work in a context with adult support. Peers could be included by delegating positions of responsibility to "neutral" students. These students could help other children solve problems on the playground when teachers are not readily available. An example of this type of intervention is the Peacemakers program.[22]          37

In summary, the general findings in the Toronto survey match those in the British and Scandinavian survey, where the same anonymous self-report questionnaires were used: boys were more involved than girls, young children were more victimized than older ones, and bullying was more common in school than outside. Many teachers and parents were unaware of individual children's involvement and children reported that teachers infrequently intervened in bullying. The number of students involved in bully-victim problems in this Toronto survey, one in three students, was similar to rates in Great Britain, but higher than in Scandinavia. Bullying is common among Canadian school children. Interventions designed to address the hidden violence of bullying in the schools must be ecological in design and comprehensive in scope.          38

■ ■ ■

## *Pre-teens Consider It Cool to Bully Weaker Playmates (abstract)*

CHRIS HENDRY

Schoolyard bullies may actually be popular with their schoolmates. In examining 452 boys in Grades 4 through 6, researchers at Duke University found that approximately a third of the boys were popular when exhibiting anti-social behaviours. Peers, thinking schoolyard ruffians to be cool, anti-social and athletic, may actually contribute to the wayward students' negative behaviours: the bullies may then internalize a connection between violence,          1

---

[21] D. Olweus, "Bully/Victim Problems," *op. cit.*

[22] Tom Roderick, "Johnny Can Learn to Negotiate," *Educational Leadership* 45:4 (1988), pp. 86–90.

popularity and control. Though the antics of bullies might be socially beneficial in the short run, researchers are unsure about the effects of such behaviours in the long term. (C.H.)

## Teaching Children Peacekeeping to Avoid Violence in the Schools and in the World (speech)

HETTY ADAMS

We all share a common bond through the children in our lives. I am sure that    1
all of us hope that they may live their lives to the absolute fullest in a world
that is continually learning better ways to deal with the conflicts we face—
whether they be local or global.

My own experience has been primarily with young people in the school    2
system, although I am a member of the Federal Human Rights Tribunal, a
panel created by the Government of Canada to conduct inquiries to determine
whether the Canadian Human Rights Act has been contravened. The Tribunal
has jurisdiction over matters that come within the legislative authority of the
Parliament of Canada. It has quasi-judicial powers and the legal authority to
stop discriminatory practices. For enforcement purposes, a Tribunal order is
made an order of the Federal Court of Canada.

Most of the panel members have a background in law, but there are also    3
a few ordinary people, such as me. My nomination came as a result of my
work with mediation within our public school system and my strong personal commitment to peacemaking.

I consciously use the word commitment as opposed to involvement. To    4
understand the difference, I'd like you to think about a plate of bacon and
eggs. It's easy to appreciate that in creating the bacon and eggs, the hen was
simply involved while the pig was definitely committed. That's the level of
my commitment.

My commitment has its roots in a personal tragedy. My 14-year-old son    5
died five years ago while in school as a result of an act of aggression by
another student. In order to help myself cope with the loss, I decided to do
whatever I could to teach other children alternatives to violence within my
own world, which was a kindergarten classroom at the time.

My approach was to create a curriculum in peacemaking which I call    6
*Lessons in Living.* These are basically lessons to enlighten young people to
believe in themselves—to believe that they can be a powerful influence for
bringing about needed changes in our society and in the world at large.
Lessons in Living includes teaching such skills as co-operation, effective communication, tolerance, empathy, and conflict resolution, including mediation. I truly believe that if the youth can be empowered by a combination of

factual knowledge of the world situation while being convinced of their own ability to change that situation for the better, your jobs will be a lot easier.

I used to ask myself this question: If peace is what every government says  7
it seeks and it is the yearning of every heart, then why are we not teaching it and studying it in schools?

I believe that many educators have arrived at the conclusion that we  8
must now teach our children peacemaking skills. We recognized that we cannot change behaviour simply by creating behaviour codes, any more than a country can eliminate crime by creating more law. In both cases it would be much like hanging a poster of Einstein on your bedroom wall in the hope that this will make you brilliant.

The skills you have learned here over the past weeks should be a part of  9
our education. Why didn't we learn these skills in school?

Students in our schools today do not have to wait until they are adults to  10
realize that there are effective alternatives to violence. In my own school, every student receives Lessons in Living. We have students trained in mediation who handle most of the conflicts that occur between students. Our school is a safe and peaceful place, and as a result our students enjoy being there. As a principal, I feel that the first assurance I need to make to parents is that their children will feel safe in school, and then I know that learning will take place.

I am reading a book by Neil Postman about the current state of education  11
in America. He examines alternative strategies that we can use to instill our children with a sense of global citizenship. I'd like to share with you a fable that appears in this book. (I have shortened it just a bit.)

## A CLASSROOM FABLE

Once upon a time in the city of New York, civilized life very nearly came to  12
an end. The air and rivers were polluted, and no one could cleanse them. The schools were rundown and no one believed in them. Each day brought new hardships. Crime and strife, intolerance and disorder were to be found everywhere. The young fought the old. The poor fought the rich. The politicians fought with everyone.

When things came to the most desperate moment, the mayor declared a  13
state of emergency. Our city, he said, is under siege like the ancient cities of Troy and Jericho but our enemies are indifference, hatred and violence.

One of the mayor's aides, in order to prepare for his exodus from the city,  14
began to read Henry David Thoreau's *Walden*, which he had been told was a useful handbook on how to survive in the country. While reading the book he came upon this passage: Students should not play at life or study it merely while the community supports them at this expensive game, but earnestly live from beginning to end. The aide explained to the mayor that the students in the public schools who had heretofore been part of the general problem, with some imagination and a change of perspective might easily become part of the general solution.

But how can we use them? asked the mayor. What would happen to their    15
education if we did?

To this the aide replied, They will live their education in the process of    16
trying to save our city. As for their lessons, we have ample evidence that the
young do not exactly appreciate them and are now even turning against their
teachers and schools. The aide pointed out that the city was spending $1 mil-
lion a year merely replacing broken windows and nearly one-third of all students enrolled in the schools did not show up on any given day.

The Emergency Education Committee and the state at once made plans    17
to remove 400 000 students from their dreary classrooms and their even
drearier lessons so that their energy and talents might be used to repair their
desecrated city. When these plans became known to the teachers, they complained that their contract made no provision for such unusual procedures. To
this the aide replied, "It is not written in any holy book that an education
must occur in a small room with chairs in it." And so, the curriculum of the
public schools of New York became known as Operation Survival, and all the
children became part of it.

Here are some of the things they were obliged to do:    18

First, the students cleaned up their neighbourhoods. They swept and    19
painted, cleaned and tidied. They planted flowers and trees and even repaired
rundown buildings, starting with their own rundown schools. Some students
were given responsibility to assist in hospitals, some helped with the elderly.
They published a newspaper to include good news. They helped in day care
centres, in food banks, and in libraries. Students trained in mediation helped
ease the burden of the court system. They helped register voters, organized
seminars and lectures. The city began to come alive.

Amazingly, the students soon learned that while they did not receive an    20
education, they were able to create one.

They lived their lessons in social studies, geography and communication    21
and many other things that decent and proper people know about. It even
came to pass that the older people, who had regarded the young as unruly and
parasitic, came to respect them. There followed a revival of courtesy and a
decrease in crime. Now it would be foolish to deny that there were not some
problems attending this adventure. For instance, thousands of children who
would otherwise have known the principal rivers of Uruguay had to live out
their lives in ignorance of these facts. Hundreds of teachers felt that their
training had been wasted because they could not educate children unless it
were done in a classroom.

But the mayor promised that as soon as the emergency was over, every-    22
thing would return to normal. Meanwhile, everyone lived happily ever after.

The moral of this fable might be that a sense of responsibility for the    23
planet is born out of a sense of responsibility for one's own neighbourhood.
It is also important that we look at the things we are teaching young people
and that we begin to reexamine our priorities. We cannot afford to waste the
energy and potential idealism of the young. We need to continually look for
ways to encourage youthful participation in social reconstruction.

Last week when I was working with a group of five-year-olds in my  24
school, I told them that I would be coming here and that I would have an
opportunity to meet some adult peacekeepers who might find themselves in
situations of conflict and danger. I asked if they had any advice for you.
Some of the advice reflects that even at the age of five, children can be very
wise. I call this Words of Wisdom for Peacekeepers.

### WORDS OF WISDOM FOR PEACEKEEPERS
(from the Primary Students of William King Elementary School)

Make sure you don't make any deals so you won't join sides.
Be careful, because in a war, even the people on the good team could get hurt.
Run away and when the coast is clear, come out and help. If you can't run
fast, use a Jeep.
Always bring a guard with you.
Talk it out. They might listen if you are peaceful.
When a gun shoots, duck.
Give the job to somebody else.
Hide behind a rock or a tree or a haystack.
Watch out for swinging swords.
Don't bring guns into countries.
Plant flowers.
Keep up the good work.

## ALTERNATIVES TO VIOLENCE

I have often been accused of being an optimist. Although I realize that vio-  25
lence, civil strife, and even war may never be totally eliminated, I do believe
that we can make great strides towards that goal if we continue to teach both
young people and adults in positions of authority and power that there are
alternatives to violence.

To cynical people who say that we are wasting our time, I remind them  26
that, in our society, there are many things that we have been able to make
totally unacceptable. From drinking and driving to smoking in public places,
from slavery to segregation, we have made great progress. Why, then, can't
we make senseless acts of violence and ultimately war, universally shameful?

I realize that there are both opponents and proponents of the thesis that  27
humankind is naturally aggressive. Certainly man has a potential for violence
that cannot be denied—but human nature only makes war possible, it does
not make war inevitable.

Over the course of the past 4000 years of experimentation and repetition,  28
warmaking has become a habit. For our own survival, we now need to
unlearn this habit which we have taught ourselves.

In my optimism, I see this as being a hopeful time in human history—a  29
time of effective disarmament and a time of the adoption of humanitarianism
as a principle in world affairs. The majority of people in all parts of the
world spend their days in a spirit of fellowship and seek to avoid discord and
to diffuse confrontation.

I feel a deep sense of pride that Canada has a strong commitment to    30
peacekeeping and Canada's leadership in this role is incontestable. By its historic association with peacekeeping, Canada is universally recognized as a
prime mover in putting United Nations peacekeeping capacities on a more
solid footing.

The world community needs, more than ever before, skilled and disci-    31
plined peacekeepers—protectors of civilization.

When I think of peacekeepers, I think of men and women who dress like    32
soldiers, organize like soldiers, live like soldiers, and are often equipped like soldiers, but in terms of traditional images, they behave in an unsoldierly way: they
prefer compromise to conquest, and persuasion and prevention to punishment.

The example you set for our young people and the potential for creating    33
partnerships between military peacekeepers and non-military peacekeepers, no
matter how small or seemingly insignificant, is reason enough to be optimistic.

Recently, I was honoured to be chosen as this year's recipient of the    34
YMCA Peace Medal. The YMCA Statement on Peace says:

> Peace has many dimensions. It is not only a state of relationships among
> nations. We cannot expect to live in a world of peace if we are unable to live
> in peace with those close to us—even those who differ from us.

The responsibility for peace begins with each person, in relationships    35
with the family and friends, and extends to community life and national
activities. There are no simple recipes.

Because of my work in promoting the need for teaching our students    36
skills in peacemaking, I often get calls from parents and teachers who are
faced with a serious problem. Recently I got a call from a mother whose 13-
year-old son lay in a coma in the hospital after a senseless beating by some of
his peers. This boy was different from his classmates and for them this seemed
to be enough of a reason to beat him. This mother was looking for a quick fix
or a simple solution to the problems in her son's school. I had to tell her that
there is no easy answer. But there is a solution—one that takes time and commitment (there's that word again). That solution is for us to create a climate
in our schools where aggression of any kind is totally unacceptable.

Within my own school, and now on a broader scale, I work with stu-    37
dents, teachers, and parent groups to introduce them to the skills of peacemaking. As you know, some schools can be extremely intimidating with
gangs and bullies tyrannizing the playground.

In some ways, the world is like a big schoolyard where we often feel    38
powerless to stop fights or keep the bullies from hurting each other or innocent victims. With bullies in school, and possibly with global bullies as well,
we need to look at the underlying causes of insecurity and aggression.

Children today are saturated with violence—from games to television and    39
movies, to schoolyards, the streets, and homes. The sad part is that often we
don't recognize it. Because of this, children become desensitized to violence.
The average young person in North America watches 22 hours of television
per week. By high school graduation, a young person will have witnessed over

18 000 murders on TV. In an effort to balance this, I feel, therefore, that it is incumbent upon us to saturate these young people with more peaceful ways of living together.

If young people have become more violent in recent years, then unfortu- 40 nately this is our legacy to them. Children are born into a world not of their own making. We all recognize that children are not born with a compelling urge to hurt others, whether verbally or physically. This is a behaviour they learn.

But on the positive side, it is also possible to unlearn such behaviours, and 41 this is how I see my role as an educator.

In our mediation training, there is one activity that carries a strong mes- 42 sage in its predictable outcome. It's an activity where we break the students into three groups and send each of the groups off with a task. The first group is asked to make a list of the things children typically argue or fight about, and how they handle these conflicts. The second group does the same, but they look at the things adults argue or fight about. The third group deals with world leaders. When they finish this task and return to the group, we examine the commonalties among the three groups. Are there things that all three groups fight about? Are there ways in which all three groups handle their conflicts in the same manner? Inevitably, there are many commonalties. Sadly enough, when we ask the question, So, what have we learned about handling conflict from childhood, through adulthood and even to positions of world power? The answer is always a resounding, Nothing!

I think we would all agree that conflict is a normal, unavoidable part of 43 life. Human beings are continually involved in conflicts. However, our response to that conflict is what determines its outcome. We can either respond in a confrontational, adversarial way, or attempt to resolve conflict in a more positive, creative manner. The list from the third group of students often cites war as a common way that world leaders handle conflicts. Some of these leaders believe (and perhaps deserve credit for the intensity of their beliefs) that violence is the only way to stop violence.

Gwynne Dyer, author and narrator of the television series *War*, said: 44

> Some generation of mankind was eventually bound to face the task of abolishing war, because civilization was bound to endow us, sooner or later, with the power to destroy ourselves. We happen to be that generation though we did not ask for the honour and we do not feel ready for it. There is nobody wiser who will take responsibility and handle this problem for us. We have to do it ourselves.

I am not suggesting that we can dismiss a country's legitimate security 45 needs, but plainly, a military response forms only a small part of that security. A deeper level of security is assured if a network of valued relationships can be formed. A peaceful, relationship-building international approach is as much a national defence strategy as war, weapons, or confrontation.

Ordinary people, solving problems effectively, build the conflict-resolving 46 community, and conflict-resolving communities are the building blocks of a peaceful world.

Peacekeepers, both at a school level as well as an international level, 　47
need to reach beyond confrontation to remove the causes as well as the symptoms of violence and strife.

In teaching tolerance, anger management, and conflict resolution skills to 　48
young people, we are equipping them with the tools to do that. We are providing them with the attitudes, knowledge, and skills to become responsible,
fully-participating members of society. Tolerance, especially, is essential to the
realization of human rights and the achievement of peace.

Our classrooms are microcosms of the cultural diversity of the global 　49
economy. Cross-cultural understanding has become a primary requirement of
a healthy learning climate, in schools and around the world.

We have a quote by Lester B. Pearson in our school: 　50

> We are now emerging into an age when different civilizations will have to
> learn to live side by side in peaceful interchange, learning from each other,
> studying each other's history, ideals, arts and culture; mutually enriching
> each other's lives.

My guess is that much of that has been happening here over the past few 　51
weeks. I have written a book, *Peace in the Classroom,* in which I devote a
chapter to ideas for classroom activities to promote acceptance of differences. If we do not diligently address the problem of intolerance we are destined to live with stereotyping, prejudice, scapegoating, discrimination,
bullying, and segregation. We need to educate children and young people with
a sense of openness and comprehension toward other people, their diverse cultures and histories, and their fundamental, shared humanity.

I dream sometimes. I think it goes with the territory of being an optimist. 　52
I dream that one day, each school across this nation, and maybe even the
world, will have earned the right to proudly fly a flag from its flagpole declaring itself to be a peaceful school. What if, one day, every nation on this
planet could fly such a flag? Part of my vision would require that all people
inheriting or elected to positions of political power would be required to
have some formal training in mediation and negotiation.

The young people learning mediation skills in our school system will be 　53
entering society as adults well equipped with the tools needed to resolve conflict with a sense of fairness, patience, and compromise.

Earlier, I read to you some advice from five-year olds. Now I will read a 　54
letter from one of my 11-year-old students who is also a mediator.

Dear Peacekeepers:

> I am 11 years old and I am a mediator in my school.
>     Sometimes it is hard to be someone who helps out. People don't always
> listen, but when they do and we get through to them it's a wonderful feeling
> to know you helped someone.
>     What you are doing in the world is brave and awesome. You are doing a
> good job trying to stop people from making war. I wish there was not a need
> for peacekeepers but we all know that there are many things in the world that
> need to change first. Things like hunger and racism.

War seems so pointless. What does it prove? That one country is better at fighting than the other? If only the whole world could learn mediation.

My advice to you is to keep your eye on the goal of world peace. Thanks    55
for trying to make the world a better place for us. I wish you all the best in the future.

■ ■ ■

# School Killers Give Bad Name to Youth Outcasts (news story)

MARLENE HABIB

Since the days of leather-clad James Dean in *Rebel Without a Cause*, we've    1
questioned and demanded answers about youth alienation.

But while young outcasts in the 50s hopped on motorcycles and hid behind    2
their eyeglasses, the recent Taber, Alta., and Colorado school shootings have put the spotlight on the killing capabilities of today's taunted and teased victims.

Why these real-life deadly revenges of the "nerds," where kids get even    3
when they don't get help?

Rev. Dale Lang is the father of teen Jason Lang, who was killed    4
Wednesday when a 14-year-old "loner" fired a sawed-off rifle at W. R. Myers high school in Taber. The Anglican minister prayed for "this broken society."

Society, which includes families, schools and communities, has indeed    5
become fragmented, bullying researcher Ahmed Motiar said Friday.

"Twenty years ago we had a great set of networking taking place because    6
of the structure of the extended family," says Motiar, a former teacher of kids with behavioural problems and author of *Defanging a Bully*, a book that examines youths' response to injustice.

"Back then, even if a kid was alienated from others in their school, they    7
had a sizable number of kids in their extended family who wouldn't leave them out."

Emotional and social support was more readily available, making it less    8
likely they'd vent anger in an extreme way, says Motiar.

Most isolated youth don't do themselves or others harm. Many even    9
channel their loneliness into constructive outlets like art or music.

These days, however, more kids turn to computer, TV and video friends    10
for comfort, because mom and dad are working late or just squeezing in "quality time." They see images of pain and suffering in the media which can trigger deadly ideas in a sick mind.

Where, for instance, were the parents of the teen trenchcoat killers who    11
killed a dozen students and a teacher in Columbine, Colo., before turning their rifles on themselves?

Kids who are troubled and depressed don't realize the finality of death,    12
say experts.

Those with emotional problems who don't feel wanted are most likely to     13
take revenge on the communities and institutions that "wronged them," says
Thomas Fleming, a University of Windsor, Ont., professor who researches
serial mass murderers.

Fleming points to the recent school shootings, Marc Lepine who a decade     14
ago killed 14 women at the Montreal University where he had wanted to
study, and Ottawa's Pierre Lebrun who gunned down four former transit co-
workers before shooting himself.

"Often with a mass murderer, they've been kicked out of the 'in' group     15
and want to take others out of it," Fleming said on Global TV's *Bynon* talk
show Friday. "They're isolated individuals who feel they've been wronged
by others."

School cuts have harmed counselling programs, and kids fear being     16
labelled wimps so they don't turn to the counsellors who are available. In
schools and communities, families in need have to take a number and wait in
line for counselling.

"Our school has a psychologist but a lot of kids don't know that," says     17
Jasmine Khattab, a Grade 11 student at Harbord Collegiate in Toronto.
"You may have to wait a week and by that time it may be too late."

In this quick-fix society, no kid with simmering psychological issues     18
wants to wait, so their agony deepens—festering sometimes for years—before
they lash out, says Motiar.

"It's become a *me* society: I want it now, I'm going to get it, even if it's     19
not the right way."

Much of what goes on at school reflects family life, says Kim Zarzour, a     20
children's issues researcher.

That can be violence or physical abuse by the parents, or even just "inef-     21
fective" parenting, says Zarzour, author of *Battling the Schoolyard Bully*
(HarperCollins).

Some experts feel both the bullies and the kids they pick on likely devel-     22
oped insecure attachments to their parents during the first few years of life,
when a child's brain is "wired."

Outcasts raised with little guidance, few limits and without moral values     23
then see themselves in a war against others, says Motiar.

"When a child labels others as the enemies, he does not feel remorse for     24
undertaking a violent act."

That may also include harming "bystanders," like teachers, whom out-     25
casts view as accomplices to whoever did them harm, adds Motiar.

Motiar urges parents and teachers to nip bullying in the bud. Some     26
schools and boards have anti-violence programs. Activists are working on
ways to get kids out shooting hoops and playing street hockey, instead of getting only mental exercise from "mind-altering" computer images.

Basically, though, parents, teachers and the community have to show     27
kids they care, even if it means placing limits, says Motiar. He advocates spiritual teachings.

"Society wants to tell me I have absolute freedom; I say no. If you're going    28
to put somebody down and hurt them, that's the limit of my freedom."

Parents, caregivers and teachers should watch out for these warning signs    29
that kids may be bullies or victims:

Victims:
- A child is not his or her usually happy self.
- Shows sudden change in eating habits.
- Seems to have low self-esteem.
- Displays excessive shyness.
- Is very defensive. Denies there is any problem.
- Demonstrates increased anxiety.
- More withdrawn and quiet.
- Is vulnerable to peer pressure or influences.
- Tends to brood a lot.
- Comes home with damaged clothes, builds walls around himself or herself.
- School grades drop.
- Receives abrupt phone calls.
- Associates increasingly with younger kids.
- Doesn't want to go to school or develops sudden dislike for school.

Bullies:
- Becoming more aggressive towards siblings, parents, others.
- Changes his or her way of dressing.
- Becomes more secretive.
- Uses unusual greeting code or sign with "certain" friends.
- Exhibits low frustration tolerance.
- Leaves house immediately when "certain" friends call.
- Stays out late.
- Adopts an "I don't care" attitude.
- Loyalty to group friends takes priority over family members.
- Peer activities seem to dominate child's life.
- School grades may drop.
- Gets involved in fights.

Source: *Defanging a Bully*, by Ahmed Motiar (Education 2000).

■ ■ ■

## How to React? (magazine article)

JULIAN BELTRAME WITH KEN MacQUEEN
AND JOHN DeMONT

From the beginning, it was a story too incredible to believe. In November, a    1
gentle, sensitive boy, subjected to taunts and a vicious beating at the hands of
school thugs, reads out a story for his Grade 11 drama class. Titled *Twisted*,

it is a story of a boy "at the brink of insanity and sanity," who envisions blowing up his school. A couple of weeks later, the 16-year-old is arrested for uttering threats, kept in jail for more than a month, while the thugs who his parents claim beat him up go unpunished. Meanwhile, his 14-year-old brother is also arrested for issuing threats after being taunted on a school bus about his sibling. With little else known, the older brother becomes a cause célèbre. PEN Canada, the organization of writers, declares it is "shocked that a piece of fiction" has landed a teenager in jail. Adds the boy's lawyer, Frank Horn: "We're living in a scary world."

Last week, the world got a little less frightening for Canada's most cele-      2
brated anonymous author. Cornwall Justice of the Peace Basile Marchand released the youth, who cannot be identified, into the custody of his parents while he awaits trial. One condition of the release was that he steer clear of Tagwi Secondary School in Avonmore, a small town 15 km north of Cornwall where he has been registered since September. But the case that on its surface appeared to be an Orwellian overreaction by police and school officials got more complicated. There were also allegations that the youth graphically threatened three classmates after he wrote his now infamous short story. Insisted school-board trustee Art Buckland: "We were not going to bring in the police simply because of a dramatic monologue of fiction."

Even the boys' father concedes school officials were handed a terrible sit-      3
uation. He told *Maclean's* both his sons were receiving psychological treatment for anger management before the arrests. He described his sons as troubled teens who feel like outcasts. His eldest son, who he said had no friends in the new school, was subjected to taunts because of a slight speech impediment. In mid-November, he added, his son came home bloodied after being kicked and punched by a group of bullies. Both sons had spent almost a year in a foster home in 1987 after he was convicted of breaking his daughter's wrist, an incident he believes contributed to the Crown attorney's reluctance to release the boys to his custody. On the other hand, a police search of the home found no weapons or explosives. "I think [the school officials] were afraid if they made the wrong decision and this is that one-in-a-million case where something happens," the father said, "they're going to be on the hot seat."

The Avonmore incident clearly illustrates the damned-if-you-do,      4
damned-if-you-don't dilemma facing schools today. Following a spate of shootings in U.S. schools in the 1990s—culminating in the slaughter of 12 students and a teacher at Columbine high school in Colorado in April, 1999, and the killing of a youth in Taber, Alta., a week later—most schools in Canada adopted zero-tolerance policies towards violence. Noting that many students had exhibited warning signs of antisocial behaviour before striking out, the policies call for school officials to intervene at the first indication of trouble. "In today's world, we have to take every sign, every complaint, every issue seriously," says Michael Jordan, principal of Ottawa's Cairine Wilson high school, where last April a 15-year-old stabbed four classmates and a staff member. In some cases, in-school counselling may be sufficient.

In others, students can face suspension or the involvement of the police. "The bottom line in our school is if you hit somebody you're suspended," Jordan said. "No question."

Still, the record of zero-tolerance policies is sketchy at best. Violent incidents continue to mount, from the fatal stabbing of a 17-year-old student in Calgary last November to last month's incident in Collingwood, Ont., where a seven-year-old threatened two classmates with a knife. Invariably, school officials say they are left to defend their failure to anticipate violence, or, as in the case of Tagwi, fend off charges of overreaction. Doug Hadley, spokesman for the Halifax regional school board, recalls the ridicule directed at school authorities when a Halifax-area student was suspended last year for throwing snowballs. "We have 58 000 students and we have to balance the individual's rights with the overall rights of the students to learn in a safe environment," he said.

The problem with zero-tolerance policies is not the intent but the execution, says York University psychologist Debra Pepler. Often communities lack the resources to counsel troubled students who exhibit antisocial behaviour. And in most cases, she adds, authorities fail to detect the underlying cause of school violence—the bullying and teasing that drives victims to lash out against their tormentors. "Bullying is a serious problem in every school and the tragedy is that victims feel they have no place to turn," says Pepler. "In most cases, they're right, because if they report it, they can be subjected to more bullying."

Dawn-Marie Wesley felt that way. But instead of striking back, she chose an extreme and tragic response. In November, the Grade 9 student at Mission Secondary School in Vancouver wrote her parents a short note, then hanged herself. "If I try to get help, it will get worse," she wrote. "They are always looking for a new person to beat up and they are the toughest girls." She was not alone in believing suicide was preferable to continued victimization. A British Columbia study of 15 teenage suicides in 1997 and 1998 found that five had been victims of bullying. Pepler, director of the LaMarsh Centre for Research on Violence and Conflict Resolution, says her study of about 200 students in schoolyard situations found that teachers detect and halt only about four per cent of bullying incidents. Yet adult intervention is critical, she says. "Children are incapable of solving the problem because it's about power, and each time a bully picks on someone, the bully's power is enforced," Pepler explained. "It's understandable when victims strike back."

Was the young author of *Twisted* near the breaking point? Horn says a trial will reveal his young client is guilty at most of an overactive imagination, and that allegations he made death threats will prove unfounded or exaggerated. "This is a typical kid," he said. "If they're going to put him in jail, there's a lot of other kids who will go to jail." Either way, the father vows to leave the community as soon as he can sell his home. He wants to move somewhere where his family will feel accepted, and his son can resume his passion for writing: "We need a fresh start."

# A Murder of Bullies, An Outrage of Writers (newspaper essay)

TIM WYNNE-JONES

There is nothing ironic in Pistol's avowal of affection for the noble Harry (in    1
*Henry V*) when he says: "I kiss his dirty shoe, and from my heartstring/I love
the lovely bully." In Shakespeare's England, a bully was a fine fellow, a
sweetheart, from the Dutch *boel*, meaning lover. It was only later that it
came to mean a blustering menacer, a swaggering coward. As a boy, I knew
a "sweetheart" or two, and on more than one occasion I found myself kiss-
ing a dirty sneaker.

There was the ruffian in Grade 3 who blacked my eye because I spoke    2
with an English accent. How was I supposed to know that in Canada,
"garage" didn't rhyme with "carriage," but with "barrage"? Which is what
I received for this dialectic gaffe, in the form of a knuckle sandwich.

Then there was Mr. Egbert, my Grade 4 principal who, enamoured of his    3
own large shadow, loved to loom. He did so over me one day while I stood
trembling beside my desk and stuttered my way through the alphabet while
simultaneously peeing my pants. We called him The Egg-Beater. Sometimes
words are all you have.

The kid in the next seat persecuted me for a month about that ignomin-    4
ious moment of incontinence. Bullying begets bullying.

Then, in Grade 7, there was Howie. Howie lived on my block. His father    5
was a brain surgeon. There were rumours that he practised procedures on his
son. Anyway, Howie was huge and he took to me in a big way, usually in the
park on the way home from school. He had a proclivity for pinning me down
with his knees and drooling great long strings of spittle on my face.

I wrote about this in the story *The Clark Beans Man*. In my fictional    6
account, the milquetoast narrator, Dwight, loves to memorize poetry. Talk
about asking for trouble! Howie just stayed Howie but in the story he got his
comeuppance. No, Dwight didn't suddenly develop superhuman, psychoki-
netic powers or befriend some carnivorous life form with a penchant for
white meat. Dwight finally overthrew his mountainous nemesis by reciting
Wordsworth at him in the voice of Donald Duck. Broke him up. Who can
resist Donald Duck?

*The Clark Beans Man* is a fantasy, like *Carrie* but without the prom    7
scene. By that, I mean joking a ruffian out of his nasty ways is probably about
as fantastical a solution as blowing him up. But Story helps. The story, at
least, gets resolved.

There is an anecdote about Steven Spielberg, when he was a kid, getting    8
a bully off his back by giving him a part in his next movie. Genius, however,
is not a commodity in wide supply amongst 12-year-olds; I would have happily settled for some muscle. But I was a back-of-the-comic-book weakling;
my biggest muscle was my mouth. You don't raise any welts with your
mouth, not when you are a kid, at least. When you escape from your pum-

melling and run off and there's a playground between you and Bluto and his bloodlust is sated for the moment, that's when you turn and let him have a salvo or two.

"I'll kill you!" you scream. "You just wait!" you warn. "You're on my hit list, Bluto!"     9

Like, Bluto thought I was serious?     10

But we're talking 30 to 40 BC, that is, 30 to 40 years Before Columbine. These days, who's to say that the little puke you've been terrorizing in the locker room isn't secretly building a hydrogen bomb in his basement? A bully had best think twice, which might be a stretch when thinking once was already a challenge. Best to go to the authorities. There are codes of behaviour. There are protocols to follow. No parent is likely to disagree with such intervention. We are all a little bit haunted. It's a disease. A pathology of fear perverts our better instincts.     11

And, anyway, it's supposed to work both ways, isn't it? The code of behaviour, the zero tolerance—that's in place for everyone, surely. Sadly, even in a school with a proactive, anti-violence initiative in place, there are those who fall through the cracks. Maybe they lack the confidence to come forward, or fear reprisal if they start naming names.     12

Maybe the words are hard to get out. Or maybe they just suspect that this is just how things are: You, down on the ground, with some swaggering menacer dribbling a Jackson Pollock on your face.     13

I have called this piece *A Murder of Bullies*. No one will suppose that I am proposing anything of the kind. I'm not about to get incarcerated over saying it. Context is everything. I am, after all, only alluding to the nomenclature of group identification, as in "a murder of crows." You could hardly call it a "gaggle" of bullies, or a "covey." How about a "pride"? Not likely. My guess is that the typical bully must suffer from debilitating self-esteem issues. He'll either get over it or develop it into a management style.     14

Because, let's face it, we don't leave bullydom behind when we leave school. The surly customs guard, the neighbour who won't return your child's ball, the meaty guy who accuses you of stealing his parking spot: The eyes spark, the fingers curl into a fist, the voice shifts into high gear *and this kid inside you is right back up against the school yard fence.*     15

A murder of bullies dominates the news: goons on skates turning the hockey arena into an abattoir; greedy and thuggish transnationals riding roughshod over our sovereign rights in the name of globalization; special-interest groups clamouring and complaining and holding democracy hostage. The kid stands on the other side of the playground, against the fence, watching all this, out of breath and nursing a scraped arm. "I'll kill you," he wants to scream. "You just wait. You are on my hit list, Bluto."     16

Instead, you put a comic spin on it, apply a patina of erudition, employ a vocabulary that has become over time your entire panoply, your armour and your sharpest weapon. You convince yourself that the pen is mightier than the sword. Bully for you.     17

■　■　■

# Dangerous Encounters:
## Violence in the Schools (case study)

BILL HOWE

### THE CASE OF LACOMBE HIGH SCHOOL

On the afternoon of October 10, 1995, after enduring "relentless teasing" and name-calling, a young 17-year-old student at Lacombe, High School, Alberta, finally retaliated. The article in the *Edmonton Journal* two days later explained how other students reported that he had been teased throughout Grade 10 the year before. He was considered different and students referred to him on various occasions as a tweek and a spaz. As one classmate commented, "Nobody liked him. . . He only had a couple of friends and they were geeks too." Others described the boy as a loner who mostly kept to himself. On the day of the incident, he clearly exploded, years of taunting welling up into a single act of physical aggression.                                                    1

Considering how common name-calling and teasing are in schools, several questions arise:                                                                     2

1. Is there such a thing as innocent teasing? At what point does name calling or teasing go too far? Are there legal grounds for action against those who tease others? Are there grounds for action under the Alberta School Act or other provinces' school legislation? Are physical reactions by the victim ever justified on grounds of self-defence?                                                      3

2. If the teasing escalates to physical contact or threats of violent actions on or off the school grounds, how do the consequences change?            4

The news reports explained how, on the afternoon of the incident, during the last block English 23 class, the harassment had "reached a peak." While the teacher had left the room for a few minutes, as many as six students took turns shooting spitballs. Apparently, after returning to the classroom, the teacher was unaware of what had taken place in his absence. When the bell rang, during the few chaotic moments of dismissal, the boy rose out of his desk, walked to the back of the class and approached one of the boys responsible for the taunting, and struck him in the stomach. Though at first, it was thought that he had merely punched him, moments later it was discovered that he had stabbed the boy with a 10-cm blade.                                  5

During the police investigation, the principal of the school offered some background to the incident. "He [the accused] expressed before a sense of being picked on and we obviously didn't teach him well how to deal with the pestering. One of the continuing battles we fight is to teach them all to get along with each other."                                                              6

An *Edmonton Journal* article on November 5, 1995 stated that the victim of the stabbing was released from a Red Deer hospital five days later, and returned to school the next week, "where some classmates greeted him as a returning hero."                                                                  7

The boy was charged and pleaded guilty to aggravated assault. His foster     8
parents planned to relocate to Calgary to give the boy a chance to start over
with a "new life."

Given the aftermath of the incident, questions of culpability are extreme-     9
ly complex.

3. Considering the facts so far in this incident, how would you go about     10
laying blame for the events of the afternoon? Assuming that each of the following parties that might have been implicated, explain what responsibility
you would assign to each on a scale of one to ten? Rank them in order of culpability (that is, blame).

- the accused who stabbed his provoker in the stomach     11
- the students involved in firing the spitballs
- the teacher in charge
- the bystanders: other students who watched but were not directly
  involved either at the time of this incident or throughout the years of
  teasing that preceded it
- the parents of the students involved in the relentless teasing
- the parents of the boy who stabbed the other in the stomach
- the principal in charge of the school
- the school board
- the province
- the structure of the education system
- society

4. Legally or judicially, it is unlikely that many of these parties will ever     12
be held responsible or be obligated to respond. Often there are certain parties
to a criminal action that are ignored or dismissed either because of the futil-
ity of enforcing expectations or the difficulty in naming them and dealing with
them personally? Morally, or philosophically, however, the incident suggests
a number of strong directives that might be aimed at such parties. From the
list above, or others that might have been missed, which individuals or groups
do you feel should be held responsible, but are likely never to be held accountable for the incident? Describe that responsibility. What message(s) would you
send to them?

5. Are there effective ways to deal with pestering? What could have been     13
or should have been taught to this boy that might have prevented the incident
from happening? What could have been taught to the others? Would students
be inclined to listen to such advice? What do you suggest might be an effective approach to the problem?

The article on November 5, 1995 explained the boy's history in more     14
detail. Apparently, at a very young age, the boy had been living with an alcoholic mother and may have suffered from fetal alcohol syndrome. As one of
the classmates at the Lacombe high school explained to reporters, "The cops
told us that when he was swimming in his mama, his mama was swimming in
a bottle. So he has some kind of disease."

Added to an already troubled childhood, at the age of nine, his mother    15
died after being stabbed 21 times by an ex-boyfriend in southeast Calgary.
The boy had no contact with his natural father and was subsequently placed
in the care of foster parents.

The article also quoted the mother of one of the boys who had shot the    16
spitballs: "Even if he was harassed or bullied, what he did wasn't justified by
that. Knowing some of the kids that were in there, I don't think it was meant
to hurt him emotionally."

During the first court appearance, the Crown prosecutor ". . .character-    17
ized the boy's violent outburst as a stress-related reaction and said that despite
the stabbing the boy posed little risk to the community."

This raises additional questions:    18

6. To what extent should an individual's background be taken into    19
account in the sentencing of young offenders? Is a prior history of teasing
enough to exonerate a student from a physical act of aggression? Is the history
disclosed in this case enough to exonerate the boy? Do you agree with the
statement made by the mother of one of the boys responsible for the teasing?
What if the stabbing victim had died?

## ADDITIONAL ACTIVITIES

1. Given the opportunity to legislate new laws or develop policies in the    20
area of schools and bullying, what guidelines would you suggest are necessary
to adequately deal with the problem?

2. Write a one-page journal entry from the point of view of someone    21
involved in the case as she or he might have responded to the events of the
afternoon:
   a. the mother of the perpetrator
   b. the mother of the victim
   c. the police officer who arrived at the scene
   d. the principal
   e. the teacher in the classroom
   f. one of the other students who watched the incident

3. Create a scene, which might take place in your own school, that    22
involves teasing or bullying. Make it as realistic as possible. In your skit,
demonstrate how you think the problem should be resolved if everyone
involved accepted their responsibilities.

# ADDITIONAL RESOURCES

## Articles

Barry, John, "Bullies—you can't beat 'em," in *The Edmonton Journal*,
    February 13, 1994.

McConnell, Rick. "Kids called loner 'tweek' and 'spaz' until he snapped," in *The Edmonton Journal,* October 12, 1995.

McConnell, Rick. "Out in the Cold," in *The Edmonton Journal,* November 5, 1995.

Gibbs, Nancy. "The Monsters Next Door: A Special Report on the Colorado School Massacre" in *Time Magazine* (May 3, 1999).

Hall, Vicki, "Taber Grieves for Lost Son" in *The Edmonton Journal,* April 30, 1999.

*Teasing and Bullying: Unacceptable Behaviour,* The Institute for Stuttering Treatment and Research, University of Alberta, Telephone 492-2619.

*Bullying—What You Can Do About It,* The Alberta Teachers' Association.

## Literature

"Long, Long After School"—Ernest Buckler / short story
"The Bully Asleep"—John Walsh / poem
"Zelda"—Emily Rodda / short story
"The Bully"—Gregory Clark / short story
"On the Bridge"—Todd Strasser / short story
"The School Yard Bully"—Peg Kehret / short story
"Along the Snake Fence Way"—Vicki Branden / short story

## Films

*The War*
*The War of the Buttons*

■ ■ ■

# *Violence in Schools: Strategies for Intervention (article from professional magazine)*

CAROL MARTIN AND JOANNE CLOSE

If we consider schools a microcosm of society, it is little wonder that its student members are, in increasing numbers, exhibiting the cost our society extols on its population. More children are born into poverty than in past generations, and the families of these children are more likely to stay poor. The high cost of living—basic expenses such as housing, clothes, food—necessitates that in many two-parent families both parents must work, some in difficult circumstances. The stresses that we face, with (one hopes) established coping patterns, are then passed to our children, children who have little in the way of strategies to help them deal with modern stressors. 1

Schools are witness to the effects these factors have on children. Brian    2
Morris is a Superintendent with the Toronto Catholic District School Board.
The board, with a student population of more than 100 000, serves the inner
city of Toronto as well as surrounding areas such as North York and
Scarborough. Its student population is as varied as the communities it serves,
and student behavioural problems, as in many boards across the country, are
a pressing problem in some schools. To combat this, says Morris, the board
has taken, at both elementary and secondary levels, a multipronged approach
to peace education and violence prevention that seems to be paying off.

The board's initiatives include the Second Step program, a preventative    3
program that is used by the teacher with all students in a class and a host of
proactive in-school campaigns managed by principals and staff. "For about
five or six years, many principals in our school system have been committed
to peace education, which has a number of components. The overall goal,
though, is to help students to develop the understandings and skills necessary
to handle anger and conflict appropriately. The principal and staff are what
make these programs successful."

As a part of peace education, selected students at the grades 5 to 7 level    4
are trained in conflict resolution. The students act as conflict managers in the
school yard, intervening in potential situations of conflict. The program has
been a great success in some schools, to the extent that it has withered because
of a lack of need. Morris contends that board initiatives, such as a "zero tolerance" policy, mean little without active support at the school and societal
levels. "The reality is that it's much easier to come up with a policy in a
boardroom than it is to work with it at an eye to eye level."

In recent years, what has particularly alarmed educators like Morris are    5
the behavioural issues exhibited by students as young as four or five years old.
"We've always had challenging kids at the intermediate level," he says. "Our
big concern now is children at the primary level. If you have a child that is
acting out at the kindergarten or grades 1–3 level, that's a concern. A lot of
effort in this board has gone to inservicing teachers on handling aggression."

Morris's group of schools is starting a pilot project aimed at reaching chil-    6
dren at the junior kindergarten level. A kindergarten teacher and a child care
worker will work with principals and teachers to assess junior-kindergarten
children throughout the Toronto east area. Ten students determined to have
potentially serious behavioural problems will be enrolled in the project in
January. After a year and a half, the students will enter regular grade one
classrooms in their home schools. There is a strong parent component to the
program. "Our experience has been that if you have a child who is acting out
all our best efforts will produce few results without some level of parent support and involvement," says Morris.

Morris's belief that a multifaceted approach is needed to combat negative    7
behaviour is echoed by Sandy McCaig, who is Director of Student Support
Services for Winnipeg School Division #1. Like the Toronto Catholic District
School Board, the board has in place a host of programs, including students
trained as conflict managers and peer mediators, a program called Developing

Capable People, which promotes positive self-esteem and sound decision-making, the Lion's Quest program, which helps students from kindergarten through grade 12 develop decision-making skills, crisis planning workshops that will be delivered on a board-wide basis, early intervention programs, bully proofing programs, and a program called Discipline with Dignity, which focuses on building a positive classroom environment. "Our major thrust," says McCaig, "is to create positive classrooms through prevention, and provide students with alternative ways to solve problems—many students don't know how to solve problems or they need to practise strategies."

McCaig, too, has witnessed a rise in serious behavioural problems in the early grades. "More students are being identified at a younger age, and emotional behaviours are on the increase. We are piloting the First Steps to Success program in kindergarten classes to help us identify students with behavioural issues. We put into place a program that involves the families. . . . We look at the classroom and the whole aspect of family and community."   8

While both boards are running early intervention programs and fostering positive attitudes in the class, neither board is ignoring the serious behavioural problems displayed by more senior students. The Toronto Catholic District School Board has in place a program for emotionally disturbed students that is supported by board psychologists, as well as social workers and psychiatrists, while the Winnipeg board is in its third year of running the Choices Youth Program for students at the grades 6 to 8 level. The pilot program, the only one of its kind in Canada, is aimed at the 15 percent of students who have been identified as at risk for behavioural problems.   9

The program is a joint effort among law enforcement, corrections, area schools, community groups, and parents. The goal of the program is to help at-risk students develop a positive self-image, become successful in their academic and personal lives, and become contributing members of society. While these goals may seem lofty, Winnipeg educators believe they are attainable when specific goals such as the following are achieved:   10

- less substance abuse,
- more academic success,
- fewer dropouts, decrease in delinquent behaviours, including those associated with gangs,
- improved social and life skills,
- increased social competency,
- increased communication among parents, the school, and the community.

The board's staff works with the police and justice department to develop a curriculum that will aid in the elimination of the behaviours. Police and probation officers teach the social skills curriculum, and work with the students in their class environment, providing instruction in topics such as conflict resolution, anger-management, coping-skills, positive family and peer relations, and academic success strategies. Other components include a wilderness component, which offers students the chance to enhance their self-efficacy by   11 participating in physically and emotionally challenging activities; a mentoring program where, for at least two hours each week, mentors help their partners deal with academic and social issues; a parent program that encourages parents to learn new skills with their children through activities designed to encourage interaction, facilitates the establishment of support networks, and includes individual home visits on a monthly basis; and, finally, follow-up clubs where students pursue a recreational activity of their choice and where existing community-based organizations provide time and resources so that students can practise their sport after school and on weekends.

McCaig reports that early results are promising. Students enrolled in the   12
program appear to be less likely to be involved in gang activities and are considered less at-risk than peers not involved in the program. "When we build
in all those factors [support from police and probation staff, community
involvement, mentoring aspect] we're more successful."

Both boards, then, have adopted an approach that treats violence in   13
schools on a variety of levels and with a variety of partners. Support for this
type of initiative is increasingly reflected in the community at large. Look, for
example, at policing practices which have moved, in many cities across
Canada and the U.S., to a more community-based level. What we finally
seem to have realized is that violence is a product of our society—to treat it
we have to draw on resources in that society, including fellow staff members,
our students, parents, trained professionals such as social workers and psychologists, police departments, and the community at large.

Among services available to schools in the Greater Toronto area is Lisa   14
Morden's Alternative Solutions. A behavioural consultant with 14 years of
experience, Morden works with a child's parents, caregivers, and teacher to
provide a consistent, constructive program aimed at curbing negative, sometimes violent behaviour.

Much of her training has come from working with deaf and/or blind stu-   15
dents at the four provincial schools—Ernest C. Drury, Robarts, Sir James
Whitney, and W. Ross Macdonald. In an effort to decrease the level and
amount of more disturbed behavioural problems evidenced by some of the
schools' children, Morden put into place a pilot program four years ago.
Rather than focusing on violent and/or non-compliant behaviour, she instituted a system that rewarded compliance. "It was outstanding what happened in the classroom. The kids were policing themselves—they were a
community—and the teacher could spend time on the curriculum."

The success of the pilot program strengthened Morden's belief that   16
a component of many behavioural problems may stem from the reward—
attention—a child receives for non-compliant behaviour. "Families, residential placements, and schools are busy places. These environments generally
operate under the assumption that children will cooperate and comply.
Compliance is an expectation that is not typically reinforced. We expect it,
but we do not reward it. Conversely, when a child is non-compliant, they will
undoubtedly receive a negative consequence. Most often, the non-compliant
child receives far more attention than the compliant child."

Given the limited amount of time many parents have to spend with their   17
children, Morden contends that non-compliant behaviour gets many children what they want, namely their parents' attention. By turning the tables on
what is rewarded in the home, parents can help to control emotional distur-
bances. The same rule holds true in classrooms where teachers can recognize
positive behaviour. "Sensitive good kids watch non-compliant kids get attention," says Morden, "and that is mortifying for them. In a way, we're teaching that if you want my attention this is what you have to do."

Morden now serves a client base that includes children who are deaf and   18
hard of hearing, children who have violent tendencies, multichallenged children, and children who have been diagnosed with disorders such as autism
and attention deficit hyperactivity disorder. She works with the family and
school staff to set up a behavioural program, and establishes effective modes
of communication to ensure that there is carry over between the home and
school. In addition, Morden presents workshops to parents and educators
that focus on curbing negative behaviour through simple, effective means—
promoting positive behaviours, setting limits, and being consistent—in and
out of the classroom.

■　■　■

# What a Seriously At-Risk Student Would Really Like to Say to Teachers About Classroom Management (scholarly article)

JULIA ELLIS

If we read the practices of teaching as the practices of culture, we can clearly   1
witness our culture's limitations when we examine the collective response of
schools and society to "difficult" students in our classrooms. In recent years,
alarm about youth violence in schools in Canada has escalated. We struggle
to understand the nature of this social problem and we search for helpful
ways to respond.

I began my own search for helpful ways to think about the situations of   2
"behaviourally difficult" children and youth after knowing troubled children
from disrupted families. Hearing their stories changed my story. Initially my
search led me to large-scale longitudinal research,[1] which had documented the
devastating and persistent effects of divorce on children. These studies concluded that children do better in households that are orderly and predictable and
which have regular bedtimes, less television, hobbies, and after-school activities.

---

[1] J. Guidibaldi, et al., "The Role of Selected Family Environment Factors in Children's Post-
divorce Adjustment" *Family Relations* 35 (1986); and J. S. Wallerstein and S. Blakeslee,
*Second Chances: Men, Women, and Children a Decade After Divorce* (New York: Ticknor
and Fields, 1989).

When writing about troubled children and youth it is common to comment     3
on the important functions of families. Galston[2] has observed that families are
best at instilling discipline, ambition, respect for the law, and regard for others
and that schools can't do it as well. Nightingale & Wolverton[3] have restated the
widely held understanding that students' self-esteem devolves from secure,
loving relationships and success at tasks. Where children have done well in spite
of apparently inadequate family support systems, many researchers have determined that such youngsters were naturally endowed with social competence,
problem-solving skills, autonomy and sense of purpose.[4]

In my search for understanding about the question of troubled children     4
I also encountered writers such as Lindquist & Molnar[5] who linked youth
violence to societal troubles such as poverty, disintegrating home environments, child abuse, violent culture, materialistic culture, and pressures to
achieve. Such critiques can show the way in which not only children, but parents themselves, can be victims of our culture. We need more critiques of this
kind to get beyond the commonsense ideology that parents simply need to be
more motivated or better educated to do their job properly.

I finally found a most adequate interpretive account of the situations of     5
troubled children and youth in the work of Brendtro and Long.[6] They begin
by acknowledging that children's troubles arise most basically from broken
social bonds between adults and children and that children who are securely
attached to adults do learn trust, competence, self-management, and pro-
social behaviour. They go on, however, to remind us that, in the past, extended families or tribes provided social bonds. Having lost our tribes, we now
rely on "a tiny nuclear family of one or two overstressed parents,"[7] to do the
whole job. Brendtro and Long remind us that when the adults' lives are
chaotic they can't manage their children's activities and affiliations. They
point out that schools are being asked to become the new tribes, and that if
they won't, prisons are the only alternative institutions for re-education.

In commenting on schools' responses to this new expectation, Brendtro     6
and Long acknowledge that although many schools do work to create safe,
inclusive environments for all students and to resocialize and reclaim troublesome students, other schools, which insist on "zero tolerance," further
estrange already alienated students through their emphasis on punishment

---

[2] W. A. Galston, "Putting Children First," *American Educator* 16:2 (Summer 1992), pp.
8–13.

[3] E. O. Nightingale and L. Wolverton, "Adolescent Rolelessness in Modern Society,"
*Teachers College Record,* Spring 1994, pp. 473–486.

[4] Northwest Regional Educational Laboratory, Fostering Resiliency in Kids: Protective
Factors in the Family, School, and Community (Portland, OR: NREL, 1991).

[5] B. Lindquist and A. Molnar, "Children Learn What They Live," *Educational Leadership,*
February 1995, pp. 50–51.

[6] L. Brendtro and N. Long, "Breaking the Cycle of Conflict," *Educational Leadership,*
February 1995, pp. 52–56.

[7] *Ibid.,* p. 53.

and exclusion. Students with difficult lives need the school to be a place of refuge for putting their lives back in balance. They could benefit from surrogate bonds with understanding teachers and other adults. Their behaviour, however, usually drives most adults away and as a last resort troubled students are often placed in specialized alternative programs, which may sometimes provide little more than a curriculum of control.

Brendtro and Long also gave an overview of promising approaches developed by people working with troubled children and youth. These are programs and practices that serve to fight delinquency rather than the delinquents themselves. They are characterized by a preventive public health approach and are growth-centred. There are different kinds of programs focusing on all age groups from early childhood to parenthood. Many entail collaborations among education, mental health, justice, social agencies and lots of volunteers. Brendtro and Long describe these approaches as belonging to a new reclaiming paradigm, which attempts to develop strength and resilience instead of simply trying to control deficit and deviance. These programs and practices attempt to work from an understanding of children's situations and to find ways to meet their developmental needs for attachment, achievement, autonomy, and altruism.     7

I began reading and learning about these programs and practices after talking with a 12-year-old at-risk student about his views on classroom management. He had been in some "trouble" on a number of occasions and was seen to be at risk of getting into more. I will call him Terry. I knew the family and Terry had known me for a long time. Terry had the job of keeping me company for an hour until his mother returned from an errand. Searching for a conversation topic, Terry asked me what I taught at university. I said that I taught classroom management to student teachers. He asked me what classroom management was and I said that it was "attention signals." He replied that he knew what those were and then proceeded to talk non-stop for an hour telling me all the things that I should tell student teachers. What Terry shared offered me a window into how he had made sense of the school system support for or response to his difficulties. I asked him to write down his ideas and offered to pay him for his work in doing so. He was very excited about the money and went directly to his computer and generated four double-spaced pages of text.     8

I have studied Terry's writing on the subject of classroom management. I have also shared it with a small group of graduate students who have a broad range of experience in schools. They were a valuable discussion group for exploring the meaning and significance of what Terry wrote. Stories often mean more than they can say.[8] To understand stories we must actively and creatively search for the meanings, purposes, and intentions behind the expressions.[9]     9

---

[8] D. P. McAdams, *The Stories We Live By: Personal Myths and the Making of the Self* (New York: William Morrow and Co., Inc., 1993).
[9] J. K. Smith, *After the Demise of Empiricism: The Problem of Judging Social and Educational Inquiry* (Norwood, NJ: Albex Publishing, 1993).

As a first response, all of us were surprised, in fact, quite taken aback, to   10
hear our institutional language coming back to us from the keyboard of a 12-
year-old. The writing was peppered with words and phrases like motivation,
self-esteem, hyperactive, starving for attention, broken glass theory, socialize,
large-class situations, bullies and class clowns. Some questioned whether the
boy actually knew or believed the ideas he was writing or whether he was
simply parroting back the lingo he had heard. Yet this is the language the
school has given him to think with. How could he so masterfully appropriate
the language and yet not use it to think about his own circumstances? And
how could he draw upon this language with such facility if it had not come to
hold some meaning for him? The language available to us both facilitates and
limits our understanding.[10]

What I heard most poignantly in Terry's writing were his pleas for attach-   11
ment and belonging. Terry made the following suggestion about how teachers should respond to problems in a child's life.

> If there are problems at home it is better to help yourself. [Otherwise] kids
> will probably be more unmotivated and less productive and it could scar
> them for life. Only when the problem is out of hand do you call a social
> worker. And make sure you never leave someone out. That will probably help
> the kid to a better life.

At first I was surprised to find this suggestion, since Terry wasn't known   12
for having great relationships with lots of his teachers. Perhaps this is Terry's
way of telling his teachers not to take his rebellion too seriously. He may also
be reminding us that whether the place is good or bad it is the child's "somewhere." To send a child alone to see the official stranger is to send him away
from his "somewhere" to a "nowhere."

In Terry's writing, he tells us in a number of ways that a positive con-   13
nection with the teacher and a positive inclusion in the class are very important to him. These are some of the suggestions he made that were related to
this theme. These were his comments about class clowns.

> When dealing with class clowns, either they are starving for attention or they
> are hyperactive. When they need attention let them read the answers to the class
> when they are correcting their papers. It could make a world of difference.

On the topic of bullies, he wrote:   14

> If the bully wants to be a leader, let him solve problems for you. Pretend he is
> the class president or vice-president and let him solve a bunch of problems. If
> the bully is unpopular, teach him that the best way to make friends is to be nice.

The following were his words about noticing and including kids posi-   15
tively in a large class.

---

[10] D. G. Smith, "Hermeneutic Inquiry: The Hermeneutic Imagination and the Pedagogic
Text," in E. C. Short (ed.) *Forms of Curriculum Inquiry* (New York: SUNY, 1991), pp.
187–209; and J.K. Smith, *op. cit.*

When kids are in a large class sometimes kids are left out . . . A kid thinks that the teacher never notices him so he can cause trouble. Other bad kids will be doing the same. That's where kids switch from good kids to bad kids and it can start around grade 3 or 4. You can even it out by . . . letting these kids take attendance down to the office. Everyone should be able to do it a couple of times, not just the good kids. Everyone counts. Calling kids bad or good could affect them, so be careful what you say and what other kids say.

Terry related the following classic solution for kids who fight with each   16
other.

When a kid does something bad, let's say hitting someone, sit down with the kids. Let one say what the other guy's problems are and what his are, and do the same for the other. If they're unwilling to solve their problem, tell them that if they don't solve it they will spend two days in the office and if they are friends they will be rewarded. And have each person say three nice things about each other and what they have in common. When punishing kids you kill their motivation and self-esteem. When you kill a kid's self-esteem he will probably stop working and either be a bully or a class clown.

In our graduate student discussion group, one of the members wondered   17
whether, through this story, Terry wasn't expressing his wish that someone might say something nice about him and, in spite of his school difficulties, recognize something they had in common. Although the topics of the above passages vary from class clowns, to fighting to large classes and bullies, the solutions are related thematically to connection with the teacher and positive inclusion in the class.

In his writing, Terry also asked that the school not be a factory where stu-   18
dents simply conform to the control and power of others. In his own way, he was asking that the adults in schools start with the students themselves rather than with a prepackaged program.

On the topic of calming kids down, he suggested:   19

Have the door open when the kids are coming in. Stand at the door and talk to the kids. Speak on their level and they will understand you and they'll stop making fun of you after school. Take a little time to talk about what they did last night or what they did during lunch hour.

On the topic of motivation, Terry wrote:   20

Lots of kids have a hard time getting motivated. When trying to get a kid motivated do not ask them what motivates them. You won't get an answer. You should ask what their hobbies are, do they like where they're sitting, can they see everything, is anyone bothering them, are there any problems at home, are they working on any projects, and what would they like to improve about themselves.

I think that in these two passages Terry is saying: "Start with me, start   21
with us, start with where we are. Really be with us." Be the "pedagogue who walks the child to school and learns what's on the child's mind." Be connected.

Be attached. Make this a "somewhere where we all belong and learn to be together in a satisfying way."

Terry also addressed achievement and autonomy by sharing some well known procedures for supporting students' academic growth and responsibility. By relating these procedures I think he was telling us that achievement and autonomy are important to him too.   22

Terry knows a lot about classroom management. He knows well that it's part of everything teachers do from greeting students, to daily routines, to planning instruction, to modifying homework assignments. Terry's a bit of an expert. He's run the gamut of school district-wide provisions for behaviour-problem students in a major city in Alberta. Terry knows what he'd like teachers to do. He and we also know that teachers can't do it all. We can't place tribe-making responsibilities entirely on the shoulders of every teacher in every classroom. As a culture, as a community, we have to stop blaming parents, stop blaming kids, and stop blaming teachers. Instead, we have to recognize what all kids need, how impossible it is for all parents to do it, and re-vision ways for all adults to more collectively care for all kids.   23

■ ■ ■

## ■ SYNTHESIS AND RESEARCH ACTIVITIES

1. This chapter covers topics as far afield as poverty, teachers as participants in oppressive systems, and physical abuse in residential schools. Although the authors do not make the connections explicitly, all of these topics can be seen as related aspects of the abuse of power in the school system. Using some of these readings as source material, write an essay from the perspective that all of these are symptomatic of a more general problem in the way schools work in and for our society.

2. The readings in this chapter are one-sided in the sense that they do not include the perspectives of educators, students, or parents who believe that many schools fulfill their mandates very well indeed by offering students an education that prepares them for post-secondary education and the workplace. Write an essay in which you critique the liberationist outlooks of some of the readings in this chapter. Develop the position that schools should be in the business of preparing students to succeed in society as it is, not of disturbing the status quo.

3. Research the issue of residential schools in more depth, including legal documents, scholarly articles and books that present the testimonies of former students. Write a research essay in which you try to account for the cruelties, both official and unofficial, of the residential school system.

4. Aboriginal Canadians are not the only people to have been colonized under British rule. Find research sources on the topic of the education of indigenous peoples in another part (or parts) of the former British

Empire: Africa, Asia, Australia, New Zealand, India, or the Caribbean. Write an essay in which you compare and contrast the Canadian residential school system to the systems of education established elsewhere under British colonial rule.

5. Some people argue that the residential school system was a product of its time, a time when schooling was not only racist but harsh in its treatment of all students. Investigate the validity of this claim by finding sources about the treatment of students in the Canadian public school system in the first part of the 20th century and comparing that system with the residential school system.

# 12

# The Brave New World of Biotechnology

What is biotechnology? Broadly speaking, biotechnology encompasses "all the studies and techniques that combine the ideas and needs of biology and medicine with engineering" (Grolier's *Academic American Encyclopedia*). In the public mind, however, biotechnology has mainly come to be associated with a range of controversial applications in the areas of genetic engineering, medicine, human genetics, crop and food production, and the forensic use of DNA. In this chapter, we will focus on some of these controversies—on the science behind them and on the ethical, social, political, and legal issues that make them important.

Genetics, the science of inherited characteristics, has figured in human history (in a rough and ready way) for thousands of years—in the breeding of domesticated plants and animals to obtain desired types. Formal scientific studies in genetics, however, date only from the experiments of the Austrian botanist Gregor Mendel (1822–1884). Mendel established some of the basic laws of inheritance by crossbreeding plants with certain characteristics and noting how those characteristics were distributed in subsequent generations. But the means for understanding the molecular basis of those laws was not developed until 1953, when James Watson, an American, and Francis Crick, a Briton, published a landmark article in the scientific journal *Nature* that first elucidated the molecular structure of DNA (deoxyribonucleic acid). It had been known for some time that DNA is the chemical compound forming the genetic material (chromosomes and genes) of all organisms, but understanding how DNA functions in the process of inheritance required knowledge of DNA's molecular structure. Watson and Crick showed that DNA has the structure of a double helix—that is, two interconnected helical strands.

Each of the two strands of the DNA molecule consists of a sugar-phosphate "backbone" and sequences of nucleotides, or bases, attached to the backbone. The bases pair up in specific ways to connect the two strands. In most organisms, DNA is present in all cells in the form of chromosomes gathered in the cell's nucleus. Genes are parts of chromosomes—that is, they are segments of DNA. Each gene is a sequence of bases that governs the production of a certain protein, so the sequence of bases that forms a gene can be viewed as a "code" for producing a protein; hence, the term *genetic code*. Acting separately and together, the proteins produced by the genes determine many of the organism's physical and behavioural characteristics, including the way in which the organism progresses through its life cycle. And because genes are passed along from one generation to the next, they are the basis for heredity.

Watson and Crick's discovery and the subsequent advances in genetics provided the foundation for genetic engineering, and the techniques developed for genetic engineering made possible the controversial applications in medicine, human genetics, and food production, that are the focus of this chapter.

Genetic engineering (a branch of biotechnology) is "the application of the knowledge obtained from genetic investigations to the solution of such problems as infertility, diseases, food production, waste disposal, and improvement of a species" (Grolier's *Academic American Encyclopedia*). Genetic engineering is also known as "gene splicing" and as "recombinant DNA technology" because it involves combining the DNA (that is, splicing together the genes) of different organisms. For example, a gene with a certain desired function (e.g., that of generating a particular antibody) could be taken from the cells of one person and inserted into the cells of a person lacking that gene, thus enabling the second person to produce the desired antibody.

In another kind of application, genes that generate desired products can be inserted into the DNA of bacteria or other types of cells that replicate rapidly. When the "engineered" cells replicate, they copy the foreign genes along with their own and generate the products specified by those genes. Populations of such cells can function as "factories" to produce large quantities of useful products.

> Career competition in the 21st century will be tough. The prizes will go only to those with the right combination of high-level physical and mental attributes. Why take a chance? You can guarantee that your unborn child will have what it takes to succeed in this demanding environment. Our highly trained medical staff stands ready to assist you in designing and executing a genetic profile for your offspring. Call today for an appointment with one of our counsellors.
>
> —GenePerfect, Inc.

The above ad hasn't appeared anywhere yet; but many people are afraid that something like this could result if the revolution in biotechnology continues, unchecked by ethical considerations.

The moral dilemmas now enveloping biotechnology would not be so hotly debated if the technology itself were not so remarkable—and effective. Thanks to its successes so far—in making possible, for instance, the cheap and plentiful production of such disease-fighting agents as insulin and interferon—numerous people have been able to live longer and healthier lives. Its promise in improved agricultural production is exciting. And even without considering the practical consequences, we have the prospect of a new world of knowledge about life itself and the essential components of our own humanity, our own individuality, as revealed in our distinctive genetic codes.

Gene splicing can be done by means of special enzymes ("restriction enzymes") that can split DNA from one organism into fragments that will combine with similarly formed fragments from another organism, thus forming a new DNA molecule. Copies of this new molecule can be obtained by inserting it into a host cell that replicates the molecule every time it divides, as

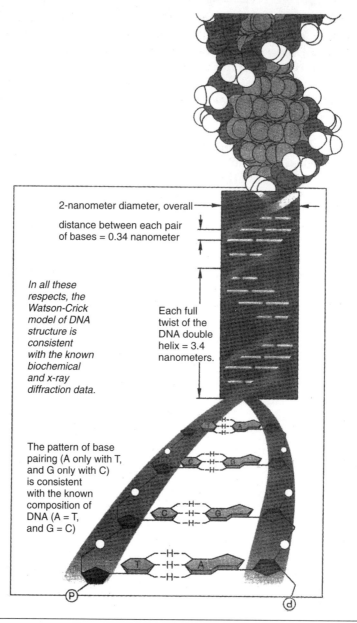

2-nanometer diameter, overall

distance between each pair
of bases = 0.34 nanometer

*In all these
respects, the
Watson-Crick
model of DNA
structure is
consistent
with the known
biochemical
and x-ray
diffraction data.*

Each full
twist of the
DNA double
helix = 3.4
nanometers.

The pattern of base
pairing (A only with T,
and G only with C)
is consistent
with the known
composition of
DNA (A = T,
and G = C)

The double helix structure of DNA (deoxyribonucleic acid). The "backbone" of each strand is composed of sugar-phosphate molecules. Nucleotide bases are attached to the backbones, and the two strands are linked by pairs of these bases. There are four different bases in DNA—the nucleotides adenine (A), cytosine (C), guanine (G), and thymine (T)—and they pair up in a highly restricted way: A pairs only with T, and C pairs only with G. Each unit of three successive base pairs (i.e., a "triplet") governs the production of an amino acid. Proteins are composed of amino acids. Thus, a gene is a sequence of triplets governing the production of a protein that consists of the amino acids specified by those triplets.

Cecie Starr & Ralph Taggart, *Biology: The Unity and Diversity of Life*, used later in chapter.

in the examples just described. In 1985, however, a more efficient method of gene splicing was developed, called *polymerase chain reaction* (PCR), done in a test tube rather than with living cells. PCR allows the double helix of the new DNA molecule to be split into its two complementary strands. When mixed with DNA polymerase from certain bacteria, the two strands function as templates for the generation of two copies of the new molecule. Thus PCR allows a repeated, rapid doubling in the number of desired molecules.

Gene splicing experiments began in the early 1970s, at first involving DNA exchanges between unicellular organisms, such as viruses and bacteria. But recipients of "foreign" DNA soon included more complex organisms, such as fruit flies and frogs (although no humans, at this stage). During this early period of experimentation, some began to worry about the possibility of a genetic disaster. What if some newly engineered microbes escaped from the lab and caused an epidemic of a new and unknown disease, for which there was no known cure? What if the delicate ecological balance of nature or the course of evolution were drastically affected? (Fears of DNA experimentation gone haywire were expertly—and thrillingly—exploited by Michael Crichton's novel [and Steven Spielberg's movie] *Jurassic Park*, in which a new race of rampaging dinosaurs is cloned from ancient DNA and spliced with frog DNA.) Some proposed an outright ban on genetic engineering experiments. At an international conference in Asilomar, California, in 1975, scientists agreed on a set of guidelines to govern future research.

In time, these early fears turned out to be groundless, and the restrictions were eased or lifted. Meantime, considerable strides were made in genetic engineering, with new applications discovered in agriculture, pollution control, and the fight against a host of diseases. Genetic engineering became big business, as many scientists abandoned the academy to found and work for firms with names such as Genentech and Genex.

But reservations persist. Some are uncomfortable with the fact of genetic engineering itself, considering it an unwarranted intrusion by human beings into the fragile structure of Nature, with too little knowledge or care about the consequences. Others have no philosophical objections to genetic engineering but worry about its effects on the environment and on humans. Or they worry about the kind of ethical problems raised by the new field of *genetic therapy*—the kind of problems suggested by the imaginary ad at the beginning of our introduction. Of course, this is an extreme example. Most people would have no problem with using genetic therapy to cure life-threatening diseases or conditions. For example, in a pioneering experiment in 1992, genes were injected into the blood cells of three infants lacking an enzyme whose absence prevented their bodies from fighting off potentially deadly viral and bacterial infections. Three years later, the infants' cells appeared to be producing the enzyme that is crucial to their survival.

There is little controversy over such forms of genetic therapy. But should genetic therapy be conducted to "correct" left-handedness? Nearsightedness? Baldness? Or even to *detect* such potential conditions? A recent survey for *Redbook* magazine revealed that while only 18 percent of respondents disapproved of *genetic testing* and manipulation to discover whether a child would have a disease or disability, an overwhelming 86 percent disapproved of using such a tool to select the sex of a child; 91 percent, to increase the child's IQ; and 94 percent, to improve the child's athletic ability. (Of course, such figures could change dramatically when the possibilities become real instead of abstract.)

There are other troubling aspects of biotechnology. Genetic testing may be used as a *screening* device by employers and insurance companies—in other words, it may be used as a means of genetic discrimination. Employers may be disinclined to hire prospective employees for whom genetic screening has revealed a present or potential health problem, such as heart disease. Since many genetic traits are linked to race or sex, genetic discrimination could be another form of racial or gender discrimination. Another area of concern is the *Human Genome Project*, a massive scientific undertaking begun in the late 1980s (and initially directed by James Watson) to determine the complete genetic makeup of human chromosomes. Armed with the knowledge of what each gene does and where it is located, scientists (it is feared) would be able to manipulate human cells to create individuals with qualities considered desirable, while eliminating qualities considered undesirable. For many, such possibilities bring to mind the notorious Nazi eugenics programs aimed at creating an Aryan "master" race and exterminating "inferior" races. And as the O. J. Simpson trial has dramatically demonstrated, there is controversy over the *forensic* use of DNA—the use of DNA testing in legal proceedings to determine guilt. While many suspects—and some convicted persons—have been exonerated as a result of DNA testing, some defence attorneys have contested the validity and reliability of DNA evidence when it is used by the prosecution.

For most, then, the problem is not so much biotechnology itself as its possible abuses. This chapter explores the controversies surrounding the application of genetic engineering in the areas of human health and agriculture. In our first readings, related to genetics and human biology, we begin with the opening chapter of Aldous Huxley's dystopian novel *Brave New World*, which for more than sixty years has served as an unforgettable warning of the dark side of scientific progress. Here we see human ova fertilized outside the womb, the embryos and fetuses conditioned and then decanted (born) from bottles, prepared to do specific jobs and to be contented and productive citizens in a stable society. Huxley's dark vision is followed by Cecie Starr and Ralph Taggart's "Recombinant DNA and Genetic Engineering," which explains the mechanics of genetic engineering as well as some of the ethical problems involved in its use. From here, we look at several largely supportive responses to genetic engineering. Canadian scientist Henry Friesen expounds the view that this work will improve life in Canada and the developing countries, and American scientist James D. Watson contends that it may lead to cures for devastating human illnesses, like cancer and Alzheimer's. Next, journalist Virginia Postrel defends genetic therapies from the libertarian perspective that the rights of individuals should come first. She argues that professional ethicists and government should stay out of the business of mandating which genetic therapies are socially acceptable. The needs of patients and the services of physicians and surgeons—that is, the free market—should determine which services, including cloning, should become available.

Other authors add a note of skepticism in reviewing the developing field of biogenetics. Jeremy Rifkin has long opposed rushing genetic technologies to market without first thoroughly debating their potential for helping—and hurting—the human race. In "The Ultimate Therapy: Commercial Eugenics on the Eve of the Biotech Century," he raises a cautionary flag about the profit motive in genetic research. In "Perfection, But at What Price?" Michael Valpy consults an international panel of medical researchers who comment on the areas of promise and danger in biogenetics. In "The Still Unread Book of Life," Margaret Munro warns that the genome draft may excite unrealistic expectations, and the author of the editorial "Blindly Into Biotechnological Era" treats biogenetic advances as a double-edged sword. Finally, Mark Nichols examines how cloning pigs may result in spare parts for organ transplants in humans.

On the subject of genetics and plant science, we begin with an article by Katharine Partridge that appeared in *Today's Parent* Magazine, "Splicy Food: Are You Unwittingly Eating Doctored Corn and Patented Tomatoes?" which looks at the availability of GM (genetically modified) foods and the costs associated with them. The last two authors take a more positive view of the GM food industry, with David T. Dennis defending the practices used in developing GM seed, crops and foods, and Barry Came examining some of the economic advantages for Canada of continued production.

## Brave New World

ALDOUS HUXLEY

*The title of Aldous Huxley's novel* Brave New World *(1932) derives from a line in Shakespeare's final comedy,* The Tempest. *Miranda is a young woman who has grown up on an enchanted island; her father is the only other human she has known. When she suddenly encounters people from the outside world (including a handsome young prince), she remarks, "O brave [wondrous] new world that has such people in it!" Shakespeare used the line ironically (the world of* The Tempest *is filled with knaves and fools); and almost three hundred years later, Huxley employed not only the language but also the irony in labelling his nightmare society of* A.F. *632 (After [Henry] Ford).*

*In comparison with other dystopias, like George Orwell's* 1984, *Huxley's brave new world of creature comforts seems, at first glance, a paradise. People are given whatever they need to keep happy: unlimited sex, tranquilizers, and soothing experiences. No one goes hungry; no one suffers either physical or spiritual pain. But the cost of such comfort is an almost total loss of individuality, creativity, and freedom. Uniformity and stability are exalted above all other virtues. The population is divided into castes, determined from before birth, with the more intelligent Alphas and Betas governing and managing the society, while the less intelligent Deltas, Gammas, and Epsilons work at the menial tasks. Epsilons are not unhappy with their lot in life because they have been conditioned to be content; and, in fact, they are incapable of conceiving anything better. Love, art, and science are suppressed for all castes because they lead to instability, and instability threatens happiness. Idle reflection is discouraged for the same reason; and, to avoid the effects of any intense emotions, positive or negative, the inhabitants of this brave new world are given regular doses of the powerful tranquilizer "soma."*

*Huxley's brave new world, then, is a projection into the future of tendencies he saw in his own world that he thought were disturbing or dangerous. In the context of our present chapter on biotechnology, we are most interested in Huxley's portrait of a "hatchery," where human ova are removed from the womb and fertilized, and where the embryos and fetuses grown in bottles are programmed before "birth" to produce an assortment of the kind of people who will be most desirable to society. In the following passage, the first chapter of* Brave New World, *we are taken on a tour through the Central London Hatchery and Conditioning Centre, where we follow an egg from fertilization through conditioning. To many people today, Huxley's dramatic portrait of the manipulation of human germ cells is uncomfortably close to what modern genetic engineers are beginning, with ever greater facility, to make possible: the substitution of "more desirable" for "less desirable" genes in order to create "better" people.*

*Born in Surrey, England, Aldous Huxley (1894–1963), grandson of naturalist T. H. Huxley, intended to pursue a medical career; but after being stricken with a corneal disease that left him almost blind, he turned to literature. Among his works are* Crome Yellow *(1921),* Antic Hay *(1923),* Point Counter Point *(1928), and* Eyeless in Gaza *(1936). Huxley moved to the United States in 1936, settling in California. In the latter part of his life, he tended toward the mystical and experimented with naturally occurring hallucinogenic drugs—the subject of his* Doors of Perception *(1954).*

A squat grey building of only thirty-four stories. Over the main entrance the   1
words, CENTRAL LONDON HATCHERY and CONDITIONING CENTRE, and, in a
shield, the World State's motto: COMMUNITY, IDENTITY, STABILITY.

The enormous room on the ground floor faced towards the north. Cold   2
for all the summer beyond the panes, for all the tropical heat of the room
itself, a harsh thin light glared through the windows, hungrily seeking some
draped lay figure, some pallid shape of academic gooseflesh, but finding only
the glass and nickel and bleakly shining porcelain of a laboratory. Wintriness
responded to wintriness. The overalls of the workers were white, their hands
gloved with a pale corpse-coloured rubber. The light was frozen, dead, a
ghost. Only from the yellow barrels of the microscopes did it borrow a certain
rich and living substance, lying along the polished tubes like butter, streak
after luscious streak in long recession down the work tables.

"And this," said the Director opening the door, "is the Fertilizing Room."   3

Bent over their instruments, three hundred Fertilizers were plunged, as  4
the Director of Hatcheries and Conditioning entered the room, in the scarcely breathing silence, the absent-minded, soliloquizing hum or whistle, of
absorbed concentration. A troop of newly arrived students, very young, pink
and callow, followed nervously, rather abjectly, at the Director's heels. Each
of them carried a notebook, in which, whenever the great man spoke, he desperately scribbled. Straight from the horse's mouth. It was a rare privilege.
The D.H.C. for Central London always made a point of personally conducting his new students round the various departments.

"Just to give you a general idea," he would explain to them. For of course  5
some sort of general idea they must have, if they were to do their work intel-
ligently—though as little of one, if they were to be good and happy members
of society, as possible. For particulars, as every one knows, make for virtue and
happiness; generalities are intellectually necessary evils. Not philosophers but
fret-sawyers and stamp collectors compose the backbone of society.

"To-morrow," he would add, smiling at them with a slightly menacing  6
geniality, "you'll be settling down to serious work. You won't have time for
generalities. Meanwhile . . ."

Meanwhile, it was a privilege. Straight from the horse's mouth into the  7
notebook. The boys scribbled like mad.

Tall and rather thin but upright, the Director advanced into the room. He  8
had a long chin and big, rather prominent teeth, just covered, when he was
not talking, by his full, floridly curved lips. Old, young? Thirty? Fifty? Fifty-
five? It was hard to say. And anyhow the question didn't arise; in this year of
stability, A.F. 632, it didn't occur to you to ask it.

"I shall begin at the beginning," said the D.H.C. and the more zealous  9
students recorded his intention in their notebooks: *Begin at the beginning.*
"These," he waved his hand, "are the incubators." And opening an insulat-
ed door he showed them racks upon racks of numbered test-tubes. "The
week's supply of ova. Kept," he explained, "at blood heat; whereas the male
gametes," and here he opened another door, "they have to be kept at thirty-
five instead of thirty-seven. Full blood heat sterilizes." Rams wrapped in
thermogene beget no lambs.

Still leaning against the incubators he gave them, while the pencils scurried  10
illegibly across the pages, a brief description of the modern fertilizing process;
spoke first, of course, of its surgical introduction—"the operation undergone
voluntarily for the good of Society, not to mention the fact that it carries a
bonus amounting to six months' salary"; continued with some account of the
technique for preserving the excised ovary alive and actively developing; passed
on to a consideration of optimum temperature, salinity, viscosity; referred to
the liquor in which the detached and ripened eggs were kept; and, leading his
charges to the work tables, actually showed them how this liquor was drawn
off from the test-tubes; how it was let out drop by drop onto the specially
warmed slides of the microscopes; the eggs which it contained were inspected
for abnormalities, counted and transferred to a porous receptacle; how (and he
now took them to watch the operation) this receptacle was immersed in a

warm bouillon containing free-swimming spermatozoa—at a minimum concentration of one hundred thousand per cubic centimetre, he insisted; and how, after ten minutes, the container was lifted out of the liquor and its contents re-examined; how, if any of the eggs remained unfertilized, it was again immersed, and, if necessary, yet again; how the fertilized ova went back to the incubators; where the Alphas and Betas remained until definitely bottled; while the Gammas, Deltas and Epsilons were brought out again, after only thirty-six hours, to undergo Bokanovsky's Process.

"Bokanovsky's Process," repeated the Director, and the students under-   11
lined the words in their little notebooks.

One egg, one embryo, one adult—normality. But a bokanovskified egg   12
will bud, will proliferate, will divide. From eight to ninety-six buds, and
every bud will grow into a perfectly formed embryo, and every embryo into
a full-sized adult. Making ninety-six human beings grow where only one
grew before. Progress.

"Essentially," the D.H.C. concluded, "bokanovskification consists of a   13
series of arrests of development. We check the normal growth and, paradoxically enough, the egg responds by budding."

*Responds by budding.* The pencils were busy.   14

He pointed. On a very slowly moving band a rack-full of test-tubes was   15
entering a large metal box, another rack-full was emerging. Machinery faintly purred. It took eight minutes for the tubes to go through, he told them.
Eight minutes of hard X-rays being about as much as an egg can stand. A few
died; of the rest, the least susceptible divided into two; most put out four
buds; some eight; all were returned to the incubators, where the buds began
to develop; then, after two days, were suddenly chilled, chilled and checked.
Two, four, eight, the buds in their turn budded; and having budded were
dosed almost to death with alcohol; consequently burgeoned again and
having budded—bud out of bud out of bud—were thereafter—further arrest
being generally fatal—left to develop in peace. By which time the original egg
was in a fair way to becoming anything from eight to ninety-six embryos—a
prodigious improvement, you will agree, on nature. Identical twins—but not
in piddling twos and threes as in the old viviparous days, when an egg would
sometimes accidentally divide; actually by dozens, by scores at a time.

"Scores," the Director repeated and flung out his arms, as though he were   16
distributing largesse. "Scores."

But one of the students was fool enough to ask where the advantage lay.   17

"My good boy!" The Director wheeled sharply round on him. "Can't   18
you see? Can't you see?" He raised a hand; his expression was solemn.
"Bokanovsky's Process is one of the major instruments of social stability!"

*Major instruments of social stability.*   19

Standard men and women; in uniform batches. The whole of a small fac-   20
tory staffed with the products of a single bokanovskified egg.

"Ninety-six identical twins working ninety-six identical machines!" The   21
voice was almost tremulous with enthusiasm. "You really know where you
are. For the first time in history." He quoted the planetary motto.

"Community, Identity, Stability." Grand words. "If we could bokanovskify indefinitely the whole problem would be solved."

Solved by standard Gammas, unvarying Deltas, uniform Epsilons. Millions   22
of identical twins. The principle of mass production at last applied to biology.

"But, alas," the Director shook his head, "we *can't* bokanovskify   23
indefinitely."

Ninety-six seemed to be the limit; seventy-two a good average. From the   24
same ovary and with gametes of the same male to manufacture as many batches of identical twins as possible—that was the best (sadly a second best) that they could do. And even that was difficult.

"For in nature it takes thirty years for two hundred eggs to reach matu-   25
rity. But our business is to stabilize the population at this moment, here and now. Dribbling out twins over a quarter of a century—what would be the use of that?"

Obviously, no use at all. But Podsnap's Technique had immensely accel-   26
erated the process of ripening. They could make sure of at least a hundred and fifty mature eggs within two years. Fertilize and bokanovskify—in other words, multiply by seventy-two—and you get an average of nearly eleven thousand brothers and sisters in a hundred and fifty batches of identical twins, all within two years of the same age.

"And in exceptional cases we can make one ovary yield us over fifteen   27
thousand adult individuals."

Beckoning to a fair-haired, ruddy young man who happened to be pass-   28
ing at the moment, "Mr. Foster," he called. The ruddy young man approached. "Can you tell us the record for a single ovary, Mr. Foster?"

"Sixteen thousand and twelve in this Centre," Mr. Foster replied without   29
hesitation. He spoke very quickly, had a vivacious blue eye, and took an evident pleasure in quoting figures. "Sixteen thousand and twelve; in one hundred and eighty-nine batches of identicals. But of course they've done much better," he rattled on, "in some of the tropical Centres. Singapore had often produced over sixteen thousand five hundred; and Mombasa has actually touched the seventeen thousand mark. But then they have unfair advantages. You should see the way a negro ovary responds to pituitary! It's quite astonishing, when you're used to working with European material. Still," he added, with a laugh (but the light of combat was in his eyes and the lift of his chin was challenging), "still, we mean to beat them if we can. I'm working on a wonderful Delta-Minus ovary at this moment. Only just eighteen months old. Over twelve thousand seven hundred children already, either decanted or in embryo. And still going strong. We'll beat them yet."

"That's the spirit I like!" cried the Director, and clapped Mr. Foster on   30
the shoulder. "Come along with us and give these boys the benefit of your expert knowledge."

Mr. Foster smiled modestly. "With pleasure." They went.   31

In the Bottling Room all was harmonious bustle and ordered activity.   32
Flaps of fresh sow's peritoneum ready cut to the proper size came shooting up in little lifts from the Organ Store in the sub-basement. Whizz and then,

click! the lift-hatches flew open; the bottle-liner had only to reach out a hand, take the flap, insert, smooth-down, and before the lined bottle had had time to travel out of reach along the endless band, whizz, click! another flap of peritoneum had shot up from the depths, ready to be slipped into yet another bottle, the next of that slow interminable procession on the band.

Next to the Liners stood the Matriculators. The procession advanced; one     33
by one the eggs were transferred from their test-tubes to the larger containers; deftly the peritoneal lining was slit, the morula dropped into place, the saline solution poured in . . . and already the bottle had passed, and it was the turn of the labellers. Heredity, date of fertilization, membership of Bokanovsky Group—details were transferred from test-tube to bottle. No longer anonymous, but named, identified, the procession marched slowly on; on through an opening in the wall, slowly on into the Social Predestination Room.

"Eighty-eight cubic metres of card-index," said Mr. Foster with relish, as     34
they entered.

"Containing *all* the relevant information," added the Director.              35

"Brought up to date every morning."                                          36

"And co-ordinated every afternoon."                                          37

"On the basis of which they make their calculations."                        38

"So many individuals, of such and such quality," said Mr. Foster.            39

"Distributed in such and such quantities."                                   40

"The optimum Decanting Rate at any given moment."                            41

"Unforeseen wastages promptly made good."                                    42

"Promptly," repeated Mr. Foster. "If you knew the amount of overtime          43
I had to put in after the last Japanese earthquake!" He laughed good-humouredly and shook his head.

"The Predestinators send in their figures to the Fertilizers."               44

"Who give them the embryos they ask for."                                    45

"And the bottles come in here to be predestinated in detail."                46

"After which they are sent down to the Embryo Store."                        47

"Where we now proceed ourselves."                                            48

And opening a door Mr. Foster led the way down a staircase into the          49
basement.

The temperature was still tropical. They descended into a thickening        50
twilight. Two doors and a passage with a double turn insured the cellar against any possible infiltration of the day.

"Embryos are like photograph film," said Mr. Foster waggishly, as he         51
pushed open the second door. "They can only stand red light."

And in effect the sultry darkness into which the students now followed      52
him was visible and crimson, like the darkness of closed eyes on a summer's afternoon. The bulging flanks of row on receding row and tier above tier of bottles glinted with innumerable rubies, and among the rubies moved the dim red spectres of men and women with purple eyes and all the symptoms of lupus. The hum and rattle of machinery faintly stirred the air.

"Give them a few figures, Mr. Foster," said the Director, who was tired      53
of talking.

Mr. Foster was only too happy to give them a few figures.                    54

Two hundred and twenty metres long, two hundred wide, ten high. He 55
pointed upwards. Like chickens drinking, the students lifted their eyes
towards the distant ceiling.

Three tiers of racks: ground floor level, first gallery, second gallery. 56

The spidery steel-work of gallery above gallery faded away in all direc- 57
tions into the dark. Near them three red ghosts were busily unloading demi-
johns from a moving staircase.

The escalator from the Social Predestination Room. 58

Each bottle could be placed on one of fifteen racks, each rack, though 59
you couldn't see it, was a conveyor travelling at the rate of thirty-three and a
third centimeters an hour. Two hundred and sixty-seven days at eight metres
a day. Two thousand one hundred and thirty-six metres in all. One circuit of
the cellar at ground level, one on the first gallery, half on the second, and on
the two hundred and sixty-seventh morning, daylight in the Decanting Room.
Independent existence—so called.

"But in the interval," Mr. Foster concluded, "we've managed to do a lot 60
to them. Oh, a very great deal." His laugh was knowing and triumphant.

"That's the spirit I like," said the Director once more. "Let's walk round. 61
You tell them everything, Mr. Foster."

Mr. Foster duly told them. 62

Told them of the growing embryo on its bed of peritoneum. Made them 63
taste the rich blood surrogate on which it fed. Explained why it had to be
stimulated with placentin and thyroxin. Told them of the *corpus luteum*
extract. Showed them the jets through which at every twelfth metre from zero
to 2040 it was automatically injected. Spoke of those gradually increasing
doses of pituitary administered during the final ninety-six metres of their
course. Described the artificial maternal circulation installed on every bottle
at Metre 112; showed them the reservoir of blood-surrogate, the centrifugal
pump that kept the liquid moving over the placenta and drove it through the
synthetic lung and waste-product filter. Referred to the embryo's troublesome
tendency to anaemia, to the massive doses of hog's stomach extract and fetal
foal's liver with which, in consequence, it had to be supplied.

Showed them the simple mechanism by means of which, during the last 64
two metres out of every eight, all the embryos were simultaneously shaken
into familiarity with movement. Hinted at the gravity of the so-called
"trauma of decanting," and enumerated the precautions taken to minimize,
by a suitable training of the bottled embryo, that dangerous shock. Told
them of the tests for sex carried out in the neighbourhood of metre 200.
Explained the system of labelling—a T for the males, a circle for the females
and for those who were destined to become freemartins a question mark,
black on a white ground.

"For of course," said Mr. Foster, "in the vast majority of cases, fertility 65
is merely a nuisance. One fertile ovary in twelve hundred—that would really
be quite sufficient for our purposes. But we want to have a good choice. And
of course one must always leave an enormous margin of safety. So we allow
as many as thirty per cent of the female embryos to develop normally. The
others get a dose of male sex-hormone every twenty-four metres for the rest

of the course. Result: they're decanted as freemartins—structurally quite normal ("except," he had to admit, "that they *do* have the slightest tendency to grow beards), but sterile. Guaranteed sterile. Which brings us at last," continued Mr. Foster, "out of the realm of mere slavish imitation of nature into the much more interesting world of human invention."

He rubbed his hands. For of course, they didn't content themselves with merely hatching out embryos: any cow could do that.    66

"We also predestine and condition. We decant our babies as socialized human beings, as Alphas or Epsilons, as future sewage workers or future . . ." He was going to say "future World controllers," but correcting himself, said "future Directors of Hatcheries," instead.    67

The D.H.C. acknowledged the compliment with a smile.    68

They were passing Metre 320 on rack 11. A young Beta-Minus mechanic was busy with screwdriver and spanner on the blood-surrogate pump of a passing bottle. The hum of the electric motor deepened by fractions of a tone as he turned the nuts. Down, down . . . A final twist, a glance at the revolution counter, and he was done. He moved two paces down the line and began the same process on the next pump.    69

"Reducing the number of revolutions per minute," Mr. Foster explained. "The surrogate goes round slower; therefore passes through the lung at longer intervals; therefore gives the embryo less oxygen. Nothing like oxygen-shortage for keeping an embryo below par." Again he rubbed his hands.    70

"But why do you want to keep the embryo below par?" asked an ingenuous student.    71

"Ass!" said the Director, breaking a long silence. "Hasn't it occurred to you that an Epsilon embryo must have an Epsilon environment as well as an Epsilon heredity?"    72

It evidently hadn't occurred to him. He was covered with confusion.    73

"The lower the caste," said Mr. Foster, "the shorter the oxygen." The first organ affected was the brain. After that the skeleton. At seventy per cent of normal oxygen you got dwarfs. At less than seventy eyeless monsters.    74

"Who are no use at all," concluded Mr. Foster.    75

Whereas (his voice became confidential and eager), if they could discover a technique for shortening the period of maturation what a triumph, what a benefaction to Society!    76

"Consider the horse."    77

They considered it.    78

Mature at six; the elephant at ten. While at thirteen a man is not yet sexually mature; and is only full-grown at twenty. Hence, of course, that fruit of delayed development, the human intelligence.    79

"But in Epsilons," said Mr. Foster very justly, "we don't need human intelligence."    80

Didn't need and didn't get it. But though the Epsilon mind was mature at ten, the Epsilon body was not fit to work till eighteen. Long years of superfluous and wasted immaturity. If the physical development could be speeded up till it was as quick, say, as a cow's what an enormous saving to the Community!    81

"Enormous!" murmured the students. Mr. Foster's enthusiasm was 82 infectious.

He became rather technical; spoke of the abnormal endocrine coordina- 83 tion which made men grow so slowly; postulated a germinal mutation to account for it. Could the effects of this germinal mutation be undone? Could the individual Epsilon embryo be made a revert, by a suitable technique, to the normality of dogs and cows? That was the problem. And it was all but solved.

Pilkington, at Mombasa, had produced individuals who were sexually 84 mature at four and full-grown at six and a half. A scientific triumph. But socially useless. Six-year-old men and women were too stupid to do even Epsilon work. And the process was an all-or-nothing one; either you failed to modify at all, or else you modified the whole way. They were still trying to find the ideal compromise between adults of twenty and adults of six. So far without success. Mr. Foster sighed and shook his head.

Their wanderings though the crimson twilight had brought them to the 85 neighbourhood of Metre 170 on Rack 9. From this point onwards Rack 9 was enclosed and the bottles performed the remainder of their journey in a kind of tunnel, interrupted here and there by openings two or three metres wide.

"Heat conditioning," said Mr. Foster. 86

Hot tunnels alternated with cool tunnels. Coolness was wedded to dis- 87 comfort in the form of hard X-rays. By the time they were decanted the embryos had a horror of cold. They were predestined to emigrate to the trop- ics, to be miners and acetate silk spinners and steel workers. Later on their minds would be made to endorse the judgment of their bodies. "We condition them to thrive on heat," concluded Mr. Foster. "Our colleagues upstairs will teach them to love it."

"And that," put in the Director sententiously, "that is the secret of hap- 88 piness and virtue—liking what you've *got* to do. All conditioning aims at that: making people like their unescapable social destiny."

In a gap between two tunnels, a nurse was delicately probing with a 89 long fine syringe into the gelatinous contents of a passing bottle. The students and their guides stood watching her for a few moments in silence.

"Well, Lenina," said Mr. Foster, when at last she withdrew the syringe 90 and straightened herself up.

The girl turned with a start. One could see that, for all the lupus and the 91 purple eyes, she was uncommonly pretty.

"Henry!" Her smile flashed redly at him—a row of coral teeth. 92

"Charming, charming," murmured the Director and, giving her two or 93 three little pats, received in exchange a rather deferential smile for himself.

"What are you giving them?" asked Mr. Foster, making his tone very 94 professional.

"Oh, the usual typhoid and sleeping sickness." 95

"Tropical workers start being inoculated at Metre 150," Mr. Foster 96 explained to the students. "The embryos still have gills. We immunize the fish against the future man's diseases." Then, turning back to Lenina, "Ten to five on the roof this afternoon," he said, "as usual."

"Charming," said the Director once more, and with a final pat, moved          97
away after the others.

On Rack 10 rows of next generation's chemical workers were being             98
trained in the toleration of lead, caustic soda, tar, chlorine. The first of a batch
of two hundred and fifty embryonic rocket-plane engineers was just passing
the eleven hundred metre mark on Rack 3. A special mechanism kept their
containers in constant rotation. "To improve their sense of balance," Mr.
Foster explained. "Doing repairs on the outside of a rocket in mid-air is a tick-
lish job. We slacken off the circulation when they're right way up, so that
they're half starved, and double the flow of surrogate when they're upside
down. They learn to associate topsyturvydom with well-being; in fact, they're
only truly happy when they're standing on their heads.

"And now," Mr. Foster went on, "I'd like to show you some very inter-        99
esting conditioning for Alpha Plus Intellectuals. We have a big batch of them
on Rack 5. First Gallery level," he called to two boys who had started to go
down to the ground floor.

"They're round about Metre 900," he explained. "You can't really do any     100
useful intellectual conditioning till the fetuses have lost their tails. Follow me."

But the Director had looked at his watch. "Ten to three," he said. "No      101
time for the intellectual embryos, I'm afraid. We must go up to the Nurseries
before the children have finished their afternoon sleep."

Mr. Foster was disappointed. "At least one glance at the Decanting         102
Room," he pleaded.

"Very well then." The Director smiled indulgently. "Just one glance."        103

■   ■   ■

## Review Questions

1. What is the Bokanovsky Process? Why is it central to Huxley's "brave
   new world"?
2. How does Huxley comment sardonically on the racism of the Hatchery's
   personnel—and of Europeans in general?
3. What is the difference—and the social significance of the difference—
   among Alphas, Betas, Deltas, Gammas, and Epsilons?
4. What technological problems concerning the maturation process have the
   scientists of *Brave New World* still not solved?

## Discussion and Writing Suggestions

1. How does the language of the first two paragraphs reveal Huxley's tone,
   that is, his attitude toward his subject? For example, what is the function
   of the word "only" in the opening sentence: "A squat grey building of
   only thirty-four stories"? Or the adjectives describing the building?
2. What does the narrator mean when he says (paragraph 5) that "particulars, as every one knows, make for virtue and happiness; generalities are

intellectually necessary evils. Not philosophers but fret-sawyers [opera-tors of fretsaws, long, narrow, fine-toothed hand saws used for orna-mental detail work] and stamp collectors compose the backbone of society"? To what extent do you believe that such an ethic operates in our own society? Give examples of the relatively low value placed on "philosophers" and the relatively high value placed on "fret-sawyers."

3. Throughout this chapter, Huxley makes an implied contrast between the brisk, technological efficiency of the Hatchery and the ethical nature of what takes place within its walls. What aspects of our own civilization show similar contrasts? (Example: We are now able to build more tech-nologically sophisticated weapons of destruction than ever before in his-tory.) Explore this subject in an essay, devoting a paragraph or so to each aspect of our civilization that you consider.

4. In the Hatchery, bottled, fertilized eggs pass into the "Social Predesti-nation Room." In that room, their future lives will be determined. Is there an equivalent of the Social Predestination Room in our own society? (In other words, are there times and places when and where our future lives are determined?) If so, describe its features, devoting a paragraph to each of these features.

5. Foster explains how the undecanted embryos are conditioned to adapt to certain environments—for instance, conditioned to like heat so that, years later, they will feel comfortable working in the tropics or working as miners; or they may be conditioned to improve their sense of balance, so that they will be able to repair rockets in midair. What evidence do you see in our own society that people are or will be subject to condi-tioning to "like their unescapable social destiny"? Consider, for example, the influence of the conditioning exerted by parents, siblings, teachers, friends, or various social institutions.

6. As we noted in the headnote, Huxley's *Brave New World* (like much sci-ence fiction) is a projection into the future of contemporary aspects of culture that the author finds disturbing or dangerous. Select some present aspect of our culture that *you* find disturbing or dangerous and—in the form of a short story, or chapter from a novel, or section from a screen-play—dramatize your vision of what *could* happen.

## *Recombinant DNA and Genetic Engineering*

CECIE STARR
RALPH TAGGART

*Many of the public policy dilemmas of our modern world—the use of nuclear weapons, for example, or the debate about when to "pull the plug" on persons near death, or the debate about privacy from electronic snooping—have arisen as a direct result of scientific breakthroughs. Much of this chapter will deal with various aspects of the public policy debate surrounding biotechnology. But we thought it would be illuminating to precede these discussions with a scientific description of just what is entailed in a key aspect of the new field—genetic engineering.*

*In the following selection, reprinted from a textbook widely used in introductory university-level biology courses, the authors survey the field of genetic engineering, describe some recent developments in the field, and conclude by discussing some of the social, legal, ecological, and ethical questions regarding its benefits and risks.*

*Cecie Starr is a science writer who lives in Belmont, California. Ralph Taggart teaches biology at Michigan State University. This passage is from their textbook* Biology: The Unity and Diversity of Life *(8th ed., 1998).*

## MOM, DAD, AND CLOGGED ARTERIES

Butter! Bacon! Eggs! Ice cream! Cheesecake! Possibly you think of such foods    1
as enticing, off-limits, or both. After all, who among us doesn't know about
animal fats and the dreaded cholesterol?

Soon after you feast on these fatty foods, cholesterol enters the blood-    2
stream. Cholesterol is important. It is a structural component of animal cell
membranes, and without membranes, there would be no cells. Cells also
remodel cholesterol into various molecules, including the vitamin D that is
necessary for the development of good bones and teeth. Normally, however,
your liver synthesizes enough cholesterol for your cells.

Some proteins circulating in the blood combine with cholesterol and    3
other substances to form lipoprotein particles. The *HDLs* (high-density
lipoproteins) collect cholesterol and transport it to the liver, where it can be
metabolized. *LDLs* (low-density lipoproteins) normally end up in cells that
store or use cholesterol.

Sometimes too many LDLs form, and the excess infiltrates the elastic    4
walls of arteries. There they promote formation of abnormal masses called
atherosclerotic plaques. These interfere with blood flow and narrow the arte-
rial diameter. If the plaques clog one of the tiny coronary arteries that deliver blood to the heart, the resulting symptoms can range from mild chest
pains to a heart attack.

How your body handles dietary cholesterol depends on what you inher-    5
ited from your parents. Consider the gene for a protein that serves as the cell's
receptor for LDLs. Inherit two "good" alleles of the gene, and your blood
level of cholesterol will tend to remain so low that your arteries will never get
clogged, even with a high-fat diet. Inherit two copies of a certain mutated
allele, however, and you are destined to develop a rare genetic disorder called
*familial cholesterolemia.* With this disorder, cholesterol builds up to abnor-
mally high levels. Many affected individuals die of heart attacks during childhood or their teens.

In 1992 a woman from Quebec, Canada, became a milestone in the his-    6
tory of genetics. She was thirty years old. Like two of her younger brothers
who had died from heart attacks in their early twenties, she inherited the
defective gene for the LDL receptor. She herself survived a heart attack when
she was sixteen. At twenty-six, she had coronary bypass surgery.

At the time, people were hotly debating the risks and promise of **gene**    7
**therapy**—the transfer of one or more normal or modified genes into an individual's body cells to correct a genetic defect or boost resistance to disease.
Even so, the woman consented to undergo an untried, physically wrenching
procedure designed to give her body working copies of the good gene.

Medical researchers removed about 15 percent of the woman's liver.    8
They placed liver cells in a nutrient-rich medium that promoted growth and
division. *And they spliced the good gene into the genetic material of a harm-*
*less virus.* That modified virus served roughly the same function as a hypo-
dermic needle. The researchers allowed it to infect the cultured liver cells and
thereby insert copies of the good gene into them.

Later, the researchers infused about a billion of the modified cells into the    9
woman's portal vein, a major blood vessel that leads directly to the liver.
There, at least some cells took up residence, and they started to produce the
missing cholesterol receptor. Two years after this, between 3 and 5 percent of
the woman's liver cells were behaving normally and sponging up cholesterol
from the blood. Her blood levels of LDLs had declined nearly 20 percent.
Scans of her arteries showed no evidence at all of the progressive clogging that
had nearly killed her. At a recent press conference, the woman announced she
is active and doing well.

Her cholesterol levels do remain more than twice as high as normal, and    10
it is too soon to know whether the gene therapy will prolong her life. Yet the
intervention provides solid proof that the concept of gene therapy is sound,
and hopes are high.

As you might gather from this pioneering clinical application, recombi-    11
nant DNA technology has truly staggering potential for medicine. It also has
great potential for agriculture and industry. The technology does not come
without risks. With this chapter, we consider some basic aspects of the new
technology. At the chapter's end, we also address some ecological, social, and
ethical questions related to its application.

## RECOMBINATION IN NATURE—AND IN THE LABORATORY

For more than 3 billion years, nature has been conducting uncountable numbers    12
of genetic experiments, through mutation, crossing over, and other events that
introduce changes in genetic messages. This is the source of life's diversity.

For many thousands of years, we humans have been changing numerous    13
genetically based traits of species. By artificial selection practices, we produced
new crop plants and breeds of cattle, birds, dogs, and cats from wild ances-

tral stocks. We developed meatier turkeys and sweeter oranges, larger corn, seedless watermelons, flamboyant ornamental roses, and other useful plants. We produced splendid hybrids, including the tangelo (tangerine x grapefruit) and mule (horse x donkey).

Researchers now use **recombinant DNA technology** to analyze genetic changes. With this technology, they cut and splice DNA from different species, then insert the modified molecules into bacteria or other types of cells that engage in rapid replication and cell division. The cells copy the foreign DNA right along with their own. In short order, huge populations produce useful quantities of recombinant DNA molecules. The new technology also is the basis of **genetic engineering**, by which genes are isolated, modified, and inserted back into the same organism or into a different one.   14

## Plasmids, Restriction Enzymes, and the New Technology

Believe it or not, this astonishing technology originated with the innards of bacteria. Bacterial cells have a single chromosome, a circular DNA molecule that has all the genes they require to grow and reproduce. But many species also have **plasmids**, or small, circular molecules of "extra" DNA that contain a few genes.   15

Usually, plasmids are not essential for survival, but some of the the genes they carry may benefit the bacterium. For instance, some plasmid genes confer resistance to antibiotics. (*Antibiotics*, remember, are toxic metabolic products of microorganisms that can kill or inhibit the growth of competing microorganisms.) The bacterium's replication enzymes copy and reproduce plasmid DNA, just as they copy chromosomal DNA.   16

In nature, many bacteria are able to transfer plasmid genes to a bacterial neighbor of the same species or a different one. Replication enzymes may even integrate a transferred plasmid into the bacterial chromosome of a recipient cell. A recombinant DNA molecule is the result.   17

Infectious particles called viruses as well as bacteria dabble in gene transfers and recombinations. And so do most eukaryotic species. As you might imagine, viral infection does a bacterium no good. Over evolutionary time, bacteria developed an arsenal against invasion by harmful genes. They became equipped with many types of **restriction enzymes**, which are able to recognize and cut apart foreign DNA that may enter a cell. Eventually, researchers learned how to use plasmids *and* restriction enzymes for genetic recombination in the laboratory.   18

## Producing Restriction Fragments

Each type of restriction enzyme makes a cut wherever it recognizes a specific, very short nucleotide sequence in the DNA. Cuts at two identical sequences in the same DNA molecule produce a fragment. Because some types of enzymes make *staggered* cuts, some fragments have single-stranded portions at both ends. Sometimes these are referred to as sticky ends:   19

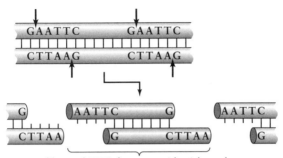

liberated DNA fragment with sticky ends

By "sticky," we mean the short, single-stranded ends of a DNA fragment    20
will have the chemical capacity to base-pair with any other DNA molecule
that also has been cut by the same restriction enzyme.

For example, suppose you use the same restriction enzyme to cut plas-    21
mids *and* DNA molecules that you have isolated from a human cell. When
you mix the cut molecules together, they base-pair at the cut sites. After this,
you add **DNA ligase** to the mixture. DNA ligase is an enzyme that seals
DNA's sugar-phosphate backbone at the cut sites, just as it does during DNA
replication. In this way, you create "recombinant plasmids," which have
pieces of DNA from another organism inserted into them.

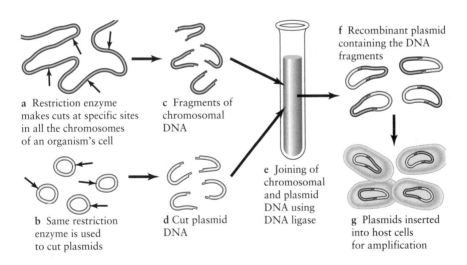

**a** Restriction enzyme makes cuts at specific sites in all the chromosomes of an organism's cell

**b** Same restriction enzyme is used to cut plasmids

**c** Fragments of chromosomal DNA

**d** Cut plasmid DNA

**e** Joining of chromosomal and plasmid DNA using DNA ligase

**f** Recombinant plasmid containing the DNA fragments

**g** Plasmids inserted into host cells for amplification

**FIGURE 1**

(**a-f**) Formation of a DNA library—a collection of DNA fragments, produced by restriction enzymes and inserted into plasmids or some other cloning tool. (**g**) Plasmid insertion into host cells to form cloned DNA, or multiple, identical copies of the DNA fragments.

You now have a **DNA library**. It is a collection of DNA fragments, pro-    22
duced by restriction enzymes, that have been incorporated into plasmids, as
illustrated in Figure 1.

## WORKING WITH DNA FRAGMENTS

### Amplification Procedures

A DNA library is almost vanishingly small. To obtain useful amounts of it,    23
biochemists resort to methods of **DNA amplification,** by which a DNA library
is copied again and again. One such method uses "factories" of bacteria,
yeasts, or some other cells that can reproduce rapidly and take up plasmids.
A growing population of these cells can amplify a DNA library in short
order. Their repeated cycles of replication and cell division yield cloned DNA
that has been inserted into plasmids. The "cloned" part of this name refers to
the multiple, identical copies of DNA fragments.

The **polymerase chain reaction,** or **PCR,** is a newer method of amplifying    24
fragments of DNA. The reactions proceed in test tubes, not in microbial factories. First, researchers identify short nucleotide sequences located just before
and just after a region of DNA from a cell of the organism that interests them.
Then they synthesize **primers.** These short nucleotide sequences, recall, will
base-pair with any complementary sequences in DNA. And the replication
enzymes called **DNA polymerases** recognize them as START tags.

For PCR, a DNA polymerase from a bacterium  that lives in hot springs,    25
even water heaters, is the enzyme of choice, because it remains functional at
the elevated temperatures necessary to unwind DNA and also at the lower
temperatures necessary for base pairing. Researchers mix together the
primers, the polymerases, all the DNA from one of the organism's cells, and
free nucleotides. Next, they expose the mixture to precise temperature cycles.
During each cycle, the two strands of all the DNA molecules unwind from
each other. And primers become positioned on exposed nucleotides at the targeted sites according to base-pairing rules (Figure 2). With each round of reactions, the number of DNA molecules doubles. For example, if there are 10
such molecules in the test tube, there soon will be 20, then 40, 80, 160, 320,
640, 1,280, and so on. Very quickly, a target region from a single DNA molecule can be amplified to *billions* of molecules.

In short, *PCR amplifies samples that contain even tiny amounts of DNA.*    26
As you will see in the next section, such samples can be obtained from fos-
sils—even from a single hair or drop of blood left at the scene of a crime.

### Sorting Out Fragments of DNA

When restriction enzymes cut DNA, the fragments they produce are not all    27
the same length. Researchers can use **gel electrophoresis** to separate fragments from one another according to length. This laboratory procedure
employs an electric field to force molecules through a viscous gel and to sep-

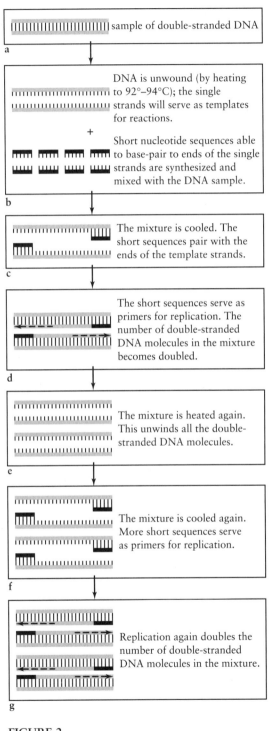

a. sample of double-stranded DNA

b. DNA is unwound (by heating to 92°–94°C); the single strands will serve as templates for reactions.

+

Short nucleotide sequences able to base-pair to ends of the single strands are synthesized and mixed with the DNA sample.

c. The mixture is cooled. The short sequences pair with the ends of the template strands.

d. The short sequences serve as primers for replication. The number of double-stranded DNA molecules in the mixture becomes doubled.

e. The mixture is heated again. This unwinds all the double-stranded DNA molecules.

f. The mixture is cooled again. More short sequences serve as primers for replication.

g. Replication again doubles the number of double-stranded DNA molecules in the mixture.

## FIGURE 2

The polymerase chain reaction (PCR).

arate them according to physical and chemical properties. For DNA, size alone affects how far the molecules move. (For proteins, remember, a molecule's size, shape, and net surface charge are the determining factors.)

A gel that contains DNA fragments is immersed in a buffered solution, and    28
electrodes connect the solution to a power source. Apply voltage, and negatively charged phosphate groups of the fragments respond to it. The fragments move toward the positively charged pole at different rates and thereby become separated into bands according to their lengths. Again, how far they migrate depends only on their size; the larger fragments cannot move as fast through it. After a predetermined period of electrophoresis, fragments of different length can be identified by staining the gel [Figure 3 on pp. 521 and 522].

## DNA Sequencing

Once DNA fragments from a sample have been sorted out according to    29
length, researchers can work out the nucleotide sequence of each type. The Sanger method of DNA sequencing, as detailed in Figure 3, will give you a sense of one of the ways this can be done.

## MODIFIED HOST CELLS

### Use of DNA Probes

Recombinant plasmids are not much use in themselves. They must be mixed    30
with living cells that can take them up. So how do you find out which cells do this? You can utilize **DNA probes**: short DNA sequences synthesized from radioactively labeled nucleotides. Part of a probe must be designed to base-pair with some portion of the DNA of interest. Any base pairing between nucleotide sequences (that is, RNA as well as DNA) from different sources is called **nucleic acid hybridization**.

The challenge is to "select" the cells that have taken up recombinant plas-    31
mids and the gene of interest. One way to do this is to use a plasmid containing a gene that confers resistance to a particular antibiotic. You put prospective host cells on a culture medium that has the antibiotic added to it. The antibiotic prevents growth of all cells *except* the ones that house plasmids with the antibiotic-resistance gene.

As the cells divide, they form colonies. Assume the colonies are growing    32
on agar, a gel-like substance, in a petri dish. You blot the agar against a nylon filter. Some cells stick to the filter at sites that mirror the locations of the original colonies. You use solutions to rupture the cells, fix the released DNA onto the filter, and make the double-stranded DNA unwind. Then you add DNA probes, which hybridize only with the gene region having a complementary base sequence. Probe-hybridized DNA emits radioactivity and allows you to tag the colonies that harbor the gene of interest.

• • •

One of the methods used for sequencing DNA, as first developed by Frederick Sanger. The method is employed to determine the nucleotide sequence of specific DNA fragments, as this example illustrates.

**a** Single-stranded DNA fragments are added to a solution in four different test tubes:

All four tubes contain DNA polymerases, short nucleotide sequences that can serve as primers for replication, and the nucleotide subunits of DNA (A, T, C, and G). Each tube contains a modified, labeled version of only one of the four kinds of nucleotides. We can show these as A*, T*, C*, and G*. The labeled form is present in low concentration, along with a generous supply of the unmodified form of the same nucleotide. Let's follow what happens in the tube with the A* subunits.

**b** As expected, the DNA polymerase recognizes a primer that has become attached to a fragment, which it uses as a template strand. The enzyme assembles a complementary strand according to a base-pairing rules (A only to T, and C only to G). Sooner or later, the enzyme picks up an A* subunit for pairing with a T on the template strand. The modified nucleotide is a chemical roadblock—it prevents the enzyme from adding more nucleotides to the growing complementary strand. In time, the tube contains labeled strands of different lengths, as dictated by the location of each A* in the sequence:

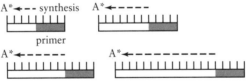

**FIGURE 3**                                              (continued on next page)

## BACTERIA, PLANTS, AND THE NEW TECHNOLOGY

Many years have passed since foreign DNA was first transferred into a plasmid, yet that transfer started a debate that will continue into the next century. The issue is this: *Do the benefits of gene modifications and gene transfers outweigh the potential dangers?* Before you personally come to any conclusions, reflect upon a few examples of the work with bacteria, then with plants. **33**

The same thing happens in the other three tubes, with strand lengths dictated by the location of T*, C*, and G*.

**c** DNA from each of the four tubes is placed in four parallel lanes in the same gel. Then the DNA can be subjected to electrophoresis. The resulting nucleotide sequence can be read off the resulting bands in the gel. Look at the numbers running down the side of this diagram.

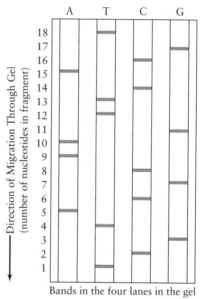

Bands in the four lanes in the gel

Start with "1" and read across the four lanes (A, T, C, G). As you can see, T is the closest to the start of the nucleotide sequence; it has migrated farthest through the gel. At "2," the next nucleotide is C, and so on. The entire sequence read from the first nucleotide to the last, is

TCGTACGCAAGTTCACGT

And now, by applying the rules of base pairing, you can deduce the sequence of the DNA fragment that served as the template.

---

## Genetically Engineered Bacteria

Imagine a miniaturized factory that churns out insulin or another protein having medical value. This is an apt description of the huge stainless steel vats of genetically engineered, protein-producing bacteria.   34

Think of *diabetics*, who need insulin injections for as long as they live. The pancreas produces insulin, a protein hormone. Medical supplies of insulin once were obtained from pigs and cattle, although some diabetics developed allergic reactions to foreign insulin. Eventually, synthetic genes for human   35 insulin were transferred into *E. coli* cells. (Can you say why the genes had to be synthesized?) This was the start of huge bacterial factories that manufacture human insulin, hemoglobin, somatotropin, interferon, albumin, and other valuable proteins.

In addition, in research laboratories around the world, certain strains of   36
bacteria are now being engineered to degrade oil spills from tankers, to manufacture alcohol and other chemicals, to process minerals, or to leave crop plants alone. The strains are harmless to begin with. The ones meant to be confined to the laboratory are "designed" to prevent escape. As added precautions, the foreign DNA usually includes "fail-safe" genes. Such genes are silent *unless* the engineered bacteria somehow are exposed to conditions that occur in the environment. Exposure will activate the genes, with lethal results for the bacteria.

For example, foreign DNA may include a *hok* gene next to a promoter of   37
the lactose operon. If an engineered bacterium does manage to escape to the environment, where sugars are common, the gene will trip into action. The protein the gene specifies will destroy membrane function and so destroy the cell.

Even so, some people worry about the possible risks of introducing genetically engineered bacteria into the environment. Consider how Steven Lindow   38
engineered a bacterium that can make many crop plants resist frost. A protein at the bacterial surface promotes formation of ice crystals. Lindow excised the ice-forming gene from some cells. As he hypothesized, spraying his "ice-minus bacteria" on strawberry plants in an isolated field prior to a frost would make plants less vulnerable to freezing. Even though Lindow deleted a *harmful* gene from an organism, it triggered a bitter legal battle over releasing engineered bacteria into the environment. In time, the courts did rule in favor of allowing such a release, and researchers sprayed a small strawberry patch. Nothing bad ever happened. Since then, the rules governing the release of genetically engineered species have become less restrictive.

## Genetically Engineered Plants

A HUNT FOR BENEFICIAL GENES   Currently, botanists are combing the world   39
for seeds and other living tissues from wild ancestors of potatoes, corn, and other plants. They send their prizes—genes from a plant's lineage—to a safe storage laboratory in Colorado. Why? *Farmers now rely on only a few strains of high-yield crop plants that feed most of the human population.* The near-absence of genetic diversity means our food base is dangerously vulnerable to many disease-causing viruses, bacteria, and fungi. It is a race against time. Our population has reached an astounding size. People, bulldozers, and power saws are encroaching on previously uninhabited areas; hundreds of wild plant species disappear weekly.

The danger is real. Recently a new fungal strain that rots potatoes entered   40
the United States from Mexico. In 1994, crop losses from the resulting *potato blight* topped $100 million. Pennsylvania farmers had little to harvest. Possibly laboratory-stored, fungus-resistant strains of potato plants will save crops in the future.

PLANT REGENERATION Botanists also search for good genes in the laboratory.    41
Years ago, Frederick Steward and his coworkers cultured cells of carrot plants
and induced them to grow into small embryos, some of which grew into
whole plants. Other species, including many crop plants, are regenerated
today from cultured cells. The methods raise mutation rates, so cultures are
a source of genetic modifications.

Researchers can pinpoint a useful mutation among millions of cells.    42
Suppose a culture medium contains a toxic product of a disease agent. If a few
cells have a mutated gene that confers resistance to the toxin, only they will
live in the culture. If cells regenerate whole plants that can be hybridized with
other varieties, the hybrids may get the good gene.

METHODS OF GENE TRANSFER   Now genetic engineers insert genes into cul-    43
tured plant cells. For example, they insert DNA fragments into the "Ti" plasmid from the bacterium *Agrobacterium tumefaciens*, which can infect many
species of flowering plants. Some plasmid genes invade a plant's DNA and
induce formation of abnormal tissue masses called crown gall tumors. Before
introducing the Ti plasmid into plants, researchers first remove the tumor-
inducing genes and insert desired genes into it. They grow the modified bacterial cells with cultured plant cells, then regenerate plants from the cells that
take up the genes. In some instances, the foreign genes have been expressed in
plant tissues, with observable effects.

*A. tumefaciens* can only infect beans, peas, potatoes, and other dicots.    44
However, wheat, corn, rice, and many major food crops are monocots, which
the bacterium cannot infect. In some cases, genetic engineers can use electric
shocks or chemicals to deliver modified DNA into protoplasts. (Protoplasts
are plant cells stripped of their walls.) At this writing, regenerating some
species of plants from protoplast cultures is not yet possible. But researchers
have had some success in delivering genes into cultured plant cells by actually shooting them with pistols. Instead of bullets, they use blanks to drive
DNA-coated, microscopic particles into the cells.

ON THE HORIZON Despite many obstacles, improved varieties of crop plants    45
have been developed or are in the works. For example, genetically engineered
cotton plants now resist worm attacks without any help from pesticides,
which have the disadvantage of also killing off beneficial pest-eating insects.    46

Also on the horizon are engineered plants that can serve as factories for
pharmaceuticals. A few years ago, genetically engineered tobacco plants that
make human hemoglobin, melanin, and other proteins were planted in a field
in North Carolina. Ecologists later found no trace of foreign genes or proteins
in the soil or in other plants or animals in the vicinity. Recently, mustard plant
cells made plastic beads in a Stanford University laboratory. (Plastics are
long-chain polymers of identical subunits.) The plant DNA incorporates three
bacterial enzymes that are able to convert carbon dioxide, water, and nutri-
ents into inexpensive, biodegradable plastic.

## GENETIC ENGINEERING OF ANIMALS

### Supermice and Biotech Barnyards

The first mammals enlisted for experiments in genetic engineering were lab-    47
oratory mice. Consider an example of this work. R. Hammer, R. Palmiter, and R. Brinster corrected a hormone deficiency that leads to dwarfism in mice. Insufficient levels of somatotropin give rise to the abnormality. The researchers used a microneedle to inject the gene for rat somatotropin into fertilized mouse eggs. After the eggs were implanted in an adult female, the gene was successfully integrated into the mouse DNA. Later, the baby mice in which the foreign gene was expressed were $1\frac{1}{2}$ times larger than their dwarf littermates. In other experiments, researchers transferred the gene for human somatotropin into a mouse embryo, where it became integrated into the DNA. The modified embryo grew up to be "supermouse."

Today, as part of research into the molecular basis of Alzheimer's disease    48
and other genetic disorders, a few human genes are being inserted into mouse embryos. Besides microneedles, microscopic laser beams are used to open up temporary holes in the plasma membrane of cultured cells, although such methods have varying degrees of success. Retroviruses also are used to insert genes into cultured cells, which may incorporate the foreign genes into their DNA. But the genetic material of retroviruses can undergo rearrangements, deletions, and other alterations that shut down the introduced genes. And if the virus particles escape from laboratory isolation, they may infect organisms.

Animals of "biotech barnyards" are competing with bacterial factories as    49
genetically engineered sources of proteins. For example, goats produce CFTR protein (for treating cystic fibrosis) and TPA (which diminishes the severity of heart attacks). Cattle may soon produce human collagen for repairing cartilage, bone, and skin. Also, in 1996 researchers made a genetic duplicate of an adult ewe. They reprogrammed one of her mammary gland cells so all of its genes could be expressed. They fused that cell with an egg (from another ewe) from which the nucleus had been removed. Signals from the egg cytoplasm triggered the development of a cluster of embryonic cells, which was implanted into a surrogate mother. The result was a clone, a lamb named *Dolly*. At this writing, the clone is thriving. The experiment opens up the possibility of producing genetically engineered clones of sheep, cattle, and other farm animals that can supply consistently uniform quantities of proteins, even tissues and organs, for medical uses and for research.

### Applying the New Technology to Humans

Researchers around the world are working their way through the 3.2 billion    50
base pairs of the twenty-three pairs of human chromosomes. This ambitious effort is the **human genome project**. Some researchers focus on specific chromosomes. Others are deciphering certain gene regions only. For example, rather than studying the noncoding sequences (introns), J. Venter and Sidney Brenner

isolate mRNAs from brain cells and use them to make cDNA. By sequencing only cDNAs, they have identified hundreds of previously unknown genes.

About 99.9 percent of the nucleotide sequence is the same in all humans     51
on Earth. The remaining 0.1 percent—about 3,200,000 base pairs—are mutations and other sequence variations sprinkled throughout the genome. They account for *all* genetic differences in the human population. Therefore, completion of the project should give us the ultimate reference book of human biology and genetic disorders. What will we do with all of that information? Certainly we will use it in the search for treatments and cures for genetic disorders. Of the 2,000 or so genes studied so far, 400 have already been linked to genetic disorders. And the knowledge opens doors to gene therapy, the transfer of one or more normal or modified genes into the body cells of an individual to correct a genetic defect or boost resistance to disease.

But what about forms of human gene expression that are neither dis-     52
abling nor life-threatening? Will we tinker with them, also? . . .

### Focus on Bioethics: Regarding Gene Therapy

This [discussion] opened with a historic, inspiring case, the first proof that     53
gene therapy can help save human lives. It closes with questions that invite you to consider some social and ethical issues related to the application of recombinant DNA technology to our rapidly advancing knowledge of the human genome.

To most of us, human gene therapy to correct genetic abnormalities     54
seems like a socially accepted goal. Let's take this idea one step further. Is it also socially desirable or acceptable to change certain genes of a normal human individual (or sperm or egg) to alter or enhance traits?

The idea of of selecting desirable human traits is called *eugenic engi-*     55
*neering.* Yet who decides which forms of a trait are most "desirable"? For example, what happens if prospective parents start picking the sex of a child by way of genetic engineering? In one survey group, three-fourths of the people who were asked this question said they would choose a boy. What would be the long-term social implications of a drastic shortage of girls?

As other examples, would it be okay to engineer taller or blue-eyed or     56
fair-skinned boys and girls? Would it be okay to engineer "superhumans" with amazing strength or intelligence? Suppose a person of average intelligence moved into a town of 800 Einsteins. Would the response go beyond muttering of "There goes the neighborhood"? Are there people narcissistic enough to commission a clone of themselves, one that has just a few genetically engineered "improvements"? Researchers can alter genes now, and they have already cloned a sheep from a fully differentiated cell.

There are those who say that the DNA of any organism must never be     57
altered. Put aside the fact that nature itself alters DNA much of the time, and has done so for nearly all of life's history. The concern is that *we* do not have the wisdom to bring about beneficial changes without causing great harm to ourselves or to the environment.

When it comes to manipulating human genes, one is reminded of our    58
human tendency to leap before we look. When it comes to restricting genetic modifications of any sort, one also is reminded of the old saying, "If God
had wanted us to fly, he would have given us wings." Yet something about
the human experience has given us a capacity to imagine wings of our own
making—and that capacity has carried us to the frontiers of space.

Where are we going from here with recombinant DNA technology, this    59
new product of our imagination? To gain perspective on the question, spend
some time reading the history of the human species. It is a history of survival
in the face of all manner of new challenges, threats, bumblings, and sometimes
disasters on a grand scale. It is also the story of our connectedness with the
environment and with one another.

The basic questions confronting you today are these: Should we be more    60
cautious, believing that one day the risk takers may go too far? And what do
we as a species stand to lose if the risks are not taken?

■ ■ ■

## Review Questions

1. For how long have genetic experiments been proceeding in nature?
2. What role do humans now play in genetic experimentation?
3. What do researchers do with recombinant DNA technology?
4. What three activities lie at the heart of recombinant DNA technology?
5. What is the basic procedure, and the basic goal, of genetic engineering?
   Provide one example of genetic engineering.

## Discussion and Writing Suggestions

1. Write a one-page summary of this selection.
2. This selection originally appeared in an introductory university biology text.
   To what extent did you find it difficult to comprehend? Locate those passages that gave you particular trouble. Does the problem lie in the terminology Starr and Taggart employ? The scientific concepts under discussion?
   The organization or writing style? See if your instructor or other, more scientifically inclined students can throw light on these troublesome sections.
3. Toward the end of this selection Starr and Taggart discuss genetic engineering at the bacterial, plant, animal, and human levels. To what extent
   do you see a different set of ethical standards operating from one level to
   another? Taking into account the kind of considerations discussed at
   the end of the passage, what kind of ethical standards do you believe
   should operate at the level of human gene therapy? To what extent do
   you believe that it will be possible or practical to maintain such standards? For example, who has an interest in imposing such standards?
   Who has an interest in resisting them?

4. Describe (if possible, in scientific report format) an experiment that you conducted in high school, or that you are conducting now in chemistry, physics, or biology. Write in language that your non-scientific readers will be able to follow.

## Canada and the Genomic Revolution

HENRY FRIESEN

*After acquiring post-graduate medical training as an endocrinologist in Boston, Dr. Friesen entered the Department of Medicine at McGill University, where he carried out research on human growth hormone (HGH) that enabled successful replacement therapy in hormone-deficient children. Further endocrine research led to the isolation and purification of the hormone prolactin; and in collaboration with researchers in the pharmaceutical industry, Dr. Friesen developed the drug Bromocryptine, which proved to be effective in the treatment of infertility in women.*

*As an administrator, Dr. Friesen served on the Medical Research Council of Canada for 20 years, and was its President from 1991 to 2000. He was appointed an Officer of the Order of Canada in 1992.*

*What follows is the transcript of a speech delivered by Dr. Friesen to the Canadian Club in Toronto. The event was co-sponsored by the Club and the Gairdner Foundation, an organization that funds medical research.*

Two thousand years ago, the great Chinese philosopher, Lao Tzu, observed that "each leaf is a tree." Since then, modern science has confirmed the truth of this ancient wisdom, not only as allegory, but as fact. We know that in the cells of each leaf there is, indeed, the genetic pattern for an entire forest.     1

Now, with the mapping of the human genome, we have been given, quite literally, the language of life itself—the pattern not simply for a forest, but for every living thing on earth.     2

For the first time, we are on the verge of understanding the biological basis of our shared humanity—of understanding the tiny genetic differences that contribute to the colour of our eyes, the shape of our mouths or our susceptibility to certain diseases.     3

Today, I would like to talk very briefly about what genomics can mean to our society—about the potential it offers and the challenges it presents. And I want to tell you why I believe it is so important that Canada become a leader in genomic research.     4

But first, some definitions. I suppose it's inevitable that new areas of scientific research bring with them their own specialized vocabulary, designed to confound the public and professionals alike.     5

So I thought it might be useful to provide you with some of the key buzzwords that you will be hearing more and more in the days ahead.     6

First, "genome." Genome is not the mapping, or sequencing that was     7
announced a few months ago. That was the Human Genome Project.
"Genome" is simply all of the genetic information stored within our cells.

I say "simply," but in fact it is a tremendous amount of information. If     8
the genome was a book, it would be the equivalent of 800 Bibles. And if I
were to start reading it to you at the rate of one "word" per second, for eight
hours a day, we would all still be sitting here 100 years from now!

The truly amazing thing is that all of this information is held inside the     9
microscopic nucleus of a cell so tiny that it could easily fit on the head of a pin.

And this is information that our bodies are constantly producing, divid-     10
ing and replicating. In the next 60 seconds, as you sit here, your body will
produce enough new DNA that if it was linked together, would stretch
100 000 kilometres. One hundred thousand kilometres in 60 seconds!

And every bit of information—every instruction that keeps us growing,     11
thinking and breathing—must be reproduced precisely. That is the miracle
of DNA.

Perhaps equally remarkable is the similarity of our individual genomes.     12
Humans have about 80 000 genes and 99.9 per cent of them are identical.
That means that only one chemical letter in a thousand is different in the
genome of, say Tie Domi and Albert Einstein. Makes you want to treat Tie
with a little more respect, doesn't it?

We're also discovering that our genes are remarkably similar to those of     13
other life forms. For example, about 40 per cent of the genes found in worms
are also found in humans. The genetic overlap between mice and humans is
almost 75 per cent. And chimps share more than 98 per cent of our DNA.

That's important because finding similar genes in simpler organisms can     14
save scientists thousands of hours of rummaging through our own—much
larger—genome.

So that's the "genome"—an amazing concentration of genetic informa-     15
tion printed on the DNA inside the nucleus of every cell in our body.

As you know, our DNA is made up of four molecules, identified as A, T,     16
C and G. Just four letters, over and over, in random order. More than three
billion of them.

It was the researchers' job to put them in the right order. That's akin to     17
being handed a dictionary and told to reproduce the works of Shakespeare.
But they did it.

Now we have an idea of the sequence, but there's still much more to learn.     18

It's like knowing the street address and telephone number of every person     19
in Canada. That's important information, but it doesn't tell us what those
people do or how their society is structured.

Similarly, having the human genome mapped out doesn't tell us how     20
genes function or interact, only their location along our DNA.

Moreover, genes themselves are not the big players in molecular process-     21
es. They're more like a text book, providing information that the cell refers to.

The real work horses are proteins. Which leads me to the next word-of-     22
the-day: proteomics.

"Proteomics" is part of genomics and is just a fancy way of saying "cat-    23
aloguing proteins and studying what they do in the body."

Why is this so important? Well, as I've said, proteins are the key players,    24
responsible for every chemical reaction essential to life.

They are the hormones that course through our veins, the guided missiles    25
that target infections; they're the enzymes that build up and break down our
energy reserves and the circuits that power movement and thought.

Little wonder, then, that proteomics is often referred to as "the next big    26
thing" in biotechnology.

What they do depends on their shape and their shapes are complex; their    27
surface covered with bumps and grooves sort of like popcorn.

The interesting thing is that these bumps and grooves are perfectly    28
formed to receive molecules, just as a lock receives a key.

By knowing the exact shape and form of each protein, we should be able    29
to develop drugs that will fit into their grooves and either activate them or
prevent them from being activated. And by doing this, we will really be able
to control disease and a host of other chemical functions inside our bodies.

Well, enough definitions. Let me give you a sense of what genomics    30
might mean to you and me in our daily lives.

But before I do, one caveat: predictions can be perilous—especially when    31
trying to extrapolate current trends into future events. Just consider that in
1972, there were 457 Elvis impersonators in the United States. By 1993, that
number had grown to 2700. If this trend continues, it will mean that by
2005, one out of every four Americans will be an Elvis impersonator!

So we have to be careful when we look ahead and make predictions    32
about what genomics can do. That said, the potential really is remarkable.

Indeed, we are already starting to reap the benefits.    33

We've made enormous progress, for example, in the area of single-gene    34
diseases. Here in Toronto, Dr. Lap-Chee Tsui discovered the gene responsible for cystic fibrosis and Dr. Ron Worton identified the gene tied to muscular dystrophy.

While we haven't been able to translate these discoveries into cures, at    35
least now we know the target we're aiming at—an enormous step forward.

In addition, the hepatitis B vaccine, the growth hormone for children,    36
new treatments for breast cancer and MS patients are all products of biotechnology that are in our clinics now and helping Canadians today.

One of the areas where genomics has tremendous potential is drug ther-    37
apy. This is because the drugs we consume today are based on average
responses. Clinical trials measure how well a drug works on a group of
people in general, not on how it will work on you, in particular.

Take hypertension. This is one of the most common health problems of    38
modern life and, as a result, anti-hypertensive drugs are the single most prescribed medication group—over $1 billion worth in Canada alone.

These drugs are very effective at preventing heart attacks, but some    39
research shows that as many as 40 per cent of those receiving conventional
therapy either don't respond or suffer side effects leading to hospitalization or

even death. In fact, severe side-effects from these drugs are the fifth largest cause of mortality in the United States. The problem is we don't know which people will respond positively, or worse, negatively.

Genomic researchers are working hard to find the genetic markers that will tell us if you're in that 40 per cent group. Think of the benefits to the individual of avoiding months of treatment that may be doing more harm than good. And think of the savings to the health system by avoiding hospitalization of these patients.　　40

A few years ago, a major international team which included Dr. Johanna Rommens here in Toronto and Dr. Jacques Simard at Laval discovered BRCA I and BRCA 2—two gene mutations that greatly increase the likelihood of breast cancer, particularly in younger women.　　41

By identifying the women with BRCA 1 or 2, we can monitor them more closely, detect the cancer sooner and begin treatment earlier—all key elements to improving their care and enhancing their lives.　　42

More generally, it is estimated that 10 to 40 per cent of people taking medication—any medication—respond less than perfectly to it. As a result, two million Americans are hospitalized for adverse reactions every year and 100 000 die.　　43

Genome research will also revolutionize the way medicine is practised. It will tell us which genes turn on when a wound heals, when a baby cries, when a head becomes bald or a brow wrinkled, when a song is learned or a memory recalled, when hormones surge or stress overwhelms—and they will learn how to manipulate these genes.　　44

Think of the typical check-up at your doctor's. Today, it's like going to a mechanic who diagnoses your car by listening to the engine. If the engine sounds good, the mechanic says the car is fine. But internally, the car could be on the verge of a major collapse. As you drive away, your brakes could fail, or your steering wheel could come off.　　45

Similarly, a physical exam consists of tests such as taking a blood sample or determining your blood pressure. What's actually happening in your body, at the genetic and molecular level, is completely unknown. Even after having an electrocardiogram, you could still have a fatal heart attack as you leave the doctor's office.　　46

But imagine going into your doctor's office and handing her a CD-ROM with your complete DNA sequence. She could then determine if you have any of the roughly 5000 known genetic diseases or are likely to get them.　　47

Based on this information, she could recommend preventive measures, years before any symptoms appear. Think of that—*before any symptoms appear!* This is early detection with a difference!　　48

This would also allow your doctor to determine, for example, whether or not you are likely to contract a particular disease that has run through your family for generations—and if so, what to do now to prevent it or at least minimize its effects.　　49

And it could also mean avoiding preventative measures—such as a mastectomy—where your genes say you're unlikely to contract a particular disease.　　50

Quite simply, your personalized DNA sequence will be the foundation for    51
the treatment you receive.

This will revolutionize how doctors practise medicine because diagnoses    52
will become biology-based, not symptom-based, ushering in a whole new
era of individualized medicine.

In other words, we are moving from reactive to proactive medicine, from    53
intervention based on what your doctor sees to intervention based on what
your DNA says.

Well, the possibilities of genomics on health and health care are mind-    54
boggling, and I could talk about them for hours, but let me just touch on one
other area where genomics could have a dramatic effect on our lives and our
society and that's agriculture.

Through genomics, we will be able to dramatically increase the volume of    55
food and fibre grown. Working in laboratories, in tissue cultures in giant bacteria baths, we will be able to produce more food, at a fraction of the cost,
than growing staples on land.

This will have enormous consequences for poorer nations, allowing them    56
to advance from mere subsistence to true development.

And by developing disease resistant crops, farmers in all parts of the    57
world will benefit. Hunger may indeed go the way of polio or smallpox.

So there is little doubt that genomics holds the power to transform our    58
lives, from the drugs we receive to the food we eat.

It is also a vital component of the new, "knowledge" economy.    59

Genomics is a classic example of the new economy. It puts a premium on    60
invention and imagination. It requires special skills and higher education.

And it is extremely knowledge-intensive. Indeed, the tidal wave of data    61
which genomics is producing is giving rise to a whole new discipline—bio-
informatics, which applies the power of information technologies to classifying, analyzing and organizing the more than three billion bits of information
in the genome.

■ ■ ■

## Discussion and Writing Suggestions

1. Friesen is a scientist like James D. Watson (whose essay follows), who is
   enthusiastic about the promises of genetic research. Compare some of
   their claims about some of the advantages of genetic research.
2. Friesen is optimistic about the outcome of genetic research. Are there
   points where he engages the opposition and responds to the serious concerns many have raised about the problems associated with genetic
   research? Friesen is giving a speech to businessmen, some of whom may
   contribute to funding his research project. In this situation, would he
   sound defensive or unsure of himself if he were to devote a lot of attention to addressing concerns and complaints about his work?

# The Human Genome Project:
## A Personal View

JAMES D. WATSON

*One of the most monumental scientific undertakings of our time is the Human Genome Project, launched in 1988.\* A genome is the complete set of genes in the chromosomes of organisms (humans have twenty-three pairs of chromosomes in the nucleus of each cell); and the purpose of the Human Genome Project is to identify, locate, and sequence all of the genes in human chromosomes. As a* Time *magazine article explained, "Encoded in the genome, the DNA in the . . . 46 chromosomes, are instructions that affect not only structure, size, coloring and other physical attributes, but also intelligence, susceptibility to disease, life-span and even some aspects of behavior. The ultimate goal of the Human Genome Project is to read and understand those instructions." Among the instructions that scientists are most eager to understand are those that determine human diseases, many of which are genetic in origin.*

*In the following article, James D. Watson, the first director of the Human Genome Project, offers a "personal" perspective on this project and its meaning for him. One of the most influential scientists of modern times, Watson, together with Francis Crick, discovered the double-helix structure of the DNA molecule, a discovery that won them the 1962 Nobel Prize and that has been the basis of almost all subsequent genetic research. Born in 1928, Watson earned his doctorate in biology from Indiana University. In 1951, while conducting research at the Cavendish Laboratory at Cambridge University, Watson met Francis Crick, and the two began their epoch-making studies into the molecular basis of heredity. Watson and Crick's paper, announcing their discovery, was published in the journal* Nature *in 1953.*

*Watson taught at Harvard University from 1955 to 1976, and starting in 1968 served as director of the Cold Spring Harbor Biological Laboratories, working primarily on cancer research. In 1989 Watson was appointed director of the National Institutes of Health's (NIH) Human Genome Project. Watson's books include* The Double Helix *(1968), an account of the discovery of DNA structure;* The Molecular Biology of the Gene *(1965); and* Recombinant DNA *(1985; with John Tooze and David T. Kurtz). This article first appeared in an anthology,* The Code of Codes: Scientific and Social Issues in the Human Genome Project *(1992), edited by Daniel J. Kevles and Leroy Hood.*

When I was going into science, people were concerned with questions of     1
where we came from. Some people gave mystical answers—for example, "the
truth came from revelation." But as a college kid I was influenced by Linus
Pauling, who said, "We came from chemistry." I have spent my career trying
to get a chemical explanation for life, the explanation of why we are human

---

\*For its first five years the Genome Project was headed by DNA pioneer and Nobel laureate
James D. Watson.

beings and not monkeys. The reason, of course, is our DNA. If you can study life from the level of DNA, you have a real explanation for its processes. So of course I think that the human genome project is a glorious goal.

People ask why *I* want to get the human genome. Some suggest that the reason is that it would be a wonderful end to my career—start out with the double helix and end up with the human genome. That *is* a good story. It seems almost a miracle to me that fifty years ago we could have been so ignorant of the nature of the genetic material and now can imagine that we will have the complete genetic blueprint of man. Just getting the complete description of a bacterium—say, the five million bases of *E. coli*—would make an extraordinary moment in history. There is a greater degree of urgency among older scientists than among younger ones to do the human genome now. The younger scientists can work on their grants until they are bored and still get the genome before they die. But to me it is crucial that we get the human genome now rather than twenty years from now, because I might be dead then and I don't want to miss out on learning how life works.

Still, I sometimes find myself moved to wonder, Is it ethical for me to do my job? A kind of backlash against the human genome project has cropped up from some scientists—good ones as well as not so good ones. What seems to have outraged many people was that, in 1990, against the proposed increase of 3.6 percent in the president's budget for all NIH funds, the human genome project was proposed for an increase of 86 percent—from roughly $60 million to $108 million. Feeling dispossessed, some scientific groups have begun to behave like postal workers' unions. The biological chemists, the molecular biologists, and the cell biologists have hired a lobbyist, a former congressman from Maine, to get the overall NIH appropriation increased. If such moves succeed, then maybe we won't have this terrible situation of really good scientists claiming that they are not getting funded because all the money is going to the human genome project.

In the meantime, hate letters have made the rounds, including the rounds of Congress, contending that the project is "bad science"—not only bad, but sort of wicked. The letters say that the project is wasting money at a time when resources for research are getting threatened: If good people are failing to get grants, why go ahead with a program that is just going to spend billions of dollars sequencing junk? In 1990, someone in my office tried to get a distinguished biologist to help peer-review a big grant application. The biologist said, "No, not the human genome!" as though he were talking about syphilis.

The biologist sent me a fax asking me to explain why he should not oppose the human genome program. I called him up and said that, though I couldn't prove it, Congress actually seemed to *like* the human genome program because it promised to find out something about disease. Congress was excited that maybe we scientists were worried about disease instead of just about getting grants. The primary mission of the National Institutes of Health is to improve American health, to give us healthier lives, not to give jobs to scientists. I think that the scientific community, if it wants to be ethically responsible to society, has to ask whether we are spending research money in a way that offers the best go at diseases.

The fact is that understanding how DNA operates provides an enormous advantage over working only with proteins or fats or carbohydrates. The best illustration of this advantage has been tumor viruses. If we had not been able to study cancer at the level of the change in DNA that starts it, the disease would still be a hopeless field. Every time a new enzyme was discovered, hope would rise that it was the cause of cancer. Cancer used to be considered a graveyard for biochemists, even good ones, many of whom wanted to cap their careers by solving cancer but failed. Not until the genetic foundation for cancer was identified could you really begin to say what goes wrong to make this terrible human affliction.   6

A similar example is Alzheimer's disease. Are we going to find out what Alzheimer's is and why it causes brain failure without getting the genes that we know predispose certain people to the disease? Maybe we will, but I would not bet on it. But if we can get the gene or genes implicated in the disease, I am confident that we will save hundreds of millions of dollars, if not billions, that would have been spent on worthless research.   7

Every year, Congress passes a bill for even more money to study Alzheimer's. Congress is voting for good goals, but we do not really know how to use the money. It is not as if all the federal budget for health and all the basic research grants add up to good research. All the study sections in the National Institutes of Health do not receive applications of equal value; they often endorse research projects or programs because they address important problems. The programs themselves are not terrible, but they often have a low probability of paying off. I am sure that half the NIH budget is spent on good intentions rather than on a realistically high probability that a research program will have a direct impact on one of the major human diseases.   8

The pressure is enormous to do something about mental disease because it can be terrible, as anyone knows who has a friend or family member suffering from it. We do spend a vast amount of money studying mental diseases, yet the effort yields very little. Manic-depressive disease leads to great moments of mania—perhaps the successful careers of a number of scientists can be attributed to it—but it also leads to depression, tragedy, and suicides. Lithium relieves some of the symptoms, but a drug is not the complete answer, as any psychiatrist will tell you. It is pretty clear that manic depression has a genetic cause. Several scientists thought they had located the gene on a chromosome. But then it got lost, and so long as it is lost, we are lost.   9

It is also pretty clear that alcoholism bears some relationship to genes. This view comes from studies on identical twins adopted and raised by different families. There *are* alcoholic families. It is not likely that their members are morally weak; they just cannot tolerate alcohol chemically. But no one has found the gene or genes for susceptibility to alcoholism, and the chance of finding the genetic sources are probably low until a much more sophisticated   10 human genetic community exists—plus the money to get the pedigrees and all the genetic markers.

Some diseases are not going to be easy to crack. For a long time, people    11
have been trying to discover the cause of schizophrenia by looking for chemical differences in the urine or the blood, a research strategy that has not been successful. It is not going to be easy to find the genes behind schizophrenia either, because reliable pedigree data[1] are difficult to compile and the condition is hard to diagnose. Thus both directions offer low probabilities, but it is still better to waste your money doing genetics because genetics lies at the heart of so much. Of course scientists should find out what the brain is. I believe in neurobiology and have tried to help raise money to support the field. But I do not believe that its current approaches will necessarily lead to the real, deep cause of manic-depressive disease.

In 1989 Congressman Joe Early said to me, "I'm tired of putting fingers    12
in dikes!" In combating disease, genetics helps enormously if it is a bad gene that contributes to the cause. Ignoring genes is like trying to solve a murder without finding the murderer. All we have are victims. With time, if we find the genes for Alzheimer's disease and for manic depression, then less money will be wasted on research that goes nowhere. Congressmen can only feel good if they are spending money on good things, so we have to convince them that the best use for their money is DNA research.

The human genome project is really trying to push a little more money    13
toward DNA-based research. Since we can now produce good genetic maps that allow us to locate culprit chromosomes and then actually find the genes for disease (as Francis Collins found the gene for cystic fibrosis), genetics should be a very high priority on the agenda of NIH research. We are extremely lucky that when James Wyngaarden was director of NIH, he saw to the establishment of what is now a permanent division within NIH called the Center for Human Genome Research. I doubt that I convinced the biologist who sent me the fax, but I may eventually, since he is very bright. I want to convince as many people as I can of the merits of the human genome project, but not to cap my career and have something that sounds good in my obituary. I can make best use of my time by trying to mobilize the country to do something about diseases that have hit my family and many others. I am sort of a concerned parent for whom things have not gone completely right. So, I am trying to enlist a group of people who will help us get these genes, and do what I think Congress wants us to do.

The ultimate objective of the human genome program is to learn the    14
nucleotide sequence of human DNA. We want the program completed in roughly fifteen years. By completed we do not mean every last nucleotide sequence. If we get 98 percent of the regions that are functional, that will probably be the end of it. We will not worry about spending infinite amounts of money trying to sequence things we know probably contain little infor-

---

[1] *pedigree data:* data that establish the genetic lineage of a particular trait or defect; the process involves gathering genetic information about the parents, grandparents, and so on.

mation. We could define the end of it to be the identification of all the human genes—that is, we will be done when we have located the coding sequences and can declare that human beings on the average contain, say, 248,000 genes, with variations such that some individuals, for example have a gene present in four copies and some in three, and that for some the gene is nonessential. It has recently been learned that only a third of yeast genes are essential. Knock out two-thirds of them and the yeast will multiply. Studying things that are not essential will keep the people in the yeast world going for a long time. I think we can safely say the project will be over when we can identify the genes.

We probably will be unable to identify the genes until we get most of the   15
DNA sequenced, because we will not know where they are. It would be nice if the whole program could be done by copy DNA (cDNA)—that is, by purely functional DNA[2]—so that we would not have to sequence all the junk, but we will never know whether we have all the cDNAs. This is not to say we should not do cDNA; we will actually fund grants for people trying to find better techniques for getting rare cDNA in tissue-specific places. But I think that we have got to sequence the whole thing.

In the first five years, we will push to achieve three major objectives. First,   16
we will try to get good genetic maps, so that each chromosome has enough genetic markers[3] on it actually to locate a gene if a pedigree is available. Currently, we have only about 150 markers that are sufficiently informative for assigning the location of genes. We have started a crash program to persuade people to make a lot of markers and to put them into a public repository made available to the whole world. We want to change the current practice among researchers of not sharing their markers because they want to be the first to find a gene and encourage everyone to make markers available to everyone.

The second objective is to make overlapping fragments of DNA available   17
so that anyone looking for a gene in a particular piece of a certain chromosome will be able to get it by paying some nominal sum. The fragment will not be totally free, but it will certainly be there for anyone who seriously wants it. Techniques for doing this seem to be available now; it should not require more than $10 million to stockpile overlapping fragments of a given chromosome. To put this figure into perspective, Francis Collins has said that finding the cystic fibrosis gene was expensive—between $10 million and $50 million. If all the markers had been available, it would have cost only $5 million. I think we can establish an overlapping fragment library for the entire human genome for a couple of hundred million dollars, which will certainly reduce the costs of subsequent disease hunts. We will end up with a map of overlapping fragments, each one identified by three or four DNA sequences

---

[2] *DNA:* Watson considers "functional DNA" only that kind of DNA that copies the messenger RNA molecules that contain instructions for synthesizing proteins.

[3] *genetic marker:* genetic "signposts"—differences in a complementary pair of chromosomes—that help locate particular genes.

along it called sequence tag sites. With PCR,[4] researchers will be able to pull out all the human DNA that may be wanted.

The third major objective is to support scientists trying to do megabase[5]    18
sequencing in one place in a reasonable period of time. An example of this type of project is a proposal from Walter Gilbert to sequence a mycoplasma, which is really a small (800 kilobases) bacterium. Gilbert's proposal, whether he lives up to it or not, is to do a million bases a year within two years. We want to encourage people to do sequencing of megabases with the aim of reducing the cost—so that within a couple of years it will fall to about a dollar a base pair, and then perhaps even to fifty cents. We will not accept a grant application from someone who proposes to sequence some DNA the old fashioned way, with graduate students or postdoctoral fellows, at the current cost—five to ten dollars a base pair—just out of curiosity about it. . . .

The NIH genome project will also try to get some real data on model    19
organisms. I will be happy if we get ten quite different bacteria sequenced up through yeast. We are now supporting a joint program between the Medical Research Council, in England, and the Laboratory of Molecular Biology in Cambridge, and the group in St. Louis that has developed yeast artificial chromosomes to sequence the genome of a roundworm. The roundworm community is eager to do it because they've already got the overlapping DNA fragments. We hope to get the sequence out in ten years. It's about the equivalent of an average human chromosome—about a hundred megabases—but with less repetitive DNA, and so probably with fewer problems. There is also an effort to sequence a plant genome, arabadopsis, which we hope will be led by the National Science Foundation with help from other agencies, including ourselves. This is roughly seventy megabases, and the project should be a real boon to botany. Except for perhaps one bacterium, none of this probably would ever have been funded in the absence of the human genome program.

Among the reasons for wanting to find bacterial genes is to help find the    20
human ones. People ask, How are you going to identify a gene if it is interspersed with so much junk and you lack a cDNA? How are you going to know you have it? That is obviously going to be hard in some cases, but if you have obtained the corresponding bacterial gene without many repetitive sequences and if you are clever, you ought to be able to spot the differences. I can imagine that typical work for undergraduates will be to find the gene once all the sequences have been obtained. Professors could tell their students: If you can identify a gene, we will let you go on to graduate school and do real science.

The human genome project is sufficiently justifiable so that if no other    21
country wants to help fund it, the United States should do the whole thing. We are rich enough to do it. But I doubt that we will be allowed to do it alone, because others are going to worry that it might actually be commer-

---

[4] *PCR:* polymerase chain reaction; a powerful technique for amplifying a gene sequence, for obtaining a large amount of DNA from a small amount.
[5] *megabase:* one million base pairs.

cially interesting, and they will worry that we will be disinclined to distribute the data very fast if we have paid for it ourselves. It is my hope that we can spread out the cost of sequencing and data distribution over many countries. As soon as a gene has been identified, it should be thrown into an international data base.

But there are problems that I don't see how to get around. If a stretch of   22 DNA is sequenced in an academic laboratory, a university lawyer will say, "That looks like a serotonin receptor. Patent it!" Mutant forms of the cystic fibrosis gene have been patented by the universities of Toronto and Michigan. They will get some royalties and maybe build better student unions with the revenues. I am at a loss to know how to put valuable DNA sequences in the public domain fast when a lot of people want to keep them private. I just hope that other major nations come in. The Japanese will not let anyone who doesn't pay for it see their work. I figure that strategy might work. People might actually pay for sequence information if that is the only way to get to see it. So I have to seem a bad guy and say: I *will* withhold information that we generate if other countries refuse to join in an open sharing arrangement. But, in truth, it would be very distasteful to me to get into a situation where we were withholding the data for reasons of national advantage.

The acquisition of human DNA information has already begun to pose   23 serious ethical problems. I think that somehow we have to get it into the laws that anyone's DNA—the message it gives—is confidential and that the only one who has a right to look at it is the person herself or himself. Still, the ethics get complicated if you can spot a gene in a newborn child that produces a disease for which no treatment exists. Sometimes these defects will be hard to spot, but sometimes, as in muscular dystrophy, they can be very easy to detect. As we begin to get data of this kind, people are going to get nervous and some are going to be violent opponents of the project unless they can feel that they or their friends will not be discriminated against on the basis of their DNA. If someone can go look at your DNA and see that you have a deletion on one of your anti-oncogenes and that you will be more liable to die of cancer at an early age, then you might be discriminated against in, say, employment or insurance coverage.

Laws are needed to prevent genetic discrimination and to protect rights   24 that should not be signed away too easily. If you are poor, it will be highly tempting to say, "Yes, look at my DNA because I want the job in the asbestos factory." If you have no money, a job in an asbestos factory is better than no job. Issues like these demand a lot of discussion, at least so that DNA-related laws are not enacted prematurely. For that reason, we are putting more than 3 percent of the genome project money into an ethics program; and we will put more into it if we find that it needs more.

We have faced up to this challenge already with DNA fingerprints. The   25 National Center for Genome Research has given $50,000 to the National Research Council–National Academy of Sciences study on DNA fingerprinting, which has lawyers and judges advising it. The police want a DNA register of sex offenders; other people may want one of dishonest accountants. People will want DNA fingerprints to prove that a politician's children are really his. At a meeting in Leicester, England, Alec Jeffries showed a slide of a letter from a woman who runs a small hotel in Wales and who wrote that it would be a good idea to have a DNA fingerprint register of bedwetters. Different people will want different information—the possibilities are unlimited. I don't think *anyone* should have access to anyone else's DNA fingerprints.

We need to explore the social implications of human genome research   26 and figure out some protection for people's privacy so that these fears do not sabotage the entire project. Deep down, I think that the only thing that could stop our program is fear; if people are afraid of the information we will find, they will keep us from finding it. We have to convince our fellow citizens somehow that there will be more advantages to knowing the human genome than to not knowing it.

■ ■ ■

## Review Questions

1. Why do some scientific researchers oppose the Human Genome Project, according to Watson?
2. Why does Watson believe that DNA research, including the Human Genome Project, should be of the highest priority?
3. What are the immediate objectives of the Human Genome Project?
4. According to Watson, what are some of the ethical problems associated with DNA research?

## Discussion and Writing Suggestions

1. Watson concludes, "we have to convince our fellow citizens somehow that there will be more advantages to knowing the human genome than to not knowing it." Has Watson convinced you that the Human Genome Project is both a good thing in itself and a useful expenditure of public funds? If so, which arguments made the greatest impression on you, and why? If not, what are your chief concerns? Should the project be cancelled? Should restrictions be placed on genetic research? If so, what kind of restrictions?
2. To what extent, if any, does Watson's own personal stake in the success of the Human Genome Project (and in the success of biotechnology, in general) affect the way that you read this article and accept his arguments? Explain.
3. Watson is a scientist trying to persuade people (both his fellow scientists and others interested in scientific matters) that the project he heads is a vital one. Setting aside for the moment your own views of the genome project, to what extent do you think Watson has done a good job of explaining this

scientific project? In particular, did you find this article difficult to follow because of the language in which Watson explained genetic concepts? If so, how might he have made his explanations easier to understand?

4. Watson argues that information gleaned from the Human Genome Project should be made available to all interested parties and that whatever has been discovered in one country should be made available to an international database. A genetic cure for a particular disease might be discovered more rapidly if more than one group of scientists were attacking the problem. But private companies might argue that they are entitled to the patents and financial profits from their own discoveries—that without such rights and rewards, they have no incentive to invest large amounts of money in research. What are your views on this subject? How can the fruits of genetic research be made widely available, while the rights of companies to earn reasonable profits from their research are protected?

# *Fatalist Attraction: The Dubious Case Against Fooling Mother Nature*

### VIRGINIA POSTREL

*Jeremy Rifkin and others challenge the wisdom of "defying" Nature by tinkering with the genetic blueprints of life. But as Virginia Postrel points out, Nature in its unmodified state can be a brutal breeding ground of illness, suffering, and disease. What genetic researchers are doing now is not so very different (at least in intent) from what medical researchers have done for centuries: that is, sought ways to block the development of disease and to offer patients long and healthy lives. If patients are willing to create "demand" for new medial techniques (even human cloning) and researchers are willing to deliver them, than what role—if any— should medical ethicists and government administrators play in deciding whether these techniques should go to market?*

*Virginia I. Postrel is editor of* Reason *magazine, in which this selection appeared in July 1997.* Reason *presents a libertarian perspective that advocates against government interference in personal affairs. (The magazine's signature phrase is "Free Minds and Free Markets.") Postrel also writes commentaries for other national publications and appears regularly as a commentator on national television.*

Twenty years ago, the bookstore in which I was working closed for a few 1 hours while we all went to the funeral of one of our colleagues. Herbie was a delightful guy, well liked by everyone. He died in his 20s—a ripe old age back then for someone with cystic fibrosis. In keeping with the family's wishes, we all contributed money in his memory to support research on the disease. In those days, the best hope was that scientists would develop a prenatal test that would identify fetuses likely to have C.F., allowing them to be aborted. The thought made us uncomfortable. "Would you really want Herbie never to be?" said my boss.

But science has a way of surprising us. Two decades later, abortion is no     2
longer the answer proposed for cystic fibrosis. Gene therapy—the kind of auda-cious high-tech tool that generates countless references to *Brave New World* and *Frankenstein*—promises not to stamp out future Herbies but to cure them.

This spring I thought of Herbie for the first time in years. It was amid the     3
brouhaha over cloning, as bioethicists galore were popping up on TV to demand that scientists justify their unnatural activities and Pat Buchanan was declaring that "mankind's got to control science, not the other way around."

It wasn't the technophobic fulminations of the anti-cloning pundits that     4
brought back Herbie's memory, however. It was a letter from my husband's college roommate and his wife. Their 16-month-old son had been diagnosed with cystic fibrosis. He was doing fine now, they wrote, and they were opti-mistic about the progress of research on the disease.

There are no Herbies on *Crossfire*, and no babies with deadly diseases.     5
There are only nature and technology, science and society, "ethics" and ambi-tion. Our public debate about biotechnology is loud and impassioned but, most of all, abstract. Cowed by an intellectual culture that treats progress as a myth, widespread choice as an indulgence, and science as the source of atom bombs, even biotech's defenders rarely state their case in stark, personal terms. Its opponents, meanwhile, act as though medical advances are an evil, thrust upon us by scheming scientists. Hence Buchanan talks of "science" as distinct from "mankind" and ubiquitous Boston University bioethicist George Annas declares, "I want to put the burden of proof on scientists to show us why society needs this before society permits them to go ahead and [do] it."

That isn't, however, how medical science works. True, there are research     6
biologists studying life for its own sake. But the advances that get bioethicists exercised spring not from pure science but from consumer demand: "Society" may not ask for them, but individual people do.

Living in a center of medical research, I am always struck by the people     7
who appear on the local news, having just undergone this or that unprece-dented medical procedure. They are all so ordinary, so down-to-earth. They are almost always middle-class, traditional families, people with big medical problems that require unusual solutions. They are not the Faustian, hedonis-tic yuppies you'd imagine from the way the pundits talk.

And it is the ambitions of such ordinary people, with yearnings as old as     8
humanity—for children, for health, for a long and healthy life for their loved ones—of which the experts so profoundly disapprove. As we race toward what Greg Benford aptly calls "the biological century," we will hear plenty of warnings that we should not play God or fool Mother Nature. We will hear the natural equated with the good, and fatalism lauded as maturity. That is a sentiment about which both green romantics and pious conservatives agree. And it deserves far more scrutiny than it usually gets.

Nobody wants to stand around and point a finger at this woman [who     9
had a baby at 63] and say, 'You're immoral.' But generalize the practice and

ask yourself, What does it really mean that we won't accept the life cycle or life course?" Leon Kass, the neocons' favorite bioethicist, told *The New York Times*, "That's one of the big problems of the contemporary scene. You've got all kinds of people who make a living and support themselves but who psychologically are not grown up. We have a culture of functional immaturity."

It sounds so profound, so wise, to denounce "functional immaturity" and   10
set oneself up as a grown-up in a society of brats. But what exactly does it mean in this context? Kass can't possibly think that 63-year-olds will start flocking to fertility clinics—that was the quirky action of one determined woman. He is worried about something far more fundamental: our unwillingness to put up with whatever nature hands out, to accept our fates, to act our ages. "The good news," says Annas of human cloning, "is I think *finally we have a technology that we can all agree shouldn't be used.*" (Emphasis added.) Lots of biotech is bad, he implies, but it's so damned hard to get people to admit it.

When confronted with such sentiments, we should remember just what   11
Mother Nature looks like unmodified. Few biotechnophobes are as honest as British philosopher John Gray, who in a 1993 appeal for greens and conservatives to unite, wrote of "macabre high-tech medicine involving organ transplantation" and urged that we treat death as "a friend to be welcomed." Suffering is the human condition, he suggested: We should just lie back and accept it. "For millennia," he said, "people have been born, have suffered pain and illness, and have died, without those occurrences being understood as treatable diseases."

•   •   •

Gray's historical perspective is quite correct. In the good old days, rich men   12
did not need divorce to dump their first wives for trophies. Childbirth and disease did the trick. In traditional societies, divorce, abandonment, annulment, concubinage, and polygamy—not high-tech medicine—were the cures for infertility. Until the 20th century, C.F. didn't need a separate diagnosis, since it was just one cause of infant mortality among many. Insulin treatment for diabetes (highly unnatural) didn't exist until the 1920s. My own grandmother saw her father, brother, and youngest sister die before she was in middle age. In 1964 a rubella epidemic left a cohort of American newborns deaf.

These days, we in rich countries have the wonderful luxury of rejecting   13
even relatively minor ailments, from menstrual cramps to migraines, as unnecessary and treatable. "People had always suffered from allergies. . . . But compared to the other health problems people faced before the middle of the twentieth century, the sneezing, itching, and skin eruptions had for the most part been looked at as a nuisance," writes biologist Edward Golub. "In the modern world, however, they became serious impediments to living a full life, and the discovery that a whole class of compounds called antihistamines could control the symptoms of allergy meant that allergic individuals could lead close to normal lives. The same story can be told for high blood pressure, depression, and a large number of chronic conditions."

Treating chronic conditions is, if anything, more nature-defiant than    14
attacking infectious diseases. A woman doesn't have to have a baby when
she's 63 to refuse to "accept the life cycle or life course." She can just take
estrogen. And, sure enough, there is a steady drumbeat of criticism against
such unnatural measures, as there is against such psychologically active drugs
as Prozac. We should, say the critics, just take what nature gives us.

In large part, this attitude stems from a naive notion of health as the nat-    15
ural state of the body. In fact, disease and death are natural; the cures are artificial. And as we rocket toward the biological century, we will increasingly
realize that a bodily state may not be a "disease," but just something we wish
to change. Arceli Keh was not sick because her ovaries no longer generated eggs;
she was simply past menopause. To say she should be able to defy her natural
clock (while admitting that mid-60s parenthood may not be the world's greatest idea) doesn't mean declaring menopause a disease. Nor does taking estrogen,
any more than taking birth control pills means fertility is a sickness.

"The cloned human would be an attack on the dignity and integrity of    16
every single person on this earth," says German Research Minister Juergen
Ruettgers, demanding a worldwide ban, lest such subhumans pollute the
planet. (The Germans want to outlaw even the cloning of human cells for
medical research.) Human cloning is an issue, but it is not *the* issue in these
debates. They are really about whether centralized powers will wrest hold of
scientists' freedom of inquiry and patients' freedom to choose—whether one
set of experts will decide what is natural and proper for all of us—and
whether, in fact, nature should be our standard of value.

Ruettgers is wildly overreacting and, in the process, attacking the human-    17
ity of people yet unborn. As Ron Bailey has noted . . . human cloning is not
that scary, unless you're afraid of identical twins, nor does it pose unprecedented ethical problems. No one has come up with a terribly plausible scenario of when human cloning might occur. Yet judging from the history of
other medical technologies, the chances are good that if such a clone were created, the parents involved would be ordinary human beings with reasons
both quite rare and extremely sympathetic. We should not let the arrogant
likes of Ruettgers block their future hopes.

■  ■  ■

## Review Questions

1. According to Postrel, who should control decisions regarding which technologies medical researchers (and patients) should pursue?
2. What distinction does Postrel make between "natural" and "unnatural"
   interventions in human health?
3. Postrel claims that professional ethicists and politicians tend to make
   their objections to high-tech medicine in abstract, not personal, terms.
   Postrel sees this as a problem. Why?

## Discussion and Writing Suggestions

1. To what extent do you see human cloning as a difference in degree or in kind from the medical research that has been done in the past? Researchers have developed elaborate techniques, for instance, to help infertile couples conceive and give birth. In what ways is cloning a radical departure from this kind of science?

2. How comfortable are you in allowing someone—or some government entity—to decide which medical investigations and technologies ought to be permitted? To take a particular case, should it be the government's decision to restrict or ban research on human cloning? Explain your answer.

3. Explain the significance of Postrel's title for this selection. What is a "fatalist" attraction? What is the case against Mother Nature? Why is this a "dubious" case?

4. What, in your view, is the distinction between healing a diseased person naturally versus unnaturally? What would be an example of each type of treatment? Explain the distinctions between the natural and the unnatural treatments.

5. "For millennia," writes Postrel, quoting the British philosopher John Gray, "people have been born, have suffered pain and illness, and have died, without those occurrences being understood as treatable diseases." In Gray's view of the life cycle, what is the function of medicine and what is the role of medical research?

6. If the decision to make genetic interventions (whether in one's own body or, perhaps, in that of a child or embryo) were left to individuals, as Postrel advocates, some observers (see the Rifkin article) predict that two classes, if not species, of humans would inevitably arise—one that insisted on being "natural" and the other that freely made genetic "enhancements." To what extent does this prediction argue for decisions about genetic intervention being made *not* by individuals but by broader cultural authorities—governments, say, or international bodies of scientists?

# The Ultimate Therapy: Commercial Eugenics on the Eve of the Biotech Century

JEREMY RIFKIN

*From its beginnings in the early 1970s, genetic engineering has been surrounded by controversy. Initial fears focused on the nightmare scenario of newly engineered microorganisms escaping from the lab and causing uncontrollable damage to other organisms in the environment. Some scientists proposed a moratorium on*

*gene splicing experiments; and in 1975, during a landmark international confer-
ence at Asilomar, California, scientists agreed to strict guidelines governing all
future research.*

*During the past decade, the science-fiction scenarios have subsided, but the con-
troversy over genetic engineering continues—focusing now on the ethical aspects of
manipulating the genetic code for our own utilitarian and commercial purposes.
Repeatedly, critics associate bioengineering with eugenics, the infamous pseudo-
science practised by the Nazis in their efforts to perpetuate the "Aryan" races and to
exterminate "inferior" races. Then, as now, critics have wondered, Who should
determine what is "superior" (or normal) and what is "inferior" (or defective)?*

*For some years, the most vocal critic of biotechnology has been Jeremy Rifkin,
a philosopher and environmental activist involved in science and technology
issues. Through his publications, his lectures, his congressional testimony, and his
Foundation for Economic Trends, Rifkin has been tireless in attacking both the
practices and the underlying premises of genetic engineering. He has also been successful in halting or delaying the testing of several newly developed microorganisms with agricultural applications.*

*Born in 1945, Rifkin attended the Wharton School of Business and then
earned a degree in law and diplomacy from Tufts University. His first book on
biotechnology was* Who Should Play God *(1977), co-authored with Ted Howard.
This was followed by* Entropy *(1980), which sold more than 750 000 copies
worldwide. In 1985, he followed with* Algeny *(the title is a wordplay on alchemy).
The present selection (from* Tikkun, *May/June 1998) is adapted from his 1998
book,* The Biotech Century: Harnessing the Gene and Remaking the World.
*Throughout his career, Rifkin has maintained a consistent theme: the genetic tech-
nologies we now pursue are so powerful, and the changes they herald so far-reaching,
that we must thoroughly debate the benefits and dangers of this new science before
proceeding. In this chapter, Jeremy Rifkin defines one pole of that debate.*

While the twentieth century was shaped largely by the spectacular break-        1
throughs in the fields of physics and chemistry, the twenty-first century will
belong to the biological sciences. Scientists around the world are quickly
deciphering the genetic code of life, unlocking the mystery of millions of
years of biological evolution on Earth. Global life science companies, in turn,
are beginning to exploit the new advances in biology in a myriad of ways,
laying the economic framework for the coming Biotech Century.

Genes are the raw resource of the new economic epoch and are already        2
being used in a variety of business fields—including agriculture, animal hus-
bandry, energy, bioremediation, building and packaging materials, pharmaceuticals, and food and drink—to fashion a bio-industrial world. Nowhere is
the new genetic commerce likely to have a bigger impact, however, than in
human medicine. For the first time in history, scientific tools are becoming
available to manipulate the genetic instructions in human cells. Human gene
screening and therapy raise the very real possibility that we might be able to
engineer the genetic blueprints of our own species and begin to redirect the

future course of our biological evolution on Earth. The new gene splicing techniques will make it potentially possible to transform individuals and future generations into "works of art," continually updating and editing their DNA codes to enhance physical and mental health. Breakthroughs in genetic technology are bringing us to the edge of a new eugenics era with untold consequences for present and future generations and for civilization itself.

In less than seven years, the global life science companies will hold patents    3
on most of the 100,000 genes that make up the human race as well as patents on the cell lines, tissues, and organs of our species, giving them unprecedented power to dictate the terms by which we and future generations will live our lives. The concentration of power in the global pharmaceutical industry has already reached staggering proportions. The world's ten major pharmaceutical companies currently control 47 percent of the $197 billion pharmaceutical market. The implications of a new market-drive eugenics are enormous and far reaching. Indeed, commercial eugenics could become the defining social dynamic of the new century.

## FRIENDLY EUGENICS

Over the next ten years, molecular biologists say they will locate specific    4
genes associated with several thousand genetic diseases. In the past, a parent's genetic history provided some clues to genetic inheritance, but there was still no way to know for sure whether specific genetic traits would be passed on. In the future, the guesswork will be increasingly eliminated, posing a moral dilemma for prospective parents. Parents will have at their disposal an increasingly accurate readout of their individual genetic make-ups, and will able to predict the statistical probability of a specific genetic disorder being passed on to their children as a result of their biological union.

To avoid the emotional anguish of such decisions, some young people are    5
likely to opt for prevention and avoid marrying someone of the wrong "genotype" for fear of passing along serious genetic diseases to their offspring. Already, part of the Orthodox Jewish community in the United States has established a nationwide program to screen all young Jewish men and women for Tay-Sachs disease. Every young Jew is encouraged to take the test. The results are made available in an easily accessible database to allow young eligible men and women to choose their dating partners with genotype in mind.

Some ethicists argue that such programs will become far more common-    6
place, placing a "genetic stigma" on young people. There's ample precedent for concern. Researchers report that when sickle cell anemia was screened for in Greece, nearly 23 percent of the population was found to have the trait. Fearing stigmatization, many of the carriers concealed their test results, believing that public exposure would seriously jeopardize their marriage prospects.

When researchers at the Johns Hopkins Medical Center recently discov-    7
ered a genetic alteration in one out of every six Jews of Eastern European ancestry that doubles their risk of getting colon cancer, many in the Jewish

community began to express their concern that the Jewish population might be singled out and made the object of discrimination. The news of the "Jewish" cancer gene came on top of other discoveries linking breast and ovarian cancer, cystic fibrosis, Tay-Sachs, Gauchers, and Canavan's disease to Jewish blood lines. Of course, scientists point out that other groups are likely to have just as many genetic links to specific diseases, but that the Jewish population has received the most attention to date because "they constitute a well defined, easily identifiable and closely related community—exactly the kind that allows geneticists to start identifying disease-causing genes." Still, the explanations of the researchers were not enough to calm an anxious Jewish community who began to vent their feelings publicly. Amy Rutkin, the director of American affairs for Hadassah, the nation's largest Jewish membership organization, reported that in the aftermath of the colon cancer discovery, the organization has been "receiving phone calls indicating a certain amount of fear and confusion." Rutkin said that "people are asking, is too much research focused on the Jewish community and are we at risk of stigmatization?"

8   Health professionals worry about genetic stigmatization and especially the prospect of selecting potential mates based on genotyping, but argue that it is still less onerous than selective abortion or sentencing a newborn to premature death or a life of chronic or debilitating illness. Not surprising, there is increasing talk of government mandated genetic testing of couples seeking marriage licenses. Even without a government requirement, it's likely that a growing number of potential marriage partners will want their future partner screened before committing themselves to a life-long relationship.

9   While genetic screening is already here, human genetic engineering— gene therapy—is just around the corner. Genetic manipulation is of two kinds. In somatic therapy, intervention takes place only within non-sex (somatic) cells and the genetic changes do not transfer into the offspring. In germ line therapy, genetic changes are made in the sperm, egg or embryonic cells, and are passed along to future generations. Somatic gene surgery has been carried out in limited human clinical trials for more than seven years. Germ line experiments have been successfully carried out on mammals for more than a decade and researchers expect the first human trials to be conducted within the next several years.

10   Despite years of favorable media reports on various somatic gene therapy experiments and the high expectations voiced by the medical establishment and the biotech industry, the results have, thus far, been so disappointing that the NIH itself was recently forced to acknowledge the fact and issue a sober warning to scientists conducting the experiments to stop making promises that cannot be kept. In an extensive survey of all 106 clinical trials of experimental gene therapies conducted over the past five years involving more than 597 patients, a panel of experts convened by the NIH reported that "clinical efficacy has not been definitively demonstrated at this time in any gene therapy protocol, despite anecdotal claims of successful therapy." Even Dr. Leroy B. Walters, a philosophy professor at Georgetown University and

the chairperson of the NIH oversight committee that reviewed and approved all of the clinical trials, remarked in a moment of candor that he and the committee had not seen "any solid results yet" after years of experiments. Still, many of the staunchest supporters of the new gene therapies remain convinced that the techniques will bear fruit as methodologies and procedures are honed and new knowledge of the workings of the genes become more available to researchers and clinicians.

Far more controversial is the prospect of conducting human germ line therapy. Debate over genetic manipulation of human eggs, sperm, and embryonic cells has raged for more than fifteen years. In 1983, a cross-section of the nation's religious leaders and prominent scientists announced their opposition to such experiments, on eugenics grounds, and urged a worldwide ban. (The coalition was put together by The Foundation on Economic Trends.) 11

Programming genetic changes into the human germ line to direct the evolutionary development of future generations is the most radical human experiment ever contemplated and raises unprecedented moral, social, and environmental risks for the whole of humanity. Even so, a growing number of molecular biologists, medical practitioners, and pharmaceutical companies are anxious to take the gamble, convinced that controlling our evolutionary destiny is humankind's next great social frontier. Their arguments are couched in terms of personal health, individual choice, and collective responsibility for future generations. 12

Writing in *The Journal of Medicine and Philosophy*, Dr. Burke Zimmerman makes several points in defense of germ line cell therapy over somatic cell therapy. To begin with, he argues that the increasing use of somatic therapy is only likely to increase the number of survivors with defective genes in their germ lines—genes that will continue to accumulate and further "pollute" the genetic pool of the species, passing an increasing number of genetic problems onto succeeding generations. Secondly, although somatic therapy may be able to treat many disorders in which treatment lies in replacing populations of cells, it might never prove effective in addressing diseases involving solid tissues, organs, and functions dependent on structure—for example the brain—and therefore, germ line therapy is likely the only remedy, short of abortion, against such disorders. 13

Zimmerman and other proponents of germ line therapy argue for a broadening of the ethical mandate of the healing professions to include responsibility for the health of those not yet conceived. The interests of the patient, they say, should be extended to include the interests of "the entire genetic legacy that may result from intervention in the germ line." Moreover, parents ought not to be denied their right as parents to make choices on how best to protect the health of their unborn children during pregnancy. To deny them the opportunity to take corrective action in the sex cells or at the early embryonic stage would be a serious breach of medical responsibility. Proponents of germ line therapy ask why millions of individuals need to be subjected to painful, intrusive, and potentially risky somatic therapy when the 14 gene or genes responsible for their diseases could be more easily eliminated from the germ line, at less expense, and with less discomfort.

Finally, the health costs to society need to be factored into the equation,   15 say the advocates of germ line therapy. Although the costs of genetic intervention into the germ line to cure diseases are likely to remain high in the early years, the cost is likely to drop dramatically in the future as the methods and techniques become more refined. The lifetime cost of caring for generations of patients suffering from Parkinson's disease or severe Down's syndrome is likely to be far greater than simple prevention in the form of genetic intervention at the germ line level.

## GENETIC RESPONSIBILITY

In the coming decades, scientists will learn more about how genes function.   16 They will become increasingly adept at turning genes "on" and "off." They will become more sophisticated in the techniques of recombining genes and altering genetic codes. At every step of the way, conscious decisions will have to be made as to which kinds of permanent changes in the biological codes of life are worth pursuing and which are not. A society and civilization steeped in "engineering" the gene pool of the planet cannot possibly hope to escape the kind of ongoing eugenics decisions that go hand in hand with each new advance in biotechnology. There will be enormous social pressure to conform with the underlying logic of genetic engineering, especially when it comes to its human applications.

Parents in the biotech century will be increasingly forced to decide   17 whether to take their chances with the traditional genetic lottery and use their own unaltered egg and sperm, knowing their children may inherit some "undesirable" traits, or undergo corrective gene changes on their sperm, egg, embryo, or fetus, or substitute egg or sperm from a donor through *in vitro* fertilization and surrogacy arrangements. If they choose to go with the traditional approach and let genetic fate determine their child's biological destiny, they could find themselves culpable if something goes dreadfully wrong in the developing fetus, something they could have avoided had they availed themselves of corrective genetic intervention at the sex cell or embryo stage.

In the Biotech Century, a parent's failure to correct genetic defects *in*   18 *utero* might well be regarded as a heinous crime. Society may conclude that every parent has a responsibility to provide as safe and secure an environment as humanly possible for their unborn child. Not to do so might be considered a breach of parental duty for which the parents could be held morally, if not legally, liable. Mothers have already been held liable for having given birth to crack cocaine addicted babies and babies with fetal alcohol syndrome. Prosecutors have argued that mothers passing on these painful addictions to their unborn children are culpable under existing child abuse statutes, and ought to be held liable for the effect of their lifestyle on their babies.

Proponents of human genetic engineering argue that it would be cruel   19
and irresponsible not to use this powerful new technology to eliminate serious
"genetic disorders." The problem with this argument, says *The New York
Times* in an editorial entitled, "Whether to Make Perfect Humans," is that
"there is no discernible line to be drawn between making inheritable repair of
genetic defects and improving the species." The *Times* rightly points out that
once scientists are able to repair genetic defects, "it will become much harder
to argue against additional genes that confer desired qualities, like better
health, looks or brains."

If diabetes, sickle cell anemia, and cancer are to be prevented by altering   20
the genetic makeup of individuals, why not proceed to other less serious
"defects": myopia, color blindness, dyslexia, obesity, short stature? Indeed,
what is to preclude a society from deciding that a certain skin color is a disorder? In the end, why would we ever say no to any alteration of the genetic
code that might enhance the well-being of our offspring? It would be difficult
to imagine parents rejecting genetic modifications that promised to improve,
in some way, the opportunities for their progeny.

It is likely that as new screening technologies become more universally   21
available, and genetic surgery at the embryonic and fetal stage becomes more
widely acceptable, the issue of parental responsibility will be hotly debated,
both in the courts and in the legislatures. The very fact that parents will
increasingly be able to intervene to ensure the health of their child before
birth, is likely to raise the concomitant issue of the responsibilities and obligations to their unborn children. Why shouldn't parents be held responsible for
taking proper care of their unborn child? For that matter, why shouldn't parents be held liable for neglecting their child's welfare in the womb in cases
where they failed to or refused to screen for and correct genetic defects that
could prove harmful to their offspring?

With Americans already spending billions of dollars on cosmetic surgery   22
to improve their looks and psychotropic drugs to alter their mood and behavior, the use of genetic therapies to enhance their unborn children also seems
a likely prospect. According to a 1992 Harris poll, 43 percent of Americans
"would approve using gene therapy to improve babies' physical characteristics." Many advocates of germ line intervention are already arguing for
enhancement therapy. They contend that the current debate over corrective
measures to address serious illnesses is too limited and urge a more expansive
discussion to include the advantage of enhancement therapy as well. As to the
oft heard criticism that genetic enhancement will favor children of the rich at
the expense of children of the poor—as the rich will be the only ones capable
of paying for genetic enhancement of their offspring—proponents argue that
the children of well-off parents have always enjoyed the advantages that
wealth and inheritance can confer. Is it such a leap, they ask rhetorically, to
want to pass along genetic gifts to their children along with material riches?
Advocates ask us to consider the positive side of germ line enhancement, even
if it gives an advantage to the children of those who can afford the technology.

"What about . . . increasing the number of talented people. Wouldn't society be better off in the long run?" asks Dr. Burke Zimmerman.

Perhaps not. Despite the growing enthusiasm among molecular biologists    23
for engineering fundamental changes in the genetic code of human sex cells, it should be emphasized that treating genetic disorders by eliminating recessive traits at the germ line level is far different from treating genetic disorders by way of somatic gene surgery after birth. In the former instance, the genetic deletions can result, in the long run, in a dangerous narrowing of the human gene pool upon which future generations rely for making evolutionary adaptations to changing environments.

We learned, long ago, that recessive traits and mutations are essential    24
players in the evolutionary schema. They are not mistakes, but rather variations, some of which become opportunities. Eliminating so-called "bad" genes risks depleting the genetic pool and limiting future evolutionary options. Recessive gene traits are far too complex and mercurial to condemn as simple errors in the code. We are, in fact, just beginning to learn of the many subtle and varied roles recessive gene traits play, some of which have been critically important in ensuring the survival of different ethnic and racial groups. For example, the sickle cell recessive trait protects against malaria. The cystic fibrosis recessive gene may play a role in protecting against cholera. To think of recessive traits and single gene disorders, then, as merely errors in the code, in need of reprogramming, is to lose sight of how things really work in the biological kingdom.

Somatic gene surgery, on the other hand, if it proves to be a safe, thera-    25
peutic way to treat serious diseases that can not be effectively treated by more conventional approaches, including preventive measures, would appear to have potential value.

Many biotech libertarians, however, disdain such distinctions. *The*    26
*Economist* suggested, in a recent editorial, that society should move beyond old fashioned hand-wringing moralism on the subject and openly embrace the new commercial eugenics opportunities that will soon become available in the marketplace. The editors asked,

> What of genes that might make a good body better, rather than make a bad one good? Should people be able to retrofit themselves with extra neurotransmitters, to enhance various mental powers? Or to change the color of their skin? Or to help them run faster, or lift heavier weights?

*The Economist* editorial board made clear that its own biases lay firmly    27
with the marketplace. To them, the new commercial eugenics is about ensuring greater consumer freedom so that individuals can make of themselves and their heirs whatever they choose. The editorial concluded with a ringing endorsement of the new eugenics:

> The proper goal is to allow people as much choice as possible about what they do. To this end, making genes instruments of such freedom, rather than limits upon it, is a great step forward.

Dr. Robert Sinsheimer, a long standing leader and driving force in the   28
field of molecular biology, laid out his eugenics vision of the new man and
woman of the biotech century:

> The old dreams of the cultural perfection of man were always sharply con-
> strained by his inherited imperfections and limitations. . . . To foster his
> better traits and to curb his worse by cultural means alone has always been,
> while clearly not impossible, in many instances most difficult. . . . We now
> glimpse another route—the chance to ease the internal strains and heal the
> internal flaws directly, to carry on and consciously perfect far beyond our
> present vision this remarkable product of two billion years of evolution. . . .
> The old eugenics would have required a continual selection for breeding of
> the fit, and a culling of the unfit. . . . The horizons of the new eugenics are in
> principle boundless—for we should have the potential to create new genes
> and new qualities yet undreamed. . . . Indeed, this concept marks a turning
> point in the whole evolution of life. For the first time in all time, a living crea-
> ture understands its origin and can undertake to design its future. Even in the
> ancient myths man was constrained by essence. He could not rise above his
> nature to chart his destiny. Today we can envision that chance—and its dark
> companion of awesome choice and responsibility.

## PERFECTING THE CODE

While the notion of consumer choice would appear benign, the very idea of   29
eliminating so-called genetic defects raises the troubling question of what is
meant by the term "defective." Ethicist Daniel Callahan of the Hastings
Center penetrates to the core of the problem when he observes that "behind
the human horror at genetic defectiveness lurks . . . an image of the perfect
human being. The very language of 'defect,' 'abnormality,' 'disease,' and
'risk' presupposes such an image, a kind of prototype of perfection."

The all consuming preoccupation with "defects" or "errors" among   30
medical researchers and molecular biologists puts them very much at odds
with most evolutionary biologists. When evolutionary biologists talk of
"mutations," they have in mind the idea of "different 'readings' or 'versions'" of a relatively stable archetype. James Watson and Francis Crick's discovery of the DNA double helix in the 1950s, however, brought with it a new
set of metaphors and a new language for describing biological processes
which changed the way molecular biologists perceive genetic mutations. The
primary building block of life was described as a code, a set of instructions,
a program, to be unraveled and read. The early molecular biologists, many of
whom had been trained first as physicists, were enamored with what they
regarded as the universal explanatory power of the information sciences.
Norbert Weiner's cybernetic model and modern communications and information theory provided a compelling new linguistic paradigm for redefining
how we talk about both physical and biological phenomena. It is within the
context of this new language that molecular biologists first began to talk of

genetic variation as "errors" in the code rather than "mutations." The shift from the notion of genetic mutations in nature to genetic errors in codes represents a sea change in the way biologists approach their discipline, with profound repercussions for how we structure both our relationship to the natural world and our own human nature in the coming Biotech Century.

The very idea of engineering the human species—by making changes at    31
the germ line level—is not too dissimilar from the idea of engineering a piece of machinery. An engineer is constantly in search of new ways to improve the performance of a machine. As soon as one set of defects is eliminated, the engineer immediately turns his attention to the next set of defects, always with the idea in mind of creating a more efficient machine. The notion of setting arbitrary limits to how much "improvement" is acceptable is alien to the entire engineering conception.

The new language of the information sciences has transformed many    32
molecular biologists from scientists to engineers, although they are, no doubt, little aware of the metamorphosis. When molecular biologists speak of mutations and genetic diseases as errors in the code, the implicit, if not explicit, assumption is that they should never have existed in the first place, that they are "bugs," or mistakes that need to be deprogrammed or corrected. The molecular biologist, in turn, becomes the computing engineer, the writer of codes, continually eliminating errors and reprogramming instructions to upgrade both the program and the performance. This is a dubious and dangerous role when we stop to consider that every human being brings with him or her a number of lethal recessive genes. Do we then come to see ourselves as miswired from the get-go, riddled with errors in our code? If that be the case, against what ideal norm of perfection are we to be measured? If every human being is made up of varying degrees of error, than we search in vain for the norm, the ideal. What makes the new language of molecular biology so subtly chilling is that it risks creating a new archetype, a flawless, errorless, perfect being to which to aspire—a new man and woman, like us, but without the warts and wrinkles, vulnerabilities and frailties, that have defined our essence from the very beginning of our existence.

No wonder so many in the disability rights community are becoming    33
increasingly frightened of the new biology. They wonder, if in the new world coming, people like themselves will be seen as errors in the code, mistakes to be eliminated, lives to be prevented from coming into being. Then again, how tolerant are the rest of us likely to be when we come to see everyone around us as defective, as mistakes and errors in the code.

Already, genetic information is being used by schools, employers, insurance    34
companies and governments to determine educational tracks, employment prospects, insurance premiums, and security clearances, giving rise to a new and virulent form of discrimination based on one's genetic profile. Even more chilling, some genetic engineers envision a future with a small segment of the human population engineered to "perfection" while others remain as flawed reminders of an outmoded evolutionary design. Molecular biologist Lee Silver of Princeton

University writes about a not-too-distant future made up of two distinct biological classes which he refers to as the Gen Rich and Naturals. The Gen Rich, which account for 10 percent of the population, have been enhanced with synthetic genes and have become the rulers of society. They include Gen Rich businessmen, musicians, artists, intellectuals, and athletes, each enhanced with specific synthetic genes to allow them to succeed in their respective fields in ways not even conceivable among those born of nature's lottery.

At the center of this new genetic aristocracy are the Gen Rich scientists  35
who are enhanced with special genetic traits that greatly increase their mental abilities, giving them the power to dictate the terms of future evolutionary advances on Earth. Silver says that:

> With the passage of time, the genetic distance between Naturals and the Gen Rich has become greater and greater, and now there is little movement up from the Natural to the Gen Rich class. . . . All aspects of the economy, the media, the entertainment industry and the knowledge industry are controlled by members of the Gen Rich class. . . . In contrast, Naturals work as low-paid service providers or as laborers. . . . Gen Rich and Natural children grow up and live in segregated social worlds where there is little chance for contact between them . . . [eventually] the Gen Rich class and the Natural class will become the Gen Rich humans and the Natural humans—entirely separate species with no ability to cross breed and with as much romantic interest in each other as a current human would have for a chimpanzee.

Silver acknowledges that the increasing polarization of society into a Gen  36
Rich and Natural class might be unfair, but he is quick to add that wealthy parents have always been able to provide all sorts of advantages for their children. "Anyone who accepts the right of affluent parents to provide their children with an expensive private school education cannot use unfairness as a reason for rejecting the use of reprogenetic technologies," argues Silver. Like many of his colleagues, Silver is a strong advocate of the new genetic technologies. "In a society that values human freedom above all else," writes Silver, "it is hard to find any legitimate basis for restricting the use of reprogenetics."

If Silver's predictions about where the new technologies are heading are  37
correct, we face the very real possibility of journeying into a Huxlian world populated by Alphas, Betas, Gammas, and Deltas. In the new scenario, however, it's the global marketplace and consumer desire, not an oppressive government, that will likely be the ultimate arbiter of the new biology. In the final analysis, commercial eugenics, controlled by global life science companies and mediated by consumer sovereignty, might prove every bit as dangerous to the future prospects of our species as the shrill cries on behalf of purifying the best blood of the Aryan race more than half a century ago in Hitler's infamous Third Reich.

The question, then, is whether or not humanity should begin the process  38
of engineering future generations of human beings by technological design in the laboratory. What are the potential consequences of embarking on a course whose final goal is the "perfection" of the human species?

Today, the ultimate exercise of power is within grasp: the ability to con-    39
trol, at the most fundamental level, the future lives of unborn generations by
engineering their biological life process in advance, making them a partial
hostage of their own architecturally designed blueprints. I use the word "partial" because, like many others, I believe that environment is a major contributing factor in determining one's life course. It is also true, however, that
one's genetic makeup plays a role in helping to shape one's destiny. Genetic
engineering, then, represents the power of authorship, albeit limited authorship. Being able to engineer even minor changes in the physical and behavioral
characteristics of future generations represents a new era in human history.
Never before has such power over human life even been a possibility.

Human genetic engineering raises the very real spectre of a dystopian    40
future where the haves and have-nots are increasingly divided and separated
by genetic endowment, genetic discrimination is widely practiced, and traditional notions of democracy and equality give way to the creation of a gene-
tocracy based on one's "genetic qualifications." The driving force of this new
bioindustrial world are giant life science companies whose control over genetic resources and the new transformative biotechnologies give them the clout
to act as commercial agents for a new eugenics era.

## COMPETING BIOTECH VISIONS

Many in the life sciences field would have us believe that the new gene splic-    41
ing technologies are irrepressible and irreversible and that any attempt to
oppose their introduction is both futile and retrogressive. They never stop to
even consider the possibility that the new genetic science might be used in a
wholly different manner than is currently being proposed. The fact is, the corporate agenda is only one of two potential paths into the Biotech Century. It
is possible that the growing number of anti-eugenic activists around the world
might be able to ignite a global debate around alternative uses of the new science—approaches that are less invasive, more sustainable and humane and
that conserve and protect the genetic rights of future generations.

While the global life science companies favor the introduction and wide-    42
spread use of gene therapy—genetic engineering—to cure diseases, and
enhance the physical, emotional and mental well-being of individuals, a
growing number of holistically minded geneticists and health practitioners
are beginning to use the new data being generated by the human genome
project in a very different way. They are exploring the relationship between
genetic mutations and environmental triggers with the hope of fashioning a
more sophisticated, scientifically-based understanding and approach to preventive health. More than 70 percent of all deaths in the United States and
other industrialized countries are attributable to what physicians refer to as
"diseases of affluence." Heart attacks, strokes, breast, colon and prostate
cancer, and diabetes are among the most common diseases of affluence.
While each individual has varying genetic susceptibilities to these diseases,

environmental factors, including diet and lifestyle, are major contributing elements that can trigger genetic mutations. Heavy cigarette smoking, high levels of alcohol consumption, diets rich in animal fats, the use of pesticides and other poisonous chemicals, contaminated water and food, polluted air and sedentary living habits with little or no exercise, have been shown, in study after study, to cause genetic mutations and lead to the onset of many of these high profile diseases.

43    The mapping and sequencing of the human genome is providing researchers with vital new information on recessive gene traits and genetic predispositions for a range of illnesses. Still, little research has been done, to date, on how genetic predispositions interact with toxic materials in the environment, the metabolizing of different foods, and lifestyle to affect genetic mutations and phenotypical expression. The new holistic approach to human medicine views the individual genome as part of an embedded organismic structure continually interacting with and being affected by the environment in which it unfolds. The effort is geared toward using increasingly sophisticated genetic and environmental information to prevent genetic mutations from occurring. (It needs to be emphasized, however, that a number of genetic diseases appear to be unpreventable and immune to environmental mediation.)

44    Some would argue that, in the case of medicine and any number of other fields, there is no reason why both approaches to applied science can't live side by side, each complementing and augmenting the other. In reality, the commercial market favors the more reductionist approach for the obvious reason that for now, at least, that's where the money is to be made. While there is certainly a growing market for preventive health practices, programs, and products, far more money is invested in "illness" based medicine. That could change, but it would require a paradigm shift in the way we think about science and its applications, with awareness of and support for a science founded in systems thinking and sensitive to the twin notions of diversity and interdependence.

45    While it might seem highly improbable, even inconceivable, to most of the principal players in this new technology revolution that genetic engineering, with all of its potential promise, might ultimately be rejected, we need remind ourselves that just a generation ago, it would have been just as inconceivable to imagine the partial abandonment of nuclear energy which had for years been so enthusiastically embraced as the ultimate salvation for a society whose appetite for energy appeared nearly insatiable. It is also possible that society will accept some and reject other uses of genetic engineering in the coming biotech century. For example, one could make a solid case for genetic screening—with the appropriate safeguards in place—to better predict the onslaught of disabling diseases, especially those that can be prevented with early treatment. The new gene-splicing technologies also open the door to a new generation of lifesaving pharmaceutical products. On the other hand, the use of gene therapy to make corrective changes in the human germ line, affecting the options of future generations, is far more problematic. Society may well say yes to some of the genetic engineering options and no to others.

After all, nuclear technology has been harnessed effectively for uses other than creating energy and making bombs.

Even rejection of some genetic engineering technologies then, does not 46 mean that the wealth of genomic and environmental information being collected couldn't be used in other ways. While the twenty-first century will be the Age of Biology, the technological application of the knowledge we gain can take a variety of forms. To believe that genetic engineering is the only way to apply our new knowledge of biology and the life sciences is limiting and keeps us from entertaining other options which might prove even more effective in addressing the needs and fulfilling the dreams of current and future generations.

The biotech revolution will affect every aspect of our lives. The way we 47 eat; the way we date and marry; the way we have our babies; the way our children are raised and educated; the way we work; the way we engage in politics; the way we express our faith; the way we perceive the world around us and our place in it—all of our individual and shared realities will be deeply touched by the new technologies of the Biotech Century. Surely, these very "personal" technologies deserve to be widely discussed and debated by the public at large before they become a ubiquitous part of our daily lives.

■    ■    ■

## Review Questions

1. Summarize Rifkin's position on the commercial control of research into the human genome.
2. What is eugenics?
3. How might research into the genetic markers of some population groups be used as a stigma?
4. What is the difference between somatic gene therapy and germ line therapy?
5. What are the arguments *for* conducting germ line therapy?
6. What is the "underlying logic of genetic engineering"? What is the significance between describing particular genetic structures as "defects," as opposed to "mutations"?
7. What kind of debates may emerge regarding parental responsibility in the Biotech Century?
8. According to Rifkin, what are the dangers of treating genetic disorders by "eliminating recessive traits at the germ line level"?
9. Why is it possible that corporate interests, and not a malevolent government (as in Huxley's *Brave New World*), might become responsible for creating a genetically segmented society?

## Discussion and Writing Suggestions

1. In previous centuries, the Earth provided the raw materials—the iron ore and the coal and the crops—on which to build economic and social progress. In the near future, writes Rifkin, the raw materials on which progress will rest will be the human genome, the knowledge of which will create the potential to cure disease and engineer future generations. Is there any difference, in your view, between industry's exploitation of raw materials of the 19th and 20th centuries and the raw materials of the 21st and beyond?

2. To what extent do you feel we are approaching a new and momentous juncture in human history? Do you share Rifkin's sense of foreboding?

3. We say it is "natural" for birds to fly, for bees to build hives, for lions to hunt their prey. Define the word "natural" with respect to the human enterprise. For instance, is it "natural" for humans to develop technology? Is it "natural" for humans to put the materials of nature to use for human ends? When does a "natural" effort for humans cross into the "unnatural?" Based on your definition, discuss how "natural" it is for humans to manipulate their own genetic structures. (An additional question might help you think through an answer: When critics claim that genetic tinkering or cloning is "unnatural," how are they defining "natural?")

4. Reread the quoted passage from Robert Sinsheimer (paragraph 28). What is the distinction he is making between the "old eugenics" and the "new eugenics"? How do you respond to this distinction? Do you support Sinsheimer's enthusiasm for bioengineering?

5. Given a free-market choice to safeguard the health of and prospects for their unborn children, parents in the (near) future may elect to boost their children genetically. If such genetic manipulation occurs, what would prevent a class system of Gen Rich and Naturals from emerging, as described by Lee Silver (paragraphs 34–37)? Given the chance to enhance your unborn child, what would you do? From the child's point of view, would you prefer to be a Gen Rich or a Natural?

6. Reread paragraph 23. Explain its rhetorical/structural function as an important pivot point in the article.

7. Rifkin is hardly neutral in his views on the commercialization of the human genome. Still, he presents the views of proponents of commercial exploitation of genetic research. On balance, how fair do you find Rifkin's presentation? In developing your answer, point to specific passages as evidence.

## Human Genome Projection

G. CLEMENT

*Source:* G. Clement/*National Post*. Reprinted with permission.

## Perfection, But at What Price?

MICHAEL VALPY

*Michael Valpy began his journalism career at* The Vancouver Sun *in 1961 and went on to serve as national affairs columnist. For* The Globe and Mail, *he has been a member of the editorial board, Ottawa national affairs columnist, Africa correspondent and deputy managing editor.*

*He has produced numerous public affairs documentaries for CBC Radio, received community awards for his writings from organizations such as Daily Bread Food Bank, the Ontario Psychological Foundation, and the Canadian Nurses Association, and won three National Newspaper Awards. In 1997, Trent University awarded him an honorary doctorate of letters for his work.*

*He is co-author of two books on the constitution,* The National Deal *(1982) and* To Match a Dream *(1998), and a co-author with Judith Maxwell and others of* Family Security in Insecure Times *(1994).*

*In the following article, "Perfection, But at What Price?", Valpy consults an international panel of medical researchers to canvass their opinions on various issues of biogenetics.*

## THE PANEL

**Dr. Alan Bernstein** has been a molecular and medical genetics professor at the University of Toronto since 1984. He has made key contributions to the study of embryonic development, hematopoiesis, cancer, the cardiovascular system, gene therapy, and mammalian development. He is the president of the Canadian Institute for Health Research. [1]

**Dr. Peter Doherty**, who originally studied veterinary medicine in Australia, is now chairman of the department of immunology at St. Jude Children's Research Hospital in Memphis and a pathology professor at the University of Tennessee, Memphis. He won a Gairdner Award in 1986 and the Nobel Prize for physiology in 1996. [2]

**Dr. Judah Folkman** developed the first implantable pacemaker and discovered anti-angiogenesis, the eradication of tumours by cutting off their blood supply. Before devoting himself to research, the Cleveland native became a professor of surgery at Harvard Medical School in 1967 and served as surgeon-in-chief at Children's Hospital Medical Center in Boston for 14 years. He received the Gairdner in 1991. [3]

**Dr. Judith Hall** is a clinical geneticist and the head of the pediatrics departments at the University of British Columbia and B.C.'s Children's Hospital. Born in Boston, her main areas of research are human congenital anomalies, including the genetics of short stature and monozygotic (identical) twins. She is an officer of the Order of Canada. [4]

**Dr. Joseph Martin**, born in Bassano, Alta., is the dean of Harvard Medical School. His specialties include the molecular genetics of neurodegenerative disease. His early work led to the discovery of the genetic marker for Huntington's disease. He won the Abraham Flexner Award for distinguished service to medical education in 1999. [5]

**Sir Keith Peters** is the Regius Professor of Physic (medicine) at the University of Cambridge. His research interests include diseases of the kidneys and blood vessels and immunological mechanisms in disease. He is a fellow of Christ's College, Cambridge, and served on the Advisory Council on Science and Technology from 1987 to 1990. [6]

## THE GAIRDNER FOUNDATION

**Dr. John Dirks** is president of the Toronto-based Gairdner Foundation, which presents an annual international award for excellence in medical science. A native of Winnipeg, he became the dean of medicine at U of T in 1987 and is currently a professor emeritus of medicine there. His work is concentrated in renal pathophysiology. He has served on the Medical Research Council of Canada and received the medical award of the Kidney Foundation of Canada in 1985. [7]

• • •

Scientists in Britain received parliamentary approval this week to create 8
human embryos for research into treating disease. In two words, therapeutic
cloning.

It is the first legal green light given to the Western world's biomedical 9
community to actually create human life. The terms are stringent: The
embryos must be destroyed after 14 days; they must never be allowed to
grow into human beings; a select parliamentary committee is to come up with
detailed regulatory controls before the first research licences are granted.

Now, from the moral principles of Westminster's lawmakers, let's travel 10
to this month's issue of *Wired* magazine, the widely read periodical of the
North American software industry, a sort of *New England Journal of
Medicine* for computer nerds. The cover story is about the Creator and the
Client. It is not fiction.

The Creator is described by writer Brian Alexander as "an intense dark- 11
haired man in his thirties [who] looks a little like Peter Lorre in *The Beast
With Five Fingers.*"

He has a PhD in molecular biology, a list of peer-reviewed publications, 12
a research job at a major U.S. university, an entrepreneurial spirit and a
shortage of ethical scruples. He has "just enough skill to make human cloning
work," Mr. Alexander writes.

And he has attracted a customer—the Client—a businessman living in 13
Western Europe whose son died from disease a year ago. The Client found
him by cruising the underworld of the Internet.

The Client wants the Creator to clone his dead son. He has consulted 14
experts and keeps tissue samples from the body stored in liquid nitrogen and
paraffin blocks. The Creator has found an in vitro fertilization laboratory that
can do the work, with a compliant director skilled in the handling of human
eggs and the IVF embryo manipulations that closely resemble the techniques
used in cloning.

At last report, Mr. Alexander writes, the Creator and the Client had 15
fallen to bickering over whether the Creator could guarantee success.

Then there is the story of the Quebec-based New Age cult, the UFO 16
worshipping Raelians, and their project, Clonaid. They announced last year,
through much salacious press coverage around the world, that they had found
a U.S. couple ready to pay $500 000 to have their dead baby cloned from
saved tissue.

The cult said it has the medical know-how to do the job. It, too, may 17
have found the Creator and his lab.

"The Creator's spirit," Mr. Alexander writes, "has been awakened by the 18
historical moment we're in right now, a convergence of under-the-radar pro-
cloning agitation, falling taboos, and the inexorable march of science.

Or, as Dr. Joseph Martin, the Alberta-born dean of Harvard University's 19
school of medicine, explains: "The technology isn't that difficult and it will
happen probably before we'd like it to.

"Cloning of the monkey has already been done. So the possibility of reproducing ourselves, humankind, within the next few years is really not a question of whether or if you can, but a question of 'who does it.'" 20

•  •  •

And so here we have the chills travelling up the world's spine. 21

Hidden from view in corporate-financed research laboratories, human-cloning experiments already may be well under way, Dr. Martin told a recent breakfast gathering attended by some of the world's outstanding clinical and basic-science researchers in genetics, immunology and molecular biology. 22

The Globe and Mail had invited the scientists to talk about the morals and ethics required to frame the relentless advance of biomedical research. 23

Britain has now taken the step to the leading edge. The U.S. National Institutes of Health has just begun to finance research using surplus human embryos from in vitro fertilization clinics (manufacturing embryos remains prohibited), which the new Bush administration is being strongly lobbied to halt. 24

The Canadian government, wishy-washy to a fault, twice has backed away from regulatory legislation of any kind, relying on a voluntary moratorium by the biomedical community that may well have served to drive research underground. In any event Canadian scientists have described human embryo-cell research in the country as having gone nowhere. 25

The publicly funded Canadian Institutes of Health Research (the reincarnated Medical Research Council) has a committee working on research guidelines. A Health Canada discussion paper given media attention this week says the government may permit therapeutic cloning similar to the British model when it finally gets around to making laws to govern human reproductive technology. 26

Religious groups, with the Roman Catholic Church in the forefront, immediately announced their opposition. 27

A brief look at the science before we get to The Globe's breakfast: 28

Dolly the sheep was cloned in Scotland four years ago. This month, scientists announced the cloning of ANDi the rhesus monkey (named for "inserted DNA") in Oregon. Mice and other forms of life have been cloned in university and private labs around the world. 29

This is how it works: The nucleus is removed from a fertilized egg to be replaced by a new cell nucleus from the tissue of the "parent" animal (or "brother" or "sister"—the language hasn't yet found the right comfortable word) in a process called somatic cell nuclear transfer. The new cloned egg is then grown into an embryo. 30

Within the embryo are stem cells, the body's master cells that go on to diversify into organs, bones, nerves, muscles, skin and blood. Researchers want to understand, using the knowledge of genetic codes, how stem cells can be grown into new organs and body parts that can replace those that are diseased or genetically disordered. 31

In Britain, before the House of Lords passed amendments this week to    32
the Human Fertilisation and Embryology Act, scientists were restricted to
research on fertilization, contraception and congenital disorders using existing, surplus embryos.

British researchers are still expected to rely on surplus embryos rather    33
than to create new ones. But the legal authority now exists, and the limits on
research have been lifted.

Against this backdrop is an engulfing debate over both the ethical issues    34
of creating life as "disposable organic material"—as one British church
leader has termed it—and the scientific issues of whether devoting so many
resources to genetic research is going down the wrong path and raising
invalid public expectations.

And, of course, there is the worry about the Creator and for-profit cor-    35
porate interest in what can be done with our bodies.

To date, private companies, universities and charitable organizations    36
working to eradicate various diseases and disorders have filed patents on
127 000 genetic bits of the human body—the gene sequences and chemical
codes that are the software of life. The race to buy life, it has been called.

• • •

The scientists who met *Globe* journalists for breakfast were in Toronto    37
to serve as jurors for medical science's prestigious Gairdner Award, known as
the Baby 'Bel because many winners subsequently receive the Nobel Prize.

The group included Harvard medical dean Joseph Martin; Australian    38
immunologist Peter Doherty; Sir Keith Peters, regius professor of physic (medicine) at Cambridge University; Harvard surgeon Judah Folkman; Judith
Hall, clinical geneticist at the University of British Columbia; and Alan
Bernstein, president of the Canadian Institutes for Health Research, the pre-
eminent agency for funding medical research in Canada.

John Dirks, president of the Gairdner Foundation and former dean of    39
medicine at University of Toronto, was also at the breakfast.

The job of the Gairdner Award jurors, Dr. Dirks said, "will be to decide    40
what ideas are important and what will last." It will be interesting to speculate on what values are embodied in the selection of this year's winner, whose
name will be announced this spring.

What they had to say, in sum, was this:    41

- The biggest obstacle to growing cloned embryos into human beings is that    42
  there is not a mass market for it. Yet. Which is not the same as saying
  there isn't a market.
- It is not the role of scientists to determine the ethical limits to research or    43
  the application of genetic knowledge to the delivery of public health.
  That is the role of legislatures and the public. The job of scientists, Dr.
  Bernstein said, is to be canaries in the coal mine, saying: "Hey, there's an
  issue coming up here, and we should have a full discussion."

- The public and the news media generally have an inaccurate and exaggerated—the best word might be naïve—idea of where genetics research is leading and what can be accomplished in treating and eradicating disease and other human imperfections. [44]
- The debate over stem-cell research will probably end, or at least become more muted, once researchers learn how to work usefully with adult stem cells and no longer need embryos. [45]
- The primary ethical issue for medical scientists is not about genetics and cloning but the rapidly widening gulf between the developed and developing worlds in the availability of medical knowledge and treatment. [46]

The market for genetics research will be created by the demand for genetically engineered human tissue (preferably a person's own) or genetic pharmacology to replace or compensate for diseased and disordered parts of the body. To that end, private corporations have invested billions of dollars in biotechnology and applied for tens of thousands of patents (one French company alone holds more than 38 000). [47]

But the reality, Sir Keith Peters said, is that the market for cloning embryos for human life is not absent. [48]

"In most Western societies, there's a tremendous amount of hand-waving about how human cloning is not going to happen, it's absolutely unacceptable, the society will reject it. [49]

"And then I ask the question of my friends: 'Okay, your only child, age 21, is killed in a motor accident and you had a chance to take a little tissue from him or her and you're beyond reproductive age yourself almost certainly—would you like to have another child, [because we] have this technology?' And I've yet to come across an answer no." [50]

"I think there are all kinds of reasons why we should not do that. But when people are faced with it as a real possibility, the answer is yes." [51]

Why should science not do that? Because genetic determinism, however much it comes eventually to be understood, will never replicate a human being. [52]

The parents who want their dead 21-year-old cloned will get a 21-year-old, Sir Keith said. But they won't get back the 21-year-old child who died. [53]

Patricia Baird, the University of British Columbia geneticist whose report from the 1993 Royal Commission on New Reproductive Technologies has been left by Ottawa to gather dust, pointed out in a public Vancouver lecture this month that genetic constitutions—even if they could be exactly replicated—can never overcome human nurture, human experience and the million and one other environmental factors that from conception give shape to a human being. [54]

• • •

What of genetic manipulation, or the application of transgenic technology? What do scientists say about therapies to deal with, for example, the genetic mutation for cystic fibrosis identified in a human embryo? [55]

The CF gene has been known for 11 years, since it was discovered by    56
University of Toronto geneticist Lap-Chee Tsui.

To date, there is no proven gene-based therapy to correct it, to replace the    57
mutated gene with one that is not.

Dr. Bernstein asked whether a couple wanting a child free of the muta-    58
tions would be willing to undergo all the required genetic manipulations,
most of which would fail. Maybe one in 50 would succeed. Dr. Doherty
said. It took 300 tries to get Dolly.

Dr. Bernstein posed further questions. Should genetic screening or the    59
mutation become required? Do we move to some sort of social consensus that
all fetuses identified with the mutation should be routinely aborted?

And what would that say to people living with cystic fibrosis—the people    60
with a mutation that wasn't identified?

To date, 950 mutations of the cystic-fibrosis gene have been identified,    61
only 30 of which are routinely screened for in laboratories. In 1 to 15 per cent
of affected patients, the mutation is not identified either during a natural pregnancy or before an in vitro embryos implanted.

Dr. Bernstein said: "It's not up to the research community to decide    62
whether fetuses with the cystic fibrosis gene should be aborted. It's for the
public through their lawmakers to either regulate or legislate.

Those questions, Dr. Doherty said, rest with the community values and    63
ethical considerations in a particular society.

The scientists at the *Globe* breakfast spoke enthusiastically about revo-    64
lutionary advances in genetics-based medical knowledge. They talked about
developments in genetic pharmacology leading to drugs that will compensate
for genetic disorders.

They predicted major therapeutic advances in the next few years for    65
cancer, diabetes, muscular dystrophy, coronary diseases and neurological disorders such as Alzheimer's.

They also repeatedly tempered their enthusiasm with warnings against    66
unreal public expectations.

"One of the things we've learned from the genetic revolution . . . is the    67
uniqueness of every individual and how much environment plays a role," Dr.
Hall said. "So although we can talk broadly about Alzheimer's, there are
major environmental factors and there will be individual susceptibilities
because of the interaction of various biochemicals."

Dr. Baird, in her public lecture, put the issue succinctly with two exam-    68
ples: There are 256 different identified risk factors for heart disease, and a
B.C. study of one million individuals followed from birth to age 25 found that
single-gene disorders occur in only 3.6 per 1000 live births.

"The vast majority of illnesses in humans are the result of complex inter-    69
actions, over time, between their genetic constitutions and [their environ-
ment]," she said. "The evidence is overwhelming that the determinants of the
common chronic diseases of modern life are complex, interrelated, act over
time and are embedded in a social context."

Which suggests that the breakthroughs in the treatment of humanity's 70
horrible disorders are not going to come from genetic discoveries alone but
from a partnership of medical scientists doing both basic and clinical research.

Harvard's Judah Folkman said: "I continue to be fascinated by the 71
absolute, unexpected and surprising discoveries that come when clinicians work
with basic scientists which would not come at all if their work was separate."

He cited as an example the isolation by basic researchers of an enzyme in 72
hemangiomas—benign facial tumours that appear at birth and usually disappear by age 7 or 8. Clinical researchers then discovered that these tumours
destroyed thyroid hormones and are a leading factor in causing mental retar-
dation in children.

Then Dr. Folkman spoke of the moral issue that is most in his mind: "All 73
our arguments about cloning and ethics will pale before the fact that we will
be judged by not worrying about places . . . that can't afford the treatments
we discover."

He recalled one of his medical residents who returned from working in a 74
children's hospital in New Delhi. The resident described how every morning
there were 20 children on the hospital's doorstep who had died overnight
from simple diarrhea.

"They don't do the fancy surgery we do," Dr. Folkman said. The assaults 75
on the frontiers of medical science have not been matched by assaults on
miserly foreign aid.

Sir Keith said the endemic presence of diseases such as AIDs in Africa— 76
where, in countries, 40 per cent of women arriving in clinics and hospitals
for childbirth are HIV-positive—puts all other medical ethical issues on the
back burner.

(In an article in *The Globe and Mail* yesterday, Stephen Lewis, former 77
Canadian ambassador to the United Nations, called AIDs in southern Africa
one of the greatest human tragedies of our age on which the West is willful-
ly turning its back.)

Dr. Doherty spoke of recently visiting the University of California's vet- 78
erinary school and seeing dogs on dialysis at a cost of $7000 a year. "Think
about it. It's these people's money. They could just as well spend the money
on a new Cadillac every year, but they choose to spend it on their dog.

"Ethically, it's appalling. Look at AIDS. In this country and in Australia 79
and in the U.S., everyone gets triple drug therapy. In Africa, . . . they can't
afford these drugs.

At a guess, there will be more public fuss in the West about the Creator. 80

■ ■ ■

## Discussion and Writing Suggestions

1. Of the panelists, who seems the most supportive of biotechnology? Who
   seems most critical? Who do you think makes the best case? What is the
   strongest argument?

2. Define the word "ethics" using a dictionary. Then look at the way medical researchers define ethical issues. Does the term shift as it is applied by individuals?

3. Valpy consults a panel of experts, in the sense that they are medical researchers. What do you think would occur if Postrel or Rifkin were added to a panel like this? Would Postrel be "out of her league," on the basis of her article that indicated that she was working with, at best, a generalist knowledge-base of biotechnological issues? Would Rifkin seem overly philosophical and pessimistic?

## The Still Unread Book of Life

MARGARET MUNRO

*Margaret Munro is the science reporter for the* National Post, *and has written widely on a variety of scientific and ecological issues. She has won numerous awards for her writing and has been nominated for the Governor General's Award for public service journalism. She is the author of* The Story of Life on Earth, *and is a member of the Canadian Science Writers' Association.*

*The following article, which appeared in the* National Post *in June of 2000, makes the case that some of the claims about the potential of genetic research may be inflated.*

To listen to gene merchants tell it, we will soon have our chromosomes read    1
as part of routine medical checkups.

Our genetic foibles—the mutations linked to dozens of disorders ranging    2
from Alzheimer's to heart disease—will be laid out for close inspection. And
we will all be the better for it.

Craig Venter, who heads the leading U.S. genetics firm Celera, is so keen    3
on the idea he talks of launching an Internet-based service to read millions of
people's genes and then tailor drugs to their individual needs.

Francis Collins, head of the $5-billion international consortium that has    4
just completed its draft of the human genome, also speaks of the benefits of
routine gene checks. He says knowing our genetic weaknesses in advance
should prompt us to cut out factors—such as smoking and lousy diets—that
might trigger disease-causing genes. Either that, he says, or we will be able to
take special drugs to stop the bad genes from kicking in.

Dream on, say the critics, who are more than a little wary of the hype sur-    5
rounding the deciphering of the human genome.

It is a scientific milestone, they agree. But one that is so misconstrued    6
there is a real danger billions of dollars are going to be misspent on needless
genetic tests that exploit people's fears about having imperfect children and
faulty genes.

"It is certainly not something that is going to change things in the next       7
few years at all," says Patricia Baird, a medical geneticist and distinguished
professor at the University of British Columbia. "It's just a stage along the
way. A milestone in a long journey, and I'm afraid it may take us where we
don't want to go."

She is so worried about the destination, she stood up at a recent meeting       8
of the Genetics Society of America and listed a litany of concerns about the
burgeoning genetics business. They range from fears of consumer exploitation
by gene promoters to the need for university geneticists to declare their growing conflicts of interest.

The human genome is said to contain the recipe for life, the biochemical        9
instructions that control everything from the colour of your eyes to production of the neurochemicals that make you think.

But scientists do not yet know how to interpret the genome, or its vast        10
stretches of seemingly useless "junk" DNA. Nor are they sure how many
genes there are in the genome. Estimates vary from 34 000 to 120 000. And
they do not have a clue about what most of the human genes do, or what
turns them on and off.

Bill Gelbart, a leading Harvard researcher, thinks the word "gene" is so        11
misleading that he recently suggested it should be banned. It would be more
accurate, he says, to speak of the compounds actually generated by different
stretches or regions of DNA. This is because many "genes" produce different
biochemical products depending on how they are tweaked by the various factors at work inside cells.

All of which makes the popular notion that genes cause disease more            12
than a little simplistic. Or an "overly naïve interpretation," as Baird puts it.

It is true that there are a handful of rare diseases, such as Huntington        13
Disease, which are triggered by a single mutation on a known gene. People
who inherit these disease-causing genes from their parents will eventually get
the disease.

But most genetic factors involved in disease are much more subtle. More        14
than a thousand different gene mutations have been linked with cystic fibrosis, Steve Jones, a British geneticist at University College in London, points out
in a critique of the genome hype. And researchers, he notes, are years away
from figuring out how to repair any of them.

He agrees completing the draft of the genome is a milestone. "An aston-        15
ishing piece of research in micro-anatomy," he says. A breakthrough on a par
with "Vesalius' dissection of the heart in 1543."

But do not hold your breath waiting for the medical revolution and pay-        16
back promised by the genome "hyperbolists," says Jones. "Don't expect it for
a while, not 400 years, maybe; but in my estimate nearer 40 than four."

He, like Baird, stresses that the big killers, such as cancer and heart dis-    17
ease, are triggered by a myriad of interacting factors including stress, pollution, diet, lifestyle and genes.

And there is plenty of evidence that the social and environmental com-        18
ponents are more powerful—and more treatable—than the genetic factors,
says Baird.

Genes no more cause heart disease, she says, than a high-stress job, a        19
high-fat diet or a couch potato lifestyle, she says.

Baird chaired the Royal Commission on New Reproductive Technologies        20
that assessed several emerging technologies, including genetics. In 1993, she
and her fellow commissioners urged the federal health minister to introduce
legislation to protect the public.

Baird is still waiting, saying the need is more urgent than ever given the        21
way the biotech industry is gearing up to market and push its genetic wares.

The federal government and Allan Rock, the Health Minister, she says,        22
have a responsibility to act to protect the well-being of the people of Canada.

"It would be the enlightened and principled and right thing to do," she        23
says. "If we as a rich country don't start addressing this kind of thing it's
simply going to be wide open internationally."

The threat, she says, is very real. And consumers are ripe for exploitation        24
by the genetics industry that keeps growing, fuelled with big money and big
expectations.

U.S. biotech companies raised US$8-billion a year through much of the        25
1990s and the investment is climbing. And enterprising companies like Celera,
which has spent a fortune sequencing genes, are now looking for a return on
their investments.

Biotech companies are expected to follow the promotional strategy that        26
has worked so well for the pharmaceutical industry. It spends close to 24% of
income on marketing, and has a sales force that visits doctors 30 million times
a year to peddle its products, says Baird. The Internet is giving the companies
an even broader reach, and Canadians are already availing themselves of the
proliferating genetic tests that can be ordered over the Web.

As evidence of problems she points to the growing use of a $3850 test to        27
determine whether a woman has inherited genes linked to breast cancer.

Increasingly, she says, American doctors believe they should test all        28
women, not just those with a family history of the disease.

Yet a negative test in no way guarantees a cancer-free life. Baird says        29
fewer than 5% of all breast cancers are now thought to occur in women carrying the genes that can be picked up by the test.

She stresses that she is not against offering the test in families known to        30
be at high risk of breast cancer. What concerns her is the commercial drive
to use the test. "Inappropriate overuse is likely if low-risk women's anxiety
is capitalized on by commercially oriented testing labs," says Baird, who
wants the government to stipulate how and when such tests should be used
and make sure they are accompanied by high-quality counselling and
follow-up. MDS Laboratory Services started offering the $3850 test in
Canada in March, but there is no national consensus on who should have
the test and who will pay for it. "It's a bit of a dog's breakfast," says Brian

Harling, of MDS, referring to the way some provincial medical plans will pay for the test and others will not. He says he would welcome a standard Canadian approach.

Baird also worries about companies promoting genetic tests for human     31
embryos.

In 1997, a Toronto fertility clinic, IVF Canada, started offering a service     32
to screen human embryos for risk of 27 genetic diseases before they are implanted in mothers' wombs. In this $7000 test, a sample is taken from a very early embryo that is probed to see whether it carries undesirable genes.

The test has been promoted as "the beginning of the end of genetic dis-     33
ease," says Baird. "Hyperbole," she says, that could lead to misuse. "Most people would like to have healthy children, and marketing of this technology could play into that goal in an exploitive and misleading way."

Academic geneticists are also increasingly entering into lucrative collab-     34
orations with big genetic companies or starting firms to promote their discoveries. "This means the opinions of academic researchers with investments in those firms, or with appointments on boards, or as consultants, can't necessarily be accepted as objective," says Baird, who wants scientists to be more up-front about their connections with industry.

"The blurring of academia with industry means a societal resource—a     35
body of independent scientists without commercial affiliation—has been lost," she told the genetics meeting. "They may not provide objective input and opinion when society has to deal with choices posed by genetic technology."

Despite her long list of concerns, Baird says: "I'm not anti-genetic."     36
Unravelling the genetic forces at work in disease will, she says, be very beneficial and, in some cases, lifesaving.

What she wants to see are safeguards to ensure that people are not misled     37
and exploited and that genetics does not claim an inappropriately big slice of public research and health-care spending.

She also worries about framing, or defining ill health in a way that pushes     38
problems back on to the individual: "It allows awkward questions on social and health policies or inappropriate workplace organization to be avoided," says Baird, who points to studies showing that social and environmental factors, not genes, account for the recent and rapid changes in the incidence of breast cancer, heart disease and colon cancer.

"If ill health is defined as genetic, innate and simply unfolding, then     39
social supports, good early nurturing, narrowing economic gaps and appropriate workplace organization are less likely to be underwritten by society," she says.

As for Craig Venter's musing that he will one day offer gene scans to the     40
masses over the Internet, she doubts such a service will help "a bloody bit."

Only one-third of patients now follow their doctor's directions and at     41
best 50% routinely take medications prescribed for their chronic medical problems. The idea that healthy people will take drugs for years on the basis of a genetic test and a future disease risk is likely to be low, she says. A persistent

and irrational element in human nature appears to be stacked against such notions of mass genetic servicing.

■ ■ ■

## Discussion and Writing Suggestions

1. What are the strongest points of concern that Munro raises?
2. Are these concerns Munro's (developed on the basis of her interpreting the evidence), or are they those that have been raised by experts?
3. Munro and Valpy are both interested in problems that may arise as biotechnology advances. How would you describe some of the differences between their approaches to the topic?

## *Blindly Into Biotechnological Era*

*WINNIPEG FREE PRESS* EDITORIAL

In 1997, when Prime Minister Jean Chrétien called an election three-and-one-half years into his five-year mandate, Manitobans were most annoyed that the election was called in the middle of a flood that made it difficult, if not impossible, for many people to vote.                                                    1

That became a bit of a controversy, but the chief electoral officer of Canada finally agreed with Mr. Chrétien that it did not matter much whether Manitobans could vote or not, and the election went ahead.          2

In Manitoba at the time, that was a bit of a sore point, although Mr. Chrétien, in the end, was right—the Liberals managed to elect six members of Parliament here. Even so, the arrogance of that election has not been forgotten. What has been forgotten is something that ultimately will matter far more than how many flood stricken Manitobans did not get to vote in 1997.          3

When Mr. Chrétien called that early election, there was a bill that died on the order paper that dealt with the regulation of reproductive technology. The recommendations included in that bill were the result of long research by a federal commission. Dolly, the artificial sheep, had just been cloned; new and different and sometimes disturbing ways of reproducing Canadians were being announced; the technology to choose the sex of a child was already on the market; the cloning of humans was a distinct possibility.          4

Today, there is no law in Canada to regulate this new and remarkable technology. Last week, when Prime Minister Chrétien, three-and-one-half years into another five-year mandate, again called an election, there was not even a bill dealing with reproductive technology or genetic engineering on the order paper that could be left to die, nothing that could be seen even as a portent of good intention. In two mandates, adding up potentially to 10 years of legislative authority, the federal government could not bring a single regulation into law.          5

Canada now, as it has under the last two terms of Liberal government,     6
heads into this new age of biotechnology flying blind. There are a few advantages to that. Lack of any kind of regulation gives a free hand to researchers
and that absence of impediment might lead to new discoveries that might not
otherwise be made. It has more disadvantages, in the lack of moral and ethical guidelines for that research and its ultimate implementation. The implications of how the results of that research should be implemented should concern
all Canadians, even if it seems to be of no interest to their government.

An American cult recently announced its intention to clone a human     7
being. The technology exists for this to be theoretically possible—as humbling
as it is, there is not a great deal of difference in the technology required to
clone a sheep or a pig and that required to clone a person.

One obvious difference is that sheep and pigs do not choose to be cloned,     8
but people can, which is where the moral and ethical issues arise. The U.S. cult
has the money, it says, from someone who wants to clone a dead child.
Human cloning, however, is illegal in the United States and in most of Europe.
The cultists may want to come to Canada, then, to do the job, because this
country has almost no regulations restricting the use of biotechnology. We
can regulate almost every other aspect of Canadian existence, from guns to
gumdrops, but we have yet to address as a society the fundamental issues that
the new technologies present.

Scientific discoveries often come about by accident, and they can bring     9
with them tremendous benefits. Penicillin was discovered quite accidentally by
Sir Alexander Fleming in 1928, and, since the 1940s, has saved more lives
than perhaps any other drug in the history of humanity. Beyond the requirement that it be delivered by a doctor's prescription, however, it has not been
regulated, and the abuse of it by doctors and their patients has resulted in new
generations of bacteria that have become immune to penicillin and to succeeding generations of new antibiotics.

Penicillin was a "miracle" drug. If its use had been more closely controlled,     10
perhaps the miracle that it worked would have lasted longer; perhaps fewer
germs today would laugh at it as they work their way through a human body.

The analogy may not be exact, but biotechnology today offers us the pos-     11
sibility of many miracles—children for infertile couples; children for same sex
couples; organs from animals for people who need transplants; organs grown
in factories for transplants. It also poses serious ethical and moral questions.
Is it right to use a human embryo to sustain or improve the life of another
person? What is the risk of introducing deadly diseases hitherto unknown in
people through the use of animal transplants? Should we clone people for
spare parts? Dare we even ask ourselves the question: How long is it necessary
to prolong the life of one person through the cloning and transplanting and
stem cell growing of another?

The line of doubts that the new biotechnology raises is at least as long as     12
the line of the hopes that it inspires.

■  ■  ■

## Discussion and Writing Suggestions

1. How would you describe some of the differences between the way the writer of the editorial approaches the task of questioning the advances of genetic research and the way Munro and Valpy approach the task of preparing science columns for a newspaper?

2. Do you agree with the stance taken in this editorial? Can you amplify one of its arguments?

3. If you came across this editorial in your local newspaper, would you read it? Would you expect it to contain cutting-edge facts or unimpeachable arguments? Why do you think people write (and read) editorials?

# Organs on Demand

MARK NICHOLS

With at least 180 000 people around the globe, including more than 3500    1
Canadians, awaiting organ transplants, and with donor organs in short supply, animals are an obvious possible alternative source of spare parts for humans. The mammal that has organs closest in size and function to *Homo sapiens* is the humble barnyard pig. And when researchers are certain porcine organs can be used safely, cloned pigs could provide a bountiful supply of identical, genetically modified hearts, kidneys, livers and other organs for transplantation. But despite scientists' successes in cloning sheep, mice, cattle and goats, turning out carbon-copy pigs proved frustratingly difficult—until now. In reports published last week, research teams from the United States and Japan explained how they produced six cloned female piglets, whose wriggling, snout-nosed existence brought pig-to-human transplants a little nearer to reality.

Scientists celebrated the clonings as a major advancement. "It's a key    2
step," said Dr. Robert Zhong, a London, Ont., transplant surgeon and immunologist, "towards an eventual revolution in organ transplantation." But formidable difficulties remain. Another study published by scientists in La Jolla, Calif., showed that pig viruses can infect human cells—raising the prospect that transplanted animal organs could spread new diseases among humans. Moreover, scientists are still searching for ways of dealing with organ rejection that is certain to occur when animal tissue is implanted in humans. "It could be years before the problems are solved," cautioned a spokesman for the British biotechnology giant Novartis. "We don't want to raise unrealistic expectations—especially among people on transplant waiting lists."

The two cloning teams produced piglets using complex procedures cen-    3
tring on fetal and ovary cells, and using electrical jolts to initiate cell division and the growth of early-stage embryos, with the results being implanted in surrogate mother pigs. The result: five piglets produced in Blacksburg, Va., by Edinburgh-based PPL Therapeutics in March, and another born in Japan earlier this year and named Xena—short for xenotransplantation, the scientific name for organ transplants between species.

Before pigs' organs can help keep humans alive, scientists will have to    4
solve the rejection problem. The solution could come from research by
Canadian scientists who are working with genetically altered white pigs raised
at the University of Guelph, about 60km west of Toronto. Bred by the
Novartis subsidiary Imutran Ltd. of Cambridge, England, the pigs are not
clones—researchers created the transgenic animals by injecting a human gene
into pig embryos and letting the pigs produce successive generations through
normal breeding. Imutran scientists think the pigs' human gene can trick
transplant recipients immune systems into accepting pigs' organs—instead of
responding with hyperacute rejection, the massive attack the human immune
system usually launches against alien tissue.

But rejection could still occur, notes Zhong, who is part of the Imutran    5
research program, and the pigs will probably need further genetic modification to avoid that. As well, he added, "we are looking for new drugs to suppress the immune response—the existing ones aren't going to do it when
pigs' organs are involved." At the same time, researchers will have to be sure
that none of the scores of viruses lodged in pigs' genetic makeup, known as
PERVs, will infect humans. "It's possible," said Ian Wilmut, leader of the
Scottish team that cloned Dolly the sheep in July, 1996, that "there are pig
viruses we don't know about that could be released into the human population." A possible solution, says Imutran's medical director, Khazal Paradis,
might involve genetic tinkering to remove the DNA sequences in pigs that give
rise to viruses. Given the problems that remain, he predicted, it could be "at
least several years before we feel comfortable enough about our program to
consider testing it in humans." If pig-to-human transplants are to be the solution to organ waiting lists, that day lies still further in the future.

■ ■ ■

## Discussion and Writing Suggestions

1. Does Nichols raise some issues that make you uncomfortable with the
   procedure of cloning animals?
2. Do some further research into the debate over whether cloning animal
   parts holds promise for people in need of organ replacement.

# Splicy Food: Are You Unwittingly Eating Doctored Corn and Patented Tomatoes?

KATHARINE PARTRIDGE

*Katharine Partridge is a communications professional based in Cobourg,
Ontario, specializing in sustainability and stakeholder issues. A journalist for
15 years, she is a regular contributor on health and science issues to* Today's
Parent *magazine.*

*In the following article, she raises questions about the degree of control consumers have over the foods they buy and eat, many of which contain GM ingredients.*

Is supper simmering as you read this? Maybe you're in line at the grocery store checkout. Well, here's some food for thought: Your grocery cart and family's dinner plates are chock full of genetically modified (GM) morsels—foods made from crops that are engineered to kill insects, tolerate herbicides or ripen more slowly. Since the first GM crops were planted in Canadian farm fields in the mid-1990s, they have made their way into more than 60 per cent of processed foods—some 30 000 products. Given that they are found in everything from infant formula to pancake mix, cereals, soups, pasta and potatoes, odds are you're feeding your family genetically modified products morning, noon and night. 1

The problem is you probably don't know what's GM and what's not. That's because the federal government figures the 43 varieties of GM corn, canola, soybeans, squash, potatoes, tomatoes, flax, wheat and cotton it has approved are so like their forebears there's no reason to label them. 2

It may get easier to spot them in the next year, however. A federally led committee of some 55 government, industry and consumer stakeholders has been wrangling since last fall over what food companies should voluntary disclose on their products' labels about genetically modified ingredients. But this is a mere appetizer in the GM food fight—a fracas fed by the ethical and environmental concerns of activists, the confusion and discontent on the family farm and the threats of trade sanctions from GM-free nations across the Atlantic. 3

Indeed, for some, the labelling issue is nothing more than a stalling tactic to divert discussion from the more profound issues of long-term threats to human health and the globe's ecosystems. Those effects can't be predicted with certainty, but critics argue that whatever happens will be irreversible. Once genetically modified organisms are released, they can't be controlled—or recalled. 4

Parents like Denise Stapleton are equally disturbed by the lack of independent, long-term research into GM foods. Stapleton, who last December helped found Gene Action, a grassroots advocacy group, regards the entire enterprise as a colossal and potentially catastrophic corporate experiment. And she's concluded that the Canadian government, which approves and regulates GM crops on the one hand and funds the multi-billion dollar agricultural biotech industry to the tune of more than $100 million annually on the other, is in cahoots with agribusiness. 5

"Canada is usually really strict with things like what medications they allow into the country," says the Toronto mother, "but they're not with something as revolutionary as this. It's food, and we eat it every day. And it's a technology that can reproduce itself. Maybe you get some results in a lab but there are millions of microorganisms in our soil that the crops are reacting with, and in our air, the birds and bugs and everything. They just don't know enough about it—the environmental implications, the health implications." 6

Those unknown implications also concern Kathryn Deiter, whose five-year-old son, Troy, is allergic to nuts. Deiter first became aware of GM foods 7 last fall when, through her work as a research librarian in Hamilton, Ontario, she came across an article describing how the protein from a Brazil nut had been genetically engineered into a soybean. The experiment was aborted when researchers discovered they'd inadvertently transferred the Brazil nut's allergenic trait to the soybean. The bean never made it to market, but the article made Deiter sit up and take note. "Are there hidden ingredients in our cereal that may be potentially harmful?" she asks.

Health Canada says Canadians needn't be concerned because it tests all    8
GM crops for allergenic properties and toxicity. But critics like Torontonian Elisabeth Abergel, who this fall will give her doctoral dissertation on the ecological risks of growing GM crops, charge that Health Canada's testing for known allergens is inadequate and for new allergens, non-existent. "It's known that one of the side effects of genetic engineering might be the unintended introduction of allergens into the diet. And, as well," notes Abergel, "we're talking about introducing some fairly toxic proteins with insecticide and herbicide resistance." There is some concern, she says, that children, whose immune systems are not fully formed, would be more susceptible.

When Jane Thornthwaite puts on her registered dietitian hat, the potential    9
for allergies tops her list of concerns. "We're introducing foreign genes, that have never been consumed, into the diet. How do we know we won't have allergic reactions?" she asks. When she switches hats, the Vancouver mother of three says that the question parents are asking is, "Is this stuff safe for my kids?" Her answer, from both perspectives, is an unequivocal "We don't know."

That conclusion is shared by a host of dissenting international organiza-    10
tions, including the British Medical Association, which has called for a moratorium on commercial planting of GM crops in the U.K. The 50 000-strong Union of Concerned Scientists in the U.S. and, at home, the Council of Canadians and the Canadian Association of Physicians for the Environment also have grave misgivings.

So do the majority of Canadians who are familiar with GM foods.    11
According to an Environics poll released last March, 75 per cent express concern about the safety of foods made with GM ingredients and more than half are not confident that the federal government is able to protect their health and safety with respect to GM products.

Health Canada and the Canadian Food Inspection Agency (CFIA), the    12
federal bureaus that approve and regulate GM foods, think these concerns are misplaced. They believe the GM foods they've OK'd to date simply fall along a continuum of agricultural innovation. After all, back in 1871, Massachusetts farmer Luther Burbank used cross-pollination to create the Russet-Burbank potato (otherwise known as the Idaho potato). Genetic engineering, the regulators reason, is an extension of that. Scientists can now excise a single gene that carries a specific trait—say, the ability to resist a particular insect—from one organism and put it in another where the trait will be advantageous.

Thus, just as Burbank used traditional breeding to create a spud able to    13
resist the Irish potato blight, scientists today have transferred a gene from a soil bacterium called Bacillus thuringiensis (Bt), which produces a natural pesticide able to fend off the ravaging Colorado potato beetle.

The difference is that, unlike traditional techniques, genetic engineering  14
allows scientists to transfer attributes across formerly impenetrable species
barriers. It is this aspect of genetic modification, widely publicized with stories of cold-resistance genes being transferred from salmon into strawberries,
that has prompted critics to dub the new products "Frankenfoods."

So far, no such fabulous creations have crossed the approvals desk of  15
Canadian regulators. Indeed, the 43 varieties that Karen McIntyre, associate
director of the federal bureau of food policy integration, and her colleagues
have seen are comparatively simple, involving single-trait transfers that are of
benefit to farmers—things like protection from insects or viruses, as with the
Bt potato, or herbicide resistance, so that farmers can spray weeds without
harming their cash crop.

To approve these new varieties, explains McIntyre, Canada follows an  16
internationally recognized protocol known as "substantial equivalence." It
says this: Because the GM plants look, smell and taste the same as the unmodified varieties that they are derived from, and because we've eaten the
unmodified varieties for centuries with no ill effects, the only things that need
to be looked at are the characteristics of the newly introduced trait.

McIntyre says that no independent federal studies are conducted. Rather,  17
the evaluations of these new traits are handled just like pre-market assessments for new drugs and food additives, by reviewing the studies submitted
by the company seeking approval. Unlike pharmaceuticals, however, clinical
trials are not required.

That will change, McIntyre predicts, as genetic modifications in foods,  18
promising such nutritional benefits to consumers as cholesterol-reduced oils,
become more complex. "Substantial equivalency has been a very flexible and
useful tool so far," she says. "But if you have a new product that has been
substantially altered, it's going to have to be tested in a different way."

What those new tests might entail is a hot topic among world health  19
organizations. At home, an expert panel of the Royal Society of Canada has
been directed by the federal government to cast its eye 10 years into the
future to ensure that the country will have the necessary policies, regulations
and scientific resources to adequately govern new GM products.

That promise of future safeguards offers little comfort to Ann Clark, a  20
pasture scientist at the University of Guelph and founder of Genetic
Engineering Alert, a group of 40 Canadian academics and government scientists. Clark has made a mission of understanding GM products, and she's concluded that the safety protocol Canada currently follows is seriously flawed.

Its fundamental assumption, says Clark, is that gene transfer is a precise  21
science: When you transfer a gene, you affect one and only one trait. But
Clark has seen plenty of evidence that gene transfers can produce unexpected results.

Take those Bt potatoes, for example. Prior to one new Bt variety being  22
released on the market, the gene that was successfully helping the potato
resist those pesky Colorado beetles was discovered to have inadvertently
"turned off" an unrelated gene that was essential to combatting an equally

devastating pest common in New York State. That slip-up was caught before the seeds were put on sale, but after the potato variety was approved.

While turning off a gene can be problematic, turning on the wrong gene can 23 also create havoc. That's the quandary with the commonly used Cauliflower mosaic virus (CaMV) promoter. This indispensable powerhouse doesn't endow a modified plant with a new trait. Rather, it is sent in alongside the new trait to switch it on. The problem, according to Clark, is that the promoter has the potential to "disengage itself from where you stick it and re-engage itself else-where." Since that elsewhere is entirely unpredictable, the indiscriminate CaMV may unwittingly turn on a gene that, for example, produces a toxin or another virus. Clark says this can easily translate into concerns about food safety.

That's not how Gord Surgeoner sees it. Surgeoner presides over Ontario 24 Agri-Food Technologies, a biotech advocacy coalition of universities, farm organizations and industry. He measures Clark's concerns as the risks that must be managed to harness the potential of genetic engineering, and he points to the millions of commercial animals that have been fed with GM soy and corn without effect. Nor, he notes, "have we yet to see any evidence of a problem in humans."

It's an argument that makes Clark snort. How could you identify a prob- 25 lem, she asks, with no one independently studying the outcomes before the seeds are approved, or monitoring the impact on health after the fact? And neither could they, since GM harvests in Canada—which, remember, have so far been considered "substantially equivalent"—are freely mixed and shipped with non-GM varieties.

This, in fact, is the issue central to the labelling debate. How can you 26 label foods containing GM ingredients when all crops are shipped as one? It concerns parents like Kathryn Deiter. "I rely on labels. We read every label on every product that we buy every time we buy it," she says. "I think I can safely say that I'm confident in our North American labelling. But hovering out there on the edge of my consciousness is that genetically modified foods have sort of snuck onto our table without the same labelling expectations."

The same issue frustrates such organizations as the Council of Canadians, 27 Greenpeace, FoodShare and the Registered Nurses Association of Ontario, which have all refused to join Ottawa's labelling discussions. They think mandatory labelling is the only way the health impact of GM foods can be tracked. Current discussions focus on a voluntary system that will not only be ineffectual in that regard but, they argue, will shift the burden of labelling to non-GM food manufacturers and the cost to those consumers who are forced to buy in a non–GM-food niche market.

Surgeoner also wonders how far you can extend labelling requirements. 28 Do the chicken fingers you pick up for your kids from the fast-food joint need to be labelled because the coating contains GM ingredients? Besides, he argues, consumers do have a choice. "I agree with choice. If you are concerned, you can buy organic. People will say it's more expensive. Well, that is your choice."

You do have a few others. Some food giants—McDonald's, Heinz baby 29 foods, the makers of some soy-based infant formulas—are quietly bowing to public pressure and making the switch to non-GM ingredients (see "The Corporate Stance," below). As well, most fresh produce is not genetically engineered. (Boundaries are blurring, though. At least one big GM-seed company in the United States has used traditional breeding techniques to transfer the engineered attributes from its genetically modified squash to a zucchini variety. The GM squash was reviewed by U.S. federal regulators, but because the zucchini was created using traditional techniques, it has bypassed the review process.)

Warren Bell, a family doctor in Salmon Arm, B.C., and president of the Canadian Association of Physicians for the Environment, reassures parents that the food we are feeding our children is safe. "It doesn't contain actual poison, nor does it have food-related qualities that render it dangerous in acute terms. The short-term danger is not there, no question." 30

When it comes to long-term dangers, Bell is more cautious. The consumption of GM foods today, he argues, "sanctions the production of many more foods of that type, which become increasingly unpredictable and which have unpredictable effects both on humans and on other segments of the ecosystem." 31

Already, farmers are seeing weeds that are resistant to the herbicides that have been engineered into some varieties of corn and soy. At the same time some GM crops are threatening to transform themselves into invasive agricultural weeds that will upset the balance of natural habitats. 32

Bell has a second concern that is more profound: the patenting of the food you put on your table by a handful of multinationals. Until recently, he says, the extension of property rights onto the world's food supply has been rigorously resisted. But now, "with the genetic modification of ordinary foodstuff, the possibility of taking over the entire area and turning it into a commodity for which the industry can charge whatever price the market will bear is an enticing, even seductive, opportunity that [agribusiness] has been slavering at the chops to take for a long time." 33

And who's acting as watchdog? The Canadian government, after all, makes federal research dollars available only to those companies and associations that can come up with matching funds; it also cheerleads the biotech industry with information supplements in consumer magazines. 34

This is the biggest conundrum of all. The short supply of unbiased information certainly makes it tough to decide what to feed your kids. Even more troublesome, perhaps, is that its scarcity nurtures a distrust that just may propel the GM pendulum too far the other way, torpedoing the possibility of beneficial new products. Food for thought, indeed. 35

## The Corporate Stance

You won't find labels telling you the foods you buy are free of GM ingredients until standards are in place. And contrary to earlier reports, Loblaws will not be removing GM foods from its stores. However, a few manufacturers are bending to public demand and sourcing non-GM ingredients for their products. 36

## *Heinz: Baby Foods, Pablum* 37

- position in Canada is the same as in Europe: baby foods, including Pablum, do not contain GM ingredients
- no status report available on such big-kid tasties as Pokemon Pasta

## *Gerber: Baby Foods* 38

- despite Gerber being owned by GM-seed giant Novartis, it has eliminated use "whenever possible" (corporate-speak in lieu of standards) of GM ingredients in its baby foods. Gerber says it doesn't think it's fair that the controversy be fought over baby food, and by eliminating GM ingredients, it's removed its products from the debate

## *Abbott Laboratories: Isomil* 39

- genetic engineering is sound science, they claim. Still, in response to consumer demand, soy-based Isomil formula will be GM-free by end of year

## *Mead Johnson: ProSobee* 40

- in North America, soy-based ProSobee formula is under review
- no changes to milk-based Enfalac formula

## *Hostess Frito-Lay: Potato Chips, Corn Chips* 41

- asked its contract farmers not to plant GM potatoes and corn for the 2000 growing season, but still buys ingredients on the open market

## *Kraft: Easy Mac Dinner, Shake 'n Bake* 42

- has conferred with Health Canada and is assured that GM products are safe. Does not have a policy specific to GM ingredients

## *Kellogg: Cereals, Pop Tarts* 43

- sources ingredients on the open market, so grain supply likely from GM crops
- continues to explore a wide variety of food innovations, including biotechnology

## *McDonald's* 44

- doesn't have a GM policy per se, but its fries are GM-free this year as a result of its supplier's decision

## McCain: French Fries    45

- in May 1999, McCain asked its suppliers not to plant GM potatoes so that it could respond to European demands for GM-free products

## Unilever: Lipton Chicken Noodle Soup, Sidekicks    46

- UniLever uses any and all ingredients approved for use in Canada whether they are GM or not

## WHAT'S IN STORE TODAY . . .

Close to 10 per cent of North American farmland is planted with genetically   47 engineered crops, and Canada is the world's third-largest grower, after the U.S. and Argentina. Genetic engineering is also used in other processes. Bovine growth hormone, which was banned by Canadian regulators last year, is used to increase milk production by about 10 per cent in U.S. dairy herds. A genetically engineered enzyme is widely used in cheese production.

Forty-three GM-food products have been approved here. You might   48 find GM foods, including potatoes, squash and sweet corn, in your store's produce section. (Three varieties of GM tomatoes have been approved but are not grown in Canada or the U.S. The much-touted FlavrSavr variety was a failure commercially.)

But the real GM food production is in canola (more than 50 per cent of   49 crops), corn (35 per cent) and soybeans (20 per cent). While most of the corn and soybeans are used for animal feed, plenty of all three cash crops make their way into processed foods, in the form of vegetable oils, sweeteners (corn syrup, fructose, dextrose, glucose), potato flour, cornstarch and soy lecithin.

## . . . AND IN THE FUTURE

Scientists say that commercial possibilities for biotechnology are limitless.   50 Here are some we may see in the future:

Nutritionally enhanced foods: rice with increased lysine to help combat   51 blindness, varieties for people who are allergic to rice; oils with less saturated fats; higher-starch potatoes that absorb less oil during frying.

Cold-hardy crops: a gene from wild broccoli has been transferred into   52 grapes to increase cold tolerance. Field trials are underway in Canada.

Edible vaccines: cholera genes spliced into potatoes that help provide   53 immunity to cholera. An edible rabies vaccine for raccoons to eat has been approved in the U.S.

Livestock, poultry and fish: livestock engineered for leaner meat; sheep   54 and goats engineered to secrete substances useful for drug production in their blood, urine or milk; pigs to produce transplant organs; chickens that can resist avian diseases; fish and shellfish with hormones to accelerate growth.

Insects: honeybees and other beneficial insects that tolerate pesticides.   55

## THE GLOBAL PICTURE

### Europe and the U.K.

The outbreak of mad cow disease a few years back prompted U.K. and   56
European Union consumers and regulators to take a hard look at food
safety. They found GM foods wanting. A half-dozen grocery store chains have
pulled GM foods off their shelves. E.U. parliamentarians have put a moratorium
on GM approvals and require GM food products to be labelled. The Cartagena
Protocol on Biosafety that was agreed to last January granted countries the
right to refuse GM crops. Canada lobbied against granting these rights.

### Japan

A mandatory labelling policy is expected to come into effect next spring.   57
Labelling will be required for processed foods if GM ingredients are among
the top three or represent five per cent of the product by weight (tofu, corn-
based snacks, beer and cornstarch products, for example). Some products will
be exempt, for example those whose GM components are removed during
processing (as with vegetable oils and soy sauce).

### Australia / New Zealand

In July, Australia and New Zealand health ministers agreed that all foods con-   58
taining GM ingredients must be clearly labelled. (Take-out and restaurant
foods are exempt.)

### U.S.

Last spring, President Clinton announced a process to develop guidelines for   59
voluntary labelling, and regulations that require companies intending to
market new GM seeds to inform federal regulators. These measures in effect
bring the U.S. up to speed with Canada.

■ ■ ■

## Discussion and Writing Suggestions

1. This article appeared in *Today's Parent* magazine. Should parents tell
   young children about the way that foods are being doctored and changed?
   Should they tell them, for example, that some tomatoes have been made
   resilient by adding the genes of fish, or should a tomato be a tomato?
2. If we don't tell children about our concerns with the way foods are being
   restructured, can we expect much protest as changes continue to be
   made? Do you think this process of developing GM foods will continue
   to evolve, so that some of the food we eat in 20 years may look nothing
   like the food we eat today?

# Why GM Foods Aren't So Scary

DAVID T. DENNIS

*Dr. Dennis started his career as a research manager at Unilever Ltd. in England. He then joined the faculty at Queen's University, where he built a research laboratory studying plant metabolism. His impressive scientific contributions have been published widely, resulting in a Fellowship of the Royal Society of Canada. He then turned his attention to the Biology Department at Queen's, during which time the department gained an international reputation for research excellence. This calibre of research provided the technologies that started Plant-Based Technologies Company (incorporated in 1995), of which Dennis is a co-founder, president, and CEO.*

*Dennis has been active in promoting the biotechnology to farmers and the general public and provided leadership in business development, forming a product development association with Dow Agrosciences.*

*In the following article, he defends GM foods and makes the case that the processes used to develop them are no less natural than those used in the development of many common food products.*

Some environmentalists want genetically modified foods to be specially    1
labelled and eventually banned. This may sound sensible, but isn't.

The plants we see around us evolved at the time of the dinosaurs, about    2
100 million years ago. They evolved for their own benefit, not ours, and
filled all the planet's ecological niches. For the past 10 000 years, mankind has
been modifying a small number of these plants to serve our own needs, not
those of the plants, and we have changed them dramatically. Over the past 50
years, new breeding techniques have ushered in the "green revolution."

Most foods, including organically grown foods, are the result of intense    3
genetic modification. The tomato started out as a small red berry from South
America that was considered toxic and was grown solely as an ornamental
plant. The kiwi fruit was, until recently, a tiny, bitter Chinese gooseberry. The
original oil from the rapeseed was an inedible industrial lubricant used in
ships during the Second World War. Genetic modification transformed it
into a health-friendly cooking oil: canola.

Activists argue that "traditional" breeding is natural. It is, if you mean    4
that—like biotechnology—it involves working with nature. But it is not, if
you mean that breeders only achieve what nature might have, if left to itself.
In fact, generations of breeders have crossed crop plants with wild relatives
and disparate other species to form unnatural hybrids such as nectarines,
seedless bananas and now the pluot, a cross between a plum and an apricot.

The public's fear of biotechnology often focuses on the perceived prob-    5
lems with copying a gene from one species and inserting it into another. But
in this "transgenic" process, biotechnologists copy only a minute fraction of
an organism's DNA. Because every organism contains up to 40 000 or more
genes, inserting one gene does not transfer the character of one organism to

another. Every gene contains a region that switches the gene on and off and a region that encodes a template for a protein that the gene produces when it is on. This latter region is what scientists copy to make transgenic plants.

Despite many similarities in the codes for proteins in different organisms, some differences can be used to improve crops. For example, the herbicide glyphosate (Roundup) inactivates an essential process in normal plants and kills them. "Roundup Ready" soybeans, corn and canola were produced by inserting a copy of a bacterial gene with an identical function to the plant gene, but that is unaffected by glyphosate. Farmers can now kill weeds without affecting their crops.          6

Not all genetic modifications use genes from non-plant sources. In many cases, the genetic manipulation involves the plant's own genes, the most celebrated of which are tomatoes in which the gene that causes them to go soft when ripe is turned off. The juice from these tomatoes is thicker and cheaper than juice from conventional tomatoes.          7

Biotechnology is simply another tool in the breeders' tool chest for increasing the diversity of their breeding lines to produce plentiful, high-quality foods for our tables. Everyone can see why farmers might welcome these new tools, but Greenpeace and organic farmers should also welcome them. Biotechnology is producing plants that require less pesticides and fertilizer, and conserve water and soil. Increased yields could reduce the amount of land under cultivation and preserve more wilderness areas.          8

Activists argue that genetically modified organisms (GMOS) are not tested fully. This is a misconception. It takes up to seven years and millions of dollars for a GMO to gain approval. The first criterion for acceptance is "substantial equivalence," meaning the company that manufactures the new GMO must show that the new product's composition is essentially the same as the normal product. The turmoil in the U.K. about GMOs was triggered by research on GM potatoes by a Dr. Arpad Pusztai in Aberdeen. Unfortunately, he prematurely communicated his data to the media and caused confusion that still persists. In reality, these potatoes should have been thrown out because they did not meet the "substantial equivalence" test.          9

If a new product is found to be substantially equivalent to the non-GM product, regulators consider the nature of the modification. For example, if the product may cause an allergic reaction in susceptible individuals, regulators demand full allergenic testing, including animal feeding trials. The company that produced the new product performs these tests—cause for concern among some activists who have no faith in corporate integrity. However, most people would not want their taxes to pay for testing all these products. In addition, the company is legally responsible for the safety of its product. If it did indeed falsify data and the product was found to be defective, the legal costs to even the largest company would be disastrous. Harming one's customers is not a valid business strategy.          10

For consumers who wish to know more about GM foods, information is available on the Web sites of the Canadian Food Inspection Agency, the U.S. Food and Drug Administration and the U.S. Department of Agriculture (see          11 below). For independent accounts of the technology, consumers can read the science and ethics reviews posted on the Web sites of the U.K.'s Nuffield Foundation or one of the world's oldest debating forums for science issues, the U.K.'s Royal Society. The Web site of my biotech company, Performance Plants, also provides information on biotechnology.

The majority of researchers in Performance Plants were, until recently,    12 university biologists. We came to this business through a fascination for the science of plants and, more generally, the science of life, and we were a little surprised by the hostility we met when our industry began producing products. We believe that sooner or later, the message about the benefits of these technologies will be evident.

Greenpeace and related organizations have a role to play in monitoring    13 developments in plant biotechnology, but this role could be enhanced without the rhetoric and antagonism that has characterized the debate so far. Much more could be achieved through an effective dialogue between these organizations and biotechnologists. Here is a list of the Web sites referred to in this article:

> The Canadian Food Inspection Agency: **www.cfia-acia.agr.ca/**
> The U.S. Food and Drug Administration: **www.fda.gov**
> The U.S. Department of Agriculture: **www.nal.usda.gov/bic/**
> The Nuffield Foundation: **www.nuffield.org/bioethics/publication/**
> The Royal Society: **www.royalsoc.ac.uk/stpol4O.htm**
> Performance Plants: **www.performanceplants.com**

■ ■ ■

## Discussion and Writing Suggestions

1. Contrast some of the arguments against GM foods in the article by Partridge to those advanced by Dennis in favour of it.
2. How does Dennis treat the opposite or alternative views?

## The Food Fight: Canada Faces Big Losses as Consumers Reject Genetically Modified Crops

BARRY CAME

In keeping with the message, the medium was suitably high-tech: a transat-    1 lantic encounter conducted live by television satellite. Up on the giant screen in the London conference hall, Robert Shapiro, chief executive officer of the Monsanto Co., listened patiently as the American biotechnology conglomerate he heads was raked over the coals by Peter Melchett, the British aristocrat who is executive director of the environmental organization Greenpeace in Britain. Lord Melchett accused Monsanto of "bullying" an ever more anxious public into reluctant acceptance of a wide range of genetically modified foods, everything from soybeans to corn to Canadian canola oil. Shapiro's response, however, was not quite what has come to be expected from the boss of the most aggressive biotech firm on the planet. "If I'm a bully," he ruefully noted, "then I'm not a very successful bully."

The candid remark drew murmurs of satisfaction from the gathering of     2
environmental activists, organized by Greenpeace. For it marked a significant victory for the country's ecological warriors, the first high-profile acknowledgement that the world's biotech industry, based largely in the United States, is losing the global battle to convince the public of the benefits of genetic engineering. Instead, consumers are increasingly fearful that there could be unknown side-effects. "We have irritated and antagonized more people than we have persuaded," Shapiro admitted to his London audience. "Our confidence in biotechnology has been widely seen as arrogance and condescension. Too often we forgot to listen."

The result has been a spreading public rejection of what is known in     3
Europe as GM—genetically modified—foods and elsewhere often as GE—genetically engineered—products. The implications for North American farmers are huge—Canada and the United States are becoming the only markets where GM foods can readily be sold, and that may not last. Anti-GM activists have already launched a campaign to rally Canadian consumers.

The evidence of the turnaround is everywhere, from British supermarket     4
shelves, where GM goods are increasingly rare, to Indian cotton fields, where outraged peasants have torched crops mistakenly believed to have been genetically altered. The 15 nations of the European Union are implementing regulations calling for the labelling of all products with even a trace of GM ingredients. Last summer, Japan's two leading breweries, Sapporo and Kirin, announced they would stop using genetically modified corn by the year 2001. Monsanto itself pledged, shortly before Shapiro's satellite debate, that it would not market controversial "terminator" crop seeds that in future could produce lucrative, one-season-only plants. "The message is scary," said Germany's Deutschebank in a recent report on genetically modified organisms, or GMOS, prepared for the bank's clients. "GMOs increasingly are, in our opinion, becoming a liability to farmers. We predict that GMOS, once perceived as the driver of the bull [market] case for this sector, will now be perceived as a pariah."

That process is already well under way in both the United States and     5
Canada, where a two-tier market for grains is fast developing. Increasingly, genetically "improved" crops are trading at deep discounts, while European processors have been willing to pay premiums of as much as $1.50 a bushel for non-GM crops. In September, the huge U.S. grain processing corporation, Archer Daniel Midland, advised American grain farmers to begin segregating GM and non-GM crops. At the same time, the two main U.S. baby food manufacturers, Gerber Products Co. and H. J. Heinz Co., declared they would no longer use genetically modified corn or soybeans in any of their products.

Canada's canola farmers have been hardest hit by the trend. In 1994,     6
Canadian exports to the European Union of canola seed, destined for crushing into oil, peaked at $425 million. "Now there's squat," says Ian Thomson, agricultural counsellor at the Canadian High Commission in London. "What's happened is that we have completely lost a market that was worth

close to half a billion dollars annually in good years." Part of the problem lies in the farming techniques of canola producers in Canada, where between 60 and 70 per cent of the annual crop is genetically engineered to render it resistant to weed killer. Canadian producers do not segregate their crop, making it virtually unsalable in Europe. If the trends continue, a similar fate may await future Canadian crops in the country's three other major markets for canola seed—the United States, Japan and Mexico, all of which are also experiencing rumblings of unease about GM products.

The problem is as much about public perceptions as it is about science. In     7
Europe, the anti-GM battle has been waged against the backdrop of a series of European food scares that began with BSE, or "mad cow" disease, in Britain and has escalated with scandals over carcinogenic dioxins in Belgian poultry and dairy products and the use in France and elsewhere of sewage slurry in animal feeds. The aggressive stance of U.S.-based agribusiness giants has not helped. The U.S. government, responding to pressure from the powerful agribusiness lobby in Washington, has taken the Europeans to court at the World Trade Organization, winning successive decisions against Europe's restrictions on Caribbean bananas and growth hormone additives in beef. The Americans have threatened similar challenges to European resistance to the free import of genetically engineered grains.

The combined effect has been to shatter Europeans' confidence in what     8
they are eating and drinking as well as fostering deep resentment about the unrestrained power of U.S. multinational corporations. "There has been an unprecedented, permanent and irreversible shift in the political landscape," Greenpeace's Lord Melchett told Shapiro last week. "People are increasingly aware and mistrustful of the combination of big science and big business."

Even the normally apolitical Prince Charles has entered the debate. The     9
much-maligned heir to the British throne gave a major boost to the campaign in June with a fierce attack on the safety of GM crops, evidently sparked by Prime Minister Tony Blair's contemptuous dismissal of the "ayatollahs" leading the GM opponents. The Prince, who operates his own lucrative organic farming business, posed what he termed 10 unanswered questions in a widely disseminated newspaper article. "What I believe the public's reaction shows," wrote Charles, "is that instinctively we are nervous about tampering with nature when we can't be sure that we know enough of the consequences."

The Prince's concerns are shared by many. It is no accident, for example,     10
that in his first major address to the European parliament last week, the newly elected president of the European Commission, Italy's Romano Prodi, singled out food safety as the top priority of his infant administration. He proposed a pan-European food agency to deal with issues such as those involving British beef, Belgian chickens and U.S. genetic modifications. "We have to provide answers," he said, "to those who are wondering if official information can be trusted these days, or is it all being manipulated for economic and political purposes?" On farms across the globe, the answers may be blowing in the wind.

■ ■ ■

## Discussion and Writing Suggestions

1. When issues of human health and ethics are at stake, how would you rank the importance of financial considerations?
2. Is the author simply reporting facts for our information, or does he seem impassioned by his side of the argument?


## ■ SYNTHESIS ACTIVITIES

1. Suppose you are writing a survey article on biotechnology for a general audience magazine, such as *Time* or *Maclean's*. You want to introduce your readers to the subject, tell them what it is and what it may become, and you want to focus, in particular, on the advantages and disadvantages of biotechnology. Drawing on the sources you have read in this chapter, write such an article (i.e., an explanatory synthesis). For background information on the subject you can draw on sources such as Starr and the introduction to this chapter. Other sources, including those by Watson, Rifkin and Postrel, offer many case studies illustrating advantages and disadvantages. And, of course, Huxley serves as a dark example of the kind of thing that *could* happen if biotechnology is used for unethical purposes.

2. Write an editorial (i.e., an argument synthesis) arguing that additional regulations need to be placed on biotechnology. Specify the chief problem areas, as you see them, and indicate the regulations needed in order to deal with these problems.

   You may want to begin with a survey of biotechnology (in which you acknowledge its advantages) but then narrow your focus to the problem areas you choose to emphasize. Categorize the problem areas (e.g., problems for prospective parents, for the workplace, for the courtroom, for the commercial applications of biotechnology). The suggested regulations—and explanations of why they are necessary—might be discussed throughout the editorial or saved for the end.

   In developing your editorial, devote one paragraph to Virginia Postrel's position (that the free market, not government regulations, should determine which genetic technologies get used). Devote another paragraph to rebutting her position.

3. *Brave New World* represents one artist's view of how scientific knowledge might be abused to ensure social stability and conformity. Huxley focused on the possibility of dividing fertilized human ova into identical parts and then conditioning the ova before "birth." Write a short story (or a play or screenplay) that represents your own nightmare vision. You may want to focus on other aspects of genetic engineering: the problem of forced genetic testing, of eugenics (creating "perfect" people or eliminating "imperfect" ones), of fostering uniformity among the population, of some fantastic commercial application of

bioengineering, or even of some aspect of cloning (among the films dealing with cloning are Woody Allen's *Sleeper* and Steven Spielberg's *Jurassic Park*).

Decide whether the story is to be essentially serious or comic (satirical)—or something in between. Create characters (try to avoid caricatures) who will enact the various aspects of the problem, as you see it. And create a social and physical setting appropriate to the story you want to tell.

4. Write an article for a magazine such as *Maclean's* or *Time* on the current status of biotechnology—as of August 2050. Try to make the article generally upbeat (unlike the nightmare vision called for in the previous question), but be frank also about the problems that have been encountered, as well as the problems that remain. Refer, at some point in your article, to views of biotechnology from the late 1980s and the early 1990s to establish some basis for comparison between what they thought "then" and what they think "now." You might model your article on the piece by Margaret Munro (which appeared in *The Globe and Mail*) or by Katharine Partridge (which appeared in *Today's Parent* magazine), or on any contemporary news magazine article of comparable scope. The language should be lively and vivid, and you should include as many "facts" as you can think of. Study your model articles for ideas about how to organize your material.

5. Genome research is made possible by the investments of pharmaceutical companies, which bet that research will reveal the genetic foundations of certain diseases that can then be corrected with specially designed drugs. Certainly, without private investment, human genome research would proceed far more slowly than it is proceeding at present. How comfortable are you with the commercial direction that human genome research has taken? Is the DNA map that researchers seek "larger" than the interests of particular pharmaceutical companies? What kinds of profits (if any) should companies be making in this field? Write an essay in which you take a position on this topic, drawing especially on the selections by Watson, Rifkin, Postrel, and Friesen.

## ■ Research Activities

1. The main focal points of the debate over genetic engineering and testing have been (1) whether the new biotechnologies are safe and ethical; (2) whether they will benefit agriculture and food processing; (3) whether they require stricter regulation (and if so, what kind); (4) whether genetic testing (or the use of genetic testing) by employers and insurance companies is ethical; (5) whether genetic testing of fetuses is ethical; (6) whether work should proceed on the Human Genome Project and/or the Human Genome Diversity Project; (7) whether geneticists should work on biological weapons. Select *one* of these areas and research the current status of the debate.

In addition to relevant articles, see Jeremy Rifkin, *Declaration of a Heretic* (1985); Joseph Fletcher, *Ethics of Genetic Control* (1988); Gerald R. Campbell, *Biotechnology: An Introduction* (1988); Charles Pilar and Keith R. Yamamoto, *Gene Wars* (1988); David Suzuki and Peter Knudtson, *Genetics* (1989); Andrew Linzey, *Slavery: Human and Animal* (1988); Monsanto Company, *Agriculture and the New Biology* (1989); Daniel J. Kevles and Leroy Hood, *The Code of Codes: Scientific and Social Issues in the Human Genome Project* (1992); and Ingeborg Boyens, *Unnatural Harvest* (1999).

2. In August 1992, researchers announced that they had managed through genetic engineering to produce mice that developed cystic fibrosis. Scientists believed that by studying the course of this disease in mice, they would be able to devise new therapies for the treatment of this usually fatal disease in humans. Follow up on either this development or some other development involving the genetic engineering of laboratory animals to further medical research. Describe what is involved in the procedure, how it was developed, the results to date, and the ethical debate that may have ensued about its practice.

3. Research and discuss some aspect of the early history of genetic engineering as it developed in the 1970s. Begin with a survey of Watson and Crick's work with DNA in the early 1950s, describe some of the early experiments in this area, discuss some of the concerns expressed both by scientists and laypersons, and cover in some detail the Asilomar (California) Conference of 1975 at which scientists worked out guidelines for future research.

4. Research some of the most significant recent advances in biotechnology, categorize them, and report on your finding. You may wish to narrow your topic by dealing with biotechnology in relation to human health, agriculture, or the law. Focus on what is currently being done, on who is doing it, on the obstacles yet to overcome, and on the anticipated benefits on the research and development.

5. In 1989 James D. Watson was appointed to head NIH's Human Genome Project. Watson's appointment and his subsequent work as director of the project generated some controversy. Research Watson's professional activities since his discovery with Francis Crick of the structure of DNA, focusing on his more recent activities. See especially, the article on Watson, "The Double Helix," which appeared in *The New Republic*, July 9 and 16, 1990. How do Watson's professional colleagues—and others—assess his more recent work?

6. Write a paper on biotechnology critic Jeremy Rifkin and the critical reaction to his activities and his books. Consult the *Reader's Guide to Periodical Literature* and locate important articles by and about Rifkin during the past decade or so. Locate Rifkin's books and survey them. Most importantly, look up reviews of Rifkin's books, starting with the listings in *Book Review Digest*. (This is an annual index that lists reviews during a given year and provides brief excerpts from the most important reviews.)

Begin your paper by summarizing Rifkin's life and work thus far. (Your introductory paragraphs should probably focus on the controversy surrounding Rifkin.) Then focus on the reaction to his work. You may want to divide your paper into sections on positive and negative reactions; or you may want to organize by critical reviews of his various books and activities. At the conclusion, develop an overall assessment of the significance and value of Rifkin's work.

7. Research the current status of either the Human Genome Project or the Human Genome Diversity Project. To what extent has the project you selected made progress in achieving its goals?

8. Research one of the recent cases involving DNA evidence in a Canadian court case. Explain how DNA matching was a significant factor in the presentation and outcome of the case, or in a subsequent appeal. *Or* review several cases in which DNA was a factor, and focus on the relationships between them, in terms of the use of genetic testing and matching.

9. Recently, our Parliament has debated regulating biogenetic research with particular interest in curtailing stem-cell research on human embryos that may lead to curing some serious illnesses but that sets off ethical alarm bells. Research and report on some of the most significant regulations imposed on the biotechnology industry, consider the views of critics and of scientists themselves, and indicate your own position (and possibly some of your own proposals) on existing and additional regulations.

10. If your college or university has scientists on its faculty who are working on DNA research, interview them to find out what they are doing. Ask them how they feel about some of the ethical issues covered in this chapter. Ask them to recommend references in the professional literature that will enable you to understand more fully the aims of their research; then consult some of these references and use them to provide context for your discussion of this research.

11. Conduct and write a summary report on student attitudes to some facet of biotechnology and write a report based on this survey. Devise questions that focus on the main areas of controversy (see Research Activity 1). Phrase your questions in a way that allows a range of responses (perhaps on a scale of 1 to 5, or using modifiers such as "strongly agree," "agree somewhat," "disagree somewhat," "strongly disagree"); don't ask for responses that require a yes/no or approve/disapprove response. (See "Interviews and Surveys," Chapter 3.) Attempt to correlate the responses to such variables as academic major, student status (lower division, upper division, graduate), gender, ethnic background, geographical area of origin (urban, suburban, rural). Determine whether respondents personally know someone with a disease for which a genetic cure is either possible or under consideration. Determine also how much prior knowledge of biotechnology your respondents have.

# 13

# Fairy Tales: A Closer Look at "Cinderella"

"Once upon a time. . . ." Millions of children around the world have listened to these (or similar) words. And, once upon a time, such words were magic archways into a world of entertainment and fantasy for children and their parents. But in our own century, fairy tales have come under the scrutiny of anthropologists, linguists, educators, psychologists, and psychiatrists, as well as literary critics, who have come to see them as a kind of social genetic code—a means by which cultural values are transmitted from one generation to the next. Some people, of course, may scoff at the idea that charming tales like "Cinderella" or "Snow White" are anything other than charming tales, at the idea that fairy tales may really be ways of inculcating young and impressionable children with culturally approved values. But even if they are not aware of it, adults and children use fairy tales in complex and subtle ways. We can, perhaps, best illustrate this by focusing primarily on a single tale—"Cinderella."

"Cinderella" appears to be the best-known fairy tale in the world. In 1892, Marian Roalfe Cox published 345 variants of the story, the first systematic study of a single folktale. In her collection, Cox gathered stories from throughout Europe in which elements or motifs of "Cinderella" appeared, often mixed with motifs of other tales. All told, more than 700 variants exist throughout the world—in Europe, Africa, Asia, and North and South America. Scholars debate the extent to which such a wide distribution is explained by population migrations or by some universal quality of imagination that would allow people at different times and places to create essentially the same story. But for whatever reason, folklorists agree that "Cinderella" has appealed to storytellers and listeners everywhere.

The great body of folk literature, including fairy tales, comes to us from an oral tradition. Written literature, produced by a particular author, is preserved through the generations just as the author recorded it. By contrast, oral literature changes with every telling: The childhood game comes to mind in which one child whispers a sentence into the ear of another; by the time the second child repeats the sentence to a third, and the third to a fourth (and so on), the sentence has changed considerably. And so it is with oral literature, with the qualification that these stories are also changed quite consciously when a teller wishes to add or delete material.

The modern student of folk literature finds her- or himself in the position of *reading* as opposed to hearing a tale. Writing his version of "Cinderella" in 1697, Charles Perrault appears (according to Bruno Bettelheim) to have "freed it of all the content he considered vulgar, and refined its other features to make the product suitable to be told at court. His version of the tale is included here, along with the Walt Disney version of the story based on Perrault.

We hear from Bruno Bettelheim, who, following psychoanalytic theory, finds in "Cinderella" a "Story of Sibling Rivalry and Oedipal Conflicts." The chapter includes two feminist perspectives on "Cinderella": historian Karol Kelley examines two filmed versions of Perrault's rendering of the tale, Disney's animated version (1949) and *Pretty Woman* (1990); and Nobel laureate Toni Morrison, in an address at Barnard College, calls on her women listeners to treat one another more humanely than the stepsisters treated Cinderella.

In "And She Lived Happily Ever After," Kay Stone explores how heroines that many of us might criticize as being figures oppressed by others and circumstance can also be understood as being active and fulfilled. For example, it is possible to emphasize that a character like Cinderella achieves her dreams amid difficult circumstances, and with perseverance and hope sets herself up to live happily ever after.

Looking at the phenomena of "reality t.v.," and specifically at the program about women in a contest to marry a millionaire, Judy Rebick returns to critiquing the Cinderella story by considering how our culture continues to thrive on dreams that are oppressive of individualism. Looking more broadly at the relation between children's stories and cultural values, Cathy Maio discusses how Disney recreates folk takes that maintain oppressive stereotypes.

A note on terminology: "Cinderella," "Jack and the Beanstalk," "Little Red Riding Hood," and the like are commonly referred to as fairy tales, although, strictly speaking, they are not. True fairy tales concern a "class of supernatural beings of diminutive size, who in popular belief are said to possess magical powers and to have great influence for good or evil over the affairs of humans" (*Oxford English Dictionary*). "Cinderella" and the others just mentioned concern no beings of diminutive size, although extraordinary, magical events do occur in the stories. Folklorists would be more apt to call these stories "wonder tales." We retain the traditional "fairy tale," with the proviso that in popular usage the term is misapplied. You may notice that the authors in this chapter use the terms "folktale" and "fairy tale" interchangeably. The expression "folktale" refers to *any* story conceived orally and passed on in an oral tradition. Thus, "folktale" is a generic term that incorporates both fairy tales and wonder tales.

## Cinderella

### CHARLES PERRAULT

*Charles Perrault (1628–1703) was born in Paris of a prosperous family. He practised law for a short time and then devoted his attentions to a job in government, in which capacity he was instrumental in promoting the advancement of the arts and sciences and in securing pensions for writers, both French and foreign. Perrault is best known as a writer for his* Contes de ma mère l'oie *(Mother Goose*

Tales), *a collection of fairy tales taken from popular folklore. He is widely suspected of having changed these stories in an effort to make them more acceptable to his audience—members of the French court.*

Once there was a nobleman who took as his second wife the proudest and    1
haughtiest woman imaginable. She had two daughters of the same character,
who took after their mother in everything. On his side, the husband had a
daughter who was sweetness itself; she inherited this from her mother, who
had been the most kindly of women.

No sooner was the wedding over than the stepmother showed her ill-    2
nature. She could not bear the good qualities of the young girl, for they made
her own daughters seem even less likable. She gave her the roughest work of
the house to do. It was she who washed the dishes and the stairs, who cleaned
out Madam's room and the rooms of the two Misses. She slept right at the top
of the house, in an attic, on a lumpy mattress, while her sisters slept in pan-
elled rooms where they had the most modern beds and mirrors in which they
could see themselves from top to toe. The poor girl bore everything in
patience and did not dare to complain to her father. He would only have
scolded her, for he was entirely under his wife's thumb.

When she had finished her work, she used to go into the chimney-corner    3
and sit down among the cinders, for which reason she was usually known in the
house as Cinderbottom. Her younger stepsister, who was not so rude as the
other, called her Cinderella. However, Cinderella, in spite of her ragged clothes,
was still fifty times as beautiful as her sisters, superbly dressed though they were.

One day the King's son gave a ball, to which everyone of good family was    4
invited. Our two young ladies received invitations, for they cut quite a figure
in the country. So there they were, both feeling very pleased and very busy
choosing the clothes and the hair-styles which would suit them best. More
work for Cinderella, for it was she who ironed her sisters' underwear and gof-
fered their linen cuffs. Their only talk was of what they would wear.

"I," said the elder, "shall wear my red velvet dress and my collar of    5
English lace."

"I," said the younger, "shall wear just my ordinary skirt; but, to make    6
up, I shall put on my gold-embroidered cape and my diamond clasp, which is
quite out of the common."

The right hairdresser was sent for to supply double-frilled coifs, and    7
patches were bought from the right patch-maker. They called Cinderella to
ask her opinion, for she had excellent taste. She made useful suggestions and
even offered to do their hair for them. They accepted willingly.

While she was doing it, they said to her:    8

"Cinderella, how would you like to go to the ball?"    9

"Oh dear, you are making fun of me. It wouldn't do for me."    10

"You are quite right. It would be a joke. People would laugh if they saw    11
a Cinderbottom at the ball."

Anyone else would have done their hair in knots for them, but she had a    12
sweet nature, and she finished it perfectly. For two days they were so excited
that they ate almost nothing. They broke a good dozen laces trying to tight-

en their stays to make their waists slimmer, and they were never away from their mirrors.

At last the great day arrived. They set off, and Cinderella watched them until they were out of sight. When she could no longer see them, she began to cry. Her godmother, seeing her all in tears, asked what was the matter. [13]

"If only I could . . . If only I could . . ." She was weeping so much that she could not go on. [14]

Her godmother, who was a fairy, said to her: "If only you could go to the ball, is that it?" [15]

"Alas, yes," said Cinderella with a sigh. [16]

"Well," said the godmother, "be a good girl and I'll get you there." [17]

She took her into her room and said: "Go into the garden and get me a pumpkin." [18]

Cinderella hurried out and cut the best she could find and took it to her godmother, but she could not understand how this pumpkin would get her to the ball. Her godmother hollowed it out, leaving only the rind, and then tapped it with her wand and immediately it turned into a magnificent gilded coach. [19]

Then she went to look in her mouse-trap and found six mice all alive in it. She told Cinderella to raise the door of the trap a little, and as each mouse came out she gave it a tap with her wand and immediately it turned into a fine horse. That made a team of six horses, each of fine mouse-coloured grey. [20]

While she was wondering how she would make a coachman, Cinderella said to her: [21]

"I will go and see whether there is a rat in the rat-trap, we could make a coachman of him." [22]

"You are right," said the godmother. "Run and see." [23]

Cinderella brought her the rat-trap, in which there were three big rats. The fairy picked out one of them because of his splendid whiskers and, when she had touched him, he turned into a fat coachman, with the finest moustaches in the district. [24]

Then she said: "Go into the garden and you will find six lizards behind the watering-can. Bring them to me." [25]

As soon as Cinderella had brought them, her godmother changed them into six footmen, who got up behind the coach with their striped liveries, and stood in position there as though they had been doing it all their lives. [26]

Then the fairy said to Cinderella: [27]

"Well, that's to go to the ball in. Aren't you pleased?" [28]

"Yes. But am I to go like this, with my ugly clothes?" [29]

Her godmother simply touched her with her wand and her clothes were changed in an instant into a dress of gold and silver cloth, all sparkling with precious stones. Then she gave her a pair of glass slippers, most beautifully made. [30]

So equipped, Cinderella got into the coach: but her godmother warned her above all not to be out after midnight, telling her that, if she stayed at the ball a moment later, her coach would turn back into a pumpkin, her horses into mice, her footmen into lizards, and her fine clothes would become rags again. [31]

She promised her godmother that she would leave the ball before mid-  32
night without fail, and she set out, beside herself with joy.

The King's son, on being told that a great princess whom no one knew  33
had arrived, ran out to welcome her. He handed her down from the coach and
led her into the hall where his guests were. A sudden silence fell; the dancing
stopped, the violins ceased to play, the whole company stood fascinated by
the beauty of the unknown princess. Only a low murmur was heard: "Ah,
how lovely she is!" The King himself, old as he was, could not take his eyes
off her and kept whispering to the Queen that it was a long time since he had
seen such a beautiful and charming person. All the ladies were absorbed in
noting her clothes and the way her hair was dressed, so as to order the same
things for themselves the next morning, provided that fine enough materials
could be found, and skillful enough craftsmen.

The King's son placed her in the seat of honour, and later led her out to  34
dance. She danced with such grace that she won still more admiration. An
excellent supper was served, but the young Prince was too much occupied in
gazing at her to eat anything. She went and sat next to her sisters and treated them with great courtesy, offering them oranges and lemons which the
Prince had given her. They were astonished, for they did not recognize her.

While they were chatting together, Cinderella heard the clock strike a  35
quarter to twelve. She curtsied low to the company and left as quickly as
she could.

As soon as she reached home, she went to her godmother and, having  36
thanked her, said that she would very much like to go again to the ball on the
next night—for the Prince had begged her to come back. She was in the
middle of telling her godmother about all the things that had happened, when
the two sisters came knocking at the door. Cinderella went to open it.

"How late you are! she said, rubbing her eyes and yawning and stretch-  37
ing as though she had just woken up (though since they had last seen each
other she had felt very far from sleepy).

"If you had been at the ball," said one of the sisters, "you would not have  38
felt like yawning. There was a beautiful princess there, really ravishingly
beautiful. She was most attentive to us. She gave us oranges and lemons."

Cinderella could have hugged herself. She asked them the name of the  39
princess, but they replied that no one knew her, that the King's son was
much troubled about it, and that he would give anything in the world to
know who she was. Cinderella smiled and said to them:

"So she was very beautiful? Well, well, how lucky you are! Couldn't I see  40
her? Please, Miss Javotte, do lend me that yellow dress which you wear about
the house."

"Really," said Miss Javotte, "what an idea! Lend one's dress like that to  41
a filthy Cinderbottom! I should have to be out of my mind."

Cinderella was expecting this refusal and she was very glad when it  42
came, for she would have been in an awkward position if her sister really had
lent her her frock.

On the next day the two sisters went to the ball, and Cinderella too, but   43
even more splendidly dressed than the first time. The King's son was constantly at her side and wooed her the whole evening. The young girl was enjoying herself so much that she forgot her godmother's warning. She heard the clock striking the first stroke of midnight when she thought that it was still hardly eleven. She rose and slipped away as lightly as a roe-deer. The Prince followed her, but he could not catch her up. One of her glass slippers fell off, and the Prince picked it up with great care.

Cinderella reached home quite out of breath, with no coach, no footmen,   44
and wearing her old clothes. Nothing remained of all her finery, except one of her little slippers, the fellow to the one which she had dropped. The guards at the palace gate were asked if they had not seen a princess go out. They answered that they had seen no one go out except a very poorly dressed girl, who looked more like a peasant than a young lady.

When the two sisters returned from the ball, Cinderella asked them if   45
they had enjoyed themselves again, and if the beautiful lady had been there. They said that she had, but that she had run away when it struck midnight, and so swiftly that she had lost one of her glass slippers, a lovely little thing. The Prince had picked it up and had done nothing but gaze at it for the rest of the ball, and undoubtedly he was very much in love with the beautiful person to whom it belonged.

They were right, for a few days later the King's son had it proclaimed to   46
the sound of trumpets that he would marry the girl whose foot exactly fitted the slipper. They began by trying it on the various princesses, then on the duchesses and on all the ladies of the Court, but with no success. It was brought to the two sisters, who did everything possible to force their feet into the slipper, but they could not manage it. Cinderella, who was looking on, recognized her own slipper, and said laughing:

"Let me see if it would fit me!"   47

Her sisters began to laugh and mock at her. But the gentleman who was   48
trying on the slipper looked closely at Cinderella and, seeing that she was very beautiful, said that her request was perfectly reasonable and that he had instructions to try it on every girl. He made Cinderella sit down and, raising the slipper to her foot, he found that it slid on without difficulty and fitted like a glove.

Great was the amazement of the two sisters, but it became greater still   49
when Cinderella drew from her pocket the second little slipper and put it on her other foot. Thereupon the fairy godmother came in and, touching Cinderella's clothes with her wand, made them even more magnificent than on the previous days.

Then the two sisters recognized her as the lovely princess whom they had   50
met at the ball. They flung themselves at her feet and begged her forgiveness for all the unkind things which they had done to her. Cinderella raised them up and kissed them, saying that she forgave them with all her heart and asking them to love her always. She was taken to the young Prince in the fine clothes which she was wearing. He thought her more beautiful than ever and a few days later he married her. Cinderella, who was as kind as she was beau-

tiful, invited her two sisters to live in the palace and married them, on the same day, to two great noblemen of the Court.

# Walt Disney's "Cinderella"

### ADAPTED BY CAMPBELL GRANT

*Walter Elias Disney (1901–1966), winner of thirty-two Academy Awards, is world famous for his cartoon animations. After achieving recognition with cartoon shorts populated by such immortals as Mickey Mouse and Donald Duck, he produced the full-length animated film version of* Snow White and the Seven Dwarfs *in 1937. He followed with other animations, including* Cinderella *(1950), which he adapted from Perrault's version of the tale. A* Little Golden Book, *the text of which appears here, was then adapted from the film by Campbell Grant.*

Once upon a time in a far-away land lived a sweet and pretty girl named 1
Cinderella. She made her home with her mean old stepmother and her two stepsisters, and they made her do all the work in the house.

Cinderella cooked and baked. She cleaned and scrubbed. She had no 2
time left for parties and fun.

But one day an invitation came from the palace of the king. 3

A great ball was to be given for the prince of the land. And every young 4
girl in the kingdom was invited.

"How nice!" thought Cinderella. "I am invited, too." 5

But her mean stepsisters never thought of her. They thought only of 6
themselves, of course. They had all sorts of jobs for Cinderella to do.

"Wash this slip. Press this dress. Curl my hair. Find my fan." 7

They both kept shouting, as fast as they could speak. 8

"But I must get ready myself. I'm going, too," said Cinderella. 9

"You!" they hooted. "The Prince's ball for you?" 10

And they kept her busy all day long. She worked in the morning, while 11
her stepsisters slept. She worked all afternoon, while they bathed and dressed. And in the evening she had to help them put on the finishing touches for the ball. She had not one minute to think of herself.

Soon the coach was ready at the door. The ugly stepsisters were pow- 12
dered, pressed, and curled. But there stood Cinderella in her workaday rags.

"Why, Cinderella!" said the stepsisters. "You're not dressed for the ball." 13

"No," said Cinderella. "I guess I cannot go." 14

Poor Cinderella sat weeping in the garden. 15

Suddenly a little old woman with a sweet, kind face stood before her. It 16
was her fairy godmother.

"Hurry, child!" she said. "You are going to the ball!" 17

Cinderella could hardly believe her eyes! The fairy godmother turned a 18
fat pumpkin into a splendid coach.

Next her pet mice became horses, and her dog a fine footman. The barn　19
horse was turned into a coachman.

"There, my dear," said the fairy godmother. "Now into the coach with　20
you, and off to the ball you go."

"But my dress—" said Cinderella.　21

"Lovely, my dear," the fairy godmother began. Then she really looked at　22
Cinderella's rags.

"Oh, good heavens," she said. "You can never go in that." She waved　23
her magic wand.

> "Salaga dolla,
> Menchicka boola,
> Bibbidi bobbidi boo!" she said.

There stood Cinderella in the loveliest ball dress that ever was. And on　24
her feet were tiny glass slippers!

"Oh," cried Cinderella. "How can I ever thank you?"　25

"Just have a wonderful time at the ball, my dear," said her fairy god-　26
mother. "But remember, this magic lasts only until midnight. At the stroke of
midnight, the spell will be broken. And everything will be as it was before."

"I will remember," said Cinderella. "It is more than I ever dreamed of."　27

Then into the magic coach she stepped, and was whirled away to the ball.　28

And such a ball! The king's palace was ablaze with lights. There was music　29
and laughter. And every lady in the land was dressed in her beautiful best.

But Cinderella was the loveliest of them all. The prince never left her side,　30
all evening long. They danced every dance. They had supper side by side. And
they happily smiled into each other's eyes.

But all at once the clock began to strike midnight, Bong Bong Bong—　31

"Oh!" cried Cinderella. "I almost forgot!"　32

And without a word, away she ran, out of the ballroom and down the　33
palace stairs. She lost one glass slipper. But she could not stop.

Into her magic coach she stepped, and away it rolled. But as the clock　34
stopped striking, the coach disappeared. And no one knew where she had
gone.

Next morning all the kingdom was filled with the news. The Grand　35
Duke was going from house to house, with a small glass slipper in his hand.
For the prince had said he would marry no one but the girl who could wear
that tiny shoe.

Every girl in the land tried hard to put it on. The ugly stepsisters tried　36
hardest of all. But not a one could wear the glass shoe.

And where was Cinderella? Locked in her room. For the mean old step-　37
mother was taking no chances of letting her try on the slipper. Poor
Cinderella! It looked as if the Grand Duke would surely pass her by.

But her little friends the mice got the stepmother's key. And they pushed　38
it under Cinderella's door. So down the long stairs she came, as the Duke was
just about to leave.

"Please!" cried Cinderella. "Please let me try."                    39

And of course the slipper fitted, since it was her very own.        40

That was all the Duke needed. Now his long search was done. And so  41
Cinderella became the prince's bride, and lived happily ever after—and the
little pet mice lived in the palace and were happy ever after, too.

*[handwritten: Bettelheim, B. (1976). "Cinderella": A story of sibling Rivalry and Oedipal Conflicts. In L. Behrens, L.J. Rosen, J.M. Rogers, & C. Taylor (Eds.), Writing and reading across the curriculum (Cdn ed.), pp. 601-604. Toronto: Longman.]*

# "*Cinderella*": A Story of Sibling Rivalry and Oedipal Conflicts

## BRUNO BETTELHEIM

*Considering that there are so many variants of "Cinderella," you may have won-
dered what it is about this story that's prompted people in different parts of the
world, at different times, to show interest in a child who's been debased but then
rises above her misfortune. Why are people so fascinated with "Cinderella"?*

*Depending on the people you ask and their perspectives, you'll find this ques-
tion answered in various ways. As a Freudian psychologist, Bruno Bettelheim
believes that the mind is a repository of both conscious and unconscious elements. By definition, we aren't aware of what goes on in our unconscious;
nonetheless, what happens there exerts a powerful influence on what we believe
and on how we act. This division of the mind into conscious and unconscious
parts is true for children no less than for adults. Based on these beliefs about the
mind, Bettelheim analyzes "Cinderella" first by pointing to what he calls the
story's essential theme: sibling rivalry, or Cinderella's mistreatment at the hands
of her stepsisters. Competition among brothers and sisters presents a profound
and largely unconscious problem to children, says Bettelheim. By hearing
"Cinderella," a story that speaks directly to their unconscious, children are given
tools that can help them resolve conflicts. Cinderella resolves her difficulties; children hearing the story can resolve theirs as well: This is the unconscious message
of the tale.*

*Do you accept this argument? To do so, you'd have to agree with the author's
reading of "Cinderella's" hidden meanings; and you'd have to agree with his
assumptions concerning the conscious and unconscious mind and the ways in
which the unconscious will seize upon the content of a story in order to resolve
conflicts. Even if you don't accept Bettelheim's analysis, his essay makes fascinating reading. First, it is internally consistent—that is, he begins with a set of
principles and then builds logically upon them, as any good writer will. Second, his
analysis demonstrates how a scholarly point of view—a coherent set of assumptions about the way the world (in this case, the mind) works—creates boundaries
for a discussion. Change the assumptions and you'll change the analyses that
follow from them.*

*Bettelheim's essay is long and somewhat difficult. While he uses no subhead-
ings, he has divided his work into four sections: paragraphs 2–10 are devoted to*

*sibling rivalry; paragraphs 11–19, to an analysis of "Cinderella's" hidden mean-*
*ings; paragraphs 20–24, to the psychological makeup of children at the end of*
*their oedipal period; and paragraphs 25–27, to the reasons "Cinderella," in par-*
*ticular, appeals to children in the oedipal period.*

*Bruno Bettelheim, a distinguished psychologist and educator, was born in*
*1903 in Vienna. He was naturalized as an American citizen in 1939 and served as*
*a professor of psychology at Rockford College and the University of Chicago.*
*Awarded the honour of fellow by several prestigious professional associations,*
*Bettelheim was a prolific writer and contributed articles to numerous popular and*
*professional publications. His list of books includes* Love Is Not Enough: The
Treatment of Emotionally Disturbed Children *(1950),* The Informed Heart *(1960),*
*and* The Uses of Enchantment *(1975), from which this selection has been excerpt-*
*ed. Bettelheim died in 1990.*

By all accounts, "Cinderella" is the best-known fairy tale, and probably also   1
the best-liked. It is quite an old story; when first written down in China during
the ninth century A.D., it already had a history. The unrivaled tiny foot size as
a mark of extraordinary virtue, distinction, and beauty, and the slipper made
of precious material are facets which point to an Eastern, if not necessarily
Chinese, origin.[1] The modern hearer does not connect sexual attractiveness and
beauty in general with extreme smallness of the foot, as the ancient Chinese
did, in accordance with their practice of binding women's feet.

"Cinderella," as we know it, is experienced as a story about the agonies   2
and hopes which form the essential content of sibling rivalry; and about the
degraded heroine winning out over her siblings who abused her. Long before
Perrault gave "Cinderella" the form in which it is now widely known,
"having to live among the ashes" was a symbol of being debased in comparison to one's siblings, irrespective of sex. In Germany, for example, there were
stories in which such an ash-boy later becomes king, which parallels
Cinderella's fate. "Aschenputtel" is the title of the Brothers Grimm's version
of the tale. The term originally designated a lowly, dirty kitchenmaid who
must tend to the fireplace ashes.

There are many examples in the German language of how being forced to   3
dwell among the ashes was a symbol not just of degradation, but also of sibling rivalry, and of the sibling who finally surpasses the brother or brothers
who have debased him. Martin Luther in his *Table Talks* speaks about Cain
as the God-forsaken evildoer who is powerful, while pious Abel is forced to
be his ash-brother (*Asche-brüdel*), a mere nothing, subject to Cain; in one of
Luther's sermons he says that Esau was forced into the role of Jacob's ash-
brother. Cain and Able, Jacob and Esau are Biblical examples of one brother being suppressed or destroyed by the other.

---

[1] Artistically made slippers of precious material were reported in Egypt from the third century on. The Roman emperor Diocletian in a decree of A.D. 301 set maximum prices for different kinds of footwear, including slippers made of fine Babylonian leather, dyed purple or
scarlet, and gilded slippers for women. [Bettelheim]

The fairy tale replaces sibling relations with relations between step-siblings—perhaps a device to explain and make acceptable an animosity which one wishes would not exist among true siblings. Although sibling rivalry is universal and "natural" in the sense that it is the negative consequence of being a sibling, this same relation also generates equally as much positive feeling between siblings, highlighted in fairy tales such as "Brother and Sister."

No other fairy tale renders so well as the "Cinderella" stories the inner experiences of the young child in the throes of sibling rivalry, when he feels hopelessly outclassed by his brothers and sisters. Cinderella is pushed down and degraded by her stepsisters; her interests are sacrificed to theirs by her (step)mother; she is expected to do the dirtiest work and although she performs it well, she receives no credit for it; only more is demanded of her. This is how the child feels when devastated by the miseries of sibling rivalry. Exaggerated though Cinderella's tribulations and degradations may seem to the adult, the child carried away by sibling rivalry feels, "That's me; that's how they mistreat me, or would want to; that's how little they think of me." And there are moments—often long time periods—when for inner reasons a child feels this way even when his position among his siblings may seem to give him no cause for it.

When a story corresponds to how the child feels deep down—as no realistic narrative is likely to do—it attains an emotional quality of "truth" for the child. The events of "Cinderella" offer him vivid images that give body to his overwhelming but nevertheless often vague and nondescript emotions; so these episodes seem more convincing to him than his life experiences.

The term "sibling rivalry" refers to a most complex constellation of feelings and their causes. With extremely rare exceptions, the emotions aroused in the person subject to sibling rivalry are far out of proportion to what his real situation with his sisters and brothers would justify, seen objectively. While all children at times suffer greatly from sibling rivalry, parents seldom sacrifice one of their children to the others, nor do they condone the other children's persecuting one of them. Difficult as objective judgments are for the young child—nearly impossible when his emotions are aroused—even he in his more rational moments "knows" that he is not treated as badly as Cinderella. But the child often feels mistreated, despite all his "knowledge" to the contrary. That is why he believes in the inherent truth of "Cinderella," and then he also comes to believe in her eventual deliverance and victory. From her triumph he gains the exaggerated hopes for his future which he needs to counteract the extreme misery he experiences when ravaged by sibling rivalry.

Despite the name "sibling rivalry," this miserable passion has only incidentally to do with a child's actual brothers and sisters. The real source of it is the child's feelings about his parents. When a child's older brother or sister is more competent than he, this arouses only temporary feelings of jealousy. Another child being given special attention becomes an insult only if the child fears that, in contrast, he is thought little of by his parents, or feels rejected by them. It is because of such an anxiety that one or all of a child's sisters or brothers may become a thorn in his flesh. Fearing that in comparison to them he cannot win his parents' love and esteem is what inflames sibling rival-ry. This is indicated in stories by the fact that it matters little whether the sib-lings actually possess greater competence. The Biblical story of Joseph tells that it is jealousy of parental affection lavished on him which accounts for the destructive behavior of his brothers. Unlike Cinderella's, Joseph's parent does not participate in degrading him, and, on the contrary, refers him to his other children. But Joseph, like Cinderella, is turned into a slave, and, like her, he miraculously escapes and ends by surpassing his siblings.

Telling a child who is devastated by sibling rivalry that he will grow up to do as well as his brothers and sisters offers little relief from his present feelings of dejection. Much as he would like to trust our assurances, most of the time he cannot. A child can see things only with subjective eyes, and comparing himself on this basis to his siblings, he has no confidence that he, on his own, will someday be able to fare as well as they. If he could believe more in him-self, he would not feel destroyed by his siblings no matter what they might do to him, since then he could trust that time would bring about a desired rever-sal of fortune. But since the child cannot, on his own, look forward with con-fidence to some future day when things will turn out all right for him, he can gain relief only through fantasies of glory—a domination over his siblings—which he hopes will become reality through some fortunate event.    9

Whatever our position within the family, at certain times in our lives we are beset by sibling rivalry in some form or other. Even an only child feels that other children have some great advantages over him, and this makes him intensely jealous. Further, he may suffer from the anxious thought that if he did have a sibling, his parents would prefer this other child to him. "Cinderella" is a fairy tale which makes nearly as strong an appeal to boys as to girls, since children of both sexes suffer equally from sibling rivalry, and have the same desire to be rescued from their lowly position and surpass those who seem superior to them.    10

On the surface, "Cinderella" is as deceptively simple as the story of Little Red Riding Hood, with which it shares greatest popularity. "Cinderella" tells about the agonies of sibling rivalry, of wishes coming true, of the humble being elevated, of true merit being recognized even when hidden under rags, of virtue rewarded and evil punished—a straightforward story. But under this overt content is concealed a welter of complex and largely unconscious mate-rial, which details of the story allude to just enough to set our unconscious associations going. This makes a contrast between surface simplicity and underlying complexity which arouses deep interest in the story and explains its appeal to the millions over centuries. To begin gaining an understanding of these hidden meanings, we have to penetrate behind the obvious sources of sibling rivalry discussed so far.    11

As mentioned before, if the child could only believe that it is the infirmi-ties of his age which account for his lowly position, he would not have to suffer so wretchedly from sibling rivalry, because he could trust the future to right matters. When he thinks that his degradation is deserved, he feels his plight is utterly hopeless. Djuna Barnes's perceptive statement about fairy    12 tales—that the child knows something about them which he cannot tell (such as that he likes the idea of Little Red Riding Hood and the wolf being in bed together)—could be extended by dividing fairy tales into two groups: one group where the child responds only unconsciously to the inherent truth of the story and thus cannot tell about it; and another large number of tales where the child preconsciously or even consciously knows what the "truth" of the story consists of and thus could tell about it, but does not want to let on that he knows. Some aspects of "Cinderella" fall into the latter category. Many children believe that Cinderella probably deserves her fate at the beginning of the story, as they feel they would, too; but they don't want anyone to know it. Despite this, she is worthy at the end to be exalted, as the child hopes he will be too, irrespective of his earlier shortcomings.

Every child believes at some period of his life—and this is not only at rare    13
moments—that because of his secret wishes, if not also his clandestine actions, he deserves to be degraded, banned from the presence of others, relegated to a netherworld of smut. He fears this may be so, irrespective of how fortunate his situation may be in reality. He hates and fears those others—such as his siblings—whom he believes to be entirely free of similar evilness, and he fears that they or his parents will discover what he is really like, and then demean him as Cinderella was by her family. Because he wants others—most of all, his parents—to believe in his innocence, he is delighted that "everybody" believes in Cinderella's. This is one of the great attractions of this fairy tale. Since people give credence to Cinderella's goodness, they will also believe in his, so the child hopes. And "Cinderella" nourishes this hope, which is one reason it is such a delightful story.

Another aspect which holds large appeal for the child is the vileness of the    14
stepmother and stepsisters. Whatever the shortcomings of a child may be in his own eyes, these pale into insignificance when compared to the stepsisters' and stepmother's falsehood and nastiness. Further, what these stepsisters do to Cinderella justifies whatever nasty thoughts one may have about one's siblings: they are so vile that anything one may wish would happen to them is more than justified. Compared to their behavior, Cinderella is indeed innocent. So the child, on hearing her story, feels he need not feel guilty about his angry thoughts.

On a very different level—and reality considerations coexist easily with    15
fantastic exaggerations in the child's mind—as badly as one's parents or siblings seem to treat one, and much as one thinks one suffers because of it, all this is nothing compared to Cinderella's fate. Her story reminds the child at the same time how lucky he is, and how much worse things could be. (Any anxiety about the latter possibility is relieved, as always in fairy tales, by the happy ending.)

The behavior of a five-and-a-half-year-old girl, as reported by her father,    16
may illustrate how easily a child may feel that she is a "Cinderella." This little girl had a younger sister of whom she was very jealous. The girl was very fond of "Cinderella," since the story offered her material with which to act out her feelings, and because without the story's imagery she would have been hard

pressed to comprehend and express them. This little girl had used to dress very neatly and liked pretty clothes, but she became unkempt and dirty. One day when she was asked to fetch some salt, she said as she was doing so, "Why do you treat me like Cinderella?"

Almost speechless, her mother asked her, "Why do you think I treat you like Cinderella?"    17

"Because you make me do all the hardest work in the house!" was the little girl's answer. Having thus drawn her parents into her fantasies, she acted them out more openly, pretending to sweep up all the dirt, etc. She went even further, playing that she prepared her little sister for the ball. But she went the "Cinderella" story one better, based on her unconscious understanding of the contradictory emotions fused into the "Cinderella" role, because at another moment she told her mother and sister, "You shouldn't be jealous of me just because I am the most beautiful in the family."    18

This shows that behind the surface humility of Cinderella lies the conviction of her superiority to mother and sisters, as if she would think: "You can make me do all the dirty work, and I pretend that I am dirty, but within me I know that you treat me this way because you are jealous of me because I am so much better than you." This conviction is supported by the story's ending, which assures every "Cinderella" that eventually she will be discovered by her prince.    19

Why does the child believe deep within himself that Cinderella deserves her dejected state? This question takes us back to the child's state of mind at the end of the oedipal period.[2] Before he is caught in oedipal entanglements, the child is convinced that he is lovable, and loved, if all is well within his family relationships. Psychoanalysis describes this stage of complete satisfaction with oneself as "primary narcissism." During this period the child feels certain that he is the center of the universe, so there is no reason to be jealous of anybody.    20

The oedipal disappointments which come at the end of this developmental stage cast deep shadows of doubt on the child's sense of his worthiness. He feels that if he were really as deserving of love as he had thought, then his parents would never be critical of him or disappoint him. The only explanation for parental criticism the child can think of is that there must be some serious flaw in him which accounts for what he experiences as rejection. If his desires remain unsatisfied and his parents disappoint him, there must be something wrong with him or his desires, or both. He cannot yet accept that reasons other than those residing within him could have an impact on his fate. In this oedipal jealousy, wanting to get rid of the parent of the same sex had seemed the most natural thing in the world, but now the child realizes that he cannot have his own way, and that maybe this is so because the desire was wrong. He is no longer so sure that he is preferred to his siblings, and he begins to suspect that this may be due to the fact that *they* are free of any bad thoughts or wrongdoing such as his.    21

---

[2] *Oedipal:* Freud's theory of the Oedipus complex held that at an early stage of development a child wishes to replace the parent of the same sex in order to achieve the exclusive love of the parent of the opposite sex.

All this happens as the child is gradually subjected to ever more critical 22 attitudes as he is being socialized. He is asked to behave in ways which run counter to his natural desires, and he resents this. Still he must obey, which makes him very angry. This anger is directed against those who make demands, most likely his parents; and this is another reason to wish to get rid of them, and still another reason to feel guilty about such wishes. This is why the child also feels that he deserves to be chastised for his feelings, a punishment he believes he can escape only if nobody learns what he is thinking when he is angry. The feeling of being unworthy to be loved by his parents at a time when his desire for their love is very strong leads to the fear of rejection, even when in reality there is none. This rejection fear compounds the anxiety that others are preferred and also maybe preferable—the root of sibling rivalry.

Some of the child's pervasive feelings of worthlessness have their origin in 23 his experiences during and around toilet training and all other aspects of his education to become clean, neat, and orderly. Much has been said about how children are made to feel dirty and bad because they are not as clean as their parents want or require them to be. As clean as a child may learn to be, he knows that he would much prefer to give free rein to his tendency to be messy, disorderly, and dirty.

At the end of the oedipal period, guilt about desires to be dirty and disorderly becomes compounded by oedipal guilt, because of the child's desire to 24 replace the parent of the same sex in the love of the other parent. The wish to be the love, if not also the sexual partner, of the parent of the other sex, which at the beginning of the oedipal development seemed natural and "innocent," at the end of the period is repressed as bad. But while this wish as such is repressed, guilt about it and about sexual feelings in general is not, and this makes the child feel dirty and worthless.

Here again, lack of objective knowledge leads the child to think that he 25 is the only bad one in all these respects—the only child who has such desires. It makes every child identify with Cinderella, who is relegated to sit among the cinders. Since the child has such "dirty" wishes, that is where he also belongs, and where he would end up if his parents knew of his desires. This is why every child needs to believe that even if he were thus degraded, eventually he would be rescued from such degradation and experience the most wonderful exaltation—as Cinderella does.

For the child to deal with his feelings of dejection and worthlessness 26 aroused during this time, he desperately needs to gain some grasp on what these feelings of guilt and anxiety are all about. Further, he needs assurance on a conscious and an unconscious level that he will be able to extricate himself from these predicaments. One of the greatest merits of "Cinderella" is that, irrespective of the magic help Cinderella receives, the child understands that essentially it is through her own efforts, and because of the person she is, that Cinderella is able to transcend magnificently her degraded state, despite what appear as insurmountable obstacles. It gives the child confidence that the same will be true for him, because the story relates so well to what has caused both his conscious and his unconscious guilt.

Overtly "Cinderella" tells about sibling rivalry in its most extreme form:    27
the jealousy and enmity of the stepsisters, and Cinderella's sufferings because of
it. The many other psychological issues touched upon in the story are so covertly alluded to that the child does not become consciously aware of them. In his
unconscious, however, the child responds to these significant details which
refer to matters and experiences from which he consciously has separated himself, but which nevertheless continue to create vast problems for him.

■ ■ ■

## Review Questions

1. What does living among ashes symbolize, according to Bettelheim?
2. What explanation does Bettelheim give for Cinderella's having stepsisters, not sisters?
3. In what ways are a child's emotions aroused by sibling rivalry?
4. To a child, what is the meaning of Cinderella's triumph?
5. Why is the fantasy solution to sibling rivalry offered by "Cinderella" appropriate for children?
6. Why is Cinderella's goodness important?
7. Why are the stepsisters and stepmother so vile, according to Bettelheim?
8. In paragraphs 20–26, Bettelheim offers a complex explanation of oedipal conflicts and their relation to sibling rivalry and the child's need to be debased, even while feeling superior. Summarize these seven paragraphs, and compare your summary with those of your classmates. Have you agreed on the essential information in this passage?

## Discussion and Writing Suggestions

1. One identifying feature of psychoanalysis is the assumption of complex unconscious and subconscious mechanisms in human personality that explain behaviour. In this essay, Bettelheim discusses the interior world of a child in ways that the child could never articulate. The features of this world include the following:

All children experience sibling rivalry.
The real source of sibling rivalry is the child's parents.
Sibling rivalry is a miserable passion and a devastating experience.
Children have a desire to be rescued from sibling rivalry (as opposed to res-
cuing themselves, perhaps).
Children experience an oedipal stage, in which they wish to do away with the
parent of the same sex and be intimate with the parent of the opposite sex.
"Every child believes at some point in his life . . . that because of his secret
wishes, if not also his clandestine actions, he deserves to be degraded,
banned from the presence of others, relegated to a nether world of smut."

To what extent do you agree with these statements? Take one of the statements and respond to it in a four- or five-paragraph essay.

2. A critic of Bettelheim's position, Jack Zipes, argues that Bettelheim distorts fairy-tale literature by insisting that the tales have therapeutic value and speak to children almost as a psychoanalyst might. Ultimately, claims Zipes, Bettelheim's analysis corrupts the story of "Cinderella" and closes down possibilities for interpretation. What is your view of Bettelheim's psychoanalytic approach to fairy tales?

*[handwritten: Kelley, K. (1994). Pretty woman: A modern Cinderella. In L. Behrens, L.S. Rosen & S. M. Rogers & C. Taylor (Eds.), Writing and reading across the curriculum (Cdn ed.), (pp. 609–618).]*

# Pretty Woman: *A Modern* Cinderella

## KAROL KELLEY

*Karol Kelley (1927–1995), a professor of women's history at Texas Tech University when this piece was written, brings a feminist perspective to two filmed versions of the* Cinderella *story: Disney's animated* Cinderella *(1949) and* Pretty Woman *(1990), starring Julia Roberts. Forty-one years separate these remakes of the Charles Perrault* Cinderella, *during which time the women's movement prompted many changes in American culture. Working an extended comparative analysis based on feminist concerns, Kelley finds the films remarkably alike in their attitudes toward gender roles. Why, given the presumably changed roles and status of women and men in our society, are the movies so similar? As you read, note the feminist principles on which Kelley bases her analysis, and consider using these principles to critique other (written) versions of the tale presented in this chapter. As you read, you may want to consider how representative Kelley's conclusions are of Hollywood movies made during the 1990s. This article originally appeared in the* Journal of American Culture *(Spring 1994).*

In modern society fairy tales are still compelling. Found in oral, written and filmed versions, the stories may serve a pleasurable purpose for individuals or a cultural purpose for academics. Fairy tales have been studied to produce typologies and methodologies in folklore, to examine societal similarities and differences, and to identify changes in values over time. On the one hand these stories have been criticized for supporting the status quo; on the other, their motifs have provided acceptable plot elements for hundreds of Hollywood motion pictures. 1

Cinderella is one of the best liked of these tales, measured both by the number of variations of the story and by the scholarly and popular interest in them. There are some 700 versions of Cinderella. It has been recorded in every area of the world, in written form in China as early as the ninth century CE (Bettelheim 236). Marian Roalfe Cox published her study of 345 variants of Cinderella in 1893 (Cox). Since that time folklorists have continued to study the story, as have literary historians, psychologists, and feminists. The most popular version in recent years in the United States has been that of Charles 2

Perrault, which was compiled in France in 1697. In roughly the past 40 years in America, elements of his story have appeared in a full-length Walt Disney cartoon, two shorter cartoon videos and some pastiches, a stage musical filmed for television and made into a video, and dozens of Hollywood films. Of the latter, *Pretty Woman* is the most obvious Perrault derivative.

The first and last of the above-mentioned film variations, the Disney 3 *Cinderella* and *Pretty Woman*, have certainly been very successful. The Disney cartoon has been reissued repeatedly in theaters since its creation in 1949 and is for sale or rent as a home video. It was Oscar-nominated in 1950 for Best Sound, Song, and Musical Scoring and has been reviewed as having "an adult following as well as a children's following" (*Greatest Movies* 88). *Pretty Woman* appeared early in 1990 and by November of that year had earned $178.4 million at the box office (Shearer 24). It has continued to sell well as a video and to earn even more money from home rentals. Julia Roberts won an Academy Award nomination as Best Actress for her role of Vivian.

Given the major changes in American society that took place during the 4 40 years between the making of these two films, differences in social values might be expected, especially concerning gender roles. Beginning with the women's movement in the 1960s there have been demands for information about women, sexuality and gender. The scholarly studies since that time have produced a better factual knowledge of women, the development of a number of feminist ideologies, and a new awareness of how gender stereotypes are created and also what their costs to society are. This data has resulted in a number of societal changes.

Politically in the past 30 years the interest in women's issues has meant 5 alterations in many laws in the United States that applied to women and the passage of an Equal Rights Amendment to the Constitution. This caused serious discussion even though it was never ratified. For the first time in American history large numbers of women openly asked for political, economic and social equality with men.

The demand for equality is one conception of feminism. A more thorough 6 definition has been provided by Nannerl O. Keohane, the former president of Wellesley College. She says that feminism

> embraces the belief that no one of either sex should be channeled into (or out of ) a particular life course by gender. Each person should have the opportunity so far as possible, to pursue her own visions, hopes, and dreams—to prepare herself to realize her own ambitions and to define her own identity, untrammeled by stereotypical expectations about what men or women can or cannot, should or should not, do. (23)

This statement implies that feminism requires self-acceptance as well as tolerance, that is, the acceptance of others' dreams and decisions for themselves.

The fields of history, psychology, and literary history have also been 7 affected by the recent concern for gender issues. There is the new area of women's history with differing sources, methodologies, time divisions and subjects of investigation. Today there are dozens of excellent books on topics not previously considered: changes in women's work and organizations, courtship and marriage patterns, sisterhood, sexuality, birth control, rape, and prostitution, among others. There are psychological studies identifying differences in male and female development, in gender perceptions and language, and in men's and women's behavior and values. Both psychologists and literary historians have begun to look at fairy tales in different ways, refuting the Jungian view that these stories are universal and the Freudian idea that they aid children's oedipal development. The more recent views criticize all tales, especially Cinderella.

In 1981 Colette Dowling published *The Cinderella Complex*. In this work    8 she argues that the gender expectations and the promises of the Cinderella story are psychologically harmful to women. ". . . [G]irls, from the time they are quite young are trained *into* dependency, while boys are trained *out* of it." Girls therefore expect that "there will always be someone to take care of them," and this feeling becomes more intense with age (101). Because being dependent is identified with femininity, women accept this attitude for themselves. Unfortunately, dependence also produces feelings of fear. Instead of trying to create a life for themselves, females search for a man to give them protection, a sense of identity, and the proof that they are loved (56, 141). To cope with their anxieties when lacking a man, many women become what Dowling calls "counterphobic." Outwardly they insist, "I don't need anybody. I can take care of myself." Inwardly they are fearful of becoming responsible for themselves and are terrified of being alone (67, 80). Dowling finds that

> Feeling helpless and frightened is so threatening to these women that they devote all their energies to constructing a life—and a style—calculated to throw everyone (themselves included) off the track. They may become racing-car drivers. Or actresses. Or prostitutes. (72)

Recent literary scholars have reacted to fairy tales in the same ways that    9 psychologists have. In 1982 Jennifer Waelti-Walters attacked the traditional folk stories for presenting girls as objects and as passive victims (1). She calls the reading of fairy tales "one of the first steps in the maintenance of a misogynous sex-role stereotyped patriarchy" (8).

Jack Zipes, in a book published in 1983, takes a historical and not a psy-    10 chological perspective. His interest is in the origins of the literary fairy tale for children in seventeenth century France and how over time the motifs, characters and themes were rearranged or eliminated to reflect the changing values of society (6–7). Zipes argues that fairy tales "have always symbolically depicted the nature of power relationships in a given society" (67). He contrasts the older version of Cinderella with Charles Perrault's adaptation and finds a shift from a matriarchal to a patriarchal point of view. In the earlier story Cinderella is a strong independent woman who rebels against the hard labor forced upon her and uses her wits and her dead mother's help to regain her upper class status in society. She does achieve her goal, which is not marriage but recognition. Perrault, on the other hand, wrote to socialize the children of the bourgeoisie, that is, to prepare them for the roles he believed they should play in society. He sexualized society, providing clear gender stereotypes. Thus Perrault's Cinderella is beautiful, polite, graceful, industrious, obedient and passive. She does not threaten men either by coquetry or intelligence. She waits patiently for the right man to come along to recognize her virtues and to marry her. Perrault's male characters must be active, intelligent, and ambitious. Not necessarily good-looking, they must be courteous and courageous. Social success and achieving are more important to these heroes than winning a wife. Thus due solely to their sex, Perrault heroines have a very limited range of opportunities, dreams, and possible behavior (Zipes ch. 2).

Like Zipes, Ruth Bottigheimer takes a historical perspective in her 1987      11
study of fairy tales, *Grimm's Bad Girls and Bold Boys*. She also seems to support the feminist point of view that fairy tales are not beneficial to women. She looks at the Grimm brothers' works as historical documents and investigates both changes over time and gender differences. She discovers that as the nineteenth-century progressed, females increasingly lost their power in the tales, as measured: by their speech, which is direct for males and indirect for females; by their silence, as compared with males; and by their punishments, which are harsher for females and occur after one transgression, while males can offend three to five times before retribution.

Recent academic work thus reflects the ideas of the women's movement.      12
What of the popular culture? Apparently it does not. Perrault's gender role stereotyping remains unchanged in both *Cinderella* and *Pretty Woman*. The latter uses current fashions and artifacts and ignores the older sexual taboos, thus giving the film a modern appearance. Despite this, *Pretty Woman* does not illustrate any major changes in gender expectations and is unaffected by any form of feminist ideology.

*Cinderella* could not be expected to be a feminist film. Disney chose to      13
use the Perrault story and adapted that to the rhetoric of an era firmly anchored in the feminine mystique. The characters are ranked and segregated by sex. Traditional gender stereotypes and not personal choice determine the behavior, life courses, and dreams that are shown in the cartoon. The same may be said of *Pretty Woman*, and, in addition, there is more ambivalence concerning the family and friendship and more acceptance of the traditional male values of competition and revenge than in the Disney film.

In both *Cinderella* and *Pretty Woman* the male sex is ranked higher in      14
wealth, occupation, and status than the female sex. A class society prevailed in the earlier time period of the cartoon. The Prince's family is not only wealthy but royal, making him the future king and future ruler of his country. He therefore has the highest possible status. Cinderella comes from a gentry family which has financial problems due to the death of her father and the selfishness of her stepfamily. Cinderella is forced to do the work of a scullery maid. Her status can be raised only through marriage, when she will take the position of her husband.

In *Pretty Woman* Edward Lewis is the hero. He is fabulously wealthy,      15
able to indulge his every materialistic desire. Given the Yuppie generation of

the 1980s, Edward's occupation as a successful and wealthy corporate raider gives him the highest possible status. Vivian Ward is the heroine of *Pretty Woman*. As the picture opens she lacks the money to pay her rent and has a pin holding up her boot. She is a prostitute, a job defined as "debasing oneself for money." Near the ending of the movie she considers raising her status herself, but she, too, chooses to marry. Edward's background is far superior to Vivian's. His father had been rich, and his mother, a trained musician. Edward is well-educated and sophisticated. His manners are impeccable, and he is accustomed to elegant places, to formal clothing, and to upper class amusements such as polo and the opera. Vivian is the product of a lower class family from a small town in Georgia. She is intelligent but uneducated, reaching only the eleventh grade in school. She throws her gum on the sidewalk, is ignorant of table manners and how to dress, loves television, movies and popular songs, and calls an orchestra "a band."

(Kelley, 1994, p 613).

In *Cinderella* the hero and heroine are equal at least in manners, and education is not mentioned. In *Pretty Woman* education and manners help to determine status, and Vivian ranks far below Edward. The gender stereotypes in popular romances give heroes a higher status than their heroines. This is found to be true in both of these films.                                                          16

In addition, gender clearly determines occupations and activities. Obtaining money is not a problem for the Prince, and he hunts and travels. Cinderella remains at home and does housework, which is properly feminine but is also dirty, physically demanding and demeaning. Life is even sex-differentiated for the mice. The males go to obtain food and have exciting adventures. When a male mouse wants to help make Cinderella's dress for the ball, a female mouse says, "Leave the sewing to the women; You go get the trimmin'."                                                          17

Edward is a businessman working with male executives, lawyers, bankers and senators. Of course his telephone operator is female. Vivian provides female services for men. Lacking job skills she is unable to support herself by any other kind of work open to her, and she must struggle to keep some control over her own body and out of the hands of male pimps. The hotel and store managers are men; the sales clerks are women. The expectations presented are that women are supposed to work, but that men are to hold the superior and better-paying jobs.                                                          18

In both movies males have much more power and are the rescuers of females. In *Cinderella* the King has the power of life or death. Granted, Disney sentimentalizes the scenes with the King's imaginary grandchildren. The male desire to see his line and name carried on is a traditional one, however. Although the Disney cartoon ends with the marriage of the Prince and Cinderella, presumably they will have the children to fulfill the King's hopes. Males are seen as rescuers; females are more passive. The male mice and dog free Cinderella from her locked room. By marrying her the Prince saves Cinderella from her family's abuse and from her domestic chores. Even the stepsisters hope to be rescued from their daily routine by husbands.                                                          19

Women who have power are presented in the Disney film as either evil or 20
silly. The wicked stepmother controls her household and the three young
women in her charge. The true nature of the stepmother was revealed only
after the death of Cinderella's father, whose authority presumably restrained
the stepmother's behavior. The fairy godmother has enormous magical
power. This is trivialized by her silliness, her song Bibbidi Bobbidi Boo, and
by her absentmindedness: she can't find her wand, or remember her magic
words, or even notice that Cinderella needs a dress to wear to the ball.

The hero of *Pretty Woman* also has the power of life and death, at least 21
over the continuance of various corporations and over the jobs of the people
working there. He is able to set up a billion dollar deal to take over Morse
Industries. Borrowing a necklace worth a quarter of a million dollars is a
minor transaction in his life. Edward can influence Senate committees and
bank officials. Because of his enormous financial power, he has only to ask to
receive the services he desires. Vivian has neither power nor identity.
Abandoned by the man who brought her to Los Angeles, she could not support herself. Her friend Kit talked her into becoming a prostitute. Vivian
cried but was powerless to do anything else. Her feisty personality indicates
counterphobia, a fear of being helpless, rather than independence. She lacks
identity in repeatedly being ready to be called by any name a man likes or by
being ready to do anything a man asks of her. Crying "Nobody will help me,"
she is unable to buy a dress by herself. She has to be rescued by Barney
Thompson, the hotel manager, or by Edward and his credit card. In addition,
Edward saves Vivian from being raped by Phil, his lawyer. She is also helped
by Mr. Morse, the elevator man, and the hotel chauffeur.

Interestingly, the women in *Pretty Woman* have even less power than 22
those in *Cinderella*. The snobbish salesladies have some control. They can
order Vivian to leave the store. Later they are punished by losing commissions, and their roles are small. More significantly, the part of the fairy godmother is transformed into a male role. Not a woman but a man enables the
Cinderella character to achieve her dreams. Barney helps Vivian to get her
first ladylike dress, teaches her the table manners she needs to know, and
finally unites the couple by informing Edward that the chauffeur knows
where Vivian lives, and that Edward is making a mistake. Barney tactfully
says, "It must be difficult to let go of something so beautiful." Ostensibly he
is talking about the necklace, but they both know he is referring to Vivian.
The latter does give advice and financial aid to her friend but is simply passing on Edward's words and money—his power and not hers.

Thus in neither movie do females partake of any of the stereotypical 23
male behavior. It is the men who rank higher in wealth, occupation, status,
power and action. What of the women? Once again the stereotypes prevail.
Traditionally women are to be beautiful, feminine, dependent, devoid of negative emotions but fully expressive of all positive ones. Females exist to fulfill
male needs.

Both heroines are beautiful, but both need the right clothing to make 24
them marriageable. When Cinderella is dressed like a princess, the prince

*(Kelley, 1994, p 614).*

only has to see her to fall in love. An item of apparel, her glass slipper, iden-tifies her as the woman the Prince really wants to marry. Clothing has the same powerful effect on Vivian. When she is dressed like a hooker, she can be one. Given elegant and ladylike clothing, Vivian feels cheap when proposi-tioned and eventually decides to give up her life on the streets.

Both heroines are seen as very feminine. Femininity includes beauty and appearance, the aforementioned dependence and helplessness, and also emo-tions. Traditionally anger and censoriousness are not feminine. The negative characters can express anger. The ugly stepsisters fight with each other and tear Cinderella's dress to shreds. Fear, sadness and self-pity are permissible for good women, as are the positive emotions of compassion, friendship, love and happiness.        25

Given the situations of both heroines, anger and resentment would appear to be logical reactions. This is not portrayed in either film. Cinderella is obedient to her stepfamily but lives in dreams merely saying, "Well, they can't order me to stop dreaming." Unable to attend the ball, she can cry in self-pity, "It's just no use . . . I can't believe any more." Hope and dreams are restored by her fairy godmother's magic, however. At a later time when there is more openness to emotions, Vivian's anger also seems very restrained. Finding her rent money gone, she is forced to sneak out of her building to avoid the rent collector. All she says to Kit, who took the money, is "I can't believe you bought drugs with our rent money." Edward reveals to Phil that Vivian is a hooker, and although she is ready to walk out, refusing her pay, she stays, saying only, "You hurt me . . . Don't do it again." Her feeling of self-pity in Barney's office is much clearer than her resentment.        26

Cinderella is usually portrayed with positive emotions. She is kind, help-ful, sympathetic, and loving, and by implication, pure and good. She is con-cerned with relationships, a real female value, even trying to persuade Bruno, the dog, and Lucifer, the evil cat, to get along together. These qualities, plus her beauty, youth, restraint, and lovely singing voice will make her a good enough wife for a future king.        27

The Prince, unlike Cinderella, is vulnerable internally. He is cut off from his feelings. She is outwardly oppressed, kept from the ball and locked in her room by her family and thus must be rescued by another. Nevertheless, Cinderella can fulfill the Prince's needs. He wants a wife and an escape from his boredom. Cinderella's appearance and her adoration of him activate his feelings and involve him in a love relationship. He has found a female to com-plement himself—she has the emotions that he lacks. Cinderella has a man to give her an identity (she is his wife), the love she has always been dreaming of to compensate for her victimization, and someone to take care of her for the rest of her life. We are told that "they lived happily ever after." *Cinderella*, therefore, clearly defines the male and female stereotypes, and pictures a suc-cessful conclusion to both male and female dreams.        28

Vivian, also, is usually presented with positive emotions. She is helpful, ready to run and answer the door for Edward; grateful, making a point of thanking Barney; sympathetic, expressing concern and compassion for        29

Edward and Morse; and loving, especially to Kit and to Edward. She is good to the extent of being honest and generous with her friends, wanting to pay her bills, and not using drugs. Phil clearly sees her as having a moral influence on Edward, a traditional female stereotype.

Where *Pretty Woman* is modernized is in the openness toward sex.  30 Nevertheless, there is some ambiguity. Sexuality in 1950 was covertly implied in the thought of having children within marriage. With a heroine who is a prostitute, sex in the 1990 film can be blatant. Most scenes are erotic. Vivian can be sexy and at the same time shown as anxious to leave the red light district and to become a proper wife, the traditional female goal.

Amy Kaminsky, in her study of two Argentinean women authors, makes  31 some comments that seem to be applicable to *Pretty Woman*. Agreeing with Simone de Beauvoir that the prostitute "exists as a projection of male fantasy," Kaminsky points out that the male perceptions of paid sexual encounters are of eroticism and pleasure (119). The prostitutes on the other hand, see the interaction as "devoid of sexual content, the better to demonstrate that prostitution is more about humiliation and submission to power than it is about sex" (130). Both views are found in the film. Obviously, the sexual relationship of the two central characters is supposed to be wonderful. Vivian also says, "I just do it. I'm like a robot," and this is after sexual encounters with Edward. The scenes between Vivian and Phil support the idea that prostitution is about abasement and power and not sensuality.

There are other modernizations. Edward is even more inwardly vulnera-  32 ble than the Prince. The hero of *Pretty Woman* is a compulsive worker who is unable to get in touch with his own feelings. Spending 10,000 dollars on therapy has enabled Edward to express his anger toward his father. His fear of heights, his incapacity to maintain personal relationships, and his inability to share his musical gifts with others or to take the time to relax and enjoy his life all indicate additional emotional problems. Vivian lacks the education, knowledge and background to help herself, but she can give to Edward everything he needs. She can laugh out loud; she can be spontaneous; she knows about taking days off; she is able to have fun; she can "veg-out" and relax. Despite Kit's coaching in how not to feel, Vivian allows herself to kiss Edward on the mouth and to fall in love with him. He is slower in his response, but he does begin to enjoy himself, to feel and to care, and, finally, to love. Like Cinderella and her Prince, Vivian succeeds in awakening Edward's dormant emotions.

The movies include a number of sex-segregated fantasies. There is the male  33 dream of making all the money a man could want and of winning out over all competitors. There is the fantasy of the beautiful, willing, submissive woman, as when Vivian says, "Baby, I'm going to treat you so nice you'll never want to let me go." There is the vision of great sex with a beautiful woman, with no responsibilities beyond financial ones. An old theme in popular literature and the theater is that of the rich, royal, or upper class man who wants to be loved for himself alone. None of Edward's friends (the people he "spends time with") really care, but Vivian cannot help herself. She falls in love with Edward despite all her resolves never to mix business and pleasure.

Vivian's fantasies are also stereotypical. The heroine being treated to all   34
the new clothes that she wants is a common theme in modern romances.
Perhaps the male apology for having hurt the woman is a female dream. The
prostitute's fantasy of a rich, good-looking, non-twisted client merges into
Vivian's childhood dream of a knight on a white horse coming to rescue her
from her locked tower. She, like Cinderella, wants a man to give her identity, proof that she is loved, and protection/marriage.

Respect for both sexes and the family may be found in feminist works. If   35
the family is criticized, alternatives are suggested. In *Cinderella* all of the
human characters are bumbling and ridiculous or greedy and evil. The stepmother and stepsisters have no love for Cinderella, only jealousy and hatred.
Her family abuses Cinderella. The King is willing to push his son into any
marriage. These ideas are even more emphatic in *Pretty Woman*. In the opening scene Phil puts his wife down. "My wife went to a lot of trouble [for this
party]—she called a caterer." Despite 10,000 dollars worth of therapy,
Edward was not there when his father died. They had not spoken in 14 years.
Little information is given about Vivian's family, but her mother does not
sound nurturing. She often locked her daughter in the attic, despite the fact
that it did not change Vivian's behavior. Her mother also called her daughter
"a bum magnet," which may have been a self-fulfilling prophesy. Only the
hero and heroine in *Cinderella* are attractive characters. In *Pretty Woman*
Barney and Mr. Morse perhaps provide the "good" father figures that neither
Vivian nor Edward had. In both films the family is denigrated, while, ironically, only heterosexual love and marriage are offered as a solution to the
problems of life caused by families.

Recent academic work has stressed the importance of sisterhood for   36
women. This topic does not appear in *Cinderella*. Instead, women are shown
as competing for men. Cinderella's friends, who often help her, are all birds
and animals, which in a hierarchical society are of an even lower rank than
herself. Vivian and Kit, her friend, do keep saying, "Take care of you,"
another modernization. Kit still doesn't seem to be a very good friend. She
steers Vivian into prostitution, urges her to deny her feelings, which increases anxiety, and takes the rent money for cocaine. Although they may be
thrown out of their apartment, and Vivian actually has the rent money, it
takes Kit three days to come and collect it. Vivian is loving, but Kit is irresponsible and uncaring in her behavior. She sees no reason to leave the red
light district, even after the dead body of Skinny Marie is found in a dumpster.

Revenge is not a feminist idea. The only revenge displayed in *Cinderella*   37
is between animals. Although the wicked cat torments everyone, it is the dog
who is responsible for Lucifer's death. Revenge is more common in *Pretty
Woman*. Vivian tells the snobbish salesladies of the commissions they lost.
Edward repaid his father for leaving his mother by destroying his father's corporation. Phil loves "the kill." He blames Vivian for his losing a great deal of
money and tries to rape her in retaliation.

Two scenes raise the question of feminism. Vivian explains to Kit that she   38
is going to a different city to finish school, find a good job and establish a life

for herself. As in Keohane's definition, Vivian seems ready to "pursue her own visions" and "prepare herself to realize her own ambitions and to define her own identity" (23). Unfortunately, such ideas disappear instantly when Edward climbs up her fire escape to rescue her. In a final scene Edward asks about the ending of her dream, what the Princess did after the Knight rescued her. Vivian replies, "She rescued him right back." This *sounds* like a peer relationship, the equality of feminism, but it is not. Both the Knight, the Prince, and Edward have real power. The Princess, Cinderella, and Vivian do not. They have the capacity to have children, and they possess their sexuality, which can stir repressed emotions. As has often been said, men are human beings; women are females. This is reiterated in both films.

   *Cinderella* expresses the gender expectations of the 1950s. *Pretty Woman*    39
demonstrates that feminist ideas are not necessary in a popular movie of the 1990s. Both movies start with the concept of dreams; both promise that dreams can come true. The question is, do we really want all of those same old tired dreams?

## WORKS CITED

Bettelheim, Bruno. *The Uses of Enchantment: The Meaning and Importance of Fairy Tales.* New York: Vintage, 1977.

Bottigheimer, Ruth B. *Grimms' Bad Girls and Bold Boys: The Moral and Social Vision of the Tales.* New Haven: Yale UP, 1987.

*Cinderella.* Dirs. Wilfred Jackson, Hamilton Luske, and Clyde Geronimi. Disney, 1949.

Cox, Marian Roalfe. *Cinderella: Three Hundred and Forty-five Variants.* London: Nutt, 1893.

Dowling, Colette. *The Cinderella Complex: Women's Hidden Fear of Independence.* New York: Pocket, 1981.

*The Greatest Movies of All Times.* Blockbuster Video. 2nd. ed. N.p.: Blockbuster Entertainment, 1991.

Kaminsky, Amy. "Women Writing about Prostitution." *The Image of the Prostitute in Modern Literature.* Eds. Pierre L. Horn and Mary Beth Pringle. New York: Ungar, 1984.

Keohane, Nannerl O. "Dear Alumnae and Friends of the College." *Wellesley* Fall 1990: 23–24.

*Pretty Woman.* Dir. Garry Marshall. With Richard Gere and Julia Roberts. Touchstone, 1990.

Shearer, Lloyd. "Intelligence Report." *The Lubbock Avalanche Journal* 24 Feb. 1991. *Parade Magazine*: 24.

Waelti-Walters, Jennifer. *Fairy Tales and the Female Imagination.* Montreal: Eden, 1982.

Zipes, Jack. *Fairy Tales and the Art of Subversion: The Classical Genre for Children and the Process of Civilization.* New York: Wildman, 1983.

■  ■  ■

## Review Questions

1. With what key question does Kelley begin her comparative analysis of *Cinderella* and *Pretty Woman*?
2. How does Kelley answer this question? What is her thesis?
3. What is a "Cinderella Complex"?
4. In paragraphs 6–11, Kelley refers to the work of several feminist writers: Keohane, Dowling, Waelti-Walters, Zipes, and Bottigheimer. What purposes do these references serve? From these references, to what topic does Kelley make a transition?
5. What are some key similarities between Disney's *Cinderella* and *Pretty Woman*?
6. What are some key differences between Disney's *Cinderella* and *Pretty Woman*?

## Discussion and Writing Suggestions

1. Outline Kelley's article, sketching its main sections. Pay especially close attention to the location of her thesis. How does Kelley lead up to the thesis? How does she organize her discussion after the thesis?
2. Reread Nannerl Keohane's definition of feminism in paragraph 6. Observe how Kelley introduces the definition early in the selection and then refers to it in paragraph 38. Read Colette Dowling's discussion of the Cinderella complex in paragraph 8; again, observe Kelley's reference back to Dowling in paragraph 21, where she describes Vivian's behaviour as an example of "counterphobia." Explain Kelley's strategy in using Keohane's and Dowling's material in this way.
3. To understand Kelley's comparative analysis fully, the reader needs to view both Disney's *Cinderella* and *Pretty Woman*. Arrange to see both movies, which are readily available in video rental stores. Then reread Kelley's selection and write a response. Is her analysis fair and accurate? Do you agree with her specific points of comparison and contrast? More broadly, do you agree with Kelley's conclusion?
4. Assume that Kelley is correct in the similarities she finds between views on the role of women 40 years ago and views today, as expressed in popular movies. Do these similarities surprise you? Why would we *not* see changes concerning gender roles in a movie like *Pretty Woman* but then see changes in the work of academic writers?
5. Kelley identifies as pivotal the scene in *Pretty Woman* in which Edward climbs a fire escape to "rescue" Vivian, who was planning to move to another city and become respectably self-sufficient. Kelley (paragraph 38) argues that Vivian is *not* Edward's equal even though the movie tries to argue that she is. Assuming you've seen *Pretty Woman*, respond to Kelley's analysis of the scene.
6. Kelley is critiquing two movies, only. Can you think of recent movies that feature strong heroines with minds of their own—movies that provide

counter examples to or that cast doubt on Kelley's conclusion about Hollywood's attitude toward women? (Consider, for example, *Ever After* and some of the more recent Disney movies such as *Beauty and the Beast, Pocahontas,* and *Mulan.*) What perspective does Kathi Maio add to Kelley's?

Morrison, T. A Cinderello's Stepsisters. In L. Behrens, L.J. Rosen, J.M. Rogers, (1979) & C. Taylor (Eds.), Writing & Reading across the curriculum (Cdn. ed.),

## Cinderella's Stepsisters (pp. 620-621).

### TONI MORRISON

*Toni Morrison (b. 1931), an African American novelist of such acclaimed works as* The Bluest Eye *(1970),* Song of Solomon *(1977),* Tar Baby *(1981), Pulitzer-prize winning* Beloved *(1987),* Jazz *(1992), and* Paradise *(1998), received the Nobel Prize for literature in 1993. Critics have hailed her work as being at once both mythic, in its themes and characters, and intensely realistic in its depictions of the sorrows, struggles, and hopes of black people. The selection that follows is excerpted from an address Morrison delivered at Barnard College. In it, she exhorts her women listeners to treat their "stepsisters" more humanely than Cinderella's stepsisters treated her.*

Let me begin by taking you back a little. Back before the days at college. To nursery school, probably, to a once-upon-a-time time when you first heard, or read, or, I suspect, even saw "Cinderella." Because it is Cinderella that I want to talk about; because it is Cinderella who causes me a feeling of urgency. What is unsettling about that fairy tale is that it is essentially the story of household—a world, if you please—of women gathered together and held together in order to abuse another woman. There is, of course, a rather vague absent father and a nick-of-time prince with a foot fetish. But neither has much personality. And there are the surrogate "mothers," of course (god- and step-), who contribute both to Cinderella's grief and to her release and happiness. But it is her stepsisters who interest me. How crippling it must have been for those young girls to grow up with a mother, to watch and imitate that mother, enslaving another girl.

I am curious about their fortunes after the story ends. For contrary to recent adaptations, the stepsisters were not ugly, clumsy, stupid girls with out-size feet. The Grimm collection describes them as "beautiful and fair in appearance." When we are introduced to them they are beautiful, elegant women of status and clearly women of power. Having watched and participated in the violent dominion of another woman, will they be any less cruel when it comes their turn to enslave other children, or even when they are required to take care of their own mother?

It is not a wholly medieval problem. It is quite a contemporary one: feminine power when directed at other women has historically been wielded in what has been described as a "masculine" manner. Soon you will be in a position to do the very same thing. Whatever your background—rich or poor— whatever the history of education in your family—five generations or one—you have taken advantage of what has been available to you at Barnard and you will therefore have both the economic and social status of the stepsisters *and* you will have their power.

*(Morrison, 1979, p621).*

I want not to *ask* you but to *tell* you not to participate in the oppression of your sisters. Mothers who abuse their children are women, and another woman, not an agency, has to be willing to stay their hands. Mothers who set fire to school buses are women, and another woman, not an agency, has to tell them to stay their hands. Women who stop the promotion of other women in careers are women, and another woman must come to the victim's aid. Social and welfare workers who humiliate their clients may be women, and other women colleagues have to deflect their anger.    4

I am alarmed by the violence that women do to each other: professional violence, competitive violence, emotional violence. I am alarmed by the willingness of women to enslave other women. I am alarmed by a growing absence of decency on the killing floor of professional women's worlds. You are the women who will take your place in the world where *you* can decide who shall flourish and who shall wither; you will make distinctions between the deserving poor and the undeserving poor; where you can yourself determine which life is expendable and which is indispensable. Since you will have the power to do it, you may also be persuaded that you have the right to do it. As educated women the distinction between the two is first-order business.    5

I am suggesting that we pay as much attention to our nurturing sensibilities as to our ambition. You are moving in the direction of freedom and the function of freedom is to free somebody else. You are moving toward self-fulfillment, and the consequences of that fulfillment should be to discover that there is something just as important as you are and that just-as-important thing may be Cinderella—or your stepsister.    6

In your rainbow journey toward the realization of personal goals, don't make choices based only on your security and your safety. Nothing is safe. That is not to say that anything ever was, or that anything worth achieving ever should be. Things of value seldom are. It is not safe to have a child. It is not safe to challenge the status quo. It is not safe to choose work that has not been done before. Or to do old work in a new way. There will always be someone there to stop you. But in pursuing your highest ambitions, don't let your personal safety diminish the safety of your stepsister. In wielding the power that is deservedly yours, don't permit it to enslave your stepsisters. Let your might and your power emanate from that place in you that is nurturing and caring.    7

Women's rights is not only an abstraction, a cause; it is also a personal affair. It is not only about "us"; it is also about me and you. Just the two of us.    8

■ ■ ■

## Discussion and Writing Suggestions

1. Cinderella "is essentially the story of household—a world, if you please—of women gathered together and held together in order to abuse another woman." Do you agree with Morrison's characterization of the story?

2. Morrison finds *Cinderella* to be a story that teaches girls unhealthy ways of treating other girls—their "stepsisters." The assumption is that fairy tales, heard while young, can have a lasting influence on attitudes later in life. Do you accept the assumption?

3. In paragraph 5, Morrison writes: "Since you will have the power to [wield influence over others], you may also be persuaded that you have the right to do it." What is the difference between having the power to take an action and assuming that you have the right to take that action? Specifically, in the terms of this essay, what does Morrison mean?

4. Morrison writes that she is "alarmed by the violence that women do to each other: professional violence, competitive violence, emotional violence." Is it your sense that the "violence" women do to one another is different in degree or kind than the violence they do to men—or that men do to men?

5. Morrison suggests an opposition between women's ambition and their "nurturing sensibilities." First, what are "nurturing sensibilities?" Are they learned (from fairy tales, for instance)? Are they inborn? What is the difference between ambition and nurturing sensibilities? How might this difference manifest itself in the workplace? In the Perrault version of Cinderella? In the Grimm version?

6. In Morrison's view, female power differs from male power. How so?

7. Why should women be any less likely "to participate in the oppression" of other women than they are in the oppression of men? Do women owe it to other women to show special consideration? Why?

8. What is your response to this address, delivered at Barnard College? If you're a woman, what do you take from this selection? If you're a man, what do you take? Do you suppose that responses to the address will differ along gender lines? Explain.

# And She Lived Happily Ever After?

KAY STONE

*Kay Stone is a folklorist and professional storyteller who has written extensively about women and folktales. Now retired from the University of Winnipeg, where she taught courses in storytelling, she has recently published a book on contemporary storytellers:* Burning Brightly: New Light on Old Tales Told Today.

*In the following article, "And She Lived Happily Ever After?" Stone explores the issue of female heroism, and reminds us that stories are complex:*

*"Language as artistic communication is a delightfully complex expression that offers myriad paths of interpretation." It may be simplistic, she argues, to dismiss a female character as passive if we witness her go through and survive an ordeal that tests her strength on all levels. She allows us to consider how folktale heroines may still demonstrate heroic qualities and behaviour, even if they do not engage in swashbuckling action.*

In 1994 a Toronto storyteller, Carol McGirr, told me a story as part of an interview I was conducting with her. She chose a Russian variant of "The Singing Bone" (AT 780): a woman is murdered and buried by her own sisters, found by a shepherd, resuscitated by her father, and then married to the tsar. Carol is an independent and assertive woman and a quietly compelling performer who favours bold heroic stories, so I wondered why she had selected a folktale with an apparently passive victim. Carol herself did not see this heroine as weak at all, but as dynamic and resourceful in her quiet yet resolute efforts to live happily ever after.[1]

1

I could recall a few other women whose similarly puzzling responses caught my attention in the interviews on fairy tales I conducted in the early 1970s, but since this did not seem to be a strong pattern I dismissed these as anomalies, so much in the minority that I merely noted them in passing but did not examine them in depth. After hearing Carol's story I not only recalled these early interviews, I also remembered listening to another storyteller, Susan Gordon, tell a particularly brutal Grimm tale, "The Handless Maiden," in 1982.[2] Susan, too, presented the abused daughter in a heroic light.

2

This brief essay poses the question of how these women could view apparently victimized protagonists positively. I will present Carol's and Susan's stories and remarks, and compare these with the words of those I had heard 20 years earlier. Carol McGirr and Susan Gordon are experienced performers. The other women were readers, not storymakers, but we learn from them that reading (and listening) are not passive acts. The tale told by the teller may not necessarily be the story perceived by the listener. This raises the issue of the constant negotiation (largely unconscious) that occurs as stories are told, heard, and read.

3

Fairytales have been justifiably criticized by feminists for their narrow portrayal of women as passive objects, as romanticized innocents, as victims of mental and physical abuse. I was initially inspired by an early article (Lieberman 1972) that examined passive heroines in the folktales edited by Andrew Lang in the late 1880s. My doctoral dissertation and first published article (Stone, *Romantic Heroines* and "Walt Disney") covered the popular collections of the Grimm Brothers, Andrew Long, and Hans Christian Andersen, as well as scholarly collections from Britain and North America. I sorted the heroines into four neat categories: the persecuted heroines who were not only passive but, like the woman in McGirr's story, were actually murdered or mutilated; passive heroines (Cinderella and Sleeping Beauty, for example) who took little action on their own behalf; tamed heroines (i.e. "King Thrushbeard") who began quite assertively but ended as submissive

4

wives; and a very few heroic heroines who took charge of their lives and their fates ("Molly Whuppee," for example).

Later feminist writers focused almost entirely on the passive and victim-ized heroines, ignoring those who belied the stereotype of the placid princess. Maria Tatar, for example, characterized the fairytale in general as a melo-dramatic "account of helplessness and victimization" (Tatar 1987, xx-xxi). Her reminder that heroes are also victimized downplays the fact that many heroines undergo more violent and extended persecutions, and that they are often rescued by someone else. This was underlined by Ruth Bottigheimer, who detailed the many ways that heroines in the Grimm tales were made to suffer, most often in silence (Bottigheimer 1987).

My interviews on folktale heroines reiterated the strong position passive and persecuted heroines held in the popular imagination (Stone 1975a). When I asked girls and women for their favourite stories they named the well known victims: "Cinderella" was mentioned 93 times, "Snow White" 57 times, and "Sleeping Beauty" 28 times.[3] It is not coincidental that these three stories were further popularized by Wait Disney, who had in fact chosen them because they were already prevalent in printed collections.

I also asked if they remembered any women who were more heroic than usual and many could recall such stories—for example, "The Peasant's Clever Daughter" and "Molly Whuppee." However, a few women chose protago-nists who were—by my scale of heroism—dubious. For example, my own mother surprised me by regarding Cinderella as "adventurous" because she disobediently went to the ball. "I would never have done that," she said admiringly. More surprising to me were the few who rejected passivity in the interviews, but chose as their favourites heroines who were even *more* afflict-ed than the popular victims. "The Goose Girl" and "The Six Swans" were among those cited as heroic stories, though these protagonists seem to accom-plish their goals through bitter suffering. I was to learn, after hearing Carol McGirr and Susan Gordon many years later, that my own perceptions of what was heroic and what was not were in need of transformation.

I first met Carol McGirr in Toronto in February of 1984 when I was attending the Toronto Storytelling festival.[4] Carol, one of the featured tellers, had been active in the Toronto storytelling community since the early 1970s.[5] As I attended festivals over the next decade I heard Carol perform lengthy Arthurian tales, Norse myths, and episodes from the Icelandic sagas. Many of her folktales were also long and complex. She seemed to favour heroic pro-tagonists, male and female. I wanted to know more about her preference for strong women in particular and her development as a storyteller in general. I asked if I could interview her formally some time in the future and she agreed—but it took another few years before we finally managed to carry this out in Fredericton, New Brunswick, where we were both performing at the annual Storyfest in 1994.

I taped two sessions with Carol over that week, the first a 60 minute dis-cussion of her storytelling in general and the second a 90 minute conversation that developed around her telling of "The Rosy Apple and the Golden Bowl," a Russian folktale she had learned from a book (Riordan, 1976: 138–143). Here is my summary:

### The Rosy Apple and the Golden Bowl

A father asks his daughters what gifts they want when he returns from the market; the first two want velvet and silk but the youngest, who stops to ponder, wants "a rosy apple in a golden bowl" that had been described to her by a beggar woman she met and befriended. Each gets what she asked for. The older sisters mock the younger until they see the beautiful images that form in the bowl when she rolls the apple in it and chants a song. They contrive to steal the bowl; they take their sister to the woods to pick strawberries where they kill her, bury her under a silver birch tree, and return home with bowl and apple. A shepherd passes by the tree, sees reeds growing there, and makes himself a flute, which reveals the murder in its song. The father later hears the flute, finds where his daughter is buried, and goes to the tsar for the healing water. She is revived, marries the tsar, and begs him not to kill her sisters. Instead they are exiled to a distant island, and the tsar and tsarina live on happily.

Carol described this as her "keynote story," a favourite of hers and of  10
many listeners in the Toronto area. It had been one of the first she began to tell, and one she was still most often asked for and enjoyed telling. I asked why she was so fond of it and she said she was first attracted to the story by the evocative imagery of the golden bowl that filled with images, and by the silver birch tree where Tania is buried. It seemed that the heroine herself was not the primary focus of the tale for Carol.

This heroine seemed to be the very opposite of the bold women in Carol's  11
lengthier stories. When I asked why she had chosen that particular story, she responded that she wanted to tell a relatively brief narrative so that it would not dominate our interview. She did not regard it as substantially different from her other stories in terms of character portrayal; she did not see her heroine, Tania, as a helpless victim at all. She viewed it as a profound story, one that offered a positive metaphor for human endurance under impossible conditions. Also, because it did not follow the usual "happily ever after" pattern (it ends with the exile of the sisters), it struck her as more convincing as well.

She recalled one of her students who wanted to hear the story over and  12
over again because it was "more real," because the heroine "was really dead" and not just prettily asleep like Snow White and Sleeping Beauty. In other words, this was not a Disneyesque story of light escapist fantasy, but a deeper story of transformation.

I thought about the story, about Carol's stated reasons for telling it, and  13
this particular student's reaction to it, and I wondered why Tania still seemed to me a problematic heroine. Yes, she was "really dead," and yes she was later resuscitated (unlike her less fortunate counterpart in a well-known ballad[6]). But how could Tania be regarded as positively heroic when she did not say a word to her parents about her mistreatment by her sisters, nor even challenge them? She certainly did not show much mental acuity when she followed her cruel sisters into the forest, and foolishly took out the golden bowl and sang the magic chant. How could she not know that her sisters were listening, that

they coveted this wondrous bowl and were willing to kill for it? It was only after she was murdered that she began to assert herself enough to have her story, told—but only indirectly through a reed.

I asked Carol how she felt about Tania as a heroine. At first Tania   14
seemed to be of lesser importance to Carol, who was more involved in the evocative images of the golden bowl and of the silver birch tree. I pressed her a bit, suggesting that Tania seemed very placid and unassertive, not the bold heroine of Carol's sagas and legends. She remarked:

> Actually I see her as being *very much* her own person, where same people would see her as taking all that from her sisters. But she does it all without complaining, because I think she's in her own world. She knows what she wants and eventually she *gets* what she wants. She gets the king and the kingdom, *and* the rosy apple and the golden bowl (interview 1994).

I suggested that Tania avoids the intolerable situation of her own "real" life and escapes into the fantastic world of the golden bowl instead of standing up to her covetous and cruel sisters. Only in death does she finally speak out—and then only indirectly—to reveal how she has been mistreated and murdered.

She disagreed. The younger sister remained heroic, so much so that Carol   15
had not even given her a thought until I asked her to look more closely at Tania's situation and apparent lack of control over herself. For the next few months we would continue to discuss this issue by an exchange of letters.

When I returned to Winnipeg I checked my dissertation for the words of   16
two women who were as insistent as Carol that their heroines were indeed heroic, though I had placed these particular stories in my category of "Persecuted Women." The first, a lively and articulate 17-year-old working as a summer volunteer at a daycare centre, chose Hans Christian Andersen's "The Little Mermaid" (definitely *not* the cloying Disney version). She told me that "one of the most aggressive women I remember was *The Little Mermaid.* She actually *did* something, she went out to get a prince" (Stone 1975a, 378). "And," she added as she recalled more of the story, "of course she sacrificed herself for him." Indeed she did—she died at the end of the story. But even this did not cancel out the mermaid's heroism for this reader, because the mermaid actively seeks out what she wants and—for a while—she achieves it.

The second woman was in her late twenties and worked as a live-in   17
counsellor in a group home for disturbed adolescents. She frankly rejected the more popular heroines as too passive but saw her outcast heroine in a Grimm tale as bold and resourceful:

> Those two, "Cinderella" and "Snow White," were pretty much the same type of character, but the sister in "The Seven Swans" was different. They just sat around, more or less, and let things happen to them. But *she* went out actively, like when she had to pick the nettles, and she won their freedom (Stone 1975, 313).

Her title ("The Seven Swans") neatly combines three Grimm tales ("The Twelve Brothers," "The Seven Ravens," "The Six Swans").[7] She seems to favour the first, in which the sister is very slightly more active. Bottigheimer notes that the sister becomes progressively more mistreated and silent with each edition of the Grimm collection (Bottigheimer 1987, 37–38). She also suggests that this story embodies many motifs of Grimm heroine tales: an innocent powerless girl, a wicked stepmother, threat of death, and last minute rescue by male character(s) (Bottigheimer, 39).

One significant motif connects all three Grimm versions: the sister is for-   18
bidden to speak *or even to laugh* for several years while she makes the magical shirts with which to disenchant her brothers. Thus she is unable to save herself from death because she cannot tell her own story. In each tale she is rescued by a male character at the last moment. The woman I interviewed earlier, who favoured this complex of stories, did not mention either the imposed silence or the impending death; she focused instead on the girl's decision to go out and seek and eventually disenchant the brothers. This woman connected the story with her own life:

> As I said, the story I remember particularly is the one with the girl and the seven brothers, or "The Seven Swans," probably because it fitted my life. I was the oldest and responsible for the other kids. I really remember that girl, how she worked to free her brothers (Stone 1975a, 313).

For these two women, the beleaguered sister and the love-struck mermaid   19
are favourites because they are *active*. This seems far more memorable to them than the heroines' self-inflicted pain (weaving for several years in silence with sharp nettles that draw blood in the swan/raven tales; accepting imposed silence and gaining human feet that are agonizing to walk on in "The Little Mermaid"). This seems to be the key—not their suffering but the fact that they *go out and do something* about it instead of "just sitting around and letting things happen to them." These two women focus on the contrast between action and inaction.

This seems to be the case for Carol as well, though Tania in "The Golden   20
Bowl" is far less active. She is, however, aware of the existence of the magical bowl and apple, manages to obtain it (however indirectly) and to bring out its magic. Her sisters fail to do this even when they possess it. For Carol, like the other two women, silence, abuse, and even murder are cancelled out by firm resolve and—most important—by eventual victory.

Another woman who found heroism in a victimized protagonist is Susan   21
Gordon, who uses folktales in therapeutic contexts. In her article on "The Handless Maiden," she discusses the boldness of the woman who is mutilated by her father, sets out in self-imposed exile, marries a king who gives her silver hands, and eventually gains her own hands back in a second exile (Gordon 1993). Susan, like the other women mentioned here, does not dwell on the woman's suffering but on her decisive acts of self-salvation—her refusal to remain in her father's house, her *commanding* a tree to feed her, and finally the miraculous restoration of her hands not by a divine act but by her own action—reaching into the water to save her child from drowning. For Susan this heroine is clearly valiant.

This attention to active transition from victim to heroine and the empha-   22
sis on strength in the midst of seeming helplessness seems to be the thread
weaving through all four examples discussed here. The two women I interviewed for my dissertation stress action over abuse in "The Little Mermaid"
and "The Seven Brothers [Swans]." They do not *deny* victimization, they
simply do not credit it as the driving force in these stories. The protagonists
go after what they want. This is exactly what Carol says of "The Rosy Apple
and the Golden Bowl," where Tania asks for what she wants and knows how
to use it, and even manages to sing herself back to life.

All four women *perceive* these protagonists as heroic. The two listeners   23
recall the stories positively but relatively passively, since they are not storytellers.
The two tellers, Carol and Susan, are able to transform their perceptions into
interpretations when they retell the stories. One way they accomplish this is to
give their heroines more to say. Let us look at how the stories change subtly but
decisively with a shift in speaking patterns, keeping in mind Bottigheimer's
assertion that women have less of a voice than do male protagonists.[8]

Susan Gordon provides a very clear example of the importance of direct   24
dialogue. She not only gives "The Handless Maiden" more to say instead of
having the story speak for her, she also changes the nature of that dialogue.
The daughter does not sweetly submit to her father as she does in the Grimm
tale; she challenges him to take responsibility for his own actions.[9] When he
fails to do so she boldly refuses to remain with her parents for fear that she
might "become just like you" (257). In the forest she does not merely "think"
(as in the Grimm tale) but speaks, not prayerfully but *commandingly* to the
king's pear tree, calling out, "My God I'm so hungry! Give me some fruit."
The tree obeys, without the intervention of God or an angel. The angel of the
Grimm tale, who takes care of the maiden during her wanderings, disappears
from Susan's story altogether.

During the heroine's second exile (in which the Grimm tale has her   25
almost completely silent), she teaches her young son about the natural world
around them. Later when her husband finds her again but wonders how she
has regained her hands, she answers by *telling* her son to get the silver hands
as proof of her identity. Susan also ends the story with considerably more
forcefulness than the Grimm tale, which concludes abruptly with a second
wedding and a "happily ever after" formula. Susan places the queen on horse-
back and has her use her own hands to control the horse as the three (wife,
husband, son) return home.

Carol's method is less obvious because she does not dramatically alter the   26
text of the story. Following the library tradition in which she was trained, she
stays so close to the wording of the printed tale that at first I could not find any
difference when I read the published story that Carol used as her source. I listened again to the taped story, with Carol's firm voice bringing the tale to life.
In Carol's voice Tania did seem more assertive than the printed text alone
reveals. I also *heard* two small but vital ways in which Tania's voice is strengthened. First, Carol brings Tania's chant to life as an evocative song while in the
printed text it seems barely more than a secretive whisper. Next, Carol has

Tania clearly articulate a resounding "No" when her sisters ask her tauntingly if she will use the golden bowl to feed the ducks. This "no" continues to echo through the story, coming to full fruition when Tania's voice speaks through the reed to tell her story to the shepherd and to her father, and then instructs her father to ask the tsar for the healing water that will revive her.

In addition to these changes, Carol's strong voice and firmly centred presence invoked a heroine who did not merely submit to her sisters' cruelty. As I noted earlier, Carol often tells heroic tales in which both women *and* men face the difficulties of their lives with bravery. Her style of narrating is much the same for the heroic tales as for "The Rosy Apple and the Golden Bowl." That is, she is completely centred in her stories, telling them with comfortable authority in a strong, calm voice that often verges on a chant. She uses few gestures or facial expressions—her clearly spoken words carry the story. She is not merely repeating the words but calling them fully to life. Tania's chant, for example, could be a plaintive appeal for help, but in Carol's voice it is a strong statement of what has been and what will be; she has been murdered, but will be revived.[10] Carol does much less than Susan in terms of expanding the heroine's character through altering the text of the story, yet the little she does is very effective.

I began this essay by asking how listeners and tellers could perceive seemingly passive female protagonists as heroic. The question might also be reversed: how did I, the researcher, fail to see what the others had seen in these heroines? It seemed that we were all speaking a different language. We meant different things by "heroic." The easy answer is that good stories, and particularly traditional folk-tales, are open to oppositional interpretations; in many ways we are indeed speaking different, personalized languages based on our own varied interests and experiences. Thus these four women saw what I had missed. They emphasized the competent acts of the heroines, their unwillingness to give in and accept their abusive situations, and their success in actively escaping them.

We can see another aspect of language in operation here as well, one that we as readers are not always aware of: written and spoken stories work on us in different ways.[11] A printed text, which seems fixed and forever unchanging, does not have the benefit of the storyteller's face-to-face personal style of presentation, much of which is non-verbal. Listening to Susan Gordon tell "The Handless Maiden" is more effective than reading her text. But in this case even reading her story is forceful, since the language in her printed story has evolved from the more abusive Grimm text. The experiences of reading and hearing Carol McGirr's story were more dramatically contrasted because her spoken language remained closer to the original text of the Russian tale. I had to listen to the taped story again to remember how Tania came to life in Carol's strong voice.

Language as artistic communication is a delightfully complex expression that offers myriad paths of interpretation. There is no one right way to view a story (and there is also no end of writers who suggest otherwise). A teller, or a writer, for that matter, cannot control how her artistic creations are received. And of course it is easy to forget that the first audience for a story is the teller herself. The centre of the story is what the teller sees or feels, the place where the story comes most alive for her and where she will bring it more fully to life for listeners. For Susan the story centre was the daughter/wife who refused to remain in abusive situations, and thus Susan's story is about her heroic development. Because Carol accepts Tania without question as heroic, she is *not* the centre of her story. For Carol it is the sounds and imagery—the magical chant Tania sings; the golden bowl and the images her chant calls up; the silver birch tree that evokes the tall Ontario birches from Carol's childhood; the reeds that grow from her grave; the chants she sings through them. Tania is not in need of heroic development, since she is already undaunted.

As I said at the beginning of this essay, the balance between teller, tale, 31 and listeners is always a delicate one that undergoes frequent and usually unconscious renegotiation. This occurs not only for tellers and listeners but for the tellers themselves, as their understanding of a story shifts and evolves. This is one of the many ways that old stories continue to be renewed, to meet the needs and interests of different audiences and the ever-changing perceptions of the teller herself, as she attempts to bring her heroines to a meaningful place in the "happily ever after" realm of traditional storms.[12]

## Notes

1. Carol bases her telling on a text in the Afanasiev collection (Riordan 1976, 138–143).
2. Susan and I were participating in a week-long storytelling residency at the Eugene O'Neill Theater Center in 1982.
3. These figures are taken from my interviews. See Appendix XI, "Popularity of Heroines," in my dissertation (Stone, *Romantic Heroines*).
4. This was a weekend festival held at Trinity Church in the last week of February 1984. It featured mostly local Ontario tellers, some of whom (like Carol) were experienced professionals and others who were in various stages of casual storytelling.
5. In 1979, several tellers who performed stories at a local cafe every Friday night decided to organize a festival and storytelling "school" that offered non-credit classes. Carol has been a regular performer at the festival and a frequent teacher at the school, as well as offering her own workshops and performances.
6. In the British (most often Scottish) ballad of "The Two Sisters" the resentful elder sister want the man who has chosen her younger sister and pushes the younger into the sea in order to remove the competition. The body is found and a harp made of her rib bones and hair; the harp sings the song of the murder but the victim most often remains unrevived.
7. It was unclear (and she herself did not recall) whether she meant "The Six Swans," "The Seven Ravens," or "The Twelve Brothers." The Grimms included three separate variants of the same basic folktale, classified by folklorists as tale type 451 in the Aarne-Thompson Index, "The Maiden Who Seeks Her Brothers."

8. Bottigheimer stresses that silenced heroines are particularly favoured in the Grimm tales: "In *Grimms' Tales* silence prevails where in other tale traditions speech had carried the day" (80).

9. When the father in Susan's tale says helplessly that he has no choice but to cut off her hands (in order to save his own life), she responds: "No choice? No choice? Oh, my God. I would give almost anything in the world not to be your daughter, but I am. *I am*. So do with me what you will."

10. When I saw Carol a year later in Toronto, she was still intrigued with the issue of Tania's character. She had read an early draft of this essay and wanted to say more about why she found Tania to be heroic: "It's because she never relinquishes hope! And she's not *made* to work—she does it for joy. Her sisters are lazy so she does her work *and* theirs." She repeated what she had said earlier, that Tania is "just biding her time. She has her visions in the bowl." She also observed that it was "a very lean story" with little time spent on description, motivation, or moralizing, "so that audiences have space for their own images" (Toronto, 24 February 1995).

11. I oversimplify the issue for lack of space. In fact even printed texts are not unchanging in terms of our active reading of them, as exemplified by the two women I quote here from interviews for my dissertation.

12. It is my firm contention, much too complex to be debated here, that "happily ever after" is not a Disneyesque state of romantic bliss, but a deeper spiritual or, if you prefer, psychological state. This transformative potential of folktales continues to draw contemporary tellers and listeners, as we see in this essay.

## REFERENCES

Bottigheimer, Ruth. Grimms' *Bad Girls and Bold Boys: The Moral and Social Vision of the Tales*. New Haven: Yale University Press, 1997.

Gordon, Susan. "The Powers of the Handless Maiden." *Feminist Messages: Coding in Women's Folk Culture*. Ed. Joan Radner. Urbana, Ill: University of Illinois Press, 1993. 252–88.

Lieberman, Marcia K. "'Some Day My Prince Will Come': Female Acculturation Through the Fairy Tale." *College English* 34 (1972): 383–95.

Riordan, James. Tales From Central Russia (vol. 1). Hammondsworth, Middlesex: Kestrel Books, 1976.

Stone, Kay. *Romantic Heroines in Anglo-American Folk and Popular Literature*. Unpublished doctoral dissertation. Indiana University, 1975.

—."Things Walt Disney Never Told Us." *Women and Folklore*. Ed. Claire Farrer. Austin: University of Texas Press, 1975. 42–50.

Tatar, Maria. *The Hard Facts of The Grimms' Fairy Tales*. Princeton: Princeton University Press, 1987.

■  ■  ■

## Discussion and Writing Suggestions

1. Is Stone arguing that all interpretations of any story are subjective and equally convincing? Or is she suggesting that interpretations vary depending on the emphasis we place upon certain evidence?
2. What do you think of these storytellers calling these female heroes active and alert, when they appear to be oppressed by others and circumstance? Can you apply this dual interpretation to Disney's Cinderella figure?
3. Compare the ways Stone and Kelley define female heroism.

# Cinderella's Not Dead, Yet

JUDY REBICK      \99ᵇ · ᵖ9

*Judy Rebick is one of Canada's best-known social activists and political commentators. Through the 1990s, she hosted CBC Newsworld's* Straight from the Hip *and* Face Off. *She was President of the National Action Committee on the Status of Women from 1990 to 1993. She is the author of two books, most recently* Imagine Democracy *(Stoddart), which outlines a radical new vision of society. She is the publisher of* rabble.ca, *a new online interactive magazine, and also writes monthly columns for* Elm Street Magazine *and* CBC Online.

*Published in the* Ottawa Citizen *(February 2000), the following article critiques the cultural implications of a television network that created controversy when it aired* Who Wants to Marry a Multimillionaire? *Although in the annals of television history, the show is more notable for the fiasco that arose when the unsavoury history of the bride and groom came to light than for its format, Rebick captures the concerns a number of feminist viewers expressed at the time the show aired about the "princess-awaiting-prince" theme.*

"It's official, Judy, feminism is dead," were the first words I heard Wednesday morning on arriving at CFRB, a private Toronto radio station where I work as a commentator. The guys had watched *Who Wants to Marry a Multimillionaire* the night before and they were all talking about it. For those who don't know, *Who Wants to Marry a Multimillionaire* is Fox's attempt to rip off the wildly successful *Who Wants to Be a Millionaire.*   1

"It was like watching a train wreck," said *Toronto Sun* Editor Lorrie Goldstein, who is also a CFRB commentator. "I couldn't stop watching it." The Sun was so enamoured, they ran it on their front page. "I'd watch it again if it is on again," said one of the young producers. All guys, different ages, all excited about this incredibly stupid show.   2

Then I went to lunch with the staff of *Straight from the Hip*, all women, also different generations and they too had watched the show and loved it. It was so bad it was good. They didn't interpret it as the death of feminism but they too couldn't stop talking about it.   3

The staff of CFRB and the staff of *Straight from the Hip* rarely have any-     4
thing in common except the fact that they work in journalism. It is true that
journalists enjoy watching a train wreck more than most but somehow I think
the enthusiasm for the show reflected something else. *Who Wants to Marry a
Multimillionaire* takes a little of every escapist fantasy in the book and puts
them all together in one cheesy package. No doubt it will be a megahit.

The beauty pageant, a thankfully dying institution, was revived by the 50     5
potential brides parading in bathing suits first, cocktail dresses next and for
the five finalists, wedding dresses. Instead of judges, there was one single man,
whom we saw from the back, watching the procession of women, all parading for his benefit alone. He got to choose the one he liked the best. It was not
hard to understand why the CFRB guys were into it.

Then there is the Cinderella fantasy. In my childhood one of the most     6
popular shows was *Queen for a Day,* where a woman was chosen to receive
celebrity treatment for one day. Her life story was told, she was fussed over
and she got great gifts. *Who Wants to Marry a Multimillionaire* seems to me
like the *Queen for a Day* of the 21st century. What's depressing here is that
the Cinderella fantasy of escaping the drudgery of everyday life into the arms
of a rich and handsome prince is still so powerful.

Of course, *Who Wants to Marry a Multimillionaire* also feeds the same     7
fantasy as *Who Wants to Be a Millionaire*, lottery tickets and gambling—
instant riches. No one talked about the pre-nup.

Then there's the Jerry Springer appeal of feeling terribly superior to the     8
people on the show who are exposing so much of themselves to us. I actually found most of the women to be fairly dignified, under the circumstances,
and the groom tried his best to sound like a sensitive kind of guy. "It's not fair
that only I get to ask the questions and decide," he said. Right.

The appeal of shows like *The Dating Game* is also here. The difference is     9
that all the power is given to the rich man, kind of like real life.

So many people these days are meeting their partners on the Internet,     10
through personal ads and matchmaker agencies, why not on television? My
niece told me about speed dating. Six women and six men meet in a restaurant, talk to one person for eight minutes and then move on to the next
person. At the end of the session, each person writes the name of the person(s)
they are willing to go out with. If the person you choose has also chosen you,
then you go out. My niece's description produced a long, intense discussion
in our family. How to meet a mate is a topic of endless fascination, usually
starting with the expression, "I could never do that." But no one wants to be
left poor or alone. *Who Wants to Marry a Multimillionaire* is the uber-
straight version of a solution.

Karl Marx called religion the opiate of the people. Our opiates are the     11
promise of instant riches, celebrity and romance. *Who Wants to Marry a
Multimillionaire* is not so much a sign of the death of feminism as a sign of
how much work is left to do.

However much equality we have achieved at work, as long as in our fan-    12
tasies we are still waiting for Prince Charming, and in their fantasies they are
hoping to have enough money to buy the girl of their dreams, we have a long
way to go.

■ ■ ■

## Discussion and Writing Suggestions

1. Judy Rebick is a well-known Canadian feminist. Does she seem unduly
   outraged by the phenomenon of "bride-buying" on TV, or does she ask
   some reasonable questions?
2. Reality TV continues to be relatively popular (with *Survivor* and our
   more historically-oriented Canadian *Pioneer Quest* and *Quest for the
   Bay*), and many contestants agree that they are motivated by the twin
   desire to test themselves and to win money. To what extent are these the
   twin motives of Cinderella and of contestants trying to marry a multimillionaire? Are these motives admirable? Are they the motives of a practical realist, or do they reflect the materialism and self-promotion rampant in our culture?
3. Can you remember the tawdry outcome of the *Millionaire* marriage? To
   some degree, both bride and groom were revealed as sham figures who
   quickly fell out of "love" in highly publicized wrangling that took place
   in the aftermath of the show. Comment on how this outcome provides an
   ironic reading of the "Cinderella" myth in exposing the vanity of the
   hope that someday a good guy will come along and make everything
   better for a nice girl who has suffered too long.

## Disney's Dolls

KATHI MAIO

*Kathi Maio is a feminist film critic who lives in Boston. She is the film editor
of* Sojourner: The Women's Forum, *and she is also film columnist for the*
Magazine of Fantasy and Science Fiction. *Her film criticism has also appeared
in publications like* Visions, Ms., *and* New Internationalist. *She is the author
of two books of film essays,* Feminist in the Dark: Reviewing the Movies *and*
Popcorn & Sexual Politics.

    *In the article that follows, Maio takes a critical look at the way Disney
portrays female heroism. She suggests that even when several recent Disney
productions have attempted to appeal to contemporary values by serving up
female action figures, many elements in the story line continue to assume
that society should be organized as a patriarchy.*

It is more than a little ironic that the Walt Disney Company's current ani- 1
mated feature, *Mulan*, retells an age-old legend about the Chinese successfully fighting off a foreign invasion. The American media giant chose to make
this particular story into its 36th animated feature precisely because it was the
perfect vehicle for a strategic incursion into the Chinese film market.

The legendary woman warrior, Hua Mu-Lan, who bravely fought off 2
alien onslaughts has now herself become an agent of a U.S. conglomerate's
ambition to dominate the culture of Asia—and the entire globe.

It's a heavy burden for one young, doe-eyed heroine to bear. But so it is 3
for all of the young women Disney has co-opted for the screen. They aren't
simply cartoons. They are symbols of the times—and one company's measurement of how their target audiences want to see women.

Disney's first animated feature, *Snow White and the Seven Dwarfs* 4
(1937), set a standard for full-length animation and established a pattern for
later Disney heroines to follow. Snow White is young, virginal, pretty, sweet-
natured and obedient. Domestic drudgery doesn't faze her since she is sure
that a handsome owning-class chap will, someday soon, come and save her.

Meanwhile, when faced with danger she runs away on tiny high-heeled 5
shoes and then falls in a weeping heap. She finds a shelter in a dusty and
dishevelled cottage and immediately feels compelled to clean it from top to
bottom (since the owners, a group of full-grown, if quite short, miners, obviously don't have a "Mother" to clean for them).

Snow White's one adversary is her wicked and powerful stepmother, the 6
Queen. Like most Disney crones, the Queen is eventually destroyed. But not
before feeding her lovely stepdaughter a poisoned apple that places her in a
death-like coma. Snow White is lovingly waked by her housemates who place
her on a bier. But she is awakened only when Prince Charming comes and
plants one on her rosy lips. Back among the living Snow White rides away
with her new boyfriend, with nary a second thought for her short friends.

It's prototypical Disney. Young women are natural-born happy home- 7
makers who lie in a state of suspended animation until a man gives them a
life. Older women are the enemy, especially if they seek power. And the
working class (hardworking, but dirty and uncivilized) are there to serve the
rich and privileged, never questioning their subordinate position.

Although the Disney team made use of different fairytales over the years, 8
the basic formula for telling women's stories through animated features changed
very little from *Snow White* to *Cinderella* (1950) to *Sleeping Beauty* (1959).

Then came the sixties: Uncle Walt died in 1966. And Disney's animation 9
teams fell into years of disarray and second-rate work. Some felt the Disney
studio would never again produce a "classic." They were wrong. Several
years after management of the studio was assumed by Michael Eisner the
company made an impressive comeback with *The Little Mermaid* (1989).
With its vibrant animation and music *The Little Mermaid* proved that the
Disney studio still knew how to make a first-rate cartoon feature. The movie

*not*
*persuasive*
↓
*group of*
*like*
*minded*
*women*

also proved that old attitudes towards women die hard. Looking at the film you'd never know that the women's movement ever happened.

Disney's take on Hans Christian Andersen is the "same old, same old." Except, for the first time, there is a new nymphet quality to the virginal heroine. Above her green tail Disney's Ariel wears only a string bikini top made from a couple of sea shells. And as innocent, wide-eyed and flipper-tailed as she is, there is something distinctly sexy about her too. Her image may not be informed by feminism, but it has most certainly been informed by the eroticizing of the pubescent female so common in Western advertising and popular culture.　　10

Like Disney heroines before her, Ariel is looking for a romantic solution to the yearning in her heart. (Andersen's mermaid looks for human love only as a means of achieving her true desire: an immortal soul. Disney's mermaid sees a cute fella as her be-all and end-all.) Ariel will do anything to have the bland handsome Prince fall in love with her. She'll disobey her stern but loving father, King Triton. She'll even make a bargain with the devil—played by a corpulent, whitehaired seawitch named Ursula. Again, the older, powerful woman (representing evil) must be annihilated. The young Prince, who embodies a healthier form of (inherited patriarchal) power, finishes the witch off. But not before she makes big trouble for our lovelorn heroine.　　11

Ursula gives Ariel a set of shapely legs, but takes her voice in trade. Hence, in *The Little Mermaid,* we are given a female protagonist who is literally silenced by her desperate need for male approval. "Shut up and be beautiful," the movie seems to tell young girls. (Books like *Reviving Ophelia* have argued that this is a message pre-teen girls constantly get from their society. Why not from their cartoons?)　　12

Since *The Little Mermaid* is a Disney flick, Ariel gets her voice back and she gets the guy. But she is nevertheless forced to abandon completely her sea world (her family and friends) for the land-locked kingdom of her Prince. In the end, Ariel is a woman without a social support system, investing her entire life in a romance. Not a situation that I've ever found to have "happily ever after" written all over it.　　13

And many women agreed. Stung by the criticism, Disney promised to show more sensitivity towards gender issues in their next movie, a retelling of *Beauty and the Beast* (1991). The company hired a woman, Linda Woolverton, as screenwriter. And they put their PR department into overdrive—promoting their new heroine, Belle, as "modern," "active" and even "feminist."　　14

It worked with most critics. But, as far as I could tell, the most feminist thing about Disney's Belle was that she liked to read. Like the 18th-century folktale's Beauty, this Belle remains a self-sacrificing daughter of a silly and cowardly father (switching places with her papa when the Beast takes him prisoner). Still, Disney's idea of an "independent" woman didn't bother me half as much as their concept of a male romantic hero.　　15

The original fairy-tale (and all the retellings I've ever read or seen, from Cocteau's 1946 movie masterpiece to the cult late-1980's American TV show) portrayed the "Beast" of the story as a big teddy bear. He looked fierce and　　16 strange, but was really kind, tender—and hopelessly devoted. The moral: Don't judge a book by its cover. An ugly exterior can hide a loving heart.

But Disney admitted that they went out of their way to create a hero with 17 a "very serious problem." Their Beast is well, beastly. He terrorizes his household staff. And he intimidates his lovely prisoner, as well. Although he isn't violent with Belle, that always seems a distinct possibility. It is her poise and exquisite beauty that tame his savagery.

The problem? Disney's reworking of the old fable implies that women 18 are responsible for controlling male anger and violence. If a woman is only pretty and sweet enough, she can transform an abusive man into a prince— forever. If only it were true. But this is a blame-the-victim scenario waiting to happen. In a realistic sequel, Belle would seek refuge at the village's battered women's shelter.

No matter its sexual politics, Disney's *Beauty and the Beast* was an inter- 19 national hit, spawning an equally successful stage musical. Disney's cartoon features were back in the groove and they proved it again with 1992's *Aladdin.* It's hardly worth mentioning the portrayal of women in this translation of an "Arabian Nights" tale. The only significant female character is Princess Jasmine, who is nothing more than a comely pawn bandied back and forth between the hero Aladdin, the evil vizier and the sultan who just happens to be her foolish father.

More interesting is the obvious racism and ethnic stereotyping in the 20 story. The dastardly characters (like Jafar, the vizier) are decidedly Arabic looking, while the hero, Aladdin, looks and sounds ("Call me Al") like a fresh-faced American. And then there were the song lyrics, the most insulting of which went like this: "I come from a land . . . where they cut off your ears, if they don't like your face. It's barbaric, but hey, it's home."

Obviously, Disney never means to offend anyone. That would be bad busi- 21 ness. But even animators and songwriters internalize racism. And the "imagineers" at Disney obviously look to reinforce cultural assumptions and push a few buttons in their audience members, if for no other reason than it's the most efficient way to tell a story. Boyish Tom Cruise look = Good guy. Swarthy, hook-nosed Basil Rathbone look = Villain. Most audience members don't even notice when this happens. It is simply the undertow of the "Disney Magic."

Some of that same undertow can be felt in the most successful animated 22 feature of all time, a Hamlet fable in fur called *The Lion King.* Here, despite the African locale the young hero is voiced by All-American white actors (Jonathan Taylor Thomas, Matthew Broderick), while disloyal, vicious hyena baddies are given street-jive dialogue and voiced by actors like Whoopi Goldberg and Cheech Marin.

Women don't fare well in this story either. Although Simba's childhood 23 playmate, Nala, can kick his butt in a mock-fight, when Simba runs away, Nala and the other lionesses are powerless to resist the oppressive rule of Scar (a crypto-homosexual villain, another Disney favourite).

With the tremendous success (over $766 million in worldwide box office) 24 of *The Lion King,* Disney plunged whole-heartedly into its own "Wonderful

World of Multiculturalism." The next animated feature, *Pocahontas,* blended their traditional all-for-love Princess tale with a true story from Native American history. And there lies the outrage: Pocahontas is not a fictional character to be casually re-interpreted. She was a real woman, who deserved better than the cartoon portrait Disney painted of her.

There's no room in this article to list all the inaccuracies in this 1995 film. Suffice it to say that Disney's buckskin Barbie bears little resemblance to the pre-pubescent girl who first met John Smith. Her real name was Matoaka and her "saving" of Smith from "execution" was probably nothing more than a tribal adoption ceremony. There was no romance between the two. She called him "father" when she met him again, years later.                                                25

In an attempt to put a cheery spin on what amounts to genocide, Disney ends their film with peace achieved between the natives and colonists. No mention is made of the eventual decimation of the Powhatan nation. And neither in this movie, nor its 1998 straight-to-video hit sequel, *Pocahontas II: Journey to a New World,* is any mention made of the fact that Pocahontas was kidnapped, held hostage, forcibly "civilized" and converted to Christianity, then married off to a colonist who viewed her origins as "accursed."                              26

Later, as a publicity gimmick for the Virginia colony, she was taken to England where she sickened and died. It's hard to make two upbeat cartoon adventures out of such a tragic story. So Disney didn't try. Instead, they drew a barefoot babe and gave her cute, comical animal sidekicks and a penchant for falling in love with hunky anglos. Sadly millions of people around the world saw Pocahontas not only as a colourful cartoon but as a palatable history lesson.                                                                                        27

In the newest animated film, *Mulan,* Disney has laid claim to a Chinese hero who, although real, lived so long ago that her story has passed into myth. The basic legend tells of a young woman who—to protect her disabled veteran father—enters the imperial army, fighting bravely for many years. As you'd expect, Disney has declared its good intentions and its sincere respect for this Chinese national hero. In fact the distortion level in Disney's *Mulan* equals that of *Pocahontas.*                                                              28

In Disney's version the woman warrior is discovered after she is injured in battle and sentenced to die. But her handsome commanding officer, Shang (a Disney invention), cannot kill her. Instead, he expels her from the army. In the legend, Hua Mu-Lan isn't discovered until after the war when her comrades visit and find her in women's attire. In the Disney version, Shang, (Mulan's would-be executioner) shows up after the war to court his former buddy—to the delight of her family and her. The real Mulan had no interest in romance.                                                                                  29

So, even though Mulan is a brave, strong hero, her motivation for entering the army has nothing to do with her own ambitions and everything to do with serving patriarchy (represented by her father and her emperor). Disney makes it clear that men still command Mulan and they always retain the power of life-and-death over her. But not to worry, all they really want to do is marry her and turn her into a Disney happy homemaker.                                   30

By looks alone, kick-boxing Mulan would seem to have little in common 31
with dainty Snow White. But looks are deceiving. Disney has changed only
the trappings and in recent cases the skin colour of its heroines. At heart, they
still all identify with male authority instead of seeking their own empowerment. And in the end a good-looking boyfriend remains the truest measure of
feminine happiness and success.

As I write this, the Chinese Government has still not given its permission 32
for a mainland theatrical release for *Mulan* (although the film is already a hit
in Taiwan, Hong Kong and other Asian markets). Chinese officials are
engaged, as the *Sunday Telegraph* put it, in a "wider struggle to suppress
foreign-backed interpretations of the country's literary heritage."

More power to their struggle. But there may just be no stopping the
cultural tsunami called the Walt Disney Company.

■ ■ ■

## Discussion and Writing Suggestions

1. Did Maio expose a nasty side of any of your favourite characters, or at
   least reveal a weakness you had overlooked? If so, does this influence
   your feelings about the character or the show?
2. Are people who create children's entertainment responsible for ensuring
   that it contains positive values and role models?
3. How does Maio's argument support Kelley's?

## ■ SYNTHESIS ACTIVITIES

1. In 1910, Antti Aarne published one of the early classifications of folktale types as an aid to scholars who were collecting tales and needed
   an efficient means for telling where, and with what changes, similar
   tales had appeared. In 1927, folklorist Stith Thompson, translating
   and enlarging Aarne's study, produced a work that is now a standard
   reference for folklorists the world over. We present the authors'
   description of type 510 and its two forms 510A ("Cinderella") and
   510B. Use this description as a basis on which to compare and contrast the two versions of "Cinderella."

   510. *Cinderella and Cap o' Rushes.*
   I. *The Persecuted Heroine.* (a) The heroine is abused by her
      stepmother and stepsisters, or (b) flees in disguise from her
      father who wants to marry her, or (c) is cast out by him
      because she has said that she loved him like salt, or (d) is to
      be killed by a servant.
   II. *Magic Help.* While she is acting as servant (at home or
      among strangers) she is advised, provided for, and fed (a) by

her dead mother, (b) by a tree on the mother's grave, or (c) a supernatural being, (d) by birds, or (e) by a goat, a sheep, or a cow. When the goat is killed, there springs up from her remains a magic tree.

III. *Meeting with Prince.* (a) She dances in beautiful clothing several times with a prince who seeks in vain to keep her, or she is seen by him in church. (b) She gives hints of the abuse she has endured, as servant girl, or (c) she is seen in her beautiful clothing in her room or in the church.

IV. *Proof of Identity.* (a) She is discovered through the slipper-test, or (b) through a ring which she throws into the prince's drink or bakes in his bread. (c) She alone is able to pluck the gold apple desired by the knight.

V. *Marriage with the Prince.*

VI. *Value of Salt.* Her father is served unsalted food and thus learns the meaning of her earlier answer.

Two forms of the type follow.

A. *Cinderella.* The two stepsisters. The stepdaughter at the grave of her own mother, who helps her (milks the cow, shakes the apple tree, helps the old man). Threefold visit to church (dance). Slipper test.

B. *The Dress of Gold, of Silver, and of Stars. (Cap o' Rushes).* Present of the father who wants to marry his own daughter. The maiden as servant of the prince, who throws various objects at her. The threefold visit to the church and the forgotten shoe. Marriage.

2. Speculate on the reasons folktales are made and told. As you develop a theory, rely first on your own hunches regarding the origins and functions of folktale literature. You might want to recall your experiences as a child listening to tales so that you can discuss their effects on you. Rely as well on the variants of "Cinderella," which you should regard as primary sources (just as scholars do). And make use of the critical pieces you've read—Stone, Bettelheim, Kelley, and Morrison—selecting pertinent points from each that will help clarify your points. *Remember:* Your own speculation should dominate the paper. Use sources to help you make *your* points.

3. What is your opinion of the critical work you've read on "Cinderella"? Writing from various perspectives, authors in this chapter have analyzed the tale. To what extent have the analyses illuminated "Cinderella" for you? (Have the analyses in any way "ruined" your ability to enjoy "Cinderella"?) To what extent do you find the analyses off the mark? Are the attempts at analysis inappropriate for a children's story? In your view, what place do literary critics, anthropologists, historians, and psychologists have in discussing folktales?

In developing a response to these questions, you might begin with Thompson's quotation and then follow directly with a statement of your thesis. In one part of your paper, critique the work of Bettelheim, Kelley, and/or Morrison as a way of demonstrating which analyses of folktales (if any) seem worthwhile to you. In another section of the paper (or, perhaps, woven into the critiques), you'll refer directly to the variants of "Cinderella." For the sake of convenience, you might refer to a single variant.

4. Review the Perrault and Disney versions of "Cinderella" and consider whether you would read either of these to your child. In an essay, justify your decision. If you admire the heroine, you might consult Stone's article to support your interpretation.

5. Try writing a version of "Cinderella" and setting it on a college or university campus. For your version of the story to be an authentic variant, you'll need to retain certain defining features, or motifs. See Aarne and Thompson—Synthesis Activity 1. As you consider the possibilities for your story, consider Thompson's point that the teller of a folktale borrows heavily on earlier versions; the virtue of telling is not in rendering a new story but in retelling an old one and *adapting* it to local conditions and needs. Unless you plan to write a commentary "Cinderella," you should retain the basic motifs of the old story and add details that will appeal to your particular audience: your classmates.

6. In her 1981 book *The Cinderella Complex*, Colette Dowling wrote:

> It is the thesis of this book that personal, psychological dependency—the deep wish to be taken care of by others—is the chief force holding women down today. I call this "The Cinderella Complex"—a network of largely repressed attitudes and fears that keep women in a kind of half-light, retreating from the full use of their minds and creativity. Like Cinderella, women today are still waiting for something external to transform their lives.

In an essay, respond to Dowling's thesis. First, apply her thesis to the variants of "Cinderella." Does the thesis hold in each case? Next, respond to her view that "the chief force holding women down today" is psychological dependency, or the need for "something external" (i.e., a Prince) to transform their lives. In your experience, have you observed a Cinderella complex at work? How do Rebick's observations about our culture fit here?

7. Discuss the process by which Cinderella falls in love in the Perrault and Disney tales. Pull your observations together and make a statement about Cinderella's falling in love. What is the significance of what you've learned? Share this significance with your readers.

8. Write an explanatory synthesis in which you attempt to define a feminist perspective on "Cinderella" as this is expressed by Kelley and Morrison. If you are feeling ambitious, you can write a second part to this essay where you consider Maio's essay, which provides a feminist response to other characters in Disney's children's movies.

# ■ RESEARCH ACTIVITIES

1. Research the fairy-tale literature of your ancestors, both the tales and any critical commentary that you can find on them. Once you have read the material, talk with older members of your family to hear any tales they have to tell. (Seek, especially, oral versions of stories you have already read.) In a paper, discuss the role that fairy-tale literature has played, and continues to play, in your family.

2. Locate the book *Morphology of the Folktale* (1958), by Russian folklorist Vladimir Propp. Use the information you find there to analyze the elements of any three fairy tales of your choosing. In a paper, report on your analysis and evaluate the usefulness of Propp's system of classifying the key elements of fairy-tale literature.

3. Bruno Bettelheim's *Uses of Enchantment* (1975) generated a great deal of reaction on its publication. Read Bettelheim and locate as many reviews of his work as possible. Based on your own reactions and on your reading of the reviews, write an evaluation in which you address Bettelheim's key assumption that fairy-tale literature provides important insights into the psychological life of children.

4. Locate and study multiple versions of any fairy tale other than "Cinderella." Having read the versions, identify—and write your paper on—what you feel are the defining elements that make the tales variants of a single story. See if you can find the tale listed as a "type" in Aarne and Thompson, *The Types of Folk-Tales*. If you wish, argue that one version of the tale is preferable to others.

5. Apart from critics like Maio and Morrison included here, various critics, such as Madonna Kolbenschlag and Jack Zipes, author of *Breaking the Magic Spell* (1979), have taken the approach that fairy tales are far from innocuous children's stories; rather, they inculcate the unsuspecting with the value systems of the dominant culture. Write a paper in which you evaluate an interpretation of fairy-tale literature. In your paper, explicitly address the assumption that fairy tales are not morally or politically neutral but, rather, imply a distinct set of values.

6. Write a children's story. Decide on the age group that you will address, and then go to a local public library and find several books directed to the same audience. (1) Analyze these books and write a brief paper in which you identify the story elements that seem especially important for your intended audience. (2) Then attempt your own story. (3) When you have finished, answer this question: What values are implicit in your story? What will children who read or hear the story learn about themselves and their world? Plan to submit your brief analytical paper, your story, and your final comment.

7. Videotape, and then study, several hours of Saturday morning cartoons. Then locate and read a collection of Grimm's fairy tales. In a comparative analysis, examine the cartoons and the fairy tales along any four or five dimensions that you think are important. The point of your comparisons and contrasts will be to determine how well the two types of presentations stack up against each other. Which do you find more entertaining? Illuminating? Ambitious? Useful? (These criteria are suggestions only. You should generate your own criteria as part of your research.)

8. Arrange to read to your favourite young person a series of fairy tales. Based on your understanding of the selections in this chapter, develop a list of questions concerning the importance or usefulness of fairy-tale literature to children. Read to your young friend on several occasions and, if possible, talk about the stories after you read them (or while you are reading). Then write a paper on your experience, answering as many of your initial questions as possible. (Be sure in your paper to provide a profile of the child with whom you worked; to review your selection of stories; and to list the questions you wanted to explore.)

# 14

# The Beast Within: Perspectives on the Horror Film

The ego represents what we call reason and sanity, in contrast to the id, which contains the passions. . . . [T]he ego has the task of bringing the external world to bear upon the id and its tendencies, and endeavors to substitute the reality-principle for the pleasure-principle which reigns supreme in the id.

—Sigmund Freud, "The Ego and the Id"

In the climactic sequence of Wes Craven's *Scream* (1997), the terrified heroine flees from a knife-wielding fiend in a Halloween cloak and mask, finding protection in the arms of a friend, himself grievously wounded. They briefly open the door of the remote farmhouse to admit a panicked young man, who cries, "Stu has gone mad!" The friend, a crazed half-smile on his face, intones, "We all go a little mad sometimes!" He raises his gun, shoots the other young man, and the heroine realizes in horror that the person she has trusted is a murderous psychopath. In the scene that follows, blood spills upon gore, with the heroine at one point turning the tables upon her attacker by donning the Halloween gear, bursting out of a closet, and impaling the killer with the sharp end of an umbrella. (Of course, he's far from finished.)

The sequence is noteworthy for several reasons. First, much of its dramatic impact derives from one of the most enduring motifs in the horror genre: the psychopathic monster who, at least part of the time, looks and acts like a normal person. Sometimes the monster can control his transformation; sometimes he can't. The implication, of course, is that much of the time you can't tell monsters from normal people because their true nature is concealed beneath a civilized facade. Second, after the psychopath says, "We all go a little mad sometimes," he credits the line to Anthony Perkins in *Psycho*. He also admits that the "blood" on his shirt is corn syrup, just like the pig's blood in *Carrie*. The characters in *Scream* are aware that they're in a horror film, and as the action develops, they tick off the various conventions of the genre. When the killer lies lifeless on the floor, the young man warns the heroine to be careful because "This is the moment where the supposedly dead killer comes back to life for one last scare." ("Not in my movie!" retorts the heroine, after finishing off the killer.) In other words, let's not take the situation too seriously, folks, because we're just playing out an established formula. Our clever twist is that we know it and we're hip about it.

*Scream* is therefore a film about the monstrous nature of apparently ordinary people, but it's also a film about horror films; it relies upon the audience's awareness of typical situations and plot patterns in the genre. It is a genre that has been fascinating audiences since the silent film era. Early examples include F. W. Murnau's vampire film *Nosferatu* (1922) and Robert Wiene's celebrated expressionist classic, *The Cabinet of Dr. Caligari* (1919). Tod Browning's *Dracula* (1931) with Bela Lugosi, though not the first Dracula film, popularized the vampire motif and inspired an endless string of sequels. James Whale's *Frankenstein* (1931)—with Boris Karloff as the monster—was also followed by a host of sequels, most notably *The Bride of Frankenstein* (1935), composed of equal parts of horror, wit, and pathos. Karloff was also the first bandaged monster in a series of *Mummy* films.

The original werewolf film, *The Werewolf of London* (1935), was followed by the more well-known *The Wolf Man* (1941) with Lon Chaney, Jr., who reprised his role in a series of lesser sequels. Shameless producers milked the genre to its limit by creating such unnatural hybrids as *Frankenstein Meets the Wolf Man* (1943) and *Abbott and Costello Meet Frankenstein* (1948). Another horror classic, *The Invisible Man* (1933), with Claude Rains, was fortunate in spawning only one sequel. *Dr. Jekyll and Mr. Hyde* had many incarnations, though these were not sequels but remakes. In more recent years, prestigious directors have made expensive remakes of the horror classics: Francis Ford Coppola (*The Godfather*) made *Bram Stoker's Dracula* (1992); Kenneth Branagh (*Hamlet*) made *Mary Shelley's Frankenstein* (1994); Mike Nichols (*The Graduate*) made *Wolf* (1994).

Horror films have more commonly been "B" movies, however, and the kind of film that Wes Craven's *Scream* is both re-creating and mocking draws upon the pulp genre represented by *The Thing* (1951), *The Invasion of the Body Snatchers* (1956), *The Night of the Living Dead* (1968), *The Texas Chainsaw Massacre* (1974), *Halloween* (1978), *Friday the Thirteenth* (1980), and Craven's own *Nightmare on Elm Street* (1985). Most of these films—and their sequels—updated the classic horror movie into the contemporary "slasher" subgenre, in which a group of helpless, isolated victims is systematically stalked and dispatched by a fiendish killer.

But why are horror films so enduringly popular? Why should a significant portion of the moviegoing public pay money to be terrified? And why should horror movies be worth studying in a college or university course?

Actually, the first question begins to answer to the last one. The fact that so many people in our society enjoy horror films raises interesting questions about popular culture and about the psychology of entertainment—questions that are taken up by some of the authors in this chapter. For now, we can suggest that any phenomenon that engages so many people in a culture can reveal significant aspects of that culture, can provide clues about its values, its professed ideals, its deepest fears. On a psychological level, the horror film dramatizes our nightmares, so that we can confront them and—from the safety of a darkened theatre—laugh at them. So we get a thrill out of being scared (some of us, anyway!) as long as we know that as spectators we'll be perfectly safe.

One of the most popular of the horror subgenres is what some have called the "transformation" film and what we call the motif of "the beast within." James Iaccino, drawing upon the work of psychoanalyst Carl Jung, calls it the "shadow archetype." The shadow represents the dark side of our nature. As Iaccino notes, the "giant monsters, from massive insects to huge dinosaurs and even incredibly sized aliens, are all reflections of the shadow blown up to outrageous proportions." In a narrower sense (one without external monsters), the shadow represents the bestial, primeval instincts that lurk just beneath our civilized, law-abiding facades, instincts that sometimes break to the surface in irrational and murderous fury. Werewolf films are a prime example of the shadow archetype, as are the numerous Dr. Jekyll and Mr. Hyde films.

Of course, the horror genre is not confined to movies. The fertile imagination of novelists and dramatists has long provided a wide variety of approaches to the motif of "the beast within." In *Midsummer Night's Dream* (1594–95) and in *The Tempest* (1610–11), Shakespeare shows us men transformed into beasts. The gothic novelists of the 18th century supplied British readers with hearty portions of horror, chains rattling in the attic, and screams in the night. In *Heart of Darkness* (1899) Joseph Conrad creates a physical, spiritual, and psychological journey into the heart of darkness in each of us— epitomized in a highly educated European, Kurtz, who reverts to savagery in the jungle after being long isolated from civilization. In William Golding's *Lord of the Flies* (1954), civilized British schoolboys stranded on an island after their plane crashes turn into savages within a few short weeks, intent on killing all who refuse to join their tribe. Whether transmitted orally by storytellers, through the writing of novelists, or through the lens of filmmakers, the horror story has entertained—and terrified—its audiences.

We begin by considering the psychological dimensions of the horror film, with an essay by horror novelist Stephen King, who asks why we should be so drawn to such horrible stuff. He takes this as his starting point: "I think that we're all mentally ill. . . ." Next, Tim Dirks provides a brief historical survey of horror films, including a list of the greatest examples of the genre. Jay Boyar describes some of the ways contemporary horror movies have changed, so that in some of the best current films there is more going on than a bath of blood and gore. Vinay Menon shifts ground from analyzing the psychological influences of horror to describing some of the ways that watching these films makes us respond physically. Robert Haas's article is a largely positive assessment of the achievement of contemporary Canadian filmmaker David Cronenberg. Haas explores the figure of the cyborg and considers how this represents a new form of the monstrous.

Next, Stanley Solomon examines the distinctive and characteristic features of "The Nightmare World," drawing distinctions between good and bad examples of the genre. In "Blowing the Lid Off the Id," psychoanalyst Harvey M. Greenberg explores both the conscious and unconscious aspects of the tortured protagonists of films such as *Cat People, The Wolf Man, Dr. Jekyll and Mr. Hyde,* and *Forbidden Planet.*

## Why We Crave Horror Movies

STEPHEN KING

*To think of modern horror fiction is to summon the name of Stephen King. Author of such best-selling novels as* Carrie: A Novel of a Girl With a Frightening Power *(1974),* The Shining *(1977),* Pet Sematary *(1983), and* Misery *(1987), King has devoted a career to exploring our nightmares and making them come alive. His novels sell in the millions; the movie adaptations based on them play to packed (screaming) houses—all testament to King's mastery of a form that prompts a simple but mystifying question: Why do people pay good money to be scared? Over his career, in various interviews and essays, King has observed that we seek out and respond to horror in fiction as a strategy for contending with the horrors and insanity of our daily lives. In the essay that follows, he observes how a good horror story lets us keep the "alligators" lurking in our psyches fed. The premise is clear: Each of us maintains both a civilized, public face and then something altogether nastier that we keep hidden but must nonetheless "feed." Good horror stories and movies do just that.*

I think that we're all mentally ill; those of us outside the asylums only hide it     1
a little better—and maybe not all that much better, after all. We've all known
people who talk to themselves, people who sometimes squinch their faces into
horrible grimaces when they believe no one is watching, people who have
some hysterical fear—of snakes, the dark, the tight place, the long drop . . .
and, of course, those final worms and grubs that are waiting so patiently
underground.

When we pay our four or five bucks and seat ourselves at tenth-row     2
center in a theater showing a horror movie, we are daring the nightmare.

Why? Some of the reasons are simple and obvious. To show that we can,     3
that we are not afraid, that we can ride this roller coaster. Which is not to say
that a really good horror movie may not surprise a scream out of us at some
point, the way we may scream when the roller coaster twists through a complete 360 or plows through a lake at the bottom of the drop. And horror
movies, like roller coasters, have always been the special province of the
young; by the time one turns 40 or 50, one's appetite for double twists or 360-
degree loops may be considerably depleted.

We also go to re-establish our feelings of essential normality; the horror     4
movie is innately conservative, even reactionary. Freda Jackson as the horrible melting woman in *Die, Monster, Die!* confirms for us that no matter
how far we may be removed from the beauty of a Robert Redford or a Diana
Ross, we are still light-years from true ugliness.

And we go to have fun.                                                                    5

Ah, but this is where the ground starts to slope away, isn't it? Because this       6
is a very peculiar sort of fun indeed. The fun comes from seeing others men-
aced—sometimes killed. One critic has suggested that if pro football has
become the voyeur's version of combat, then the horror film has become the
modern version of the public lynching.

It is true that the mythic, "fairytale" horror film intends to take away the        7
shades of gray. . . . It urges us to put away our more civilized and adult penchant for analysis and to become children again, seeing things in pure blacks
and whites. It may be that horror movies provide psychic relief on this level
because this invitation to lapse into simplicity, irrationality and even outright
madness is extended so rarely. We are told we may allow our emotions a free
rein . . . or no rein at all.

If we are all insane, then sanity becomes a matter of degree. If your          8
insanity leads you to carve up women like Jack the Ripper or the Cleveland
Torso Murderer, we clap you away in the funny farm (but neither of those
two amateur-night surgeons was ever caught, heh-heh-heh); if, on the other
hand your insanity leads you only to talk to yourself when you're under
stress or to pick your nose on the morning bus, then you are left alone to go
about your business . . . though it is doubtful that you will ever be invited to
the best parties.

The potential lyncher is in almost all of us (excluding saints, past and pre-     9
sent; but then, most saints have been crazy in their own ways), and every now
and then, he has to be let loose to scream and roll around in the grass. Our
emotions and our fears form their own body, and we recognize that it
demands its own exercise to maintain proper muscle tone. Certain of these
emotional muscles are accepted—even exalted—in civilized society; they are,
of course, the emotions that tend to maintain the status quo of civilization
itself. Love, friendship, loyalty, kindness—these are all the emotions that we
applaud, emotions that have been immortalized in the couplets of Hallmark
cards and in the verses (I don't dare call it poetry) of Leonard Nimoy.

When we exhibit these emotions, society showers us with positive rein-      10
forcement; we learn this even before we get out of diapers. When, as children,
we hug our rotten little puke of a sister and give her a kiss, all the aunts and
uncles smile and twit and cry, "Isn't he the sweetest little thing?" Such coveted
treats as chocolate-covered graham crackers often follow. But if we deliberately slam the rotten little puke of a sister's fingers in the door, sanctions
follow—angry remonstrance from parents, aunts and uncles; instead of a
chocolate-covered graham cracker, a spanking.

But anticivilization emotions don't go away, and they demand periodic      11
exercise. We have such "sick" jokes as, "What's the difference between a
truckload of bowling balls and a truckload of dead babies?" (You can't
unload a truckload of bowling balls with a pitchfork . . . a joke, by the way,
that I heard originally from a ten-year-old.) Such a joke may surprise a laugh
or a grin out of us even as we recoil, a possibility that confirms the thesis: If
we share a brotherhood of man, then we also share an insanity of man. None

of which is intended as a defense of either the sick joke or insanity but merely as an explanation of why the best horror films, like the best fairy tales, manage to be reactionary, anarchistic, and revolutionary all at the same time.

The mythic horror movie, like the sick joke, has a dirty job to do. It delib- 12 erately appeals to all that is worst in us. It is morbidity unchained, our most base instincts let free, our nastiest fantasies realized . . . and it all happens, fittingly enough, in the dark. For those reasons, good liberals often shy away from horror films. For myself, I like to see the most aggressive of them—*Dawn of the Dead*, for instance—as lifting a trap door in the civilized forebrain and throwing a basket of raw meat to the hungry alligators swimming around in that subterranean river beneath.

Why bother? Because it keeps them from getting out, man. It keeps them 13 down there and me up here. It was Lennon and McCartney who said that all you need is love, and I would agree with that.

As long as you keep the gators fed. 14

■ ■ ■

## Review Questions

1. What relationship does the statement "we're all mentally ill" have, in King's view, to the appeal that horror movies hold for us?
2. Why do we go to horror movies, according to King?
3. In what ways might horror movies offer "psychic relief"?

## Discussion and Writing Suggestions

1. Do you agree with the initial proposition that "we're all mentally ill"?
2. What does King mean when he writes that by going to horror movies, "we are daring the nightmare"? What *is* the nightmare?
3. Does King's discussion of how horror films act upon us reflect your own experience in both watching and enjoying horror films? Explain your response, focusing upon one or more particular examples of films that you think were especially effective in keeping "the gators fed."
4. How can nightmares "manage to be reactionary, anarchistic, and revolutionary all at the same time"? [A "reactionary" view is one that values an old, well-known (if flawed) system over present-day systems; an "anarchistic" view is one that rebels against any system or order; a "revolutionary" view is one that seeks to replace the current system or order with a new one.]
5. King asserts (as have others, including Freud) that being civilized exacts its psychological toll. In your own life, have you seen this to be true? What have you sacrificed in order to play by the rules and be praised? At what cost? Do you see any relationship between the parts of yourself you are denying and the way you respond to horror movies?

6. King claims that "the potential lyncher is in almost all of us." Do you agree? If you're skeptical, see the chapter on Obedience to Authority in this text for more on this theme. In explaining how ordinary people could carry out Hitler's "Final Solution" and kill millions of innocent people, psychologist Stanley Milgram offers much the same analysis as King. (Milgram very carefully re-creates the conditions that lead the so-called normal person to commit acts of atrocity.)

# Horror Films

TIM DIRKS

*In the following selection Tim Dirks provides a useful historical survey of horror films since the silent era, and offers a list of the most important examples of the genre. He begins his discussion by focusing upon some of the key features of horror films.*

*Dirks, author and manager of an award-winning website, "The Greatest Films" http://www.filmsite.org/, which includes reviews and commentaries of many classic American movies, has been watching and studying films his entire adult life. Formerly a history teacher, Dirks currently serves as online course manager at a technology training centre in the Bay Area of Northern California.*

Horror films are designed to frighten and to invoke our hidden fears, often   1
in a terrifying, shocking finale, while captivating and entertaining us at the same time in a cathartic experience. Horror films effectively center on the dark side of life, the forbidden, and strange and alarming events. They deal with our most primal nature and its fears: our nightmares, our vulnerability, our alienation, our terror of the unknown, our fear of death, loss of identity, or fear of sexuality.

Whatever dark, primitive, and revolting traits that simultaneously attract   2
and repel us are featured in the horror genre. Horror films are often combined with science fiction when the menace or monster is related to a corruption of technology, or when Earth is threatened by aliens. The fantasy and supernatural film genres are not synonymous with the horror genre.

Horror films, when done well and with less reliance on horrifying special   3
effects, can be extremely potent film forms, tapping into our dream states and the horror of the irrational and unknown, and the horror within man himself. In horror films, the irrational forces of chaos or horror invariably need to be defeated, and often these films end with a return to normalcy and victory over the monstrous.

Of necessity, horror films are generally set in spooky old mansions or   4
fog-shrouded, dark locales, with "unknown," supernatural or grotesque creatures, ranging from vampires, madmen, devils, unfriendly ghosts, monsters, "Frankensteins," demons, zombies, evil spirits, arch fiends, satanic

villains, the "possessed," werewolves and freaks, even the unseen, diabolical presence of evil.

Horror films developed out of the tradition of Gothic novels from Europe by way of Mary Shelley or Bram Stoker. The first Frankenstein monster film (a 10-minute version) in the US was made as early as 1910 by the Edison Studios, starring Charles Ogle as the monster. The earliest horror pictures, now-forgotten "vamp" pictures (films featuring devilish captivating ladies) in one-reel or full length features, were produced in the US from 1909 to the early 1920s, making the horror genre one of the oldest and most basic. The first genuine vampire picture was produced in Europe—F. W. Murnau's *Nosferatu* (1922), a film adaptation from Bram Stoker's novel *Dracula*.

Other European filmmakers contributed to the genre, producing a number of horror films based upon old folktales, fables, and myths. One of the more memorable of the early films was Germany's silent expressionistic classic, *The Cabinet of Dr. Caligari* (1919). The shadowy, disturbing, nightmarish quality of "Caligari" was brought to Hollywood in the 1920s, and continued into the classic period of horror films in the 1930s. Before then, Hollywood was reluctant to experiment with the themes of true horror films. Instead, the studios took popular stage plays and emphasized their mystery genre features, providing rational explanations for all the supernatural and occult elements.

One actor who helped pave the way for the change in outlook and acceptance of the genre was Lon Chaney, known as "the man of a thousand faces." He starred in numerous silent horror films beginning in 1913, including the early *The Hunchback of Notre Dame* (1924) and his most memorable portrayal of Erik, the disfigured bitter composer of the Paris Opera in the groundbreaking, vividly-frightening film, *The Phantom of the Opera* (1925).

Many of these early silent classics would be remade during the talkies era. For example, John Barrymore starred in the first version of the Jekyll/Hyde story, a silent film titled *Dr. Jekyll and Mr. Hyde* (1920). It was later remade in two noteworthy versions: Fredric March's Oscar-winning portrayal of the transformed scientist in director Rouben Mamoulian's *Dr. Jekyll and Mr. Hyde* (1932), and Victor Fleming's MGM production of *Dr. Jekyll and Mr. Hyde* (1941), starring Spencer Tracy in the title role and Ingrid Bergman as the "wicked" girlfriend.

By the early 1930s, horror entered into its classic phase in Hollywood— the Dracula and Frankenstein Eras. The studios took tales of European vampires and undead aristocrats, mad scientists, and invisible men and created some of the most archetypal creatures and monsters ever known for the screen. The studio best known for its pure horror films and its classic horror stars, Bela Lugosi and Boris Karloff, was Universal Pictures.

With Tod Browning's direction, Universal produced a film version of Lugosi's Broadway success about a blood-sucking vampire named *Dracula* (1931), released early in the year. The film adaptation of Bram Stoker's novel played upon fears of sexuality, blood, and the nebulous period between life and death. The first Dracula film was followed closely by James Whale's masterful monster/horror film of Mary Shelley's novel, *Frankenstein* (1931), the quintessential combination of science fiction and horror in a "mad doctor" thriller. Boris Karloff's poignant portrayal of the Monster's plight gave a personality to the outcast, uncomprehending creature.

Without resorting to an existing literary horror figure, such as       11
Frankenstein, Dracula, Dr. Jekyll and Mr. Hyde, or The Invisible Man, Universal also created a new and "original" creature—the werewolf—in two films. The first werewolf film was *The Werewolf of London* (1935). The second and most famous was the excellent B-grade film *The Wolf Man* (1941), with Lon Chaney, Jr. in his first appearance. The "transformation" scene from man-to-wolf, involving complicated cosmetic/makeup artistry, is remarkably realistic. Unfortunately, the Wolf Man role hopelessly typecast Chaney, Jr. for life—he was forced to star in a series of very poor sequels, teamed up with other Universal horror stars in B-grade films including *Frankenstein Meets the Wolfman* (1943), and in two films adding Dracula to the mix: *House of Frankenstein* (1944) and *House of Dracula* (1945). The worst ignominy suffered by Chaney, Jr. was in Universal-International's comedy *Abbott and Costello Meet Frankenstein* (1948).

Other classic horror films of the 1930s and early 1940s include Tod       12
Browning's unusual *Freaks* (1932), Claude Rains as *The Invisible Man* (1933) in Universal's critically acclaimed film version of H.G. Wells' novel, Charles Laughton as the horribly deformed bellringer in the excellent *The Hunchback of Notre Dame* (1939), and Claude Rains again in the remake of *Phantom of the Opera* (1943). Notable films with living dead, "zombie" plots included Universal's classic *The Mummy* (1932) with Boris Karloff in the title role—his second Monster role success (and Lon Chaney, Jr., in the title role in 40s sequels), Bela Lugosi's performance in *White Zombie* (1932) and Val Lewton's B-masterpiece production *I Walked With a Zombie* (1943) (see below). One of the best adventure/horror films of all time is the "beauty and the beast" classic *King Kong* (1933).

Dracula films and sequels, although more common, were less successful       13
than many of the superb Frankenstein sequels. Universal Studios churned out more Dracula sagas in the 30s and 40s, including the first sequel *Dracula's Daughter* (1936) featuring a female vampire, and Robert Siodmak's *Son of Dracula* (1943), with Lon Chaney, Jr. in the starring role as the vampire. Britain's Hammer Studios, as they did with Frankenstein sequels in the 50s, reinvigorated the Bram Stoker novel by remaining faithful to the material in a spectacular Technicolor sequel. Talented director Terence Fisher (with Christopher Lee as the reclusive Count Dracula and Peter Cushing as Dr. Van Helsing) created the classic *The Horror of Dracula* (1958).

The witty Frankenstein sequel *Bride of Frankenstein* (1935), directed by       14
James Whale, outdid the original—it was a marvelous mixture of humor, classic terror, and unforgettable images—including Elsa Lanchester as the spectacular bride. Together, Lugosi and Karloff starred in three films together, the best being *The Black Cat* (1934). Karloff's last film as Frankenstein's Monster was *Son of Frankenstein* (1939)—it was one of the best sequels before many

inferior creations in the 1940s and 50s, such as *The Ghost of Frankenstein* (1942), starring Lon Chaney, Jr. as the Monster, or the campy *I Was a Teenage Frankenstein* (1957).

The first of six installments of Frankenstein sequels from Britain's 15 Hammer Studios (pairing actor Peter Cushing in the starring role as Baron von Frankenstein with director Terence Fisher), *The Curse of Frankenstein* (1957), was soon followed by *The Revenge of Frankenstein* (1958) and *The Evil of Frankenstein* (1964). The fourth and best of the Peter Cushing/ Frankenstein movies was *Frankenstein Created Woman* (1967).

Val Lewton, using a more subtle, suggestive, eerie approach in a number 16 of atmospheric, sophisticated horror/suspense films, produced eleven low-budget films for RKO Studios in the 1940s, directed first by Jacques Tourneur, and then by Mark Robson and Robert Wise. Lewton's first film, directed by Tourneur in his feature-film debut, was the suspenseful horror classic *The Cat People* (1942), possibly the first horror film to never show its monster. Through 1948, Tourneur also contributed *I Walked With a Zombie* (1943), *The Seventh Victim* (1943), *Ghost Ship* (1943), *Bedlam* (1945), and *Isle of the Dead* (1945). (Years later, Tourneur returned only once to the horror genre with *Curse of the Demon* (1957), a film which demonstrated Lewton's influence. Tourneur is most famous for the film noir classic *Out of the Past* (1947).) The most influential of Lewton's directors was Robert Wise, who created such classics as *The Curse of the Cat People* (1944) and *The Body Snatcher* (1945), and then later in his career directed *The Haunting* (1963). One of the best ghost/supernatural films ever made is *The Uninvited* (1944).

Many of the films in the horror genre from the mid-1930s to the late 17 1950s were B-grade movies, inferior sequels, or atrocious low-budget gimmick films. In the atomic age of the 1950s, most of the monster films were cheaply made, drive-in, grade-Z films. A few American-made monster/horror films of the time, however, effectively capitalized on terrorizing threats that were extraterrestrial powers, such as the alien found in the Arctic in *The Thing (From Another World)* (1951), the aberrant or alien threat in Don Siegel's classic *Invasion of the Body Snatchers* (1956), or the unusual monsters in *The Creature From the Black Lagoon* (1954), a film originally shown in 3-D, *The Blob* (1958) and *The Fly* (1958).

Horror films branched out in all different directions in the 1960s and 18 after, especially as the Production Code disappeared and film censorship was on the decline. Horror could be found in the dark shadows of the human soul itself as in the psychopathic Bates Motel operator in *Psycho* (1960), in the modern gothic thriller starring two aging Hollywood actresses, *What Ever Happened to Baby Jane?* (1962), in the preacher with "love" and "hate" tattooed on his hands in *The Night of the Hunter* (1955), in writer Stephen King's story of a schoolgirl possessed with telekinetic powers in director Brian de Palma's film *Carrie* (1976), or in the crazed husband in a hotel closed and snowbound for the winter in another Stephen King tale, *The Shining* (1980), masterfully directed by Stanley Kubrick. Horrible conflicts could occur with supernatural monsters as in *Alien* (1979) necessitating a superhuman power or effort to destroy the threatening evil. Roman Polanski's *Rosemary's Baby* (1968) dared to show the struggle of a young pregnant woman against witches and the forces of the devil, culminating in her delivery and mothering of the devil's child. Some of the better devil-possession sequels include: *The Omen* (1976), *The Amityville Horror* (1979), and *Poltergeist* (1982).

The horror genre has recently been subject to violence, sadism, brutality,   19
victims of possession, and blood-and-gore tales. Some of the most effective box-office successes include George Romero's unrelenting, low-budget cult classic, *Night of the Living Dead* (1968), the camp classic *It's Alive!* (1974), Tobe Hooper's exploitative cult film *The Texas Chainsaw Massacre* (1974), the manipulative *The Exorcist* (1973) with a devil-possessed young girl, *Halloween* (1978), Brian DePalma's suspenseful, Hitchcock-like *Dressed to Kill* (1980), *Friday the 13th* (1980) (which produced seven more sequels), and Wes Craven's *A Nightmare on Elm Street* (1985). Many of these films told tales of a vengeful murderer motivated by some past misdeed or sexual perversity.

These successful horror films spawned many inferior, sickening slasher   20
films which highlight shock, violence, and usually a homicidal male psycho who commits a string of gruesome murders of female victims (where brutal killing/slashing/hacking metaphorically substitutes for a rape). Examples include *Mother's Day* (1980), *Motel Hell* (1980), *Prom Night* (1980), *He Knows You're Alone* (1981), *I Spit On Your Grave* (1981), *My Bloody Valentine* (1981), the comedy parody *Student Bodies* (1981), *Sorority House Massacre* (1986), and all the *Halloween*, *Poltergeist*, and *A Nightmare on Elm Street* sequels.

## SELECTION OF GREATEST HORROR FILMS
GREATEST EARLY CLASSIC HORROR FILMS:
*The Phantom of the Opera* (1925)
*Dracula* (1931)
*Frankenstein* (1931)
*Dr. Jekyll and Mr. Hyde* (1932)
*Freaks* (1932)
*The Mummy* (1932)
*The Old Dark House* (1932)
*White Zombie* (1932)
*The Invisible Man* (1933)
*King Kong* (1933)
*The Black Cat* (1934)
*Bride of Frankenstein* (1935)
*The Hunchback of Notre Dame* (1939)

OTHER GREATEST HORROR FILMS:
*The Wolf Man* (1941)
*The Cat People* (1942)
*I Walked With a Zombie* (1943)
*Phantom of the Opera* (1943)
*The Uninvited* (1944)
*The Body Snatcher* (1945)

*The Picture of Dorian Gray (1945)*
*The Thing (From Another World) (1951)*
*House of Wax (1953)*
*Creature From the Black Lagoon (1954)*
*The Night of the Hunter (1955)*
*Invasion of the Body Snatchers (1956)*
*The Fly (1958)*
*Psycho (1960)*
*The Innocents (1961)*
*What Ever Happened to Baby Jane? (1962)*
*The Birds (1963)*
*The Haunting (1963)*
*Repulsion (1965)*
*Night of the Living Dead (1968)*
*Rosemary's Baby (1968)*
*The Exorcist (1973)*
*It's Alive! (1974)*
*The Texas Chainsaw Massacre (1974)*
*Jaws (1975)*
*Carrie (1976)*
*Halloween (1978)*
*Alien (1979)*
*Dressed to Kill (1980)*
*Friday the 13th (1980)*
*The Shining (1980)*
*The Howling (1981)*
*The Evil Dead (1982)*
*Poltergeist (1982)*
*Gremlins (1984)*
*A Nightmare on Elm Street (1985)*
*The Fly (1986)*
*Evil Dead 2: Dead by Dawn (1987)*
*Beetlejuice (1988)*
*Misery (1990)*
*The People Under the Stairs (1991)*
*Buffy the Vampire Slayer (1992)*
*Body Snatchers (1994)*
*Scream (1996)*

■   ■   ■

## Review Questions

1. How do science fiction films differ from horror films, according to Dirks?
2. What is the literary origin of the horror film genre?

## Discussion and Writing Suggestions

1. In the first part of his discussion, Dirks focuses on the power of horror films to both frighten and entertain us. "They deal with our most primal nature and its fears," he writes, "our vulnerability, our alienation, our

terror of the unknown, our fear of death, loss of identity, or fear of sexuality." To what extent does this conclusion—and other parts of Dirks's discussion—accurately describe your own experience with horror films? Refer to particular films and particular scenes in these films, and explain how they derive their power.

2. Select one or two films that did not make Dirks's list of great horror films (or which were made too recently to make the list) and explain why you believe they should be added to the list. What, in your view, makes a great horror film—as opposed to a merely good or competent one? As an alternative to this assignment, select one or two films that did make Dirks's list, but shouldn't have, in your opinion. Explain your reasoning.

3. Rent and view one of the films listed as a classic by Dirks. Then, critically review it, focusing in particular upon how it works (or does not work) its power. Try to cast your discussion in the terms used by Dirks in the first three paragraphs of his essay. For example, what kind of "vulnerabilities" in us does a film such as *Invasion of the Body Snatchers* or *The Fly* target? How does a film such as *Rosemary's Baby* tap into "the horror within man himself"?

## Horrors, They're Back

### JAY BOYAR

*Jay Boyar has been the movie critic of the* Orlando Sentinel *since 1982. His reviews also appear on MSNBC, E! Entertainment Television and National Public Radio (the non-commercial U.S. counterpart to Canada's CBC) as well as in major U.S. magazines and newspapers. Boyar also teaches film studies and his critical work has been recognized in the form of awards from the Associated Press, the Florida Society of Newspaper Editors and the Society of Professional Journalists, as well as a Pulitzer Prize nomination.*

*In this article from the* Montreal Gazette *(1998), he explains how horror movies changed with* Scream, *moving on from the cliches of the slasher movies which had been popular in the eighties.*

At first, a slight shifting of soil. A rat, perhaps? Or the wind? Then, suddenly, a big clump of earth is shoved aside as a gaunt, icy arm stretches out from the grave.   1

It's back—back from the dead!   2

The horror movie is back!   3

What do you mean, you didn't know it was dead?   4

Well, somewhere in the mid-'80s, horror films were killed off—or, at least, thoroughly marginalized—largely by their own repetitiousness. Cheap, exploitative sequels to slasher flicks like *Halloween* (1978), *Friday the 13th* (1980) and *A Nightmare on Elm Street* (1984) lost much of their bloody zing, even for their ghoulish core audience.   5

"If you do sequels to *Halloween,* there's really no more of a story,"  6
complained *Halloween* director John Carpenter, who feels that his deliberately vague, suggestively supernatural villain, Michael Myers, was "kind of ruined" in the sequels. "All you're going to do is expose the fact that it (the original) was a very delicate dance."

But two years ago—just when you thought it was safe to go back to  7
the movies—*Scream* premiered. Directed by Wes Craven (*A Nightmare on Elm Street*), it shocked many industry observers by promptly becoming a blockbuster.

"*Scream* really revitalized the genre," said Carpenter, who dubs it a  8
"know-it-all" teen movie. "It recast horror for a very cynical, postmodern generation of young kids. . . . It let them be superior to the narrative."

According to author James B. Twitchell, much of that film's appeal was  9
based on its implicit assumption that the horror audience was knowledgeable about, and even fed up with, the cliches of slasher movies—the lunatic killers, the scary masks, the cheesy "danger" music, etc. So even as it served up fresh shocks, *Scream* also made fun of those stale devices.

## WINK-WINK, STAB-STAB

"*Scream* makes a lot of wink-wink jokes that say, 'You've seen it all before,'"  10
observed Twitchell, whose books include *Dreadful Pleasures: An Anatomy of Modem Horror* and *Living Dead: A Study of the Vampire in Romantic Literature.* "There's a lot of wink-wink and a lot of stab-stab."

The all-but-inevitable *Scream 2* soon followed, along with *I Know What*  11
*You Did Last Summer* (written by *Scream* scripter Kevin Williamson). And now, on Halloween weekend, the aftershocks of *Scream*'s success are really being felt. There are eight horror or semi-horror movies currently in theatres or just about to open—nine if you count *The Rocky Horror Picture Show* (1975), which always seems to be playing some place or other.

The list includes John Carpenter's *Vampires, Halloween: H20* (which,  12
like the other *Halloween* sequels, Carpenter did not direct), *Bride of Chucky, Blade, Urban Legend* and at least parts of *Beloved, Practical Magic* and *Apt Pupil.* Coming up in the next several months, we can look forward to *I Still Know What You Did Last Summer,* remakes of *Psycho* and *The Mummy,* a biopic about James Whale (the director of the 1931 *Frankenstein*) called *Gods and Monsters,* and, no kidding, *Freddy vs. Jason.* Talk about a revival.

When it comes to horror flicks, there are two kinds of people in this  13
world—those who believe that any horror movie that has managed to shock, jar, startle or gross them out, however briefly or superficially, must be a masterpiece, and those who hold out for a deeper, more profoundly disturbing level of terror. In the former category are mostly teenagers and early twenty-somethings, said Twitchell—people with insecurities, psychosexual and otherwise, that often find expression in trashy tales from the cinematic crypt. Carpenter agrees. "There's a lot of fear that goes with moving into adulthood," he reflected. "All those things are dealt with in a horror film... . . .

They're presented to young audiences in a way that doesn't affect them directly, couched in a theatrical, horror idea.

"You see, that makes it safer."     14

As far as this youthful, thrill-seeking crowd is concerned, the bloodier     15
and less artful the horror is, the better. "The horror film, at one level, is always a roller coaster," said Twitchell, who added that the clientele for the cheap-thrill flicks is almost identical to that for thrill rides.

Janet Leigh does not belong to the "roller coaster" crowd. And she certainly     16
ought to know something about horror movies, having starred in Alfred Hitchcock's great classic, *Psycho* (1960), and having appeared in the single most famous horror scene of all time, the dazzling shower sequence from that very film.

"If it's a cheap shot, then it's a cheap shot," said Leigh, whose witty, self-     17
referential appearance as a school administrator in *Halloween: H20* (starring daughter Jamie Lee Curtis) was that movie's most gracious grace note. The actress has little patience for any filmmaker whose motto is, as she puts it:

"All we're going to do, here, now, is we're going to make this as bloody     18
as possible."

The glut of those bloody films in the late '80s and early '90s so devalued     19
the term "horror movie" that some of the best examples of the form seemed forced to fly under other colours.

"*The Silence of the Lambs* (1991) was a horror film that did extremely     20
well," said Carpenter. "*Fatal Attraction* (1987) was a horror film. I mean, those are big-budget, big-star horror films that don't appear to be horror films."

"It may have been just a marketing decision," speculated Twitchell, who     21
teaches at the University of Florida in Gainesville. "They didn't think the market was there, so they called them something else."

Adults did go to these kinds of films, but these were the exceptions. In     22
fact, Carpenter suspects that the older we get—and the closer we get to death—the less standard horror films have to say to us. "As we get older, we confront the fact that there is an end out there," he said. "We see it in our friends, maybe some of our loved ones, our parents.

"We become less interested in movie horror because real-life horror is all     23
too present."

True cinematic horror—the kind that gets into your bones and keeps you     24
up nights—is as rare as it is disturbing. Director Bryan Singer (*The Usual Suspects*), who describes his new film, *Apt Pupil,* as "very much a horror movie," is on the same page with Janet Leigh when it comes to what he calls "thrill ride" films.

"You don't really ever really, really get scared" at them, said Singer,     25
whose *Apt Pupil* is based on a Stephen King novella. The director prefers what he calls "the real horror films," like *The Shining* (1980, another King adaptation), *The Exorcist* (1973) and *The Innocents* (1961, based on the Henry James novella *The Turn of the Screw*).

## GOOD AND EVIL

"Movies like that really scare me," said Singer, whose new film concerns the 26
evil influence of a Nazi war criminal on a fresh-faced suburban teen.

For Leigh, the credibility of the characters is a key issue—whether the 27
movie is a horror picture or a comedy or a film noir like her newly re-edited
and reissued *Touch of Evil* (1958). "If you believe the person, then the situation will be there and the audience will react to the situation like the person
does," she said. "If it's phony, then it's not going to take at all, whatever genre
that you're portraying."

In the case of a specially well-established horror sub-genre, like the vam- 28
pire movie, film-makers sometimes become so distracted by playing around
with the trappings of the form and the newest glitzy special effects that they
lose sight of the characters and the story. With *Blade,* which he co-produced
and starred in, Wesley Snipes tried to keep his eye on the larger dimensions of
his film.

"It's a movie about good and evil," he said. "Very classic, simple story. . . . 29
We've got great visuals, great special effects—that's all good. But if you don't
have a story that people can relate to and vibe with, they're not going again."

Like the filmmakers of the late '80s and early '90s who avoided the 30
horror label, Snipes doesn't even call *Blade* a vampire movie. Carpenter also
resists that classification for his latest effort, even though it is titled John
Carpenter's *Vampires.* "There's a little biting and some fangs, but it's a
Western," he said. *"The Wild Bunch* meets *Vlad the Impaler:* Whaddaya think?"

Perhaps the main problem with most exploitation flicks is simply that 31
they're not suggestive enough. That, anyway, is the conclusion of Melanie
Griffith, who starred in one of the most unsettling films of the '80s, Brian De
Palma's *Body Double* (1984).

"Where they go wrong, is when they show too much," offered Griffith, 32
whose mother, Tippi Hedren, was Hitchcock's leading lady in *The Birds* and
*Marnie.* "Like with Hitchcock, that was all in your imagination. ... Obviously,
you saw certain things. But a lot of it has to do with how much a director can
leave up to the audience's imagination."

Now that the creature—the horror movie—once again roams the Earth, 33
this might be worth bearing in mind.

■ ■ ■

## *Discussion and Writing Suggestions*

1. Look up the term "postmodern" in a current dictionary and jot down a
   working definition. How does your definition fit with the one implied by
   the article?
2. Do you agree with the author that audiences want more than blood
   and gore?

3. The author says that real cinematic horror—"the kind that gets into your bones and keeps you up nights"—is rare. Can you name a truly frightening movie and provide several reasons to explain your choice?

## It's Our Brains That Scare Us

VINAY MENON

*Vinay Menon started writing for* The Toronto Star *in 1994 and has been its pop culture reporter since 1998. The following article was published in* The Toronto Star *in 1999. Rather than emphasizing the psychological appeal of horror, he examines how the experience of watching horror films stimulates physical reactions that account for viewer interest.*

Hidden in foreboding shadows, the killer clutches a serrated butcher knife and creeps toward his unsuspecting victim.   1

The musical score—swirling minor notes and jarring, off-tempo beats— intensifies. You swallow hard. He moves behind his female prey and slowly raises his weapon. Your heart rate accelerates.   2

Suddenly, she spins around and sees the intruder. Her eyes get saucer-big. You start to sweat. She lets out a piercing, guttural scream. Adrenaline rushes into your blood.   3

He slashes downward, thrusting the cold steel into her warm flesh. Your breathing gets shorter. She shrieks. The hairs on the back of your neck stand up. You're afraid.   4

And just like that, the symbiotic relationship between horror movies and viewer physiology is, again, successfully tested.   5

"Horror movies are all about the physiology of fear," explains James Twitchell, a professor of English at University of Florida and author of *Dreadful Pleasures: An Anatomy of Modern Horror.*   6

"It really is a physical sensation. It's about getting to that state where you think, 'Oh, my God, I'm in danger.'"   7

And in darkened theatres throughout North America this summer, limbic systems and other neurostructures are being treated to an endless array of fear-arousing stimuli. Everything from the subliminal power of dark suggestion in *The Blair Witch Project* to more traditional explorations of the paranormal in *The Sixth Sense* and *The Haunting.*   8

And whether they realize it or not, horror genre directors and script writers are all hoping to connect with a viewer's amygdala—an almond-shaped mass of gray matter in the brain's temporal lobe.   9

"That area becomes active when you are frightened," says John Yeomans, a professor of psychology at the University of Toronto who studies neural pathways and the startle reflex.   10

When something unexpectedly happens onscreen—a crashing sound, say, 11
or a masked face suddenly appearing from behind a closet door—the amygdala can get activated.

Connected to the amygdala are descending neural pathways which can, 12
in turn, activate other brainstem pathways.

"It's known that startle is activated by a set of giant neurons in the 13
brainstem," explains Yeomans.

"And these big neurons then activate a whole series of motor neurons 14
throughout the brain stem and spinal chord. And that makes you jump."

And whether it's caused by a possessed Linda Blair speaking in tongues 15
in *The Exorcist* or Jamie Lee Curtis shrieking with abandon in *Halloween*,
another physiological sign of fear is horripilation—or "the lifting of the hairs
on the nape of the neck," as Twitchell defines it.

Clark McCauley, professor of psychology at Bryn Mawr College in 16
Pennsylvania, says teenagers are particularly drawn to the genre's engrossing,
visceral sensations because they allow them to engage in "mastery testing."

"Young people, whether they realize it or not, often want to sit through 17
a film without closing their eyes to see if they can do it."

And young couples—a mainstay in horror film lineups—often watch 18
horror films to play out socially constructed gender roles.

"Males are supposed to be strong and unresponsive and females are sup- 19
posed to be upset and dependent. This is called the 'snuggle theory.' And
horror movies give both sides a chance to do a little snuggling," says
McCauley, adding that the key in all of this is simulated risk. "After all, if
people really thought that the terrible things happening on screen were really
going on, they would be up out of their seats calling for the Marines."

Says Twitchell: "The key, always, is that one part of your brain knows 20
you are not at risk and the other part knows you are running the risk."

For young viewers, especially children who have not developed a stable 21
world view, these risks can transcend simulation and become all too real.

"It's an age-dependent thing," says Yeomans. 22

"Young children are not at all attracted to frightening things. If it's really 23
frightening, they don't want anything to do with it."

■  ■  ■

## Discussion and Writing Suggestions

1. Menon emphasizes that what we see influences how we feel—our bodily
   sensations. Does this argument help to explain why some people enjoy
   and some loathe horror films?
2. Have you had any of the physical reactions Menon describes while
   watching horror cinema? Are the feelings the author describes rewarding
   on some level?

# The Cronenberg Monster: Literature, Science, and Psychology in the Cinema of Horror

ROBERT HAAS

*Robert Haas is the author of a book entitled* Haunted Mind: The Supernatural in Victorian Fiction. *His article appeared in a 1995 special issue of the American scholarly journal* Postscript, *on Canadian filmmaker David Cronenberg. In it, he explores some of the ways in which Cronenberg has presented the integration of human and machine as disastrous or monstrous.*

Over the past 20 years, the films of David Cronenberg have remained remark-    1
ably consistent in subject matter and theme. Exploring his own conception of the nature of horror (often with bloody excess), his initial films are at first dismissed as grade "z" horror films, relegated to second feature drive-in status. However, over the past 20 years, Cronenberg's films have matured; evolved, perhaps even mutated into complex examinations of the human condition. And, while the visceral nature of his early films may have been largely stripped away in his later work, his original vision and perspective regarding the nature of horror have been maintained, mostly through a creative decision to remain independent of the Hollywood system. Whether one likes his work or not, ultimately it demands attention. Contemporary film and cultural scholars are approaching Cronenberg's films from remarkably diverse critical perspectives, observing that his work is often free of the conventions and limitations that plague directors ensconced in Hollywood franchises and studio politics. Everyone, it seems, has something to say about Cronenberg and his films, even Cronenberg himself. In an interview from the book *Dark Visions*, David Cronenberg is asked what led him to remake *The Fly*, a film first released in the 1950s through the Hollywood system. He replies:

> Immediate thoughts of remaking the original *Fly* would lead you to think that maybe I'd do some type of campy film and maybe get Vincent Price to do a cameo, which I believe another production was going to do. That would make it something else, not bad, but not something that I would be interested in. It was really reading the script I was given that had some elements in it that really struck me as being very powerful and very much me. (Wiater 37)

The idea that a David Cronenberg film must be, according to the director    2
himself, "very much me," is a key to understanding the unique and independent body of work that Cronenberg has amassed. Because Cronenberg's professional career spans almost 25 years, special emphasis must be placed on multiple perspectives addressing issues concerning who Cronenberg is and how that relates to his work. Is there a conscious renewal in each film of Cronenberg's original theme of the visceral nature of human beings? Does this theme evolve with each new film or does it stagnantly repeat itself? Does a

diminution of blood diminish this theme in his later work? Is Cronenberg a misogynist? Given that Cronenberg was originally a literature major at the University of Toronto, do literary allusions permeate his work? Indeed, what is the influence of classical literature on this distinctly modern (and often post-modern) director? How has his use of language evolved throughout his career? What about Cronenberg's reliance on psychology? Is he able to translate abstract psychological concepts into screen images? Can visceral and surreal-istic images coexist on screen? While there are many approaches to answering these questions, one consistent element occurs within all of Cronenberg's work. In the films of David Cronenberg, these themes revolve around the role of the monster: a being so conventionalized in past films that it becomes prob-lematic and an area of discovery for both the director and the audience.

## THE MONSTERS AND THEIR MAKER

With respect to the narratives of Cronenberg and specifically the role of the monster(ous) in those narratives, many of Cronenberg's films rely largely on the conventions of classical gothic fiction, but with a difference: none of his films maintain the romantic ideology concerning man and his relationship to nature and God so often found in other films dealing with gothic monsters. Also, although many Cronenberg monsters maintain a strong connection to the great gothic monsters of early '30s films (especially *Frankenstein* and *Dr. Jekyll and Mr. Hyde*), and employ various conventions of gothic cinema throughout the narrative, Cronenberg still manages to create a purely post-modern creature—a combination of that easily recognized cinematically gothic monster and an infinitely more complex monster: a cyborg in the Harawayian sense, by which I mean one who is able to move beyond the boundaries of classically structured gothic narratives, psychological analysis, mythology, science, medicine and sexual identity, one who can operate within the blurred boundaries of all of these disparate elements.

    Any notion of Cronenberg's films being throwbacks to the classic gothic horror films of the '30s is in fact not necessarily an inaccurate description of his work. After the glut of post–World War II nuclear monster films, the Hammer series of Dracula and Frankenstein films from England, and the low-budget gothic visions of Roger Corman and William Castle, Cronenberg, like the earlier gothic film makers, emphasizes grotesque elements, the mys-terious, the desolate environment, the horrible, the ghostly, and ultimately, the abject fear that is aroused in the viewer. Additional gothic conventions within Cronenberg's film include the sense of enclosure as events occur within the confines of a warehouse laboratory (*The Fly*), a self-contained apartment complex (*They Came From Within*), or the inner recesses of one's own mind (*Naked Lunch*), causing the viewer to be removed from everyday environ-ments (a tactic Poe would have been all in favour of). One of the primary aims of the gothic narrative is to create the single effect of an eerie and ghostly atmosphere, and to do so the narrative emphasizes the physical aspects of var-ious structures: the vastness of the warehouse-factory filled with machinery and experimental equipment in *The Fly*, the sterile environment of the Mantle Twins' apartment in *Dead Ringers*, or the "interiorized" set-like quality of Interzone in *Naked Lunch*. Finally, like most gothic monsters, Cronenberg's characters are often at first super-sensitive heroes who cannot function in conventional society. Johnny Smith (*The Dead Zone*), Seth Brundle (*The Fly*), Beverly Mantle (*Dead Ringers*), and Bill Lee (*Naked Lunch*) all attempt to share their super-sensitivity to the point of maladjustment, but due to physical appearance, supernatural mental abilities or instabilities often induced by experimental drugs, these attempts always ultimately fail.

However, more than just recreating the gothic, Cronenberg rethinks   5 what it means to be a monster in an age of postmodernism. *The Fly* is the only Cronenberg "monster" film in any traditional sense (unless you count the cheesy looking slug of *They Came From Within* as a monster). But, even then the approach to creating any monster for Cronenberg could never be simplistic or conventional. In fact, Brundlefly, the monster in *The Fly,* is a heterogeneous combination of many conventions, including gothic, classic '50s science fiction, contemporary science fiction, and cyberpunk, combined with Cronenberg's own visceral conception of the body turned against itself and inside out (graphically foreshadowed by the bloody baboon found in the telepod after one of Brundle's early experiments).

Now there is a tendency by many to retain a firm belief in Brundlefly as   6 a pure extension of gothic symbolic imagery. Another perspective regards the monster of *The Fly* as a creature solely from the domain of science fiction. Some critics see simplistic combinations of both of these elements. Thomas Dougherty in his *Film Quarterly* review of *The Fly* states that "patched though the director's own transmission devices, *The Fly* fuses old time science fiction with new age sexual friction" (39). Ultimately, Brundlefly works best, I think, as a fusion of many disparate elements. A combination of insect, human, and machine; sexless; driven by instinct but possessing some semblance of intellect up to the end; suffused with a mimetic sense of humanity and pathos, Cronenberg's monster transcends conventional and contemporary representations of monsters. It is not undead, not an alien, not a mad demonic slasher. It is a gothic cyborg, existing only as a fiction but imbued with science fact, medical relevance, and psychological musings concerning what it means to be a man or a bug in contemporary society.

Now, to say that all of Cronenberg's monsters are cyborgs is not entire-   7 ly accurate either. Implicit in any definition of a cyborg is the idea that it is a "successful" integration between machine and flesh. Brundlefly is not. Max Renn in *Videodrome* is not. The integration between human and animal and machine, between science and nature, between the mind and the body is, in fact, disastrous in every Cronenberg film.

## CRONENBERG'S CYBORG CINEMA

Horror and science fiction films have never been too particular concerning   8 definitions of monsters (or cyborgs); they include a wide range of types and can be found in a vast number of films spanning the 85 years since Thomas Edison's "one reeler" *Frankenstein* (1911) and Karel Capek's play *R.U.R.* (1920). From *Metropolis* (1925), and *Dr. Jekyll and Mr. Hyde* (1931), to *Alien* (1979), *Blade Runner* (1982), *The Terminator* (1984), and even *The X Files,* many films (and television shows) have effectively developed the public's multi-dimensional conception concerning the intersection between science and horror. However, this intersection, especially in relationship to humans, has never been especially complex, whether they appear malicious, beneficent, or something in-between flesh and machine.

By "successful," I mean that the cyborg as represented on film is, regard-   9
less of motivation, somehow superior to the human(s) who created it. James Whale's Frankenstein Monster is physically a haphazard collection of carrion and metal bolts. Yet it displays superhuman physical abilities, resiliency, and (through Karloff's performance) a sympathetic connection with the audience that qualify it as a successful creation. Likewise, Ridley Scott's Roy Batty, the genetically replicated, programmed, and manufactured off-world slave leader from *Blade Runner*, displays superiority not only through his physical accomplishments, but also through his emotional and ethical development. Harrison Ford's Decker becomes a mere cipher through which the audience watches the development and the destruction of a better human than the humans.

Cronenberg's cyborgs are unusual, for rarely do they advance morally or   10
even physically beyond human limitations; here the cyborg more often regresses and, through accident and chance, can meld both animal and machine to create a genetic monster (the "new flesh" of *Rabid, Videodrome,* and *The Fly*), or the mind and the body to create neither man nor animal nor machine, but something "other" (*The Brood, Scanners, The Dead Zone, Dead Ringers,* and *Naked Lunch*).

Therefore Cronenberg's genetically or psychically altered scientists, doctors,   11
writers and teachers can only be considered as an alternative to conventional images of the cyborg. However, these images not only allow for unsuccessful meldings of flesh and machine, but also allow for disaster. Only here do they become closely allied with other cinematic representations of cyborgs.

Historically, the cyborg has stood for the radical anxiety of human con-   12
sciousness about its own embodiment, at the moment embodiment appears almost fully contingent. Cyborg anxiety has stood for an oscillation between the "human" element associated with affections, eros, error, innovation (projects begun in the face of mortality) and the "machine" element (the desire for long life, health, physical impermeability, self-contained control processes, dependability, and hence the ability to fulfill promises over the long term) (Csisery-Ronay 399).

Throughout the history of cinema, the cyborg has fit into two distinct   13
roles, largely stemming from this anxiety, anxiety that is in no small way bound up with romantic and gothic assertions concerning humans and their relationship with God: the first is the physically superior but morally inferior superman and the second is the tragic technological monster (albeit still

functionally superior to humans). In *Frankenstein,* the monster is destroyed for the sake of humanity, demonstrating, "through sentimental nostalgia, the superior value of God's favorite creature just the way He made him" (Csisery-Ronay 398). This romantic/religious sentiment is easily identifiable. An idealistic scientist reflects on God and nature early on in the narrative and by the end, before he places his head under the drill press, or is thrown off a windmill, declares through tried and true cliche that "there are some things mankind shouldn't tamper with."

Another typical definition of a cyborg insists that there is all exaggeration    14 of the body/intellect dualism plugged into a form of cinematic prosthesis. In *Blade Runner,* the replicants (cyborgs) generate and absorb dread, possibly because human beings, without knowledge of the original conditions of their construction, have no way of knowing the degree to which the body and mind can be considered distinct (if they can at all). Additionally, humans have no other way to approach the "renegade replicant" problem other than through retirement (termination). This solution is ultimately ironic and inevitably parodic, since cyborgs already present difference even as they are despised for their similarities to humans.

A possible way to accept the gothic cyborg in Cronenberg as a monster    15 is to recognize the conflict between traditional examples of cyborgs so often found in science fiction cinema from *Frankenstein* to *Blade Runner* and the cyborg as defined by Donna Haraway in her essay "The Cyborg Manifesto: Science, Technology, and Socialist-Feminism in the Late Twentieth Century." Haraway's cyborg is not classically superhuman or necessarily monstrous, although it can assume monstrous proportions. Her cyborg is a theoretical object for which the schizo-physical body is not necessary, in the same way that Alan Turing, in *Mechanical Intelligence,* considered a machine to be "a set of operations, relations, algorithms, not necessarily a physical object" (254). Her cyborg is simultaneously object and subject, free of the conventional dialectics or narratives of power, yet constantly concerned with the machinations of power. Once the distinction between Cronenberg's character and the conventional cyborg in other science fiction films is recognized, then "Brundlefly" can be placed more specifically on the boundary between Haraway's theoretical cyborg, a creature that also lies on the boundaries of societal community, and the cinema's gothic monster creation.

Cronenberg's development of a creature both traditionally monstrous    16 and possessing qualities of a Harawayian cyborg is explored in *The Fly* through the techno-nightmare of the protagonist, Seth Brundle (Jeff Goldblum). A unique way of accomplishing this is created through an approach that rejects the phallocentric perspective normally associated with high-tech science fiction cyborg narratives. Cronenberg consistently dehumanizes the male protagonist, deemphasises the male perspective, and deobjectifies the female persona. So, in an attempt to move beyond the boundaries of monolithic perspective and narrative, the images chosen in *The Fly* often reject the empathetic relationship between audience and male hero/protagonist or audience and cyborg (although both relationships exist in the film).

Instead, they maintain an (inconsistent) reliance on alternatives proposed by Haraway, especially in her theories concerning cyborgs:

> The cyborg is a hybrid creature, composed of organism and machine. But, cyborgs are compounded of special kinds of machines and special kinds of organisms appropriate to the late twentieth century. Cyborgs are post Second World War hybrid entities made of, first, ourselves and other organic creatures in our unchosen "high-technological" guise as information systems, texts, and ergonomically controlled, labouring, desiring, and reproducing systems. The second essential ingredient in cyborgs is machines in their guise, also, as communications system, texts, and self acting, ergonomically designed apparatuses, (1)

## THE MIND-BODY SPLIT: THE FLY AND THE CRONENBERG SOLUTION

To best illustrate the idea of the monstrous cyborg as employed by David Cronenberg, let's look at one film: *The Fly*. In the world of Cronenberg's film, the fly becomes a pedagogical translation (or simulation) of Haraway's hypothetical definition of the cyborg as a "promising [gothic] monster": human, animal, and machine are literally spliced together on screen using the forms of Seth Brundle and the fly and the telepod that transports them. This new creation is methodically and painfully dehumanized over the course of the film— appendages fall off, food must be vomited on in order to be consumed, and superior intelligence is replaced by raw emotion. **17**

Presence and self-presence have been called into doubt by technology and subversion of gothic and science fiction conventions. According to the old school of scientific thought, or as Haraway calls it "the old boys of science," fusion, especially between narrative and boundary creature, is a bad strategy of positioning when attempting to envision the future. Yet, the character of Seth Brundle, in the narrative *The Fly*, places himself in the exact position: a boundary creature who transports himself through the telepods, a machine aptly described as a "designer phone booth," and, like the baboon who is turned inside out, is fused, but at the same time split into distinct (though not immediately obvious) selves: the scientist (the cyborg/man) and Brundlefly (the cyborg/monster). **18**

Central to the divergent concept of Brundlefly as cyborg/man and cyborg/monster in society is the split between Brundlefly and society. According to Haraway, "monsters have always defined the limits of community in western imaginations." (180) While this split is not nearly so clearly defined in *The Fly*, splitting in the context of *The Fly* should be about heterogeneous multiplicities that are simultaneously necessary and incapable of being squashed into isomorphic slots or cumulative lists. Brundle, the intellectual scientist, has noble passions for his work, for the betterment of society, as well as romantic passions for Ronnie. Brundlefly desperately attempts to retain some elements of reason in an effort to transform itself back into Brundle or a combination of Brundle, Ronnie, and their unborn child. **19**

To emphasize the loss of his humanity, Brundlefly even has moments of 20 poetic sadness as it recognizes its relationship to Kafka's dung beetle from "The Metamorphosis": "I was an insect who dreamed of being human, but now the dream is over." In the film's most moving scene, Brundlefly longs to be the first insect politician, the compassionate fly, but realizes that it is declining into raw instinct. It is an attempt to become a Haraway cyborg that fails. Faced with the impossibility of its desire, Brundlefly begs Ronnie to run away before she is hurt.

Even when man, fly, and telepod are all successfully "spliced," the self 21 and other still exist. The creature that falls from the telepod at the film's climax is a tripartite creation of intelligence, passion, and technology—connected yet obviously separate. Brundle's quest for unity has failed and he remains forever apart from and outside of humanity. However, Cronenberg isn't entirely ready to do away with monolithic perception. With his body and mind completely transformed, Brundle painfully communicates his desire to die; this is a unique human decision and allows the audience a certain pathetic acknowledgment of Brundle's position. For a brief cathartic moment, the audience sees themselves mirrored in Brundle's suffering and then he is killed. Yet Brundle/Brundlefly maintains a unique place in cinema. He/it is a polymorphous, postmodern creation that exists neither in the gothic tradition nor in the boundaries wherein traditional boundary creatures lie. This monster exists outside the boundaries of both monster and cyborg. Cronenberg's Brundlefly is a creature never filmed before: a monster as failed cyborg.

## Works Cited

Csisery-Ronay, Istvan, Jr. "The Science Fiction of Theory: Baudrillard and Haraway." *Science Fiction Studies* 18.3 (1991): 387–405.

Dougherty, Thomas. "The Fly." *Film Quarterly* 40.1 (1987): 38–40.

Haraway, Donna J. "A Cyborg Manifesto: Science, Technology, and Socialist-Feminism in the Late Twentieth Century." *Simians, Cyborgs, and Women*. New York: Routledge, 1991. 149–182.

—. "Situated Knowledges: The Science Question in *Feminism* and the Privilege of Partial Perspective." *Simians: Cyborgs, and Women*. New York: Routledge, 1991. 183–202.

Mulvey, Laura. "Film and Visual Pleasure." *Film Theory and Criticism: Introductory Readings, Third Ed.* Gerald Mast and Marshall Cohen, Eds. New York: Oxford UP, 1985. 803–817.

Wiater, Stan. *Dark Visions: Conversations With the Masters of the Horror Film*. New York: Avon, 1992.

■ ■ ■

## Discussion and Writing Suggestions

1. The Fly is part human, part insect and part transformer pod, or machine. Can you think of other creatures that develop from this monstrous

recipe? Do any of them represent forces of good in the films or shows in which they appear? If so, how have they escaped doing the will of powers of evil, given their monstrous make-up?

2. Can you cull several points from this article that you might use to defend the genre of horror movies from the charge that they are strictly mindless "Grade B" entertainment?

# The Nightmare World

STANLEY J. SOLOMON

*In "The Nightmare World," Stanley J. Solomon defines the horror film as a safe environment in which to confront the violence and fear that pervade our lives. A film scholar and professor of English, Solomon provides a careful overview of the horror genre, defining its principal elements and distinguishing it from science fiction cinema—with which it shares some similarities. Like Stephen King and others in this chapter, though from an entirely different perspective, Solomon speaks to the duelling impulses in each of us. Horror movies give us a chance to recognize these impulses; in* The Wolf Man, *for instance, we see ourselves in the character who, on the rising of the full moon, becomes a werewolf. This selection appeared originally in Solomon's book-length study of cinema,* Beyond Formula: American Film Genres *(1976).*

[T]he horror genre, ultimately, is a major genre because major artists of our    1
time have worked seriously in it and produced notable films that range beyond the depiction of the horrific event to probe the nightmare world hidden in all of us. The conjuring up of monsters of the mind and the objectifying of them in the cinema is a symbolic form of exorcism, which very likely the general public intuitively grasped from the genre long before William Friedkin's *The Exorcist* (1973) popularized the subject. In an era that intellectually gives little credence to devils, witches, and monsters, but lives continuously with massive violence, perversion, and nihilism, the horror film provides us with a protected access to a nightmare world otherwise shunted outside of civilization by the twentieth-century forces of sophistication, science, and sociology.

The cinema of horror concretizes this nightmare world—our abstract fears    2
of destruction and death. The midnight visits of vampires, the laboratory-induced reincarnations, the skull deformities, the murders in the fog—these visual images of the genre may be the symbols of our fears rather than the psychological source of them, but terror without a body is terror deprived of a means of menacing us. Nevertheless, it is lamentable that along with the whole modern movement toward cinematic explicitness in all genres, the horror genre should in recent years have lost much of its suggestive power. The giant shark rising from the ocean in Steven Spielberg's *Jaws* (1975) is merely a familiar creature of the sea, and the havoc it creates confined to the physical world and sub-

ject to the laws of nature; it will not leave the beach with us. In contrast, Carl Dreyer's Danish film *Vampyr* (1932), a tour de force of implicit horror, seems only a remote ancestor of the blood-lust films of the seventies. However, the genre is still open to creative talents who can give form to the explicit materials demanded by producers for financial success, and still suggest the unlimited terrors lurking in the recesses of our nightmare world.

If the depiction of archetypal fears is one aspect of the genre, the process    3
whereby these fears become dramatic incidents in a film reveals at least two other genre traits: the degree of unpreparedness on the part of the endangered victim, and the vitality or strength of the source of horror. The source is never, for instance, merely a human murderer. It may turn out to be so later in the film, but when it strikes, it is either supernaturally empowered (psychotics always have great energy in the cinema and usually the strength of several men), or simply a supernatural creature, a Frankenstein monster, a zombie, an immortal force likely to return for another killing (or worse, a film sequel). As for the characteristic of unpreparedness, Hitchcock[1] himself has elaborated on the distinction between the kind of suddenness typical of ordinary films and his own brand of suspense, which plays on the gradual development of the potential horror in a situation—known to the audience, but beyond the film character's awareness. And certainly Hitchcock is right in the psychological sense, as well as in the esthetic sense: murder in a dark alley, which he has often discounted, is less effective than murder in a crowded, well-lit U.N. Building. But even so, we will always have ordinary films with us, and if filmmakers cannot pull off the Master's style of suspense, mere shock will be used instead. Often the duration of an incident designed to shock is prolonged foolishly past the point where the audience fully expects it; for example, the never-exhausted use of the situation of the innocent young woman exploring the darkened, murder-filled house (which originated in the eighteenth-century gothic novel in England and was so overused even then that Jane Austen, in the 1790s, wrote one of her early novels parodying it). In such sequences our common sense tells us of the immediate danger of which the woman seems entirely unaware.

It is worth reflecting on the motif of exploration in the house of horrors.    4
There are two types of exploration in such situations; one is the relatively logical procedure involved when the searcher does not know that some horror is lurking in the house. In this aspect of the search motif, the levels of irony reinforce the element of terror in the sequence. A second type of exploration far more common in the genre occurs when the character actually is aware of great danger, even when the threat is ambiguous. This intrusion into the haunted house by a fearful yet determined figure, often a defenseless woman, almost always establishes an identity between the searcher and the audience; we may not know exactly what evil will befall the searcher, but we sympa-

---

[1] *Hitchcock:* Alfred Hitchcock (1899–1980), the "master of suspense" who directed such film classics as *The Lady Vanishes* (1938), *Notorious* (1946), *Strangers on a Train* (1951), *North by Northwest* (1957), *Vertigo* (1958), *Psycho* (1960), and *Frenzy* (1972).

thize with him or her at each turn of the perilous corridors and at the opening of each squeaking door (in many low budget horror films, one can of oil
would convert all the eccentric mansions into normal houses).

Yet if we sympathize with the irrational pursuit of the nightmare—when
a telephone call to the police station or waiting until daylight would diffuse
the inherent terror of the place—what does this say about our own involvement in the situation? It does not seem to be some insatiable curiosity, for that
could be satisfied by the characters' examining the threatening situation.

It seems that as frightened as we are of the dark horrors ahead of the
searcher, we must force ourselves to explore them, to continue on toward that
confrontation with whatever ultimate form the nightmare can take. But it perhaps goes even further than that. The final horror is extremely limited in its
possibilities. And do we not know in advance what the worst of these possibilities are? An unusually brutal man, halfman, or full monster with a knife,
either lunging at our back or jumping from the shadows at our face. There are
some other alternatives, ghosts of indescribable forms, but essentially, for the
horror to be as unbearable as we hope it is when we purchase our tickets, it
has to represent death—the death of the searcher, and indeed the death of our
surrogate self. Perhaps the ultimate irrationality of this typical moment of
horror in the nightmare film represents our own subconscious desire to confront our inevitable dread: to meet death before we really die. Or looked at
another way, such moments of horror are cathartic, symbolic suicides, speaking directly to our hidden wish to attempt everything and to survive unaltered,
to get murdered without being murdered.

## THE CINEMA OF REASON AND NIGHTMARE

The nightmare world, with which we all have a personal and very private
acquaintance, derives from the suppressed fears within every individual and
differs for each of us, at least in its details. Some very clever illustrators and
makeup artists design movie monsters that are effective in capturing some universal idea of horror but of course strike us as original all the same. A monster readily visualized by everyone is probably not very monstrous, though
there do seem to be a few images derived from certain real "monstrosities"
that have permeated the unconsciousness of the human race (prehistoric animals and huge spiders, rats, bats, roaches, and so on). Nevertheless, the
depiction of the horrific represents a major challenge to filmmakers, for by its
nature the cinema objectifies and externalizes abstract concepts so that they
take on a visual embodiment. If the horror film is to succeed, some care must
be taken that the essence of whatever is supposed to be the horrible object
remains suggestively terrifying. A monster once seen becomes rather quickly
assimilable into the environment of the film and correspondingly less intimidating. Its mere physical appearance will not do for long.

This is the basic reason for the lack of success of so many films that concern the threat of some outside force such as a monster or a creature from
another planet. Once the force is visualized, we feel that it then can be han-

dled and destroyed sooner or later, and during the process the threat loses its initial impact. Science fiction films differ from true horror films, though they both frequently employ monsters, in that the implicit danger in the former is supposed to originate in the outer world and to be dealt with accordingly, whereas the dangers in the world of the horror film are symbols of our nightmares, projections of our inner reality—even though the necessity of the cinematic form requires, in most cases, some overtly corporeal menace. The horror film aims at psychological effects, the science fiction film at logical possibilities. Many aspects of both genres overlap, certainly, since the minor examples of both aim for sensational depictions of terror with little regard for the sense of good science fiction or the sensibility of the real horror film.

When worked out properly, the science fiction film is premised on　9
people's ability to handle things that intrude into their comfortable physical reality. For example, in the Howard Hawks-Christian Nyby science fiction film *The Thing* (1951), the strange vegetable monster is destroyed by electrocution (that is, it is fried), and even though the film ends with a warning that earth may be repeatedly invaded by other monsters or civilizations, we can hardly worry about that possibility as long as we have electricity. But in the nightmare world, dreams recur; fears sometimes take on new shapes but seldom disappear entirely (if they did, so would the practice of psychiatry). The stake is inevitably thrust into Dracula's heart—over and over again. Dracula returns, not merely for crass commercial reasons, but because he has become rooted in the psychology of modern moviegoing society. The monsters that spring from our own psyche are either the zombies we constantly recreate or symbolic archetypal figures of evil. At the end of a science fiction film, order is restored—the spaceship crew or earth itself is saved, permanently. When we awaken from the nightmare world, we have only a temporary reprieve; another dream may follow on the next night. In that case, all that has happened has been an evaporation of a monster, which simply returns to its spiritual or disembodied form, to be picked up by our brainwaves and re-embodied sometime in another film.

The nightmare genre is thus not entirely suited to rational explanations,　10
since its primary thrust is toward the exploration of emotional states—horror and the more or less irrational response to it. If the source of the horror were itself entirely rational (for instance, an escaped lion on a city street), an irrational response to it would reveal no more than outrage or cowardice, but rational plot patterns run counter to the basics of the genre. It is necessary, in those horror films where at least a rational explanation is offered, to postpone that logical moment until all the usual effects of the genre have been achieved. But it is not at all necessary—though it usually does happen—that the source of the horror be logically categorized by the end of the film. The critical dumbfoundedness that greeted Hitchcock's *The Birds* (1963) resulted from the filmmaker's failure to provide any ultimate explanation of the bird attacks. Had Hitchcock been working in the realm of science fiction, some explanation would have been needed to finish the film, but such a requirement is irrelevant to the horror genre, even if it could have been supplied. Hitchcock

reveals no interest in how the situation came about; what matters is the depiction of the rebellion of birds, a usually pleasant aspect of nature. Surely this is not a sensible theme for us to ponder in the way that we might ponder the possibilities of an invasion of flying saucers. We might be invaded by inhabitants of another planet—that is within the realm of scientific possibility; but to speculate about disruptions of nature is to engage in nightmares with an unlimited scope of possibilities beyond the laws of science and the evidence of our senses. *The Birds* is a masterpiece of another type, a probing into the response of various people to a reversal of the natural order. It is beyond the issue of plausibility.

## ROMANTIC ISOLATION

Eventually the zombies of the mind can be battered down, and if not perma- 11
nently laid to rest, at least buried in crypts that might remain sealed for decades to come. But there are other fears engendered by the horror genre that do not readily subside because they are by nature nothing more than an extension or alteration of the hero. This type of horror film usually gains its peculiar effectiveness by making the hero into a monster and eventually leading us to relate to the monstrous condition, which points toward the hero's inevitable doom. This type of film relies almost equally on our underlying pity as well as on our usual fears.

The werewolf is perhaps the best representative of this ambivalent placing 12
of the beast within the body of the hero, though the actual American appearances of the character have not been notably successful (such as Stuart Walker's *The Werewolf of London* [1935], George Wagner's *The Wolf Man* [1941], Eric Kenton's *House of Frankenstein* [1944]). The werewolf, a good man who turns periodically into a creature of violence, cannot prevent himself from killing when, under the influence of the full moon, he becomes a huge deadly wolf. Considered from a psychological perspective, the werewolf is just the archetypal schizophrenic man, with uncontrollable impulses toward evil. We share with him these impulses, but watching him on screen we undergo a purgative experience as he acts out for us the process of inevitable doom awaiting the person who loses control, who destroys in a moment of madness or passion. He is a cousin to Dr. Jekyll, the difference typically being that the doctor (that is, the mad scientist) willingly brings about his own downfall by his overweening scientific pride or curiosity. Turning into Mr. Hyde, he becomes temporarily a mad monster, his lucidity restored for shorter and shorter lengths of time when he can revert to his normal self. The Jekyll-Hyde category of the horror genre is rich in attempts to devise new insights into this simple Robert Louis Stevenson story of the split personality within all of us, and it has attracted filmmakers from Jean Renoir to Jerry Lewis.

Werewolves and Hydes are also related to a larger group of horror films 13
that deal with the obsessed maniac, but in most cases the maniac is so depraved we cannot identify with him. Psychotic killers can hardly be expected to pass as acceptable members of society even when their need to kill has

been temporarily satisfied. For this reason, the werewolf turned back into his normal self, the urbane Count Dracula (in the daytime) and Dr. Jekyll, are far more frightening figures of the nightmare world than their more realistic kin, the diabolical murderer. Although the monster may have chemical or physiological causes for his murders, we can often interpret his motives as a kind of temporary insanity, though not in the legal sense. On the surface he murders because as a monster he has to, but on another level—not really a disguised level either—he kills because he finds it gratifying. We in the audience never yield to the equivalent temptation, yet we note how often the first murder committed on screen is against a somewhat unsympathetic character. Viewers are thus led toward plausible identification with the monster, even though as the crimes increase all pretense toward moral sympathy on a rational plane disappears. We remain horrified, but we persist in feeling sympathetic toward the monster as he succumbs to his terrifying worse self.

In a relatively few but memorable instances, the nightmare genre has been   14 able to achieve a sense of the pathetic as strong or stronger than a sense of the terrifying. It might seem that the combination of pathos and horror would not work, but we should remember that the genre as we know it today derives from a branch of nineteenth-century literary romanticism that was much more at home with pathos than with horror. The theme of the savage or misfit or monster in romantic literature is not easily duplicated in film today because the physical appearance of the movie monster would probably need to be toned down to generate sympathy, thereby becoming more human and less horrible. Nevertheless, the existence of some classic portrayals of pathetic monsters indicates that the nightmare world is much broader and more complex than it appears in the majority of its films which present a horror lurking somewhere "out there." Watching Dr. Frankenstein's laboratory-created monster, the audience identifies with the pursued creature driven to destruction by a frenzied mob.

James Whale's *Frankenstein* (1931) is usually among the first films that   15 come to mind when this aspect of the genre is discussed, along with his *The Bride of Frankenstein* (1935), Tod Browning's *Dracula* (1930), Ernest Schoedsack and Merian C. Cooper's *King Kong* (1933), and a number of other masterful contributions of the 1930s. *Frankenstein* is one of the most romantic films Hollywood ever turned out, and Whale might well have achieved major status as a filmmaker had he directed films with more normal, respectable surfaces. But below the surface of Whale's expressionistic fantasies, yet there in the most palpable way, are the themes of isolation and the desire to be loved, material that often seems the stuff of films that have greater pretensions to art, though few films of the era had greater claims to cinematic art. Boris Karloff's impersonation of the monster is so filled with humanity that despite the creature's clumsiness and a temper readily provoked to violence, there is no point at which we do not feel for the monster and oppose his persecutors, the townspeople, who in their uncomprehending fear chase and destroy the creature without communicating with him or learning of his gigantic potential for goodness. Though unnamed in the film, the monster has been from that time on named after his creator, Dr. Frankenstein, by the general public. The banal framing story of the overambitious scientist creating a living thing that goes out of control, escapes, and in various ways punishes the scientist for trying to be a god, was less important than the brief biography of the monster. Left to himself, the monster seeks only to establish some human contact—that is, to be loved on the level of his understanding, which is that of a big pet dog. He is, for thematic purposes, less the creation of the laboratory than the "natural man," a large, lumbering animal that fights only when he is cornered or tormented. He cannot speak in the film, though he learns to do so in the sequel, *The Bride of Frankenstein.* In the latter film he finally forms his sole friendship—with a blind hermit—though that too is doomed by interlopers who represent society and civilization. But for most of both films, the monster himself is the most frightened character.

With *Frankenstein* the motif of romantic isolation almost immediately   16
became a dominant influence in the development of the genre—though it had appeared in at least one classic instance as early as 1925 in Rupert Julian's *Phantom of the Opera.* In this film the disfigured madman lives a subterranean existence because of his terrifying face, emerging only because he has fallen in love with a woman he determines to abduct. After *Frankenstein,* numerous films depicted humans or monsters isolated in an alien environment, though the motives for that existence varied with the horror figure's degree of intelligence. In 1933, for example, *King Kong* followed directly the *Frankenstein* pattern of an innocent creature destroyed by a world that will not respond with understanding at a moment of implicit danger. In the same year, Whale turned out another classic of the genre in *The Invisible Man,* which features a scientist who has taken a drug that produces not only his invisibility but a growing insanity that leads him to try to conquer the world. And in Michael Curtiz's *Mystery of the Wax Museum* (1933) we find another sort of archetypal figure of romantic isolation: the artist. In this case, the artist has been driven insane by a fire that ruined his wax statues and made his face hideous. Designing a mask for himself, he is able to exist within society in an outwardly unremarkable way, but nursing a desire for revenge and committing murders; he is a variant on both the *Phantom of the Opera* motif and the Jekyll-Hyde split personality.

■ ■ ■

## Review Questions

1. Reread the selection's first paragraph and identify Solomon's thesis, or claim. Paraphrase this sentence.
2. Identify three traits of the horror film genre.
3. "It seems that as frightened as we are of the dark horrors ahead of the searcher, we must force ourselves to explore them." What two reasons

does Solomon offer for our desire to search (as the character in the film searches) the haunted house?

4. What qualities must a monster maintain, once it is shown on the screen, if it is to remain horrifying?

5. What is the key difference between a science fiction movie and a horror movie, according to Solomon?

6. Solomon calls the werewolf "the archetypal schizophrenic man" in whose downfall we (ordinary theatre-goers) find a "purgative experience." What does Solomon mean, and how is the werewolf related to Dr. Jekyll and Mr. Hyde?

7. Why are movie monsters of the werewolf/Dracula/Jekyll-Hyde type more sympathetic to us than movies about psychotic killers?

## Discussion and Writing Suggestions

1. Discuss Solomon's assertion that our era gives "little credence to devils, witches, and monsters, but lives continuously with massive violence, perversion, and nihilism." First, do you agree with his assessment of our era? Solomon means to contrast, or set up a tension between, our apparent disbelief in devils (for instance) and our daily exposure to violence. Explain this contrast or tension.

2. Solomon suggests that the horror film's objectifying—making objects out of—our inner demons on the screen "exorcises" these demons. What is your experience in watching horror films? Do you feel in any way relieved on leaving?

3. Think of a horror film you've seen—one that scared you. Was there a "search" scene, in which the main character must search through a haunted house (ship, hotel, . . .)? What was the search scene's effect on you? If the search made you tense, why did you watch? (Does Solomon's explanation—see Review Question #3, above—satisfy you?)

4. Solomon suggests that we all have suppressed fears that give rise to a "nightmare" world and, moreover, that this nightmare world is highly specific: different people are horrified by different thoughts and images. Is this generalization true for you?

5. Recall a horror movie that, momentarily at least, terrified you. What, in fact, was so terrifying about the monster? How well does Solomon's account of how horror movies affect us explain your reactions to the movie? For instance, in retrospect, did you find that the movie in any way gave you "protected access to a nightmare world otherwise shunted outside of civilization"?

6. What is your reaction to the serious study of horror films as a genre, or distinctive type of film? Solomon, for instance, is a scholar of the horror genre, as are many others who write articles and books. To what extent, in your view, do horror movies justify such scholarly attention? Is there in these movies the substance needed for serious study?

7. Solomon asserts that we identify with the werewolf and with the Jekyll/ Hyde character. Do you find these movie monsters sympathetic? Why?

## Blowing the Lid Off the Id

HARVEY GREENBERG

*As a psychoanalyst, Harvey Greenberg attributes outward behaviour and feelings to interior states. The view that there are subconscious and unconscious aspects to personality that determine conscious thought and action derives, in modern times, from Sigmund Freud. Freud believed in mental processes that are not directly accessible to consciousness. Some of these mental processes are instincts, urges, or desires (the "id") that have been repressed from the conscious mind (the "ego") by the "censor" (the "superego") because they are shameful or antisocial. It is in this Freudian context that Greenberg writes of horror movies "Blowing the Lid Off the Id"—of giving direct access, at least during the course of a particular movie, to our usually repressed and shameful impulses.*

*Here, Greenberg applies the principles of psychoanalysis (which he does for a living in New York City) not to human patients but to an artifact of human culture: movies—and, in this section of his book* Movies on Your Mind *(1975), the horror film. Greenberg writes of interior "beasts" just as others do in this chapter. As you contemplate the connections among the chapter's fiction writer (King), the film historian and theorist (Solomon), the various film critics, and the psychoanalyst (Greenberg), you might ask: Are the interior states—the beasts—that these writers describe identical? Do you recognize these states in yourself? in others? Are these interior states elements of human personality that we can even acknowledge consciously?*

When he heard I wanted to become a psychoanalyst, an old general practitioner vehemently warned—"Son, stay away from the crap—when you stir a stink, all you get is a bigger stink!" The ancient injunction against stirring up the seething cauldron of the unconscious (cf., Pandora, Oedipus and other mythic meddlers with the psychic peace) rests squarely upon the anxiety we feel before the often alarming strength of our own emotions.

It is written that in a certain African tribe, when an individual falls ill, his relatives and friends are forced on pain of death to reveal their dreams to the shaman. If evil intent towards the afflicted one be discerned therein, the dreamer is labeled a witch, and cast out into the wilderness. To the primitive, the child and many neurotics, intense aggressive and sexual feelings are particularly reprehensible, carrying as much weight as an actual criminal deed such feelings might motivate, and laying the guilty party open to the retribution of the gods, the tribal Judges, or the remorseless Superego.

We are repeatedly admonished in weird cinema that even the gentlest of men may bare fangs and bay at the moon when his passions are kindled. The movie monster thus represents the destructive forces unleashed when reason and civilized morality are overthrown by our unruly instincts. The mutable lycanthrope is but another version of Hobbesian man, the naked ape bellowing in the wilderness, Fred C. Dobbs[1] in Wolf Man's Clothing!

Weird cinema often lays the blame for blowing the lid off the Id within   4
the unquiet spirit of the candidate for monsterdom, and/or upon malignant outside spirits. . . . The heroine of Val Lewton's 1942 film *Cat People* (played by the memorably feline Simone Simon) has emigrated from her obscurely Transylvanian origins. She marries an apple-pie and ice-cream American oaf; when her husband develops an "innocent" relationship with a female coworker as square as he, her jealousy turns into rank paranoia, and she turns into a panther. The film is noteworthy for its xenophobia: we are led to believe that hubby bedded an alluring pussycat from across the sea, and got a tiger in his tank[2] instead.

On closer scrutiny, the husband proves far from innocent. He provokes   5
the incipient cat lady with stinging allusions to the charm and competence of his "pal," while the latter, despite her demonstrations of queasy solicitude about her rival's tenuous emotional state, is palpably out to break up the marriage. Hollywood's characteristic disguise of an immoral reality places the responsibility for infidelity, seduction and the taunting unto madness of a vulnerable waif upon the festering rage of the attained foreigner.[3]

In Universal's *The Wolf Man* (1941), another guiltless *naif*, Lawrence   6
Talbott, loses his humanity with the eruption of his jealousy. Like the catwoman, Talbott is a rejected outsider, returning to the English village of his birth after years of self-imposed exile (never explained) in America. He is called back by his aristocrat father after his obviously preferred older brother's death. The cruel father treats him like Cain, with ill-disguised hostility even after their formal reconciliation.

While wandering on the moors, Talbott slays a werewolf, but is bitten in   7
the fight. Later, at a village carnival, he meets the young woman he has been wooing unsuccessfully, with her fiancé. The two men compete at a shooting gallery. Talbott performs well until he freezes at the toy image of a wolf. His adversary contemptuously blasts it down. "You win," Talbott groans.

---

[1] *Fred C. Dobbs:* The prospector (portrayed by Humphrey Bogart) in John Huston's *Treasure of the Sierra Madre* (1948), who, after finding gold in the mountains of Mexico, becomes crazed with greed and murderous paranoia as he suspects his partners of trying to rob him.

[2] *tiger in his tank:* In the 1960s, an ad campaign by Exxon Oil featured a cartoon "tiger in your tank" to dramatize the power of its gasoline.

[3] Which does not, of course, diminish *Cat People's* shock value. Lewton was one of those gifted directors who could scare an audience witless by altering the substance of the ordinary into pure menace. Take the famous sequence in which the heroine changes into her panther persona at a hotel swimming pool, where the other woman treads water, alone and achingly vulnerable. The quiet lapping of the wavelets, the confused lights, shadows and echoes rebounding off the tiled walls combine to produce an atmosphere of exceptional disquiet. One longs for this subtlety at a time when the horror film, caught up in pervasive cinematic sadism, so frequently leaves the sensibilities glutted with gory surfeit. [Greenberg]

Subsequently he catches the girl alone, tries clumsily to tell her of his love. She rebuffs him, and directly thereafter he changes into a werewolf, howling out his pain on the lonely moors. Talbott has lost an implicit Oedipal battle—the Oedipal motif appears virtually undisguised later in the film, when the father, after persistently denying his son's lycanthropy, is responsible for Talbott's escape. Father then encounters son changed to Wolf Man, about to assault his lost love on the moor. The father kills him with the same silver-headed cane which Talbott wielded against the werewolf that infected him! (I shall have more to say about the monster as adolescent Oedipus presently.)

The Pandora's box of the unconscious is frequently opened by the "mad" 8 scientist, a misguided humanitarian or a demented egomaniac seeking vengeance against the world that has derided his genius. By tampering with the natural order, the good/bad doctor inadvertently releases the Id-monster within himself, like Dr. Henry Jekyll (*Dr. Jekyll and Mr. Hyde*), Dr. Janos Rukh (*The Invisible Ray*), or Dr. Morbius (*Forbidden Planet*).

*Dr. Jekyll and Mr. Hyde* has been brought to the screen more often than 9 any other weird tale. The persona of Jekyll actually changes little from one film to the next: thoroughly dedicated, genteel and priggish, Jekyll remains the essence of the repressed Victorian. But Hyde's gargantuan appetite for evil has elicited a wider range of interpretation: it is, once again, the old story of Lucifer being more interesting than God! The rarely exhibited Rouben Mamoulian version (1932) remains the favorite of most critics, myself included. The fabulous transformation scene, to the accompaniment of Mamoulian's own recorded muffled heartbeat, has never been equalled. The director steadfastly refused to reveal the lighting and makeup effects that turned Frederic March's handsome features into a brutish parody of humanity. I prize the film especially for its tasteful, yet pointed evocation of Hyde's exuberant carnality (elsewhere it is Hyde's non-sexual sadism that is emphasized). Violence and eroticism are skillfully blended when Hyde lures a young barmaid into his web, goads her into a frenzy of lubricious terror, then strangles her off-camera in what is clearly intended to be an orgiastic substitute.

In Universal's *The Invisible Ray* (1933) a latter-day Jekyll, Dr. Janos 10 Rukh (Boris Karloff out of monster drag) ignores his beautiful young wife to search for "Radium X," a meteoric element with mysterious curative powers thought to have fallen to earth eons ago. Rukh recovers the lost substance in Africa, but after exposure to its intense radioactivity, develops the ability to kill at a touch or a glance. He drops out of sight and is presumed dead. Within a few years a colleague has mastered the dangers of Radium X, reaps fame and honor, while Rukh's wife falls in love with a younger man. Then Rukh resurfaces; the radioactivity seething in his brain has driven him mad, and he commences murdering everyone connected with his humiliation. Before he can kill his wife and complete the cycle of his vengeance, his strength ebbs. His older mother crushes the vial containing the antiserum that maintains his fragile hold on life, and the glowing Rukh hurls himself out a window, to be instantly reduced to ashes by the unchecked poison raging within him.

In real life, no Radium X would be required to catalyze Rukh's obses-     11
sional tendencies into a full-blown paranoid state. I have elsewhere indicated
that paranoids often provoke the very maltreatment and rejection they fear.
The clinician marks Rukh as chronically afraid of closeness, more at home
with his grandiose fantasies than the small pleasures of genuine intimacy. Men
like Rukh often sicken in their declining years, when the earlier promise of
success has not been fulfilled, and death no longer seems a distance possibility. They drive themselves into emotional exile, thrusting away those who
might love them with their coldness, nagging and jealous tantrums. Like
Rukh, they end up as mad isolates, consumed by bitterness and envy. One
notes that Rukh's mother is his executioner. She reproaches him for his misdeeds and failures, and the film implies that she has a legitimate right to do so:
actually, the mothers of these obsessional-paranoid types are wont to blame
and shame their sons to death with no justification save their own rancor.

As Hyde is to Jekyll, so the radioactive Rukh is to his former rational self.     12
Either the mad scientist converts his ego into the horrid image of his lustful,
envious Id, or he constructs a fearful projection of his "monstrous" desires
and sets it loose to burn and pillage, often consciously unaware that the
monster is the agent of his repressed wishes. The monster may thus be likened
to the delinquent who is covertly encouraged to act out one parent or another's unconscious antisocial impulses. The parent in these cases has *superego
lacunae*, i.e., a conscience as full of holes as a Swiss cheese. The adult projects
his or her disavowed criminality upon the child, who can then be "safely"
labeled as the bad seed! While the law may fail to recognize this subtle brand
of complicity, at least in the movies the chickens always come home to roost.
However noble or craven his conscious motivation, the mad scientist's complicity in the misdeeds of this "offspring" is acknowledged and punished
when monster turns upon master and destroys both.

The mad scientist's Id-monster usually appears disguised in fur and claws     13
or encased in metal, but there is one remarkable film in which the Freudian Id
itself is the Technicolor monster bred out of is creator's bad dreams—MGM's
1956 science fiction extravaganza, *Forbidden Planet*.

An interstellar space ship lands on the planet Altair IV to recover sur-     14
vivors of an ill-fated colonizing expedition. Only two of the original group
remain: Morbius, a philologist of formidable intellect, and his naive, overripe
daughter, Altaira. Morbius explains to the intrepid Commander John Adams
that he and his family care to cherish life on Altair IV, whereas the other
members of the expedition could not adjust, and were either torn limb from
limb by an invisible monster that prowled the night, or were vaporized with
their ship on lift-off after they were unable to persuade Morbius to leave.
Since then, Morbius' wife died of natural causes, he and his daughter have
lived unmolested for nearly twenty years—"yet always in my mind, I seem to
feel the creature is lurking somewhere close, sly and irresistible. . . ." Morbius
refuses to disclose the nature of his studies on Altair IV, but he has surrounded himself with technological marvels that are obviously beyond the
competence of a linguist.

He warns his would-be rescuers to go before they, too, suffer the fate of     15
his companions. Commander Adams senses something amiss, and refuses to
depart. That night his ship is invaded and disabled by the planet's reawakened
invisible menace. Altaira develops a crush on the handsome commander who,
in the tradition of Space Opera is irritated at her innocent provocation of his
men with her lush endowments until he himself takes the fall.

Morbius is pressured to reveal the secret of the forbidden planet to     16
Adams and the eggheaded ship's doctor. Millennia ago, Altair IV was the seat
of a great culture—the Krel, vastly superior to man in every way. Having vanquished crime and disease, they stood poised "on the threshold of some
supreme accomplishment which was to have crowned their entire history."
Then, "this all but divine race perished in a single night," leaving as enigmatic
legacy an enormous web of underground machinery, still monitoring and
maintaining itself after 200,000 years!

With his knowledge of linguistics and an electronic I.Q. boost from the     17
Krel "plastic educator," Morbius acquired the barest fraction of their
wisdom, but enough to become a scientific wizard and also inflate his ego
beyond mortal bounds. He proposes to release the results of his research in his
own godlike good time. Adams objects that mankind is entitled to the Krel
data without Morbius' regency. As Morbius waxes angrier at his daughter's
infatuation and the intruders' insistence that he return to Earth, the depreda-
tions of the invisible monster escalate; during one attack, Morbius is discovered stirring in a troubled slumber at his desk (Morbius = Morpheus!) while
the Krel machinery registers an astronomical power drain. Here is the only
instance when *Forbidden Planet*'s impressive special effects falter by violating
a central canon of weird cinema—never show the audience too much. Caught
in the beams of the spacemens' blasters, the Id-monster looks like a cartoon
fugitive from Disneyland. Better to have left it forever unseen![4]

---

[4] The naked face of Thanatos is best revealed sparingly. Like the dim member of repressed
trauma, that which is most frightening is likely to be half-glimpsed, seized and reinvented
by each viewer's uniquely personal intuition of doom, like the room in Orwell's *1984*
where political prisoners were confronted with their most private fears of death. Indeed,
what made the great radio horror shows so much more terrifying than the average horror
flick was precisely that so much was left to the febrile imagination. I still can remember an
episode of Arch Obler's *Lights Out!*, in which a giant chicken heart was swallowing up New
York. The announcer yelled that it was sprouting tentacles. *Tentacles*, for God's sake!! I
didn't know what they were, but trying to screw up the mind's eye to get a better look
scared me out of my eighth year's growth!

Laughter is a necessary ingredient of the horror experience, but it must be carefully
mixed with fear. Jury-rigged horror, like the Mexican vampire cheapies that starred popular wrestlers, or the Disneyesque Id-demon of *Forbidden Planet*, ridiculously displays its
seams and stitches, and the willing suspension of disbelief is itself suspended. On the other
hand, horror beyond psychological tolerance cancels enjoyment and nullifies catharsis. The
film becomes a nightmare from which it is impossible to awaken after leaving the safety of
the theater, an unmastered trauma that continues to plague the mind. Pictures like *The
Exorcist* or *Night of the Living Dead* have been supremely effective in spawning raw panic,
but they also irrevocably violate our childlike faith in the movies not to harm us.

The egghead doctor slips into the Krel laboratory, and uses the plastic 18 educator to match his wits with Morbius. He is mortally injured, but manages to warn Adams before he dies: ". . . the big machine . . . no instrumentality, true creation, but the Krel forgot one thing . . . monsters, John, monsters from the Id!" And Adams realizes that *Morbius* is the predator of the forbidden planet! The Krel machine enabled that proud race to transcend the need for physical tools, to change thought instantly into force and matter. But just as the benevolent ego of each Krel was linked to their fantastic creation, so was the Id of each, with its primitive lust and hatred. In one night, every Id-monster of the Krel summoned up the machine's illimitable power, and the race literally self-destructed.

But still the machine carried on. Morbius unwittingly entered into the 19 mindlock that had blown the lid off the collective Id of the Krel. While he slept, Morbius' Id savaged his companions because they wanted him to leave Altair IV. And twenty years later, he has sent out his inner beast against Adams, his crew, yes, even his daughter when she throws in her lot with the spacemen. In one stroke, the "mindless primitive" of the lofty-minded Morbius would remove his rival and the source of their rivalry, his own flesh and blood.

At first, Morbius frantically denies what he already partly knows, but as 20 with any hallucinating psychotic, his Id bursts into his waking life. The invisible monster appears outside his citadel, smashes down one supposedly unbreakable defense after another, and begins to melt down the last barrier—"solid Krel metal, twenty-six inches thick!"

"Guilty! Guilty!!" Morbius screams, "My evil self is at that door, and I 21 have no power to stop it! I deny you! I give you up!!" Miraculously, the unseen horror recedes. Morbius is disengaged from the Krel machine. Like Prospero in *The Tempest* (*Forbidden Planet* is often compared with Shakespeare's play), he breaks his staff, buries his book. But like Faustus, that other Promethean overreacher and meddler in dangerous arcana, he must pay a mortal price for his hubris. He has been physically consumed by the gigantic mental effort expended in putting his Superego back on the ascendant. This retelling of Genesis cleaves the figure of our first ancestor in twain: Morbius, eater of the forbidden fruit of the Krel knowledge, must stay behind and die, while Commander Adams(!) will be allowed to quit the tainted Eden of Altair IV.

Morbius bids Adams take his daughter and go in peace. Rather touch- 22 ingly, he calls the Commander "son," acknowledging the psychological basis of their rivalry, and activates an atomic reactor that turns the planet into a supernova after the Earthmen have departed. Watching from deep space, Adam consoles Altaira, his new Eve:

> ADAMS: About a million years from now, the human race will have crawled up to where the Krel stood in their great moment of triumph and tragedy; your father's name will shine again, like a beacon in the galaxy . . . it's true, it will remind us that we are, after all, not gods!

In supernatural cinema, these lines—"there are secrets better for man not 23 to know!"—are usually spoken by an elder scientist surveying the havoc left by the deceased monster. Reminiscent of my old mentor who warned me away from the big stink of psychoanalysis, this venerable antique stands appropriately humbled before the inscrutable turnings of the universe, in contradistinction to his presumptuous younger colleague who has either been killed by his creation or shot down in his Id-disguise to reemerge as his better self after death, like Dr. Jekyll, or Dr. Collins in *The Invisible Man*. But whether the setting be gothic or galactic, the "secrets of nature" pursued by the mad doctor to his inevitable ruin are often metaphors for the turbulent emotions locked within the secret recesses of the troubled heart.

■　■　■

## Review Questions

1. For Greenberg, the movie monster is not simply a monster but a representation of something inside us. What, for Greenberg, does the movie monster represent?
2. What qualities, both in terms of story line and psychology, do the Cat Woman, the Wolfman, and Dr. Jekyll and Mr. Hyde share, according to Greenberg?
3. Writing in reference to the Id-monster in *Forbidden Planet*, Greenberg offers "a central canon of weird cinema—never show the audience too much." Why offer this so-called rule? To what problem is this rule a response?
4. To what does the "stink" refer in Greenberg's opening paragraph, and what role does this stink play in horror movies?

## Discussion and Writing Suggestions

1. What are some of the forces that the individual and society bring to bear to keep unconscious emotions in check—that is, *un*conscious? What is so dangerous about these emotions?
2. It is a cliché that even the most mild-mannered man or woman conceals an "animal" within—an inner beast that, once provoked, can completely overrun the mild personality. In what contexts have you seen this cliché at work? Does your experience confirm it?
3. Reread this article, focusing on Greenberg's Freudian analysis of specific movies. Freud's theories form a well-developed, complex system of thought that seeks to explain (among other things) the causes of human fear and unhappiness. Select *one* of Greenberg's Freudian critiques—preferably of a movie you have seen, and respond. How useful do you find the analysis in helping you understand and appreciate the movie?
4. Following Freud, Greenberg assumes the existence of a vast, but unconscious, sea of inner emotions. When this inner sea is confused and espe-

cially stormy, the "surface" life of a person can be disrupted and, in extreme cases, be made monstrous. Offer a competing reason for the appearance of monsters, perhaps a reason that has nothing to do with inner emotions.

5. To what extent do you accept as valid the transferring of psychoanalysis—a practice meant for application to human patients—to movies? Can movies, or characters in movies, be analyzed the same way a patient on a couch can be analyzed? Explain.

## ■ RESEARCH ACTIVITIES

1. Select three or four films that comprise a subgenre of the horror film, as indicated in Tim Dirks's article—for example, *Dracula* or *Frankenstein* films, or some of the more recent "slasher" films. If you're interested in werewolf films, consider, in addition to the ones in Dirks's piece, *The Howling* (1980), *An American Werewolf in London* (1981), *Wolfen* (1981), *Ladyhawke* (1983), and *An American Werewolf in Paris* (1998).

   Rent and view these films. Then, research (1) the conventions of this particular subgenre and (2) comments by reviewers and critics. In addition to conducting a subject search of horror films in both print and electronic (Web and CD-ROM) sources, you might find the following books particularly helpful: Stanley J. Solomon, *Beyond Formula* (1976), Thomas Schatz, *Hollywood Genres* (1981), Barry Keith Grant, ed. *Film Genre Reader* (1986) and *Film Genre Reader II* (1995).

   For critical commentary and reviews of individual films, see *Film Index International on CD-ROM* (covers films from 1930 to the present), *Film Review Annual* (collections of film reviews, 1981 to the present), *The New York Times Film Reviews* (1913 to the present), *International Index to Film Periodicals* (1972 to the present), *Film Literature Index* (1973 to the present), *Variety Film Reviews, Magill's Cinema Annual* (1982 to the present), and film review listings (alphabetically listed under "Moving Pictures" or "Motion Pictures") in the *Reader's Guide to Periodical Literature*. Three useful web sources on film include Cinemachine **www.cinemachine.com/**, Cinemania **cinemania.msn.com**, and The Internet Movie Database (IMDb) **us.imdb.com/**.

   In your paper, relate the particulars of individual films to the conventions of the genre or subgenre. Show how a particular event, or motif, for example, follows the convention or varies it. Compare and contrast what happens in one film to a corresponding event in another, giving reasons for the differences, and discussing the effects of these variants. To sharpen the focus, you may want to confine your attention to just one crucial or representative scene in each film (for example, the first appearance of the "beast" or its ultimate defeat).

2. Focus your attention on a single horror film, one covered in this chapter, or another that you particularly like, or one that you would like to see. Using some of the sources suggested in the previous exercise, research the critical reviews and commentary upon this film. Categorize the main focal points of critical comment and compose an explanatory synthesis on the critical reception of this film.

3. Select a horror film based on a novel. Read the fictional work, view the film, and write a paper comparing and contrasting the two versions of the same story. Locate some critical reviews of both fiction and film and integrate these sources into your discussion.

   Examples: *Frankenstein* (novel by Mary Shelley, 1818); *Dr. Jekyll and Mr. Hyde* (novel by Robert Louis Stevenson, 1886); *Dracula* (novel by Bram Stoker, 1897); *The Invisible Man* (novel by H. G. Wells, 1897); *Psycho* (novel by Robert Bloch, 1959); *Rosemary's Baby* (novel by Ira Levin, 1967); *The Shining* (novel by Stephen King, 1977).

4. View at least two film adaptations of the same story—for example, the Fredric March version of *Dr. Jekyll and Mr. Hyde* (1932) and the Spencer Tracy version (1941); or James Whale's *Frankenstein* (1931) and Kenneth Branagh's (1994). Researching some of the critical commentary on these films, write a paper comparing and contrasting the two or more versions. As with Research Activity 1 above, you may want to sharpen your focus by concentrating your attention upon just one or two key sequences in each film.

5. As Dirks points out in his selection, the theme of some horror and science fiction films concerns either a misuse of scientific research—and, as a corollary, the arrogance of scientists—or a corruption of technology. Many of the early horror films include some variation of the line, "I/you have meddled in things that man should leave alone!" *Frankenstein* is the most obvious example of this motif; other films in which the scientist is the bad (or at least misguided) guy include *The Invisible Man* (1933) and the two versions of *The Fly* (1958, 1986). The arrogant Dr. Morbius overreaches in *Forbidden Planet* (1956). An atheistical scientist is the villain in *Fantastic Voyage* (1966). Many of the monster movies of the 1950s (and most recently, the 1998 *Godzilla*) blame nuclear testing for the creation of gigantic city-stomping lizards.

   Research this particular aspect of horror films—the motif of the scientist or of technology as malign, dangerous, or even blasphemous (that is, encroaching on areas that belong rightfully to the deity). Use some of the sources listed in Research Activity 1 above, focusing particularly on those that deal to some degree with the ways that horror or science fiction films imply or dramatize attitudes toward science and technology.

6. If you'd like a change from horror, select another standard film genre: for example, the Western, the detective film, the gangster film, the *film noir*, the musical, the science fiction film, the war film, the screwball comedy, the black comedy, the family drama, the social problem film.

Using some of the sources suggested in Research Activity 1 above, write a paper showing how two to four examples of this genre make use of its conventions.

7. Horror films have sometimes come under attack from people who believe that they can be bad influences upon young or impressionable viewers. Objections have focused on the high level of graphic violence in many horror films, as well as the underlying rape implications in many of the older horror films (advertising material often featured a scantily clad young woman being carried off by the beast). The 1950s saw a reaction against excessively grisly horror comic books and, to a lesser extent, horror films. Research one or more of these anti-horror campaigns and report on your findings. You may also want to look into the work of social scientists (such as Edward Donnerstein and Elizabeth Rice Allgeier) who have researched the links between violence in films and violent proclivities in males. Keep in mind that the question is not only whether horror films are likely to inspire imitation of the violent actions portrayed, but also whether repeated exposure to horror films may help foster an increased tolerance of violence as an acceptable way of releasing anger or frustration.

# Literary Credits

"Winter Organization" in Patricia Curtis *Biology*, 2nd Ed. New York: Worth, 1976. pp.822–823.

Robert Hutchins, "Gate Receipts and Glory," *The Saturday Evening Post*, December 3, 1983.

From: *Biomedical Ethics: Newsletter of the European Network for Biomedical Ethics*, Vol. 1, No. 1, 1996.

Jane Yolen, "America's 'Cinderella,'" APS Publications, Inc. in *Children's Literature in Education* 8, 1977, pp.21–29.

Excerpt from "Toward an Intelligence Beyond Man's" from *Time*, February 20, 1978. Copyright ( 1978 Time Inc. Reprinted by permission.

"The Nature and Meaning of Data" from *The Integrity of Intelligence: A Bill of Rights for the Information Age."* By Bryan Glastonbury and Walter Lamendola, September, 1982, Palgrave Publishers. Reprinted with permission of Macmillian Ltd.

"Too Much Privacy can be Hazardous to the Person." Reprinted by permission of the author, Lawrence Solomon.

"Why is there a Wal-Mart in my Backyard and how did it get there?" by Christopher Leo. From: Canada Centre for Policy Alternatives – Manitoba. 309–323 Portage Avenue Winnipeg MB, R3B 2C1

"Wal-Mart to Build, Abandon City Malls," by Aldo Santin, copyright ( *Winnipeg Free Press*, June 11 2000. Reprinted with permission.

"Mall Owners Vent Anger at Wal-Mart," by David O'Brien, copyright ( *Winnipeg Free Press*, January 12, 2000. Reprinted with permission.

"Roll Back the Red Carpet for the Boys," by Donna Laframboise. Reprinted with permission of the author.

"Our Daughters, Ourselves," by Stevie Cameron. From *The Act of Writing: Canadian Essays for Composition*, Fifth Edition, by Ronald. Conrad. Reprinted with permission of the author.

"Left, Right and Centre," From *Introduction to Politics A Conceptual Approach 5th edition*, by M. Dickerson and T. Flanagan copyright (

1998. Reprinted with permission of Nelson Thomson Learning a Division of Thomson Learning. Fax (800) 730-2215.

The Canadian Charter of Rights, Copyright her Majesty the Queen in the Right of Canada.

"I'm Tired of being a Slave to the Church Floor," by Jack Stackhouse, from the *Globe and Mail*, December 22, 1999. Reprinted with permission of the *Globe and Mail*.

"The Homeless: Are we Part of the Problem?" by Jack Layton, from the *Globe and Mail*, December 22, 1999. Reprinted with permission of the author.

"Life on the Streets," by Thomas O'Reilly Fleming, from Down and Out in Canada. Canadian Scholars' Press, 1993. ( 1993 Thomas O'Reilly-Fleming. Reprinted by permission of Canadian Scholars' Press. The article is an excerpt of a chapter from a book published in 1993 called *Down and Out in Canada: Homeless Canadians*. In the excerpt, the author examines some of the causes of homelessness by looking at several specific cases that document the plight of individuals. Dr. Fleming is chair, Applied Arts and Health Sciences, Seneca College and has taught at the University of Windsor, University of Toronto, York University, Ryerson Polytechnic University and many other schools in Canada. He has published ten books on subjects including crime, law, juvenile crime, multiple murder, the environment and homelessness.

"No Room of her Own," by Sylvia Novac, J. Brown, and C. Bourbonnais from *No Room of her Own: A Literature Review of Women and Homelessness*. Ottawa: Canada Mortgage and Housing Corporation, 1996.

"Now they're Killing the Homeless," by Kathy Hardill. Reprinted by permission of the Author.

"The Stones Missed the Real Target," by Pat Capponi, from the *Globe and Mail*. Copyright Pat Capponi c/o Beverley Slopen Agency.

"Children of Poverty," by Mark Nichols, *Maclean's* June 26, 2000.

"The Scientific Mystique: Can a White Lab Coat Guarantee Purity in the Search for

# Index of Authors and Titles